existence

ROBERT CUMMINGS NEVILLE

existence

PHILOSOPHICAL THEOLOGY

VOLUME TWO

State University of New York Press

Cover art: *Existence* by Beth Neville
Graphite pencil and colored pens on Bristol board paper, 10"x10", January, 2013

Published by
STATE UNIVERSITY OF NEW YORK PRESS, ALBANY

© 2014 State University of New York

All rights reserved

Printed in the United States of America

No part of this book may be used or reproduced in any manner whatsoever without written permission. No part of this book may be stored in a retrieval system or transmitted in any form or by any means including electronic, electrostatic, magnetic tape, mechanical, photocopying, recording, or otherwise without the prior permission in writing of the publisher.

For information, contact
STATE UNIVERSITY OF NEW YORK PRESS, ALBANY, NY
www.sunypress.edu

Production, Laurie Searl
Marketing, Kate McDonnell

Library of Congress Cataloging-in-Publication Data

Neville, Robert C.
 Existence : philosophical theology / Robert Cummings Neville.
     pages cm
 "Volume two."
 Includes bibliographical references and index.
 ISBN 978-1-4384-5331-6 (hc : alk paper) 978-1-4384-5332-3 (pb : alk paper)
 1. Theological anthropology. 2. Philosophy and religion. 3. Ontology.
I. Title.
 BL256.N48 2014
 218—dc23   2013046365

for Nikolas Zanetti

The art on the cover of this volume is by Beth Neville, my wife, who has provided art for many of my SUNY Press books. She has my great thanks, as I said in the first volume of this *Philosophical Theology*. Like the cover art she did for *Ultimates: Philosophical Theology Volume One*, the colored-ink drawing for this volume's cover symbolically expresses its central themes. Though a square, the linear orientation is horizontal, indicating that this volume is about the human condition. The strongest horizontals are the two double cones pointing left and right with their longest ends. The human condition is of interest here because of the bearing it has on what is ultimate, symbolized most strongly by the touching of the tips of the short ends of the cones in the middle. The fact that the drawing has mirror images of left and right sides reflects the balanced importance of the two main topics of the human condition considered under the aspect of ultimacy, namely, human predicaments and ecstatic fulfillments. One of the main compositional elements is the strong horizontal thrusts of lateral semi-circles whose apexes are in the opposite side of the drawing from that in which their ends leave the picture. There are four of these semi-circles on each side, symbolizing the four cosmological ultimates that function in human predicaments and ecstatic fulfillments, respectively. Given that their arms cross one another, they inscribe four almond shapes in the center, indicating ultimacy, while they extend beyond their embrace to point to what lies beyond any finite harmony. On each side of the drawing are two portions of smaller semi-circles that originate in that side but extend outward without crossing to the other side, calling to mind the influence on any thing of other things outside it, and vice versa. Thus each thing is shown to harmonize its own components while including among those components the influences of other things and in turn influencing the others; nothing stands without internal integrity and external reference. The emotional and value intensity of the human condition has some cooling moments, but more red-hot connections, and at the center, the yellow fire of ultimacy. The argument of the book elaborates this symbolism.

Contents

Cross References	xiii
Preface	xv
Introduction	1
I. The Existential Dimensions of Religion	1
II. The Human Condition, Suffering, and Semiotics	9
III. Universality of Religion	15
IV. Ontological Ultimacy: Death and Life	18

Part I
Ultimate Boundary Conditions

Part I. Preliminary Remarks	25

Chapter One
Form as the Condition of Obligation — 31

I. Form and Human Possibility	32
II. Value	34
III. Obligation	36
IV. Obligations: Moral, Social, Personal, and Natural	43

Chapter Two
Components as the Condition for Grounded Wholeness — 49

I. Deference and Integration	50
II. Mythos: Orientation to Wholeness	52

III. Some Contemporary Christian Re-Mythologies	54
IV. Compartments: Appropriation, Deference, Negotiating Change, Realism	62

Chapter Three
Existential Location as the Condition for Engagement — 71

I. The Cosmology of Existential Location	72
II. Contours, Value, and Otherness	73
III. Human Engagement across the Existential Field	77
V. Modes of Engagement: Awareness, Appreciation, Courage, Love	79

Chapter Four
Value-Identity as the Condition for Meaning — 85

I. The Cosmology of Value-Identity	85
II. The Eternity of Value-Identity	88
III. The Symbolism of Meaning	90
IV. Modes of Achievement: Personal Goals, Contributions to Nature and Society, Facing Suffering, Relating to Ultimacy	96

Part I. Summary Implications — 101

Part II
Predicaments and Deliverances

Part II. Preliminary Remarks — 107

Chapter Five
Guilt and Justification — 113

I. Failure of Obligation: Damnation, Betrayal, Existential Refusal, Blood Guilt	114
II. Brokenness of Obligation	121
III. Deliverance from Moral and Social Guilt: Redemption and Restoration	125
IV. Deliverance from Personal and Natural Guilt: Sagacity and Purification	131

Chapter Six
Disintegration and Centeredness 135

    I. Disintegration: Alienation, Arrogance,
        Suffering, Delusion 136
    II. Centeredness: Deliverance from Disintegration 139
    III. Deliverance from Alienation and Arrogance:
        Healing and Humility 141
    IV. Deliverance from Suffering and Delusion:
        Comfort and Enlightenment 144

Chapter Seven
Estrangement and Connection 149

    I. Estrangements: Denial, Distortion, Despair, Hate 150
    II. Connection 153
    III. Deliverance from Denial and Distortion:
        Acceptance and Purgation 155
    IV. Deliverance from Despair and Hate:
        Faith and Reconciliation 160

Chapter Eight
Meaninglessness and Happiness 167

    I. Destruction of Meaning: Impotence, Isolation,
        Apathy, Non-Being 169
    II. The Ambiguity of Absolute Value-Identity 171
    III. Deliverance from Impotence and Isolation:
        Renunciation and Dedication 173
    IV. Deliverance from Apathy and Non-Being:
        Submission and Affirmation 177

Part II. Summary Implications 183

Part III
Ecstatic Fulfillments

Part III. Preliminary Remarks 189

Chapter Nine
Ecstatic Meaning in Time 195

    I. Meaning in Life 195
    II. Historical Apocalyptic 198

  III. Cosmic Apocalyptic   201
  IV. Time within Eternity   204

CHAPTER TEN
Ecstatic Life in Eternity   209
  I. The Problem of Ultimate Meaning   209
  II. Mapping the Infinite onto the Finite   212
  III. Eternal Life and Its Temporal Maps   216
  IV. The Truth of Finite Symbols of Ultimate Meaning   220

CHAPTER ELEVEN
Ecstatic Love   225
  I. Gratuity   226
  II. Arbitrariness   229
  III. Undeservedness   232
  IV. Surprise   234

CHAPTER TWELVE
Ecstatic Freedom   239
  I. Cosmological Freedom   239
  II. Release from Attachment to Finding Meaning   244
  III. Freedom in Becoming a Sign of Ultimacy   247
  IV. Freedom to Love   249

Part III. Summary Implications   253

PART IV
Engagement and Participation

Part IV. Preliminary Remarks   257

CHAPTER THIRTEEN
Ritual   261
  I. Anthropological Understandings of Ritual   261
  II. A Ritual Analysis   266
  III. Confucian Understandings of Ritual   274
  IV. Ritual Engagement   277

Chapter Fourteen
Commitment   279
    I. Bio-Developmental Dimensions of Commitment   280
    II. Religious Commitment and Worldviews   283
    III. Intensity of Religious Commitment   287
    IV. Sharing of Religious Commitment   290

Chapter Fifteen
The Life of Faith   293
    I. Preparation   293
    II. Presence and Action   297
    III. Relationships   300
    IV. Faith Enduring Change and Death   304

Chapter Sixteen
Inhabitation of a Sacred Worldview   307
    I. Sacred Worldviews   307
    II. Inhabiting Absolute Value-Identity   311
    III. The Ontological Shock of Creation   314
    IV. Chaos and Containment   316

Part IV. Summary Implications   319

Notes   323
Bibliography   337
Index   353

Cross References

As a systematic work, the three volumes of *Philosophical Theology* involve much cross-referencing among its parts. Although each of the volumes has a primary title—*Ultimates*, *Existence*, *Religion*—the cross-references are to the volumes by number. Cross-references are in endnotes on the occasion where commentary is required; otherwise they are in the text. The general rubric for cross-referencing is this: Cross-references will always be in *italics*, and this means that they refer to volumes of *Philosophical Theology*; the first roman numeral refers to the volume. If the reference is to a chapter, the volume number will be given first, followed by a comma, then the chapter number as an arabic number, and perhaps if needed a comma followed by a section number in lower-case roman numerals. So, "Volume II, Chapter 3, Section IV" would be *II, 3, iv*. If the reference is to a part in the volume, the roman volume number is first, followed by a comma and "pt" for part and an arabic numeral for the number of the part. So, "Volume II, Part III" would be *II, pt. 3*. Often a part is referred to as a whole; but if the reference is to the "preliminary remarks" or the "summary implications," which are always keyed to parts, not chapters, then the referent to the part would be followed by a comma and "pr" and/or "si." So, "Volume III, Part IV, preliminary remarks and summary implications" would be *III, pt. 4, pr, si*. If a reference does not indicate a volume number, this means the volume referred to is the one in which the reference is made. The text spells out titles of the three volumes when it discusses them directly.

Preface

The title of this second volume of *Philosophical Theology* is *Existence*, and the term is used in the sense associated with existentialism or the "philosophy of existence." The volume's overall thesis is that the existential reality of religion is engaged in two primary and sometimes overlapping ways: confronting ultimately important human predicaments and confronting ecstatic ultimate human fulfillments. The "existential reality of religion" is a pregnant phrase that cannot be defined so much as built up and illustrated. Its philosophic work arises from the background of existentialism in late Western thought and was contextualized in the Christian theologies of Rudolph Bultmann and Paul Tillich, among others. The influence of existentialism on construing religion in existential ways was not limited to its Western sphere. Keiji Nishitani and others in Japan, formulating a late-modern form of Buddhist philosophy or theology, dealt explicitly with the existentialist literature.[1] Following Tillich's language, we can delimit "the existential reality of religion" as those things that define a person ultimately. This is the primary meaning of the title, *Existence*; Nishitani explicitly used the term *Existenz*, as did Karl Jaspers.

Ultimates: Philosophical Theology One described these things that define a person ultimately as pertaining to "anthropological ultimates" (I, intro.; I, 5). The thesis here is that there are two kinds of things that define a person ultimately: engagements with ultimate predicaments of the human condition, and engagements with ultimate realities that ecstatically deliver a person beyond personal self-definition and into definition in terms of the ultimate realities themselves. From the perspective of ecstatic fulfillment, the human predicaments are not as important as they sometimes seem. Nishitani and Tillich agreed that the ecstatic relation to the ground of finite beings is the most fundamental reality of human beings and their most profound fulfillment, relativizing all others.

Existence: Philosophical Theology Two is an essay in theological anthropology. "Theological anthropology" is a Christian term for reflections on human nature, its conditions, and its processes insofar as they bear upon matters of ultimate significance. The bearing on matters of ultimate significance is what makes these topics religious and thus of theological interest. All long-reflecting and literate religious traditions have works in the genre of theological anthropology, whatever they call it, even if there is no reference to divinity (*theos*) in their symbols of ultimacy, as there is not in Buddhism. *Philosophical Theology One*, introduction, Section II defined religion as various human symbolic engagements of ultimacy expressed in cognitive articulations, existential responses to ultimacy that give ultimate definition to the individual and community, and patterns of life and ritual in the face of ultimacy. One dimension of the distinction between the three volumes of *Philosophical Theology* is that *One* deals with cognitive articulations, *Two* with existential responses to ultimacy, and *Three* with religious patterns of life. *One* studies ultimacy, ultimate reality, and similar cognates in detail, and some of the results of that study are summarized here and at other places in this volume. Theological anthropology thus deals with the religious dimensions of human nature, its conditions, and processes. *Philosophical Theology Three* elaborates hypotheses in detail that attempt to articulate salient characters of religion and religions.

To have a central portion of *Philosophical Theology* be a theological anthropology is particularly timely because of the recent publication of two extraordinary essays in theological anthropology, David H. Kelsey's *Eccentric Existence: A Theological Anthropology* (2009) and Wesley J. Wildman's *Science and Religious Anthropology: A Spiritually Evocative Naturalist Interpretation of Human Life* (2009).[2] In one sense, it would be hard to imagine two more diametrically opposed approaches. Kelsey's is a work within Christian theology, aimed at developing a cutting-edge Christian theological anthropology that addresses the concerns of contemporary people from the standpoint of his careful articulation of Christian revelation. Wildman's is a work designed to understand first what science has discovered (and where it is tentative, or mistaken, or lacking in attention or proper tools) about human nature and second to say how this reveals religious depths, which he articulates in terms of ultimacy. From Kelsey's standpoint, he himself is an insider to the Christian faith, and Wildman's anthropology is that of an outsider (although Wildman is an ordained Christian minister whose job is at a United Methodist theological school). From Wildman's standpoint, he himself is an insider to the broad secular academy that includes science and the humanities within the public to which he is accountable, whereas Kelsey is a particular confessional theologian whose basic Christian premises are nonnegotiable. Kelsey writes,

> I suggest that the claims about human beings that are nonnegotiable for Christian faith are claims about how God relates to human beings. These claims are as follows: (a) God actively relates to human beings

to create them, (b) to draw them to eschatological consummation, and (c) to reconcile them when they are alienated from God.[3]

Compare this with Wildman's assertion that the ultimate is not a God who is a determinate being who "does things," such as create, save, or reconcile. The virtues he claims for his account are:

(i) [I]t properly registers universal or near-universal components of the human condition, from the cultural to the biological; (ii) it integrates every discipline and level of understanding about the human condition and human nature; (iii) it naturally relates these components of human life to the depths of natural reality in such a way that the determinate character of those ecstatic depths is disclosed; (iv) it renders more conceptually consistent the religious schemas that govern the interpretation of symbols of the human condition that arise within cultural and religious spheres of wisdom; and (v) while it does not appeal to everyone, it is profoundly intellectually illuminating and spiritually rewarding for those drawn to it.[4]

These are extremely different approaches to theological anthropology and, in the current theological context in America, represent opposing, sometimes hostile, positions.

Yet they share important similarities. Both, for instance, explicitly write out of a self-affirmed particular intellectual tradition. Kelsey writes as a Christian and has an eloquent defense of particularity.[5] Wildman is equally clear that, although he might have written as a Christian theologian given his own background and religious life, he is writing as a member of the secular academy, albeit the topic is religion.[6] The disciplinary humility of particularity is evident in both, even though Kelsey's topic is the implications of the Christian God for all humanity and Wildman's is the nature of all humanity (or at least most) as referred to the ultimate. Another similarity is that both believe that theological anthropology is hypothetical, not deductive in any sense.[7] For Kelsey, the particularism of the Christian context entails that certain Christian principles are nonnegotiable, even though all are subject to interpretation of the daring sort in which Kelsey engages. For Wildman, even though no religious premises are nonnegotiable because such nonnegotiable premises would have to come from a supernatural or supranatural source that he rejects, that very point is nonnegotiable as a commitment of the secular academy and especially of his naturalistic religious philosophy, a direct parallel of nonnegotiability relative to a particular context commitment.[8]

The most striking, and intellectually fruitful, difference between them is what they leave out. Kelsey writes with only a little mention of what modern science has learned about human nature, although what he says is sensitive and sometimes detailed. It is as if contemporary science only gives up-to-date ways of saying what theologians should say about human nature as determined by other considerations. Wildman, by contrast, devotes the predominant weight of his book to analyzing the findings of science in a host of areas of human life, extracting from them the religiosity that allows him to argue for his main thesis: that to be human is to be *Homo religiosus*. For his part, however, Wildman pays almost no attention to what might be wrong with the human condition such that, as Kelsey would put it in Christian terms, people abort their creaturely status, miss their eschatological mark, and need reconciliation. Wildman's presentation of human nature is that it is filled with troubles but few existential contradictions save those of evolutionary immaturity and mis-fit to the environment.

Philosophical Theology Two's theological anthropology pitches its tents in a middle ground between Kelsey and Wildman, embracing both to a very large extent, although set in a context of global religions that is appreciated but not inhabited by either here to any great extent.[9] Like Kelsey, it tracks a worm within the human condition that gives religion a special place, not just as an evolved phenomenon as analyzed in *Philosophical Theology Three* but as a response to deep flaws in the human condition. Also like Kelsey, it tracks religious ecstatic fulfillment, which Kelsey names in Christian terms as "eschatological consummation." Ecstatic fulfillment or eschatological consummation is obviously a function of experience in some respect, and Wildman has devoted an entire volume to the subject, *Religious and Spiritual Experiences*. But Wildman's study carefully delimits itself to the qualities and causes of the experiences, avoiding in principle any question of how the "religious and spiritual experiences" are definitive of human life in relation to ultimate reality or realities, although he does assess their (fallible) cognitive reliability. *Philosophical Theology* takes ecstatic fulfillment to be definitive for how human beings can relate to ultimate reality. The term "ecstasy" in the phrase "ecstatic fulfillment" takes its penumbra of connotations from the work of Robert S. Corrington, who calls his position "ecstatic naturalism."[10] The capacity for ecstatic religious fulfillment is just as important for defining people religiously relative to the ultimate as the pervasive problematics of religious predicaments. *Philosophical Theology* holds that the various personal and cultural ways in which this ecstatic fulfillment is experienced are somehow less important than the ways by which they relate human beings to ultimacy.

The two central parts of this volume deal directly with the existential reality of religion, with Part I being something of a philosophical prologue and Part IV being an afterword examining practice. Part II, Predicaments and Deliverances, discusses the flaws relative to ultimacy in human life and remedies religion offers for these flaws. The flaws are understood as types relative to each of the ultimate boundary conditions described in Part I with their mutual implications, and the remedies are relative to these types of flaw. The boundary conditions themselves are understood in terms of the cosmological ultimates examined in *Philosophical Theology One*. The chapters of both Part I and Part II here follow the order of those cosmological ultimates:

form, components formed, existential location, and value-identity. Existential theologians such as Tillich and Nishitani construe the human predicament(s) to be the principal factor in the human condition. Both see something like ecstatic fulfillments as ways of solving the problems of the predicaments. The validity of their point is acknowledged here. But the argument of Part III is that ecstatic fulfillments are religious venues of their own partially independent of the predicaments. Some people can find ecstatic fulfillment without resolving their predicaments much at all. Part III, Ecstatic Fulfillments, has four main themes: fulfillment or ecstatic meaningfulness in time, ecstatic life in eternity, ecstatic love, and ecstatic freedom, each the subject of a chapter. This part does not strictly follow the symmetry of Parts I and II in the order of the cosmological ultimates. Therefore the structural architectonic of Part III is not as obvious as that of the earlier parts. At a slightly greater metaphorical distance, however, they do follow the architectonic of the cosmological ultimates. Meaningfulness in time is tied to choices relative to possibilities as people live out their temporal lives. "Living in eternity" is a function of how the components of life are integrated, the ultimate venue of wholeness. "Ecstatic love" is first and foremost an orientation toward others in the existential field, although its ultimate venue is all the created things insofar as they are together: the cosmological field of mutual relations is possible only because of the ontological field of mutual relevance, explained at length in *Philosophical Theology One*, Part III. "Ecstatic freedom" is found in the venue of achieved value-identity, a somewhat ironic point because what one has already achieved in life is something one no longer has the freedom to change.

An unusual organizational character of Kelsey's *Eccentric Existence* is that it places the discussion of eschatological consummation before its discussion of redemption or what it calls "reconciliation." The standard Christian form for systematic theologies is "creation, fall, and redemption," and Kelsey reverses the last two. *Philosophical Theology Two* very well could have followed Kelsey's model: the positive engagement of ultimacy, resulting in ecstatic fulfillment (or eschatological consummation), could be treated before the negative engagements of ultimate predicaments. In some ways it would be more natural to explore how human life can be given ultimate significance by its positive engagements of ultimacy before tackling the problems of how that relation to ultimacy is flawed. In this volume, however, the more usual order is followed, mainly because both ultimate predicaments and ecstatic fulfillments are analyzed philosophically and the details of the philosophic analysis are more perspicuously laid out in terms of the conditions for the predicaments than would be possible in terms of the conditions for the fulfillments. Kelsey gives rhetorically controlling power to personifying metaphors for the ultimate, so that "creation," "consummation," and "reconciliation" are discussed in the rhetorical ambiance of the "will" of God, something *Philosophical Theology* would do hesitantly as only one metaphorical system among others. It agrees with Kelsey, however, that the religiously important elements of theological anthropology have to do with how we are defined in relation to ultimate reality. Wildman has not been persuaded to do this, rather using anthropological and experiential elements of the human condition only to point to ultimate reality.

Like Wildman, however, *Philosophical Theology* enthusiastically accepts the findings of science, controlling for mistakes, tentativeness, and the never-finished character of scientific inquiry. Wildman calls this the "modern secular interpretation of humanity," and claims rightly that any theological anthropology ought to be constrained to be roughly consistent with this interpretation, qualified by the ongoing fallible shifts and lacunae of the sciences. But unlike Wildman, *Philosophical Theology Two* probes the predicaments for human life that come from the nature of ultimacy and not only from the ultimately important affairs of evolution and the value structures that appear in evolutionary history. Unlike Kelsey, it holds to nothing nonnegotiable within Christian revelation and indeed accepts revelation as merely the revelation of new dimensions of reality that come from the development of better signs for interpreting it; it treats all the other religious traditions the same way.[11] Unlike Wildman, it treats allegiance to the secular academy as itself also negotiable, fearing that complacence in this matter runs the danger of scientism. But like Wildman in his epistemological theory, it construes the real public to which theological anthropology is accountable to be the array of all disciplines and perspectives that might have an interest in the matter. Unlike Wildman, *Philosophical Theology* takes in many of the perspectives that have been excluded unjustly from the academy and includes the positive arguments that might be made for the charismatic authority of traditional scriptures and founding events as subject to interpretation.[12]

At the heart of the difference between Kelsey and Wildman is the primary "object" of their discussion. For Kelsey, it is the religious individual, however much the individual is embraced within and defined by society, culture, and religious community. For Wildman it is groups that define religious traits for the individuals within them, whether the groups are evolutionary human populations; biological groups; or social, cultural, and religious groups. For Wildman, the point of theological anthropology is that human beings as a group or species are *Homo religiosus*. For Kelsey, it is how individuals are defined by their relation to God and God's particular work with them in creation, fulfillment, and redemption, given that individuals experience their condition as broken. *Philosophical Theology* addresses Kelsey's problematic mainly in *Two* and Wildman's problematic mainly in *Three* and attempts to integrate them.

Different from both Kelsey and Wildman, *Philosophical Theology Two* organizes its argument on a philosophical interpretation of ultimacy. The human predicaments and ecstatic fulfillments arise not from an action by a determinate God nor only from matters in the biocultural evolution of human beings but also from the fact that human beings universally bump up against fundamental structures of reality that are ultimate. They are ultimate, from a metaphysical point of view, as ultimate traits or conditions of anything real and, from the human point of view, in that they constitute boundary conditions for the human world. *Philosophical Theology One*, Part III argued that there is one ontological ultimate and four cosmological ultimates; the points are rehearsed in the present volume in the Preliminary Remarks to Part I. The four cosmological ultimates derive from the very structure of determinateness—anything whatsoever is determinate in being what it is and not being something else. These ultimates are: form, components formed in the determinate thing, existential location with respect to other things, and the value-identity achieved by getting these components together with this form in this existential location. From the human perspective, form appears as possibilities with alternative ways of being actualized in human choice that have different values, putting people under obligation to actualize the better. Components have values of their own that not only need to be treated with proper comportment but also harmonized so as to give wholeness to individuals' lives. Existential location puts people in relation to other people and the social and natural environments such that those should be appreciated and loved for the created values they have and might have. And people need to achieve some value in their identity that gives meaning to their lives; their value-identity consists in both the values achieved within the harmonies of their lives (subjective value) and the values they cause or affect in other things as integrated into those other things' harmonies. As to ontological ultimacy, all the aforementioned are the result of an ontological creative act that ought, from the human perspective, to be appreciated in gratitude as an affirmation of being.

The human predicaments have a roughly similar threefold character. With reference to each of these ultimates, people generally are failures; from this it is common that people proceed to downplay or even reject the normativeness of these ultimates (to be just, develop wholeness, be compassionate, accomplish something, and give grateful consent to existence itself). Then in a further, contradictory step, people tumble to reject themselves both for their failures and for their alienation from the norms of the human condition, often extending this to a rejection of existence itself. Ultimately important predicaments have some version of this three-step fall: (1) failure, (2) rejection of the norms of the human condition, and (3) rejection of the self and existence because of both of these. This scheme will be introduced more fully in the introduction and developed piecemeal throughout Part II.

Ecstatic fulfillment has many intertwining dimensions, and religious and imaginative cultures have differing symbols for all of these. *Philosophical Theology* gives a two-way analysis of this situation. One way is from the perspective of human beings on the ultimate. This perspective is itself bifocal. One lens sees the ontological act of creation from our position within time (II, 9) with all this entails about our lives as agents and patients in the midst of historical conditions; the dominant concern here is with our choices relative to what is ultimate. The other lens sees the ontological act of creation as the concrete reality, that is, the eternal reality (*II, 10*), within which our lives have meaning and identity, including the significance and insignificance of our choices; the dominant concern here is the integration of our fragmentary wholeness within the eternal whole.

The other analysis of the situation of ecstatic fulfillment is from the perspective of human identification with the ontological act, not so much relating to it but being part of it. This perspective is also bifocal. Relative to what it produces, the ontological creative act is loving, and sexual images are prevalent in expressing this dimension of ecstatic fulfillment. Of course, the ontological creative act does not produce anything that is other than itself: the act includes its products as its terminus. Human beings are always in a situation faced by others. But in various ways, identification with the ontological creative act provides at least a simulacrum of the love that results or consists in ejaculatory birthing of the other, a love that does not cast off its offspring but that does not reduce it to the lover's love either (*II, 11*). The other lens on ecstatic fulfillment from the standpoint of the ontological creative act is on the act itself, rather than mainly the product, and what this lens sees is freedom. This freedom is gracious, arbitrary, not bound by value, and surprising. To the extent ecstatic fulfillment involves identification with this freedom, we enjoy perfect freedom despite the constraints of form, our components, our existential field, and our actual achieved value (*II, 12*).

"Ecstatic fulfillment" has a peculiar bias in that it structures its network of points around people being fulfilled. Its points might be made another way, through elucidating the qualities of ultimacy grasped in experiences that are fulfilling. The strange beauty of existence in the face of all its horrors has a kind of reality that relativizes the ecstasies of specific paths and that can be grasped by people in any condition, including people far from any virtuosity of religious fulfillment. The beauty is, of course, some quality of the value that pervades any congeries of determinate things. It need not be connected with unusual experiences—only, perhaps, with the singularity of a scene that instances the singularity of the ontological act of creation itself.

A special point should be noted about value, which is construed here as a trait of anything that has form. Most kinds of Western reflection now assume that reality is only objective fact and that nothing has intrinsic value except as a function of one or another kind of human subjective valuing intentionality. This view was commonsensically preposterous from the standpoint of East Asian thought up until the recent powerful influence of Western thinking. It is also contrary to the common experience of almost everyone that the things of the world are value laden and that we can be wrong about them. Experience itself of course is shaped by many cultural and purposive factors of intentionality, and so the values recognized in the world are intended by the shaping elements of human interests. But people ordinarily suppose that their interests ought to be aimed at the things worth being interested in, not that their interests are entirely arbitrary and are the sole bestowers of values on their objects.

In accord with most common sense and most traditions other than those of the modern West, *Philosophical Theology* argues for the universality of value in anything that has form (*I, 10; III, 9*). It claims that to be determinate at all is to have value; to be is to have value. This claim for the universality of value in anything that has form makes an enormous difference in many areas of religious and moral thinking. Combined with the theory of experience as symbolic engagement (*I, 3*), the hypothesis of the universality of value properly balances the "objective" and "subjective" elements in the human experience of value in the value-laden realities of the world. Chapter 1 in this volume develops the hypothesis about the universality of value in form.

I thank the following students from the doctoral seminar in Advanced Systematic Theology 2 in the spring of 2011 for their careful reading and helpful comments on a draft of this volume: Nicholas DiDonato, Bethany Joy Floch, Sungrae Kim, Divine Mungre, Imani-Sheila Newsome-McLaughlin, and Lancelot Watson. Similar thanks go to students and colleagues in the same course offered in the spring of 2013: Yohan Go, Josh Hasler, Jong Wook Hong, Xinjun Liu, David Rohr, Bin Song, and Ulrich Winkler. This volume is intimately connected with the other two volumes of *Philosophical Theology*, and the thanks to organizations and people expressed in their prefaces hold for this volume as well. Nathaniel F. Barrett has been an important conversation partner for many years, particularly on the topic of value that pervades this volume, especially Chapter 1. Christian Polke read the whole after the first draft was finished and offered important corrections. Gratitude particularly should be repeated here for conversations and responses to this text from Wesley J. Wildman, John H. Berthrong, Christian Polke, Ray L. Hart, Robert Corrington, Rick Peters, Jay Schulkin, Beth Neville, and Nikolas Zanetti.[13]

All quotations from the Hebrew and Christian Bibles, unless otherwise noted, are from the New Revised Standard Version, copyrighted in 1989 by the Division of Christian Education of the National Council of the Churches of Christ in the United States of America. References for all other citations are in the bibliography.

This volume is dedicated to Nikolas Zanetti, who not only met with me twice a week during the years of drafting *Philosophical Theology* but exemplifies in my experience the drive to virtuosity both in coping with the central predicaments of the human condition and in celebrating its ultimate ecstatic fulfillments. He also has made me feel that I have something of intellectual worth to teach by his reception and magnification of it. No Confucian could ask for greater filiality.

Introduction

I. THE EXISTENTIAL DIMENSIONS OF RELIGION

William James, in his landmark *The Varieties of Religious Experience*, noted that two "branches" in the study of religion exist, which he called the "institutional" and the "personal." Each offers many definitions of religion, but he opted for the personal and so set up his inquiry with the following:

> Religion, therefore, as I now ask you arbitrarily to take it, shall mean for us *the feelings, acts, and experiences of individual men in their solitude, so far as they apprehend themselves to stand in relation to whatever they may consider the divine*. Since that relation may be either moral, physical, or ritual, it is evident that out of religion in the sense in which we take it, theologies, philosophies, and ecclesiastical organizations may secondarily grow. In these lectures, however, as I have already said, the immediate personal experiences will amply fill our time, and we shall hardly consider theology or ecclesiasticism at all.[1]

James, like the other pragmatists, understood the social dimensions of experience, but with regard to religion, the personal, the solitary, is most important to study, he thought.

Alfred North Whitehead was even more emphatic in emphasizing the personal. Whereas James acknowledged two branches of study of religion, Whitehead *defined* religion in personal or individual terms. His eloquence in the first chapter of *Religion in the Making* is important to quote at length.

> Religion is force of belief cleansing the inward parts. For this reason the primary religious virtue is sincerity, a penetrating sincerity. . . .

In the long run your character and your conduct of life depend upon your intimate convictions. . . . The conduct of external life is conditioned by environment, but it receives its final quality, on which its worth depends, from the internal life which is the self-realization of existence. Religion is the art and the theory of the internal life of man, so far as it depends on the man himself and on what is permanent in the nature of things. . . .

Religion is what the individual does with his own solitariness. . . .

Thus religion is solitariness; and if you are never solitary, you are never religious. Collective enthusiasms, revivals, institutions, churches, rituals, bibles, codes of behavior, are the trappings of religion, its passing forms. They may be useful, or harmful; they may be authoritatively ordained, or merely temporary expedients. But the end of religion is beyond all this.[2]

Although both James and Whitehead recognized the social dimensions of religion, they took the individual's perspective, and that in some solitariness, to be more important. Most social science approaches to religion, excluding some forms of psychology, construe this individualism to be an extraordinary Protestant Christian bias.[3] True, the Protestant existentialist Søren Kierkegaard is the epitome of inwardness, subjectivity, and individual self-determination in religion. Martin Luther's most famous quotation is "Here I stand: I can do no other." Protestantism has not been exclusively individualistic, however. John Wesley and the Methodist movement, now in several denominations, emphasized the environmental conditions for saintliness, promoting grade school, high school, and college education, for instance; Protestant liberalism developed the progressive social gospel movement in Europe and America. Nor is emphasis on the individual perspective particularly limited to Protestantism. Augustine invented the genre of the confession, and confession is the most intimate relation of an individual to whatever the individual "considers the divine," as James put it. Confession and penance are central to monastic movements, especially in their anchorite manifestations. Eastern as well as Western Christianity is extraordinarily inward in that sense, employing its social forms to focus away from the social on the individual in relation to God.

Focus on the inward and solitary is by no means limited to Christianity. Most forms of monasticism, as in Buddhism, Jainism, Daoism, and some forms of Hinduism work to bring into disciplined articulation the individual's own reality. Nishida brought this focus to his twentieth-century Buddhism. This inward emphasis is especially strong in the renouncer forms of Hinduism, which usually also have shadow realities in those forms that emphasize the dharma of domestic life. The heart of Islam is the submission of the individual to Allah, and the social dimensions of Islam, which are extremely prominent in its social presentations, are only the context and medium of that individual submission. Confucianism is known for its emphasis on social ritual, and that will be significant in *Philosophical Theology Two* and *Three*. But the emphasis on sincerity goes back to Confucius. In one way or another most Confucians would agree with Wang Yangming on the unity of thought and action. Tu Weiming explicitly connects Confucian inwardness to the Western existentialist problematic.[4]

With the help of the metaphysics developed in *Philosophical Theology One*, Chapter 10, and shortly to be rehearsed in the Preliminary Remarks to Part I, we are in a position to say with more precision than Whitehead and James why they are right about the importance of religion's interiority. According to that metaphysical hypothesis, to be determinate at all, a thing has to be a harmony of two kinds of components, conditional and essential. The conditional components are those by virtue of which the thing is related to other things so as to be determinate with respect to them. The essential components are those that integrate the conditional components so that the thing has its own reality. Without the conditional components, the thing would not be determinate with respect to other things and could not exist. Without the essential components, the thing would not exist over and above the components considered separately.

With respect to religion, in these volumes religion is defined as *human engagement of ultimacy expressed in cognitive articulations, existential responses to ultimacy that give ultimate definition to the individual and community, and patterns of life and ritual in the fact of ultimacy* (I, intro., ii). This means that religion requires among its conditions that there be semiotic systems, languages, and cultures for cognitive articulation of ultimacy, that there be ways in which individual and communities are defined, and that there be religious and social communities as such in which religion can be lived out. But all these things might be present in an individual without being integrated in such a way as actually to engage ultimate realities. In addition to these and other conditional components of religion, there need to be the essential features that deploy them so that ultimate realities and ultimate dimensions of reality are actually engaged. A religious culture with all its symbols in play and a religious community with all its religious practices being observed are not really religious unless individuals actually engage ultimate realities in and through them. This point can be deeply frustrating for social scientists who want to identify religion with cultures, traditions, or communities and yet want to avoid judging whether ultimacy is actually engaged. Not surprisingly, religion for them morphs into, or is reduced to, what is studied by anthropology, history, sociology, or some scientific variant, a point to be discussed in *Philosophical Theology Three*, Chapter 1. Critics in every religious tradition, however, have complained when the practices become hollow, the symbols lose their capacity to engage ultimacy, and communities become false to their genuine roles in hosting engagements with ultimacy. The social dimensions of religion have their own dynamics irrespective of whether they are actual vehicles for religious engagement. When they do in fact function not as mere social realities but also as religious realities, it is because the individuals within them have the essential features to organize them so as to actualize the engagement. The essential components of religion that turn the conditional components of religion into components of actual engagements of ultimacy are the interior kinds of things to which James and Whitehead allude. They are studied in Part IV here.

What can we say of the near universality of the religious stress on inwardness, particularly in light of the near universality of a tension between that and a stress on social embodiedness and the existence of what James called two "branches" of reflection on religion, the personal and the social?

Only the individual perspective allows us to make sense of the ultimate seriousness of life's brokenness and ecstatic fulfillments. Recognition from the solitary perspective of how an individual faces what is ultimately important in life is what requires, and legitimates, the interpretation of life as determined by religious predicaments and fulfillments. Therefore, the focus of this volume of *Philosophical Theology* on predicaments, religious remedies, and ecstatic fulfillments involves the central employment of the perspective of the individual.

Religion: Philosophical Theology Three focuses more on the study of religion and religions, and how individuals find or create communities of religious life together. Many of its discussions treat religions as groups, and speak of individuals primarily as members of groups. Those discussions, while important, do not have as their direct objects individuals who are religious, only patterns and problems of religiosity. *Philosophical Theology Two* sets the conditions by means of the individual perspective for interpreting the social aspects as religious instead of merely social, political, and cultural. The discussions of ritual and community in *Philosophical Theology Two* take the form of asking how individuals can participate. Religion is tied to how individuals engage ultimacy in their thoughts, practices, and existential determinations, and this individual perspective is not to be lost when we note that thoughts are framed in cultural semiotics, practices are socially learned even when solitary, and existential determinations are particular to individuals' social situations. The social dimensions are important on their own, which is why they command a whole volume in this study. But they cannot be separated from the existential solitariness of the individual perspectives on ultimacy that interpret religion as existing in response to ultimate human predicaments and ecstatic fulfillments.

The metaphysics elaborated in *Philosophical Theology One*, Chapter 10, Section I, offers what at this stage in the argument at least is a metaphor for the distinction between the interior and the other dimensions of religion. Any thing, in the present case a person, has two kinds of components, conditional and essential. The thing necessarily is a harmony of both kinds and both are necessary for the harmony. The conditional components derive from those things with respect to which the harmony (or person) is determinate, some of which are themselves necessary for the harmony to exist at all and others of which are accidental to what the harmony is. Among the conditional components for a religious individual are the social things that bear upon religion, for instance, as listed by Whitehead and James, as well as the physical and other conditions that allow the person to exist as religious. The essential components are those that integrate all the conditional components so that the person is religious, and these for the most part are the interior elements, those that appear more strongly in the solitariness of individuals. Without the essential interior elements, the person would not be religious, that is, engaging ultimate matters. All the conditional components might be there without being integrated so as to constitute religiosity. Prophets have long complained about the observance of the social and physical forms of religiosity that do not have the living waters of religion in them. Those forms might be studied on their own without any serious mention of religion. Religion is the symbolic engagement of ultimacy, and its essential components are mainly those of interior solitude while its conditional components are all the other conditions that might or must be present but would not be religious without the essential elements. Both essential and conditional components are equally necessary for religion, but the conditional components such as religious institutions can be present without being religious; the essential components are impossible without the conditional ones to integrate. This volume focuses on the essential components of religion as the symbolic engagement of ultimacy whereas *Philosophical Theology Three* focuses on some of the conditional components.

The central thesis of *Philosophical Theology Two*, Part II, in its discussion of predicaments and deliverances, is that typically if not universally something ultimately important is wrong with human life and that religion in part is the attempt to rectify, fix, or heal that wrong. This thesis is extraordinarily complex and multidimensional. *Philosophical Theology Three* studies religion as ways of life that engage ultimacy more or less well, including but not exclusively involving ways of remedying the ultimate wrongnesses of life and shaping ecstatic fulfillments. But the question for *Philosophical Theology Two* has something of a prior status: What is the work that religion does in remedying predicaments and forging paths to ecstatic fulfillment? This is related to but not identical to the question of how or why religion arose with the biological evolution of human beings. Religion obviously had some adaptive value so as to become a universal human phenomenon, but that adaptive value might be a mere side effect of religion's main work of remedying ultimately important wrongs and giving orientation to ecstatic fulfillments. *Philosophical Theology Two* focuses on what it is in the human condition that makes religion important or even necessary in the first place.

The predicament languages of "wrongness and rectification," "brokenness and fixing," "sickness and healing," and the like, are not quite right. The first carries too many moral connotations, the second seems too mechanical, and the third too organic. Moreover, metaphors like these do not convey the sense of aesthetic wonder, awe, and poignancy that religions struggle to shape as ecstatic fulfillments and without which we are inhumanly stupid. In some profound sense, religion's work is to give poetic voice to our incomprehension of the depth of the ultimate realities that define human existence. Then again, many people think the real work of religion is to cope with suffering, or guilt, or death. Furthermore, the negativity in these metaphors, appropriate as it is, is not the whole of religion: the positive side of religion is what Part III calls "ecstatic fulfillment," which strangely is compatible with unfixed brokenness. All these issues are discussed in this volume and given their due in integrated fashion. Nevertheless, none of the metaphors is ever fully adequate.

Religion becomes an existential necessity when a crisis occurs that is ultimately important in the sense of questioning an ultimate boundary condition of life. This occurs on the cultural level as well as the personal. Paul Tillich in *The Courage to Be* said that the predominant thematic crisis of the ancient Near East at the time of the rise of Christianity and Rabbinic Judaism was panic over mortality and immortality; this focused the many dimensions of human predicament through the lens of the ontological question of existence itself. Tillich said the crisis of the late medieval and early Reformation period was guilt and eternal punishment or salvation, a focus through the lens of the predicaments of obligation. The modern crisis, he thought, is the quest for meaning in a meaningless cosmos, focusing through the lens of value-identity. We can also note a strong concern, at least in developed societies, with human beings as Others and with the environment, a focus through the lens of "engaging others in the existential field." Also, there is a prominent concern in developed societies with psychological and physical healing, a focus through the lens of wholeness with regard to life's components.

Tillich was speaking mainly of Christian cultures as he understood them. In an analogous vein it can be said that the thematic crisis of ancient China was how to establish orderly rule out of social chaos; the crisis for medieval Tong and Song dynasty China was how to absorb serious foreign influences, such as Buddhism, Christianity, and Islam, and to re-Sinicize an integral Chinese culture with spiritual depth and metaphysical breadth; the contemporary problem for China is to pull all the other world cultures into its orbit so as once again to be the center.[5] The rhetorical center of gravity of Christian and Confucian traditions was taken from the thematic crises of the ancient period and modified by the concerns of later periods.

Sometimes individuals in crisis have a religious culture already in hand that scripts responses, and the practical issues are how to engage that religion appropriately and effectively. Sometimes no religion is near at hand and people go in search of religious answers, appealing to already formed religious strictures or attempting to cobble together new ones. By "religion" in this context is meant a worldview containing a sacred canopy of symbols of ultimate matters that can provide cognitive, emotional, and behavioral priorities in response to the crisis (*I, 1, 4; III, 4*).

Concerns about ultimate matters lie on a continuum (I, 5). Toward one end are people who have few if any ultimate concerns, only mundane proximate ones, with at best mild interest in the representations of ultimate matters in the religious worldviews at hand. Few people, however, can live long without some crisis or other that does raise ultimate questions, the death of a friend, for instance, or the failure of a friendship, or some traumatic dislocation or violence, or loss of a career. Religion's worldviews offer guidance about priorities in times of crisis and, as people become more concerned about ultimate matters, they take religion more seriously, perhaps engaging the religion within which they live with greater zest, perhaps seeking out a better religious worldview. The more their concern develops, the more they define the domains of their life in terms of the religious priorities, perhaps defining themselves in many if not all ways by the ideas, spiritual practices, and activities of their religious worldview. For some few people toward the other end of the continuum, religious adepts, the concern for ultimate reality slowly switches from looking for that reality to provide priorities for life to looking for how to embrace that ultimate reality more closely, to conform to it, merge with it, abandon oneself to it—the metaphors for this are legion. This extreme form of ultimate concern might take shape as ecstatic fulfillment, although ecstatic fulfillment need not be a function of a concern, strictly speaking. In this other extreme of the ultimate concern continuum, one's own life ceases to be ultimately important, only proximately important; religion's priorities may be continued as guides but not as ultimately important ones. Religion itself slides to proximate importance, relativized, treated as convention to be followed (or not) as life makes practical. This phenomenon is as prevalent in Buddhist devotees and Hindu renunciants for whom the ultimate is modeled on some extrapolation of consciousness, and in Daoist adepts and Confucian sages for whom the ultimate is modeled on emergence, as it is in Jewish, Christian, and Muslim mystics who start with a personal model of the ultimate and tip transcendence beyond all models.[6]

Philosophical Theology Two, regarding predicaments in Part II, mostly is about the need for religion in the large middle stretch of the ultimate concern continuum when existential crises make religion necessary for the sake of orientation and the prioritizing of life's domains. It is not very much about the people whose lives seem untouched by ultimate issues. Nor does it focus much until Part III on those whose religion has gone so far as to abnegate ultimate significance to personal or communal life in favor of abandoning oneself to the religious object.

The outline of *Philosophical Theology Two* is as follows. Part I analyzes the ways in which the transcendental cosmological ultimates of form, components, existential location, and value-identity constitute the human ultimate boundary conditions of obligation, wholeness, engagement, and meaning. Each boundary condition is analyzed in its own chapter, and in each case it is shown to have some kind of normative claim on human life. At the root of what it means to be human is not just to have the DNA of *Homo sapiens sapiens* and to belong to human biological and social communities: what is definitive of the human is being under obligation, needing wholeness, engaging others properly, and seeking a value in life that has meaning. These together constitute, for human beings, what it means to be creatures of an ontological act that creates the whole world. Because these transcendental traits of determinateness are the boundary conditions for any determinate thing, they would apply to all creatures if the creatures had the mental, semiotic, and voluntary capacities to take them to be normative for what they might and might not do. Paul Tillich based his *Systematic Theology* on a surprisingly obscure distinction between the "essential" conditions of life and the "existential." The normative status of the ultimate boundary conditions for human life as described in Part I might well be something like what he meant by the "essential" conditions.

Part II then studies, chapter by chapter, how each of the normative ultimate boundary conditions gives rise to failure, and that failure is an ultimate human predicament. Each chapter also discusses the fall from the predicament of failure into the deeper brokenness of the rejection of the relevant normative ultimate condition and also self-condemnation or nihilism. These constitute four kinds of ultimate human predicament. This is close to what Tillich meant by the "existential" conditions of life. Moreover, each of these cosmological kinds of predicament is a path leading to the ontological predicament: the ontological contingency of the world on the ontological act becomes for human life a reality to be affirmed in gratitude but often denied in resentment. Each chapter shows how some aspect of the ontological ultimate is revealed in each cosmological predicament. Of course, the four predicaments and their problematics overlap and interweave in complex ways. The response of religion to these four kinds of predicaments, their brokenness and fall, is sketched in each chapter. In reference to the human predicaments, religion is to be understood as the offering of deliverance, in each of the many types of predicament involved.

The emphasis on ultimate predicaments and their remedies makes it seem as if religion were only a response to problems. In contrast to the negative tone of this part of the inquiry, it needs to be stressed that religion is also a medium of ecstatic ultimate fulfillment, a joyous celebration of existence or rather many forms of ecstatic, joyous celebration. Part III argues that these forms of ecstatic fulfillment are different from and in their ways transcend other forms of human fulfillment that are not so explicitly and directly involved with engaging ultimacy. The human "justification" of religion lies only partially in its remedies for the ultimate human predicaments; indeed, so often those remedies do not work. And very often religion's remedies bring in their own consequences of violence, hatred, bitterness, and cultural oppositions to far better ways of life. The most important "justification" of religion is that it enables ecstatic ultimate fulfillment, something no other cultural enterprise can do.

Ecstatic religious fulfillment cannot be separated from ultimate predicaments and religious attempts to address them, although it cannot be reduced to extremely successful remedies of failure as Tillich and Nishitani seem to do. Only the seriousness of the engagement of the predicaments, always on the edge of ontological shock, can keep ecstatic religious fulfillment from being simply feel-good experiences. Feel-good experiences are easily manufactured by cheap religion and even by what pretends to be nothing more than entertainment. Ecstatic experiences of power, belonging, and victory can be demonic in the extreme. The signs involved in all concrete experiences have their own material quality, "how they feel" (*I, 2–3*), and that feeling might be ecstatically, orgasmically, pleasurable. But whether those experiences with ecstatic feelings genuinely engage what is ultimate, and thereby have religious significance, depends on whether they are embedded in real engagements with ultimate realities. The context of engaging ultimate predicaments, with all their negativities, is what allows for the critical connection of ecstatic feelings with ultimacy that constitutes genuine ecstatic religious fulfillment.

The reference to ultimate structures of reality and the philosophical analysis articulating them should not deflect attention from the jarring bluntness of existentially ultimate crises. Religion does not arise only or even mainly out of philosophy, although philosophy shapes what religion becomes in response to human predicaments. Rather, religion arises incrementally out of predicaments that characterize the human condition as such and out of shocking experiences of ecstatic fulfillment. At least, this is the hypothesis that is developed here, along with the philosophical hypotheses about ultimate realities.

Part IV of this volume explores some of the connections that individuals have with religion or religions, emphasizing the perspective of the individual participating in larger social realities. Anticipating some of the analyses of the organized aspects of religion to be treated in *Philosophical Theology Three*, its chapters nevertheless focus on how individuals access religion to deal with their predicaments and ecstatic fulfillments.

This quick and sketchy exposition of the hypothesis about the human condition, its predicaments and ecstatic fulfillments, and religion's role in all this, is problematic even as an introduction to what is to come. The remainder of this introduction elucidates some of its limitations.

II. THE HUMAN CONDITION, SUFFERING, AND SEMIOTICS

Let us step back and ask a question prior to the analysis of the predicaments. Why is it that the human condition should be understood as having ultimate predicaments? Why is the human condition not simply a situation for human life, with better and worse elements?[7] The hypothesis about predicaments asserts that there is something wrong in the human condition, a brokenness, a mythic fall from a better state, a failure of an ideal that should not be failed. A decisive element of the human condition is that something is wrong with it and that religion in part is the effort to fix what is wrong. This requires more introductory reflection. Is there a universal characterization of brokenness?

Sometimes the term "suffering" has been used to denominate what is "wrong." As a general notion, suffering functions as a token in theodicy discussions that ask how or why there is suffering in the world. Buddhism has used suffering systematically to indicate what is wrong and to understand how to fix it. But Buddhism has also shown how complex and many-sided suffering is. Physical suffering sometimes and perhaps always is the prime analogate behind any other sense of suffering. Everyone has felt physical pain. But suffering also is involved with loss, with aging and decay, with diseases that inhibit and end life even when they are not particularly painful in a physical sense. Being part of a biological system inherits all the kinds of suffering involved in coming to be by using the energies of others, living through transformations in which nothing lasts, and decomposing to provide resources for other things. Then there is the suffering that comes from the frustration of some expectation of human flourishing, the oppression of a person or group in a larger social order, destruction through natural processes ("catastrophes" as seen from the standpoint of those suffering), premature closure of a personal or social project, premature death. Suffering has been understood to be the divine reward for a badly lived life, perhaps extending through many subsequent painful lifetimes, perhaps for eternity. On the other side, suffering has been understood to be a condition of ordinary life for an individual or group such that the divine reward of heaven is promised to make things right in the long run.

Recent studies of traumatic suffering, such as in child abuse, natural disasters, or battle, have pointed out some of the limitations of thinking that suffering "can be made right."[8] In trauma, an early traumatic experience lies buried in subsequent experience, causing later distortions and apparently inappropriate responses to things; "treatment" of trauma involves strengthening the person to face the early trauma and learn to live with it, meliorating some of the consequent negative effects; but one does not get over the trauma or erase it—one learns at best to tame and live with it. Shelly Rambo, speaking about Christian theology, argues that the phenomenon of trauma in human experience should limit the sense in which religious responses to suffering should be viewed as "fixing it." While she is right in her critique of certain kinds of Christian triumphalism—the view that God sooner or later will make all things right (at least for some people)—there are other senses of "fixing" or "remedy" that do not give the lie to the enduring and irreversible traits of suffering of many kinds.

The rhetoric with which the human predicaments have been characterized is complicated on a deeper level by suffering, however. Andrew Sung

Park has criticized the main traditions of Christian theology for paying too much attention to sinners and too little to suffering.[9] The main example of suffering he has in mind is that of the Korean Minjung who suffer a kind of cultural trauma that renders them nearly dysfunctional when it comes to bettering their condition. He, along with trauma scholars and many liberation theologians, emphasize the point that religion should respond to suffering, remedying it where possible, rather than focusing its efforts to help sinners. When suffering comes from oppression, as in the Minjung case, religion should not pay attention first to the oppressors but rather to the oppressed. Septemmy Eucharistia Lakawa's *Risky Hospitality: Mission in the Aftermath of Religious Communal Violence in Indonesia* details the Muslim-Christian communal violence in Indonesia around the turn of the century, particularly the Muslim attack on the Christian village at Duma in 2000; her account of the Christian response, particularly that of the women, in attempts at both remembrance and reconciliation moves through just about all kinds of suffering. Christianity in its dominant Euro-American forms might very well pay attention to the sinners rather than to the oppressed and those who suffer more generally. But there are many other dimensions of Christianity and of all the other Axial Age religions that address questions of suffering, especially suffering that comes from injustice.

Nevertheless, in the presentation of the human predicaments in this volume, the predicaments are imaged as conditions to which human beings need to respond, and for which religion seeks responses. This presentation might seem to some thinkers to focus too much on the active responses and to pay too little attention to issues of suffering as such and of bearing up under it. In answer, it should be said that suffering, bearing up under it, breaking under it, and continuing its consequences in trauma-like ways are themselves religious responses insofar as suffering has ultimate significance. "Ultimate significance" here means that the suffering defines ultimate boundary conditions for human life, as it so often does. Suffering is ultimate insofar as it breaks fundamental possibilities of human flourishing. Suffering is not the only thing that does this, of course, and religion needs to respond to those other things, too. The chapters that follow discuss many different kinds of things that break the possibilities of human flourishing and that call for religious remedies. Suffering itself has at least five kinds, relative to the five ultimates: the suffering of guilt, the suffering of personal brokenness in mind and body, the suffering of loneliness and wounding others, the suffering of ruined possibilities of achievement, and the suffering of despair and hatred of existence. Each of these kinds has many forms, and a number of these are discussed herein.

Suffering is thus no ordinary general notion, and as such it is not a particularly helpful universal designation of what is wrong with the human condition that religion is supposed to remedy. The brokenness of the human condition has at least as many manifestations as there are human predicaments.

Moreover, the internal variety within those cosmological predicaments and the obvious kinds of overlap and interactions among them multiply the kinds of wrongness to an extraordinary degree.

By the same token, whatever might remedy the various kinds of brokenness in their crisis manifestations can hardly be only one kind of "salvation." S. Mark Heim has argued powerfully that religions do not mean the same thing by "salvation" and that therefore in many respects they are not in competition however much they seem to use competitive language.[10] *Philosophical Theology* appreciates the point but puts the distinctions differently. It is not so much that various religious traditions each have different central meanings for salvation as that reality has different predicaments with different kinds of brokenness each of which requires its appropriate remedy or "salvation" ("salvation" language might be too Christian a term). Thus each major tradition is likely to have some articulation of each of the main kinds of predicament and brokenness, with remedies appropriate to each however much these are expressed in the symbols of different religious cultures.

That something is wrong with the human condition and that religion is supposed to fix it is an empirical claim. One of the purposes of *Philosophical Theology Two* is to provide cumulative arguments to make it plausible and persuasive. Merely to announce that there are human predicaments is not enough. Certain points need to be made to make these claims about diverse ultimate predicaments vulnerable to empirical correction.

First is the assumption that such a thing as "the human condition" exists. After all, people are different in so many ways, biologically, culturally, geographically, and historically, to name a few. Do people in developed countries share a human condition with those who live in savage conditions of social, economic, and martial chaos? Do people of the twenty-first century share a human condition with those of the first century of the Common Era, or with our common ancestors in Africa two hundred thousand years ago?

Yes, they do. Human beings of all times and places share a common evolutionary heritage that puts us on Earth together and shapes the possibilities of life around Earth's gravity, atmosphere, and biosphere with its related ecologies. The proportion of salt in our blood is about the same as that of the salt in the ocean. Every human being bears the evolutionary results of the development of DNA, of bones, sinews, and muscles; of nervous, motor, and sensory systems; and of energetic, metabolic, and chemical exchanges with the environment. Nearly all human beings share the specific elements of DNA that allow for interbreeding. Evolutionary biology includes many interesting research projects concerned with the evolution of religion.[11]

Much more centrally important for religion about the human condition is that all human beings have evolved semiotic systems (*III, 1, iv*). The evolution of semiotic systems is concomitant to evolving far enough to interbreed as humans with a social structure for caring through long infancy and childhood. The contents of those semiotic systems are different group by group, and here the differences in culture, times, and places are important. But the very fact of having semiotic systems such as languages, gestures, and rituals *establishes the human condition to be that of having to interpret the world symbolically.*[12] Because of the universal human capacity and necessity to engage the world interpretively, the human condition involves remembering or imagining a distant past the value of which bears upon present conduct, anticipating or imagining distant possible outcomes of conduct, dealing with real things and people in the environment, cooperating so that most actions are conjoint actions, and assessing what happens not only in terms of immediate results but in terms of larger perspectives on the world.

Of course, these common elements in the human condition (and this list is by no means exhaustive) might not be very important. Why dignify the common elements as *the* human condition and associate that human condition with religion? The reason is that these common elements are associated with the boundary conditions by which human beings understand their world as meaningful and thus are ultimate human conditions. This powerful capacity for understanding is made possible simply by having semiotic systems that perhaps evolved with no more original adaptive value than just to get along in small-clan life. Collectively, these boundary conditions are symbolized through sacred canopies by which people find ultimate orientations in their lives (*I, 1, 4*). As a first pass at these ultimate orientation conditions we can associate them with the transcendental traits of determinateness itself: form/possibilities, components formed/wholeness of integration, existential location/engaging others, and ultimate value-identity/meaning.

Because all human beings face distant possibilities that differ in the value of their outcomes, some of which depend on human action, all people have at least a rudimentary sense of a need to do what is right or best. Vast cultural differences distinguish the ways people parse and evaluate their futures, as well as feel responsibilities and take authority for acting together or singly. Nevertheless having future possibilities is ultimately important and defines the human condition in an ultimate way. To be human is "to live under obligation."

Because all human beings come from somewhere (the evolutionary story told previously is a very recent account of where people come from), people understand themselves to be grounded in a past and in the ongoing diversity of things that make their lives possible. That grounding might be symbolized by a mythic sacred past (Eliade), a founding story (the Ramayana, Mahabharata, and the Hebrew Bible's historical passages), or deep connections to the earth or sea, or a heritage of sage emperors. People also need to integrate the immediate conditions and accidents of their situations. But in all of these and other kinds of symbolizations of the grounding components of human life exists an attribution of value and harm, of worthiness and perhaps evil, to things in the past, with the result that people in the present are grounded with an obligation to live up to the founding good and cope with the founding evils. The past is present in the components that make up a person's life at any moment. Of course, more than the past are among the components of a person's life: particular families, friends, and enemies, local geography, current events, the particulars of one's body and its health—all are components that need to be integrated into a life. The ultimate grounds of human life affect the ways people orient their present conduct. To be human is to find integration and wholeness to be problematic.

Because all people live in an environment with nature and other human beings, some sense of being in a larger existential field is an ultimate condition in the way the world is understood, with a problem of harmonizing with other things in the field. Cultures differ greatly in the kinds of things they imagine to be in their existential field, and hence how that field is shaped. Some small-clan cultures know only their valley while other cultures worry about their place in the cosmos. Having an existential location in a larger field, however that field is imagined to be populated, is an ultimate condition of human life. To be human is to have to engage others and other things in some appropriate way.

Because what people do makes a difference to the value of what turns out, people understand themselves rightly to have some kind of cumulative value-identity. Of course, many things distinguish the values of people, whether they are rich or poor, live here or there, are among the favored people or not, are happy or suffer greatly. Cultures evaluate things like this differently. But more than these variations in the kinds of *given* values that make up people's lives are those that come from how people respond to the diverse given conditions of their lives, over a lifetime. That response, plus the values in the conditions, constitutes a kind of cumulative value-identity, who the people really are all things considered. Sometimes this identity is taken largely from the behavior of a community or group, sometimes more from individual initiative. Nevertheless, value-identity is a universal component of any semiotic system that registers behavior with respect to what is future, past, and environing. In some symbolic scheme or other, cumulative value-identity registers in sacred canopies. This is among the factors that make death a significant event, registered in burials and funeral rites, because the person is "cumulatively summed up" by termination.

These last four observations add flesh to the earlier claim that existential crises are oriented by four cosmological ultimate realities or boundary conditions. There is a fifth, an ontological boundary condition. Because a "person" suddenly is no more when death occurs and "only the body" is left, existence itself is an ultimate condition of life. Most cultures with Axial Age sensibilities to imagine the world as a whole also symbolize the radical contingency of that world (*III, 2*).[13] But that kind of ontological speculation, however symbolized, might not register with people until the prospect of annihilation occurs in the context of death. Tillich called this "ontological shock."[14] That things, or at least oneself and one's associates, exist at all is remarkable as an ultimate condition of life, indeed a surprise.

All these aspects of a human world are necessarily registered by some signs or other in any semiotic system that articulates a symbolic future, a past and set of components, an environment, cumulative human value-identity, and contingent existence. These are the aspects of the human world that constitute "the human condition" that has ultimate significance. Religion deals with ultimacy, as argued in the introduction to *Philosophical Theology One*, and so the human condition, on this understanding, is a fundamental theological problem.

III. UNIVERSALITY OF RELIGION

The second aspect of the double claim that the human condition has something wrong with it and that part of religion's function is to fix it, and that religion mediates ecstatic fulfillments regarding ultimacy, is the assertion that there is something universal about religion. For many decades, Western scholars have been so chastened by the recognition that early scholarship in comparative religions imposed Western, usually Christian, categories on the definition of religion that they have become allergic to speaking about religion as such.[15] They would rather speak about religions, and even then say that we should separately study the various cultural phenomena previously called religions so as to develop articulations of each according to its own terms. This allergy is part of the power in postmodern analyses that would immediately presume that any attempt to characterize religion as such is the a priori imposition of parochial categories. Along with this allergy often comes the Marxist point that, by setting the terms of analysis with a theory of religion, the scholar is establishing hegemony over those studied and thereby exerting inappropriate power. To be sure, the control of discourse is an exercise of power, and sometimes that power is nothing better than the assertion of the typical claims of one's social location. But scholars also seek to control discourse so as to make it more sensitive, profound, and true, and less biased, harmful, obscurantist, and manipulative. Postmodernism itself is a self-conscious movement to control discourse and at the present time is the "hegemonic discourse" of the academy in the humanities, as it would say (*III, 1, ii*). The question is not whether the control of discourse is the exercise of power but whether the discourse is improved by this or that effort to set its terms. *Philosophical Theology* is committed to making the terms of discourse as vulnerable to correction as possible.

Having said this, whether to speak primarily of religion or religions (understood perhaps as family resemblances) is a question of purpose to be decided empirically. Precisely because of what has been argued in the previous pages, the methodological priority of religion over religions recommends itself. Despite differences in culture, time, and place, all human beings share a common biological heritage with the evolution of semiotic systems that force the envisionment of (1) future possibilities of differing value, on which people act; (2) past and present conditions that must be integrated into ongoing life; (3) an environment with other things with which one must interact and harmonize to some degree; (4) cumulative value-identity for persons and/or groups that have to do with the value they achieve; and (5) the contingency of existence itself, regardless of the unit of existence considered. These are real issues, universal to all peoples who have semiotic systems precisely because they have semiotic systems. They are parts of the real ultimate boundary conditions for human life, and they are inescapable. Any sacred canopy that is developed with much cultural depth has to find some symbols for articulating something about the forms and values of possibilities, the components that make up human life, the existential field within which it is lived, the ultimate value it has for individuals and groups, and its existence itself. Because human cultures have developed symbol systems that deal with all these ultimate conditions through the sophistication of Axial Age religions, it might be tempting to think of this as a historical accident, occasioned by the remarkable cultural ecumene of the Axial Age. But, in fact, the Axial Age only gave a kind of universalistic shape to these cultural expressions (*III, 2*). Any culture that has time to develop symbols for addressing the realities it faces needs to have something in its sacred canopy to provide orientation to these realities.

Therefore, it is at least plausible at this stage in thinking about religion and ultimacy to address the questions of religion from this philosophical perspective and to inquire how various articulate religious traditions have dealt with them.[16] Because these questions are so profound, or ultimate, or distant, or transcendent, but always immediate in terms of how they shape life, a range of possible responses exists that is most likely found within every reflective religious tradition. For instance, every tradition has debates about free will and determinism when it comes to facing possibilities. So, an interesting question for the study of religion is how these debates among ranges of initially plausible responses are to be understood and evaluated. Of course, each tradition has its own cultural forms of response; detailed, linguistically based, and culturally sensitive studies need to take account of the untranslatable singular elements in each situation. Nevertheless, it makes sense to see religion as the human species' response to the issues of ultimacy as they need to be articulated in any deep and reflective sacred canopy.

Because of this, the citation of religious beliefs, doctrines, practices, and so forth, in *Philosophical Theology* usually, although not always, selects examples that are organized by their relevance to the philosophical point at hand. This stands in contrast with the analysis of these ideas in deep connection with the other elements in the traditions from which they are taken. Only in *Philosophical Theology Three*, Part II, are religions such as Buddhism and Christianity discussed in terms of what might be called their own integrity.

Even then, the discussion there of Part II follows Chapters 3 and 4 of that volume that explain that religions are far more intermixed and not given to identities with boundaries except insofar as individuals attempt to establish boundaries. The heritages of religions are never pure, always mixed and ambiguous.

Having argued that the claim that there is something wrong in the human condition and that religion is supposed address this assumes, first and rightly, that there is a significant universal human condition and, second and rightly, that religion is universal, consider the assumption that there is something universally wrong. The third assumption is the assertion of the universality of wrongness. To speak of a human "predicament" is to affirm some near-universal wrongness. Yet the religions are by no means in agreement about what the predicament is. Most, though not all, have strong traditional strains that picture a primordial state of perfection, a paradise that somehow has been lost. Confucians and Daoists lament the loss of the influence of the sage emperors; Buddhists lament the loss of the living Dharma; Hindus lament the loss of the effective authority of the Vedas. Jews, Christians, and Muslims lament the loss of the original Eden, although they differ over what was lost and how. Most of those same traditions, however, have alternative strains that attribute the current predicament to immaturity, lack of (sacred) education, or the like. But even then, the dominant themes of the human predicament that control the rhetoric differ among the religions. West Asian religions, with dominant conceptions of a personal God, harp on disobedience; South Asian religions harp on defects of consciousness, illusion, or delusion; East Asian religions harp on disharmony that frustrates emergence. The dominance of these themes affects the rhetoric of each.

Yet the argument given so far suggests that the ultimate boundary condition of facing possibilities raises ultimate issues of righteousness or embodying the right form in life. The ultimate boundary condition of being grounded in the components of life, some of which have a distant past, raises ultimate issues of being true to what has been achieved in attaining wholeness. The ultimate boundary condition of being with others in an existential field raises ultimate issues of harmonization and engaging others in ways that are responsible to the value-possibilities involved. The ultimate boundary condition of achieving a cumulative value-identity raises issues of facing evaluation in ultimate perspective. The ultimate boundary condition of sheer existence raises questions of how to relate to radical contingency. Precisely because human beings have some degree of control over what they do, they can be wrong about possibilities, about how to relate to their grounding elements, about how to relate to others, about how to achieve the best absolute value-identity, and about how to relate to their own contingency.

Thus every sacred canopy needs symbols to articulate these five dimensions of human predicament: obligation and guilt (regarding possibilities), grounded wholeness and disintegration (regarding components), engagement and estrangement (regarding existential location), achievement and destruction (regarding value-identity), and affirmation and negation (regarding radical contingency). In related but distinct senses, each of these dimensions involves suffering but much else that is broken besides. Parts I and II discuss these in detail. The cosmological dimensions are discussed directly, the ontological indirectly.

Sacred canopies also need to be able to say how to overcome these five aspects of human predicament. This is not a simple task of identifying a single savior or saving path, or enlightenment, or spiritual exercise. Rather, this is an extraordinarily complicated distribution of any tradition's symbolic lore to address these five dimensions in some way or other, with whatever emphases the rhetorics allow.

IV. ONTOLOGICAL ULTIMACY: DEATH AND LIFE

The pattern of analysis of predicaments and ultimate fulfillments in this volume follows the four cosmological ultimates and their human boundary conditions of obligation, wholeness, engagement of others, and the achievement of meaning in value-identity. The analysis of predicaments follows the scheme more strictly than that of ecstatic fulfillments. The ontological predicament of coping with radical contingency underlies each of these in various ways, as does the ontological fulfillment of ecstatic love and freedom in the ontological creative act. But the ontological dimension is a theme on its own.

The radical contingency of the cosmos, including human life, is represented in sacred canopies in various ways that together testify to the ontological creative act and so allow it to be engaged more or less well. That act is arbitrary in the sense that there is no reason for it and its products are their own justification. Within sacred canopies, this ontological status of radical contingency is registered with symbols of awe, astonishment, humility, sudden self-recognition, perhaps gratitude, perhaps focused attention on suchness, and the like (I, 15–16; II, 10–12; III, 15–16).

The focal human predicament regarding radical contingency is death, the cessation of the radically contingent. Death has powerful metaphoric reach. It can signify the death of a star going supernova or a planet in collision, the death of the oceans, the death of a kind of human natural environment, the death of a people, of an historical project, of a way of life. But most directly it signifies the death of persons, friends and enemies, family members, one's children, one's self.

From a cosmological point of view, all these things are only changes. When Zhuangzi's wife died, his disciple, Huizi, went to offer condolences and found Zhuangzi singing and drumming, not mourning. In response to Huizi's bewilderment, Zhuangzi said,

> When she died, how could I help being affected? But as I think the matter over, I realize that originally she had no life; and not only no

life, she had no form; not only no form, she had no material force. In the limbo of existence and non-existence, there was transformation and the material force was evolved. The material force was transformed to be form, form was transformed to become life, and now birth has transformed to become death. This is like the rotation of the four seasons, spring, summer, fall, and winter. Now she lies asleep in the great house (the universe). For me to go about weeping and wailing would be to show my ignorance of destiny. Therefore I desist.[17]

One of Shiva's major traits is to be the transformer, dancing the cosmic changes of the world, the destroyer as much as the creator. In most forms of Buddhism all things are understood to be nothing more than passing moments in highly contingent confluences of causal processes, *pratitya-samutpada*, in which nothing has its own being. The nature of these processes and moments is the subject of much division and debate among schools of Buddhism. The recognition that death is only change has been less prominent within the West Asian monotheisms, because human beings are so often construed to be created for a divine purpose that would be frustrated by death. Nevertheless, they, too, recognize a profound truth in the fact that human beings come from dust and return to dust. Their divine purpose might be to die. Some strains of monotheism think that a good death will be rewarded with everlasting life, but other strains do not give much credence to continued conscious existence. Job said, "Naked I came from my mother's womb, and naked shall I return there; the Lord gave and the Lord has taken away; blessed be the name of the Lord."[18]

Nevertheless, death is not only change. It is the loss within time of eternal value-identity, to use the categories of *Philosophical Theology One*, Chapter 12. Something in the eternal identity of a person is lost to the flow of time when a person dies. This shows, within the temporal flow of events, the radical contingency of the person's life and, by implication, of everyone's life.

So it is no exaggeration to say that death is the ontological predicament that is registered in sacred canopies as the result of radical contingency. Roughly speaking, there are two fundamental interpretations of death as a human predicament. One says that death is just a commitment to another life of suffering, on and on. As the doorway to more temporal life, death in the ordinary sense is the great enemy. Death as the cessation of rebirth and the transcendence of time, on the other hand, is the great friend. A large array of different interpretations of this exists in many of the world's religions. The other interpretation of death is that it is the end of life and life is a great good, despite suffering. If death leads to nothing but quick or slow dissolution, it is ontologically sad. If it leads to resurrection in a new heavenly life, it is a welcome friend, though many religions worry that it might be the gateway to everlasting suffering. Again, a large array of variations is to be found on the theme of life after death. Johannes Brahms, in the third of his *Four Serious Songs*, voices two sentences from the apocryphal book of Sirach 41: (1) "O death, how bitter is the thought of you to the one at peace among possessions, who has nothing to worry about and is prosperous in everything, and still is vigorous enough to enjoy food"—Brahms's line is angry, descending, abrupt, and seriously bitter; (2) "O death, how welcome is your sentence to one who is needy and failing in strength, worn down by age and anxious about everything; to one who is contrary, and has lost all patience!"—Brahms's line in this section is hymnic, ascending, drawn out, and ecstatically welcoming.

Death is not the only focal point in the recognition of radical contingency. The symbol of "life" is its opposite side. Understood relative to ultimate predicaments, life can symbolize their overcoming. But life has a broader reach than the negation of death. It can symbolize also the ecstatic fulfillments that can be found relative to ultimate ontological contingency. Life, like death, has a similarly broad metaphoric reach—the life of a community, a nation, a natural environment, a planet, the dynamic universe. But its key notion is the life of an individual. Life here does not mean organic biological systems so much as the prized existence of oneself in the world. To be apprised of life's radical contingency is to be filled with life, grateful and joyous, as much as it is to be concerned with death. To say that one does not understand the deep meaning of life without understanding also death is a commonplace. The opposite is also true: one does not understand the deep meaning of death without understanding the deep meaning of life. To engage the ontological act of creation well is to "come to life" in a profound sense, even when suffering remains, death ensues, and the circumstances are tragic. The meaning of profound life includes ontological gratitude, awe, humility, surprise, joy, love, and freedom, as we discuss in this volume. This is the territory of ontological ecstatic fulfillment, connected with ontological predicaments but not merely their resolution.

Sometimes the symbol of life extends beyond the profound life of individuals who engage the ontological act well to characterizations of the act itself, especially as that act functions as the ontological context of mutual relevance. Theistic symbol systems thematize this point so as to characterize the ontological act as divine life. Thus, an individual is profoundly alive by virtue of participating in a larger divine life. In nontheistic symbol systems this extension of life to the ontological act itself is less common, although not entirely absent. For instance, in Kashmir Shaivism the understanding of Shiva is moved from personalistic theistic forms to impersonal forms of consciousness while retaining symbols of life in the pulsing of the "ontological heart." Ecstatic fulfillment of the devotee is through participation in the living, nonintentional consciousness of Shiva.

The discussion in this introduction so far has focused on the human condition, religion, and the religious predicaments and ecstatic fulfillments, as understood within sacred canopies, from the most ancient to the most recent scientific ones. These sacred canopies articulate the cosmos, variously understood, insofar as the ultimate realities of human life within the cosmos require addressing. The sacred canopies can be called "cosmological" not only because they articulate ultimate conditions for the cosmos but also, in a technical sense, because they articulate how things in the cosmos connect together according to the ultimate conditions.

Articulating sacred canopies is a function of imagination and inquiry. While ultimate conditions of human existence do exist, the symbol systems for articulating them are human constructions that are limited by the very finite respects in which they articulate the ultimate. The philosophical theory exploited here—of possibilities, components, existential location, value-identity, and radical contingency—is itself a hypothesis with a history, limitations, and an inevitable future of modification, transcendence, and rejection. Nevertheless, despite the fallibility of all sacred canopies, human beings define their identity within the boundaries they articulate.

The distinction between the ontological and the cosmological has now become more complex. In *Philosophical Theology One*, ontology referred to the being of determinate beings whereas cosmology refers to the nature of determinate beings as harmonies, roughly speaking. Thus, in *One* the ontological dimension of determinate beings as harmonies was treated in terms of the essential and conditional components by virtue of which things can be many and one within the ontological context of mutual relevance, all as created by the ontological creative act. The cosmological dimension of determinate beings was treated there as the transcendental traits of harmonies, namely, form, components formed, existential location, and value-identity. The cosmological dimension presupposes the ontological for its very existence.

In *Philosophical Theology Two*, human predicaments as defined by sacred canopies are treated as falling within the cosmological dimensions of human life, as is the array of remedies for human predicament defined by sacred canopies. Because radical contingency is something also addressed within sacred canopies, however, its predicament is something like a cosmological address to the ontological dimensions. Whereas in the chapters of Parts I and II, only the cosmological dimensions of form, components, existential location, and value-identity are treated at length, each of those is also an expression of the ontological creative act itself. Therefore, the question of ontological ultimacy in radical contingency can be raised through each of these cosmological modalities. Within the human condition, the ontological peers through the cosmological. Behind all the cosmological predicaments is the ontological predicament of death. Behind all the cosmological paths to ecstatic fulfillment is the ontological significance of life.

Part I

Ultimate Boundary Conditions

Part I

Preliminary Remarks

The philosophical hypothesis concerning human predicaments and ecstatic fulfillments builds on the already complex hypothesis concerning ultimate realities elaborated in *Philosophical Theology One*, Part III, namely, that one ontological ultimate reality and four cosmological ultimate realities constitute the ultimate or boundary conditions for human life (*II, preface, intro.*). The thesis is summarized at length in respect of theological symbols in *Philosophical Theology Three*, Chapter 4, Section II, and we recall it briefly here for the purposes of the present volume.

The ontological ultimate reality is the act of creation, the end product of which is the world in all its diversity and connectedness, its changes, its patterns, and its chaos. The ontological act of creation is not itself determinate apart from the nature it gives itself in creating. The world's temporality and spatial extensiveness are among the determinate things created, and the ontological act of creation is not itself in time or space. The created world is not separate in any sense from the ontological creative act; rather, it is the end product of that act. The contents of the created world are anything that philosophy, the sciences, other traditions of inquiry, and the breadth of civilized experience, might find them to be. Neither the ontology of the creative act nor the metaphysics of determinateness specifies anything about what the world is besides being determinately whatever it is.

Anything that is created is determinate in the sense that each thing is something rather than nothing and itself rather than everything else with respect to which it is determinate. Therefore, the conditions of determinateness as such are transcendental conditions of the world. In fact, they would be the transcendental conditions of any world to the extent it is determinate. The four cosmological ultimate realities are transcendental traits of anything and everything that is determinate. According to the hypothesis, they are form, components formed, existential location relative to other things, and the achievement of some value-identity (*I, 10*). Expressed a bit more complexly, to be determinate is to be a *harmony* that has a (1) *form* or pattern; (2) *components* of which there must be two sorts, *conditional components* by virtue of which the harmony is conditioned by and conditions the other determinate things with respect to which it is determinate and *essential components* by virtue of which it integrates the conditional components so as to have its own being relative to others; (3) *location* in an existential field constituted by the ways the determinate things condition one another; and (4) the value-identity achieved by having these components together with this form in this existential location relative to other things. The cosmological ultimate realities are ultimate conditions for any determinate thing.

These five ultimate realities constitute the ultimate boundary conditions for human life in a religiously interesting way only insofar as they relate to the semiotically meaningful structure of that life (*I, 2–3; II, intro.*). The ontological contingency of the world takes the existential form of the radical contingency of human existence and the meaningful human world, often expressed as matters of life and death. The cosmological ultimate reality of form becomes the human boundary condition of having to deal with alternate possibilities of different values, and hence of being under obligation. Having components means, for human life, having to comport oneself to the components so as to defer to them properly and achieve integration and wholeness. Being existentially located determines the ultimate boundary condition of having to engage appropriately with others. Achieving some value-identity and coming to terms with this constitutes the ultimate boundary condition of finding meaning or value in life.

Together these five ultimate boundary conditions of human life are normative for human life. To be human in some ultimate sense is to face the question whether to affirm existence as such on the ontological level and on the cosmological level to be obligated to deal righteously with value-laden possibilities, to need to find wholeness, to engage others and the rest of the world appropriately, and to find meaning in the value resulting from one's life. To express these points in such telegraphic fashion is to oversimplify them to the point of potential distortion. At this stage in the argument they are mere formulas for organizing the discussion. Moreover, this philosophic language is abstract in ways that the various religions' expressions of parallel points are not. Nevertheless, the purpose of this volume is to flesh out these systematic points with such abundant detail as to make the hypothesis plausible, persuasive, and orienting. The hypothesis of the theological anthropology of *Philosophical Theology* is that to be human is to be normatively bound to face the question of the affirmation of existence, to be under obligation, to need wholeness, to engage rightly with other things, and to achieve a meaningful identity with value.

The language of norms comes principally from the first cosmological boundary condition, form as providing possibilities, because how people relate to existence, wholeness, existential location, and meaning in significant part is a matter of choice among possibilities. Perhaps the great majority of life's conditions are simply given. But what is interestingly human, from a religious perspective, is what people do with the conditions given them. Among the possibilities with regard to which people are under obligation to choose well are those having to do with how people comport themselves toward the components of their lives, how they relate to others, how they build a life with value and meaning, and how they address the question of the affirmation and enjoyment of existence on the ontological level. Because of the need for choice, these conditions are all normative in senses that will be explored.

The five ultimate boundary conditions are different from one another, however.[1] The temptation to think that there can be only one ultimate condition needs to be resisted. The causal relation between the ontological ultimate and the four cosmological ones shows how these five fit together consistently and coherently. The ontological act of creation is not "more ultimate" than the four cosmological traits of determinateness, because its very nature as ultimate requires the determinate world as the end product of its creating. Any ontological creation would have to be of a world that is determinate, and hence implies the four cosmological ultimates. The unity of human life, such as it is, involves addressing all five boundary conditions throughout one's life and they are obviously related; many of the non-obvious ways they are related are discussed in this volume.

How do these ultimate boundary conditions constitute anything that might be called a human predicament, or the human predicament, or ultimate human predicaments? The human predicament in general is that the normative boundary conditions bind us, and yet we fail them, and then we have to cope with that failure. Each boundary condition has its own genre of predicaments of failure, as discussed primarily in Part II of this volume. In respect of each boundary condition, there are ways of rightly coping with failure according to the various religions.

The human predicaments of ultimate significance are situated within the wider human world. The ultimate realities relevant to those predicaments are therefore those that show up in the human world. The notion of "human world" is ambiguous. Peter Berger and other experts in sociology of knowledge would use the term to refer to the ways by which people symbolize reality so as to construct a public symbolic image that gives meaning to human life.[2] *Philosophical Theology One*, Chapter 1, employs Berger's theory to begin a discussion of sacred canopies. A sacred canopy is an intellectually and socially constructed set of symbols depicting the humanly relevant boundaries of reality. But on the other hand, "human world" means whatever in reality is relevant to human life so as to constitute its boundary conditions, the putative referents of the symbols in a sacred canopy. Sacred canopies can prove false, not only by internal inconsistency, but by failing to articulate some ultimately significant aspects of reality experienced in other ways and hence becoming implausible. They become inoperative to engage these realities of life because they are mistaken in part about them.

The "human world" in this discussion means primarily the ultimate realities that bear upon human life, and only secondarily the symbols through which people engage them. Therefore, the argument of this part is that the cosmological ultimates of form, components, existential location in a field with others, value-identity, and radical contingency upon an ontological creative act are relevant to human life as the boundary conditions of obligated possibilities, wholeness, appropriate engagement, meaningfulness, and the consent to and enjoyment of created being in general. The human world's boundary conditions, in this analysis, are the normative claims of obligated possibilities, wholeness, appropriate engagement, the achievement of meaning, and coming to terms with existence as such.

Over and above this sense of the human world are the symbol systems in sacred canopies that various religious traditions have developed to articulate the human world. At this level of analysis, the issues are those of comparative theology, to find where there is real similarity and real difference beneath the surface of symbols that might appear to be cognate. That all the large, literate religious traditions have symbols to deal with these issues is one strand in the defense of the hypothesis that obligation, wholeness, appropriate engagement, the achievement of meaning, and coming to terms with existence are indeed ultimate realities for human beings, constituting the boundary conditions for the human world, and hence religiosity in general.

On the other hand, that they all have symbols to articulate these humanly relevant realities does not mean that they say the same things about them. *Philosophical Theology One* claimed in fact that there are at least three great metaphoric systems that have been developed for articulating ontological ultimacy: the elaborations of metaphors of emergence, consciousness, and personhood. Each of these spawns its own varieties of ways of dealing with obligation, wholeness, engagement, meaning, and existence, and the traditions are not consistent within themselves, let alone among each other. That the philosophical categories serve to exhibit some of these important differences is another advantage of the hypothesis about the ultimate realities in the boundary conditions of the human world.

The purpose of this part is to examine in detail how the cosmological ultimates give rise to the ultimate boundary conditions of the human world: obligation, wholeness, engagement, and meaningfulness. This is done with a chapter for each. In every case the point is made that, in reference to the normativeness of each of the cosmological ultimates in human life, human beings inevitably or almost inevitably are failures, although the analysis of this failure takes place in Part II. Moreover, the cosmological ultimate realities in the human world are connected. What people do relative to one relates to what they do relative to the others. Part of the wholeness question is how these connect.

Within human life, the ontological question of existence, deriving from the radical contingency of the world on the ontological act of creation, is pervasive. But it arises in different ways with respect to obligation, wholeness, engagement, and the achievement of meaning. Each one can raise the question of whether life is worth living. The ontological predicament is examined in these particular ways in each chapter.

Chapter 1 examines the ultimate boundary condition that comes from form, namely, obligation. Chapter 2 studies the ultimate boundary condition that comes from having components, namely, groundedness and its integration into wholeness. Chapter 3 addresses the boundary condition that comes from existential location, namely, engagement. Chapter 4 takes on the ultimate boundary condition that comes from value-identity and meaning, namely, ultimate meaningfulness in value. Each of these traits presents an approach to the ultimacy of radical contingency.

CHAPTER ONE

Form as the Condition of Obligation

The first step in this theological anthropology is to reflect on the fact that human beings face possibilities about which they make decisions. This reflection covers important philosophical ground: the nature of obligation, moral worth, value, and the character of form itself. The ultimate boundary condition of form as it puts human life under obligation functions in all the other boundary conditions: people make decisions about their own integration, about engaging others, and about achieving a value-identity that gives life meaning. All the other boundary conditions have form. Within the temporal processes of human life, form determines the possibilities that might be actualized; it determines the value and structure of the things that are in fact actualized; and it is the structured value of the past. So, in all these ways the study of form and its role as a boundary condition for human life is primary and a good first step in this inquiry.

It need not be the first step, however. We could begin with a study of nature as the originating environment for human life, or with a study of human biology, social conditions, and psychology. All of these are important components of human life, and in fact return for consideration in Chapter 2, where we reflect on components as such. But in this theological anthropology, we begin with reflection on human choice because that is at the heart of the existential reality of religion.

The first section develops at some length the connection between the ultimate transcendental trait of having form and the way this is implicated in the human world.[1] The second section focuses on the sense in which form bears value, such that anything that has form has value; this topic is treated at several places in *Philosophical Theology* (I, 10; III, 9). The result of this discussion is a general theory of human life as being under obligation, the topic of Section III. The fourth section spells out a classification of obligations.

I. FORM AND HUMAN POSSIBILITY

Philosophical Theology One, Chapter 10, noted that to be a determinate thing at all is to be a harmony with form. For temporal things such as human beings, so complex and discursive through time and space in their harmonies and interactions, the *future* is form under the aspect of possibility; the *present* is the deciding among alternate possibilities as to which ones to actualize; the *past* is, with respect to form, those possibilities that have been actualized and the exclusion of those that have not. Although human possibilities are contextual in many senses, and eventually are to be understood in terms of those concrete contexts, to begin with a consideration of some of the metaphysical structures of form relative to human life is the most practical beginning. Pervasive traits often are more practical and determinative in the long run than local contextual ones.[2]

Form is the metaphysical basis of the structure of the future in temporal things. Some remarks are necessary about the metaphysics in this, dealing first with form and then with value as a function of form. According to the analysis in *Philosophical Theology One*, Chapter 12, the future is a harmony with essential and conditional components. The essential component of the future is pure unity, which, when conjoined in contrasts with the future's conditional components coming in different ways from the past and present, constitutes formal patterns as future possibilities. These patterns might unify the plurality of things given to the future as its conditional components by actualized things of the past, relative to present moments that might decide among alternatives. This analysis of future possibility strongly reflects the Neo-Confucian theme of *li*, which usually is translated "Principle" but which Stephen Angle better translates as "coherence."[3] The Neo-Confucian slogan "*li* is one, its manifestations are many" can be interpreted in *Philosophical Theology* to mean that, as one, coherence per se or "essentially" is that which would make any plurality cohere and that, as many, coherence is the pattern of any given particular plurality of things (the conditional components of form) that do cohere. Because form needs both essential and conditional components, there is no way in which form or coherence as pure unity can exist by itself, nor any way by which a plurality can exist by itself without some bare coherence.

The *form* of the future is thus a structured possibility for actualization, most likely with a structure that is vague with respect to alternative possibilities for actualization. Because of the plurality of actualized things at any moment, many decision points are involved in deciding on a given, vague future possibility. Thus the future possibility has the structure of a field of alternatives that can be decided by many decision points. In a specious present, a human agent is surrounded by many other "contemporary" agents whose decisions also affect which future possibilities are actualized. A football player, for instance, needs to be aware of what all the other players are doing and pondering as he structures how he will address the field of possibilities in a given play. And the field of possibilities is not open only to other human deciders: social institutions, movements, wars, climatic changes, changes in underlying natural conditions—all these are among the larger array of decision points that affect a person's possibilities. Between a given person in the present and the possibilities being faced, an array of intermediate decision points also exists. The person will have to keep on making decisions to carry out a present intent for a future outcome. Most if not all human choices involve conjoint actions with others, including other nonhuman factors. Sometimes conjoint actions are cooperative, sometimes antagonistic, and sometimes oblivious. Moreover, because every decision, by the person or by the other deciding processes, changes the field of possibilities, the structure of possibilities itself is constantly changing, a kaleidoscope of shifting alternatives. Given this structure of form and possibility, *an ultimate condition of human existence is to face value-laden possibilities.* The remainder of this section elaborates this thesis.

The sense of "human nature" correlative to the facing of alternative possibilities for decision is that of the decision-maker, the agent. In many important circumstances, decisive agency is a matter of spontaneous action, of freedom. Human freedom has many dimensions in addition to creative choice, but the point to stress here is that the facing of possibilities is a model for spontaneous emergence, one of the principal symbols for the ontological ultimate reality, the act of creation. In free choices, individuals create something that was not there before, a novelty that resolves a previously unresolved alternative for actualization. This human and very common sense of spontaneous emergence is important for grasping the ubiquity of spontaneous emergence as a model for the ontological ultimate. Of course, free choice is also characteristic of persons in general, and thus a part of the equally ubiquitous use of personhood as a model for the ontological ultimate. Nevertheless, the primary significance of the personhood model is the intentions that lie behind choice, the function of purposes in actions. To the extent that purposes or intentions determine the choice of a person, that choice is not spontaneous emergence; rather it is caused by the nature of the agent. True freedom of choice in the human case is personal in the sense that it includes intentions, purposes, and other motives among the antecedent factors that shape the field of possibilities. But the choice is not genuinely free unless there is also the creative emergence of a novelty. In a free choice, the novelty that emerges spontaneously, over and above all antecedent determining factors shaping possibilities, determines which of those possible antecedent motives will be decisive. A person gives himself or herself the decisive motive, purpose, or intention by choosing an action that actualizes the possible alternative determined by that motive. This is why people sometimes are surprised by their choices. Genuine free choice is more a model of spontaneous emergence than of personhood.

II. VALUE

Concerning value, a possibility has an internal structure for how the components of a harmony might be integrated. This structure has the value of integrating these components with this formal pattern in this existential situation, giving rise to the harmony's value-identity (*I, 10; III, 9*).[4] Value itself is a function of form: any formal pattern is the expression of the value of having its components together in the way of the pattern. The structure of a possibility has two principal variables, complexity and simplicity. Complexity refers to how the diversity of different components is sustained within the form, and simplicity refers to how the layering and organization of patterns within patterns gives rise to stark unified contrasts. Complexity without simplicity would be mere conjunction: a and b and c and . . . Simplicity without complexity would be mere homogeneity: a/a/a, and so forth. Any formal pattern has both complexity and simplicity of varying kinds and degrees. Patterns complex enough to be future possibilities have many layers in which things on lower levels are combined to create new entities on the higher levels, which in turn are combined to create yet new entities within the form. The value is greater the more the entities within the form at the higher levels are focused to be in contrast with one another. "Contrast," a technical term from Whitehead, obtains when two or more things with different natures just fit together.[5] The contrast is greater the more different the things are from one another. The characters peculiar to each are more focused the more they arise out of a dense hierarchy within themselves; each is itself a contrast arising from the complexity/simplicity structure of its components. Leibniz called something like this mixture of complexity and simplicity the "density of being."[6] The value of the possibility lies in the kind of mixture of complexity and simplicity the form holds and also the degree to which complexity and simplicity are maximized.

Most signs in human semiotic systems articulate things in the world that are high-level contrasts, often neglecting the underlying hierarchies. For instance, we note human beings and their actions, not the underlying biology that makes them possible. We note nutritious foods without registering their underlying chemistry in relation to our metabolism that makes them nutritious. Experience is more complex in its valuational patterns the more it does register the underlying value hierarchies at play and their relations with one another. This illustrates the point that formal possibilities for people have a character that is grasped by the people only in the respects in which people's intentional structures of interpretive experience are able to grasp them, a point that is discussed at greater length elsewhere (*III, 9–10*).

Form as possibility thus is a possible value: to actualize the form is to actualize its value. Every actual thing has form, of course, and so every actual thing has a value. Because its form is relative to the forms of other things, and its possibilities before being actualized constituted a field of possibilities for many things to actualize together, the values of things are related, including both those that are actualized and those possible values that are excluded from actualization.

This point is of enormous importance for the whole of *Philosophical Theology*. Because value is resident in any form, valuation always has an objective component. The intentional, subjective side of interpretation always is involved in selection of the respects in which to interpret things valuatively, as the Confucians have steadily pointed out. The other side of this, however, is that value is resident in the things to be valued relative to human intentionality, a point equally stressed by the Confucians. Thus there is no sense in which valuation can be completely subjective. Even when it is horribly mistaken, valuation is measured against the value in the forms of the things evaluated. This position accords with the classic Western view and the Confucian view from the earliest times that to be is to be valuable. It is at odds with the common position in modern Western philosophy that things are only facts and that to attribute value to them is somehow problematic, a matter of justifying a human prejudice.

Every possibility thus has a value. A possibility that contains alternative possibilities has alternative values. Given the kaleidoscope of shifting possibilities facing a human actor, the value differences are significant, difficult to discern and track, and very complex. No special mystery is here, however. By evolution and culture human beings are habituated to be aware of conditions that affect the value-outcomes of their own actions and the things going on around them. Even very simple animals have this capacity, although perhaps not with the power of semiotic systems to refer to distant and complicated phenomena.

Human beings have some control over their behavior.[7] This control is limited, first, by what other things do, second by the person's own potentials and capacities, third by the structure of the relevant possibilities, and fourth by the person's discernment, knowledge, and awareness of all the aforementioned. With regard to the first, it makes sense to cooperate with other people so that their opposition does not limit options and to act in harmony with nature so that our intents are not immediately frustrated. Of course, sometimes cooperation requires too much sacrifice of our own intent, interest, and good judgment so that opposition is the best recourse. Sometimes, as in the case of illness, nature seems not always to be amenable to harmony in ways that sustain our integrity, although one's integrity or wholeness itself is something that needs to be harmonized with other values in the possibilities.

With regard to the second, our potentials come from the past, and we can increase them by cultivating lives that provide rich resources. Our capacities are our habits of organizing potentials so as to be able to act effectively in situations. These can be increased by education of various sorts, a theme more steadily important in Confucian thought than in Western thinking that has sometimes supposed that democracy does not allow for demands of elite education.[8] Nevertheless, potentials and capacities are limited.

With regard to the third, the structures of the possibilities themselves, these are mainly set by circumstances beyond our control. Nevertheless, sometimes it is possible to do things that enhance our possibilities, such as getting a certain kind of education that qualifies us for possibilities otherwise closed to us or making moves in a battle that give rise to a wider range of options.

With regard to the fourth, human beings are limited by how much we understand the forces around us, our own potentialities and capacities, our possibilities, and the connections of all these. These limits can be pushed back by greater understanding, but the ironic effects of ignorance are such that often we do not know in what greater understanding would consist. Moreover, at some point in certain kinds of difficult actions, more information dilutes the effort to accomplish something, although this, too, is something that should be understood. At the end of his regime of education for political leaders in the *Republic* (in Book 7), Plato sent the graduates off to govern the provinces so that they could learn timing, not a matter of more understanding but of a habit of action.

Because human beings have some control over their behavior, within these and perhaps other limits, they determine to this degree which possibilities in their futures will be actualized and which excluded. This is an important, but not the only, sense of human freedom. Some philosophical and religious traditions have denied this freedom. Often the theological motive for denying this sense of freedom is to defend the omnipotence of the ultimate conceived as a creator God, as if the freedom and power of God were in competition with the freedom of human beings. Calvinist Christians such as Jonathan Edwards and some orthodox Muslims (in opposition to the freewill Mu'tazilites) held to this position; their opponents argued that God would be unjust for rewarding or punishing behavior for which the people themselves were not freely responsible. A more subtle understanding of the motives for denying human freedom to control behavior with respect to possibilities of different value, however, comes from understanding the limits to behavior. When other forces are overwhelming, a person is not free. When a person's potentials and capacities are inadequate for decisive action, the person is not free. When the possibilities allow of only one outcome, the person is not free. When the person's ignorance of what is needed to be understood in order to act freely is incorrigible, the person is not free. When the person is not mature in moral discernment and action, the person is not free. In many circumstances, we are not free when we would like to think we are. Nevertheless, in many other circumstances, we are indeed free within limits and to that extent are responsible for what we choose.

III. OBLIGATION

To the extent human beings are free to determine the outcome of possibilities, and the possibilities have differential value, to that extent human beings are under obligation to do the better rather than the worse. This is the very meaning of obligation: it is better to do the better than the worse. Insofar as a person's actions determine the person's character, the person becomes better or worse by doing the better or worse. To say that a person is under obligation to do something is to say that it is better to do it than not to do it or to do something that excludes it. Kant was right in the *Critique of Practical Reason* to call this sense of obligation "categorical": it has to do simply with doing the better rather than the worse. If a person is in a position to act on the matter, that person is obligated to do it, because not to do it would be to do the worse. Motive for action makes no difference, save that motives sometimes structure relevant possibilities. No matter what one might want, if there is a difference in value between the possibilities whose outcome one might affect, one is obligated to do the better. Of course, sometimes it is impossible to tell the differences in value. And sometimes there are different kinds of value for which no commensurate scaling can be found. But where there is a difference in value, and where whatever one does or does not do affects the outcome, one is under obligation.

Many thinkers resist this notion of obligation. Several kinds of objection are raised. First, some people say that to be under obligation requires that someone places you under obligation, for instance, a God, or someone in authority such as a military commander or an aristocrat to whom you owe loyalty. The difficulty with this is that it is possible simply to deny being obligated by the command. One can always reject the claim of the other to command one's obedience, and it might be possible to give reasons why obedience should be denied, for instance, that the command is to do a bad thing and that disobedience leads to the greater good. What justifies the claim of obedience in the long run is only that the commands are better than their alternatives, even if the justification moves through a long circle of justifying a social arrangement of authority, such as that in battle you should follow the commands of the ones in charge even if they are not the wisest. Obligation coming from authority is only justified if the authority is justified as the best to follow.

A second objection is that you are under obligation only if you first accept the obligation, as in accepting someone as the authority, or as in signing on to a project of a society or other body, even oneself. Without accepting the obligation in the first place, the objection goes, it is not binding upon you. But this amounts to saying that there is no real normative obligation, no categorical imperative, only obligations that follow from needing to be consistent with one's own will. Kant called these "hypothetical imperatives" because they have the form "if you want A, you ought to do B in order to get it." Kant's problematic arose out of the more general cultural view among Enlightenment scientists that nature has no value that ought to be respected. But an obligation obliges you whether or not you want to accept it—that is why it is obligatory rather than simply what you want. Obligation consists in the fact that choosing the better makes you a better chooser, and choosing the worse makes you a worse chooser. Accumulated character over time, in part, is the complex summary of better and worse choices.

A third objection is that the whole notion of obligation depends on there being some truth to the view that there are better and worse persons, better and worse choosers, better and worse ways of responding to the normative claims of being under obligation. If in fact there are no real values in things, in human beings or in the things to which they relate, then there can be no real obligation. People simply are who they are. Sometimes this view is softened to say that there are attractive and unattractive characters, a matter of aesthetic character. But aesthetic traits do not bear on moral character in any way that relates to obligation. This is the most powerful objection because it rests on denying the thesis that things have real value. To the extent the arguments given here are valid, that to have form is to have value and that the form of the human chooser has the value that comes from the value of the choices made, the objection falls to the ground. Without the thesis that things have real value, this objection to the very idea of obligation is valid.

David Hume is famous for saying that you cannot derive an "ought" from an "is."[9] By "is" he meant facts with no value character. G. E. Moore developed this argument with what he called the "naturalistic fallacy," namely, to believe that natural things have value that might imply obligation.[10] He suggested an objectivist position on value, however, namely, that "value" is a "simple, non-natural quality" that inheres in some things, as the color yellow inheres in some things. The much simpler and less arbitrary metaphysics of *Philosophical Theology* says, contrary to both Hume and Moore, that "is" always implies "ought" where it lies in the way of human choice because all facts have value.

A fundamental ultimate condition of being human, therefore, is to lie under obligation. This is part of the nature of being human in a world best understood as processes of interacting harmonies. This ultimate, natural, condition is registered in all the reflective religious traditions, although with highly varied interpretations.

One universal dimension of this is the obligation attendant upon ritual participation: the ritual obliges the participants to do certain things (*II, 13*).[11] As ritual is usually understood, pre–Axial Age religions ritualize a much wider array of life activities than Axial Age religions. But if ritual is understood in a Confucian sense, as is urged in this study, it extends to any semiotically structured activities including language. A language speaker is obliged to follow the rules of syntax and semantics if communication is to take place.

Beyond ritual, however, the great religious traditions articulate and train for the general proposition that human beings lie under obligation. The West Asian religions often express this in terms of obedience to the commands of God. Sometimes this is understood to mean that obligations are obligatory because God commands them, not because of any intrinsic distinction between better and worse. This understanding is a default position when a group wants to defend something it takes to be obligatory but that it cannot defend rationally. The contrary understanding also is operative in the West Asian religions. In the account of creation in Genesis 1, God creates the elements of the cosmos and then "sees" that they are good. Plato's *Euthyphro* is a classic examination of the dilemma: is the good good because the gods will it, or do they will it because it is good? The position of *Philosophical Theology* is that the ontological creative act creates a world in which determinate beings exist as harmonies, all of which have value in themselves and relative to each other. There can be no antecedent divine intention to create valuable things, but also there could be no creation of determinate things without them having harmonic form that ipso facto is valuable. This position is compatible with important strains in Judaism, Christianity, Islam (which particularly emphasizes obligation), and Greek and Roman Paganism.[12]

Buddhism in its various forms presents a rhetoric that seems to some to downplay obligation as too closely connected with attachments. Buddhism sometimes has been criticized for not taking seriously enough the obligations to change material conditions so as to relieve suffering. Yet nothing in the account of obligation in *Philosophical Theology* requires that people be attached to their obligations. Kant went so far as to say that obligations are purer in some sense when they run contrary to inclinations or attachments.[13] Obligation is a real objective condition that consists in the value differences among different possibilities, such that the better possibilities ought to be actualized rather than the worse. When a field of possibilities faces a group of potential actors, and that field has better and worse possibilities, someone should do something about the obligation to actualize the better. In this case it is useful to distinguish the objective obligation from the subjective responsibilities of someone or a few people to fulfill the obligation for the group. Division of labor in a society depends on people playing roles with subjective responsibility for objective possibilities that oblige everyone. Nevertheless, even when a general obligation becomes an individual's personal subjective responsibility, the fact that the person has this responsibility is not necessarily a matter of attachment. Release from attachments in Buddhism, interpreted in a variety of ways, does not mean that actions are not obligated when they might make a difference to the value of the outcome. The Eightfold Noble Path of the Buddha is an organized way of defining general personal and social obligations that people need to address in order to enter onto the path of release from the attachments that cause suffering. In various forms of Buddhism, special obligations come into play on the path toward liberation, for instance, obligations to a teacher or guru, or the obligations attendant upon the bodhisattva's vow to postpone liberation until all sentient beings are released.

The forms of Hinduism are too varied to typify in a single approach to value and the human condition of lying under obligation. Nevertheless, a background theme through most forms of Hinduism is "dharma," meaning obligations that uphold the order and value of the cosmos. The dharma obligations are different for different kinds of people, and in fact are among the essential conditions that define the differences among castes.[14] A persistent theme in many kinds of Hinduism is the obligation to perform the sacrifices that sustain the gods and their world order.

Obligation is perhaps the most conspicuous element of the Confucian philosophical-religious tradition. Obligation is interpreted, in the Doctrine of the Mean, for instance, as arising from the continuum between human beings having the normative structure of Heaven as their inner nature and the structures of all things in the human world (the "ten thousand things"), each of which has its own valuable nature to which certain responses are appropriate and others not. The Mencian line of Confucianism stresses the natural capacity of people to discern the values of things and to respond appropriately, a natural capacity that can be cultivated by removing obstacles to its habitual operation. The Xunzian line of Confucianism stresses the need for learning how to discern values and appropriate responses but still holds to the fundamental aesthetic basis of obligation. As a path toward sagehood, Confucianism emphasizes the education and personal cultivation necessary to fulfill obligations. Because of its insistence that individuals are defined in their social context, this educational and personal cultivation requires the concomitant cultivation of the institutions of society so as to facilitate the easy and complete fulfillment of obligations. Classical Daoists tend to deride the Confucian preoccupation with concerns for righteousness but offer a discipline of conforming to the Dao as a way of fulfilling obligations without effort. The contents of obligations differ significantly among schools of Chinese thought and practice.

A number of scholars involved in recent comparative Confucian-Western thought have suggested that progress is made by likening Confucianism to virtue-ethics in the Western sense as interpreted from the Aristotelian tradition by Alasdair McIntyre.[15] But this likeness can be deceptive. Virtue ethics in the West has been oriented to determining what we ought to do and stands in contrast or complement to ethical orientations such as deontological and consequentialist ethics for determining the same thing. In the Confucian case, a great deal of what has been called ethical is a function of the quest for wholeness, from the array of issues having to do with filial piety, practices of meditation, to the institutions of apprenticeship. Another large swath of Confucian issues has to do with developing ways of discerning, appreciating, and responding to other people, to social institutions, and nature; in *Philosophical Theology*, these are issues of engagement with others, and involve cultivating special skills and orientations to the world. Much of the cultivation of the Confucian ideal character has to do with orientation to these kinds of ultimacy.

But Confucians also have to figure out what to do when confronted with alternative possibilities with differing values, that is, determining obligation in the sense under discussion in this chapter. In this regard, the Confucian project seeks out the worth of things, "investigating" them, in the language of the Great Learning.[16] Certain elements of the project have to do with cultivating sincerity so that personal ego and selfishness do not get in the way—these are like virtue ethics. But in this instance the removal of selfishness is instrumental to getting a truer view of what the things are to which one might respond. Then figuring out the response, although it involves having a clear heart that intuitively responds well to the values of things, includes also learning to harmonize and bring under control the causal paths that move from the instincts of one's heart to accomplish a complex choice. As to choice among possibilities, determining what to do, Confucianism holds to an objectivist metaphysics in which things deserve to be treated certain ways because of the values of who or what they are, and personal virtue often is required to be able to see this and to act upon discerning choices. The obligation is to do the best thing, given the differently value-laden possibilities, and virtue is only instrumental for this. All in all, the Confucians, especially the Neo-Confucians, emphasize the need for study, commitment, growth, imagination, and maturation in order to be able to discern value-laden possibilities relevant for moral action. With regard to wholeness and appropriate engagement, however, virtues of certain sorts are more nearly the point of responding to the relevant ultimates, surely so in the former case.

In summary of our argument so far in this chapter, one ultimate dimension of the human condition is that we have obligations and can and do fail them and that this is recognized across religions.

Three things should be said at this point about the place of this theory of obligation relative to some competitors. The first is that this is a wholly realistic theory of value (*III, 9*). That is, value is constituted by the nature of form itself, namely, its character of combining simplicity and complexity in a hierarchy of layers of formal harmony. The values of possibilities are what they are by virtue of their forms, whether or not anyone recognizes them. This is the simplest metaphysical hypothesis about value in an array of hypotheses most of which tie value to human intentionality or purpose. Theories that attempt to derive value from the subjective side of human intentionality have insurmountable difficulty saying *why* some things should be the object of human intention and purpose. Although value is always relative to human purpose from the standpoint of human experience and decision, what makes one possibility more valuable than another is a function of what it gets together in what pattern. This value is something to be discerned relative to choice: as Peirce said, one of the most important questions for human beings is what purposes are worth having, and that is a function of the character of possible objects of purpose. Value lies in the character of form itself.

The second point to notice is that the hypothesis here always relates the future as possibilities of varying value to human beings under the intentional stance. Values are meaningless to human choice save insofar as they do relate directly or indirectly to the intentionality structure of human life. Form becomes interesting possibility when its internal possible variations are relative to human choice. In this sense, the possibilities afford options for choice. So, the *real* values need to become *objective* values in some sense, that is, objects for intentions, in order to be engaged in choice. A number of current ethical theories define value in terms of a combination of objective and subjective conditions. Of course, human valuation is always such a combination. But the hypothesis here says that value is resident in the formal possibilities per se. The intentional grasping of the possibilities by individuals involves interpreting the possible future options in terms of their own situationally determined intentionalities. So, only those aspects of the real values in the possibilities can be interpreted and thereby engaged for which the people have signs to recognize. Moreover, the deployment of signs to sort the focal things to be interpreted against a background is a function of multiple layers of valuation built in to the habits of the interpreters' culture and personal experience. In this sense, the values that function in human experience as consciously recognizable are always a combination of the subjectivity of the intentional interpreters and the real values of the possibilities that they engage. Many theories that recognize the objective-subjective interplay do not have the theory of interpretive experience as engagement among their resources, and thus are stuck trying to derive value from the interaction of possibilities and interests that still have no way of recognizing anything as having value to enter the situation. Many approaches to the reality of values in nature suffer from presupposing the split between fact and value, which sets up their task to prove that some facts have value because of their relation to human experiencers. If the framing conceptuality is that nature is merely factual, so that the problem of the naturalistic fallacy makes serious sense, then there are two deficient responses. One, made by G. E. Moore, is that value is a "simple non-natural property" that just sticks to some things and not others, as some things are yellow and others are not. The other is that human experience projects value onto what are in fact only value-neutral things because of human need, impulse, desire, or delectation.

 Third, part of the normativity of facing possibilities of different values is the meta-obligation of people to find ways of discerning what the humanly relevant possibilities are. Societies attempt to cope with this by means of cultural habits of valuation, by rituals, debates over principles, calculations of advantage and enjoyment, the development of historical projects, summary rules of what is discerning in certain circumstances, and a whole host of other theories determining what to do. One aspect of the virtue-ethics traditions that have arisen in many cultures is that they focus on the cultivation of good forms of intentionality, those aimed at the most important human values. So there is a recursive function relative to possibilities defining obligation. We engage those possibilities only insofar as we can bring them in to the ambiance of our interpreted world. But the possibilities themselves are what bear value. Therefore we need to know what that value is in order to respond to our obligations. Hence, we are responsible for understanding the possibilities insofar as they bear upon life.

IV. OBLIGATIONS: MORAL, SOCIAL, PERSONAL, AND NATURAL

The complexity of obligation can be indicated, albeit briefly, by developing a classification of some of its main loci. The distinctions drawn here are arbitrary in many ways, as is the assignment of labels. The distinctions among kinds of obligation come from the structures of possibility as these are faced by human actors. These structures are exceedingly complicated and filled with intertwining causal patterns. The labels come from the English-language traditions of moral discourse in which they have had both vaguely overlapping and also technically defined differentiated definitions. In this discussion they are assigned somewhat arbitrary meanings. Four kinds of obligation are discussed: moral, social, personal, and natural. They correspond to four kinds of fault discussed in Chapter 5, namely, moral fault, which tracks into the brokenness of moral guilt and condemnation; social fault, which falls into the brokenness of guilty betrayal; personal fault, which becomes the brokenness of existential guilt; and natural costliness, which when broken is blood guilt.

Moral obligation, as the term is used here, refers to the value-differential possibilities that relate to bringing the right or optimal order to human relations and to the natural and social contexts that underlie those relations, as these possibilities are presented for choice in quotidian situations. The boundaries of this definition become clearer in contrast to the other forms of obligation discussed. Internally, it comprises obligations to do the better in interpersonal relations with direct personal contact, in relations with others mediated by small and large group community structures, and in relations with other individuals who are anonymous and perhaps distant, although subject to being affected by one's actions. The emphasis in moral obligation is on attending to those possibilities that, negatively, respect the humanity of those involved and, positively, contribute to its enhancement. Because of complicated roles in social structure, obligations to respect and enhance humanity are of many different kinds. Moral obligation obviously involves proper engagement of others and the abilities to discern their worth, a topic concerning the ultimate reality of engagement of those within one's existential field, the topic of Chapter 3.

People are affected by one's actions through the mediations of many different causal processes. The institutions of society, for instance, are the primary carriers of moral consequences of actions that are registered in most cultural semiotic systems. Therefore, some of the most significant morally freighted possibilities are those that have to do with the goods or harms that might be done to those institutions, such as families, friendships, living communities, workplaces, and the like. When the relations among individuals are significantly affected by mediating institutions, moral obligations are often described in terms of justice. Social institutions, however, are not the only kind of mediators among persons. Natural causal structures are also important, and perhaps in the long run are more important. Care for the environment insofar as that sustains and enhances human life is a moral concern. Care for the conditions of nature that promote or harm health is another. Many aspects of nature are not susceptible to being modified by human behavior, but far more aspects are susceptible than cultural traditions had believed prior to the development of modern science. Nurturing nature for the sake of its support for the conditions of good human life is a moral concern. Any possibilities that hold differential values for human welfare in respect of protecting and enhancing humanity in individuals, including possibility structures for social institutions and natural causal foundations, provide moral obligations.

Social obligations, by contrast, are those having to do with playing roles in groups, communities, and societies. As Confucians have long stressed, perhaps more than other traditions, to be humane is to inhabit and be obliged to perfect certain fundamental roles in society, such as in family relations, friendships, local and perhaps larger community functions, and in cultural production. Societies define these roles in many different and often conflicting ways, but they include: roles in domestic life, gender identity, education, nurturance; care of the young, elderly, sick, weak, and outcast; roles in economic production, in the provision of shelter, clothing, and tools; roles in military operations, in protection against floods, droughts, fires, and barbarians; roles in government, legislation, policing, and the judiciary; and roles in the enhancement of culture and civilization in the arts and crafts, music, literature, speech, and ritual sensitivity.

Most people play many social roles. No one plays all of them, and societies are structured by the differential assignment of roles. Many social roles are age and cohort specific. Some roles are simply given, such as those having to do with family position. Others, such as leadership roles, need to be assumed, although there can be moral obligations to assume such roles. People learn to play some roles just by functioning in society as the roles dictate; other roles need to be learned through various forms of education and experience. Confucians would point out, rightly, that most roles are defined vaguely in terms of their social function, and that part of being humane is learning to individuate those roles. Parents, for instance, have social obligations to nurture and educate their children; each parent needs to individuate his or her way of caring for each of the individual children as well as the particular structure of the family. Social roles are one kind of ritual, and the playing of rituals ought to be perfected; this is a general theme of social obligations: the obligation to perfect one's ability to fulfill the obligations of one's social roles. Heroism is extraordinary devotion and skill in playing certain kinds of social roles.

In addition to playing the roles to which one is obligated, one also bears the project of integrating these roles within one's life. The diversity of roles and social relations they define constitute important components of life to which one needs to find compartments so that together they can be integrated with personal wholeness, a topic of Chapter 2. Societies differ wildly in the social roles they present to individuals, although all the social functions mentioned earlier need some roles or other to fulfill them.

The roles themselves are not morally neutral, however. Some roles are morally harmful, for instance, roles in an economic system that is oppressive, or certain familial roles in a dysfunctional family. The role of a corrupt official in a government is a bad one, and someone who is heroically successful at such a role is a villain of heroic proportions. For the most part, the obligations to judge the morality of a social role, to support good roles and to dismantle and change bad ones, are elements of moral obligation. The relevant considerations have to do with how the social roles mediate the ways by which individuals are treated in their humanity by actions within the society. The lines between social and moral obligation are blurred when certain social roles, for instance, those of legislators or political leaders, are charged with monitoring and improving the roles in a given society. In modern societies influenced by the Axial Age religions, social roles are idealized as having a moral direction in the ways they are played. But as the corrupt politician illustrates, certain social roles can be played successfully, according to the rules of the role, but without moral probity.

Social and moral obligations can come into stark conflict, as when a soldier has the social role of fighting a war that is morally wrong and that he knows to be so, or at least suspects. The plot of the Bhagavad Gita raises this dilemma in a classic way: Arjuna, the military hero and leader of his faction, is socially obligated to fight and is morally repulsed at having to kill his friends, teachers, and kinsmen. Krishna persuades him to fulfill his social obligation by saying, in effect, that the moral considerations are trivial or irrelevant (you cannot kill immortal souls), and that other issues are much more important than whether to fight or not. In contrast to the individualism of ancient military heroes, soldiers of our own time sometimes find their military obligations to be reduced to mere instruments of political decisions that they might consider immoral. At some point, many will say that their moral obligations outweigh their social obligations to the military, often with disastrous consequences. Many terrorists feel the opposite side of that dilemma, deciding that they will have to use means they know are immoral in order to fulfill their social obligation to their cause.

Personal obligation, nested in with moral and social obligation, is defined by the possibilities of different values that affect the development of the person's own character. A person's character is extremely complicated, especially as tied in with the causal structures that provide obligations of the moral and social sorts and as implicated in the quest for wholeness. One aspect or level of character development is the obligation to develop good habits and skills at fulfilling moral and social obligations. In most cultures, much of this is learned through the repeated practice of moral action and the performance of social roles. Aristotle in the *Nicomachean Ethics* stressed the importance of practice and imitation in learning to be moral and socially ethical. But in complex societies (and which society is not complex?) sometimes it is necessary to take extra pains to develop oneself into a moral person who is socially adept. Aristotle, for instance, said we deliberate about the means but not about the ends of goal-directed actions.[17] Yet often the issues are so complex that we should deliberate about the ends as well. Plato stressed the importance of innovative thinking and dialectic for the discernment of ends.[18]

On another level exist personal virtues that are not, strictly speaking, functions of moral and/or social obligations. For instance, there are moral obligations to care for people and social roles for doing this with expertise; but there is no obligation to be loving that goes beyond care. Yet the Axial Age religions advocate the personal virtue of being loving, however differently they nuance this. Other virtues are like this, such as cultivated sensitivity to others, commitment to beautify one's environment and society, a responsibility for appropriating and representing the accomplishments of the past, and so forth. Perhaps these obligations to personal enhancement can be summed up as obligations to being humane in the richest sense. Different cultures define humane virtue with some variation, and it is central to Confucianism. Yet something like that is an ideal in all cultures because the structure of possibility is such that what individuals are able to do can make them more or less humane, and they are obligated to become more humane where they can. The obligation to choose among possibilities in order to make oneself more humane is related to but not the same as cultivating proper engagement to things in one's existential environment, a different ultimate norm for human life from that of choosing well among possibilities.

Perhaps the highest kind of personal obligation is to develop the best personal value-identity that one can. This includes all the other obligations but as played back to define one's own identity. This sense of personal obligation is taken up in more detail in Chapter 4.

Natural obligation is of a different order from moral, social, and personal obligation and is paradoxical and difficult to express. Perhaps the most effective expression is in the metaphor of "being true" to nature. It is the obligation to live in such a way as to be respectful of the values in nature as these present themselves among the alternatives for choice. In this sense, it is close to the concerns of Chapter 2, having to do with how human beings relate to those things they integrate into their lives, and to those of Chapter 3, having to do with engaging others well. But natural obligation is still an obligation in the sense that it derives from the structure of possibilities with different values that are affected in their outcomes by human actions.

From the cosmos to the local environment and indeed to persons' internal environments, nature bears multitudes of interwoven values. Those values call for respect when they are affected by human behavior. This is perhaps most obvious in the environmental consciousness that has arisen in the last century in modern cultures. It is one thing, a moral obligation, to protect and enhance the natural environment so that it supports human life. It is another thing to protect and enhance it because of its own actual and potential value, and we have natural obligations to do that, too. As we learn that our influences on the environment extend far beyond direct interactions, specific obligations to nature are revealed to be very broad indeed. From concern about overfishing the lake to concern about destroying the ozone layer is a huge expansion of scale of natural obligation. From that to concern about global warming is yet a more significant expansion. What will the human reach into nature be when we start rocketing our wastes into space, and then follow with our own colonists?

This section has indicated schematically some of the types of obligation people face. But this typology is good only for calling attention to the complexity of obligation. Any given instance of facing possibilities with different values needs analysis of the many dimensions of obligation within it.

CHAPTER TWO

Components as the Condition for Grounded Wholeness

The second step in this theological anthropology is to reflect on the need for wholeness as an existential reality in part defining the human condition. The philosophical hypothesis guiding this study of human predicament is that among the ultimate boundary conditions for human life are the transcendental structures of determinateness as such: form, components, existential location, and value-identity. Because every person has many components to harmonize in his or her life, the issues of attending to the values of those components and integrating them together constitute the normative need for well-grounded wholeness. How is this to be understood in terms of engaging ultimacy?

The previous chapter investigated the ultimate human conditions that arise from the fact that every determinate thing, including each human being, has form. The most relevant aspect of form in human life is that people face possibilities that contain alternative possible outcomes over which they have some control, and about which they must choose. Because all possibilities are bearers of value, and the alternative outcomes often have different values, people lie under obligation to choose and actualize the better rather than the worse possibilities. What they choose determines the kind of value-identity they have. To choose and actualize the better, so far as lies within their powers, is to make them better agents, more responsible; to fail to do that is to make them worse people. "Better" and "worse" are not the only judgments to be made about how people define themselves by choices: the kinds of choices they make define them as kinds of people. Human predicaments with regard to form have to do with the obligation to choose the better possibilities and the common, if not necessary at least nearly inevitable, failure to do so.

Also, however, are the ultimate boundary conditions and predicaments that arise from the need to integrate the components of life. All harmonies have components that are integrated according to the possibilities actualized. These components include both conditional components and essential components (*I, 10*). The conditional components are indefinitely various, but for human life the most important ones are those having to do with the people and social institutions that make up human life, the natural biological processes that are part of life, and the roles than human beings play in the larger ecology of nature. To have a meal with one's family is to deal with all four loci of conditional components as components. The essential components are the components that have to do with the integration of the conditional components, moment by moment. They, too, are indefinitely various, but for human life the most important ones are those that have to do with how people address obligations, how they comport themselves to the components of their lives, how they engage things with which they are in important existential relation, and the value-identities they achieve. A person is not the essential components alone, but the concrete harmonic integration of the conditional and essential components that results from the essential components as well as the conditional components.

I. DEFERENCE AND INTEGRATION

Because human beings have some control over what they do and become, a problem arises as to how to comport oneself with regard to one's components. On the one hand, a harmony obviously does integrate its components according to its formal pattern. On the other hand, the components of a person's life have value in themselves (because of their own forms) and therefore deserve to be treated with respect for those values. A rock has no such problem, for it has no choice in the matter and simply is what it is. But human beings have different ways by which they can comport themselves toward their components. When they comport themselves well or authentically, they are well grounded in their components; "well-groundedness" is an important theme to be explored in this chapter. When they comport themselves poorly or inauthentically, people are not well grounded but rather somewhat alienated from some important parts of themselves. Those human predicaments having to do with components of life arise from the fact that it is an ultimate normative condition of human life to be well grounded and yet very difficult to be so.

Human comportment to the components of life looks in two directions. Facing the components, comportment addresses them as making claims in terms of their own values. Facing the function of harmonizing them, comportment needs to integrate them so as to make up the harmony of the person. The term "wholeness" here as applied to a person's life signifies the particular kind of harmony that is measured by both groundedness and integration. Integration that does not ground the person appropriately in the components, comporting itself toward them with due respect, is defectively located in the things that provide conditional components for the person's life. Integration, on the other hand, that does not bring coherence to those components so that the life has some unity in human terms is defectively harmonized. Wholeness is to be understood in this study in terms of both quality of groundedness and quality of integration.

Insofar as the ways by which human beings comport themselves toward their components are matters of choice, all the dimensions of obligation discussed in Chapter 1 are relevant to comportment as well. The rough loci of obligation also show up as loci of comportment. Human beings comport themselves toward other people and should do so morally. They comport themselves toward the social institutions that mediate human relations and have social obligations to comport themselves well. Similarly they comport themselves to their own persons and should respect the obligations involved there, and they comport themselves toward their place in the wider natural world with all the convoluted obligations involved in this. Moreover, human relations themselves are kinds of harmonies, and so the condition exists to make those relations well grounded when they are functions of conjoint actions, not of individuals alone. As semiotically organized institutions of human relations as well as interactions with the natural environment, societies themselves should be well grounded in their components. The human place in nature and the roles of individuals and societies in this also should be well grounded. Thus there exists a complex network of obligations to well-groundedness. That network of obligations for well-groundedness also poses issues of integration relative to each.

Comportment with regard to the components of life is not reduced to obligations, however. Comportment usually is the achieved and habituated disposition toward the components. It is an embodied orientation toward them that shapes how people take up their components when they deal with them, including when they deal with them under the rubrics of obligation.

Orientation was discussed in *Philosophical Theology One*, Chapters 1 and 4, in terms of worldviews providing symbols within which the various affairs of life might be contextualized with reference to one another, perhaps with regard to ultimacy. The orientation involved in comportment toward components is also symbolically shaped. Because the elements in a worldview might be more or less comprehensive and consistent, individuals employ or commit themselves to worldviews in various ways. A worldview orients elements in human life to one another according to a larger picture of reality. The orientation involved in comportment has more to do with the comporting individual, society, relationship, and human place in the natural order than it does with how the affairs in which they are involved are oriented to one another. Comportment is the integral person's orientation to his or her components, not the orientation of the components to one another. The orientation in comportment is embodied in the ways the person addresses the various kinds of components.

It would be tempting to say that comportment is an embodied orientation of the whole self to components. Nevertheless, wholeness of self is a rare achievement. Psychologists point out that we have various "self states" that often are dissociated from one another: associating them is a great achievement. Cognitive scientists point out that the neural basis of semiotically shaped human behavior involves the integration of a number of systems that do not always run well together. This element of integration, too, is an achievement. Of course, components of a harmony, including a person or a person's whole life, de facto hang together even if in terrible ways that are destructive to the components and to the forms of togetherness in the person. So often, basic components of life work against other basic components. As mentioned, however, what is ultimate in the matter of a person comporting appropriately to the components of life and integrating them well so as to have wholeness is both respect for the values in the components and elegance in the forms by which they are combined.

II. MYTHOS: ORIENTATION TO WHOLENESS

Our discussion in this chapter so far has been very abstract. The abstraction is such as to make it abundantly clear, as is illustrated copiously in the chapters of this volume, that all large religions have projects for developing wholeness. The project of becoming whole is related to but different from the project of making good decisions relative to the possibilities that people face. At this point, however, it is appropriate to introduce another instrument of analysis for the ultimate predicaments surrounding wholeness, the notion of a mythos.

Probably for most people in most cultures, identification of and comportment toward the important components of life, and the forms of their integration in life, are organized by supervening signs that derive from a mythos. A mythos is a set of stories or legends—and geographies and cosmic histories—that identify what life is about, what its joys, sorrows, and obstacles are, what kinds or shapes of persons play the important roles, and how lives are organized according to appropriate virtues and heroic acts. Mythic structures have been well analyzed by scholars, particularly classicists, for generations. But the distinguished popular historical theologian Karen Armstrong perhaps makes the best statement:

> In most premodern cultures, there were two recognized ways of thinking, speaking, and acquiring knowledge. The Greeks called them *mythos* and *logos*. Both were essential and neither was considered superior to the other; they were not in conflict but complementary. Each had its own sphere of competence, and it was considered unwise to mix the two. *Logos* ("reason") was the pragmatic mode of thought that enabled people to function effectively in the world. It had, therefore, to correspond accurately to external reality. People have always needed *logos* to make an efficient weapon, organize their societies, or plan an expedition.... *Logos* was essential to the survival of our species. But it had its limitations: it

could not assuage human grief or find ultimate meaning in life's struggles. For that people turned to *mythos* or "myth."

Today we live in a society of scientific *logos*, and myth has fallen into disrepute. In popular parlance, a "myth" is something that is not true. But in the past, myth was not self-indulgent fantasy; rather, like *logos*, it helped people to live effectively in our confusing world, though in a different way. Myths may have told stories about the gods, but they were really focused on the more elusive, puzzling, and tragic aspects of the human predicament that lay outside the remit of *logos*. . . .

The only way to assess the value and truth of any myth was to act upon it. The myth of the hero, for example, which takes the same form in nearly all cultural traditions, taught people how to unlock their own heroic potential. Later the stories of historical figures such as the Buddha, Jesus, or Muhammad were made to conform to this paradigm so that their followers could imitate them in the same way. Put into practice, a myth could tell us something profoundly true about our humanity. It showed us how to live more richly and intensely, how to cope with our mortality, and how creatively to endure the suffering that flesh is heir to.[1]

The legends, sacred geographies and cosmic histories of a mythos are proper parts of a sacred canopy (I, pt. 1). Not every sacred canopy has such mythic elements; for instance, many scientific worldviews with secularistic sacred canopies flush out mythic elements. A mythos does not function as a mythos, however, unless it affects large portions of a worldview outside the sacred canopy such that it provides models for thinking, valuing, and acting in many domains of life so that they do not act at cross purposes. In many respects, a mythos is needed to give meaningful orientation to the domains of life and prescribe proper ways to behave within them. Cumulatively, a mythos provides the symbols by which individuals, and sometimes communities, define what it means to integrate the various component domains into wholeness. A mythos might also affect other aspects of human predicament than the quest for wholeness, but its cultural center of gravity lies in the wholeness problematic. The truth of a mythos lies in its value for providing forms for wholeness, not in its representation of the nature of the ultimate as other symbols of ultimacy aim to do. People in the ancient worlds of East, South, and West Asia might not have distinguished between their mythic and their logical symbols. Modern people do make that distinction.

In *Philosophical Theology*, the mythic function of providing overarching symbols for wholeness is to be evaluated according to the spiritual success it has with regard to providing models that (1) are appropriate for grounding people in the components of their lives and that (2) integrate those components so as to enrich life beyond those components as separate from one another or barely touching. The truth questions therefore are not those of representative truth but rather are about how the mythos grounds people well or poorly in their components and how richly it integrates those components as well grounded.[2] Mythic symbols in a sacred canopy are among those responsive to the demands for intimacy in articulating the ultimate realities of human life.

The significance of mythos for wholeness can be illustrated in our time by the attempt to supply contemporary myths where traditional myths have failed to function. For comparative purposes the mythic works discussed here are taken from the Euro-American cultural tradition, with English-language expression; they have some currency outside that cultural sphere but by and large might not be forcefully intelligible outside it, unfortunately. They all are re-mythologizings of what they take to be the Christian, or a Christian, mythos.

III. SOME CONTEMPORARY CHRISTIAN RE-MYTHOLOGIES

Consider first the *Narnia* stories by C. S. Lewis. These volumes were written ostensibly for children whose mythos they were intended to become.[3] Narnia is a magical country entered by children, and in the first novel the portal is the back of a wardrobe in an English country house. Children, of course, have been taught rough and ready rules about what things are real and how they behave. In Narnia, things behave differently (for instance, many animals talk). But then, for children, the ways things work in the real world are still often different from their childish expectations and a magical land of surprises is somewhat iconic of their own experience. In the mythos of Narnia, everyday things are often much more important than they seem, and the English visitors, all children who are capable of taking magic at face value, are called upon to do heroic things that bring out powers and potentials that they did not know they had. In the Narnia stories there are forces of evil as well as powers of good. In the first novel, *The Lion, the Witch and the Wardrobe*, one of the children is seduced by the evil side, which offers tempting sweets and plays upon the boy's resentment of being ordered around by his older brother (who is usually right but immature in managing the younger brother). The boy repents of his folly and is rescued by the good people and animals around his siblings. The evil witch, however, owns his soul because he had betrayed his siblings and their friends. Aslan, the divine lion who is a surrogate for Jesus in this mythos, redeems the boy from the witch by submitting himself to be killed. But anyone who in innocence lays down his life for another comes back to life, which Aslan does, in the company of the two sisters of the condemned boy. Meanwhile, the army of the evil creatures led by the witch advance upon the army of good creatures led by the elder brother and there is a battle to the death, testing the courage of the brothers and their band, until Aslan arrives with the sisters and wins the day. The mythic background requires that Narnia be saved by the "sons and daughters of men," not by Narnia's own intelligent and verbal creatures who can only cooperate with the humans. In reward for various deeds of heroism, the four children are made kings and queens of Narnia to rule in glory, with primogeniture giving order to their royal rule.

Embedded in the stories are some powerful and perhaps unfortunate stereotypes that become powerful and usually unconscious elements of mythic consciousness. For instance, Narnian people are all white and take quickly to the English children, whereas in many of the stories the bad people are dark-skinned and have vaguely Middle-Eastern name styles. The good people carry straight swords whereas the bad ones have scimitars. In most of the stories girls are represented as well as boys, often in careful balance; but the gender roles are stereotyped to a great extent.

Nevertheless, in the mythos, virtue is associated with nobility of character to which anyone can rise, and vice is a baseness to which it is easy to fall. Courage is called for even when things look extremely bleak. Affairs are highly unpredictable, and the point is made over and over that Aslan is not a tame lion and cannot be counted on to be around when needed. Contrary to many understandings of Christianity, victory within time is not assured, and the seventh novel is in fact about the end of Narnia, which is destroyed and all the good people and creatures killed despite their heroism. No world lasts forever, it is said. In the last, deep-night battle around a bonfire, the valiant children, the last king of Narnia, and the good creatures are overwhelmed by their enemies and are driven dying through the door of a wretched stable where they emerge in a sunlit land like Narnia at its best, though more intense. The people (dwarves) who refused to take sides in the last battle between good and evil are in that suddenly revealed land but can see nothing but blackness because they lived "only for themselves." The others rush "further up and further in" to more intensely real and broader landscapes of Narnia, eventually connecting with the landscape of England, then with ever more inclusive locations of reality. The imagery of increasingly dense reality is an artful imagining of the eternal life in the ultimate as the ontological ground of mutual relevance that is described in *Philosophical Theology One*, Chapter 12, and elsewhere. The mythic themes in the *Narnia* stories include the heroic ideal of living nobly like kings and queens in the face of adversity, the expectation that the weakest might prove to be the strongest, the lesson that evil plays on human weaknesses, the conviction that evil can be redeemed but always at a cost of innocent sacrifice, and the importance of courage and fighting to the last because that is the right thing to do without expecting victory (a point that is central to the Bhagavad Gita, as well). The mythic problem that gives meaning to life, in the Narnia vision, is how to face evil and its temptations when the universe is utterly strange, magical, and unpredictable, and God (Aslan) is wild, not the always-in-charge predictable king. Human hope should lie in other-timely (or eternal) happiness, not this-worldly victory.

J. R. R. (Ronald) Tolkien was a contemporary and close friend of C. S. Lewis whose three-volume *The Lord of the Rings* came out in the early

1950s shortly before the *Narnia* books were published in 1959. Lewis, early a skeptic, was (re)converted to Christianity largely because of the influence of Tolkien, who was a Roman Catholic. Lewis returned to his Anglican version of Christianity.[4] *The Lord of the Rings*, like *The Chronicles of Narnia*, is fantasy and could never be interpreted as nonmythic theology. It is a mythic model of life set in a different world to be applied to the understanding of this world, and it has gathered an extraordinary cult following that includes many non-Christians. In fact, whereas Aslan is a thinly disguised Christ figure, there is no Christ figure in *The Lord of the Rings*, although the good wizard, Gandalf, dies in a vicious fight and comes back to life to lead his troops to victory. Tolkien maintains a strict distinction between good and evil. The plot unfolds as the good people destroy a powerful ring before it can be used by the evil forces to destroy them, and the subplot is that the ring has a seductive power tempting those who carry or wear it so that the final obstacle to its destruction is the reluctance of the hero, Frodo, to cast it into the fire that would melt it down.

Like Lewis, Tolkien distinguishes the good from the evil generally by race, with humans, hobbits, dwarves, wizards, and elves being good, and Orcs of various species and other beasts commanded by the semi-divine evil spirit, Sauron, being evil. In the films, the good people all have good teeth, and the bad creatures are bereft of dentistry. One hobbit, Gollum, is broken by the ring's seductive power and is evil, though his attempt to prevent the ring's destruction in the end actually causes it. One man, Boromir, is seduced by the ring but manages to redeem himself by an heroic defense of the good people. One wizard, Saruman, is seduced by Sauron, not by the ring, to the evil side. Tolkien is less nuanced than Lewis regarding the psychology of seduction—love of power promised by the ring is about all there is. But like Lewis with his heroic children, Tolkien's myth elevates the smallest and weakest people, the hobbits, to the positions of greatest strength and accomplishment. Far more than Lewis, Tolkien emphasizes friendship and cooperation in the struggle to destroy the ring and hence the evil Sauron. The first volume is about a "fellowship" of representatives of different races questing forth to destroy the ring in the midst of Mordor, Sauron's own territory. The fellowship is broken with some hobbits going into Mordor and the rest of the party staying on the good side of the river that separates the bad and good lands. After the separation, those on each side are deeply concerned about and act in reference to what the others might be doing. Alliances are built by both sides, with the leaders of the good side bringing both an alien nation of humans and a large army of human ghosts to their aid in the final battle. Even Sauron and Saruman have a peculiar kind of manipulative friendship. Friendship for Tolkien crosses social classes, human cultural differences, and interspecies rivalries, and the friendships are developed with great subtlety.

The main theme of *The Lord of the Rings* is the struggle of the good people against an enemy vastly superior in force. They win by courage, intelligence, and mutual help against martial opposition, the temptations of the ring, and despair—the greatest enemy. The victory is plainly historical, on a battlefield, and there is no hint of tragedy or loss. Almost no people on the good side die except heroically. Nothing of Lewis's sense of world's ending occurs in *The Lord of the Rings*, although the age of the dominance of the world by elves is shifted to the age of human beings. In this sense it is a saga of human coming-of-age and taking of responsibility. The whole of the *Rings* and its surrounding mythology is set within an extended sense of time. This contrasts with Lewis's sense that what happens within time is somehow abstract compared with its deeper reality. For both Lewis and Tolkien, in one sense the ideal for human life is the noble, the kings and queens. Actually, women have but a small place in Tolkien's story, which is at one level about Aragorn, the legitimate heir, earning the right to be the true king. In another sense, for both Lewis and Tolkien, the non-noble people can show extraordinary virtue in their courage and ability to conquer despair. Tolkien's novels are exquisitely crafted in plot and characterization so that people of nearly all ages can identify with the meaning of life that is depicted: meaning is found in having a great quest where the obstacles are mainly temptations to go over to the dark side and to give in to despair. *The Lord of the Rings* has filled the fantasy lives of several generations of readers.

The *Star Wars* films by George Lucas appeared about twenty years after the Lewis and Tolkien novels. They are more explicitly religious than Lewis and Tolkien's stories, with a main theme being the mysterious Force that binds together the entire cosmos and provides extraordinary powers to those who cultivate and rightly relate to it. Like the Chinese *qi*, the Force has Daoist resonances that are highly attractive to Westerners who find implausible the anthropomorphic images of ultimacy that abound in theism. Disaffected Jews and Christians can salute one another with "May the Force be with you!" and think of themselves as being spiritual but not religious. Rather unlike the Daoist sensibility, however, the *Star Wars* mythos centers the meaning of human life on a quest, as in *The Lord of the Rings*. The means to the quest is the cultivation of the Force in one's own powers, following the martial traditions in most cultures. Moreover, the Force can be cultivated for evil: going over to the "dark side" is language that derives from the *Star Wars* mythos. The main thematic plot of the original three *Star Wars* films is the struggle of the heroes of the Force, the Jedi Knights, against the villains of the Force. The subplot is the search of the hero, Luke Skywalker, for his father, who turns out to be the villain of the Force, Darth Vader. The original films were followed up three decades later with three more films, not sequels to the original action as might be expected, but prequels that explain how Luke's father, originally so gifted and good, could become seduced to the dark side of the force. Like Lewis and Tolkien, Lucas represents human beings as originally good but subject to seduction, and also redemption: Luke redeems his father in the end.

The mythos of *Star Wars* is that life is a battle between good and evil, and that these divisions derive from different ways of relating to and internalizing ultimate reality. Ultimate reality is in one sense the ground of all goodness because it is the Force connecting and energizing all things. But it is not intentional in any sense and can be appropriated for evil intentions. Meaning in life derives from one's roles in this battle. Unlike Tolkien, Lucas manages to give women important roles in the wars. Whereas Lewis and especially Tolkien focus greatly on psychological character development, the original Star Wars trilogy is much more one-dimensional in this regard, being limited mainly to martial cultivation. The *Star Wars* prequels are more psychologically complicated. Yet the *Star Wars* characters are defined in terms of their intriguing roles, which provide many opportunities for mythic fantasy.

In direct contrast to the *Star Wars* films, J. K. Rowling's *Harry Potter* series of books centers predominantly on psychological and spiritual development. They start with the entrance of eleven-year-old Harry Potter into a magical British preparatory school for magicians, Hogwarts, and progress one novel per year until he is seventeen. Each novel is written in language appropriate for readers of the age of Harry Potter, beginning with relatively short and accessible texts to a 759-page concluding novel. The books have been extraordinarily popular with young readers who have lined up for hours to buy the volumes the hour they come out; some critics have credited these novels with restoring the interest of young people in reading and, although excellent highly professional blockbuster films have been made of each book, reading the novels themselves has captivated not only the age-equivalent fans of Harry but others as well. They have the fascinating intricacy of nineteenth-century Russian novels.

The overarching plot is Harry's adventures to fend off the attempts to kill him by Voldemort, a socially inept and isolated young wizard of great power who aims to make himself the master of evil. Voldemort had tried to do this when Harry was an infant, killing both his parents (magical adepts and graduates of Hogwarts) and causing Harry to be raised by his totally unmagical aunt and uncle. The first novel is filled with things of interest to an eleven year old: magic tricks, athletic games on broomsticks, weird places—especially the Hogwarts campus—making new friends (Harry's friends Hermione and Ron grow with him through the novels, as do several other characters), finding mentors and parental figures, and battling for a magic talisman. Each succeeding novel gets more complicated psychologically, testing friendships, mastering crafts, and growing through the travails of puberty. The cast of characters grows in complexity. In the final novel Harry has to overcome all dependency on his friends and mentors, while coming to appreciate them for the flawed but wonderful people they are. In the end he has to will his own death in order to overcome Voldemort, who is destroying all the things Harry holds dear. In a sense, Harry is like Aslan, who has to sacrifice himself for others in order to save and redeem them. Whereas Aslan is always innocent, however, in line with the mythos of innocent blood redeeming the guilty, Harry has to die because a small part of the evil Voldemort was implanted in him when he was attacked as an infant. All along, like Voldemort Harry could speak the language of snakes, and he came to be able to read Voldemort's mind and feel his vile intentions as his own, though he steadily struggled against the part of Voldemort in himself. By letting Voldemort kill him without any hint of revival or return, Harry allows the evil in himself to be killed and so is able to choose to return without the evil that had become part of him and to kill Voldemort instead. The moral is that we have to die to the evil within us in order to live effectively according to the good in us. Even the best of us, like the hero Harry Potter, need to die in order to be reborn to that best.

In contrast to the moral and aesthetic clarity of the Lewis, Tolkien, and Lucas works, most of the people, creatures, and buildings in the Harry Potter books are ugly; toads and rats are beloved pets. The only "beautiful people" are the Malfoys, who throughout most of the novels represent opposition to Harry but turn out to be not so bad in the end. All the characters are morally ambivalent and many sided; their evil intentions come to be understandable in terms of motivation. The sneering Professor Snape is a mystery in his loyalties throughout, jealous of Harry and pining after Harry's mother whom he loved; at the end of the sixth novel he kills Harry's beloved mentor Dumbledore; at the end of the seventh this is revealed to have been part of a plot initiated by Dumbledore to prepare Harry to face Voldemort. Dumbledore himself, Harry's protector through the first six novels, turns out to have a checkered past from which he has learned hard lessons. Dumbledore greets the murdered Harry in a kind of limbo and poses to him the question whether he would like to withdraw from messy, violent, apparently hopeless affairs in death, as Dumbledore has done, or to return to take on Voldemort one last time. Harry chooses to return, accepting the moral ambiguities. Many of Harry's friends have been killed in the last great battle (in which women were just as fierce warriors as men) but Harry finally kills Voldemort. In the end, Harry marries Ron's sister and sends their children to Hogwarts, dealing with only the ordinary vicissitudes of life, having conquered his own nemesis.

Vastly more complex than the other mythic tales discussed here, Rowling's mythos is a Christian death-and-resurrection story without a transcendent or supernatural divinity like Aslan or the Force, and without a cosmic history like *The Lord of the Rings*. It beautifies nothing, and in fact finds good in the ugly and outsized. Evil, which seems like a somewhat clear oppositional element to the eleven-year-old Harry, turns out to be much more complex, composed of accidents, misfortunes, ambivalence, and many-sided motives. Evil is within oneself even when it is being resisted. It is found in all people, even the apparently heroic who sometimes are heroes in spite of it. Friendship is the deepest source of pleasure and power, but true friendship results in independence where one can act alone. Grief for one's friends and one's own death can be borne because it is good to engage life. The eschatological fulfillment is not some "higher up and further in" intensification of reality, as in Lewis's vision, but learning to live with death in doing heroic things in a muddled world.

In comparison with Lewis, Tolkien, and Lucas, Rowling's mythos is far more complex, realistic, and heroic in ways that relate to actual modern life. That it has such an appeal in modern Western life means, in part, that the simplifying escapisms of the other mythic tales are not as satisfying as life properly lived, in which the home of one's paideia is lovingly likened to warts on a hog.

In the last century, these mythic tales have functioned as orienting imaginations of what is important in human life and how those important things are to be ordered in daily living and troubled times. The cultural situation has been such that for a great many literate people in the West and other English-speaking lands, the tales of the Christian Bible cannot function as an orienting mythos. For some people, the traditional Christian imagery is taken almost literally, which means it competes with science, finds itself on the defensive, and ceases to be able to provide mythic orientation; the substitute mythos for fundamentalists is that of fighting to defend a religious culture against delegitimation, not a theme close to Christian content. Something similar holds for other forms of religious fundamentalism. For many of the nonfundamentalists, the biblical tales seem to be too supernaturalistic to be plausible in a religiously iconic sense, and so are dismissed from serious consideration. Yet those supernaturalistic symbols might very well function mythically if appeal to "magic" makes the mythos function to be non-iconic, not about what it seems to be about, but rather about how to orient life to the integration of its important components. The function of mythos can be illustrated further by a restatement of some of the mythic functions of two versions of the traditional Christian symbols.

Philosophical Theology One, Chapter 8, distinguished two major framing conceptions of theology, the narrative and the metaphysical. Although the distinction appears in most religious traditions, it is exemplified in recent Christian theology by Karl Barth and Paul Tillich, respectively. According to the narrative version of Christianity, the mythos is the story of creation, fall, and redemption, and people find meaning through their places in that narrative. Lewis's *Narnia* stories most clearly fall within that frame. Tolkien's *The Lord of the Rings* does as well, especially when set alongside others of his writings such as the *Silmarillion*: within the greater cosmic created order is the passage of ages in Middle Earth from the age of the elves to that of men. Lucas's *Star Wars* films have little sense of being set within an ultimately significant created cosmos. Nevertheless, the several-generation span of the action, from innocence to fall to redemption, attempts to give meaning to individual life within a much larger story of galactically measured historical events. Karl Barth's own theology reads more like a cosmic, mythic narrative of creation, the absolutely central importance for the cosmos of human beings, who fall, and who are redeemed by God in Christ. In Barth's narrative God in Christ is the only major player. At the same time, Barth holds that human beings have their own responsibility, a paradox in his Calvinist divine-sovereignty mythos.

An alternative Christian metaphysically framed mythos downplays the cosmic narrative (and can accept the scientific evolutionary narratives at face value) and does not refer to a battle between divine goodness and forces of evil. It affirms that creation is fundamentally good and that people are, as well. Many evils come from conflicts of goods and from plain accidents of natural, social, and personal forces. But sin as a corruption of originally good potential, or failure of the maturation of goodness, is real as well: in this mythos, the blackness of the human heart cannot be underestimated. Nevertheless, the biblical pictures of Jesus affirm that guilts of the blackest heart can be annulled so that anyone whosoever can be restored or developed into right relation with the ultimate creator and the whole of creation. Following the examples of Jesus, and guided by the symbols of the Holy Spirit, people can live with the ambiguities of life, dying to the evil within them and always ready to take the next step of life refreshed. In this metaphysical Christian mythos, redemption is always possible and there is always hope in redemption and happiness. But there is no guarantee that good (or bad) enterprises will be successful within time, no comedy in this sense. The quality of spiritual life does not depend on winning but on being in right relation with the ultimates. In the mythic Christian terms, human happiness consists in delighting in the glories of God's creation, with God often being imaged in personalistic terms, in terms of the depth of mystical consciousness, and in terms of the dynamic power in all emergence and transformation. A proper Christian mythic image of heaven would be a party in celebration of God's glory, with whatever one might find desirable in heaven. Given the biblical references to Jesus going to find rooms for his disciples, and his skill at winemaking at the marriage in Cana, Heaven might be like a great college party!

This discussion of the search for an adequate Christian mythos in the English-speaking world, in the context of the modern breakdown of the mythic function of traditional Christian symbols, is intended to illustrate the function that a mythos plays in the quest for wholeness. This function is very different from the descriptive function of religious symbols that aims to articulate what is ultimate and how that impacts sacred worldviews. Of course, that descriptive function is important in its own right. And a personal or cultural mythos is important for more than organizing the components of life so as to achieve some wholeness. But the point here is to focus on the symbolic roles of a mythos for framing the integration of the important components, and for identifying what those components are.

Other cultures have different mythic structures for these functions, some of which are discussed in what follows and in *Philosophical Theology Three*. Here it is worth pointing out that some of those structures bear resemblance to the heroic structure of the Christian mythoi, for instance, the saga of Arjuna in the Bhagavad Gita. And yet in the South Asian tradition lies another set of myths, those having to do with the ascetic or hero of consciousness. The attainment of adept powers in the purification and control of consciousness characterizes all the myths that focus on the role of the guru. In these mythic structures, the integration of the components of life comes from the centering of consciousness. Buddhist and Hindu mythic structures are different in many ways, particularly in the ways the self is modeled as relating to the components of life, relativizing them in the former cases and sometimes embracing them in the latter. Yet the meditative approach to consciousness and its deeper levels is similar in both. It provides an intimate experiential model of the ultimate reality of the ontological act of creation resulting in the plural world set in the venue of the ontological context of mutual relevance. Whereas the cosmological ultimate reality of form evokes experiences of spontaneous emergence in the case of free choice, the cosmological ultimate reality of comportment toward components can center profoundly on the experience of consciousness as the integrating factor laying out the ontological context of mutual relevance.

The next step in our analysis is to discuss four modes of authentic comportment: appropriation, deference, negotiating change, and realism.

IV. COMPORTMENTS: APPROPRIATION, DEFERENCE, NEGOTIATING CHANGE, REALISM

The first mode of comportment has to do with how a person *appropriates* the important components. Perhaps the paradigm case is filial piety in the Confucian sense. Parents, of course, are crucial components of a person's life, regardless of how well the person appropriates what the parents can give. In the Confucian understanding, however, the parents are supposed to embody a high degree of virtue that the children can appropriate so as to become virtuous themselves. Adult children are supposed to take care of elderly parents, to be sure, and this is how the social roles are organized (and not only in Confucian societies). The most important part of filial piety, however, is for the children to become sufficiently virtuous that the parents are freed of the obligation to make their children virtuous. Becoming a good person is the greatest gift a child can give parents. In the Confucian (and not only the Confucian) moral firmament, the many facets of personal goodness have to do with becoming humane. Humaneness is something learned primarily from parental humaneness. And so, the root way to become good is to appropriate the parents' virtue. Yet not all parents are particularly virtuous. Therefore, sometimes children have to reach back to more distant ancestors to find the virtues to appropriate. (Confucius was so discouraged about the virtue in his time that he reached all the way back to the legendary sage emperors to find the rituals that could carry virtue.) Carrying down and repristinating ancestral virtue thus allows children to make their parents more virtuous than they really are, which is the heart of filial piety. Many people besides parents are components of a person's life, and all should be honored by appropriating what is best in them, perhaps making them better in the process. Cultures have different models and even different mythic motifs of what parental or ancestral virtue involves.

Roughly continuous with parents, family and cultural traditions are important components of life and should be appropriated in the best ways possible. Authentic comportment toward traditions means appropriating them so as to recognize and internalize their values in the richest ways. Of course, traditions, even family traditions, are multifaceted and not always consistent. Moreover, the traditions are components of contemporary lives that are somewhat different from the lives that bore the traditions in the past, and so the traditions are transformed when appropriated anew. They need to be harmonized with new conditions. Authentic appropriation does not mean simply repeating the traditions but the judicious transformation of them so that the best in the tradition is carried over to contribute to current flourishing while the downsides of the tradition are excluded. The Christian tradition, for instance, has in the past been deeply anti-Semitic; because of the evil of anti-Semitism, that Christian tradition needs to be appropriated in ways that exclude anti-Semitism today.

A potential conflict arises between the needs to appropriate the better rather than the worse elements of the tradition and to integrate the tradition with other elements in contemporary life. A person integrating traditions into a single life has many concerns that determine the possible shape of the integration. Honoring and appropriating the best of those traditions sometimes is too high a price to pay for getting through the night. Under stress, people often push away their family traditions so as to conform to a more viable way of integrating themselves within a narrower boundary, often one that is reinforced by their present circumstances. Sometimes it is easier to appropriate the worse sides, for instance, anti-Semitism, if there are pressing reasons to find a scapegoat. Authenticity of appropriation requires honoring the valuable in the tradition rather than serving the needs of current harmonization. Sometimes this is not possible. A functional mythos, however, might provide models for appropriating traditions artfully under the press of contemporary circumstances. Or, reference to such a mythos might be a counterweight to the temptations to cut traditional baggage. Sometimes, traditions that are or should be components of a person's contemporary integrity are simply not compatible with one another except through modifications that reflect too much the contemporary needs of integration.

Countless biological processes are components of human life, including the human body and its metabolic environment. Comportment to the human biological network is authentic when the biological contributions are recognized and maximized in value. Given a choice of diet, people comport themselves authentically toward their metabolic processes by eating healthy foods. People comport themselves authentically toward their body when they exercise and optimize their physical capacities. Most religious traditions recognize physical training as part of spiritual exercises, as in yoga or martial arts. Human bodies grow through stages, each of which involves different elements of comportment and integration. Those stages take place within changing environments of family, neighborhood, and economy, all of which bear upon proper comportment to personal biology.

In addition to comporting themselves toward their own biological processes, people comport themselves toward nature as a whole insofar as that is symbolized within their consciousness. Authentic comportment toward nature involves organizing life so as to enhance nature through human roles. In this context, nature is appropriated by means of orienting human roles to support its flourishing, however that is understood. Some ancient cultures contributing to the mythos of a contemporary religion gave high priority to the integration of the human within the larger cosmos. This was particularly true of the original religions of East Asia, including Daoism, Confucianism, and Shamanism. Others had mythic representations of withdrawal from deep involvement with nature into the protections of inner consciousness. Western ancient mythic motifs sometimes emphasized the human imperative to dominate nature. Most mythoi are not consistent, however, and the motifs of natural harmonization, withdrawal, and dominance can contest with each other in cultural consciousness.

The second mode of comportment has to do with *deference* to the integrities of the important components of life. As harmonized together in a person's life, the components are often compromised, and the demands of harmony take precedence over the flourishing of the components within the limits of the components performing their functions within the harmony. In face of obligations to optimize the values in human relations, in societies, personal development, and environmental interactions, the demands of justice can compromise the integrities of components severely. Acknowledging this, authentic comportment toward components involves deference. Deference is the acknowledgment of the integrity and worth of the components on their own, irrespective of the immediate roles they play in the person's, relationship's, society's, or nature's harmonies.

The most obvious comportment of deference again is in the Confucian model. At the base of all human relations in that model is the practice of recognizing other people for who and what they are, with their specific roles, values, and needs. The practice of ritual propriety is aimed to make deference the base of all relations. But everyone is different, according to Confucian ethics, and so everyone should be deferred to as unique, even though involved in ritual relations. Part of the unique value-identity of individuals is the roles they play in complicated social networks. These include roles in reference to those who would defer to them. So, part of deference is skill in reciprocating ritual relationships so as to allow the others to be themselves in fulfilling ways. Deference to others is far more than reciprocating in rituals of deference, however. It includes all the skills of discernment that allow one to mirror the other at the same time as recognizing the difference of the other from oneself. Deference in any authentic mode requires restraint, self-control, and an ability to fit the other into one's own harmonious world in ways that reflect the other's specific humanity. Obviously, deference is difficult when the other plays instrumental roles in one's harmony. These points about ritual and deference in the Confucian vocabulary have important analogues in the general notion of dharma as duty in Hindu cultures.

Besides people, social institutions themselves are due deference, even when a person is using them instrumentally. The legal system, for instance, is an instrument for obtaining justice, and so it is made a component of one's life. In addition, however, the legal system has its own integrity, and a person using the system can comport himself or herself to the system as such by recognizing that integrity and worth, even when it might be possible to distort the system to the person's advantage.

Nature, too, contributes many components to a person's life toward which the person can be comported with authenticity. Food, for instance, is essential to the person, and eating it destroys the animal or the life cycle of plants eaten. Not to respect the animal or plants, however, not to realize that they are paying the price of one's own health and survival, is inauthentic deference. Many cultures, but especially Native American ones, ritualize deference to the things in nature that must be used for human survival and culture.

Nature as a whole, however this might be symbolized in various cultures, also is an object of deference insofar as the roles human beings play in nature are components of their own being. Authentic comportment toward nature involves finding ways of living within nature that allow its integrity to be maintained.

The third mode of comportment has to do with *negotiating change*. Change is necessary for the achievement of possible harmonies. But change also means the loss of something in achieved harmonies. One of the fundamental characteristics of Shiva is to be at once the creator and destroyer. Continuity through change means the reachievement of important elements of harmony moment by moment. Although it is conceivable that all the important components of a person's life remain the same through changing times, in point of fact the components themselves usually are changing, and the person's continuity means reaffirming, in some sense, essential components that make for the continuity. Of course, continuity is not always good or desired. In a number of senses people want to change. But in a deeper sense, people want to be sure that it is they themselves (with a continuing identity) who change.

The human predicament of negotiating change is thus extraordinarily complex, dealing with all kinds of issues of achievement, loss, and meaningful continuity through change. The ancient background cosmology of East Asian culture supposes that changes are the most basic units of physical, mental, and spiritual reality, a supposition that is seemingly at odds with Western conceptions of reality as substantial. Any kind of formed reality, in the East Asian conception, is a pattern of yin-yang changes. The metaphoric center of "yang" is the act of extension, which reaches some limit of its own power and then retreats, as "yin," to the matrix of tranquility whence extension begins again, and so on. Yang and yin are not themselves structures, as might be assumed by interpreting the long and short lines in the hexagrams of the Yijing as structures in a static diagram. Rather, those lines indicate elements of change, yang being extension, exertion, the move to more; and yin being retreat, receptivity, diminishment. Any real change is an interaction of yang and yin moves. A single such move is like a wave, rising on yang and falling on yin. Waves have amplitude (greater and lesser height) and frequency (varying speed). The differential complexity of an object is thus the structured changes happening within it. Moreover, the harmonic play of changes within an object needs to be in synchronization with the harmonic play of changes in its environment. The supposition of this cosmology of change is reflected in East Asian medicine focusing on rebalancing things so as to be in harmony with oneself and the environment, in politics and social theory focusing on rituals that bring about harmonious interactions of individuals and parties that have conflicting interests, and in relations with the natural environment focusing on acting without competition.

Within the Chinese traditions are many responses to the issues of negotiating change, especially change as so fundamental. Zhuangzi did not grieve when his wife died because he took her death to be a mere, value-neutral, change of elements. On the other hand, Daoism has other strains that are filled with attempts to extend life by finding nondecomposing harmonies for the human body, aiming at everlasting immortality. Confucianism emphasizes rituals to retain contact with the past, especially ancestors, as well as moral seriousness to deal with the issues of change in the future as they come. Confucianism also valorizes as an important human kind of change the mode of engagement with affairs, sometimes engaging with full commitment, but sometimes going into retreat when convinced that the good side will be defeated.

South Asian traditions share with the East Asian ones the fundamental assumption that life is in constant change. Instead of framing this primarily as a cosmology (although it is part of many South Asian cosmologies), they treat it as a trait of consciousness. The chief predicament is how to negotiate change in experiential consciousness, and a wide range of responses is given. Sometimes the reality of change and underlying continuity is in question, which bears upon the condition of "reality" to be discussed shortly. Sometimes the predicament takes the form of clinging to that which does not last. Other times it takes the form of learning to act freely through constant change. Through many forms of South Asian tradition, both Buddhist and Hindu, an underlying sense of change is involved in the suppositions of karma: somehow a soul is continuous in identity while changing on the basis of personal responsibility from the conditions of one lifetime to another, on and on. On the one hand, the predicament is to improve one's karma. On the other hand, the predicament is to end the wheel of lives. Generally, for the South Asian traditions, change is the primary source of suffering in one sense or another. All of these strategies have complex structures and variants.

West Asian traditions share the strong affirmation of change in concrete life. Plato reflected a deep sensibility when he said that concrete things are always becoming something else, and they never simply are. For Plato, the only things that have "being" in the sense of remaining self-identical are possibilities or logical forms; the forms are useful for identifying structures of becoming, which register as changing from one form to another. Aristotle represented another deep sensibility with his conception of things as substances in which matter and form are combined and unfold. The situating of form in things, for Aristotle, is a contribution of efficient causes that contain the actuality that gets passed on into formed substance, and this is directed by the final cause or goal or value that is realized in the substance. The identity of a substance is guaranteed by its form. Insofar as the Western traditions have been determined more by Aristotle, at least in the suppositions of their common sense, it might seem that negotiating change is not such an important predicament. Nevertheless, far more than East or South Asian traditions, the West Asian ones have emphasized conversion, a transformation of soul, a taking on of a commitment to God or to a community that requires a new way of harmonizing life. To be sure, conversion is important in the other traditions, especially in Buddhism, but not to the extent it is in Paganism, Christianity, Judaism, and Islam. Judaism does not give much prominence to the rhetoric of conversion, preferring instead to speak of purification and faithfulness. But in all the Western traditions, the predicament of change is to change the heart of one's soul, not just the conditions or ways of life but the heart itself. This stands in rhetorical contrast, if not metaphysical contradiction, to the South Asian traditions that emphasize an underlying reality that does not change and that is most real as the self.

The condition of *reality* versus illusion or unreality is the fourth mode of comportment toward components. A person is a harmony of components. What is real? The harmony? Or the components unharmonized? Of course, the answer is both. But the question becomes an ultimate human condition insofar as the person comports himself or herself toward the components. As Kierkegaard put it in playful Hegelese:

> Man is spirit. But what is spirit? Spirit is the self. But what is the self? The self is a relation which relates itself to its own self, or it is that in the relation [which accounts for it] that the relation relates itself to its own self; the self is not the relation but [consists in the fact] that the relation relates itself to its own self.[5]

The self is not just the components nor the components harmonized. The personal self has a reflexivity such that it comports itself to its components, and the components comport themselves as potentialities, to the self as a comporting-to-its-components harmony. Some thinkers attempt to reduce this self-relational comportment to consciousness and its self-reflexive subjectivity and objectivity. But it applies all across the spectrum of ways to comport the self to its components. Kierkegaard drew one important lesson from this self-reflexivity of the self, namely, that it presents a particular predicament of despair: what is really real?

South Asian traditions most often treat the changing contents of experience or consciousness as the components that make up the self. Those components are in constant change. Hindu traditions tend to say that the true self is an underlying reality of some sort, and a great many theories have been developed to express this, including dualistic and nondualistic ones. Buddhist traditions tend to say that there is no true self in this sense and that the only reality is the changing things that come and go in consciousness. Many theories have been developed within Buddhism to understand the continuity of consciousness necessary to note changes. Some forms of Madhyamaka Buddhism attack the very distinction between reality and illusion. Like Plato, many South Asian traditions assume that real reality has to remain self-identical through time and cannot change, and whether there is such a thing, and if so how to access it, is the predicament.

East Asian traditions influenced by Buddhism play the theme of reality and illusion around the sweetness of decay, the falling leaves. Other East Asian traditions play that theme around issues of scale and perspective. Is Zhuangzi dreaming of a butterfly? Or is Zhuangzi the butterfly's dream?

The Christian apostle Paul said that the good he intended he did not do and the evil he intended to avoid he did. This inserted a deep contradiction into the Christian conception of the self. Moreover, for Paul, when he did something good it was the power of God, not himself, that was at work; and when he did something evil it was the disharmonized parts of himself, not his integrated self, from which agency came. Is there no real self? Are the components of the self too wayward? Christian (and other) traditions have divided on ways to indicate the reality of the self over against God and against temptations, some holding to dualistic and others to monistic views.

However widely divergent the conceptions of grounded wholeness, religions all have ways of articulating what is important and how to relate to those important things. Most often those ways function mythically. This chapter has indicated something of how this works within English-language culture. The chapter also has pointed out how diverse the conceptions of the self are and how these are sometimes in direct contradiction, as in the Buddhist rejection of the atman theory with the conclusion that there is no self in any ordinary sense. Most theologies would attempt to work out a doctrine of the self, but that is not the project here. *Philosophical Theology* says that regardless of one's conception of the self (which should learn as much as possible from contemporary science), the self has components that need to be integrated in a well-grounded way.

Chapter Three

Existential Location as the Condition for Engagement

The third step in this theological anthropology is to consider the ultimate boundary conditions for relating to others, where "others" include other people as well as institutions and various elements in the natural environment. The transcendental traits of harmony that define the main boundary conditions for being a determinate thing take on special guises as the ultimate boundary conditions for the world as relevant to human life. The transcendental traits are (1) form, the special human relevance of which is to put us under obligation; (2) components, the relevance of which is to give us the norm of grounded wholeness; (3) existential location, the relevance of which is the issue of engaging other things in our existential field; and (4) value-identity, which constitutes the problem of human meaningfulness. The first two chapters of this volume dealt with the first two traits and this one deals with existential location. In what sense is the existential definition of human reality determined by how well we engage others?

John Donne wrote, "No man is an island, entire of itself. . . . And therefore never send to know for whom the bell tolls; it tolls for thee."[1] It sounds paradoxical. On the one hand, we customarily think of people as atoms, each independent. On the other, it is tempting to read Donne as denying the plurality of people, asserting some kind of total identity such that another person's death is my own death. Yet he is right about how we are related to other people without denying differences. The philosophical issues are profound, finding a way between atomism on the one hand and a kind of idealist denial of external difference on the other. Every religious tradition wrestles with this. Our inquiry here begins with the abstract cosmology of existential location itself and moves to an almost equally abstract consideration of the contours that delimit a harmony. Then it moves to the issues and modes of human engagement with others, all as functions of the ultimate boundary condition of being existentially located relative to others.

I. THE COSMOLOGY OF EXISTENTIAL LOCATION

Existential location is placement within an existential field, by which here usually is meant a space-time field; similar traits would hold for analogous senses of a field, however, such as a field of ideas, or a mathematical field, or a field of philosophical positions. To expand on the theory introduced in *Philosophical Theology One*, in the philosophical cosmology derivative from the theory of harmonies, an existential field is understood in the following way. The field is not an empty container in which existing things might be put. Rather, space-time extensions are constituted by determinate things, that is, by extended harmonies. Harmonies have their own internal extension as the result of the togetherness of their essential and conditional components, and the harmonies together connect up so as to constitute an existential field. Each harmony thus has its own extension and the cumulative harmonies constitute the field. This would be paradoxical if the harmonies were like atoms that have internal extension by themselves and out of relation with one another. But, to the contrary, because each harmony needs conditional components from other harmonies, each is defined in part in terms of the others. Therefore the togetherness of the harmonies in the existential field is a condition for the harmonies being anything at all. Part of the internal extension of any harmony comes from the other things that are internal to it by virtue of being conditional components.

Two different harmonies might contribute conditional components to one another, or one to the other. Insofar as the harmonies have essential components that are outside each other, each harmony has an extension that goes beyond the extension internal to the other. The existential field consists of the extensions of harmonies that are joined by conditional components and are external to one another by their essential components. The existential field thus is a vast matrix of connections of harmonies mediated to one another by other harmonies ad infinitum, whatever the character of the world's harmonies might be. The essential and conditional components of a harmony are themselves harmonies and so contain within themselves an extension constituted by their own components. Thus there is no part of any harmony, no component of a component, all the way on down, that does not itself have components and hence internal extension as well as external extension.

Of course, many kinds of components exist and their extensiveness is not necessarily of the spatio-temporal sort. Insofar as the extensiveness is indeed spatio-temporal, there can be no point that is not further divisible. But many components of things have extension that is spatio-temporal only by analogy. For instance, a human being has a physical body in a space-time location, occupying just so much space and time, and also has a set of parents and grandparents (living or dead). The extensive field relating the person's contemporary body to the culture of the grandparents involves space-time location but also a great deal more. If the maternal and paternal grandparents come from different cultures themselves, for instance, there is an extension of cultural meanings and traditions relating those cultures, which in turn impact upon the person two generations down. Cultures are related by semiotic fields constituted by the similarities and differences in their symbols, by the geographies where they flourished, and among other things by the ways they are appropriated by subsequent generations. All these relations are to be understood as extensive. This is especially important when noting that the grandparents have essential components that make them really distinct from their grandchild and vice versa.

The extension within a harmony consists of the relations among its component harmonies such that they condition one another and yet are external to one another by virtue of their differing essential components. Thus there is an existential field within each harmony, and within each harmony's component harmonies, on down ad infinitum. The character of the harmonies' harmonies determines the character of the existential field that is extensive beyond each harmony and intensive within each harmony, and extensive among the component harmonies of a harmony, and so on down. One fault of metaphysical atomism is that it assumes that atoms do not have any internal extensiveness except insofar as they are "in" a space-time field. But how can a non–space-time thing be "in" space-time? A thing needs to be spatial in order to be in space, temporal to be in time, and so forth. The theory of harmonies defines what it means to be "in something": it is to be a component in a harmony or a harmony in an existential field constituted by the mutual conditioning but external relations among harmonies. One fault of metaphysical idealism is that it assumes that nothing is really external to anything else—no essential components of things standing outside of the conditional components that are parts of other things. Thus such idealism, of F. H. Bradley's sort, cannot account for metaphysical pluralism. The theory of harmonies defines what it means to be "outside" of something while still in an existential field constituted by an assemblage of harmonies.

Although the cosmology of existential location is extremely abstract, it is crucial for understanding how human individuals relate to those things that are other than themselves but are defined in part by their relations with them. To engage others only as they are involved in our experience, and thus reduce them to elements of ourselves, is a great temptation. This chapter explores this in greater detail.

II. CONTOURS, VALUE, AND OTHERNESS

What is the boundary of a person, distinguishing what is within from what is without? The person's skin? All that is contained within the subject experience or mind of the person? Does it include all that the person causes or influences in other things? Abstract though it is, this discussion of the cosmology of extension allows for a clarification of the discussion of the cosmology of form earlier in Chapter 1, in which it is claimed that the identity of a thing is defined by the form that integrates its components in its existential location. The claim is that to have form, and identity in that sense, is to have value. What is the boundary, or profile, or contour of a harmony?[2] It is the form or pattern of the contrast within which all the harmony's conditional and essential components are together. That form has levels of integration expressing complexity and simplicity, and the value of the harmony is constituted by the hierarchies of components within components, each with its own value, and constituting new values when contrasted together with other components. Thus wherever there is extension, there is value. The internal complexity of the value of a harmony is constituted by the complexity of its internal patterns of hierarchies of integration.

Nevertheless, the value of no harmony is ever limited to the value contained within its form because many of its components, the conditional components, are other harmonies that have their own values that are partially external to the harmony. In fact, the identity of any harmony is always partly constituted by the identities of those things that condition it. In temporally dynamic harmonies such as human beings, their internal harmonies are constantly changing as their conditioning harmonies change. Moreover, their very identity changes as their component conditions change. No harmony can be defined exclusively in terms of any form for its components but also needs for its definition the references to the conditioning harmonies. Or, as Donne said, "No man is an island."

Therefore it is difficult to speak of a harmony as a thing by itself, having its own properties. Aristotle believed that things could be defined as substances, where part of the meaning of this is that the substance is a subject to which its properties apply. But the properties of a harmony, as conceived in *Philosophical Theology*, do not inhere in it as predicates in a substance. Rather, the harmony can be specified only in terms of its conditioning neighbors, and then its identity is constantly shifting as the dynamic conditions change. To put the point another way, a harmony is defined not only in itself alone but also in terms of the extensive field within which it has location. It defines that field in part and is defined by it.

It follows that the value in a harmony is not only "within" it but is also a function of the harmony in its conditioning environment. A harmony does have value in itself, but that value is defined in part by what is not within the harmony. Plato understood the complexity of this point. In many of his dialogues he had his interlocutors attempt to define a "form," that is, some concept that can be stated exactly in terms of what it includes, excludes, and puts together in some pattern.[3] In nearly every case, arguably in every case, the attempt to define the form either fails or is used temporarily and then deconstructed. The discussion in the dialogue reveals what happens when different patterns are used for the form, and different things included and excluded; often, as in the *Republic*, different premises about component parts, such as human nature, are tried out to see how they affect the form under definition, such as justice. But no form by itself is satisfactory. This is because the internal mixtures of components under discussion are functions in part of external things that are excluded in part. Every thing, to which a naming or explanatory form might be predicated, in Plato's vision, is defined in part by what is not itself. In contrast, forms, for him, simply are what they are and not some other thing; thus forms apply only obliquely to concrete things.

The result of this is that, for Plato, things are processes of change in which forms inhere partly, and usually temporarily; they never define the whole thing. For Plato, philosophy (or education in any high sense) is the art of knowing when and how forms can be used to identify things. The very task of picking out real things in the world is a matter of adroitly identifying harmonies with their forms that are defined in part by what conditions them. There are no simple logical objects, rather intentional objects defined in terms of their internal harmonies and their external conditioning relations. The logical tradition deriving from Aristotle, which assigns properties to objects, cannot be fully accurate about the world. In fact, it always pushes toward the mistake of considering logical objects outside the context of their larger conditioned identity.

Because the values of things are a function of the connections between their internal harmonies and the conditions in their existential fields, those values can be identified only by representing the situation of the things in their fields. Plato had the hope of finding mathematical ways of representing this interplay of harmonies with other harmonies in what here is called conditioning existential fields. His famous lecture On the Good, which has been lost but which was heard and reported on by many, was unintelligible because it had too much mathematics in it. Doubtless, the mathematics Plato had at his disposal was inadequate to the task of representing how the form of harmonies bears value. But Plato's ideal remains a lure, especially in the Western tradition that has accepted the scientific exclusion of value from the facts of the world. Most other traditions, especially the Confucian, have not lost the sense of the contextualized character of value as harmony; but then they have not developed a logic to rival Aristotle's, however.

The assemblage of harmonies in existential fields itself presupposes the ontological act of creation, analyzed in *Philosophical Theology One*, as the ontological context of mutual relevance in which different harmonies can be together with their essential components so as to be able to constitute an existential field. The ontological act of creation simply creates the harmonies as mutually fitting without any one including all the others. Without that ontological act, not even one thing could be determinate, because to be determinate requires genuinely different things with respect to which a thing can be determinate. The ontological creative act is the ultimate condition that constitutes the harmonies whose transcendental traits constitute the ultimate predicaments for the human world that should be registered in sacred canopies.

Existential location is in an existential field by virtue of which a person is together with other things. That togetherness is constituted by the ways by which the things condition one another. Yet this is not the only constitution of the togetherness, because the other things have essential components of their own that are not contained within the conditioning matrix. Because of these essential components, other things are other. In the case of other human beings, the otherness includes a depth of subjectivity that makes the other mysterious, elusive, and always over against our grasp.[4]

Philosophical Theology has argued throughout that the ontological act of creation, which lies behind the externality of the many things that are related to one another, has been symbolized with three main metaphorical systems, that of spontaneous emergence, that of consciousness, and that of the person. Because of the otherness in persons, the model of a person as other can be developed into a model of God who is Wholly Other, Mysterious, Elusive, and Wild. Many such models of God as Person have been developed. Most involve magnifying, to a superhuman degree, human powers such as knowledge, intention, and will; emotions such as love, hate, and mercy; and capacities to create and act. In many Jewish, Christian, and Muslim notions of God, these powers are raised to an infinite degree. God so conceived as a personal Other, must be assumed to be in an existential field with people so as to be able to act with reference to them, and different traditions imagine the existential field uniting God with the more ordinary existential field of the world in various ways. We know from the arguments of *Philosophical Theology One*, Part III, that nothing in an existential field can be truly ultimate in an ontological sense, because the connections of any existential field presuppose an ontological context of mutual relevance that allows the things indeed to be other than one another while connected. Therefore, God conceived as a person, however infinite or beyond, who is located in an existential field, however heavenly, cannot be as ultimate as the ontological act that makes the existential field possible. Nevertheless, some version of this personifying model of God is used in many sacred canopies to indicate the mystery and elusiveness of the ontological creative act in ways that are intimate to interpersonal analogies in people's own existential fields. The tension between the intimate symbols of a personifying conception of God and the more transcendent ones that place God outside of any existential location occurs in many if not all theological traditions (I, 6, 7). Paul Tillich had a classic statement of the distinction in his essay "Two Types of Philosophy of Religion," in which he characterized the conception of God as a being who is in existential connection with us as like "meeting a stranger," marking out the otherness that makes every other person a stranger in some sense; the more transcendent conception is characterized as like finding God in the depths of one's soul.[5]

The nature of the existential field, or the extensive continuum as Whitehead called it, is determined by the complex interlocking characters of the harmonies within it.[6] As noted, that field has extension among and within harmonies, and also intension within the components of harmonies. At the micro level the characters of the physical existential field are truly weird and counterintuitive, as contemporary physics has shown. That level of the existential field can only be imagined in mathematical terms. At the macro level the characters of the physical existential field are also somewhat weird, including such things as gravity acting at a distance, the constancy of the speed of light, and so forth. At the meso level, which is mostly although not entirely what matters in human affairs, commonsense notions of space and time obtain.

III. HUMAN ENGAGEMENT ACROSS THE EXISTENTIAL FIELD

Human beings obviously are harmonies existing in existential fields relating them to other things. Physically, things are extensively outside of us by being in different places in space, with a mediating connection of places between any two things. Things are extensively outside of us also by being before or after us, or overlapping us in time. For most practical purposes, although by no means all, things run alongside us for a time and with relevant proximity. The physical existential field, for most purposes, is the underlying frame within which other existential fields such as common or conflicting cultures and cooperative or competitive activities take place. One of the cosmological components of existential fields is that they are constituted by the kinds of harmonies within them. This means that human beings have physical existential location with regard to other physical things, but also have existential location with regard to all the other kinds of elements of human harmony that distinguish things, such as cultural differences, differing roles in common intentional projects, and different roles within families.

What is humanly ultimate about existential location is a dimension of all the kinds of otherness that human beings encounter with the myriad things that distinguish them. Harmonies are of too many sorts to be classified easily, even those that are important for human life. With due awareness of the arbitrariness of the boundaries and of all the senses in which they overlap, the harmonies discussed here as related to human beings in the existential field are (1) other human beings; (2) semiotically structured institutions, including communities; (3) the individual human being as existentially located relative to himself or herself; and (4) nature in a larger sense involving the biological, chemical, and physical environment and history. This is the pattern introduced in Chapter 1 to classify humanly important kinds of possibilities.

The existential condition presented by the existential field is that other things to which human beings are related, including themselves, are harmonies with their own essential components, and hence are existentially external to the individual human being (excepting self-reference). Yet those harmonies are also internally related to people by the various conditional components and mediating harmonies that connect them in the existential field. So the other things are existentially related to human individuals as genuinely Other, related but different. How does this give rise to a predicament?

A dilemma constitutes the predicament. On the one hand, a temptation exists to treat the other as reduced to the components of the other that get into the individual by virtue of perception, interpretation, understanding, and various other forms of internalization. In point of fact, this is all we have of the others—what we can know of them and feel from them as we engage in conjoint life. We do not directly know or live their own subjectivity. We do not grasp except indirectly how their own essential components function within them to integrate them as they exist alongside us. With friends we construct elaborate imaginative representations of what their subjective life is like, and can get enough feedback to make that accurate. Sometimes we understand our friends better than they understand themselves, and vice versa. But understanding through a representation, a complex sign, however correct, is not to possess the other from the inside of their essential components. When we forget this, then we do treat the other as nothing more than what is objectified within our own experience. This is to deny the genuine otherness of the other.

On the other side of the dilemma, the individual is tempted to ignore the other in significant ways, acting as if the other were not there, as if its place were empty in the important senses, and as if its various conditionings of us were only our own doing, not the other's. This kind of denial has its pragmatic limits, obviously. Yet it is amazing how far it can be taken. Think how long the integrity of environmental nature was ignored or subordinated in modern cultures. People can be oblivious to the existential footprint that they themselves have. They can ignore significant ways in which institutions contribute to their own conditions, as in the case of successful or oppressive economies, for instance. They can ignore other people as people, treating them only as functionaries and acknowledging them only when the functions obtain.

The predicament for human life that stems from existential location is how to address things as genuine others, not reducing them to components of the self, even though they are in part that, and not ignoring them as existentially significant. This point is easily grasped when the other is another human being, because we understand the problem of subjectivity in others and its inaccessibility to us. Levinas and other philosophers like to stress the point by "capitalizing" Otherness and Others.[7] In their sense, we are Others to ourselves, too. They would be reluctant to say that institutions such as families, communities, or economic systems are Others, because they do not have subjective consciousness and intentionality. But those institutions do have a harmonic structure with essential components that make them different from one another and different from individuals that might participate in them. Levinas's Continental tradition of philosophy has even less respect for nature, whose codes cannot easily be read off of human cultural semiotics. Nevertheless, institutions and nature have harmonic structures with their own essential components that make them existentially different from human individuals and from each other. Their otherness consists in the differences that give them different existential locations, and these differences result from them having their own essential components that allow them their own existential locations. Thomas Berry goes so far as to say that the cosmos should be viewed as a world of subjects, not objects.[8] He does not mean, of course, that mountains and trees have intentionality, although some Pagans hold that. Rather Berry means that each thing has its own integrity from the inside. *Philosophical Theology*'s theory of harmony renders this as the integrity that comes from each thing harmonizing itself with its essential components that place it outside of other things. If "subject" can be understood to mean being the subject of one's own becoming, as Whitehead put it, or as being the subject of one's own essential integration and thus occupying one's ownmost place and identity, then Berry's phrase is right. The existential field is filled with subjects, which are objects only for one another.

The predicament of existential location is how to treat all those significant others as subjects when all we have of them is their objectivity for us. This is to say, when we human beings as harmonies are among other harmonies in the existential field, how are we to harmonize with them? How are we to engage them? How are we to avoid estrangement from them?

All the issues of harmony in an existential field are complicated by the issues of obligation and wholeness. Of course, we *ought* to engage others properly as others. And, of course, we *need* to be grounded in others that contribute components to our lives. The issues of groundedness indeed look very much like those of engagement, deference to the integrities of those who are parts of our lives, for instance. But groundedness has to do with comportment toward things that are components of our lives, while issues of engagement (as the terms are distinguished here) have to do with things that, while components of our lives in some respects perhaps, are genuinely other, in their own places and times.

IV. MODES OF ENGAGEMENT: AWARENESS, APPRECIATION, COURAGE, LOVE

Four modes of engagement are important to study here as illustrative of the range of kinds of relations to otherness within the ultimate boundaries of existential location: awareness, appreciation, courage, and love. These terms, to be sure, each are signals of a wide range of meanings.

Awareness in this context does not primarily mean understanding, although some understanding is involved in any awareness. Rather it means awareness that something important exists in the existential field relative to the landmarks of one's own existence. This does not suppose that, without awareness, people believe that a vacuum exists in a part of the field. Rather it supposes that some token of existential place-filling is experienced rather than what is really there. Some obvious examples make the point. Financial traders are capable of understanding the various economic consequences of transactions—such as the buying and selling of home mortgages, foreclosures, and profit-making—without being aware of the human elements of those transaction in terms of the lives of the homeowners. The fiscal traits of mortgaged homeowners, their capacities or incapacities to pay mortgages at various interest rates, are tokens that are real in their own right but that substitute for any awareness of the human costs of the financial traders' transactions. The disastrous human realities of the recent Great Recession are real enough and have extraordinary causal consequences: but they were not in the awareness of the financial traders who thought that the financial realities had only to do with their attempts to make money for themselves and their clients.

Or consider tourists from rich countries who visit poor ones with outstanding sights or ruins and are unaware of the everyday lives of the people there, seeing only those people in their functions with regard to the tourist industry. Or consider people who are aware of their neighbors only in the terms that directly impact themselves, being unaware of the lives of those others on their own terms, and what the neighborhood means to them. Or consider how violent terrorists, jihadists, crusaders, and other kinds of patriots look upon whole classes of people merely as bodies in the way of their political interests, being unaware of the human realities of those whom they would kill, which might in fact outweigh any political considerations.

Or consider how it is easy to notice poor people and to contribute to their welfare by giving alms and supporting charity, without being aware of the causal economic, and perhaps political and climatic, structures that cause the poverty in the first place. Those structures are real and configure the existential field, but they are not easily brought into awareness. Sometimes lack of awareness is simply lack of signs to be able to identify realities that are present. Other times it is the result of signs that block what otherwise would be seen. Institutions are often invisible to those who engage only certain transactions within them.

Or consider how long the modern technological passion to master and exploit the environment for human purposes masked many important forms of awareness of the way nature works on its own terms. The project of sustaining natural exploitability has led to scientific understanding of some of the larger causal processes of the environment. Yet even that sometimes blocks awareness of what nature is on its own terms. Very few people are aware of the long-term evolution of the natural environment and the roles that human habitations play in affecting that. In all these examples, the existential field contains "others" that should be engaged with awareness, even though awareness is often lacking.

Appreciation is the mode of engagement that takes the values of the things engaged into account. These include values as operative in multiple contexts, such as things' intrinsic values, the roles they play in larger systems of which they are parts, the roles they play relative to affairs of human importance, and the roles they play relative to particular persons' interests. Appreciation is not just a passive skill, just keeping one's eyes open. It involves the active tasks of figuring out how to appreciate the values in the things with which a person is engaged in the existential field. Sometimes this means enhancing sensitivity to things, and many religious traditions have "yogic" practices for increasing sensitivity. It also means deconstructing the ways people organize their experience that make them insensitive to the things engaged. But most of all it means learning how to understand the values in the things engaged on their own terms and in their connections with other things. Such learning often requires long and rigorous inquiry. Perhaps Confucianism is the tradition that has focused this most thoroughly with its complicated processes of education of the sage. The Confucian sage is not only one who is clear and sincere, not blocked by selfishness, but also one who is learned and educated. People, institutions, and nature cannot be appreciated in their values today without the benefit of scientific, artistic, economic, and historical knowledge. Engaged appreciation requires hard work, often expensive work.

Courage is a mode of engagement that has been central in West Asian religions. The existential field presents human beings with things to engage that are extraordinarily threatening. Nature is not well scaled to human affairs. Other things do not always agree to human beings' need and will to consume them. The character of existence, as evidenced in the processes of the existential field, is "precarious," as Dewey said.[9] Thomas Hobbes, living in times rather like those of Confucius, delicately said that, without some superpower to hold all makers of violence "in awe,"

> Whatsoever therefore is consequent to a time of Warre, where every man is Enemy to every man; the same is consequent to the time, wherein men live without other security, than what their own strength, and their own invention shall furnish them withal. In such condition, there is no place for Industry; because the fruit thereof is uncertain; and consequently no Culture of the Earth, no Navigation, nor use of the commodities that may be imported by Sea; no commodious building; no Instruments of moving, and removing such things as require much force; no Knowledge of the face of the Earth; no account of Time; no Arts; no Letters; no Society; and which is worst of all, continuall feare, and danger of violent death; And the life of man, solitary, poore, nasty, brutish, and short.[10]

Families are often dysfunctional, friends fickle, enemies powerful, governments corrupt, and human projects fragmented, ambiguous, frustrated, and short lasting. Individuals are often their own worst enemies. Moreover, the whole meaning-apparatus of human life as expressed in worldviews with sacred canopies is a fallible human construction, at best a set of broken symbols. So with regard to engaging the field of existence, there exists a deep and abiding temptation to give up. To survive in denial of the threatening things with which people are existentially connected is always a possibility for a while. Not forever, of course, because nature kills us in the end. But people can live hunkered down with minimal engagement. To engage life's realities requires faith.

Paul Tillich interpreted the heart of Christianity, even of Western religion, as a problem of courage.[11] Faith, for him, is the courage to be in the face of the existential vicissitudes of life. Courage becomes aware of the things to be engaged, appreciates their values, including disvalues, and plunges into the engagement. Courage in this sense is not the belief that things will turn out alright with earthly victory or heavenly reward if people just keep on trying. C. S. Lewis's *Chronicles of Narnia* makes that clear. Rather courage is the will to engage in spite of failure, frustration, and eventually death: to affirm oneself as holding to an existential location in the field that includes those others, to affirm the whole created order within which human life is located. Tillich, in his existentialist days, interpreted just about the whole meaning of Christianity in terms of the project of faith that undergirds engagement.

Love is the fourth mode of engagement. Love is an extraordinarily complex mode of being or agency, and is not exhausted by its role in authentic engagement (*II, 11*). Nevertheless, its role in existential location relative to other things in the existential field is extremely important and perhaps the basis of all the other roles. Building on awareness, appreciation, and courageous engagement, love is engagement with both delight and gratitude for the others engaged.

As a dimension of a mode of engagement, delight is not the same as desire although it is compatible with desire and in some instances might lead to it. Rather, delight in this sense is a doubled form of engagement. On the one hand, it is delight in the existence and nature of the thing engaged. On the other hand, it is delight in the character of the existential field such that the thing is given in existential connection so to be able to be engaged; delight in the thing includes delight in the existential togetherness of the thing with the person or community that engages it. So, loving the thing engaged includes loving the existential world in which engagement is possible.

Love as existential delight is difficult and paradoxical because so many things are not delightful by ordinary standards. Not all people are delightful, many institutions are vicious and oppressive, and nature is red in tooth and claw, always killing us in the end. Only superficial religious sensibilities say that the world is always beautiful and that we should delight in its pretty picture. More profound and universal religious sensibilities recognize the depth of suffering in human experience even as they also recognize the good things to celebrate and perhaps even achieve ecstatic fulfillment. Love as existential delight is religiously profound because it requires delighting in the enemy, the institutionalized ways of life (even when they should be changed on moral grounds), and all aspects of nature including catastrophes, toxins, deadly diseases, aging, and death. Buddhist and Hindu images of cadaverous ascetics are objects of delight.

Not all religious traditions give central place to engagement with love, as delight in even the bad things with which people are existentially connected. The dominant forms of Confucianism, for instance, maintain an ultimate moral seriousness about promoting the good and eliminating the bad, although in the end even Confucianism blesses the world of change in which one will someday not exist. Buddhism and Christianity do give dominant place to engagement with love, however. Although Buddhism has tended to limit compassion to sentient beings, the bodhisattva in Mahayana is enjoined to have compassion even for villains. Jesus famously said to love enemies. In many difficult ways, engagement with love needs to embrace within it the moral imperatives that might include thwarting or destroying that in which delight is also taken. Arjuna's dilemma is a case in point.

Love as a mode of engagement is gratitude as well as delight. The gratitude is for the existential field that makes the engagement possible, as well as for the thing in which delight is taken. It is gratitude for the very existence of the existential field with its specific contents. Some religious traditions focus the gratitude as if to a god or to the God who creates a world with things related as others to one another in an existential field. The foundation for this, and for other directions of gratitude, is the ontological act of creation that creates determinate things that must be together as others to one another in an existential field. But the gratitude is *for* the existential field that gives connections with others (*II, 11*).

These modes of engagement of others—other persons, institutions, oneself, and nature—are not the only kinds. But they are basic conditions for all kinds: awareness, appreciation, courage, and love. They obviously are easy to fail, and this failure is explored in Chapter 7.

In some obvious ways, all religions have thematized issues of relating to others. As is explored in *Philosophical Theology Three*, Chapter 2, part of the revolution of the Axial Age religions was the insistence that all things, especially all people, be engaged with some version of awareness, appreciation, courage, and love—universal compassion. The philosophical cosmology of the existential field reflected upon in this chapter has indicated how this religious commitment to compassion (at least in principle) is a direct response to a transcendental trait of existence itself.

CHAPTER FOUR

Value-Identity as the Condition for Meaning

I. THE COSMOLOGY OF VALUE-IDENTITY

The fourth step in this theological anthropology is to reflect upon the human quest for meaning as an existential response to the ultimate boundary condition that everything has a value. The phrase "quest for meaning" is a contemporary way of putting the point, conditioned by late-modern discussions of anomie and the loss of meaning that comes from the secular destruction of traditional religious worldviews. Other ways of putting the point include the "search for identity"; "search for justification in the eyes of a judging God"; "the achievement of that which has value according to some high standard"; "the search for immortality or permanence of personal identity, experience, and value"; and "the search to eliminate the round of lives in which identity and value are always flawed." All of these and many more are ways by which religious and philosophical traditions have responded to the normative demands put upon human beings by the fact that their identities have value of some sort or another. Anything whatsoever has a value-identity, as argued here, but human beings have value that comes in part from what they have chosen, from what they have inherited from their culture and its history, and from how they have affected other things and people in their environment. People are aware that, at least in part, the value-identity they achieve or bear might have been otherwise. Indeed, most of us could be better than we are, at any point and in the long-run value-identity achieved over a lifetime. That we have value-identities means that we should do something about that. And when the deeds are past, and we are left with what we are, what is the meaning and worth of that? Having value-identity is an ultimate boundary condition of all things and of human life in particular.

Value-identity is the fourth of the transcendental traits of harmony, in addition to form, components, and existential location. This is the value achieved by harmonizing the components at hand according to the form's pattern in the existential location in the larger field (*I, 10*). A harmony's value-identity includes both the value within the harmony and all the values caused or influenced in other things by the way the harmony patterns its components in the existential field. Value-identity takes its value from the forms embodied in the harmony, which in turn are embodied in the togetherness of all the other harmonies that, through their mutual conditioning, constitute a location for the harmony in the larger existential field.

Value-identity thus has two portions: subjective value-identity and objective value-identity. Subjective value-identity is that which is contained within the contour of the harmony itself, with its own conditional and essential components. "Subjective" here does not imply consciousness, intentionality, or anything like that, except when dealing with certain dimensions of human and other animal harmonies. Objective value-identity is the value the harmony has insofar as it is among the components of other things, its values for those other things. "Objectivity" here means the harmony as an object for other things. In all these discussions of "value," negative value, disvalue, harmfulness, disastrousness, and catastrophe are all comprised under "value" along with the positive connotations. "Harmony" does not always have positive connotations. A harmony can have a value-identity that is far worse than it should be (in whatever sense of "should" is relevant), and it can be harmful to other harmonies, playing different value-roles in different things. A harmony necessarily has a value-identity, and the necessity applies to both its subjective and objective portions.

Human beings are discursive harmonies, playing themselves out over time in shifting environments. Often the important segments of human lives are harmonies in their own right with more or less integrity, and thus have their own value-identity. These segmented value-identities can reside in the roles people play, their value-identity as parents, workers, neighbors. Or they might be for a delimited time of life, such as early childhood, sophomore year in college, or retirement living. Or the segments might be relationships, institutional work, specialized interactions with nature and the environment. The pursuit of short-term and long-term goals reflects a kind of segmentation of life. Human lives have many kinds of segments that are not easily woven as components into an integrated narrative. Such segments have integrities of their own, a life of their own, although they exist within the wider frames of a person's life. Each such segment is the achievement of a value-identity that is consistent with but somewhat independent of many others of the person's segments because each has something of its own rationale. Because of the segmented character of human life, we need to speak of many achievements of value-identity. Achieving such value-identities is a transcendental trait of ultimacy in human beings.

Ultimacy is usually associated with the summary or whole identity of a person, however. A person as a whole is a harmony that stretches through time, that at any one time has an astonishingly complex mixture of important segments and components, and that includes a vast array of subharmonies with forms within forms. The overall harmony of a person's life is likely not to have the sharp contrast that the more important segments do. To represent a person's overall harmony in the form of a story is to attempt to give the life as a whole some kind of sharp contrast, where all the parts are meaningful in terms of one another as a narrative conveys meaning to incidents. Real life is much messier than what can be told in a story, nevertheless, and the actual form of a person's lifelong discursive harmony might be vastly confusing because its complexity so outweighs its simplicity.

Still, however they are organized in an overall life pattern, the cumulative achievements of a person's life constitute the person's *absolute* value-identity. Each person achieves a value-identity for life. Religions seek to find signs to signify summarily this absolute cumulative identity, signs such as narratives, community-role contributions, family position, career achievements, and so forth. Usually the religiously important symbols for absolute value-identity construe some segment's value-identity to symbolize the whole.

A person's absolute value-identity includes both subjective and objective portions. Perhaps it is easiest to identify a person's value with the harmonized components of the person's life, the subjective side. This is the main focus of an autobiography, for instance. But the objective portion of a person's value is still part of that person's ultimate identity. A person is real as a value-identity in the roles played in other things, in the lives of other people, in the effects on communities and institutions, in the contributions (including negative ones) to culture and civilization, and in the differences made to the natural and social environments. The objective value-identity of a person can be effective far away from and long after the person's own subjective life. The objective portions of the absolute value identities of Buddha, Confucius, and Jesus are far greater than the subjective portions, shaping long and richly branching traditions.

Some parts of the subjective value-identity of a person are that person's own responsibility, and these are the parts with which the moralistic components of religion are mainly concerned. People are not responsible as very young children or as addled seniors; and they are not responsible for huge accidents in their lives in which no responsible control can be exercised. But much of the rest of life is a matter of partial responsibility, and we are interested in how people respond to the components that are given them in life. This is the sense in which some strains in religion say that people are "under judgment" in some ultimate sense. Nevertheless, the real absolute subjective portion of value-identity includes much more that is achieved in a life than those things that are matters of personal responsibility.

A person's objective portion of value-identity is largely in the control of other things, including the ways other people respond to the person. A person's objective value-identity "for posterity" is very much a function of posterity and its values. But not entirely so. Serious responsibility accrues to a person to behave in such a way as to improve things rather than harm them. Sometimes a person's effects can indeed be controlled, within limits, by the person. Therefore, to some important degree, a person's objective value-identity is a matter of the person's own responsibility.

II. THE ETERNITY OF VALUE-IDENTITY

The achievement of human value-identity so far here has been described in temporal terms. In the midst of life, part of the harmony of a human being is the facing of possibilities, the making of decisions, the continued maneuvering to keep decisions on track, and the timely pursuit of the important segments of life. At the beginning of life, a child has little responsibility for facing possibilities, and toward the end of life, the possibilities narrow down and perhaps the person loses capacity. At the very end of a person's days, the temporal dimensions of life are all in the past.

But the very possibility of temporal passage depends on the eternity of the temporal modes of past, present, and future being together (I, 12). Although not at any given time, in eternity all of a person's days are future possibilities, all those days are matters of present spontaneous decision (responsible or not), and all those days are past and actualized. The eternity that holds all these together is the ontological creative act that creates things that unfold temporally. Thus a person's subjective value-identity is ultimately eternal, existing in the dynamism of the ontological creative act in which all future possibilities are shifting with reference to decisions, all present moments are creative, and all past moments are gaining new meaning and value as time actualizes more moments. In the terms of important strains in most religions, this eternal subjective value-identity is who a person is in ultimate perspective.

The objective value-identity of a person is also eternal for the same reasons. Spatially and temporally distinct things are also changing in time, in concert with the person's subjective temporal identity and often extending far beyond that. The person's value-identity as embodied in processes extending far out into the existential field is part of the eternal identities of those other things, for better and worse. Those other things are external to the person in important respects even when they are other persons who are intimately connected with the person through time. The externality of the things to one another, metaphysically rendered by the fact that each has essential components that are not components of the others, is the reason for acknowledging that the ontological creative act is the ontological context of mutual relevance that makes relevance with externality possible (I, 11, 12).

So the objective and subjective portions of a person's absolute value-identity are together only in the eternal ontological creative act. A person's true whole value-identity is to be understood only in reference to that ontological creative act upon which all determinate things are contingent.

No perspective exists within the world, no human being or any finite harmony, from which a given individual's whole absolute value-identity can be grasped, except indirectly in some symbology or through other reference to the ontological context of mutual relevance in the ultimate creative act. The human achievement of value-identity is thus ultimate not only because it is the human embodiment of the transcendental trait of value-identity in any and all harmonies, but also because it lies only within the ontological context of mutual relevance on which the entire cosmos is contingent. The whole absolute value-identity of a person is not a characteristic of the person as a harmony; that would be limited to the subjective portion of the person's value-identity. The whole value-identity of the person must include the value-identities of all the other things whose valuable components include the person, however indirectly.

This constitutes a powerful existentially demanding ultimate boundary condition that has resonated across the world religions and is a major determinant in the contemporary religious situation. In contemporary terms, it is expressed as the problem of the meaning of life. Most commentators today imagine the meaning of life to be a problem because of the decay of traditional answers to it. Thus Peter Berger, Paul Tillich, Charles Taylor, and Hubert Dreyfus and Sean Dorrance Kelly in various important and publically recognized ways have understood the collapse of Christendom in the West to have caused a problem of cultural and individual anomie.[1] To this point there is a great truth, and alternative stories need to be told about the tribulations of meaningfulness in the Islamic world, in the extraordinary transformations of traditional cultures in South Asia and differently in East Asia, as well as among indigenous peoples.[2] Nevertheless, the predicament of meaningfulness does not exist primarily because of the decay or collapse of some tradition's solution to it. Rather, the predicament of meaningfulness exists because of the character of the human relation to the ultimate condition of having absolute value-identity.

The predicament consists in the fact that a person's real absolute value-identity includes the objective elements that are parts of other things over which the individual has no essential control. A person's essential control is limited to the subjective dimensions of his or her identity, the values achieved in the integrations of the components of that person's life. Yet a person's effects on other people, on the social environments within which the person lives, and on the natural environment might be far more important, decisive, and long-lasting than those values that make up the person's own life, subjectively considered. Those effects are in large measure a function of what those other things do with the influences from the person. The only perspective from which both sides of the value-identity of the person are together is the ontological context of mutual relevance in the ontological creative act. Only within that ontological context is the full meaning of the person's life to be found.

The contemporary Western commentators are right that the predicament of meaning is a matter of anomie, of lack of identity. For, the subjective elements that make up a person's own life, integrating the components of life in a discursive harmony through all its segments, are not the full or absolute value-identity of the person. The attempt to find identity by the turn inward, so typical of contemporary Western culture but based on precedents in most other traditions as well, finds less and less identity, not more, and easily turns to narcissism. Yet, the reason this is a problem is not that the old definitions of identity have faltered. Rather, the reason is that the subjective sphere is not the whole, or even often the most important element of the person's absolute value-identity, and it is not easy to attain to the absolute perspective of the ontological context of mutual relevance.

III. THE SYMBOLISM OF MEANING

How then can that context be symbolized so that people can relate to it and identify themselves as having meaning? Three classic situations have developed among the Axial Age religions in response to this.

In much of South Asia by the eighth century BCE the religious life of people was highly determined by dharma, usually translated as duty.[3] This was a significant shift from the marauding habits of the previous centuries associated with the Aryan invasions and large population shifts. Individuals' lives came to be defined in detail by duties owed to others; to social institutions such as family, village, and ritual practices; and also to the natural environment as understood in sacred ways. The proliferation of duty relations to others was a functional way of identifying the objective forms of a person's identity so that the performance of dharma was a way of uniting the objective and subjective dimensions of absolute value-identity. South Asia was becoming a highly differentiated class society, and dharma defined differences among the classes. How people treated others within their own class according to dharma differed from how they treated people in other classes, and even the definitions of the classes were functions of parallel and interacting dharma structures. The classic distinction between the Brahmin, Kshatriya, Vaishya, and Shudra castes were defined in terms of dharma. The dharmas were different for men and women, and for people at different stages of life. The mighty influence of this tradition of dharma has continued and developed in South Asia down to this day. As an articulation of the predicament of absolute value-identity, the definition of one's relations to other people, social institutions, and the natural environment (or at least parts of it) in terms of an elaborate set of detailed duties offered a way of symbolizing the objective influences on the values of others relative to the subjective performance of dharma.

The proliferation of the details of dharma, however, seemed to drain the vital sap from the subjective elements of a person's life. By the sixth century BCE an articulation of subjective inwardness was developing with revolutionary importance. The Upanishadic movement lightened up on the importance of following dharma and developed the concept of the self as the atman, the inner presence of consciousness. The metaphors of consciousness were developed in different directions, but with the result of an identification of atman with Brahman, the ultimate reality, itself modeled in basic ways on the character of consciousness. This was important in the early Upanishads, the Brihadaranyaka and the Chandogya, and was developed in diverse ways in the following centuries throughout many of the subsequent systems of Hinduism. As a contrast to the emphasis on the dharma system, the renunciant traditions in South Asia are like the Upanishadic movement, although perhaps more extreme.[4] Sometimes these amounted to an explicit rejection of the dharmic responsibilities of family and social life and a retreat to the forest and wilderness. Perhaps these retreats were a function of a life stage following upon the fulfillment of domestic responsibilities. In many instances, they simply constituted an alternative way of life. Eventually Buddhism and Jainism developed as systematic ways of renouncing many of the dharma structures of South Asian societies and castes. They also emphasized the inward character of consciousness and its connection with ultimate reality, although they gave very different metaphysical accounts of this from the general Upanishadic tradition. As large movements, however, these renouncing religions also had to organize themselves with new forms of duties, for instance, in monastic life. And to be sure, they never completely effaced the duties of common social life.

So the predicament of absolute value-identity in South Asia was articulated as the tension between highly detailed regulations of normative relations to other people, social institutions, and nature, defining the individual in terms of dharmic duty, and a move to inward consciousness in which the individual is defined apart from those normative relations as constituted by something more basic. Throughout the centuries, this tension has been a fundamental determinant of the religious situation developing from the South Asian Axial Age.

In East Asia, the situation was similar with important differences. In the seventh and sixth centuries BCE the vitality of the Zhou dynasty had fizzled, resulting in less centralized civilization and more social chaos. In the midst of this the aristocracy and landed gentry developed a somewhat detailed ritualization of certain aspects of life, especially relations among people and among organizational and administrative offices. This ritualized life was highly aesthetic and attuned to perceptions of worth and differences in people and social roles, and to a lesser extent to the environment. Although there were class distinctions in China and the rest of East Asia, they were not codified as strictly as the caste distinctions in the dharma system of most of South Asia. The lower classes in China were probably not deeply involved in the ritual systems during the early Axial Age because of lack of leisure to pursue their aesthetic elements. The rituals had less to do with the definition of duty toward others, institutions, and nature than with how to be valuably related to them, expressing the best of human nature. Confucius in the sixth and fifth centuries began a religio-philosophical school elaborating the cosmology and morality appropriate for an aesthetically ritualized society, representing it as an antidote to the social chaos of his time. Although Confucius and his followers emphasized the importance of inner humaneness and sincerity, ritual behavior itself came to function as a symbolic way of relating to others who bear the valuable effects of one's behavior and thus to the objective elements of one's identity. Carried to the extremes of a formalism that can be taught much more easily than the subtle balances of practicing rituals with inner authenticity, Confucian ritualism became a powerful symbol of the matrix of relations with others that constitutes the ontological context of mutual relevance. Perhaps more than the Indian practice of dharma in terms of intricate duties toward others, the Confucian articulation of the Chinese ritual practice emphasized the recognition of the otherness in the others. Rituals involve extreme focus on deference to the other as other, albeit related and partially defined by social roles.

As in India, however, symbolizing absolute value-identity with a pattern of learned roles with regard to other people, institutions, and nature risks a loss of the authenticity of the inner self. In contrast to India, which sought the inner self in meditation and the purification of consciousness, the Chinese turned to inner spontaneity and the spontaneous elements of emergence to be found in nature that resist ritualization. The sophisticated Confucian philosophers always recognized this inner spontaneity. But it was what later separated as the Daoist traditions that emphasized it as an antidote to the formalism of a ritualized society. The early Daoists emphasized the spontaneity of nature, and urged individuals to find spontaneity by recovering that natural impulse within themselves. Daoism was much more than this, to be sure, and had other criticisms of the Confucian bent of their society. It also learned techniques of meditating on the bureaucratic offices among the Daoist deities (usually human adepts who had made it to a higher level of being) with strong disciplines of the control of consciousness. But even among the Shangqing Daoist adepts, the perfected consciousness was not to discover the depths of reality in consciousness itself but rather to perfect the abilities of visualization that lead to a transformation of one's own reality.[5] With the advent of Buddhism to China, yet another force for spontaneity and against formalistic ritualism was added, with its own special turns. The Sinicization of Buddhism in China included the addition of themes of spontaneous emergence to its more Indian and Tibetan emphases on consciousness per se.

An interesting difference in tone having to do with moral agency has been present between the South and East Asian approaches to the predicament of absolute value-identity. For the former, agency is very much determined by preformed duties toward others: one's dharma is set and the question is whether one will perform it, the question Arjuna faced. In reaction to dharma, the South Asian way of turning to inward consciousness has emphasized *not* acting, withdrawing from agency. In Advaita Vedanta, for instance, this goes to the extreme of wondering whether release is possible before death, because while living one cannot escape acting at least in trivial ways.[6] Some forms of Buddhism attempt to replace moral agency with observation of consciousness, although the disciplines of meditative enlightenment are built on top of the mastery of moral ways of life. In East Asia, the formalisms of ritual are not so much preformed duties as they are public, common roles by which a relation with other things can be established. Hence the problem is not so much whether to do one's duties but to learn to play the rituals well. Ritual playing, even at its most empty formalistic extreme, requires learning to do it well, to become an adept. The tensive reaction against this is to emphasize the spontaneity of decision-making, the sense in which the agent is self-constituting in learning to choose and act well. The spontaneous self whose actions emerge from within does not lose itself in some underlying indeterminate reality such as Brahman nor abandon action through time in favor of savoring the moment of suchness. Rather, it forces the emergence of the unique and particular individual in a context in which the excellence of the individual, that is, the individual's ideal absolute value-identity, is constituted by how well the individual relates to the values of the ten thousand things.

The tensions between ritualization of the relations of individuals with others and social and natural environments and the rejection of ritual formalism in the name of spontaneous emergence define the East Asian version of the predicament of relating to absolute value-identity. Spontaneous emergence by itself can be disrespectful of others, selfish, and even mean; taken to its extremes it can become narcissistic, like the South Asian focus on consciousness. In this, the wholeness of self is lost: the objective elements in others lost completely and the richness of the subjective harmonization of the components of life lost as well. At the other extreme, an aesthetically ritualized set of relations with other people, institutions, and natural environments can become so formalized as to be stultifying to the individuality of the subjective components of life. The absolute value-identity can be obscured by the loss of the subjective as well as the objective elements. How to balance these is the situation for the East Asian version of the predicament of absolute value-identity down to this day.

The West Asian Axial Age religions have responded to the absolute value-identity predicament in related but also different ways. It should be emphasized that the distinctions drawn here between the South, East, and West Asian traditions are large generalizations. They were not separate, especially during the Axial Age when there was much commerce among them. Moreover, analogous circumstances have produced analogous responses across what historians call the "ecumene" of Asia.[7] Nevertheless, West Asia has some distinctive themes.

The dominant theme for unifying the objective and subjective elements of absolute value-identity in West Asian religions has been *belonging* to the religious community. Of course, there have been religious communities elsewhere. But the West Asian religions have made participation and self-identification through that participation into a dominant theme. The emphasis on belonging has been supported by the related emphasis on theistic metaphors for ontological ultimate reality. The creator of the cosmos is a God (or committee of gods) who perhaps is like a king (or an incestuous family). So, belonging means citizenship in the divine kingdom. The cult of a god, or of Yahweh or Allah, is membership in the god's people, with a price for membership and also benefits. Who a person is in absolute perspective is interpreted as who one is as belonging to the group that constitutes the basic relation to the ontological ground. Membership in the religious community defines the person's duties toward others, of course, as in Indian religions, and involves rituals of respect as in the Chinese. But it is the membership per se that puts the person in the symbolic position of the ontological context of mutual relevance. Being in that symbolic position does not mean that the person is able to grasp his or her absolute value-identity as it is objectively in other things, except very indirectly. But it does mean that the person's absolute value-identity can be approved or made acceptable, and therefore bear an ontologically positive meaning, because of the person's membership in the community founded by God. Even if the person's life is utterly terrible, and the person's influences on other people, institutions, and the natural environment completely disastrous, the person can be forgiven with mercy and set in right relation to the ontological creative act if the person is a proper member of the divine community.

The West Asian Axial Age religions punctuate the membership differently as a symbolic way of identifying with the ontological context of mutual relevance within which both the objective and subject dimensions of absolute value-identity rest. Judaism focuses on membership in the people of Israel, the Chosen People. The fifth century BCE exiles who returned under Ezra and Nehemiah purged the people of the land to purify membership in Israel, instituted the authority of the Torah, and insisted on the importance of the Holiness Code (Leviticus 17–26). By the fourth century CE the rabbinic tradition of Judaism had claimed authority for defining the people and cleaned up the separation from the Christian movement that had itself begun as a Jewish sect. The Jewish diaspora up until the present time has kept Jewish identity fairly well marked. Contemporary Zionism is a new form of membership that for many defines the meaning of being a Jew such that people's absolute value-identity is given content by that membership. The Christian conception of belonging to the "Way" of Jesus within Judaism developed in the first century into a mainly Gentile movement that separated itself slowly over the next three centuries from Judaism and various forms of Roman religion.[8] The nature of the Christian community as a "church" developed in different ways as the movement spread through Europe, Africa, Persia, India, and China. Nowadays in at least the Western parts of the world, Christianity is often taken to be primarily membership or participation in the Christian Church, defined one way or another. The Church provides the symbol of the ontological context of mutual relevance, which is why it is so easy for some Christians to say that there is no "salvation" outside of the Church. Islam followed Judaism in thinking itself to be a special community constituted by Allah for the salvation of the world, and it followed Christianity in thinking that this community should be extended to include all people. In complicated and qualified ways, Islam recognizes the salvific power of religions other than Islam, but only because of their founding contributions to the final revelation to Muhammad.[9]

At the same time, an inward turn toward mysticism and spiritual asceticism developed within the West Asian religions, often although not always as a counterweight to the emphasis on participation in the organized religions. Greek philosophical mysticism was present in Hellenistic Judaism and thus also in Christianity. Neo-Platonism with its mystical spirituality flourished in some elements of Judaism, and rather thoroughly in Christianity and medieval Islam.[10] Sometimes the turn to inner purity took the form of separatist movements, as the Qumran community defined itself over against practicing Judaism and the monastic movement defined itself over against secular Christianity with its ecclesiastical organization. The Sufi movement within Islam brings to public expression powerful strains of mystical spirituality within Islam.

In the contemporary West, the religious situation is sharply formed by the tension between the people committed to "organized religion" and those who distance themselves from all organized religion but regard themselves as spiritual. The spiritual types are sometimes held in contempt by those who submit themselves to the disciplines of belonging to an organized community. But this is to overlook the perennial tension between, on the one hand, regarding the self's absolute value-identity—that is, salvation (for Judaism, Christianity, and Islam), to be defined by membership in the community that expresses the divine organization of holiness—and, on the other hand, regarding it to be determined by cultivated inner spiritual virtuosity. Particularly in the academic world, many people consider themselves to be Jews or Christians by culture, yet avoid participation in the organized religion in any way that would constitute self-affirming membership; they take themselves to be secular because they do not participate in organized religion, but also to be deeply spiritual.

The tension between organized religion and being spiritual characterizes the response to the ultimacy of absolute value-identity among West Asian religions, down to the present day. The predicament is the difficulty of holding both sides of this tension together.

These remarks have been generalizations about different strategies that Axial Age religions have taken to symbolizing the ontological context of mutual relevance within which both the objective and subjective aspects of absolute value-identity can be registered. These will be made more specific in other discussions in *Philosophical Theology Three*, Part II. The remainder of this chapter focuses on the kinds of achievements that must go into developing an absolute value-identity in any culture.

IV. MODES OF ACHIEVEMENT: PERSONAL GOALS, CONTRIBUTIONS TO NATURE AND SOCIETY, FACING SUFFERING, RELATING TO ULTIMACY

The bite of the ultimate boundary condition constituted by value-identity is not usually felt in reference to the whole of a person's value identity but rather mainly to those elements that involve the person's own responsibility in some way. These elements can be categorized any number of ways and, for the purpose of the analysis here, four categories of projects are discussed, noting that the boundaries between them are not fixed and that much of life falls into more than one. They are: projects of achieving personal goals; projects of public achievement in society and nature; projects having to do with facing suffering; and projects of attaining an acceptable value-identity in relation to ultimate reality. These categories of projects are themselves extremely complex and internally various, and religions have responded to them diversely.

The projects of *achieving personal goals* are oriented around the more important segments of life. These can be long-term goals such as having a satisfying career, raising a family, or mastering a spiritual discipline. Or they can be short-term goals such as succeeding in a particular career task, helping a child get through a difficult time at school, or learning to sit in the lotus position. Everyone's life is filled with countless numbers of such goals. In themselves, they are not ultimate. They have proximate worth, and when for some reason they are treated as of ultimate importance they can take on the aspect of demonic possession. Although no personal or proximate goals of this sort are of ultimate importance, it is of ultimate importance to have such goals and to achieve them to some degree because the achievement of an absolute value-identity is an ultimate condition of human life. Part of a person's absolute value-identity is to be a competent person in the kinds of personal and local goals that make up the person's life, which of course are dependent in form on historical and cultural circumstances, and on personal choices. For centuries the Hindu traditions, for instance, have hosted two competing shapes of life providing an array of goals for achievement, that of the householder and that of the renouncer. Achievement in either one is recognized as important. Other traditions as well have competing ideals for achievement.

Some people, of course, are very high achievers, the adepts and virtuosi of life. Most people are not such high achievers. What is ultimately important for value-identity is not the high degree of achievement: being "the best" or "a master" is proximately very important and might well direct efforts in a highly focused way, but it is not ultimately important. What is ultimately important regarding projects of personal and local goals is that the goals are engaged with seriousness because they constitute the main content of personal identity insofar as that results from personal responses to the givens of life.

The projects of *public achievement* are also ultimately important for value-identity. "Public achievement" here means both contributions to social life and contributions to the natural environment, contributions that overlap a great deal. Nevertheless, the recognition of both is ancient. Often the contributions to social life are articulated in terms of roles in families and communities. Sometimes they are more idiosyncratic responses to social and natural needs. Ancient religions often understood the public significance of some sacrifices to be the maintenance and nourishment of nature and its gods. In our time, as Thomas Berry has taught us, it has become imperative for human beings in all societies to undertake what Berry called the "Great Work."[11] The Great Work, negatively, means changing human ways of life that are destructive to the environment. Positively, it means doing things to enhance the environment. He had in mind the environment of the Earth. But with the increasing capacity of human beings to affect the solar system and larger cosmos, the "public" for which human beings can relevantly achieve contributions expands enormously.

The reason that the achievement of public contributions in this broad sense is a matter of absolute value-identity for individuals (and communities) is because human beings are located in a larger existential field that includes others in society as well as processes of nature that extend far beyond the individuals by themselves. The contributions, important as they might be, are not themselves ultimate. What is ultimate is the identity the persons have as committed to their contributions. When they fail, the failure might be relatively bad. But when they fail and withdraw from addressing public obligation as such, they isolate themselves as if they were not connected in the larger existential field. Of course, they are connected whether they recognize it or not and those connections have attending obligations. But they deface themselves in ultimate perspective by denying those obligated connections.

The projects of *facing suffering* are extraordinarily complicated and have been approached in many different ways. One set of projects for facing suffering is to treat it as a condition of the way life is experienced and to attempt to change that mode of bad experiencing as such. Both Buddhism and some forms of Hinduism take this as a dominant, though not exclusive, orientation toward spiritual achievement. The Buddha's Four Noble Truths articulate suffering as a pervasive trait of all experience, as something that results from a wrong attachment to things experienced, and as capable of being transcended through one or more of the many Buddhist forms of devoted life. Hinduisms of the Vedantic sort sometimes take suffering to be the result also of a wrong identification with what is unreal as if it were real. The metaphysical suppositions behind the Buddhist and Hindu approaches are quite different, and various within each tradition. Most religions have ascetic traditions that manifest some version of this project of transcending suffering by changing the ways things are experienced. Recent studies of the suffering of trauma complicate the project of amending the way things are experienced. In trauma, something disastrous experienced in the past causes subsequent experience to be deformed. To treat the present experience of suffering therapeutically, the earlier experience needs to be addressed and the experience of the disaster reformed.[12]

Another sort of project for facing suffering is to do something about the causes of suffering, not in the sense of the way things are experienced but in the sense of the conditions of experience that cause suffering, and the consequences of suffering. Suffering comes from disease, so improve medical care; suffering comes from natural catastrophes, so build earthquake-proof buildings and establish emergency relief organizations; suffering comes from famine, so develop better agriculture and storage methods and policies; suffering comes from poverty, so improve the economy and distributive justice; suffering comes from social oppression, so change deleterious class structures and bigoted consciousness. Religious traditions have long been involved in facing suffering by removing its objective causes as much as possible. Although always limited, human efforts in matters such as these are significant. A significant part of a person's value-identity can be projects that face suffering by trying to remove its causes and cope therapeutically with its consequences.

Another set of common projects for facing suffering has to do with developing compassion, care, and empathy for those who are suffering. Sometimes such compassion can lead to concrete efforts to relieve the suffering. But even when nothing can be done, development of compassion and fellow-suffering is an ultimately important goal in itself, related to engaging others with respect. To engage those who are suffering with compassion is difficult because it brings something of their suffering into one's own life. But it is a highly adaptive emotional impulse even when limited to compassion for those in one's in-group. Adepts at compassion, such as bodhisattvas, not only postpone their own liberation from the suffering of change until others too are liberated, but extend compassion to all living beings. Most religious traditions have saints of compassion.

A fourth set of projects for facing suffering consists of spiritual and other disciplines that allow one to bear up under suffering. An obvious example of this is people who learn to live with intractable illnesses. People also can learn to bear up under catastrophic circumstances, under economic and social injustices that will not be changed in the short term, under the collapse of their special projects, and under betrayal by or disappointment in friends and family. Bearing up under abandonment is a prominent way of facing suffering in religion, particularly in Judaism, Christianity, and Confucianism.

Suffering is faced in countless ways. How one faces suffering is an ultimately important project in the achievement of absolute value-identity.

The projects of *attaining an absolute value-identity* in relation to ultimate reality are those commonly associated with the goal of religious life. In the terms of the monotheistic traditions, these projects are usually articulated as determining who we are before God. Some strains of the traditions have extremely individualistic understandings of who "we" are while others put the issues more in collectivist terms. The project is to achieve an absolute value-identity in ultimate perspective that is acceptable. Part of acceptability is in being righteous, part in being whole, part in being engaged well with others, and part in being related to ultimacy or ultimate reality as such, as the previous chapters of this part have argued. "Acceptability," to be sure, is a rhetorical trope that makes sense in the context of personifying symbols for the ultimate reality, a symbolic context that *Philosophical Theology* argues is not itself metaphysically ultimate. In monotheistic practice, "acceptability" to God is understood through human projections onto ultimate reality of what people can best define as righteous, whole, and properly engaged. One need not have a monotheistic set of symbols for ultimate reality, however, for the point to hold. No matter how ultimate reality is construed—for instance, as Dao, Heaven, Brahman or some other transcendent deity, or Emptiness of consciousness, or spontaneity of emergence—the achievement of a value-identity in relation to that is a matter of ultimate importance.

One of the problems with this kind of project of achievement is to find ways to symbolize the self in relation to the ultimate, as the previous section explained. Sometimes this is done through symbolizing the self through a narrative biography. But this would embrace only part of what needs to be symbolized; it lends itself to a story of dealing with moral obligations and with personal and local goals, but not to those aspects of identity that have to do with groundedness in components or engagement with others in the existential field. Some cultures can provide identifying symbols for the self through social roles in families and communities, or through actions in historically significant situations. Late-modern cultures, however, tend to be too fragmented to offer many salient symbols for self-identity, as would be needed to achieve the absolute value-identity of being related to the ultimate. As Charles Taylor and many others have argued, the problem of the identity of the self in ultimate perspective is very confused today, so much so that individuals often do not know where they stand ultimately, regardless of the content of their absolute value-identity.[13] In old-fashioned Western language, the problem is the identity of the ultimate particular nature of each person's soul, and yet we have no consensus on how to symbolize the soul.

Nevertheless, however well the self or soul is symbolized, how that self stands in ultimate perspective is the ultimate absolute human identity. That value-identity is eternal. It comprises both the subjective and objective portions of the self, which can be integrated only in ultimate perspective. Every person has such an absolute value-identity, for better or worse. Most people are highly complex and inconsistent mixtures of positive and negative value achievements. That each person has such a value-identity means that having a good one is a fundamental, ultimate, human predicament.

PART I

Summary Implications

The four chapters of Part I have analyzed human ultimate boundary conditions in a more complex fashion than might be expected in the light of the history of theological explication. The usual expectation is to find some single most basic human condition that makes normative claims on the existential definition of the individual. But the argument here is that there are five equally basic ultimate boundary conditions, four deriving from cosmological ultimate realities and one deriving from the ontological ultimate reality of creation. In the most embracing sense, the human condition as a religious problem has to do with ultimate reality insofar as ultimacy demands some response from human individuals and societies. Religious traditions articulate ultimate reality in various symbols within their sacred canopies. These symbols represent ultimate reality in finite-infinite contrasts. On the finite side is some character of reality that constitutes an important part of the world as graspable by human beings. On the infinite side there is the situation that would obtain if the finite side were not real. So, in the main, the sacred canopies of those religions that have intellectual and spiritual breadth and depth represent ultimate traits of reality that define the boundaries of the world as graspable by human beings and indicate how they impact human life so as to constitute predicaments. Five ultimate realities are to be engaged with some symbols or other, and so five kinds of ultimate boundary conditions are to be found variously interpreted in the rich traditions of the world religions. The difficulty in engaging these boundary conditions turns them into ultimately defining predicaments, as Part II elaborates.

Nevertheless, these five normative boundary conditions and their respective predicaments are not to be addressed separately in life. Just about any complex event, any action, anything that happens to human beings within which they make responses, involves all five boundary conditions. Nearly any human reality within which people make choices involves the predicaments of obligation. Most human realities involve comportments toward the components of life as backgrounds for choices, and thus involve the predicaments associated with attaining wholeness. Nearly every human reality involves relations with others and so involves the predicaments associated with engagement of other people, social institutions, and environing nature. Most human happenings, actions, and responses affect the absolute value-identity of individuals in both subjective and objective modes and so involve the predicaments of achieving absolute value-identity. Nearly every human happening is shaped by and shapes individuals' affirmation or negation of existence as such, even when that is not given much articulate expression, and so involves the predicament of gratitude or consent to being in general.

Therefore, when theology addresses some human condition, some situation, or action, or happening, individual or social, it can and should be alert to the five dimensions of predicament. To be sure, perhaps one or a few are very important in the condition at hand and the others not important. This is an empirical matter to be determined. Sometimes issues of choice are uppermost, sometimes issues of grounded wholeness, or engagement, or achievement of value-identity. The issues of just what is important in individual cases of human realities of interest to theology are among the most important to determine in inquiry; sometimes initial impressions of importance turn out to be wrong.

The point at hand is that the five dimensions of human ultimate boundary conditions provide respects in which any human reality involving personal response can be interpreted. These respects are the ways in which any such reality is related to ultimacy, as ultimacy is understood in *Philosophical Theology*. Wars, economic structures, loyalties and betrayals, senses of purity and disgust, personal and communal lifestyles, choices about what to become, what to do, what to preserve or destroy, what to build, with whom to affiliate or disaffiliate, how to love and hate—all these and countless other human realities are subject to the fivefold theological analysis of how they bear on human predicaments.

No one boundary condition defines the human condition, because no one way exists by which human beings relate to ultimate reality, given the five ultimate realities. The scheme used in this analysis draws upon the transcendental traits of harmony analyzed in *Philosophical Theology One* to characterize whatever is determinate in any sense of determinateness. These traits are form, components, existential location, and value-identity, and the chapters of Part I have been devoted to these, respectively.

Thus, Chapter 1 analyzed the role of form in harmony in terms of pattern and value and showed that, for human beings, this means that people face possibilities with different structures and values, possibilities that in some circumstances are to be decided by what lies within human control. Therefore, human beings lie under obligation to understand and choose the better alternatives, to actualize them and to live with the values they have actualized and with the exclusion of those values they decided against. Chapter 2 analyzed issues of comportment toward the components in harmony, the things that are integrated within the harmony's form and that connect the harmony with other things with respect to which it is determinate. At the human level this means that people, as harmonies living out their lives through time and in relation to other things, comport themselves toward their components in the ways they integrate them. Authentic comportment leads to being well grounded in those components, and inauthentic comportment means being alienated from at least certain of the important components of human life, as Part II discusses in more detail. Wholeness in human life has to do with being well grounded in the components integrated into the individual's person, however those components are involved in the affairs of life with which the person is involved.

Chapter 3 analyzed the connections among harmonies in an existential field and argued that at the human level this poses the ultimate boundary condition of engaging the environment and those things in it, particularly although not exclusively human beings. Although complex and changing relationships exist among human beings as harmonies, whereas groundedness has to do with the comportment of the personal harmony as a whole to its component parts, engagement has to do with relations with things that are connected with the person but still external in important senses.

Chapter 4 analyzed how harmonies achieve a value-identity with both subjective domains, in which the value is contained within the harmony, and objective domains, in which the value-contribution of the harmony is contained within other things it affects conditionally. Most comprehensively, value-identity is registered only in relation to ultimate reality. At the human level, value-identity is an achievement of many sorts. All the affairs in which a person participates affect the absolute value-identity that person achieves.

The analyses in the chapters of Part I have distinguished several senses of each trait of ultimate boundary conditioning of human life, each demanding normative response. These senses are rough classifications and have overlapping elements and many cross-implications; the descriptive phrases are tokens for much more complicated discussions.

Response

Under Obligation:
    Moral Obligation
    Fulfillment of Social Roles
    Personal Development
    Obligation to Nature

Under Grounded Wholeness:
    Appropriation
    Deference
    Negotiating Change
    Realism

Under Engagement:
: Awareness
: Appreciation
: Courage
: Love

Under Meaningful Value-Identity:
: Personal Goals
: Contributions to Nature and Society
: Facing Suffering
: Relating to Ultimacy

This list uses code words that are explained more nearly fully in the text of the chapters. Nevertheless, even in the text it is clear that the analyses that come from these several philosophical topoi relative to the transcendental traits of harmony do not ever give a complete analysis of any of those complex notions. The list does, however, give some indication of the complexity of the human condition and what is broken about it. No quick answers to those questions can be given that address all the dimensions discussed here. This is important for Part II, as is indicated in its preliminary remarks.

The four transcendental traits of harmony provide determinate orientations to what is cosmologically ultimate. They also indicate in philosophical language elements that rich sacred canopies should include according to some symbolism or other, for they define things that are ultimate for the humanly meaningful world. Yet these traits of harmony are themselves radically contingent on a deeper ultimate reality, the ontological creative act that creates determinate things, harmonies, in the first place. The connection between that ontological creative act and its terminus—a plurality of determinate things—is complicated and intimate. There is no act without the creation of the determinate things with the transcendental traits of harmony. There are no things without the ontological act (I, pt. 3). As a consequence of this connection, each of the elements of ultimate human boundary conditions related to the traits of harmony leads into a deeper boundary condition about reality itself. The ontological boundary condition is a deep current running under all the others in any of the affairs of life in which they emerge.

PART II

Predicaments and Deliverances

Part II

Preliminary Remarks

The ultimate boundary conditions for human life place normative demands on individuals to be righteous, whole, appropriately engaged with others, and productive of a meaningful value-identity. Because we commonly fail these normative demands, these ultimate boundary conditions constitute human predicaments: the human condition is to be under obligation but often to fail it, to be whole but often in fragmented and self-alienated ways, to be engaged badly, to have value-identity that is seriously flawed. This part of *Philosophical Theology* analyzes how the ultimate boundary conditions constitute human predicaments and how religions respond to these predicaments. The predicaments are generally the same for all peoples regardless of cultures. And so there are more or less common problems to which diverse religious cultures respond in their varying ways.

Human predicaments often lead to two further ultimately significant consequences. The first is for people who fail the normative boundary conditions to reject in some way or other their normativeness, or at least to be ambivalent about it. The second common consequence, and perhaps at least tempting to most people, is self-condemnation both for the failure and for the ambivalence or rejection of the normative conditions. Human brokenness consists in these last two points, some kind of rejection of or ambivalence about the normativeness of the human condition and some kind of self-condemnation, with the result that people need religious help. Religious interventions, deliverances, and remedies are aimed at addressing this kind of brokenness. Religious worldviews address the ultimately significant crises of life by fitting them into the dimensions of human predicament for which religion offers deliverances.

"Human predicament," to use that neutral-sounding phrase, therefore is (1) to be normatively bound to the five ultimate realities, (2) to fail in those normative relations, and then (3) to be broken in response to the failure in a paradoxical way, on the one hand with denial of some aspects of the normativeness and on the other with self-condemnation for doing so.

Although the human predicaments involve coping with failure with regard to the ultimately normative boundary conditions that define human life and the depth of personhood, they do not entail in themselves that people are broken. The brokenness comes in response to failure. The human predicaments are *given* as the normative conditions of human life. Brokenness in response to the human predicaments is *typical* of the human condition as such. This brokenness occasions a deeper predicament regarding the ontological ultimate condition of radical contingency on an ontological creative act. Brokenness, therefore, often has two levels or stages as people slide deeper and deeper into it. The first is a kind of cosmological brokenness in which the person's normative relation to the cosmological ultimate—obligation, wholeness, engagement, value-identity—is weakened or denied. The second is a move into ontological brokenness in which acceptance of the being of the cosmos, including one's own being, is weakened or denied. Widespread patterns of individual brokenness can come to typify groups and societies, even cultures. Some people, of course, are far more broken than others and perhaps it is possible that some people are not broken at all.

As the human condition contains many predicaments in which human beings are broken, so religions have addressed the deliverances from these broken states with interventions. "Interventions" here is an extremely vague term, meaning only that religions present or offer things to be done about the broken states. Sometimes these are put forward as interventions that come from God or the gods, other times as services of religious experts such as priests or spiritual adepts, sometimes as salvific teachings, or special disciplines, and as a host of other modalities, many of which are discussed in this part. Livia Kohn points out that interventions can be of the sort one initiates oneself, taking on a new path, or they can be very much from the outside; the practice of Zen, for instance, is the former whereas the practice of Pure Land Buddhism is the latter, "self-power" and "other-power," respectively.[1] Religious interventions propose to change the ways people imagine and think, respond and behave, so as to be delivered from the fundamental predicaments. The interventions are specific responses to brokenness and thus are to be distinguished from more inclusive ways of religious life discussed in Part IV and in *Philosophical Theology Three*.

In some instances, the brokenness relative to ultimate predicaments renders the person incapable of self-remedy. Many kinds of ultimate predicament result in impotence so that the remedies have to come from the outside—this often is what is meant by "intervention." Of course, the interventions need to be taken up by the broken person in order to be effective. Sometimes this might be little more than becoming committed to a spiritual practice that has always been available and that, perhaps, the person had practiced in the past. Other times it might mean a more radical change. Part IV examines some of the ways by which people can access the interventions offered by religion. Part II here focuses on the need for the interventions and how they are relative to the dimensions of ultimate human predicaments that need fixing.

Relative to the individual's, and in some cases the community's, need, the interventions are sought as deliverances or salvations. "Deliverance" is the generic word preferred here to "salvation" because of the latter's close association with common but narrow Christian conceptions of salvation as a matter of getting a good afterlife. But much of the discussion in recent literature has employed the language of salvation. "Salvation" comes from the Latin roots *salvus* or *salubritas* that mean whole, well, sound, healthy, safe, and the like: it is how a goodhearted person "salutes" another. The word "salvation" has also come to have much narrower meanings in certain kinds of Christian (and Pure Land Buddhist) discourse, as in salvation from hell, destruction, or the bondage of sin. The word itself, however, has a broad enough range in a comparative context to include the fixing of human predicaments in all their dimensions. S. Mark Heim, in his important book *Salvations: Truth and Difference in Religion* argues forcefully that "salvation" can be applied to a wide variety of different religious ends or goals. In a curious way, his argument is the reverse of the one to be made here. He tries to show that the fundamental goals or conceptions of salvation in different religions are different from one another and are therefore not necessarily incompatible, even when they appear to contradict one another.

The argument here, to the contrary, is that the various forms of the human predicament appear in all human societies and hence in nearly all religions. Therefore, in some way or other, with some symbol system or other, all the religions need to present paths of deliverance that address all or most of the elements of the human predicament.

Heim is right, of course, that different traditions have their own rhetorical systems. Christians say that salvation is "associated" (in different and sometimes conflicting ways) with Jesus Christ, about whom Confucians would have nothing to say and whom certain Hindus would adopt as yet another avatar. The rhetorical center of gravity in the East Asian religious traditions typically treats deliverance in terms of harmonization or the rebalancing of that which is out of harmony. The rhetorical center of gravity in South Asian traditions typically has to do with enlightenment of consciousness in the face of illusion. The rhetorical center of gravity in West Asian religions, including Islam, typically has to do with reestablishing obedience and righteousness in the face of disobedience and unrighteousness, with appropriate rewards and punishments. Yet these rhetorical systems need to be understood as signs that connect the interpreters who live by them with reality in its many dimensions. The different symbol systems do not constitute the reality except insofar as they are deployed in a life and that life changes the realities. They serve, more or less well, to interpret reality in different respects in different contexts.

If the scheme of the argument of Part I has plausibility, there are at least four major forms of predicaments with brokenness and sixteen minor ones under them. Of course, there might be many other forms of brokenness and combinations of these that have their own natures and names. This scheme with its lists is more illustrative of religious phenomena than a pretense to be exhaustive. Whatever the rhetorical system of "salvation" or "deliverances" in a religion of civilized breadth and depth, it would need elements to address most or all of these kinds of brokenness.

Therefore, it would be highly misleading to give a simple interpretation of deliverance for any religious tradition. For a Christian, to be saved by "accepting Jesus Christ as Lord and Savior" might well be an existential moment of great significance, but its meaning is barely conveyed in that phrase. By itself it seems to suggest a feudal relation of vassalage, a political relationship that seems not to be a matter of ultimate concern. But if Jesus Christ is interpreted as "the way, the truth, and the life," and those notions were spelled out with philosophical richness, then perhaps faith in Jesus would address the brokenness of unrighteousness, alienation, estrangement, and self-destruction, each with its many elements. In this situation, the ways by which Jesus Christ is symbolically interpreted would be contextualized with respect to the kind of broken predicament at hand. For instance, it would seem that deliverance from the brokenness of unrighteousness, including blood guilt, might be addressed through the intervention of the Christological symbols of atonement and sacrifice. Deliverance from disintegration and ungroundedness might be addressed through the intervention of the Christological symbols of the historical Jesus, the man of humility and deference. Deliverance from estrangement in the existential field might be addressed through the intervention of symbols of love in the teachings of Jesus. Deliverance from self-destruction might be addressed by the intervention of the Christological symbols of Jesus as friend and also as the Cosmic Christ. Deliverance from ontological separation of the finite from the infinite might be addressed through the intervention of Trinitarian symbols of Jesus as Second Person of the Trinity. These Christological symbol systems are by no means consistent with one another as items within a code of signs. The actual "meaning" of Jesus Christ within Christianity is not one thing but all of these things and doubtless others as well.[2] A theological Christology should understand Jesus Christ not according to any one definition but in terms of reference to each of these many topics deriving from the realities of life. Similarly, a theological Buddhology should understand Gautama Buddha in reference to specific teachings, to roles as a guru to different types of people, to historical context (the "historical Buddha"), to his founding of institutions of Buddhism, to cosmic Buddha-mind, to lineages of Buddhas and bodhisattvas, to reigning over the Pure Land, and so forth. These are not consistent, as evidenced by the different denominations of Buddhism, the differing references to popular and esoteric kinds of practice, and the rest; but they and many more domains of reference are part of the religious "meaning" of Buddha. Each religious system has many contradictory variants within its historical development. Yet given the different contexts of their use, in reference to different elements of human predicament and brokenness, they might all be consistent as resonating together, and the consistency can be articulated only through a discrimination of the different realities in reference to which the symbols are developed.

The actual interventions and remedies of religions are well known: physical exercises and diets; singing and dancing; formation of the imagination through songs, scriptures, stories, theories, travel, communications; teachings through classes and guru-disciple relations; worship practices both private and communal; the special ritualization of various domains of life; various disciplines of spiritual formation, discernment, and guidance. This list could be greatly extended, developing differences among cultures and historical periods. The point of Part II is not so much to catalogue these well-known religious deliverances as to show how they are deployed to address different forms of brokenness associated with the basic human predicaments. A given deliverance might address several different predicaments, depending on circumstances. Thus a specific ritual, for instance, or a dietary requirement, cannot be understood on its own but only in reference to the various predicaments it can address as an intervention.

Each brief chapter in Part II introduces deliverances relevant to the respective predicaments of the boundary conditions. These goals of deliverance are justification, centeredness, connection, and happiness, all interpreted in ways relating to ultimate conditions of reality. Chapter 5 deals with the forms of obligation, guilt, and the restoration of righteousness and purity in justification. Chapter 6 deals with comportment, alienation from or disintegration of self, and the achievement of groundedness as wholeness through becoming centered. Chapter 7 deals with existential location and reconciliation from estrangement through connection. Chapter 8 deals with the recovery of absolute value-identity in ultimate perspective, constituting happiness.

CHAPTER FIVE

Guilt and Justification

In the commonsense view of many reflective people, especially in the West, the primary function of religion is to cope with unrighteousness and its consequences. This is particularly true when religion is viewed in its public life as civil religion. In the most general sense, unrighteousness is a failure to fulfill obligations that sometimes includes two further shadows. One is a nascent and perhaps implicit, or full-blown and explicit, rejection of the obligatoriness of obligations, which amounts to a rejection of obligation as an ultimate boundary condition normative for human life. A noble version of this is a Nietzschean transvaluation of values; a less noble version is simply a flight from obligation. The other is a rejection by the unrighteous person of the person's own self as having the dignity of being bound by obligations, which in turn amounts to a rejection of the ultimacy of human identity relative to at least one of the cosmological ultimates. Ironically, these two rejections contradict each other and yet go together in the brokenness that typically results from the human predicament constituted by having obligations. Religion is by no means exhausted in its interventions to cope with unrighteousness. Nevertheless, it is a fundamental and obvious part of religion, expressed in every religion.

The approaches to human predicament relating to ultimate obligation exhibit an astonishing variety, not only among world religions but within each one. Obligations themselves are of very many kinds, of which four were discussed in Chapter 1 and are discussed in more detail here. Any given field of possibilities with alternative values usually faces many different agents, and obligates them all in different ways. How any given agent relates to the possibilities open to the agent's choices and actions depends on the multiplicity of roles played relative to the possibilities. What the relevant agents do, and might or should know, about the alternatives is extremely complicated. Moreover the cultural differences that specify the vague category of "obligation" are vast: think of the differences among the Confucian sense of filiality, the Hindu sense of dharma, and the Jewish sense of the obligations of Torah.[1]

"Unrighteousness" applies on a continuum of failures of obligation that begins with mild mistakenness about what to do, to increasing degrees of culpability for mistakes, to increasing degrees of rejection of the obligatoriness and increasing degrees of denial of the self as defined by obligations. These last two tumbles into brokenness can be called "guilt" in a serious sense, although the term "guilt" has been used for mere error.

The fundamental predicament of obligation and guilt arises from the transcendental trait of form, which in respect of the project of human life presents itself as the ultimate condition of facing possibilities that have different values among which choices need to be made. Chapter 1 of this volume studied four kinds of obligation the failure of which are shown in Section I here to result in four kinds of guilt. The kinds of obligation are moral, social, personal, and natural, and these are associated, respectively, with four kinds of guilt: damnation, betrayal, existential refusal, and blood guilt. The present chapter in its third and fourth sections studies the senses of deliverance corresponding to these that can be symbolized as redemption, restoration, sanctification, and purification; these are given special meanings in the discussions to follow that survey some of the interventions that aim to bring them about. Together, these add up to what can be symbolized as "justification in ultimate perspective."

"Justification" is a technical term in Christian theology but is intended here in a much broader, properly purified, vague sense. It means the setting right of the double brokenness of rejecting obligation and rejecting the obligatedness of the self. This includes the Christian use of the term but is not limited to Christianity. Justification does not mean that original failures of obligation are turned over so that they are not failures. It does not mean in this usage that proper or exculpating excuses are given. Rather it means that the person is restored to standing under obligation and often failing it, but without condemnation for rejecting obligation as such or the person's own self as defined by the dignity of responsible human agency relative to possibilities for choice.

I. FAILURE OF OBLIGATION: DAMNATION, BETRAYAL, EXISTENTIAL REFUSAL, BLOOD GUILT

The human predicament regarding obligation, as registered, one way or another, in the sacred canopies of the world's religions is not only that we lie under obligation but that we fail those obligations and, according to some traditions, do so inevitably. Natural obligation is not the only kind in which failure is inevitable. Indeed, failure is likely or inevitable with respect to the human normative response to the ultimates of wholeness, engagement, and a fully meaningful life of achieved value-identity. This section deals with failures with respect to obligations regarding possibilities of differing value, which when degenerating into brokenness can be called "guilt."

Moral obligations come from the structures of possibilities regarding outcomes on people, outcomes that would be different in value. Whatever possibility is chosen from the structured field of possibilities, the others are excluded, and every possible outcome has some value or other. If your child is sick with a bacterial infection and you can give the child an antibiotic (or not), of course you should choose to give the medicine; no one will lament the exterminated bacteria. If it happens, however, that these are the last specimens of this particular kind of bacteria, then the (dis)value of eliminating the species has a kind of serious counterweight against the quick healing of the child, not that it is enough to justify withholding the medicine if the illness is serious.

Many moral choices, however, pit the goods of some individuals over against the goods of other individuals, or the goods of individuals in immediate relation to certain institutions over against the long-term good of the institutions and how they will affect others. Here it is clear that any choice entails the serious exclusion of valuable possible outcomes. Now suppose that we had some kind of moral calculus by means of which we can establish a clear sense of priorities of better and worse among the possibilities in a possibility field, and we always know the optimal choice, always gaining the most value in quantity and the best in quality (as if those could be reconciled!) and always losing the least value. Most cultural traditions suggest rules, guidelines, value hierarchies, and the like to help with this calculus, although in point of fact the supposition that we have such a calculus is vain. As the Confucians have always argued, discretion is required in the application of any rule, goal, or precedent. But supposing we had such a good calculus, and we always picked the optimum possibility, then in a sense we always make the right moral choice, tragic as that might be. This would be the best we can hope for morally.

Nevertheless, the ways possibilities are structured for choice and action in any moment do not allow for doing justice to the long-term values of the people, as well as institutions and other things involved in the possibility structure. We have obligations to all the people in our family, but when forced at specific points to choose between them we serve some at the expense of others. We have obligations to people at work as well, sometimes choosing them over family and at other times the opposite. We have obligations to friendship and leisure time for ourselves, as well as to the demands of countervailing situations. Even though at each choice point we might make the optimum choice, in the long run we partly fail our obligations to all the morally freighted dimensions of our lives just as much as we partly satisfy them. Particularly for people in midlife deeply hedged in by obligations in many directions, it seems that nearly everyone says you have not done enough for them lately, and they are right. Our obligations to the separate individuals and institutions are often deeper than the obligations to choose the optimum possibility when they are conjoined in a given possibility structure. The result is that even making the optimum choices at all the choice points, we deeply fail the people whom we should have served better. Making the best choices (which we rarely do with any consistency), we still are morally guilty. Of course, we often make less than optimum choices because of culpable ignorance (we should have chosen earlier to be better informed), inability to cooperate in conjoint decisions, selfishness, laziness, fatigue, and a host of other nonexcusing excuses.

All the ways of failing moral obligation appear as well in analogous ways in the domain of social obligation. In addition, faithful pursuit and fulfillment of social obligations that themselves are immoral result in moral failure; or the choice to be moral at the sacrifice of the social obligation to some important role, such as a warrior's role to defend his or her people, results in serious failure of social obligations. We are guilty of failing our social obligations that define us as members of the human community. Because these memberships define us, failing social obligations is a betrayal of who we are in connection with others. Not only do we betray the specific communities within which we have social roles, we betray the very sociality that defines human beings as conditioning one another through their institutions.

These moral and social kinds of common failures of obligation build in complications to personal obligations. In addition to them, we fail ourselves by despair at moral and social failure. Despair can lead to self-hate, as a result of which we do wicked and destructive things to ourselves. Self-hate can be projected onto the world or ultimate dimensions of reality so that we cultivate the personal character of positive evil. Most people are not positively evil like the world's notorious characters, but most of us feel the pull toward that sometimes. We are guilty of failing to make ourselves to be as we ought to be and this amounts to a great existential refusal to take ourselves in our moral connections as legitimate objects of moral obligation. It is a refusal of our existence and its conditions.

The paradox of natural obligation comes from the fact that human beings (like all other living things) are costly creatures. Our metabolism alone means that we prevent the nuts we eat from becoming trees, the grains from becoming new plants next season, the animal flesh from continuing in the life of the animals. Our societies need space, and that means diminishing forests and prairies. In so many other ways, too, the natural and social existence of human beings is costly to nature.

In addition, the organization of human life is costly to itself. Biologically, personally, and socially we are hierarchically organized so that higher levels dominate and control the lower. This is simple enough to see and accept when we note that our biological organ systems organize biochemical reactions. But we embody in our nervous system the responses of our ancestors as well. The reptilian part of our brain—so ready to feed, fight, flee, or fornicate—is controlled in us by higher brain systems such as the Purkinje cells to smooth out motion, the limbic system to mediate instant responses, and the frontal cortex to deliberate and decide rationally. Yet the reptilian impulses are still there, bound down tenuously by other mental functions but ready to erupt in road rage when another driver cuts us off. Human beings with highly developed executive control functions are very costly for the free expression of primitive impulses. Similarly, as Xunzi pointed out in his essay on Nature or Heaven, babies are extraordinarily self-centered and are taught to function as family members by ritualizations that relate them to the good of others and of the family system. A functional family, surely a good thing, is costly to the free expression of natural self-centeredness. Families are tight units with extraordinary powers of solidarity as in-groups in opposition to other families and out-groups. Civilized society imposes laws of citizenship, enforced by the police, on the families who are in natural competition, feuding, and often at war. This civilized pressure is costly to family integrity. The higher-level human achievements are all good and worth it: personal self-direction and control is good; functional families are good; civilization is good. But all at a price.

From the standpoint of natural obligation, the obvious responsibility is to minimize the costs of human existence while maximizing the benefits of human existence to nature at large. Religious traditions have dealt with this in various ways. Vegetarians, for instance, who are found in most religious traditions, claim that by eliminating animals from their diet they lower their metabolic cost to the rest of nature. But they have to eat a lot more vegetables than they otherwise would if they also ate meat, and they run against the evolutionary grain of human beings as omnivores. In many but not all ways, it is possible to live human life in ways that enhance the nature of which we are parts.

The price registers in the possibility structure regarding human behavior toward nature, including the internal human environment, as the possibilities excluded. In a logical sense, the actualization of any possibility containing alternative possibilities excludes all but the actualized alternative. In nature, however, there exist ongoing structures and processes that have values of their own that are constrained or destroyed by the natural existence of human beings. In one sense, the nut that becomes part of a meal simply has a different chemical career than one that grows into a tree, just as the death of Zhuangzi's wife is, in one sense, just a chemical transformation. But in another sense it is the ending of the "natural" career of the nut. Surely, reptile brains are good building blocks for sophisticated human brains; yet, the inhibition of their impulses is a frustration. The individual's self-centered interest, indeed, the individual's real good, might very well be just a contribution to the welfare of the family; yet its frustration is costly to the individual. So also with the suppression of family ambitions by the justice of the body politic. From a human standpoint, it is entirely natural to control impulses, to subordinate selfish desires, and to sublimate feuding energies into the pursuit of high civilization. It would be unnatural for human beings not to do that.

All these kinds of fault discussed here—moral, social, personal, natural—save the last are faults for which we are responsible in one way or another. By contrast, the blood guilt that comes with the price of our existence is something for which we are not seriously responsible except by being ourselves. Our very existence as individuals and communities stains us with the fault of that price that without any further serious brokenness is a kind of blood guilt. How can that guilt be borne? There is no possibility of making amends, although we can minimize the prices our existence extracts. If the blood guilt drives us to such extremes of self-condemnation and hate that we think to destroy ourselves, that still does not erase the price already paid, and most often it ruins whatever good was purchased with the price, making the price meaningless or vain.

To lie under obligation in moral, social, personal, and natural matters and to be failures almost inevitably in most of them constitutes the array of human predicaments regarding obligation. The sacred canopies of the world's religions offer at least four paradigmatic accounts of why obligations are failed when they are not inevitable, each with several alternative interpretations. The first three have to do with moral, social, and personal guilt and the last has to do with blood guilt. Most of the great traditions have versions of all four.

One account is that the common lot of human beings is to be immature or insufficiently educated in the habits and means of fulfilling obligations or both. This is the dominant theme in Confucian moral thinking. Learning, for Confucian culture, includes the slow mastery of the subtleties of ritual play that increasingly discriminate how people and institutions as well as nature should be treated in differently appropriate ways, a mastery that involves physical training as in martial arts and calligraphy, intellectual education, and cultivation of the proper emotional tones.[2] Behind this theme is the metaphysical view that Heaven imparts a proper moral sensibility to human nature and that this needs to be cultivated in order to be enacted.[3] Two main Confucian traditions interpret this differently. The Mencian tradition says that if obstacles are properly removed, human nature will slowly manifest the Heavenly impulses as the person matures. The Xunzian tradition says that rituals need to be introduced early in order to connect inbuilt human capacities with their proper outlets in action. The differences between these traditions is sometimes put as follows: for the Mencian, human nature is good and will develop well if not distorted; for the Xunzian, human nature is bad, or selfish and disorganized like an infant, if not cultivated with rituals that embody proper sensibilities.[4]

Within Judaism, the fundamental problem is that human nature is created with two impulses, one toward love, mercy, and harmony, and another toward aggression, which leads to evil but which is necessary for the energies of social life and reproduction.[5] The task of moral education is to bind these two together so that the aggressive impulses do not do bad things. Within Christianity, Irenaeus, almost alone among classical theologians, argued that Adam and Eve fell because they were immature. Within Islam, each soul is offered the chance to submit to Allah, and some theologians explain why some do not by saying that they are immature.

A second fairly common account of the failure of obligations is that for some reason or other human beings have fallen from a previous state in which obligations were steadily fulfilled. Again, Confucianism stresses this point in its claim that the ancient sage emperors knew the secrets of pure virtue and especially knew the rituals that led to the regular fulfilling of moral, social, and personal obligations. Somehow, the wisdom and practice of the ancients has been corrupted or lost. Confucius claimed that he was not teaching anything new, only passing on the virtues of the ancient sage kings in a recovered form (most scholars think that he was disingenuous in this claim and in fact was a creative genius). Daoists also frame their understanding of history as that of a fall from a primeval time of natural virtue in which obligations were fulfilled naturally and without effort.[6]

A persistent theme in Buddhist historical understanding is that a Buddha, an enlightened one, is born in each era, embodying and teaching the dharma. After his death, the living disciples have the dharma teaching, but not the Buddha. After a while, the living teaching is lost and only texts remain. All the while, the general practice of the dharma declines until the next Buddha arrives to restore the perfect teaching. Maitreya is the Buddha expected after Gautama.[7]

The most famous story in the West of the fall from paradise is that found in the early chapters of Genesis with Adam and Eve's expulsion from the Garden of Eden, followed by Cain's murder of Abel and the subsequent continual decline until Noah's flood. Christians have focused on the personal culpability of Adam and Eve, and have developed a range of theories about free will and determinism in this regard. Jews and Muslims interpret the garden state already to have tremendous tensions built into it and emphasize more the mercy of God than the culpability of human beings, although that, too, is important.[8]

The third fairly common account for the steady failure to meet obligations is that it results from a prior failure to discriminate what is real and important, a failure based on confusing personal and social interests with what is real. In India (as well as elsewhere), this account is set within a basic concern about change and the passage of time. Roughly speaking, most forms of Hinduism, in accord with basic Vedic themes, take change to be a mark of unreality or insubstantiality: the real is to be found in that which does not change, namely, the self or consciousness that observes change. In one way or another, the unchanging reality of the self is identical with the unchanging character of reality, and the perception of change is an illusion if it is regarded as really real. The Vedic expression is "Atman is Brahman." Of course, this theme of reality as unchanging is balanced with the Shaivite theme that reality is constantly changing and that the emergence of the new is facilitated by the death and dissolution of the already emerged, as Shiva dances. On the Shaivite model, the failure of obligations is caused in some way by the hankering to hold on to things that change: Shaivites would not approve of Faust's allegedly salvific plea, "Remain a while, you are so beautiful."

The Buddhist response to the disparity between change and unchanging reality is dialectically the opposite of the Hindu response, namely, the denial that there is any unchanging or even continuous self or consciousness at all. No atman exists, says the Buddhist doctrine of anatman.[9] For the Buddhists, it is not that the change is illusion and the self that has forgotten its unchanging character is real. Just the opposite. The only reality is that of the change, *pratitya-samutpada*; even the belief that there is a continuous self observing the change is in some sense the illusion for many kinds of Buddhism. Those senses vary from simply believing that the intentional self owns its perceptions, to the Yogacara view that an underlying consciousness grasps each dharma as it arises and "perfumes" its connections with other dharmas, to the Madhyamaka theory that even the continuity of consciousness is an illusion. The result regarding the failure of obligations is vaguely the same as that understood by the Hindus, however. We try to cling to changing things to keep them from changing, and this leads to attachments to illusory continuities and the suffering that comes from their inevitable loss. The texture of the Buddhist understanding of suffering is different from that of most forms of Hinduism.

The proper response to the confusion of the real and the unreal is to be enlightened. Christianity has long held that Jesus was the "light of the world" whose coming shows people for what they truly are, unmasking those who live in untruth. In East Asian traditions, the realities of the things to which one should relate are often distorted by selfish interests, and with enlightenment one can discriminate both one's selfishness and the real worth of the things to which relations are obligatory.

The fourth account of failure of obligation, this time directed toward what here is called natural obligation, is a primitive sense that, if there is not a sacrificial payback to justify social or personal existence, the balance of the cosmos will be lost. In the Vedic tradition, the proper performance of the various sacrifices is required in order to sustain the gods, without whom the world order would collapse.[10] Buddhism early on separated itself out from the culture of the Brahmanical sacrifices and, in pursuing the middle way, seemed to treat ritualized sacrifice in an external fashion. Nevertheless, the liberation of sentient beings from the bondage of attachments is the grain of the universe, for most forms of Buddhism. The bodhisattvas and certain other adepts live in personal sacrifice of themselves and their own liberation in order to devote themselves to the liberative grain of the universe. Put the other way around, unless they sacrifice themselves, the universe will be stained with the bondage of sentient beings.

Confucianism, ancient Temple Judaism, and Christianity are organized around sacrifices that have cosmic bearing. The seasonal sacrifices of the emperor are necessary for the harmony between human existence and the seasons of the year; sacrifices to ancestors are the condition for the inheritance of virtue. The ancient Israelites knew that impurity is unavoidable—walking on an unmarked grave unknowingly, killing an enemy in battle whose corpse falls on the warrior. Sacrificial purification rites are necessary just to get along day by day, let alone when the whole community stains itself with profligate worship. Christianity takes blood guilt to be more a matter of human culpability than many other traditions, although in many conflicting senses.[11] The earliest distinctive element in Christianity was the Eucharist, a ritual eating and drinking of the symbolic body and blood of Jesus, who was the sacrifice for the sins of the world, or at least for the Eucharistic communicants.[12] Some early Christian atonement symbols say that, because of blood guilt, perhaps traceable to Adam and Eve but continued in personal practice ever since, human beings stain the entire cosmos because they have sold themselves to Satan.[13] The sacrifice of Jesus Christ is the redemption that returns them to God's ownership whom they again (or for the first time since Eden) can approach with purity.

Having discussed some of the typical senses of failure of obligation and typical accounts for them in several world religions, we now turn from these predicaments themselves to how they lead further to brokenness.

II. BROKENNESS OF OBLIGATION

The predicament is twofold in the case of each of the predicaments. On the one hand, the nature of ultimate reality as expressed in the transcendental traits of harmony constitutes ultimate elements of the human world that call forth responses that define human beings ultimately: obligation with regard to possibilities for free action, grounded wholeness in the ways people comport themselves toward their own important components, engagement with other things that make up one's existential field, including oneself as existentially located, and the achievement of an absolute value-identity that defines who one is in ultimate perspective. On the other hand, the predicament is that people often or always fail in some or all of these responses, and in this sense become broken. There is no taking away the need to deal with obligatory possibilities, components, existential connections, and value-identity. But when people are broken in their responses to these ultimate conditions, they have predicaments from which they need deliverance.

The first species of human predicament arises out of the fact that human beings face possibilities that have differential value. Because the alternative possibilities are often better or worse, they lay obligations on the people who face them and have to decide how to actualize them. To fail the obligations, at least some of them, is a frequent if not inevitable occurrence. The result is that people are in normative contradiction with themselves: they are not what they ought to be. They do what they ought not do, and vice versa. In myriad ways, some of which are schematized in the previous section, people are failures with respect to obligation. The human predicament regarding the ultimacy of obligation is how to cope with this basic kind of failure.

In some obvious sense, if failure is built in to human life, the thing to do is to pick up and go on afterward, making amends where possible and searching for ways not to fail again. But because this failure is a kind of normative contradiction, it has a special normative status of something like what the monotheistic religions have called "guilt." More than being responsible for bad decisions, guilt is a kind of ontological status that leads often if not always to further brokenness.

There are two typical forms of response to guilt that lead to brokenness regarding the human state of lying under obligation. The first is an attempt to diminish the importance of, or outright to deny, the normative state of being under obligation. This is to deny the ultimacy of value-laden form as a determiner of the human condition, and beyond that to deny the ontological creative act that creates a world where all things have form and human beings face obligations regarding choice among which forms to actualize. The second is an attempt to diminish or deny the self that is guilty, to condemn that guilty self. Both deny the ultimacy in the human roles of being under obligation and also can go further to deny the ultimacy of the ontological creative act as the founding of the human self that can be guilty. Here is the way of nihilism regarding obligation. These points can be spelled out.

The inner contradiction of guilt is not a logical one. Logically, of course, it is possible to be guilty. Otherwise it would not happen. The inner contradiction is normative, a contradiction between what one ought to be and what one is.

Form is pattern or structure for unifying a plurality. Contradiction, therefore, is a corruption or abuse of form. Precisely because form bears value, the possibility of normative contradiction is inbuilt to form: one's choice excludes the better option so that the value-laden actuality and the normative excluded possibilities are in contradiction. In this way, people with obligations can and do live in formal contradiction. Because form and the facing of possibilities is an ultimate boundary condition, the internal contradiction between one's obligations and one's achievements is an ultimate kind of human predicament. Guilt is an offense against form itself as it binds the human world and gives rise to obligation.

That the human condition involves the predicament of formal normative contradiction is widely recognized and symbolized in powerful ways. The contradiction is expressed in the symbology of disharmony in many traditions, especially but not exclusively those of East Asia.[14] The contradiction is expressed in the symbols for the confusion of the real and illusory in many traditions, especially those originating in South Asia.[15] Representing the West

Asian traditions, St. Paul wrote, "For I do not do the good I want, but the evil I do not want is what I do."[16]

The first kind of brokenness that tumbles so often from this guilty contradiction is an attempt to undermine its normative status. Many ways exist to do this. One is to assert that there are no real value differences among the possibilities. This might be made as an empirical claim (which usually is in fact false). Or it might result from a sudden affirmation of a value-neutral cosmology, with the follow-up step of saying that all appearances of difference among the values of the alternative possibilities are mere subjective projections. Another way to slide down the path of denying the normative status of obligation is to say that, even if there are value differences, they cannot be known or the person is not responsible for knowing them. Ignorance is a good excuse when one is looking for an excuse. Yet another way to tumble is to admit that possible outcomes do differ in value but deny that the person at hand is the relevant agent with the responsibility. The previous section rehearses ways of denying responsibility. People fleeing the guilt of failing obligations can combine these and other strategies of de-normatizing obligation so as to escape the painful guilt of this kind of contradiction.

The more serious people are in this denial of the normativeness of obligation, the more their flight turns into a denial of the ontological status of value-laden possibilities relative to human life as part of the radically contingent ontological act of creation. If there are possibilities, and if some of them consist in alternative ways of actualization, and if there are human choosers who can make a difference, then simply to deny the normativeness of obligation is to deny the creation itself. This is one form of malevolence to being-in-general, as Jonathan Edwards would say, that denies existence and the ontological creation of the world itself.[17] Denial of the cosmological ultimate of form leads to the denial of the ontological ultimate of creation.

The second kind of brokenness falling out from the guilt of failure of obligations is apparently the opposite of the first kind, namely, the redoubling of the failure so as to condemn the self. Profound self-condemnation leads to the tortured soul so legendary in Christianity, Judaism, and Islam, and also Confucianism. When buoyed up with imagery of divine judgment, self-condemnation leads to despair. Of course, not all guilty monotheists tumble this far. In fact, the Christian Bible is clear that "judgment is mine, says the Lord." But some do, and many of these, for instance St. Paul, claim that this thorough self-condemnation is the appropriate assessment for everyone whether they know it or not.

Such existential nihilism is a denial of the self as facing alternative possibilities. Dostoyevsky's hero, Raskolnikov, in *Crime and Punishment*, begins by denying the normativeness of obligation in any form of morality and murders a woman just for the sake of doing so, the first form of brokenness. But then he moves to utter self-condemnation, the second form of brokenness, until brought to accept himself by a lover. Absent that acceptance, he would end denying himself and the ontological creation through which he came to be.

Deep down, however, even an optimally ordered life in relation to nature is costly. Human beings have a sense of this, which registers at the primitive level in the rituals to propitiate the victims that were sacrificed to make civilized life possible. Paul Ricoeur argued that the most elementary sense of evil is something like a stain, an involuntary flaw.[18] At some deep level, natural obligation can never be translated into personal responsibility. No matter how responsible we are in optimizing the possibilities we actualize, the blood cost of our existence remains. If we are "true to nature," even in acting out our natural functions, we recognize that other things have paid a price for our existence, and our own layers of organization have paid a price for our high human achievements. Beyond the obligation to optimize our possibilities in relation to nature is the obligation to recognize and grieve the price paid for our existence. In the sense of nature as ancient as that viewed in primitive society and as contemporary as the vision of evolutionary theory, we are bought with a blood price.

Natural obligation is articulated in an ultimate finite/infinite contrast that puts in question the legitimacy of our own existence. So often the ritual sacrifices practiced by our primitive ancestors, which were aimed to justify human existence in whatever form it took, were blood sacrifices, indeed human sacrifices. At some deep level, with regard to natural obligation, it is not that we could have done better: we could have not existed at all. Our primitive sense of the right to exist involves an obligation to pay back our price in blood. How else would we account for the ubiquity in world cultures of sacrifice, so often human sacrifice or its surrogates such as the symbolic cannibal ritual of the Christian Eucharist?

Natural obligation moves the discussion from an obligation tied to accountability in the sense beloved by European Enlightenment moralists to a darker sense of existential obligation that lays upon us something for which we cannot be accountable. Built in to this sense of natural obligation is the inevitability of failure and blood guilt.

Having to deal with the predicaments of obligation, that is, of possibility and choice, is one mode of the predicament of radical contingency. The predicament of radical contingency was characterized earlier as that of death. So, one meaning of death comes from the predicaments having to do with obligation, namely, condemnation or, more strongly, damnation.

Two roughly distinguished approaches to the problem of death were noted in the introduction to this volume. One, reflecting some version of karma theory, treats death as a condemnation *to* a next life based on the ways by which one did or did not fulfill obligations in this life. The ultimate goal, again envisioned in different ways, is to obtain release from the karmic effects of one's obligated life, which means no more lives. Death from the wheel of morally determined rebirths is release from the predicament of radical contingency as manifested in the problematic of form, possibility, and obligation.

The other general approach to death treats it as a termination of the chances to do better, with some kind of reward possibly coming later. Many versions of the approach are competitive, for instance, images of an afterlife rewarding the good and punishing the wicked, perhaps with a limbo or purgatory in between; or perhaps the problem is to gain an afterlife of any sort rather than simply ceasing to exist; some versions do not employ afterlife conceptions at all. The point of all, however, is to say that the way one does or does not fulfill obligations determines whether one merits life that is not limited by obligations. To be a forgiven sinner is to rise above obligations while still working at them.

This chapter so far has argued that the ultimate dimension of the human condition that consists in facing normatively differentiated possibilities constitutes an ultimately significant human predicament. The ultimacy of the facing of possibilities comes from the transcendentally constitutive character of form as part of any harmony. Other transcendental traits of harmony exist, namely, components, existential location, and value-identity. Hence, the human predicament deriving from the ultimacy of form and the contradictions to form that come from failures of obligation is not the only ultimate predicament. Each of the other cosmological ultimates poses its predicaments for human life. Yet, because form is inseparable from components, existential location, and value-identity, the predicament of normative contradiction is an element in all the other predicaments.

The following two sections discuss the interventions by which religions aim to deliver people from guilt.

III. DELIVERANCE FROM MORAL AND SOCIAL GUILT: REDEMPTION AND RESTORATION

Moral guilt can be viewed proximately and ultimately. Proximately, moral guilt falls on everyone, "inevitably if not necessarily," to use Reinhold Niebuhr's famous phrase.[19] As such, moral guilt is not a religious problem, only a problem of coping with bad behavior in oneself and others (not to minimize the importance of this!). Ultimately, moral guilt spirals into a condition that defines part of one's ultimate identity. Its ultimate dimensions heave into view when the motive for the immoral action is to be immoral as such and the immoral action thus condemns itself. It damns itself by rejecting the ontological condition of value-laden possibilities that lay one under obligation.

Augustine has been chided in the literature for taking such a trivial example of moral guilt, his adolescent theft of pears with his friends from a neighbor's tree, for his analysis of religiously ultimate moral guilt.[20] But a more serious example would have confused the issue. Augustine came to understand that incident to be motivated not by hunger or desire for pears but by the deliberate delight in doing something he and his friends knew to be wrong. Morally trivial in terms of the weight of the value consequences, that incident was an ultimately, that is, religiously, defining moment for Augustine and his friends, whose companionship was ruined by it.[21] As Chapter 1 of this volume argues, even the best intentions to be moral can be frustrated by moral ambiguity so that people turn to reject the ground of morality itself in the obligations resident in their possibilities, and will to be guilty.

Complicating this, and sometimes coming from resentment at such inevitable failures, many people react against being obligated. Often symbolized as disobedience to an ultimate law or command, a common human failing is to know the obligatory and still choose the worse. Sometimes this is motivated by egocentrism or selfishness. Other times it is sheer perversity, rejecting the obligatory as such. Moral guilt is then chosen in a profound way, so that people are doubly responsible for failing obligations. Damnation is the choice of evil for evil's sake, in some symbolic understanding of those terms. It might be symbolized by a condemning judge, or by the remorseless rewards of karma. But it is a condition of willing moral guilt. This can be symbolized as "damnation," so long as the cross-cultural breadth of that term is used. Confucianism and Daoism express this in terms of deliberate turning from the Way. The situation in India is complicated in those situations in which the universal obligatoriness of dharma is affirmed by many but rejected by the renunciants. Yet even the renunciants renounce in the name of a higher obligation or path to ultimate release. Buddhism in most of its branches agrees with most religious practices of Hinduism that fundamental moral probity is required to be mastered prior to serious efforts at enlightenment. Even when a moral terror achieves enlightenment, according to Buddhism, this treats enlightenment as an intervention that "justifies" the person with regard to the predicament of obligation.[22] Christianity and Islam are at home with notions of damnation as an external or internal judgment that consigns the damned to punishment.

Guilt is an objective condition, however, not something that can be removed by willing oneself to be innocent again. Even if one never again transgresses (in that way), and even if one does not *feel* guilty, the guilty deed eternally is what it is. Religious traditions have many different ways of registering this fact. The feeling of being guilty for something of which one is not really guilty is common and often lies at the base of psychological disabilities. A crucial element of spiritual transformation in many religious traditions is coming to understand and own up to real guilt, as opposed to false guilt, and to feel guilty where guilt is deserved.

Some traditions have versions of karma in which the moral consequences of objective guilt inexorably determine future reincarnations. Others hold to some version of ontological judgment, either by a judging God or gods, or by some nonpersonal registration of the guilt, with corresponding punishment. Because moral guilt is not merely harm done to others but is a condition of the doer, the ultimate seriousness of its reality is that retributive justice is justified.

"Retributive justice" is a broad notion with many highly technical specifications in legal and moral literature. The meaning intended here is the vague one, that moral guilt is a condition that puts a person in the position of deserving a harm that is (approximately) as great as the harm for which the person is guilty. In proximate matters, this is the basis of the punishment theory of how to respond to wrongdoing, and it has debatable merits in different contexts; Hegel argued that it is necessary in order to respect the humanity of the guilty party when the temptation is to dehumanize that person in matters of serious crime.[23] In ultimate matters retributive justice takes the form of reversing the guilty person's rejection of the ultimate conditions of obligation by separating that person from the conditions of ultimacy. This might be symbolized by some version of condemnation to a life of perpetual illusion, or separation from God, or withdrawal of rights within the community that provides personal definition, or many other ways.

How can the guilty person be set right with the ultimate conditions of obligation? This is the question of deliverance with respect to moral guilt at the ultimate level. "Redemption" is the general term used here to signify this project of intervention. The term gained currency within Christianity with a specific metaphoric base. One version of moral damnation in Christianity is that the damned person (or the whole damned human race) is separated from God by being given over to Satan or the powers of evil. Being "given over" means that Satan or evil "owns" the person and has a right to that person's life, which in turn means that the person is ultimately identified not with ultimate reality but with its opposite (however that is construed). "Redemption" is the price paid to Satan or evil that "buys back" the life of the guilty person, like redeeming an item that had been pawned. But "redemption" quickly took on much larger connotations within Christianity to mean the whole apparatus of restoring the guilty party to a right relation with God or the ultimate. That larger meaning can be applied across the sacred canopies of all religions insofar as they register the ultimacy of moral guilt to be a separation from ultimate realities that in fact define the human condition. A brief survey of some of the redemption strategies for deliverance can make the point.

One array of redemption strategies lies against the background of cosmological conceptions of karma. Although not all conceptions of reincarnation have the moral dimensions of karmic determination, those that do illustrate the principle of retributive justice: there is a real character of the moral (or immoral) life of individuals that determines in a juridical and biological way the character of subsequent lives.

Some karmic traditions believe that remaining within the wheel of reincarnations is itself the separation from ultimate reality that constitutes damnation. They entertain versions of redemption as escaping that wheel, perhaps to rejoin a deeper reality such as Brahman or Buddha-mind. Some of these versions are nondualist, as in Advaita Vedanta and the Patriarchal faith of Mahayana Buddhism (as interpreted by Sung Bae Park, for instance).[24]

According to the latter, sudden enlightenment (often resulting from dedicated koan spiritual practice) reveals that, instead of being caught within the wheel of samsara, one has been one with the Buddha-mind all along. Other versions are dualistic according to which liberation from the cycle of lives means establishing a right relation to what is ultimate. Some versions of redemption from the karmic round, instead of connecting with a deeper, nonchanging reality, focus on living into the fact that change itself is all there is, *pratitya-samutpada*, that this is the ultimate, and that any point within the change—including a self, a guilty self—is ephemeral. Other karmic traditions view the punishment and reward system as itself directly connected with the task of redeeming people from separation from ultimate reality, urging people to improve their karma so as to reach higher and higher states of reality. In all these systems, the reality of moral guilt is acknowledged and the justice of retribution is admitted. Redemption means establishing a new relation to what is ultimate, however understood, that is compatible with guilt and deserving of retribution but that transforms the retribution into a state of ultimate reality that does not ultimately suffer retribution.

Another array of redemption strategies, as noted previously, interprets the separation of the guilty person or community from ultimate reality as redeemable by sacrifice. A powerful strain in the religion of ancient Israel construes guilt to result in such stain or impurity that the person or even a whole people are prevented from entering into the presence of God.[25] Redemption comes from the performance of sacrifices ordained by God to accomplish purification. God provides for the sacrifices out of divine mercy, which is in delicate tension with divine justice. Christianity lifted this conception to a cosmic scale, arguing that all people are sinners and thus impure, and that only the sacrifice of the Son of God, Jesus Christ, could accomplish the purification. Many conflicting versions of the meaning of this atoning sacrifice have been developed within Christianity. But all aim to show how individuals can be redeemed sinners, always sinners, but still purified and brought into right relation with God.

Yet another array of redemptive responses to moral guilt symbolizes the separation of the guilty person from the ultimate in terms of the community. A person is greatly defined by roles within the community, according to some traditions, and the separation from the ultimate means that the community rejects the person in those roles. Redemption means the reordering of the person to make him or her fit or acceptable within those roles again. There are many versions of this "reordering," including enforced reeducational practices, as in some strains of Confucianism, monastic life, and sometimes punishment in penitentiaries. The Confucian case is particularly interesting because it stands at such an opposite extreme from the Christian case according to which God in Jesus Christ pays the redemptive price externally, as it were, for the guilty sinner. In the Confucian case, nothing external would avail. Rather, the person can be redeemed only by setting out on the path of becoming a sage. In the Confucian view, no matter how guilty they are and in flight from obligation and their own responsible agency, everyone is capable of becoming a sage so as to reestablish learned and effective contact with the ultimate (*li*, translated Principle or coherence). Particularly as developed by the Neo-Confucians, becoming a sage requires two kinds of cultivation and their integration. On the one hand is the cultivation of the inner self so that a person is capable of discerning the fundamental forms of coherence in the world and assessing which are ideal. On the other hand is the cultivation of action in the world so as to enhance ideal harmony or coherence. The connection between these two is extremely important. This conception of becoming a sage is based on a metaphysical analysis of the grounds of obligation in nature, namely, Principle. The conception stands in interesting contrast with the Christian metaphysical analysis of God as Creator and the divine Son as Redeemer. In both cases ultimate reality provides an intervention; in the Christian case, the intervention is performed by ultimate reality and only taken up "in faith" by the guilty sinner; in the Confucian case the intervening redemptive possibility of sagacity is present in the person from the beginning but has to be accessed and cultivated so as to actualize the connection between the ultimacy of obligation and the obligated person.[26]

These arrays of responses and others often are all found together within each of several large religious traditions, presenting many-sided approaches to problems of moral guilt and its redemption. Some religions make certain ones central to their rhetoric, but most involve all. Many of the variations reflect different ways of symbolizing ultimacy, the character of cosmic and social causation, and a host of other factors. Yet most religions do contain responses and procedures by which, for at least some people, moral guilt is both acknowledged and yet brought into compatibility with some sense of the right relation of the person to ultimate reality, including the ultimacy of obligation.

Although not all religious traditions would put it this way, the expressions and mechanisms of redemption appear as revelatory. Revelation, as characterized in *Philosophical Theology*, consists of signs or persons or interpreted events that open up some aspect of ultimate reality that is obscured without them (I, introduction). In the predicament of moral guilt and retribution, there appears to be no way out. The redemptive move—some liberation from karma, or reconciliation with God, or resetting of one's social nature in relation to ultimate reality—reveals a new possibility. That possibility is to be redeemed from some kind of spiritual separation from the ultimate ontological creative act because of guilt regarding the ultimacy of obligations stemming from the transcendental trait of having to face possibilities.

Most of the issues of moral guilts and salvific redemption carry over by analogy into the issues of social guilts and restoration. Yet there is a unique kind of guilt that comes from failing to live up to the obligations of social roles (II, 1). Although some social roles might be incidental and external to a person, many others are not. Memberships in family, communities, political and historical situations are definitive of individuals, one way or another. As *Philosophical Theology One*, Chapter 10, argues, individuals are harmonies of essential and conditional components, and social roles are among the most important conditional components.

Social guilt is not, then, something only proximate in importance, although many failures of social roles are as trivial as stealing pears is in the moral realm. When social guilt evolves to the point of rejecting the social roles as such, or certain important ones, it amounts to a rejection of the ultimate nature of the definition of human beings in social terms. Confucianism insists on this with perhaps the greatest intensity of any Axial Age religion. In terms of proximate issues of social guilt, rejection of social roles is a betrayal of the social group in which the roles should be played. But in terms of ultimate issues of social guilt, it is a betrayal of the social nature of the person, which is part of the person's ultimate ontological created nature, a rejection of sociality as such.

Deliverance from betrayal of one's ultimately social nature can be called "restoration," meaning restoration of the social identity of one's life and of solidarity with the community. As an ultimate matter, restoration as a salvific intervention is directed at healing and reaffirming the very sociality of the person. When failure at meeting social obligations results in rejection of the social obligations as such, then the person has denied a cosmologically fundamental created ultimate condition of human beings, namely, mutual conditioning through social institutions. Restoration then means restoring the person to an affirmative relation to social obligations as such, a reaffirmation of a covenant, as some traditions put it. Most forms of Judaism and Christianity affirm that people are created as human only as in a covenant with both a community and with the Creator. Being in the covenant is not a matter of choice but of ontological status as a human creature. For many forms of both religious traditions, individual moral guilt is also an offense against the communal covenant so that restoration is both to a right relation with the covenant-giving Creator and to proper membership in the community.

Restoration to an ultimate affirmation of sociality and the importance of obligatory social roles cannot be an abstract matter apart from concrete social roles. Therefore, deliverance through restoration of sociality requires restoration to good standing in the communities in which the person has important social roles. Whatever mechanisms effect the restoration must involve those actions in and by the society—somehow symbolized to indicate the ultimate connections—that accept the person back in good standing. These include social arrangements that restore the person as a social role-player in good standing.

Nevertheless, not all social roles are good (II, 1). Moreover, sometimes the obligations to fulfill certain social roles are in contradiction to moral obligations. Sometimes the failure to fulfill social obligations leading to betrayal of the ultimate condition of sociality stems from conscientious rejection of social roles in the name of some higher morality. Therefore, the restoration to sociality still might involve the rejection of certain social roles. The renouncer traditions in Indian religions, the Confucian tradition of the retreat from communal participation, and monastic traditions of various types all are special social roles that "restored" people can play that involve rejection of other social roles. These special social roles might look like the betrayal of a given community's social roles and their obligatory nature, from the standpoint of that community. The traditional tension in South Asian religions between the dharma of the Brahmanical household and the dharma of the renunciants has parallels in other traditions. At the very least, the ultimately important role of being a social critic, or a critic of the institutions within which certain roles function, should be acknowledged.

The object of social obligations is only indirectly other individuals, as they are impacted by the institutions of society. The direct object of social obligations is institutions. The various institutions of renunciation and criticism need to be recognized as institutions just as much as those more commonly identified with social organization and welfare. Restoration to the ultimacy in social obligations can come from the interventions involved in renouncing institutions as well as those more obviously recognized as constituting society-building organizations. Perhaps the most common interventions of restoration are rituals that symbolize reentrance into the social roles betrayed and abandoned, or entry into new social roles that continue the rejection of the original social order while claiming to form a new one. The important point is that the person's rejection of the ultimate significance of social roles, and of the person's own self as having a fundamentally social nature, are eliminated and the person restored to obligation to the sociality of human agency.

IV. DELIVERANCE FROM PERSONAL AND NATURAL GUILT: SAGACITY AND PURIFICATION

Section I termed the ultimate predicament that results from failure of the obligations to cultivate oneself a great "existential refusal," a refusal of the self as a moral agent. An aspect of the obligation to choose well among alternatives of differing value is the meta-obligation to cultivate the self as capable of good choice. The great existential refusal is to reject that meta-obligation. This is a person's refusal to take his or her own self as involved in moral and social obligations as a legitimate object of moral obligation. The cultivation of oneself has many dimensions beyond the moral, and is discussed in many contexts in *Philosophical Theology*. Here the general point is that one has a moral obligation to take oneself as an object of moral obligation just as one has such obligations toward other persons and institutions.

The term "sagacity" can be used for the dimension of deliverance that addresses the predicament of the great existential refusal to take oneself as an object of moral obligation, with the various aspects of self-cultivation that attend upon this. Etymologically it is affiliated with "sage," a term for an adept who develops personal cultivation to an ultimate level of worth and discriminating action. Sagacity thus has a wide range of meanings associated with different aspects of self-cultivation, and also is often taken to be associated with a graded scale of virtuosity.

The particular meaning of sagacity intended here, however, has to do with reversing the great existential refusal with an affirmation or commitment of that obligation, namely, to make oneself the best one can be in ultimate perspective. Sagacity in this sense is associated with vows of the sort that monks and nuns take, with conversion commitments, and the like, and is part of what is commonly called sanctification. In the West, sagacity was once associated with philosophy, back when "philosophy" was an alternative term for "religion." Some philosophers still think of themselves as seekers after sagacity in the sense of wisdom about what is important and the bearing of this on action. The most obvious traditional home for the projects of sagacity, however, is within Confucianism. Confucius's oft-quoted characterization of his development defining sagehood is:

> At fifteen my mind was set on learning. At thirty my character had been formed. At forty I had no more perplexities. At fifty I knew the Mandate of Heaven. At sixty I was at ease with whatever I heard. At seventy I could follow my heart's desire without transgressing moral principles.[27]

Although many contexts exist in which it is relevant to ask just how sagacious a person is according to some scale of degrees, in this context the relevant question is whether the person has abandoned the great refusal and set out on the path of attending to moral obligations to the person's own self. For deliverance consists in reaffirming the connection with ultimate reality, the ontological creative act, a connection that includes oneself as an object of moral obligation. How far one gets in the process of cultivating oneself—as a matter of moral obligation—is not ultimately important, save in matters of absolute value-identity discussed elsewhere. What is ultimately important about sagehood here is one's commitment to the process as a matter of recognition of the ultimacy of moral obligation to prepare the self for addressing ultimacy in moral and social obligations.

Religions have many salvific interventions that aim at sagehood regarding obligation as they understand it. Most of these are associated with wholeness, a much broader notion of self-achievement than sagehood considered as a remedy for the great existential refusal. Human beings can be broken in respect to obligation, to their own wholeness, to their engagements with other things and people, and to their absolute value-identity. Sagehood is that ideal for wholeness that involves commitment to developing the self as properly educated for dealing with moral and social obligations. As Stephen C. Angle has shown with respect to the Confucian ideal of the sage, this involves a commitment that carries through many phases of development and is based on the nature of human potential and nature's own value structures. Whereas guilt and betrayal come from rejecting obligatory relations into which a person is "naturally born," as it were, the great existential refusal comes from deliberate rejection of the task of cultivating the self so as to be good at the discernment and fulfillment of obligation. Even though societies might ritualize the developmental point of maturation in which a person is supposed to take over responsibility for self-cultivation in matters of obligation, a person still might refuse to make the necessary commitments. The remedies are inducements to take up that moral education, and religions have many.

Intervention to deliver from blood guilt is purification. In its ultimate aspects, blood guilt is not something for which people are morally responsible, as if they could have avoided it. Rather, blood guilt comes from the price others pay for human existence, the price paid by our internal biological and emotional processes for our controlled executive behavior, and the price individuals and family groups pay for social order. In some obvious senses, these prices are all worth it. Nevertheless, the very blood of human existence is costly in lives, resources, and freedom. As Ricoeur said, human existence is stained.

Purification is a ritual dimension to human existence that allows people to live with blood guilt. It does not erase the guilt, but allows people to live with it. Although purification takes a great many forms in religion, it has three main kinds: symbolic purgation, sacrificial displacement, and sacrificial reconstitution of the world as pure or holy.

Symbolic purgation might be literal use of purgatives—as in the peyote rite—or special diets, abstention from certain foods for a period, or fasting from certain or all foods; or ritual cleansing as in baptisms, bathing in sacred rivers or pools, or ceremonially changing from dirty clothes to clean. The purgation is symbolic because it does not really "cleanse" a person or community from the real costs of civilized existence. It symbolizes those costs as impurities that can be removed like purifying the body. Buddhist imagery of crossing to the other shore symbolizes purification in the whole of a religious quest. The power of lotus-flower imagery comes from the fact that the pure blossom arises from the mud of the lake or stream bottom. Hindu rites of bathing in the Ganges symbolize a periodic purification. Crossing the Sea of Reeds symbolized for the ancient Israelites a washing off of the stains of Egypt, and crossing the Jordan into the Promised Land marked them as purified as God's special people. Crossing the Jordan imagery in Christianity symbolizes the move from the travails of Earthly life to the pure land of Heaven. Christian baptismal imagery symbolizes dying to the impure life and rising with Jesus, who rose from the waters of the Jordan after having been baptized by John the Baptist and also from the wretched death of crucifixion to a new life sufficiently pure to be in the divine presence. Although in these examples there might be some instances in which purification addresses morally culpable sin, the purification also addresses the blood guilt that just is part of life.

Sacrificial displacement involves removing the guilt from oneself or from the community and placing it on a scapegoat. The Levitical atonement ritual is a literal rendering of this in which the priest takes the people's sins and his own and places them on a goat or lamb that is then sent into the wilderness to be absorbed by an evil spirit. Scapegoating is a metaphor for a much wider range of practices, however. Persons and communities, usually minorities, have been used as scapegoats, often to extraordinarily horrific moral effect.[28]

Sacrificial reconstitution of the world as holy was an almost universal phenomenon in ancient cultures. Modern people have tended to look on ritual sacrifice of plants, more often animals, and sometimes human beings, as attempts to appease gods, and sometimes that might be the right interpretation. But more often, the sacrifices were intended to empower the gods to keep the world in good order, however that was understood. This was so in the Mimamsa traditions of India, the imperial sacrifice cults of China, and the household sacrificial rites of the ancient Mediterranean world.[29]

The dimensions of the predicament of obligation and guilt are so intertwined that a single salvific intervention of practice, teaching, or a figure might involve many or all the dimensions. For Christians, for instance, Jesus Christ justifies sinners from the moral guilt, commits them to a social way of justice and love, leads them to learn love of self and others, and purifies them with his sacrificial death. This is to say, Jesus is not only about justifying morally guilty people, or only about establishing institutions of justice and care, or only about enabling sanctifying sagacity, or only about atonement, but about all of these. Moreover, each of these rubrics involves many lines of development, often conflicting with one another. To understand Jesus as savior, then, is to pursue all these lines in their multiple dimensions. The same is true for many of the revelatory centers of other religions.

CHAPTER SIX

Disintegration and Centeredness

In the reflective view of many people worldwide, the primary function of religion is to ease suffering, mend brokenness, and cultivate personal integration, wholeness, and serenity. Sometimes this is combined with a strong passion for justice and a sense of obligation to bring it about, insofar as injustice often has to do with suffering, brokenness, and disintegration. But the religious quest for wholeness is not the same as the quest for righteousness and the fulfillment of obligation.

The fundamental predicament of grounded wholeness and the failure to achieve it derives from the transcendental trait of every harmony having components that it integrates according to its form. For human beings, this means that individuals comport themselves well or poorly toward the important, usually ongoing, components of their lives. Comporting themselves well, they are well grounded in the things of which they are composed; comporting themselves poorly, they exhibit either a failure of integration or an impiety toward the components, or both, resulting often in disintegration of the otherwise achieved overall harmonies with the integrities of the components of their lives.

Chapter 2 argued that proper comportment to the components of human life has four modes: appropriation, deference, negotiation of change, and realism. The present chapter reflects on the ways by which disintegration regarding comportment takes the form of distorting these modes. The first section deals with these modes of inauthentic comportment. The modes of inauthentic comportment are simply ways of failing to comport properly to components of life: alienation rather than appropriation, arrogance rather than deference, suffering in several senses rather than successful negotiation of change, and living in illusion, or delusion, rather than with a sense of reality. The second section argues that deliverance from disintegration involves the religious quest for centeredness, restoring wholeness. The third and fourth sections detail deliverances from alienation and arrogance, and from suffering and illusion, respectively.

I. DISINTEGRATION: ALIENATION, ARROGANCE, SUFFERING, DELUSION

A thing could not be a component of human life unless it is given a place within it and hence is appropriated in a way or to a degree. The predicament of appropriation, however, is to appropriate the component in such a way that carries into the human life the real values in the component. Too often human beings simply forget the full reality of that which composes them. They forget their ancestors, their history, and those influential upon them. They do not pay attention to what they consume and eat. They do not treat their own responsibility as a proper component of themselves. Most people are inattentive and forgetful. Properly to appropriate the components of life requires a learned skill at living, a skill that has many forms but that is addressed in spiritual practices of nearly all the world's religious traditions. This is extraordinarily complicated because proper appropriation requires taking as much of the good as possible while leaving behind, or correcting, or making amends for, the disvalues carried by components. Livers and kidneys filter out the toxins in food, but sophisticated education is required to filter out the toxins in one's history and traditions, in family habits and community loyalties. To the extent that the components are not appropriated properly, people are alienated from those components. The components enter into the people in purely functional ways, in which the needs of the people determine what is carried over and what is filtered out. The real character of the components, whose values and disvalues are borne by the components, is denied, forgotten, left behind. People are even alienated from their own bodies whose needs they neglect in favor of other interests of the harmonizing self.

The deeper predicament that turns appropriation into alienation is that sometimes the needs for harmonizing the self prevent a rich appropriation of the components. Sometimes the self cannot stand appropriating an important component and feels itself forced to alienate itself from that. Imagine a Confucian faced with the predicament of appropriating a seriously wicked parent: after finding virtue from more distant ancestors and remonstrating as much as possible with the parent, perhaps still the Confucian needs to disown the parent or, in the extreme, to take his or her own life so as to disown the parent. Too often, the historical, cultural, and biological characters of the components of life are so threatening to the harmony of life itself that they can be included as components only in alienated ways. To that extent, however, the life is ungrounded in them, however much it results from them.

Failure to address the predicament of deference is to be *arrogant*. Arrogance comes from the will of the self to harmonize itself at the expense of its important components to which it should defer in a kind of natural piety. A self can harmonize itself in many ways, including different ways of comporting itself toward its components. The better ways include modes of life in which proper deference can be paid. When those ways of life are possible, and people choose nondeferential ways of life, as in a consumer society, there is a failure of morality in making the worse rather than better choice. But in addition there is a failure of comportment that consists in the arrogance of saying that the values chosen for the self outweigh the values to which deference should be paid.

Most spiritual traditions note that arrogance easily spirals out of control and comes to defend itself. Pride is a good thing when its objects include successful comportment. But pride can easily lead to adopting a conception of one's ego and its needs that lead to increasing failure of deference. Failure of deference leads to increasing selfishness in comportment toward the important components of one's life. We are accustomed to understanding selfishness in terms of relations to other persons. The selfish person comports himself or herself toward the other so as to get as much as possible out of the relationship, regardless—that is, without deference—of what the other might derive. Selfish behavior in a relationship with another person habituates itself and shapes the relationship as such.

Failure of deference also leads to a selfish comportment to the institutions in which people exist. Interpersonal relationships are themselves institutions and need care; they are harmed by selfish one-sidedness. Families, neighborhoods, communities, religious groups, educational institutions, social services such as police and fire protection, as well as larger institutions such as the judiciary, the arts, and the political process, all can be failed in deference by the selfish comportment of individuals and subgroups.

Most modern societies have been collectively selfish with regard to the natural environment, and have inculcated this into the sensibilities of most of their citizens. Environmental disasters resulting from this are colossal. Similarly, few people have the deference to consider the roles they are playing, and those that they should play, in the ongoing process of nature. Sometimes the selfishness in this latter respect is little more than thinking that people have no roles to play, and the human race continues its destructive ways.

Failure to defer in the predicament of negotiating change leads to suffering, as the Buddhists have emphasized, although there also are other causes of suffering such as sheer physical pain that do not have to do with change per se. The predicament of negotiating change has dimensions of creative achievement and loss, and of continuity of identity and the achievement of identity itself. When change for the better is possible, directed activity to change things for the better most often risks losing what is achieved in the status quo. A profound suffering comes from the dilemma of how much risk to take in order to achieve something better, particularly when that achievement is uncertain. In some people, this kind of risk becomes debilitating to an extraordinary degree, blocking any kind of abundant life. Deference to the possibility of achieving the better involves putting oneself and prized things, including loved ones, at risk. Although taking risks is always a judgment call, and not all risks are worth it, proper deference toward creative possibilities in life with regard to important issues requires detaching oneself from the concern to protect oneself and opening oneself again to the real possibilities of loss and gain.

Failure of deference in loss is the clinging to things that change with all the kinds of suffering detailed in the extraordinary analyses of Buddhism. Buddhists emphasize learning the lesson that the self itself is in constant change, and so the self is lost in the face of customary attempts to cling to personal identity. The self as ego is a component of the larger harmony of a person, a false component according to Buddhism when speaking of the "higher truth." Hindu traditions sharply differ in analysis of failure to defer to the losses in change, claiming according to one theory or another that there is a self that underlies the things that change but that the deepest self does not change. Attaining some kind of connection with that unchanging self is the ideal. Nevertheless, failure to defer to the significant changes in experience itself results in identification of the self with those things that change, as the Samkhyas would put it. Improper deference to loss in change results in the suffering of identifying oneself with what is, and should not be, lost. Fear of death is perhaps the most grievous suffering.

Failure to defer to the reality of components relative to the whole of human life leads to the pain of living in illusion. Perhaps some people like to live in an illusory state, even a deluded state. Many people do not want to know what is truly real. But reality has a kickback and illusions are rarely sustained for long. Of course, the traditions of South Asia give profound cosmological and phenomenological accounts of illusion, and in this sense some people's illusions are self-supporting even when reality kicks back. But according to the South Asian traditions, people with these profound illusions are desperately unhappy, even when they think they are having fun. Even the less profound senses of illusion within which people live are extremely painful to bear, especially on those occasions in which they are shown to be illusions. The pain, even in less profound senses of illusion, amounts to a felt sense that one is unreal.

Thus, failures in the predicaments occasioned by needing to comport properly to the important components of human life result in many kinds of disintegration. People so often are ungrounded in the appropriation of the goods and ills of the components of their lives, in the deference to the values of those components apart from their lives, in negotiating change through demands for achievement, loss, and continuity of identity, and in sustaining a sense of reality.

II. CENTEREDNESS: DELIVERANCE FROM DISINTEGRATION

The summary result of this discussion is that failures in comportment toward the important components in human life constitute a kind of human alienation from self. By "alienation" here is meant an internal dissonance between the components of life and the harmony they compose together. Estrangement is distinguished from alienation in the next chapter as a dissonance (or something worse) between people and the other things that make up the existential field in which they are located. Alienation, in the sense defined here, is an internal contradiction.

Alienation in the primary sense is a characteristic of the whole of a person's identity—the harmony itself—in reference to the life's components. Derivative senses exist in which the components themselves can be alienated from one another. The ego is not the whole harmony of the person but rather a functional organizing principle among the components; Freud argued that the ego can be alienated from the id and the superego. So, given the plethora of theories of "parts of the soul" among world religions, not to speak of contemporary scientific psychologists, many kinds of intra-component alienations are possible.

The significant alienation that forms an *ultimate* predicament for human life, however, consists in that of the harmony toward its components, in modes of appropriation, deference, negotiating change, and addressing reality. Much of what is said here about alienation within persons toward their components can be said by analogy about alienation within groups, institutions, and other harmonies that are shaped and partially controlled by human beings.

Being grounded is a mode of being radically contingent. When one's comportment toward life's components is alienated, one fails to achieve life in fullness. This is often called spiritual death, not the death of the body but the death of the soul. Or, with alienation from important components of life, the soul cannot achieve its full reality and does not quite come to life. The person's harmony is not quite real.

Religious interventions to cope with the failures of grounded wholeness generally have to do with centering or attaining centeredness. The metaphor of centeredness suggests a relation between the components of life arrayed out from a center that need to be arranged appropriately relative to the integration in the center. The center, of course, is created by the arrangement of the arrayed components, not by any dimensionless point. A person becomes centered by becoming well grounded with respect to this component of life, and that component, and these others. Centeredness is relative to the kinds of components that become well grounded; people can be centered in some respects but not others. The idea of grounded wholeness is addressed through interventions that create centeredness in harmonizing the components of life. In American popular religion, "centeredness" is most often associated with meditation seeking a purity of consciousness, martial exercises such as taijiquan, centering mantras such as a Buddhist chant or the "Jesus Prayer" that bring a feeling of calm and well-being. Such centering interventions are not limited to popular culture. Johann Sebastian Bach's cantata *Gott, wie dein Name, so ist auch dein Ruhm* (BWV 171) focuses in a most sophisticated way on the joys and power of praising, meditating on, and praying in the name of Jesus. These are indeed interventions that are connected also with more profound senses of centeredness.

Some of these more profound senses serve to mark off what is distinctive about the human pursuit of wholeness that is not suggested by general remarks about how persons are harmonies that need to be well grounded in their components. Although the strategy of *Philosophical Theology Two* is to apply the cosmological considerations of ultimate structures to human realities, this strategy can miss the religious force of what is distinctly human. In religious terms, the problem of wholeness is that of "soul." Some people, probably represented in most traditions, think of soul as some kind of homuncular entity that is the essence of a person and that might or might not pass from one body to another, life to life, or Earth to Heaven. That is not the meaning taken here. Here soul, like every other determinate thing, is a harmony, in this case a centered harmony of a person involving the particularities of the person's components. We should be able to say of a person's soul, relative to wholeness, that it has been lost; interventions help to find the soul. Sometimes people behave in a soulless way and sometimes societies lose their soul. A good soul is "beautiful."

Three profound senses of centering help indicate what soul is and why it is beautiful with well-grounded wholeness. Joseph Grange, in his extraordinary book *Soul: A Cosmology*, ends his discussion with a citation of James Joyce's characterization of beauty in *A Portrait of the Artist as a Young Man*.[1] Joyce has Stephen Dedalus say: "Aquinas says: *Ad pulcritudinem tria requiruntur integritas, consonantia, claritas.* I translate it so: *Three things are needed for beauty, wholeness, harmony and radiance.*" Although Joyce adduces wholeness, harmony, and radiance on the subject of beauty in art and artists, Grange rightly sees them also as special traits of soul.

Wholeness of soul, for Joyce and Grange, is what sets the person off from the background as a special person. Any harmony has a pattern integrating its components and in that sense is "whole." But because so many of the components are conditional components interplaying with other things, the boundaries or contours of the person are somewhat arbitrary. The person is in a situation and in some sense is just another part of that situation. A person with soul is so centered in the situation as to have a distinct identity, and to function with a specialness that expresses that distinct identity. The identity likely is in the midst of changing, and soul thus is always growing and adapting, finding new ways of being distinct. A person's soul foregrounds the person against the background, both for that person and for others. Such wholeness is an expression of, and is expressed through, confidence. The person has "faith with" ("confidence") personal wholeness in the midst of the streaming situation. People who are not whole cannot sustain that distinctness and engage with confidence. The remedy for them is to find centeredness that allows the person to be confident with the components as integrated. The center holds the components together so that the person manifests a whole identity relative to the situation and other things in the existential field. Interventions that bring about centeredness thus treat the problems of soul relative to wholeness.

"Harmony" (*consonantia*) in the Joyce/Grange analysis refers to the ways in which the components of life relate so as to enhance one another, to interplay creating new components, to take on new meanings through their interactions. This is analyzed in Chapter 1 of this volume in terms of the ways forms always bear value in hierarchies with simplicity and complexity. A human life "has soul" the more the main components of life serve and feed one another and do so in dynamic ways. Any harmony has some value because of the ways its form integrates its components. The dynamic harmonic interplay of human components, however, allows for a centered play with and through that dynamic harmony. A person with little soul might have a body, a job, a family, a cultural heritage, an historical watch full of important tasks, and a group of friends, but might have them merely compartmentalized. A great-souled person brings each to the enrichment of the others, and changes each in that enrichment. A truly centered person engages life and expresses soul by acting and enjoying with all the components turned on and tuned in. When a person's harmony is not well grounded and whole, centeredness is needed to bring the harmony back into the organic interplay that makes human intentional activity full of soul. The religious interventions to cultivate that kind of centeredness address the predicament of wholeness.

"Radiance" (*claritas*) is the expression of wholeness and harmony defined in the Joyce/Grange way so as to manifest uniqueness and singularity. Grange associates this rightly with Duns Scotus's "thisness" or *haecceity*. In one sense, every actualized thing is a "this," bearing in it the patterns that are also possibly common to other things. In the actions of soul, however, the thisness of the person's actions and being, standing out as a whole and dynamically functioning as a dynamic integration of components, is manifest to those who have eyes to see, including the implicit self-consciousness of the soul itself. Some people are somewhat distinct and somewhat integrated, but dull. People with soul radiate. Every person should radiate, and when the grounded wholeness discussed here is missing or mangled, the person is dull. Centeredness brings things together so that the soul is unique and operates uniquely, again confident in itself. All the religious interventions that make for centeredness serve to bring a person's soul to radiance.

III. DELIVERANCE FROM ALIENATION AND ARROGANCE: HEALING AND HUMILITY

Chapter 2 discusses four domains of grounded relations of persons to their components, with four corresponding senses of disintegration. In the language of that chapter, people should comport themselves toward their components with appropriation, deference, skillful negotiation of change, and realism. The failures of these, respectively, result in alienation, arrogance, suffering, and delusion. The modes of deliverance common in many religions to these senses of the predicament of groundedness and disintegration can be symbolized, respectively, as healing, humility, comfort, and enlightenment. The first two are discussed in this section, the last two in the following.

Healing is a major theme in many if not all religions and has important albeit diffuse roles in sacred canopies. Its metaphoric extension makes it a dimension of many senses of deliverance beyond that addressing the alienation of a person from the person's own components. "Alienation," too, is a theme that extends beyond its use here, which is controlled by the issues of failing to appropriate the value in the components of human life properly. But the philosophical sense of the current point is clear. The person needs to comport himself or herself toward the components so as to bring the components' values into the person's harmony in a proper way, lifting up the positive values and escaping, altering, or enfeebling the negative ones. When the person fails to do so, either neglecting what is positive in the components or embracing too much of the negative, the person becomes alienated from some important parts of himself or herself. To be sure, the parts are still integrated within the person—otherwise the person would not exist with them as components. Nevertheless, they are integrated in ways that set the components at odds with the value that should be embodied in the overall harmony of the person's life. To that extent, there is distortion of integration within the larger integration of the person that is poorer for it.

The root meaning of healing is the modification of parts of the body so that they do their positive job and do not inhibit the whole with their negative traits. A broken bone is to be healed so that it functions correctly within the skeleton. Its fracture is a negation that should be eliminated with splints, new growth, perhaps pins, and so on. The same holds for diseases of specific organs. They are "appropriated" into the human whole when they perform the roles that constitute their positive virtues and do not bring in deficits, such as germs or cancers that badly affect other organs. Ancient religions had much to do with "rebalancing" the parts of the body in relation to the whole, and rebalancing the body in relation to the natural processes with which the body interacts in the natural and social environment. Chinese medicine was oriented to the ancient Chinese theory of yin-yang balance, and it was connected (and still is today) with exercises undertaken for health, longevity, and martial powers.[2] In India the tradition of Ayurvedic medicine is ancient, based on Vedic texts, and elaborated through religious and cultural ways of life. Yoga plays a role in bodily centering somewhat like taiji although its principles are different and it is connected with a whole therapeutic philosophy that goes far beyond "bodily" healing. Modern medicine often has separated itself from religious or spiritual approaches to physical health; but many hospitals are sponsored by religious bodies, chaplains are in sharp demand, and more "traditional" forms of healing are proving their empirical worth.

A slightly expanded meaning of healing deals with the emotional realm where loves and hates, attachments and revulsions, tranquility and aggression all have their proper objects, places, and relations to one another. Loving good and hating evil are fine things, but loving evil and hating good are misappropriations of love and hate; and so with the rest. The long-lasting effects of trauma are being recognized now and theological means of recognizing and coping with this are being developed.[3] We are rediscovering some of the psychophysical causal interactions, such as trauma, that were suppressed under mechanistic models of medical healing. A victim of traumatic injury might be clearly healed in a bodily sense but suffers from unhealed experiences. Healing of individuals under therapeutic regimes now has a broad range of applications funded by third-party insurers!

Greatly expanded meanings of healing include the healing of individuals in their human relationships, in their relations to their careers, in the ways they relate to their families, their heritages, and the particular elements of the cultures in which they participate, and in their relations to their historical and natural places. Of course, these relationships might have many things wrong with them, and often the improvement is to change or eliminate those things radically. Such changes are not what is meant by healing. Healing is the changing of the ways by which those things function within the person so as to allow them to be appropriate in their true value for the persons or societies at issue. Healing of the person is the salvation of the comportment toward the important components of the person's life so that they bring their values (and disvalues) into the person's life appropriately.

Healing is a form of centering in that it arranges or rearranges the parts of the body, mind, emotions, and other parts of life so that they function together in an organic way. Healing makes functionally different things work together so as to create a personal identity, in some dimension or other, that allows for integration, action, contemplation, harmonization with external things. The great religious teachers were often also healers, and used therapeutic metaphors for their activities.[4]

The second dimension of the predicament of grounded wholeness and disintegration is deference and, when it fails, arrogance. The comportment of deference is to understand and respect the values ingredient in the important components of human life on their own terms, explicitly distinguishing those from the values they have within a person's life for the sake of the person's overall harmony. The person might have to eat an animal or a fruit for food but still should respect the integrity of the animal or fruit and mourn the loss of its life, deferring to it in that respect. Arrogance is the assertion of the importance of the person's own harmony to the point where deference or respect for the values of the components compromised together in the person is diminished or impossible. Arrogance is the dismissal of deference for the values of things component to human life. Arrogant comportment is an ultimate ontological mistake of thinking that things exist only for oneself, when in fact things have their own values and hold one another in mutual valuation.

Salvific intervention to cope with arrogance is the learning of humility. By humility is not meant here the taking of a subordinate place in reference to others, although sometimes the term is used that way. Rather, humility here means persons' comportment to the important components of their life—which might include their body, family, heritage, other people, institutions, and the natural environment—that recognizes the components' own needs in distinction from the needs the larger whole of the person might have for the components. The human body has needs for food, shelter, and rest, and the humble person respects those needs even though in certain circumstances those needs have to be subordinated to crises of survival. Human emotions have something of a life of their own, and the humble person recognizes this even though in certain circumstances emotions need to be suppressed in order to accomplish something. Other people play important roles in a person's life, but the humble person recognizes that the others have their own lives and play many other roles elsewhere, even if sometimes the others need to be called in to play their roles for the person.

How is humility learned so as to be salvific? Sometimes it comes from being humiliated, as happens by design in some monastic situations; but often humiliation leads to reinforced arrogance. Sometimes humility is learned through ascetic practices that beat down the ego so that the things that serve the ego can be appreciated on their own; but often ascetic practices mortify the fleshly components of life to pump up the ego's sense of control. Sometimes humility is learned by precept. All the great religions teach humility as a primary human virtue. Most often, however, humility is learned by participating in a humble way of life, following models, engaging in humble practices.

Humility is a kind of deliverance that not only builds on healing in the senses discussed previously but that constitutes a preparation for engaging others. Humility shows itself in the engagement with others. But more fundamentally it is a mode of comportment within a person by which the whole relates to the components according to their own worths in addition to the worth of their contributions to the person.

IV. DELIVERANCE FROM SUFFERING AND DELUSION: COMFORT AND ENLIGHTENMENT

Suffering has a great many forms, as noted in Chapter 2 as well as the introduction. Not all suffering is a function of change and the inadequate negotiation of change, although the South Asian traditions have strong impulses to trace all suffering to change and the way it is addressed. Certainly, alienation from the components of life is painful, and so healing in the sense discussed earlier is a way of addressing that dimension of suffering. Likewise, arrogance is a form of suffering, and the learning of humility is an important response to that kind of suffering. Of course, the causes of suffering should be eliminated as much as possible. Suffering people should be given relief as much as possible. To as great an extent as possible, past suffering should be made amends for, redeemed, and perhaps rewarded with compensation. But even when suffering is short-lived and leads to a greater justifying good, to the extent suffering is real it is a compartment toward components of oneself that is destructive to the whole of the person. The dimension of deliverance that addresses suffering per se is comfort.

Finding comfort in the face of suffering is a great deliverance. Sometimes comfort comes as balm from other people. Sometimes it comes from shared empathy with others or a deity. Sometimes it comes from one's own reserves resolving to get through. Sometimes it comes from understanding suffering and its causes, Spinoza's great vision. From a theological point of view, all these sources of comfort are expressions of the ontological creative act that also gives us the conditions of suffering in the first place. Job's "comforters" brought no comfort at all. Only Job's encounter with God in the whirlwind brought true comfort.

Comfort seems to have at least four dimensions that might occur in instances of comfort, relative to the kind of suffering at hand. First is simple relief from suffering such as (temporary at least) relief from pain, slowing down loss, postponing destruction or disaster, mitigating ill effects, and so forth. A massage, a slug of whiskey, a drink of water in a parched place, a visit when lonely or in prison—all of these bring comfort in the form of relief from immediate suffering. Many kinds of suffering cannot be relieved, however.

The second dimension of comfort is knowing that some good might come of the suffering. Grieving parents of a child who died take some comfort in knowing that medical science might have been advanced through the study of their child's case, or knowing that their child's organs might be used to help someone else. Sometimes suffering accompanies difficult work on a worthwhile project, and the worth of the project gives comfort, perhaps even justifying comfort. Sometimes the suffering comes from sacrifice that a person makes for the sake of someone else, or for some cause such as the defense of the country. That might give some comfort to the suffering of wounded soldiers or to their families who suffer for them. Voluntary suffering for altruistic purposes is well recognized in many species, including the human, and the altruism brings some comfort to those who recognize it. Knowing that some good comes from the suffering is a high ideal. Hoping that some good might come from it is more common. People also take comfort from belief that some good might come from suffering when the belief is false. The search for comfort in situations of grief often leads to powerful strains of wishful thinking, causing people to have hope in charismatic leaders, divine providence, or Heaven when those same people would be skeptical about all three in situations where suffering is absent.

The third dimension of comfort is discovering that someone cares about one's suffering. If someone cares, perhaps they can bring relief to suffering, or bring some good out of it. But even if they cannot, their simple caring can bring some comfort by itself. Why is this? If someone else cares about a person's suffering, the one who cares suffers, too, to some degree. How can this be helpful? Why are two people suffering better than just one? Perhaps the answer is that in someone caring, the person who suffers is recognized as a subject who suffers, as a person in their own right. The suffering itself—the pain, the loss, the emotional travail—can be considered merely as the condition of the person, lamentable as that is. But to be recognized as a person who is bearing through the suffering is to recontextualize the suffering to a degree. It means that the sufferer is not reduced to the suffering itself, even when it feels that way. Some theists believe that human suffering is helped when God suffers, too. Process theology, for instance, in Christianity and Judaism, stresses the healing comfort of knowing that God feels and shares in all human suffering. This seems paradoxical because it is difficult to see why that does not just make things worse—ruining Heaven with human suffering when Heaven is supposed to be beyond suffering. But the point has to do with the divine recognition of human subjectivity in suffering. Process theists stress the otherness of the divine subject recognizing the otherness of the human sufferer and being a companion.

The fourth dimension of comfort is an extension of the third, namely, that being known as a subject activates the centeredness of the person known. To know that one is known by another, one has to recognize one's own self as a subject. Indeed, it is to see oneself as a potentially centered subject—the more centered, the more being known by another is deep and dialectically self-reflective. In many ways, one becomes a centered self by seeing this reflected in another, and responding to that reflection, and to the other as reflector and also a centered self. Centeredness is an achievement for a human being, not a metaphysical given as many of the German idealists believed. Among the ways it is achieved is through being known as a subject. Being known as a subject who is suffering is being known as someone whose centering needs to take in the suffering among the important components of life. To the extent that engaging with others who know one to be suffering as a subject causes one to respond to their knowing as a centered person, the suffering itself is contextualized or organized within one's life as one component among others. Uncentered, suffering can cause chaos in a person's life, unhinging its needed habits and personal organization. But centering the suffering fits it in to the economy of a person's life so that the person gives the suffering only a place among other places. That place might be wholly destructive, as in the case of a fatal disease. But its meaning within the person's centered self takes second place to the meaning of the whole self. When the suffering is grounded as a component of life, it is just part of grounded wholeness, and that is a great comfort.

The force of extreme suffering sometimes is a loss of the ability to tell what is real. Particularly is this true to the extent suffering comes from a failure to negotiate change properly. Both Hinduism and Buddhism have dominant themes of the failure to negotiate change resulting in illusion, or delusion. Enlightenment in some sense or other is the deliverance from delusion.

Of course, enlightenment is far more than this and is a major theme in all religions. In most forms of Buddhism and many forms of Hinduism "enlightenment" is the theme that stands for just about all aspects of salvific intervention, the goal of moral striving and of the many institutions of guru-disciple relations. Enlightenment in the Confucian tradition is closely tied to the cultivation of self involved in learning how to advance morally and politically. Enlightenment is at the center of some forms of Daoism, such as the Shangqing school. In the Abrahamic traditions it is associated with many kinds of mystical, contemplative, and ecstatic practices. The fact that enlightenment means so many different if related things in so many contexts in so many religious traditions makes it a somewhat unhelpful category of salvific intervention without further specification.

Enlightenment in the sense intended in this section has to do with discovering who one really is. The philosophical background for this is discovering one's true or authentic comportment of one's overall identity to the components of life. To be sure, there is vast diversity among religious traditions concerning how this question is to be answered. We have already discussed the differences between the common Hindu theme that the true self is not the changing components but an underlying atman that is identical with changeless Brahman, a theme parsed in many different ways, and the common Buddhist theme that there is no underlying self at all, only the fleeting components. Enlightenment in some Confucian traditions, for instance that of Wang Yangming, stresses discovery of the true nature of Principle or the source of harmony deep within the soul, perhaps prior to any sensation or reaction.[5] Jesus had many parables on the theme of "waking up" to discover that one is not defined by membership in "the world" but rather in "the kingdom of God." One of the most famous is the parable of the ten bridesmaids, five of whom did not bring extra oil for their lamps and so missed the wedding celebration; Jesus concluded, "Keep awake therefore, for you know neither the day nor the hour."[6]

Religious traditions also differ widely on the means presented for enlightenment. Some employ processes that disrupt usual thought patterns, such as Jesus's parables and Zen koans. Others stress transformative special experiences, such as Paul's epiphany on the road to Damascus (recounted in Acts 9) and the sudden enlightenment experiences in some kinds of Buddhism. Yet others understand enlightenment to be the goal of a long process, sometimes with markers identifiable by spiritual advisors. Sometimes enlightenment is seen to have degrees.

Enlightenment, at least in the sense intended here and in most traditions of spiritual development, is not directly about learning something special about the world. It is about learning about one's true self in the sense of seeing how one's components relate to their overall frame within the self. Since these components are often things such as other people, communities, and natural processes that extend far beyond the person, with careers of their own in some instances, enlightenment does involve a new grasp of the world to some extent. But that grasp is focused on how one's self embraces (or does not embrace) those aspects of the world as components with special compartments.

Healing, the finding of humility, taking comfort, and attaining enlightenment are salvific themes that together address human wholeness. Wholeness is not the same as harmony. Every person is a harmony of some sort or other, good or bad. A personal harmony is in a disintegrated state when it is not well grounded with respect to its components. Among the most important forms of disintegration are alienation with respect to how the components of life should be appropriated, arrogance resulting from a failure of deference, suffering that arises from the maladroit negotiation of change, and delusions about what is really real concerning the self. Wholeness is by no means easy to attain, among other reasons because it has so many parts that might not be coordinated with one another. Most religious traditions find means for addressing most or all of the elements of wholeness, however.

CHAPTER SEVEN

Estrangement and Connection

In the reflective view of many people worldwide, the heart of religion is about treating other people well. Religions differ with respect to which people should be treated well, and much variety obtains on that score within even the Axial Age religions that say "everyone" should be treated well. But remarkable unanimity holds on rough rules of thumb about what it means to treat others well, witness the many forms of the Golden Rule.[1] Most religions say that treating others well means, at minimum, treating them justly but also at maximum treating them with some kind of love or compassion. "Others" include more than other people, of course, and perhaps the metaphors of "love" are barely appropriate for mountains and oceans, but some analogous regard is commended.[2] To be sure, we do not treat others all that well and religion aims to deliver us from that failure.

The fundamental predicament of engagement and estrangement derives from the transcendental trait of existential location, that is, the relation of human beings to other things, including other human beings, institutions, and natural systems, in an existential field. As Chapter 3 discusses, these things are genuine others, with their own kind of subjectivity resulting from having their own essential components. An ultimate element of being a person in a world with such "others" is to engage them in ways that respect their own integrity and otherness. Chapter 3 analyzes four dimensions of engagement: awareness, appreciation, courage, and love. Failure to engage well results in estrangement. The four forms of estrangement parallel to the dimensions of engagement are denial, distortion, despair, and hate, respectively.

Deliverance relative to the engagement/estrangement predicament thus has to do with connection, the making of connections that overcome estrangement. Relative to the four forms of estrangement are four themes of deliverance: acceptance overcoming denial, purgation overcoming distortion, faith overcoming despair, and reconciliation overcoming hate to make love possible.

The ultimate predicaments occasioned by the existential field cannot be separated from the predicaments of obligation occasioned by form or the predicaments of grounded wholeness occasioned by comportment to components. Obligations obtain toward other people as well as oneself, toward institutions, and toward nature in all of its scope. Many things are both other in the existential field and in certain respects are components of one's life. As a result one should comport oneself with respect to them with proper appropriation, deference, negotiation of change, and realism at the same time that one should treat them as external to oneself in the existential field with awareness, appreciation, courage, and love. Nevertheless, the dimensions of the predicament of engagement/estrangement should not be reduced to those of wholeness/disintegration precisely because things external to oneself in the existential field cannot be reduced to mere components of oneself. They might be very important components, as friends are components of one another's lives; but they are also other to one another and should be engaged as others as well as comported to as components.

I. ESTRANGEMENTS: DENIAL, DISTORTION, DESPAIR, HATE

Four modes of estrangement follow from the modes of engagement: denial, distortion, despair, and hate. These follow fairly simply from failures of engagement.

Failure to engage things with awareness on the surface is a kind of ignorance. The things are just not taken into account. Nevertheless, the things that should be engaged are real and are in existential causal connection with the people who should engage them. To be unaware of them in some sense is to structure experience so as to screen them out by substituting objectifying representations of them. As mentioned previously, it is possible to see the poor, for instance, merely as the poor, not as persons with their own lives. In this instance, they are reduced to representations, "the poor," in the experience of the people who should engage them. With respect to engagement, this objectification, the reduction of things engaged to their representations in the experience of the engager, amounts to a kind of denial.

To be sure, distinctions should be drawn concerning degrees and causes of unawareness. Objectifications that are built in to experience to prevent awareness are culpable. Lack of a microscope to see tiny things is not culpable in the same sense, although some of the tiny things cause disease and suffering and should be Cloroxed away. The spiritual disciplines involved in becoming aware include enhancing our modes of awareness with education, research, and the invention of signs and technologies that mediate existential connections in ways that can come to human awareness.

Thus a continuum exists ranging from culpable denial of others to a simple failure to have the means to be aware of things. A related continuum has to do with the kinds of value and importance borne by the various things to be engaged. Human experience always involves interpreting things with signs that stand for the objects only in certain respects. We are somewhat unaware of those aspects of things for which we do not have signs. This is unproblematic with regard to many kinds of things that we engage. For instance, we can look on a meadow and see it as a riot of colors, of blooming and buzzing things, without engaging each stalk of grass; a poet, however, can call awareness to a single stalk. The meadow as a whole has a value far greater than most of its parts taken by themselves, but in a certain sense a single stalk is incomparable. Similarly, with people, we necessarily represent them in terms that reduce them in part to roles and sometimes to mass memberships, as in crowds. But the terms by which we do that should not prevent us also from interpreting them in the ways that make up life more from their own perspectives. Serious spiritual failing comes with culpable denial of awareness.

Failure to engage with appreciation, too, might be simply the result of not having the training or the means to appreciate the values of things. Nevertheless, things are given in the existential field to appreciate, and human cultures are measured in part by what they facilitate in the way of appreciation. The challenge for modern cultures is to find ways of appreciating environing nature, for instance, and the human roles within it that have been excluded from modern life.

Because things exist in the existential field to be appreciated, however, failure to appreciate them, if there is any awareness, can only be to appreciate them with distortion. In some circumstances, this might be unimportant, although what seems unimportant in one context might be very important in another. Distortion becomes serious and religiously grievous when it results in things being harmed by distorted human engagement. Perhaps the most perspicuous examples of this are various forms of bigotry in which groups of people identified by some trait are treated in a harmful manner that has no real justification in the trait, as in racial prejudice and bigotry against homosexuals and other sexual minorities.

Failure to engage with courage leads to despair. On the surface, it is only timidity, perhaps fearfulness, with the consequent diminished capacity to engage. Fear feeds on itself, however, and deepens. Sufficient fear breeds hopelessness, hence despair. The despair is existentially crucial because of the double-sidedness of the role of faithful engagement. On the one hand, one withdraws from engaging others. But, on the other hand, those others constitute the matrix for one's own existential location. Not engaging them deeply, one fails to engage oneself. If other things become like ghosts in one's environment, what is the reality of one's own existence? Because of the causal interconnected character of the existential field as constituted by the plurality of things, one's own existential location is a function of the others and, if the others are not engaged as real, to engage oneself as real becomes seriously difficult.

Religious traditions have taken many different stands on what the reality of the self is, if any. Some, such as Buddhism, deny it entirely or almost entirely. Yet the faithless engagement of environing things puts too much pressure on (false) conceptions of the ego to make up for whatever existential reality experience is alleged to have. The Buddhist Anatman doctrine does not say that refusal to engage the self is a good thing, only that one ought to understand the *pratitya-samutpada* construction of the self, and of everything else, to be what it is. When that happens, the contents of the world, properly understood, as well as the meaning structure of the self, are intensely engaged. Buddhist faith takes the form of the courage to accept and morally engage the samsaric structure of reality.

Failure to love, of course, consists in indifference, then hostility, and then hatred. The important things of the world have their own natures and interconnections and deserve to be made objects of awareness, appreciation, and delight, even when their own values are harmful to others. Therefore a failure to love is a failure to affirm one's own place in the existential field; it is a kind of blindness, or rather, a selfishness that looks to the good of one's own existence rather than that deserved by the important things around. Not to delight in things is a kind of ignorance, or stupidity, but when ramified its consequence is to turn the failed lover into a hater. Hatred is a dangerous emotional constitution. To hate Brussels sprouts is one thing, not so dangerous so long as enough other good vegetables are welcomed into the diet. But to hate a person, or a way of life, or a community, or an environment begins to amount to a rejection of existence, because the existential field connects the hated object with the hater. Hate then redounds on the hater: hating others hardly can be kept from hating oneself.

The complication in all this is that there are many bad things that are difficult to love. The bad things should be disliked and changed, as part of moral obligation. A distinction needs to be drawn between something like liking, which should be appropriate to the object according to its relative merits, and loving, which should be appropriate to the object as an existent, and always called for. To dislike corruption in politics and corrupt politicians is morally appropriate. To hate them, however, is to attack their existence and that of the existential field in its multiple connections. Sometimes the word "hate" is used to mean only extreme dislike. But it is useful to segregate it from extreme dislike on the basis of the distinction between disliking the value-identity of the thing engaged and hating its existence and ramifications through the existential field. Disliking the value-identity takes the form of disgust at what the thing is. Hating its existence is the abandonment of gratitude for the thing's existence.

II. CONNECTION

To exist intentionally in the world is to occupy a changing existential location with the other important things in human life that constitute an existential field. The challenge is to engage those things in the modes appropriate to the existential connections, which themselves are constituted by their differing natures with essential and conditional components. Individuals, including oneself, institutions, various elements of the natural environment, and humankind's roles in the larger processes of nature, constitute a rough list of kinds of humanly important things. The modes of engagement for these kinds of things include awareness, appreciation, faith, and love, all in various forms (I, 3, iv). The human predicament is that these modes of engagement are often hard to carry off and harder to perfect with the result that they are failed. Robust engagement requires spiritual virtuosity and even then is rarely perfect. Collectively, the failures to engage can be called modes of estrangement, and deliverance from estrangement is a kind of connection, or reestablishment of connection.

Obligatory and groundedness dimensions of estrangement exist. One ought to engage things robustly in the sense that one ought to treat them as they deserve to be treated. This is an obligation. The things we engage become part of us, among our conditional components, and the engagement is an essential component of our lives. But estrangement is not merely a matter of obligation and groundedness. In the existential field other things are not mere components of a person; they are external, too, and ought to be engaged as external, particularly where that means not objectifying them, not treating them exclusively as components. Engagement means connecting with things as others, with their own essential components. In some contexts it is appropriate to say that engagement treats all engaged things as subjects, or that it fails as engagement when it does not do that. Estrangement is a condition of being false to the connections among different things in the existential field, and ultimately it involves being false to oneself. Denial, distortion, despair, and hatred are perversions of existence as that is constituted by the existential field.

Radical contingency is particularly manifest in the trait of having location in an existential field. One's actual life is contingent upon the existential forces that make it possible, or not, for one to occupy one's existential location. The existential field is the source of most forms of human suffering, particularly if relations to oneself within one's own location are acknowledged as part of the field.

Spiritual life and death are also articulated by the ways in which one is engaged or alienated. To be fully alive in the field of existence is to be well engaged with its important subjects. To be alienated is, to that degree, to be imperfectly existent in the sense of failing to occupy an existential location in a larger field as well as the person should be able to. So the predicament associated with engagement of other things in the existential field can degenerate from specific estrangements to a rejection of existence itself as that is manifest in the fields of things in the world.

This leads to the kind of brokenness that rejects the normativeness of having to engage things in the existential field at all. Of course, one cannot exempt oneself from the existential field. One's own conditional components are functions of other things interacting in defining the existential field. But one can pretend that there is no obligation to attend to others in the existential field in ways that reflect their subjective and objective worth and value-identity relative to oneself. Although most cultures teach that one should be attentive to certain kinds of "others," few teach as part of common sense that one should be attentive to most or all things according to their merit. Theistic religions often say that everything in God's creation is precious in the sight of God and thus should be loved, but without much concrete symbolization of the "everything" with the result that whole nations are exempted from proper regard, and sometimes much of the natural environment. Some religions teach that "all sentient beings" should be treated with compassion and proper regard, but usually fall short on making that concrete for much beyond the mammalian kingdom: only the most serious adepts worry about insects and microbes. The East Asian religions emphasize the harmony of all things, but concretely neglect a great deal in practice. So without much particular fault, most people are oblivious to making proper connection with many things with respect to which they are neglectfully engaged. When this is pointed out, and consciousness of the enormity of the task of properly engaging all things dawns, the temptation is to deny that there is anything normative about doing that. When it becomes clear that one should connect with someone or something that one hates, the temptation is almost impossible to resist. So not only is there the failure properly to engage, there is the fall that consists in denial that proper engagement is normative.

The irony of this is that one is a defining part of the existential field in which one exists. To deny the normativeness of engaging all those things that are other is then also to deny the normativeness of properly engaging oneself. To do this is to reject the normative status of engagement as a proper part of being a person. Immediately this turns back on a rejection of oneself as a legitimate part of an existential field with others. Whereas the first fall is to collapse back into an intentional stance of pure selfishness, at least with regard to those things one does not want to engage, this second fall is to come into existential contradiction with oneself. It is a form of denial of the worth of one's existence as a participant in the existential field, a truly serious form of brokenness.

Together, the fall into denial of the normativeness of engagement and the fall into self-contradiction constitute a rejection of the ontological act of creation that constitutes a world in which people are together with the things that constitute them in part and that transcend them in part, just as the people transcend all the external things that constitute them. The ontological context of mutual relevance is the field of fields within which determinate things can exist, and that are made to exist by the ontologically ultimate act of creation. So the failure of engagement is a rejection of the ontological act of creation itself. The remedy to estrangement is the cultivation of the proper connections so that engagement is possible and its inevitable failure possible to bear without denying their normative status or one's own status in the existential field.

Religions have developed interventions to deliver people from the forms of estrangement: denial, distortion, despair, and hate. These are acceptance, purgation, faith, and reconciliation, all forms of establishing connection. These are discussed as pairs in the following two sections.

III. DELIVERANCE FROM DENIAL AND DISTORTION: ACCEPTANCE AND PURGATION

To engage things in one's existential field it is at least necessary to be aware of them. Awareness of most things is indirect, and always mediated by the signs with which they are interpreted. Thinking of the spatio-temporal field as such, awareness of most things is through what Whitehead called "transmutation," namely, the substitution of an overall quality for a differentiated plurality, as in seeing the sky to be blue rather than to be a host of atmospheric events, or thinking of the Chinese "people" rather than each of the persons in China, or engaging a person in a particular role rather than as a player of many roles and as having a subjective life. Human experience of things in the existential field is generally transmuted to the sensual signs built in to the nervous system and to the symbolic signs within cultural semiotic systems. Yet it is possible to push back against transmutation to engage things more completely, getting to know some individuals beyond superficial roles, meeting particular Chinese individuals and getting to know them, studying some of the details of the atmosphere. Science helps to penetrate behind commonsense transmutations, and theoretical conceptualities help engage inner structures. Friendships allow for ever-deepening engagements of people.

Some lack of awareness is simple ignorance, some is perceived as a problem requiring an effort to overcome it, and some is buttressed with reasons not to be aware that constitute denial (*II, 3*). Because engaging things in the existential field is an ultimate condition of human life, awareness as such is a virtue. Nearly all religious traditions have programs for increasing awareness, at least for the spiritual virtuosi. Some of these projects aim to transmute all the cosmos with concrete embodied feelings of unity, others aim to gain perfect awareness of things just such as they are, others aim to engage things as arising out of the abyss of Non-being through the ontological creative act, and yet others aim to perfect the awareness of love (*I, 16*). Awareness in these advanced spiritual senses is an achieved virtue of a person as existing with others, indeed the whole cosmos, in an existential field. Most people are not very aware in these senses, and many people seek to increase their own awareness.

A global religious phenomenon of the last century has been the growing recognition of the need for environmental awareness. Part of the reason for this recognition has been increasing scientific knowledge of how human behavior interacts with nature causally in deleterious ways, such as in causing global warming. On the face of it, this practical interest in protecting the environment is not necessarily religious. But the new scientific knowledge also reveals more about what the elements in nature are, how they interact to form environments of various kinds, and what their own values are. These natural "others" have their own values of which people need to be aware and appreciate when they engage them. The environments include those local ecologies within which people live in their various communities, and also the larger landscapes and seascapes that have many forms of connection that are not immediate to human interests. The weather patterns of El Nino, for instance, associated with global warming produce coordinated effects in many nonadjacent parts of the world. Global warming in part is a function of the ozone layer, which in turn operates in a causal system with solar radiation. The sun's radiating power is in a causal system with all the bodies in the solar system, which itself is a locus of force on the edge of the Milky Way galaxy that spins in an elaborate, barely imaginable, dance with the other galaxies of the universe. The universe itself might be just one of many.

The night sky has been a civilizing force in human cultures for eons. An irresistible source of awe, it has been the compelling source of human understandings of regularity and order with instances of irregularity and dazzling adventitiousness. In ancient cultures across Eurasia and the Americas the night sky has stimulated mathematical speculation. To think of the heavens as divine has been a natural teacher to people who seek to make sense of things beyond the domains of direct human need. In recent centuries, however, science has allowed human beings to understand the night sky as never before, and opened up new mysteries and perplexities never imagined. As fantastic as some of the ancient speculations were, the theories of contemporary astrophysics expressed in mathematical media are a thousand times more counterintuitive. The religious significance of this is the astonishingly difficult task of becoming aware of what the others are in the world created by the ontological act of creation. The ontological context of mutual relevance contains things of worth that older traditions had not imagined. Some ask the ontological question in terms of just what world God has created, others in terms of what consciousness is capable of discriminating, others in terms of what spontaneously emerges from nothing. The answers now require scientific imagination and understanding, and anything less is impious. The ontological act can only be symbolized and thus engaged through its product, and the night sky has revealed much that had not been guessed at.

The cosmic environment of the night sky (which might be one of many universes) is related to our local galaxy, to our solar system, to our barriers against cosmic radiation, to the changing of our seasons and the patterns of our weather. These in turn affect the ecologies of our local habitations and the ways by which we and our neighbors live. To engage others within the world now includes engaging these rings of nature with their own values and reasons for being with one another. Sometimes the values of these others are for practical purposes indifferent to immediate human needs, simply to be appreciated for themselves, as Xunzi observed long ago. But now we know how human behavior can affect the environment in ever more distant rings of causal patterns.

Human awareness of the breadth and depth of the natural cosmos is increased by some obvious interventions as photographs and expressions of theories. Religions can sing new songs about the existential otherness of nature. But sometimes awareness is blocked because of entrenched religious or cultural attitudes toward nature. Often the human realm is conceived as set off from nature in some opposition, with cultural emphasis on the subordination of nature to human interests as in some versions of the Abrahamic religions, or in deep-seated concerns to tame the tigers and conquer the natural indifference of the environment to human flourishing. In these instances of resistance, awareness depends on creating openness to awareness.

Awareness of others becomes an ultimate human predicament when it is blocked by denial, which constitutes in part a denial that the person is created in an existential field with others who should be engaged. Deliverance with respect to such denial is the attainment of acceptance of whatever is denied. Fundamentally, this means the acceptance of the world for what it is when individuals would rather it be otherwise. Acceptance here does not mean that the individuals have to like the conditions, only that they accept the conditions as being what they are so that they can be aware of them and engage them properly. Very often, proper engagement means changing the things engaged.

Acceptance is closely tied to suffering. The cosmos is chaotic and not often ordered by the scale of human needs: people often deny the chaos by pretending that the cosmos is created for the sake of the human adventure—acceptance means accepting the chaos and thereby engaging it. Nature provides the context for human life but with many destructive elements: people often deny the destructiveness and need to overcome the lies they tell themselves in order to accept it and thus engage it. Human relations should be mutually beneficial, but in reality many people are enemies: conflict is often denied, and should be accepted instead so that it can be engaged realistically. Often people's ego needs cause them to screen out and deny many elements of their situation: acceptance means dropping the ego needs so that they can become aware of the situation as it is.

The religious cultivations of acceptance are multiple and they vary according to the mechanisms of denial that are at work. Deconstruction of the ego is an almost universal goal among religions, although the nature of the ego is construed variously. Many character virtues are important for being able to accept the facts of conflict and become aware of them. Denial of nature's destructiveness often requires criticism and rejection of the stories, usually promulgated by religions that superimpose happy endings on tragic situations. Acceptance of the nonhuman scaling of natural forces usually requires giving up theologies that see all things ordered by some cosmic or divine purpose that has human happiness or virtuous reward as its end.

Beyond the issues of awareness, denial, and acceptance in the engagement/estrangement predicament are the issues of appreciation and distortion. In one sense, appreciation of the value structures of the others to be engaged is merely a deepening of awareness. To be aware of something includes being aware of its values (and disvalues). But appreciation also involves the internalization of the values in the others into the interpretive frames of the person doing the appreciation. This is not to say that the interpreter becomes, agrees to, or embodies the values of the others, only that the interpreter engages the others respecting the others' values. The interpreter achieves signs that orient the interpreter to those others with respect to their values.

As opposed to ignorance or incomplete appreciation, breakdown of appreciation involves holding a distorted interpretive representation of the others that in turn distorts the engagement. Bigotry against "other" groups is perhaps the paradigm, leading to a systematic distortion of appreciation across the existential field that makes the connection. Bigotry itself is a good metaphor, however, for a wide variety of interpretive stances toward others that distort their real and otherwise accessible value because of some factor in the interpreter. The most common form of bigotry arises from the in-group/out-group distinction that is almost universal in pre–Axial Age religions and remains important in a great many social contexts (*III, 2*).

The present global religious situation involves three extremely important cases of bigotry that require purging, that of intolerance of members of other religions, that of the subordination of women, and that of rejection of homosexuals. For a long time, religious identity has been tied closely to the definition of one's in-group and of the others' out-groups. Axial Age religions relativize the in-group/out-group distinction, at least in principle, so that their practitioners should be aware of and appreciate the religious bearings of the others. The analysis in *Philosophical Theology* shows why this is so: all the great religions (and even some of the non-great ones) are forged in response to common problems of ultimacy. While not suggesting in the least that all religions are equally successful in addressing these problems, it should be knowable from any perspective how the other perspectives are attempting to address those problems, which justifies a deep measure of respect. The present global religious situation is that once again, as has happened so often in the past, religious traditions are in conflict, sometimes armed conflict. Therefore, the purging of bigotry against members of other religions is of paradigmatic importance. What is it in religious individuals that causes them to be bigoted against those of other religions? On the surface it might seem to be convictions that one's own religion is the only way to address the ultimate issues with the result that others are held in contempt. To the extent that is true, the purging of bigotry requires little more than a theology lesson in the universality of religious structures. But deeper, such bigotry expresses a feeling of defensiveness about one's own religion that stems from suspicions that the others might be right and one's own position implausible (*II, 13–14*). To purge this kind of feeling requires subtle measures.

The subordination of women is a classic form of bigotry. It attributes to a whole class of people, by virtue of their membership in the class (as women), negative traits such that they should be subordinated. This is complicated by the pressures of additional social roles and sexual attitudes. But those roles and attitudes have been formed by the pressures of bigotry as much as they have shaped the bigotry to seem natural. The women's revolution, which is at different stages in different cultures in the contemporary global religious situation, indicates how complicated the purgation of this bigotry is. As with defensiveness about one's own religion, perhaps men are defensive about their own prerogatives as men (itself a form of reverse bigotry—attributing merit to a class that has little or nothing to do with the traits of the class as such). But then women, too, hold to social bigotry about the proper subordinate roles to which they are held; is this a yet more devious and indirect form of defensiveness?

The homosexual revolution seeking recognition and appropriate rights for homosexual, bisexual, transgender, and other minorities is more recent than the women's revolution, and probably closely connected with it. Even more than bigotry against women in roles traditionally assigned to men, homophobia (and more generally any bigotry against sexual minorities) is embodied in feelings of impurity on the part of many people. Imagination of the sexual activities of such minority people fills bigoted people with disgust, although of course those activities are precisely the attractive kinds of sex to the minority people. On the surface, bigotry against sexual minorities might stem from fear and rejection of people who are different in fundamental ways, such as sexual orientation, from oneself. Deeper, however, such bigotry stems from insecurity about one's own sexual orientation, including in some cases feelings of sexual attraction that are not normatively heterosexual. Purging this kind of bigotry requires significant personal transformation in some cases.

Deliverance from such distortions in appreciation as bigotry requires purging the cause of distortion from the interpreter's structures for engagement. Religions have many symbolic and not-so-symbolic purgative procedures.

Chief among them are literal chemical purgatives and cleansing baths. Breathing exercises are often construed as purgative. Sometimes these are associated with martial disciplines used as spiritual exercises.[3] Psychedelic substances are sometimes used to jolt loose patterns of bigoted thought so that people and places can be seen more nearly for what they are.[4] Music, dancing, whirling, fasting, and other practices are employed to symbolize or perhaps cause the dislocation of distorting structures. Often, forced fraternization with the objects of bigotry, such as members of sexual minorities, is sufficient by itself to set people at ease with themselves and remove the strangeness of the other; models of sexual minorities in public life, common depictions of them in the media, and the discovery that many family members and friends have been closeted members of sexual minorities is accomplishing a significant revolution in some parts of the world. Sometimes travel through cultures and places wrongly thought hostile leads to a relearning of structures of interpretation. When those distorting structures involve the determination of interpretation by caricatures of people and places, the caricatures can be broken by engaging them in ways that deconstruct them. For instance, the example of women in positions of leadership, or of African Americans in positions of high accomplishment, or of homosexual people in ordinary situations of living, breaks stereotypes. Purgation is the right image for dealing with distortion in the sense analyzed here and in Chapter 3, because what is required for deliverance is an elimination of the distorting structure in the interpreter.

Religions employ the rituals and practices of purgation to eliminate what they believe are distortions in appreciation. Their beliefs about this might not be correct. A religious community organized around a strong in-group/out-group distinction might believe that fraternization with the out-group people is a distortion and employ purgative procedures to restore a perception of the out-group as the enemy, whereas an Axial Age religion would believe the opposite. The religious direction of purgations of such distortions needs to be guided by more advanced appreciations of what is valuable in the environment of others, and often this need is what moves the intellectual life of a community from liturgical to theological thinking.

IV. DELIVERANCE FROM DESPAIR AND HATE: FAITH AND RECONCILIATION

The third dimension of the engagement/estrangement predicament Chapter 3 discusses is the need for courage to engage the situation of things in the existential field that are threatening in important ways. So many parts of life seem hopeless when judged with reference to winning, and of course in the end everyone dies and the universe goes out. The hopelessness of life's enterprises need not turn to despair, however. Some people carry on to do their best even knowing that everyone loses in the end, as Lewis depicted in the *Chronicles of Narnia*. But the predicament is that the engagement of the existential field so easily does turn to despair, on top of denial and distortion, when the inexorable, non-human-scaled forces of life move through.

Deliverance from despair is the attainment of faith. In this context, faith is the commitment to engagement despite the hopelessness of winning.[5] Or rather, faith in this sense is the embracing of a way of life that carries on regardless of the outcome, like Arjuna's commitment to do his martial duty without regard for the fruits of his actions.[6] Faith in this sense of course has many cultural forms and dimensions that cut across the affairs of life. One dimension of faith is belief in a way of understanding things that justifies the effort of engagement. Most usually, this is belief in a sacred canopy that defines a kind of higher victory than the one that appears hopeless. Shelly Rambo argues that this kind of victory theology is of limited value in the case of trauma.[7] Sometimes faith is belief in a rewarding afterlife, or better future life, or trans-temporal eternal life.

Sometimes faith is belief in a sacred canopy that sees the turning of the wheel of time as itself a good thing, where hope at winning needs to be coupled with the expectation of change, aging, and losing, giving up on fulfilling the ambitions and projects of the age while giving way to the different ambitions and projects of the next generation. In contrast to forms of Buddhism and Hinduism that see the turning of the wheel of time as the problem to be escaped, Shaivism inculcates the worship of Shiva as both creator and destroyer, sometimes more the latter when Vishnu is associated with creation. Near Christ University in Bangladesh is a local shrine to Shiva for which the ambient legend is about Shiva's behavior after his beloved wife Parvati was killed by the other gods to stop her murderous behavior. Grieving, he carried her body on his back all across India, neglecting his duties as destroyer. Leaves would not fall, last year's crops did not die after harvest, no animals or people died, and the world became too crowded and ground to a halt. So the gods snuck up behind him and surreptitiously cut off her body parts, one after another. Shrines all across the subcontinent mark where those body parts fell. Finally, when nothing was left of her on his back, this was pointed out to Shiva, who then got back to work destroying things according to the cycles of life. The gods and people rejoiced because destruction and death are as much a part of life as birth and growth.[8] Shiva had temporarily lost faith, by reason of his grief, in that which justified his very own divine duty.

A deep dimension of faith is commitment to a way of life that shapes continued engagement in light of certain kinds of hopelessness. These ways of life are most often shaped within religious sacred canopies, and most people who are committed to them are fairly distant from any sophisticated intellectual understanding of them. The symbols of the sacred canopy do not have to be analyzed in much depth to guide people through engagements with hopelessness. If, for instance, a sacred canopy promises a rewarding life in heaven after the shades are drawn on all the projects of this life, including life itself, faith in that without further analysis might be sufficient to provide solid, faithful engagement of life's vicissitudes. Sophisticated theologians might debunk a literal view of a heavenly afterlife with good reason, but the unsophisticated faithful might find that their faith in heaven is a powerful and true indexical symbol to drive their heroic engagement. *Philosophical Theology One* argued that the truth of symbols in interpretive engagement consists in the carrying over from the object of the interpretation, the ultimate meaning of engagement of the existential field, in this instance, into the interpreter in the respects in which the symbols represent the object. The symbols might not be true iconically, as describing or mirroring the reality—there might be no literal heavenly afterlife—but they might be true indexically in the sense that they connect ultimate reality with the engaged interpreter with the result that the interpreter embraces the engagement of the literally hopeless existential field.

Faith in the sense intended here is the putting on of a religious way of life that affirms the engagement of the existential field as an integral part of a person's ultimate human reality. The religious way of life might be something articulated in the traditional world religions. Or it might be a combination of such ways of life. Or it might be a religious way of life that is rather far from any traditional religious sacred canopy, something sui generis with the individual, or the individual's local community, or with the special circumstances.

How does saving faith come about? What intervenes to promote it? Religions organize their teaching of the young so as to present the sacred canopy defining the faithful way of life in increments that can be understood and adopted. They supply real as well as legendary models of faithfulness as a kind of spiritual virtuosity. They articulate the vitality of the engagement in the face of adversity in ways that can be made habitual.

Yet there is a crucial difference between faith as taught and faith as internalized in commitment. Adolescence is a time when parental and cultural religious sensibilities are turned into objects for affirmation. Perhaps in many societies adolescence and its rites of passage mean little more than initiation into the culture's practices and beliefs of faith. The outcome of that initiation is that the adolescent defines himself or herself as the one determined by that faith, and committed to some degree to following through with it. In modern societies with pluralistic cultural patterns, there is likely to be a more complicated adolescent project of examining, affirming, and denying various elements of their native ways of faithful living. Many adolescents plainly reject their parental religious culture. Sometimes that rejection is in favor of an alternative, or an individualized construction out of many alternatives. Sometimes adolescents emerge with no faith whatsoever, which sets them up for new conversions later, or for despair when life's grim realities come home. In late-modern societies that commonly emphasize learning, adolescent commitments to faith are expected to change and grow throughout life. The major point about the acquisition of faith is not its content but the fact that it has to rest on a decision the individual makes to become the person of that faith, to live by it, to define oneself by it, in order to stay engaged in the existential field (II, 14; III, 3, 4).

Needless to say, misdirected faith can be devastatingly evil, a point brought home in a time of religious extremism that defines the content of faith in terms of murderous martyrdom. Any religion that emphasizes faith over the other elements of religion that make for *truthful* life is in a dangerous situation. Theology as inquiry into the truth about ultimate matters is absolutely crucial to balance the practices of faith that can lead to very bad engagements. Nevertheless, engagement of the existential field as such is an ultimate condition of human life. Failure to save engagement is as deep a loss as failure to save the commitment to theological truth (II, 13; III, 13, 14, 16).

When perverted or lost, the dimension of the engagement/estrangement predicament that consists in love turns to hate. Reconciling people with what they hate, the restoration of love, is the goal of interventions addressing the engagement/estrangement predicament in this point. Chapter 3 argues that love has two components, delight and gratitude. Hate thus has two components as well, delight turned to disgust, and gratitude for the other turned to murderous intent or the will to eliminate the other. The former has to do with the value-identity content of the hated things in the existential field. The latter has to do with the existence of those things. Reconciliation involves both components.

Reconciliation with things the love of which has turned to disgust is perhaps the most obvious form of reconciliation, and the most dramatic. If the other is an enemy, or a former friend who has caused pain, reconciliation involves a complicated process of coming to terms with this, cultivation of the powers of mercy, and the genuine granting of forgiveness. Religions contain conflicting views on the process of forgiveness, some requiring admission of guilt and contrition, others not. Sometimes punishment is required as a condition for forgiveness, or the payment of a price of some sort.[9]

Reconciliation with other human beings is a metaphor for reconciliation with much broader elements of the existential field, for instance, with a society containing oppressive conditions or with nature that makes one chronically ill or brings devastating calamities. Something that should be the object of delight in an ultimate sense can be turned into an object of disgust and revulsion. Reconciliation means coming to accept the value-identity of that object at some important level, even when the proper response, having accepted it, is to change it. *Philosophical Theology Three* discusses feelings of purity and impurity at greater length. The point here is that often the disgust reactions associated with taking people who are not in the in-group to be impure and local places not familiar to the in-group to be evil need to be changed for reconciliation to take place. Changing people's minds about hated things is not enough: the heart needs also to be changed. Often the interventions involve close and regular association with the hated person or place, and exercises to develop empathy and the ability to see the world from the other's position. Unfortunately, religions have in fact cultivated hate based on in-group/out-group distinctions more often than not. The Axial Age ideals were laid down on top of tribal values that were deeply internalized and stand in considerable competition with them (III, 2).

Reconciliation with the very existence of a hated object is deeper than reconciliation with its value-identity. Hatred of the existence of the object, perhaps expressed in murderous terms, implies hatred of the existential field itself, including one's place in it. Hatred of the existence of others can easily turn to hatred of oneself as an equal occupant of the existential field. This in turn amounts to a hatred of the ultimate ontological act of creation that creates things in an existential field. Many people have an underlying deep hatred for having been born into their situation, in their family, with their body, in their community and nation, and in their time. Reconciliation thus means reconciliation with one's existential placement relative to the other things in the existential field.

The predicament of love/hate is not a mere temptation to fall from an ideal. Rather, it is based on the fact that, despite the ultimate ontological relation to others that involves love as affirmation, so much of life includes what truly ought to be hated. Evil people, wicked social conditions, and a heartless nature sometimes make hate the only authentic response. Yet hate is a self-destructive way of engaging life. So in some sense true love needs to include legitimate hate within it. Therefore, reconciliation is not a return to naïve delight and gratitude. It means taking delight in things that sometimes are not delightful, but worthy of being treated as such because they are parts of creation. It means being grateful for things that one should still seek to change or eliminate. Precisely because of this enfolding of hate within love, the engagement of others is seriously ambiguous. Only the immature can fail to appreciate the many dialectical layers of emotion, thought, and behavior that are required for genuine engagement.

The result of this is that reconciliation means not only reconciliation with things within the existential field but also reconciliation with the ontological creative act that gives the field and one's location in it in the first place. Reconciliation is a central theme of the Christian tradition, but it usually has referred to reconciling the world to God. The world has turned evil and worthy of divine wrath and hate. But wrath and hate are not worthy of God who creates the world to begin with, as one line of argument goes. So, reconciliation in Jesus Christ, according to many strands of Christianity, means bringing God back to the point of delighting in and being grateful for the world despite its sinfulness. Many versions of how Jesus Christ is supposed to accomplish this in sacrifice, redemption, atonement, and the rest have been given. The point made in this chapter, however, concerns how human beings can be reconciled to the world God creates, to use the Christian term for the ultimate.

Reconciliation is thus a double-edged project. On the one hand, it means being reconciled to the things the ontological act of creation creates in the existential field to which people relate as others. On the other hand, it means being reconciled to the creator of the world as such. Love of God, to use the theistic idiom, is no easy matter, especially since God has created a world filled with suffering that kills us in the end. Perhaps Jesus's famous command to love enemies was intended as a preparatory discipline for loving God who, though lovely in awesome ways, is still an enemy at the ontological level, in fact. The idiom of consciousness expresses the double-edged project of reconciliation equally well: on the one hand, find ways of relating to the arising and ceasing of things that change and, on the other, find ways of relating to their source in the depths of consciousness (whether resting in Brahman or totally empty).

Throughout all these ideals for interventions to heal brokenness—acceptance, purgation, faith, and reconciliation—the unifying project is finding techniques for relevant senses of connection. Connection in turn is for the sake of being able to live with the ultimate ontological predicament of estrangement. Religion aims to cultivate that proper engagement, and many of its practices are aimed at making difficult connections. But religion also has to cope with the fact that some connections might be impossible and estrangement impossible to avoid. This is a deep problem for value-identity, the topic of the following chapter.

CHAPTER EIGHT

Meaninglessness and Happiness

In the reflective view of many people, the function of religion is to articulate and secure happiness in the deepest sense they can imagine. "Happiness" is a good general term for satisfaction with the values of the things that make up a person's life. These include both what the person causes and achieves, the conditions under which the achievements are made, and the value-laden elements of the person's life contributed by other people, institutions, history, and nature. All of these things make up the person's absolute value-identity. Of course, that value-identity has many elements of disvalue—suffering, failure, frustration, and the collapse of meaning of one sort or another. To the extent the person cannot be satisfied with some or all of the person's value-identity, the person is unhappy. Happiness is satisfaction in value-identity regardless of what kind of value it holds.

Chapter 4 analyzes absolute value-identity as having subjective and objective portions. The former are those elements of value-identity that are parts of the person's own life, harmonized among the patterns of the person's essential and conditional components. The latter are those elements of value-identity that are resident in other things, parts of the harmonies of those others. Obviously, many parts of value-identity, as functions of mutually exchanged conditional components, are both subjective and objective. Although value-identity has temporal existential location, its true reality is in the mode of eternity (I, 4, 10). Furthermore, there is no perspective from within the created order from which both objective and subjective portions of a person's value-identity can be registered together directly. They can be registered only from the standpoint of the ontological context of mutual relevance in which things are together as external to one another in their essential components.

The achievement of a value-identity is an ultimate condition for all human beings. Every person has a value-identity, however good or bad, fulsome or minimal. Because of the intentionality of human life, the achievement of a value-identity is something of a task for all people to the extent they have responsibility. Because the possibilities for human life are value-laden, there is an obligatory dimension to one's value and all the moral, social, personal, and natural successes and failures with respect to those obligations become part of one's value-identity. Religions with strong theistic rhetoric often thematized these elements of value-identity as standing under some kind of judgment. Similarly, the task of achieving actual grounded wholeness contributes values with respect to appropriation, deference, negotiating change, and realism. These are involved in the internal actualization of the self and have mainly to do with the subjective portions of value-identity. Religions, especially those inspired by South Asian roots, often thematize these elements under notions of the "true self." The objective portions of value-identity have mainly to do with engaging the things that define one's place in the existential field; the "others" of one's existential situation and the values achieved in perfecting awareness, appreciation, courageous faith, and love are important, as well as the objective values created in the other things. Religions thematized these elements under the rubrics of action and creativity.

The achievement of value-identity takes its main, but not exclusive, content from these predicaments of obligation/guilt/justification, of grounded wholeness/disintegration/centeredness, and of engagement/estrangement/connection. But the achievement of value-identity is an ultimate condition of human life on its own. Within temporal human life, this can be divided for illustrative analysis into achievements of personal goals, of contributions to nature and society, of finding ways of facing suffering, and of relating to ultimacy as such within the context in which one has value-identity. A person's successes and failures within these domains of achievement constitute a changing personal value-identity. These successes and failures also have ultimate significance, however, for they constitute the ultimately singular reality that persons have, whether considered to be only one lifetime or a round of many. The ultimate predicament of the achievement of value-identity concerns the ultimacy of the otherwise proximate identities that people have.

The analysis here discusses the fall from ultimate achievement into ultimate impotence with regard to personal goals, into ultimate isolation with regard to contributions to nature and society, into ultimate apathy with regard to the facing of suffering, and into ultimate non-being with regard to relating to ultimate reality. The present chapter discusses the goals of some of the corresponding forms of salvific deliverances that religion offers in various modes: renunciation to deliver from impotence, dedication to deliver from isolation, joyful submission to deliver from apathy, and total affirmation to deliver from non-being. However paradoxical it might seem at first, happiness requires renunciation, dedication, joyful submission, and total affirmation.

1. DESTRUCTION OF MEANING: IMPOTENCE, ISOLATION, APATHY, NON-BEING

The human predicament of the achievement of absolute value-identity is set by the tension between the objective and subjective aspects of identity. But it is made especially problematic by failures of achievement, which are common if not inevitable and universal. Failures of achievement are not only failures: they constitute something broken in the human condition that needs to be fixed.

Failures to achieve personal goals are common and expected, and are not ultimately important beyond their specific content. Learning to be competent in many segments of life is difficult, and the learning itself is based on failures as well as successes. Moreover, the degree of control people have over their lives is limited. Most human achievements require the cooperation of others that might not be forthcoming, or not competent if offered. Events and natural processes are not scaled to human intentions. Accidents happen. The organization of life within which projects for the achievement of goals take place is fragmented. Most human actions are ambiguous in their meaning and value. Life is too short to accomplish some things. Then again, life can be too long to hold on to what is accomplished. Strangely, Christians deified Jesus despite the fact that he had poor students, a fickle following, was abandoned by friends, was executed for political reasons that had nothing to do with what he stood for, and died even younger than Mozart: his human situation was no more felicitous than the common lot. As the Hebrew Bible's Ecclesiastes pointed out, life's projects are vanity. Nevertheless, a decently engaged, grounded, and moral person tries to achieve as much as possible, winning on some projects, losing on others, knowing that nothing good lasts forever. Such ordinary people rise to the issues on their watch for the time and in the circumstances allotted to one's life, and do so with both successes and failures.

The predicament of achievement in personal and local goals becomes a matter of human brokenness when a person rebels or retreats from the ambiguities of life. With respect to the ultimate character of the existential field, this is estrangement from being in the world. With respect to the ultimate character of value-identity, it is a double denial of one's own identity as having a situation with its demanding goals and of the ontological context that creates human beings with such fragmentation, frustration, and ambiguity. This tempts to bitterness, self-hate, ever worsening incompetence, and hatred of the ultimate reality that creates the situation. The predicament of having to achieve personal goals and failing seriously often leads to the rejection and denial of life and its contents, and one's own value-identity as defined by that. Collectively, these can be symbolized as a kind of ontological impotence: a definition of self as unable to achieve in any ultimately important sense.

Failure in projects of public achievement is as common as failure in projects of achieving personal and local goals. The failure in itself does not constitute human brokenness. Rather, the value-identity of individuals is broken when particular or seemingly universal failures lead them to reject the responsibilities to make public contributions to society, culture, nature, and all the other important meaningful connections through the existential field. This results in withdrawal from the particular publics into which people are created by means of attempts to define one's identity with excuses from the need to make public contributions. Of course, one cannot actually withdraw from public life. Even a recluse lives within a social structure with at least parents, neighbors, and social institutions defining the economic, juridical, and artistic dimensions of the context. The question is not whether the social public can be escaped: it cannot. The question is whether a person contributes what is possible and desirable, or is an unnecessary drain and cost to others. This is even more significant with respect to the natural environment and all the mixtures of social ways and natural processes. A person cannot escape a natural environment, only do it weal or harm. Ontologically, a person is defined in significant measure by the existential connections with other things in the existential field. To fail the obligations in these connections is only human. To deny the connections with their obligations is ontological isolation and self-destruction.

Denial of the ultimacy of having a public life, whether wanted or not, builds a self-contradiction into one's absolute value-identity. It seeks to isolate the individual as if the individual were not mutually defined by all the other things that constitute its social location. On the one hand, every person lives in the public of a larger existential field. On the human level the important elements of this are semiotically meaningful social relations, and causally networked natural connections. Simply to exist is to be in this larger public, and a great many things in human life press this point home constantly. On the other hand, the person who denies the ultimate seriousness of moral obligations, of the demands for integrated groundedness in the components of life, and of the rigors of existential engagement in this public, denies his or her own identity as being in the world in a profound sense. It is a denial, or existential equivocation, of the reality of one's own creation and hence absolute value-identity.

Failure at facing up to suffering leads to a similar result. Not that suffering easily can be made painless, prevented, balmed with compassion, or borne with equanimity! But efforts to face up to suffering achieve, in part, one's absolute value-identity. To turn away from the task of facing up to suffering, however, is to give in to the difficulties of life and partly to define one's value-identity as withdrawal from the realities of human experience. Religions have pointed out how the failure to face up to suffering leads to confusion and turbulence of mind, to selfishness that does not help others when it is possible to do so, to coldness of heart, and to a weak, cringing, whiny value-identity. Failure to face up to suffering in appropriate ways is a denial of the goodness of creation, of which suffering is a part, and thus of one's own goodness whatever that might be. In the most profound sense, it is apathy—denial and loss of feeling. It manifests itself as boredom, acedia.[1] Apathy is an ontological denial of a crucial ultimate condition in a person's absolute value-identity.

Every person has an absolute value-identity, most likely with mixed results regarding obligations, wholeness, and existential engagement. But in addition to these dimensions of absolute value-identity is the issue of how one responds to the predicament of achieving a value-identity as such. The predicament is that human beings need to attend to that identity itself, through all the dimensions of their morality, comportment, and engagement. If they deny the need to attend to that, which they can do through rejecting obligation, groundedness, and engagement as such, then they have not identified themselves as people in ultimate perspective. Part of being human is to identify one's humanity as including a relation of oneself to ultimate reality.

To be sure, a wide range of interpretations of this contradiction within a person's ultimate identity has been given within the many religious traditions. Some interpret the contradiction to result from pride which, when broken by circumstance, reverses to become self-hate, hatred of existence, and hatred of the ultimate grounds of existence. Others interpret the contradiction to result from too much clinging to a false sense of self. Others find the contradiction in a failure to identify the true self. Yet others find the contradiction to be best understood as a failure at individuation within ritualized social roles. Each of these enlightens some element of the ontological contradiction.

Failure to address the question of achievement results in failure to identify with an absolute value-identity, a failure of affirming existence as such.

II. THE AMBIGUITY OF ABSOLUTE VALUE-IDENTITY

One of the most important contributions of Paul Tillich to philosophical theology was to thematize the ambiguities of life.[2] He was not the first to recognize this, of course, but he was the one who brought the theme into the discourse of contemporary theology, and not just Christian theology.

Life is ambiguous on many levels. Moral options, for instance, are ambiguous in that in their complexity they do harms as well as goods; very few options are win-win. Most of the time moral deliberation settles for optimizing the goods and minimizing the harms. Moreover, most moral options are for conjoint actions with a number of different agents acting for different moral reasons, perhaps even reasons that are contradictory to one another. Some intentions are laudable and others are to be condemned or pitied, even when they all result in the same conjoint actions. Even within a given individual, an option chosen and acted upon can be motivated by many different intentions, some of which are at odds with one another; the human heart is far more effective than it is consistent.

Grounded wholeness, too, is ambiguous because, on the one hand, it respects those important components of life for what they are irrespective of what they might be made to become when appropriated in a person's or community's life. On the other hand, integrated groundedness requires appropriating the components so as to lift up what is good in them and exclude what is bad, as when a person appropriates a cultural or family heritage. An even greater ambiguity in grounded wholeness lies in the frequent dilemma of appropriating what is good for the person at hand, in a selfish sense, and what would be good for the heritage itself as carried on into the future. Any given state of grounded wholeness is likely to involve ambiguities in its comportment that reflect these diverse pulls of value.

Existential engagement, in addition to its elements of obligation and comportment, is also ambiguous. Engaging the "subjectivities" of some things often requires distancing from the subjectivities of others. Although engagement should always affirm the realities of the existential field, its causal structures so very often do not allow this to be consistent across the board. Hence people engage themselves ambiguously, affirming their existential connections in some directions while subordinating or even denying them in others. Tillich's existential theology profoundly analyzed the ambiguities of faith itself, the courage to engage and thereby affirm one's existence and that of the others.

The most profound sense of ambiguity, however, is in respect to being-itself, as Tillich called it. He wrote:

> Being, limited by nonbeing, is finitude. Nonbeing appears as the "not yet" of being and as the "no more" of being. It confronts that which is with a definite end (*finis*). This is true of everything except being-itself—which is not a "thing." As the power of being, being-itself cannot have a beginning and an end. Otherwise it would have arisen out of nonbeing. But nonbeing is literally nothing except in relation to being. Being precedes nonbeing in ontological validity, as the word "nonbeing" itself indicates. Being is the beginning without a beginning, the end without an end. It is its own beginning and end, the initial power of everything that is. However, everything which participates in the power of being is "mixed" with nonbeing. It is in process of coming from and going toward nonbeing. It is finite.[3]

Philosophical Theology has developed Tillich's ontology in far greater detail than he did, and he might not like its directions. Being-itself in his thought is largely equivalent to the ontological creative act whose power creates the determinate things or beings. The concept of the ontological creative act is a detailed rendering of his notion of being-itself as the power of being in beings. The ontological creative act is absolutely arbitrary, not coming from any prior potentialities or from any substantial nothingness. As arbitrary, the ontological act is a beginning in the sense of making that which would not be otherwise, but without a beginning; and it is an ending, in the finite determinate things of creation, that is not an ending. Every determinate thing is thus doubly ambiguous with respect to being. With respect to being-itself or the ontological creative act, there exists absolutely no justification for its existence: it simply is what it is. With respect to finite being, each determinate thing is defined in relation to the other things with respect to which it is determinate, and contains internal to itself as conditional components the relative non-being of not being each of those other things. The arbitrariness of existence with respect to being-itself is mirrored in the arbitrariness of each thing being "thrown," to use Heidegger's term, into the existential field defined by the positive and negative mutual definitions of each thing.

With respect then to a person's absolute value-identity, should the arbitrariness of existence itself and of the nature of one's defining limitations with regard to other things be accepted? To affirm them is to add to the situation received from the ontological creative act of one's own will and the consequent effort involved in all the dimensions of human life including its ultimate predicaments. This affirmation is in the face of all the ambiguities of the given situation, including one's own existence and its negations. Not to affirm the radical contingency of the world and oneself is to say No! to one's own ultimate value-identity, a negation built in to that identity itself.

Human reality is peculiar in that it involves as part of itself its own affirmation or negation. Of course, an absolute value-identity for people who negate themselves and their situations is still real. But it lacks that dimension of reality of joining in the ontological creative act, feeling its cosmic power pouring through one's finite efforts, overflowing with gratitude for existence as such, such an important ecstatic fulfillment! Despair at the ambiguities of achievement of absolute value identity leads to double brokenness. On the one hand, it leads to the denial of the normative significance of absolute value identity. On the other hand, it leads to the rejection of one's own existence and the conditions that make it possible. In some "heroes" of despair this might take spectacular form. But in most people, the despair lurks on the underside of otherwise positive intentional existence.

In the appropriately vague senses, deliverance from impotence as defined here is through renunciation, and deliverance from isolation is through dedication. The next section deals with these topics. The fourth section deals with the ways in which the remedy for apathy is submission and the remedy for the flight to non-being is affirmation.

III. DELIVERANCE FROM IMPOTENCE AND ISOLATION: RENUNCIATION AND DEDICATION

Self-identification with ontological impotence, with the inability to do anything ultimately important, is ultimately self-destructive and in nearly all circumstances a mistake. People do achieve at least some of their goals some of the time, even when it seems that everything is tumbling down around them. Nevertheless, it does not help to point this out to people who know that small achievements are not what is at stake. The major salvific theme to be found in religions is that one should renounce the claim to be identified with the accomplishment of the goals and let oneself be identified instead only with the effort. Renunciation is salvific, if it is genuine, because it makes failure with regard to personal goals to be inconsequential and still is consistent with the effort one should make toward them. True renunciation does not mean renouncing the effort, only one's identification with success.

The classic expression of this is Arjuna's dilemma in the Bhagavad Gita in which Krishna tells him that he has no right to the fruit of his actions, fighting in this case, only to the actions themselves. "To action alone hast thou a right and never at all to its fruit; let not the fruits of action be thy motive; neither let there be in thee any attachment to inaction."[4] His actions themselves are all devoted to goals, for instance, winning the battle and justifying his family. But Arjuna's ultimate identity is in the skill and purity with which he acts, not what he accomplishes. Divinity, Krishna as an avatar of Vishnu, is in everything, in all outcomes.

> Earth, water, fire, air, ether, mind, and understanding, and self-sense—this is the eightfold division of My nature. This is My lower nature. Know My other and higher nature which is the soul, by which this world is upheld, O Mighty-armed (Arjuna). Know that all beings have their birth in this. I am the origin of all this world and its dissolution as well. There is nothing whatever that is higher than I, O Winner of wealth (Arjuna). All that is here is strung on me as rows of gems on a string. I am the taste in the waters, O Son of Kunti (Arjuna). I am the light in the moon and the sun. I am the syllable *AUM* in all the Vedas. I am the sound in ether and manhood in men. I am the pure fragrance in earth and brightness in fire. I am the life in all existences and the austerity in ascetics. Know Me, O Partha (Arjuna), to be the eternal seed of all existences. I am the intelligence of the intelligent. I am the splendor of the splendid. I am the strength of the strong, devoid of desire and passion. In beings am I the desire which is not contrary to law, O lord of the Bharatas (Arjuna). And whatever states of being there may be, be they harmonious, passionate, slothful—know thou that they are all from Me alone. I am not in them; they are in Me.[5]

Speaking as the avatar of Vishnu, Krishna points out that attachment to the fruits of action is a misplaced attempt to possess what is all God in the first place.

This is related to certain interpretations of Buddhist themes of nonattachment as found in the Four Noble Truths.

> (1) Now this, O monks, is the noble truth of pain: birth is painful, old age is painful, sickness is painful, death is painful, sorrow, lamentation,

dejection, and despair are painful. Contact with unpleasant things is painful, not getting what one wishes is painful. In short, the five *khandas* of grasping are painful.

(2) Now this, O monks, is the noble truth of the cause of pain: that craving which leads to rebirth, combined with pleasure and lust, finding pleasure here and there, namely, the craving for passion, the craving for existence, and craving for non-existence.

(3) Now this, O monks, is the noble truth of the cessation of pain: the cessation without a remainder of that craving, abandonment, forsaking, release, non-attachment.

(4) Now this, O monks, is the noble truth of the way that leads to the cessation of pain: this is the noble Eightfold Path, namely, right views, right intention, right speech, right action, right livelihood, right effort, right mindfulness, right concentration. . . .[6]

These verses have been interpreted in countless ways in Buddhist traditions, but all have to do with intervening in the life of pain with renunciation of attachment.

Although many strains of Buddhism seem to emphasize a transformation of mental behavior as the salvific road to nonattachment, hence liberation from suffering, behind most of these is the theme of nonattachment to the ego interests of actions. Actions, not merely "mental dharmas," simply are what they are if the ego has renounced interests in them beyond the actions themselves. Buddhist martial arts such as gungfu are extraordinarily active, practiced, and focused, and yet are thought to be nonattached.

Renunciation is also a powerful theme in some Christian interpretations of Jesus. Jesus had aimed his mission at a purification of Israel, but it had not worked. He seemed to know that he was doomed and prayed in the Garden of Gethsemane that "this cup" would pass from him, but nevertheless that God's will be done (according to the memory of him in the early Church that produced the Gospels). That is, he renounced any hope for success, or even escape, and commended himself to God. This continued through the interrogation after his arrest and through his execution. Many Christian interpreters have argued that Jesus did this out of commitment (attachment) to a much larger goal, the deliverance of the world, or at least of some people within it. Although Jesus surely did work as a teacher of salvation, the theology interpreting his crucifixion and resurrection as salvific in that large sense came after his time. The theme of renunciation should not be forgotten.

Renunciation as a spiritual path has many forms in religions. Some come through asceticism and even mortification of the flesh, although the Buddha counseled against this. Others come through actions such as giving away one's goods, as when Jesus asked the Rich Young Ruler to renounce his wealth and follow him. Renunciation is an important dimension of monastic vows of many religious traditions.

Renunciation is not a major theme as such in Confucianism for which dedication to projects and the management of household and community is a paramount virtue. Nevertheless when things go wrong, especially in political affairs, the Confucian sage is expected to renounce his office and ambitions, perhaps to go on retreat.

The predicament of achievement/destruction that comes in respect of contributing to nature and society is that failures can lead to isolation. Contributions to nature and society are public, that is, they connect across the existential field from the agents to others, individual, social, and natural. Like the achievement of personal goals, there is nothing ultimate about most if not all public contributions. What is ultimate in the matter is the having of contributions to make as such, for this is part of what defines a person in the existential matrix of natural and social life. One's existential location provides a context in which public contributions are relevant, indeed are obligatory. Each person's situation is somewhat different, and perhaps there are no ultimately important public contributions to make. What matters in this instance is not the content of the contributions but the affirmation of the contributions as an ultimately important constituent of being a creature in the created existential field. Failure at this or that public contribution might isolate a person within an existential matrix in which he or she is expected to contribute. But that isolation is only proximate, relative to the contribution at hand.

Ultimately important isolation is not just failure at this or that contribution but the self-destructive move to deny the ontological importance of contributing to the existential public. It is self-imposed isolation, although it might be reinforced by people in the social public retaliating against failure and withdrawal.

The deliverance from this kind of isolation is dedication to the public contributions that need to be made in society and to nature more broadly conceived. Dedication is the reaffirmation of connection and commitment of one's energy and life to serving the existential connection. Dedication needs to be understood in parallel with renunciation. Renunciation separates the ego from the success of attempts at achievement, in this case the making of public contributions. Dedication is the commitment to the effort to continue at those attempts having renounced the right to their fruits. Dedication is commitment without regard for hope of success, like Jesus following the way to the cross despite it all. Dedication without renunciation is well attested in religions, but is open to a sudden turn to self-destruction in the face of insurmountable opposition or failure. Renunciation without dedication is also well attested in religion, in the many examples of hermetic withdrawal, for instance, but is open to a sudden turn to passionlessness, acedia. Many religious traditions treat renunciation and dedication in tandem, though they associate the first mostly with personal goals and the latter with public ones.

The attainment of dedication as a salvific project is the flip side of renunciation. Arjuna could not just renounce the fruits of his action, he had to lead his comrades in a great battle. The Buddhist martial artists could not merely become nonattached to winning, they had to get out and perform the exercise. Jesus could not simply give in, but had to follow through to the end.

How is the salvific form of dedication attained? Religions indeed parallel it to renunciation. The martial stories from the Bhagavad Gita and Buddhist history couple renunciation of the fruits of action with committed dedication to the action. But how does a person get there? In Arjuna's case, it was through a single conversation that was in part a philosophy lecture and in part pastoral counseling. For the Buddhists it sometimes has meant a sudden enlightenment, the result of which is the obviousness of renunciation and dedication. But more often it has to do with stages of spiritual life where vows of renunciation/dedication are taken with more and more seriousness. This is true of monasticisms in most of the traditions that practice that. Monastic vows are simultaneously renunciations and dedications.

IV. DELIVERANCE FROM APATHY AND NON-BEING: SUBMISSION AND AFFIRMATION

The human predicament of facing suffering is dealt with by at least four strategies common in religious traditions: changing the way we experience, removing the physical and other causes of suffering as much as possible, finding and giving compassion, and just plain bearing up under intractable suffering (II, 4). For the most part these strategies have at best limited success, and people commonly retreat in the face of suffering. This retreat leads to confusion and turbulence of mind, selfishness, coldness of heart, and a whiny value-identity. The result is a loss of the ability, or the will, to have feelings that might suffer, a loss of humanity. This is apathy in the extreme, acedia, boredom at reality.

Deliverance from ontological apathy in the face of suffering involves submission to the conditions of suffering and the constitution of the absolute value-identity of the self as one who submits. Submission in this sense does not mean retreat from any or all attempts to face suffering, to remove its causes, to moderate its pain, to help others or seek help in compassion, or just plainly to bear up with what cannot be avoided. All of these efforts to face suffering are good so far as they go, and, in some instances, obligatory. Submission to the conditions of suffering is salvific in the face of the ontological retreat from the life that requires that suffering be faced. Michael Raposa argues that the retreat from suffering in boredom itself makes possible a new advance in spiritual life, treated here as submission but which Raposa characterizes as peace.[7] Although submission does not lead one to like suffering one whit more, it does lead to a peculiar kind of ontological joy at being in a world that includes suffering and the predicaments of facing it.

Here is an instance in which the depths of human predicament can open into ecstatic fulfillment.

Submission is a sublimely treacherous form of deliverance, however, because it so easily slides into subservience. This is particularly true in the monotheistic traditions where submission to the created conditions of existence takes the form of submission to the God who creates them. Submission is the naming form of deliverance in Islam, and, surely, many contexts exist in which this means simply bowing down to Allah in a subservient way. The same is true in Christianity, Judaism, and some theistic forms of Hinduism. Subservience is the opposite of submission in this context, however. Subservience is the act of handing over one's responsibility to the person or deity to whom one is subservient. As such, it is an escape from adult responsibility to a kind of infantile dependence on the other for moral orders and guidance, often with the implicit (or explicit) codicil that, if one does what the other says, and things go wrong, the responsibility belongs to the other. Religious traditions that stress obedience to the will of a God, or to the dictates of scripture or some other authority, run the risk of leading people to adopt the posture of children. This risk also attends images, common in Judaism and Christianity, of people as children of God, or as sheep of His pasture. Of course, many contexts exist in which those images are appropriate. But they are wholly inappropriate if they foster the abandonment of responsibility in favor of some kind of subservience.

The very point of submission in the context of recovering from the spiritual deadness so often caused by inability to face suffering is to accept the life one is given and take responsibility for dealing with it as well as one can. The depth of the predicament of facing suffering/apathy is that it has to do with achieving an absolute value-identity as one who is created in a world that contains inevitable suffering and death. The problem in the predicament is not that some suffering cannot be overcome. The problem is that one is tempted to retreat from the ultimate existential task of facing suffering to a position that denies feeling vulnerable to suffering. The force of submission as a salvific path is that it restores the vulnerability to feel suffering as an element in one's absolute value-identity. To submit in this context is to submit to the facts that one's absolute value-identity includes being created in a world of suffering and that facing this suffering is an ultimate part of one's value-identity.

The practical consequence of submission is not collapse, quiescence, or subservience to someone else who will face suffering in one's stead. Rather it is to engage the world in ways that face suffering with all the vigor at one's disposal, removing the psychologically pathological ways of construing experience that multiply suffering, removing the external causes of suffering as much as possible, providing compassionate comfort and seeking it out, and just bearing up when suffering simply has to be borne.

Submission then means taking on the tragic dimensions of life. Tragedy itself has many dimensions, of course. There are tragedies of nonachievement among those with great potential; tragedies of malachievement among those who do grievous harm; tragedies caused by natural catastrophes, disease processes, and aging among those not finished with their intended life course; and tragedies afflicting communities and nations. A person who submits to the existential reality of having to face suffering accepts the fact that existence itself has tragic dimensions and still lives life to the fullest, renouncing certain kinds of claims on success, and dedicated to engaging the issues attending that person's watch.

How do religious traditions convey the deliverance of submission? Usually it is by emulation of an example. The hero who would make reality conform to her or his desires, discovers that it cannot be made to do so and then submits, is a model for emulation. Variations on this theme include the Daoist sage, the Confucian scholar-official, Gautama Buddha, Arjuna, Moses, Jesus, and Muhammad.

As submission is the acceptance of the tragic dimensions of life, affirmation is the acceptance of the comic dimensions. Comedy, at least in the "ultimate" sense used here, is the gratuitous, arbitrary, undeserved, surprise of existence itself. Of course, comedy has many less-than-ultimate meanings having to do with a story turning out to have a happy ending. This "happy ending" meaning carries over into the ultimate domain when existence, including persons' own lives, is given a narrative frame. Those religious traditions that provide an ultimately narrative frame for theology thus are committed to an end-of-story version of Heaven. The limits of the narrative framing are discussed elsewhere (*I, 8; II, 13*). In the ultimate domain, the primary meaning of comedy is the happy surprise at the gratuitous, arbitrary, and undeserved fact of creation itself. This surprise is grasped in a kind of total affirmation.

The affirmation in the surprise of existence itself is extremely complicated and builds upon, while including, the downsides of the predicaments discussed so far: damnation, betrayal, existential refusal, blood guilt, alienation, arrogance, suffering, delusion, denial, distortion, despair, hate, impotence, isolation, and apathy. Ultimate affirmation needs to be able to include these, and the means of including them involve, at least to some degree, their respective deliverances: redemption, restoration, sanctification, purification, healing, humility, comfort, enlightenment, acceptance, purgation, faith, reconciliation, renunciation, dedication, and submission. The affirmation of existence or the ontological creation necessarily embraces all the other predicaments and their deliverances, to some degree or another.

Of course, there are degrees of ultimate affirmation. The degrees are contingent upon the degrees of deliverance in the other predicaments, which also vary. Moreover, life is an on-again, off-again affair in many crucial respects, with spiritual progress in one dimension being offset by regress in others, good on some days, bad on others. So it is with total affirmation.

The affirmation of ultimate identity is not total in the sense that it is complete and forever locked in, although some traditions have argued that it can be so in some instances, those who admit to "totally realized" individuals. The affirmation is "total," however, in the sense that, according to some symbol or other, the totality of the creation is affirmed. The issue at stake is the predicament of having an absolute value-identity that includes a relation to ultimate reality itself, namely, the ontological act of creation and the world created. That relation is problematic for all the reasons discussed, and it constitutes a predicament when a person chooses non-being, that is, refuses an identity in relation to ultimate reality. Existence is inherently ambiguous. If response to ambiguity is rejection of the gratuitous, arbitrary, undeserved surprise of such existence, then one wills, or succumbs to, non-being, to use Tillich's language.[8] Deliverance from this willing of non-being is an affirmation of oneself within the totality of the ontological creation.

How is the totality of creation symbolized? The many religious cultures of the world have produced an extraordinarily diverse set of symbols, as is discussed throughout these volumes. Each has its own way of articulating a relation between a person's value-identity and what is symbolized as ultimate reality. According to the discussion of this volume, there should be four basic sets of symbols of ultimate reality and of the relation of individuals to them: for obligation, wholeness, engagement, and value-identity. All four further presuppose that the ultimate reality, metaphysically considered, is the ontological act of creation and that what is created are harmonies, each with form, components, existential location, and value-identity, that together constitute the existential field.

The first set of symbols for the whole of ultimate reality includes those representations of the world within which people lie under obligation, deriving from the fact that all people face possibilities of different value. The physical cosmology reflects the science or traditions of the day, but what is important is that human beings are conceived as being under obligation within that cosmology. Given the predicaments of fulfilling obligation, to be in ultimate relation to ultimate reality in this sense is to be "justified" (*II, 5*). The juridical tone of this kind of relation reflects the symbols of being under judgment, punished, forgiven, rewarded, and so forth.

The second set of symbols for ultimate reality includes those having to do with groundedness within the created world as an ultimate definition of a person. The physical cosmology reflected in this might be a naturalism like that of some Native American religions, or a modern biological sensibility like that reflected in Wesley J. Wildman's *Science and Religious Anthropology*. But what is ultimately important is that the symbols show how one's ultimate identity is whole. The wholeness is what can be obtained within the created order such as it is, and as it is symbolized.

The third set of symbols has to do with the ultimate reality of the created order as an existential field of things, including people, institutions, and nature in a larger sense, that need to be engaged. The symbols of ultimate reality have to do with the ways of symbolizing the whole cosmos and its contingency, which are many. What is important for one's absolute value-identity in this respect is symbolizing oneself as engaged. Religious traditions have pushes and counterpushes in this respect. Given the difficulties that must be embraced within this mode of affirmation, the degree to which one can affirm oneself in ultimate context depends on being able to have a somewhat pointed and stable symbol of one's own identity.

The fourth set of symbols has to do with the very project of having an absolute value-identity in relation to ultimate reality. One of the most prominent components of contemporary global culture is a suspicion that nothing is ultimate. All projects are thought to be just human projects, with nothing real to match the projections. Concern for ultimacy is sometimes taken to be an escape from concern for something proximate about which something should be done immediately. Concern for ultimacy within religious communities is often construed as concern to defend the cultural community as such, which often can mean serious bigotry. Nevertheless, the fact that there are proximate origins of symbols of the ultimate does not prove, or even suggest, there is nothing ultimate to which they refer in an effort to interpret. Given the predicament of absolute value-identity, the relation that an individual has to the ontological creative act is itself an ontologically significant element of value-identity.

In fact, this relation sets the context of ultimacy for the meaning of human life itself. All the predicaments discussed so far have focused ultimacy on something within the transcendental cosmological connections among form, components, existential location, and value-identity. The present consideration adds a focus on value-identity but shifts the whole concern from the created order to the gratuitous, arbitrary, undeserved, and surprising ontological act of creation. So deliverance here much more literally means an affirmation of being over non-being.

How does one achieve this total affirmation of the ontological creative act and all that depends therefrom? Perhaps the most efficient way, which crawls its slow motion across many if not all traditions, is that, when faced with something very important and personally defining, and then losing it, one can either rant at the loss, or fill the time and place to enjoy what was lost with gratitude. Parents who have lost children understand this best.

Absolute value-identity has both subjective and objective domains. The forms of deliverance having to do with justification and wholeness seem more to do with the subjective side, that part of value-identity contained within the person's own harmony. By contrast, the forms of deliverance having to do with connection and happiness seem more to do with the objective, the values that a person contributes to the value-identities of other things and persons. But all the predicaments and all their respective forms of deliverance derive from the transcendental traits of harmony that in turn depend on the mutual determination of harmonies with one another. So the cumulative value-identity of a person, expressed in any of the predicaments, is expressed only as a function of the ontological context of mutual relevance in which harmonies are together with their separate essential components so as to determine one another. No person possesses an absolute value-identity exhaustively within the person's own harmony. Part of that absolute value-identity consists in the ways the person's determinations of other things are taken up within the subjective harmony of those other things. No individual has an absolute value-identity by himself or herself. Every absolute value-identity exists only in the eternal life of the ontological creative act within which separate, mutually determining harmonies exist. The points made here about affirmation of ontological identity cannot be explicated fully without the discussions of individuals in community that come in *Philosophical Theology Three*.

Nevertheless, it is apparent now how happiness is fostered by renunciation, dedication, submission, and affirmation. Renunciation of the need for success and identification only with one's personal actions allows a person to live with impotence, and even with failure to do one's best. Dedication, however, is a commitment to do one's best and is part of the form of grounded wholeness; dedication overcomes the ill effects of being isolated by others, and perhaps can surmount the isolation itself. Joyful submission embraces suffering, letting it be what it is despite successful and unsuccessful attempts to relieve it; submission embraces the passage of time, and the loss of things, even the loss of one's life. Affirmation of the creation within which one comes to and leaves life internalizes into a person's value-identity all the value in the cosmos that might make a difference to that life. Of course, the values of many things are symbolized and made relevant only from a great distance, as it were: the cosmos can be grasped for affirmation (or rejection) only by means of the symbols available. Similarly, happiness is shaped by the symbols that give it specific content.

PART II

Summary Implications

The chapters of Part II provide philosophical constructs for forms of salvific intervention or deliverance that address the predicaments deriving from the ultimate boundary conditions for human life studied in Part I. Like the philosophical constructs for the predicaments, those for deliverance come from the transcendental traits of harmonies, which in turn are the determinate things created by the ontological creative act. The constructs, read through the argument of *Philosophical Theology One*, are metaphysical depictions of reality, proposed collectively as an hypothesis for understanding ultimate reality and its bearing on human life. In the discussions of Parts I and II, the philosophical constructs have been scaled to human life through comprehensible and accessible, although informal, analogies.

The arguments for the philosophical hypothesis about the metaphysical structure of reality stand on their own. But in the context of human predicaments and deliverance, the constructs within that hypothesis serve as an architectonic scaffold on which to arrange the symbolic engagements of religious traditions and can be assessed for their helpfulness in this regard. Within the argument here, a certain priority is given to the philosophical hypothesis and its arguments, for the overall claims are that religion is the human response to ultimacy and all its bearings. Religions are various historically conditioned ways by which that response is developed. The points about the predicaments and their respective deliverances have been occasions for citing ways by which some of the major religious traditions have symbolized their responses to ultimacy. The philosophical theology here is not an inductive argument from a phenomenology of religion, as attempted by Mircea Eliade. But it is given greater plausibility to the degree that it highlights how the different religious traditions address ultimate issues of the human predicament and how to fix it. The very complexity of the philosophical construct makes it possible to show how a religious tradition has a few symbols that serve widely different purposes in different contexts relative to the array of issues in the predicaments.

Whereas a phenomenology of religion studies the symbols themselves, this philosophical theology studies the engagements of ultimate reality and ultimate dimensions of experience by means of the symbols. The interpretive structure of the engagement is the religious reality, not the symbols themselves. Therefore, if every large-scale religious tradition needs to address the predicaments of obligation/guilt, grounded wholeness/disintegration, engagement/estrangement, and achievement/destruction, then the core texts and motifs of symbols in its sacred canopy need to be used to address all those, sometimes the same symbols with very different uses. The interpretive developments of religious traditions through time, leading to diverse and sometimes competing strains within the traditions, illustrate how the symbols can be used in very different kinds of engagements. Only recently has careful study in the history of religion begun to recognize the variety of communities of engagement and practice within traditions that previously had been thought to be more unified. Or rather, scholars sought to find the unifying threads, when in fact the diversity lay in different kinds of responses to engagements with different aspects of ultimate reality. Here and elsewhere throughout *Philosophical Theology* the citation of history of religion has employed three related forms: the core text and motifs, the interpretive traditions of those core texts and motifs, including the mixing of them among traditions, and the current scholarly understanding of the diversity involved.

For the sake of convenience, it is helpful to update and simplify the chart of predicaments given in the summary implications of Part I with their respective themes of deliverance:

Predicaments	Deliverances
Obligation/Guilt	**Justification**
Moral/Damnation	Redemption
Social/Betrayal	Restoration
Personal/Existential Refusal	Sagacity
Natural/Blood Guilt	Purification
Grounded Wholeness/Disintegration	**Centeredness**
Appropriation/Alienation	Healing
Deference/Arrogance	Humility
Negotiating Change/Suffering	Comfort
Realism/Delusion	Enlightenment
Engagement/Estrangement	**Connection**
Awareness/Denial	Acceptance
Appreciation/Distortion	Purgation
Courage/Despair	Faith
Love/Hate	Reconciliation

Achievement/Destruction   Happiness
    Personal Goals/Impotence   Renunciation
    Public Contributions/Isolation   Dedication
    Facing Suffering/Apathy   Submission
    Relating to Ultimacy/Non-being   Affirmation

The predicaments and deliverances discussed here lie within the sacred canopies as they are symbol systems that allow for the engagement of ultimacy. This part has attempted to lay out some of the principal ways in which the existential predicaments of reality are articulated by sacred canopies and how those sacred canopies produce a series of remedies for how to fix them. But it has not addressed the profoundly important issue of how people, individually or in groups, actually engage those remedies. Deliverances of any of the sorts discussed here so far are not merely articulated by religions: they need also be taken up, which is the topic of Part IV after the discussion of ecstatic fulfillments in Part III.

Part III

Ecstatic Fulfillments

Part III

Preliminary Remarks

Ecstatic fulfillment is an ultimately profound way of achieving absolute value-identity. The existential reality of religion identifies people in part by how it orients them to the predicaments of life occasioned by the ultimate boundary conditions. But in larger part, and for most people in their engagement of religion, its existential reality lies in how it mediates ecstatic fulfillments. In ecstatic fulfillments, the ultimates are engaged in special ways to establish a person's value-identity: that identity comes to include directly the meaningfulness of the ultimates insofar as they are engaged relative to the ontological reality of the creative act. In a cosmological sense, a person's absolute value-identity consists in the subjective and objective elements of identity and value discussed in Chapters 4 and 8. In an ontological sense, a person can also have an absolute value-identity through ecstatic fulfillments that make the person's meaning include an integral appropriation of the ontological ultimate reality and the cosmological ultimates insofar as they are part of that ontological act. Nishitani has thematized ecstatic human nature in relation to the nothingness that lies behind or in the absence of the ontological act, which he calls the "nihility" of human life as created "ex nihilo."[1] In profound senses, ecstatic fulfillments give a transcendent meaning to life, transcendent of the meaning that comes from righteousness, wholeness, engagements, and ordinarily achieved value-identity.[2]

Although it is not true for all people who are deeply involved in their religion, for many the principal motivation is the experience of being in love with the gods or God, the joy of feeling one with the Dao, the bliss of cosmic acceptance, the transport of group identification in worship or music. For many people, religion provides the venue and the symbolic forms by which they rapture at the marvel of sheer existence, perhaps in singular, blinding transcendent experiences, more likely in barely noticed glimpses as from the corner of an eye in the midst of quotidian affairs. For some, religion frames the sudden realizations of what truly matters and what does not in the struggles to deal with life, realizations that put what matters in ultimate perspective. For some, religion teaches the still point where the self is at home, perhaps as a sudden enlightenment, perhaps as a habit of realized existence. For some, religion shapes the embrace in which one experiences loving and being loved, walking in the garden when the dew is still on the roses. For some, religion provides the venues and symbolic forms for the transcendent affirmation that, when all goods and all evils have flourished and passed, when all of life passes without overcoming ambiguity, when all loves bring joy and then leave, still all is good. These are kinds of ecstatic fulfillments and they fly in the face of ultimate predicaments unresolved.

Of course, there are heroes of ecstatic fulfillment. But the ordinary people in all the world's religious traditions also engage the ultimates in these ways, with modest intensity perhaps, feeling through the symbols of bad music, cheap art and kitsch, occasioning these ecstatic fulfillments in ritualized celebrations of the seasons and life transitions of the people around them. For a great many people, it is these positive ecstatic fulfillments that give religion its importance and not so much its promise of deliverance from life's predicaments. Most of us have had moments of such transcendent serenity and have met a few people who are strangely serene as a way of being in a world that seems far from what might prompt serenity. For many people, religion as a venue for ecstatic fulfillment, ritualized and enculturated, is far more important than religion as a bearer of deliverance.

Religion thus provides the human condition not only relief from suffering and repair of brokenness. It also provides a positive value or fulfillment that differs from and in its way transcends the fulfillments available in family and communal life, in politics, art, personal excellence, and other forms of high culture. Because individuals and their communities face ultimate predicaments in the immediacy of their lives, theology has a tendency to focus on the negative and its resolution. Insofar as psychology or popular spirituality is a secular scientific form of religion, it, too, has focused on the pathological and interpreted religion as therapy. D. J. Moores, in the introduction to her *Wild Poets of Ecstasy: An Anthology of Ecstatic Verse*, likens the recovery of the importance of the positive in religion to the recent development of positive psychology. Having reflected at length on the ultimate predicaments of individuals, what can be said about their ultimate fulfillments?

Ultimate ecstatic fulfillments are not coextensive with intense religious experiences as commonly understood. The common understanding of religious experiences usually identifies them with their phenomenological content, for instance, supernatural appearances (as in William James's *The Varieties of Religious Experiences*) or a certain kind of intensity (as in Wesley J. Wildman's *Religious and Spiritual Experiences*). But the phenomenological content is a function of the semiotic system involved in interpretive activity, and the references among its items are extensional, not necessarily in intention of a real religious object

(*I, 3, iii*). The signs involved in religious experience also have a material quality, such as the feeling that comes from spinning, or from drunkenness, or peyote, or starvation, or protracted singing, or hypnotic preaching. In all these instances the sign with its material quality can be caused by a variety of factors having nothing to do with religion, but it is not part of religious experience unless it is also employed in an intentional interpretation of something ultimate. The phenomenological content and the material feeling of the signs are not necessarily religious; to be religious is for them to be employed interpretively in some real engagement of ultimacy, which cannot be determined by studying the symbolic content or the feelings alone. The good news is that because of religiously relevant symbolic content and powerful feelings with certain kinds of material qualities, there are aspects of ultimacy that can be engaged. The bad news is that the mere occurrence of these signs commonly labeled religious does not mean that one is having a religious experience. There has to be a real engagement, the validity of which is determined by examining the difference the experience makes in the life of the engaging person, as it is in other cases of determining the validity of experience. Not all experiences that involve "ecstatic" religious symbols are religious experiences. And there is no reason to think that genuinely engaged religious experiences are all at the level of being ecstatically fulfilling. Experiences with regard to the religious predicaments are religious, for instance, but rarely fulfilling. Ecstatic fulfillments are experiences or habits developed through experiences that somehow establish a proper and successful relation to the ultimate realities at issue.

So, religious fulfillments must somehow be the successful or proper engagement of ultimate realities and the ultimate dimensions of various domains of experience. Most seriously, this means the engagement of the ontological reality of the ontological act of creation. But engagement of the ontological reality is often mediated through engagements of the four cosmological realities of form/value/obligation/choice, the need for grounded wholeness, the engagement of others as others in one's existential field, and the attainment of absolute value-identity. These four singly and together in various combinations provide means for engaging the ontological act itself, and in fulfilling ways. Furthermore, to engage the cosmological realities by themselves, without taking them in their contexts as the transcendental traits of the ontological act itself, is to abstract them from what makes them ultimate. Their ultimacy comes not from their own characters per se but from the fact that they are the transcendental conditions of the ontological act. Religious fulfillments are multifarious, not only because of differences in cultural conditions and semiotic systems but also because of the plurality of the cosmological ultimates. Yet they also have a profound unity in that diversity because of their being the transcendental expression of the ontological creative act (no matter what is created, so long as it is determinate in some sense). Every religion notes this profound unity in diversity, but perhaps it is thematized best in Islam.[3]

A good term to hold steady the connotation of religious fulfillment as engaging well the ontological creative act in and through the cosmological ultimates is "ecstasy." Literally, it means "standing out of," which refers both to the cosmological ultimates out of which one stands, while standing in them, and the ontological ultimate that is not reducible to any or all of the cosmological ultimates but has no determinate reality outside them. The common associations with "ecstasy" include sex, drugs, and music, none of which need have anything to do with religion. It is not surprising, however, that sexual experience, intoxication, and music that merges the self with others have long been symbols and metaphors for religious ecstasy. Ultimate religious fulfillment is to be understood as a finite/infinite contrast where the cosmological ultimates are the finite side and the ontological ultimate the infinite side, and yet both together are wholly, if strangely, positive, even the indeterminacy of the ontological act apart from its cosmological consequences. "Ecstasy" has many meanings in religious contexts, and in some sense all or most of them find their places in the sense of ecstasy to be delineated as ultimate religious fulfillment. Paul Tillich thematized the concept of ecstasy in the third volume of his *Systematic Theology* to be the mark of genuine religious spirit in contrast to merely human senses of spirit, and Keiji Nishitani does the same thing in his *Religion and Nothingness*.

The systematic exposition of ultimate ecstasy as religious fulfillment follows the order of the cosmological ultimates, taken as paths for rightly engaging the ontological ultimate. The first of these is about lying under obligation and the necessity of responsible choice and action. What is ultimate fulfillment in what we do? This is the topic of finding ultimate meaning within time, the arena of action. Many religions have focused heavily on this in the development of apocalyptic thinking. The limits of narrative have already been discussed (*I, 8*) and are elaborated more in Chapter 9. Whatever their limits, however, religious fulfillment seeks ecstatic fulfillment within time.

The second cosmological ultimate defines the problematic of grounded wholeness for individuals. But wholeness includes not only the reality of an individual's life within the present moments in which choices are made under obligation. An individual's identity is genuinely eternal in ways that are discussed throughout *Philosophical Theology* (especially *I, 12*) and are elaborated more in Chapter 10 here. A different sense of ultimate fulfillment is found in the meaning of life from the perspective of eternity.

The third cosmological ultimate defines the individual in relation to others as involved in the existential field. Problematic as the notion is, the ultimate fulfillment with regard to others is a proper sense of love of them as expressions of the ontological creative act. Chapter 11 argues that the ecstatic fulfillment of love is love of the ontological creative act as well as, and through, the love of others.

The fourth cosmological ultimate defines the individual's absolute value-identity, which has a paradoxical quality insofar as it is an expression of the ontological creative act. Ecstatic meaning in time, ecstatic identity in eternity, and ecstatic love provide content for ultimate identity and together their fulfillments are the fulfillment of a person's identity. But in reference to the ontological creative act, any content of absolute value-identity is a matter of full participation in the ontological creative act that is perfectly free. Therefore, ecstatic freedom is the fulfillment of absolute value-identity, as Chapter 12 argues.

Ecstatic fulfillment involves a strange reversal of the direction of engagement of ultimate reality we have assumed. In the senses of engagement discussed so far and presumed in the theory of symbolic engagement, the interpreter is the active engager. Part of the meaning of ecstasy in religious fulfillment, however, is that the transition is made so that the ontological creative act is the active engager, at least in partial and symbolic ways. Religious fulfillment experiences the ontological creative act as the source of the individual's meaning within time, of identity in eternity, of love of creation itself, and of the individual's very being as free. Because of this reversal, ecstatic fulfillment engages the four cosmological ultimates with mediation through the ontological creative act, and so our discussion is structured by those cosmological ultimates in looser and more metaphorical ways than Parts I and II treated them.

CHAPTER NINE

Ecstatic Meaning in Time

I. MEANING IN LIFE

A great many people find ecstatic happiness in lives that are otherwise filled with troubles and ambiguities. Few of these people are religious virtuosi or adepts. For most, the ecstatic fulfillment is not a constant experience but happens occasionally as a "peak experience." Many people who themselves are mired in predicament and have never had anything like an ecstatically fulfilling experience still have met people who do manifest ecstatic fulfillment. The "guru culture" of South Asian religions is a strong testimony to this, calling attention to "fulfilled" or "actualized" paradigms. But there are saints of ecstatic fulfillment in the other Axial Age traditions, too, from hyperactive whirling dervishes and bouncing Hassidim to dour devotees of Calvin's radiantly glorious God and oh-so-moderate Confucian sages.

Although this volume has characterized religion first as a response to predicament, most likely the role of religion in bearing experiences of ecstatic fulfillment is more basic. The models of ecstatic fulfillment are what draw people to religion to cope with their predicaments. Patrick McNamara in his *The Neuroscience of Religious Experience* goes so far as to cite the practices of ecstasy in song, dance, and chemical inebriation of our distant ancestors as religious forms that played important roles in the evolution of the executive control functions of the *Homo sapiens sapiens* brain. Ecstatic experience whooping it up around the campfire might be a far cry from the cultivated experiences of the Axial Age religions. Surely, those distant ancestors had no Axial Age theories of ultimacy in mind, nor did they interpret their ecstatic fulfillments with much attention to orders of ultimacy. But then, the vast majority of people who find ecstatic fulfillment in their religious practices today also do not interpret those experiences with theories of ultimacy. They do, however, have symbolic systems in terms of which they interpret those experiences that might very well function indexically to make those experiences genuine ecstatic engagements of dimensions of ultimacy.

Save for a few metaphysical mystics, the symbol systems that give meaning to experiences of ecstatic fulfillment have intimate intensity, probably with little transcendent transparency. The peasant who is ecstatically fulfilled by the earth in his hands; the simple Christian whose life is shaped daily by imagined walks with Jesus in the garden when the dew is still on the roses; the chef who, like in the film *Babette's Feast*, cooks to bring happiness, reconciliation, and peace—these people have symbol systems that mediate dimensions of ultimate reality to the particularities of their lives. These are not particularly adept, but they access their religion with its symbols so that they inhabit them with the intensity of ecstatic fulfillment (*II, 13–16*).

These symbol systems work by setting the intimate details of life within a larger frame that shapes the meaning of those details. From their particular perspectives, they give the particularities of life ultimate meaning within time. Probably for most people whose lives are fulfilled ecstatically at least occasionally, the possibility that there is a nontemporal frame for life's meaning is not a conscious option. Our study here begins with the consideration of ultimacy within time as the frame connecting the particularities of life to ultimate realities.

Although ordinary people with ecstatic fulfillments at the center of their religious lives operate through highly imaginative symbol systems, our dialectical study of how such symbol systems in fact relate people to ultimate realities needs to work through the examination of adepts. Religious virtuosi are those who work through to the connections in more or less open ways, testing their traditional symbols and engaging them in critical depth. The adepts are indeed the ones in virtue of whom it is possible to say that an ecstatic experience is engagement of the genuinely ultimate.[1] The symbols in the ecstatic experiences have material qualities that are intense and shattering or enjoyable, but that might not be truly connected with ultimacy so that the experience is a true engagement. The dialectic of the adept reveals the structure of that connection.

One dimension of ecstatic fulfillment is finding the meaning of one's life as a participant, in one's historical milieu. All people have some sense of their local history; but this is not interestingly religious unless that local history is understood as part of a larger story. Usually in Axial Age religions the larger story is represented as the total historical milieu, or even cosmic history. There is a sense of ecstatic fulfillment that comes from experiencing oneself as part of an ultimate story. At least this is the claim of those whose ultimate framing structure for theology is narrative.

Much of the ordinary meaning of human life comes from the roles people play in their social groupings, natural contexts, and the narratives by which they understand acting in those roles. In a general sense, a man might find meaning in his role as a father, but in a specific sense his paternal meaning has to do with the story of how he acts as a father. Ordinary human meanings are largely a matter of the interweaving of roles and stories of what is done in and with those roles. Other aspects of human meaning might have little to do with roles or stories and these other aspects are often more important. Nevertheless, a crucial kind of ecstatic fulfillment comes from engaging the ultimate through a sense of participation in an ultimate narrative.

Ultimate human meaning can be sought in stories only if the stories are ultimate in some sense. The next two sections examine claims of ultimacy for histories that when brought to an end give ultimate meaning to the whole, and for cosmic history that stretches far beyond human history but also when brought to an end or to a significant reversal gives ultimate meaning to the whole. A preliminary consideration of what ultimacy in a story consists in needs to be made, however.

Philosophical Theology One, Chapter 8, argues that the ultimacy of story or narrative is problematic. It distinguishes two kinds of ultimate rhetorical frames for theology itself, a narrative frame and a metaphysical frame. A narrative frame, such as Karl Barth's cosmic drama of creation, fall, and redemption, puts all metaphysical relations among human beings and other creatures with the ultimate within the narrative frame; the metaphysical relations are not ultimate except as part of the larger narrative. Similarly, the Bhagavad Gita, which in itself is far more metaphysical than narrative, can be read within the larger narrative frame of the Mahabharata. On the other hand, the Mahabharata as a theology can be read as a local context within which the metaphysics of the Bhagavad Gita can be construed as the ultimate frame.

Paul Tillich, in somewhat explicit opposition to Barth, developed a "ground of being" metaphysics as the ultimate from within which he read Christian claims about history. *Philosophical Theology* sides with Tillich in its defense of its ultimate rhetorical frame for theology. Part of the reason for the rejection of narrative as the ultimate rhetorical frame is that a narrative sorts selectively among the things that exist and their relations, obscuring things and relations that do not have meaning within the narrative. So, for instance, Barth's history of creation, fall, and redemption obscures the people and ideas of the religions other than Christianity, with Judaism understood in relation to creation and the rhetorical context for Christianity for the most part.

Another element of the reason for the rejection of narrative, however, is the difficulty of defining ultimacy in exclusively narrative terms. This chapter considers in greater detail the claim that the ultimate meaning of human life might lie in the form of a story. Without doubt, stories of salvation and end-times are common symbols of ultimate meaning in many religions, perhaps all the Axial Age religions except Confucianism. The question here is whether narrative can approach literal or iconic truth about human meaning. Or is it limited to indexical truth?

Narratives that give meaning to individual and communal life in some ultimate way are apocalyptic. Ultimacy lies in apocalyptic stories. The root meaning of apocalypse, however, is "removing the veil," or, literally, "revelation." This means that the ordinary ways by which people understand their lives are "revealed" in their ultimate meaning by the symbols of ultimacy, perhaps in a narrative. Not all ways of finding ultimate meaning in one's life in time involve narrative. In karmic religions each sentient being has a history of many lives with moral formation. This can be represented as a kind of biography, as in the tales of the "previous lives of the Buddha." But these religions, mainly in South Asia, rarely view the whole present situation in which a given life takes place as having a role in an ultimate framing story so that one's participation in historical events is ultimately defining or the subject of ecstatic ultimate fulfillment. It's as if each sentient being were a story unto itself. Moreover, the connections among a sentient being's many lives are matters of moral deservingness and are not necessarily, if at all, sequences in an overarching narrative. In some of these traditions the ultimately important point is to stop the round of karma. In some, the historical aspect of living is the very problem and the ultimate meaning of a given life is the cessation of the story and connection with unchanging reality; or unchanging emptiness. Our concern in this chapter, however, is with those who find the ultimate meaning of temporal life to be itself participation in a fulfilling temporal narrative.

II. HISTORICAL APOCALYPTIC

Historical apocalyptic is the vision of the world in which human history is created by an intentional agent for a purpose that is fulfilled with some consummating conclusion. Perhaps the primary source for apocalyptic thinking in West Asia was the strain of Zoroastrianism according to which the good creator God, Ahura Mazda, struggles with his benevolent immanent power, Spenta Mainyu, against with the evil spirit, Angra Mainyu, for supremacy in human history, with cosmological embellishments. This was a dualism of primal divine powers with Ahura Mazda representing order and Angra Mainyu representing chaos. The belief was that the good God would prevail at the end of time, bringing about perfect order and reviving the dead.

The Jewish exiles in Persia were influenced by this way of thinking, introducing apocalyptic into Jewish thinking, as illustrated, for instance, in the Hebrew Bible's book of Daniel 10–12. In that book, the character Daniel dreamt he was resting by the Tigris River when he had a vision of an angel, probably Gabriel, who explained to him God's help to those who appealed to him, citing a number of wars, and promised that some people, those who supported the divine cause, would be raised from the dead in the last time (the earliest reference in the Hebrew Bible to resurrection).

The resurrection theme was central to the Christian writer, Paul, who believed that within a short time, probably within his own lifetime, Jesus would return on the Day of the Lord to raise the faithful who had died and take them as well as the living faithful up into heaven at the end of history.[2] His conception of Heaven, common in the first century, was that there are planes of existence above the plane of the Earth (and the even lower planes of hells) that have different physical properties. Aristotle, for instance, had argued that things below the orbit of the moon naturally move in straight lines, while the moon and the things in the planes above have naturally circular motion up to the planes of the stationary stars, which only spin. Paul believed that when the faithful are taken up into the heavens their bodies are transformed so as to be immortal.[3] The Christian book of Revelation, the last book of the New Testament, combined the political history of Daniel with the personal history of individuals who are faithful to Jesus Christ and persevere through persecutions, to conclude with a catastrophic destruction of the natural Earth and the creation of a new Heaven and a new Earth.

The Muslim belief in the coming Day of Judgment when all souls will be called to account builds on the Jewish and Christian apocalyptic ideas. Much of the Qur'an is devoted to the Day of Judgment, and the impossibility of knowing when it shall come. Nevertheless, the ultimate meaning of life, in Islam, is how each individual fares before Allah on that Day.

Historical apocalyptic is more prominent in the West Asian religions than in the other Axial Age religions. It has variations running from the history of individuals to the history of nations and political and religious movements. Perhaps the most common form of popular religion now in areas across the globe affected by Judaism, Christianity, and Islam is that each individual is believed to be called to judgment upon their death, and the history of their personal life in this sense has ultimate significance. A common theme in this popular religion is that people ordinarily do not think of their lives as ultimately significant—what they do, good and bad, does not matter much beyond immediate consequences. Being confronted with the vision of ultimate judgment, however, causes some people, especially in times of stress, to convert to an ultimate concern to be judged with mercy and to reassess their lives and live with an eye to judgment.

Standing individually under judgment is presented as something to be feared, especially by revivalist preachers of apocalyptic personal religions who use the fear as a motive for eliciting religious commitment. Nevertheless, the prospect of standing under judgment does give a form of ultimate meaning to life. One's life history is more than it seems because it stands under ultimate judgment.

Of course, no one has a life history alone, and conjoint histories also can be conceived to be under ultimate judgment, the histories of families, communities, nations, or particularly religious communities. For some Jews, being faithful as the community of Israel to God's promises for the Promised Land gives ultimate meaning. For some Christians, the Church, under some conception of church or other, is an ultimate unit to be judged in the history of redemption. For the early Muslims, with interpretive variations in subsequent groups, the political movement of Islam bringing Allah's order to the Earth was conceived to be Allah's own divine action in carrying out the providential divine plan.

The Muslim case illustrates the merging of the history of a community with the history of humankind with respect to its ultimate meaning. In the visions of apocalyptic thinkers such as Paul, all people on Earth are players in the cosmic drama of human fall, struggle with the powers of evil, and ultimate divine victory that ends history. Although human beings are players in the great historical drama, they are not the main players for those early apocalyptic movements. Later variations on apocalypticism reversed those emphases. Political movements such as the Christian Crusades against the Muslims and Jews in Palestine claimed divine sanction that gave ultimate meaning to the crusaders' lives. The same was true in the opposite direction for the Muslim defenders. Millennial movements have abounded in European history, identifying the culmination of history with a particular date, or a date that will occur when certain signs have been received. The great popularity in the English-speaking world of the *Left Behind* series of books illustrates the hunger of many people to find ultimate meaning in a drama in which the genuinely good souls are raptured up to Heaven while the souls who want to be good struggle against the forces of evil, including divine or demonic ones, waiting for Jesus to return and massacre the evil people and the unbelievers.[4] The apocalyptic imagery of the *Left Behind* series appeals to the folk religion of people today who are comfortable with a world filled with supernatural agents. This kind of popular religion has been reviled by many sophisticated Western thinkers since the European Enlightenment (and by Confucian thinkers for two millennia before that!). Without a trace of supernaturalism, however, the visions of Hegel and Marx have an apocalyptic structure in which individual lives are given meaning by virtue of the roles they play in a larger story of contest and change that has ultimate significance. Hegel thought of the march of Spirit in history as the Absolute, God properly conceived. Marx debunked the theological language of the Hegelians so as to say that the actual revolutions for which he called within history are the true venues of ultimate meaning.

Thomas J. J. Altizer identifies the ultimate or God with the historical process itself interpreted in an Hegelian way.[5] Thus, he ambivalently proclaims the death of God. In one sense, for him and other "death of God theologians," the death of God is the collapse of the transcendent God above history and the self-abnegation of that transcendent creator so as to be wholly embodied in history. History is thus divine and ultimately significant without reference to a transcendent God. In another sense, the advance of the late modern age has meant, for Altizer, that an ultimate significance cannot be attributed to history, that history does not hang together in narrative form the way an apocalyptic narrative must. Therefore the meaningful narrative that has been influential in the Abrahamic religions, for him, has frittered away to the end of history, the death of that apocalyptic God.

The very grave limitation of historical apocalyptic for contemporary theology is that human history itself can no longer be conceived in terms of a single meaningful narrative that seems to have purpose or univocal worth (I, 8). Narratives in history are generally imposed after the situation has past and are far too simple to indicate what really took place and what it meant. Only in terms of natural history can the human species be viewed in narrative form, and even that is likely to be an oversimplification.

III. COSMIC APOCALYPTIC

Cosmic apocalyptic gives ultimate meaning to human life by locating it within a cosmic "natural history" that extends far beyond human life but that has an ultimately significant origin and goal. Perhaps the paradigmatic form of cosmic apocalyptic was the family of traditions in ancient India according to which the cosmos arises by expansion from Hiranyagarbha, or the Golden Egg. The cosmos expands from this for a very long time, for instance 360,000,000 years, or some other large multiple of thirty-six, until it contracts again to the infinitely dense and internally simple egg. Then the process repeats. There are many variations on this. Sometimes the expanding and contracting cosmos is identified with Shiva, sometimes with Vishnu. Within the process of expansion and contraction lie stages, and in ancient India it was thought that we live in the final age, the Kali Yuga. In this final age, human beings are short-lived and often morally corrupt, a great diminishment from the heroic stature of human beings in previous ages. The ultimate meaning of human life has little to do with a person's life particulars but rather with the way those particulars get along as the universe moves toward collapse. Then again, in those ancient Indian movements, the particulars of a person's life are not as important as the way the individual is merged with a deeper reality, in this case the history of the expanding and collapsing cosmos.

Buddhism, of course, does not want to attribute ultimate significance to the particulars of personal life but rather to the abandonment of attachments to finding ultimate significance. Nevertheless, popular Buddhism and many Buddhist schools of philosophy have held to a theory of ages of history that provide the contexts for understanding the particular human situation.[6] For instance, the age during the lifetime of a Buddha is a highpoint because the Buddha embodies the dharma of enlightenment. After the Buddha's death, there still are the direct disciples who know the dharma of enlightenment as embodied. After they are gone is the age of the writings of the dharma of enlightenment and the relics of the Buddha. As the interpretation of the writings gets farther and farther from the sources, it picks up errors. Finally the world awaits the next Buddha, who will restore the living teaching. Gautama Buddha defines our period but at such a distance that many people long for the coming of the next Buddha, Maitreya. In the South Asian primal traditions, the cause of the collapse of the age is not so much human failings, as in the Noah story in Genesis, as it is the nature of the cosmic structure itself.

Although the cosmic imagination of the South Asian traditions has been vast and highly speculative, modern science has given it specificity. Whereas the ancient West Asian traditions mainly had cared about nature only insofar as it is the context for human history, and thus could tolerate the idea of the world being only a few thousand years old, the South Asian traditions thought in terms of a much vaster and more ancient cosmos. Thus the speculations of the recent scientists that the universe is about 13.6 billion years old would have seemed quite appropriate to the ancient South Asian mind.

The theory of evolution, however, is what has made it possible to tell a narrative about the cosmos. The narrative runs from the Big Bang through the evolution of stars and planets though stages of the formation of Earth and atmosphere, to the evolution of species on Earth (and possibly elsewhere). The theory of cosmic evolution allows for the prediction of cosmic dissolution. One such prediction is that the cosmos will expand so far that its massy objects will slow down and have enough residual attraction to come back together again, running backwards toward the Big Crunch. Some speculate that the Big Crunch will then explode as another Big Bang, replicating something like the Hiranyagarbha scenario.

What can the modern scientific narrative of the natural history of the cosmos determine about the ultimate meaning of human life? A number of things, two of which are mentioned here.

First, to the extent that the cosmic natural history is the ultimate frame of meaning, nothing lasts long, cosmically speaking. Therefore no ultimate meaning for human life can be found in a political arrangement, or a theocracy such as the Kingdom of God, or universal peace on Earth. Life on Earth cannot last, and the planet will fall into the sun in a few trillion years. Of course, much proximate meaning can be found in working for peace and justice, and these are ultimately important. But those efforts can never be understood as contributing to an everlasting success. Some religious thinkers can say that human beings at some point are removed from the course of natural history, perhaps to a parallel universe of Heaven or Hell. But this is to deny ultimate significance to the cosmic narrative. It is also difficult to make plausible because it seems to be an empirical claim about a parallel universe that is not empirically conceivable.

Second, the cosmic evolutionary story of modern science provides the conceptual apparatus for human beings to conceive themselves to be cosmic agents. Evolved through eons on Earth, human beings as a species are now seen to affect the Earth's own evolution. Many people see the effects of the human species to be a degradation of the richness of life on Earth, with serious interference with the cycles of atmosphere, temperature, and climate. In one sense, these disastrous changes brought about by humans on the ecological environment that is their habitat are just the results of the species expanding its niche. Many species have eaten themselves out of house and home! No natural reason exists why the human species should last or expect its habitat to last forever. In another sense, however, solid value judgments can be made about the value of biodiversity, about better and worse ways to modify the environment, and about what things to preserve and what to eliminate. As human beings are beginning to rocket vehicles, people, and waste off the Earth into the solar system and beyond, the environment of human influence has expanded into larger regions of the cosmos. Any objectivist moral theory such as has been defended in *Philosophical Theology* would support efforts to make discerning judgments about the effects of human beings on their environment and organizing efforts to produce the better rather than the worse effects.

Thomas Berry, perhaps the most acute and imaginative theological interpreter of the issues of the environment, argues that, as a species, human beings have a "Great Work."

> History is governed by those overarching movements that give shape and meaning to life by relating the human venture to the larger destinies of the universe. Creating such a movement might be called the Great Work of a people. There have been great works in the past: the great work of the classical Greek world with its understanding of the human mind and creation of the Western humanist tradition. . . . In India the great work was to lead human thought into spiritual experiences of time and eternity and their mutual presence to each other with a unique subtlety of expression. China created one of the most elegant and most human civilizations we have ever known as its great work. . . . Meanwhile the incoming Europeans committed themselves to the development of a new industrial age that was beginning to dominate human consciousness. New achievements in science, technology, industry, commerce, and finance had indeed brought the human community into a new age. Yet those who brought this new historical period into being saw only the bright side of these achievements. They had little comprehension of the devastation they were causing on this continent and throughout the planet. . . . The Great Work now, as we move into a new millennium, is to carry out the transition from a period of human devastation of the Earth to a period when humans would be present to the planet in a mutually beneficial manner. This historical change is something more than the transition from the classical Roman period to the medieval period, or from the medieval period to modern times. Such a transition has no historical parallel since the geobiological transition that took place 67 million years ago when the period of the dinosaurs was terminated and a new biological age begun.[7]

Since the termination of the dinosaurs, we have lived in what science knows as the Cenozoic Era. Berry says that the Great Work of human beings is to move into what he calls the Ecozoic Era, characterized by mutual beneficial relations between human beings and the environment.

Thus he, and many other environmentalists, say that the great significance of human life is what it does with regard to the further evolution of the cosmos, insofar as that can be affected by human action. Moreover, the great significance of individuals lies in the particular things that seem only proximate but that contribute to the development of the Ecozoic Era. Without doubt, Berry is right about the need for self-consciousness on the part of human beings about what our species is doing to the environment. The importance of attending to this might be far greater in cosmic perspective than the other particulars of what we do with our lives, including the histories of our peoples.

Yet is this an ultimate meaning for human life? As with Marx, it can be argued that there is nothing more ultimate than the revolution for which he called. Berry's might be a more important revolution than Marx's. But is such a narrative meaning ultimate? This is the topic of the next section.

IV. TIME WITHIN ETERNITY

Philosophical Theology has argued throughout that temporal, spatial, and all other kinds of differences that are determinate to some degree with respect to one another require an ontological context in which they can be relevant to one another. Although the conditional components of things contextualize the things with respect to one another in terms of relations within the cosmos, they do not provide a context within which different things, with their different essential components, can be together. The ontological context of mutual relevance does provide for that togetherness of different things, each with its own essential components. The argument has been developed throughout this work that only an ontological act of creation, the terminus of which is the created world, can be this ontological context of mutual relevance.

Narrative apocalyptic supposes that many things are related in the story, and that they occupy different times and places. Therefore, narrative apocalyptic itself presupposes a deeper ontological context of mutual relevance than it constitutes in itself and cannot be ultimate in that ontological way. This is so even when the apocalyptic narrative includes as part of the drama a divine creator who makes the world and then interacts with it to redeem it, as in the apocalypticism of many strands within the Abrahamic traditions. For, if the divine creator is determinate apart from creation, being good, intelligent, willful, and so forth, even in an infinite way, a deeper ontological context is required for the creator to be distinguished from the creatures. If it is said that the creator creates the determinate divine nature in creating the world, then that is the same as the ontological theory in *Philosophical Theology*: the ontological creative act is indeterminate apart from creating, and in creating becomes determinate as creator.

But for there to be a *narrative* of creation, redemption, and so forth, a temporal difference must exist between creator and created, and then the ontological context of mutual relevance is the locus of the creation of the creator (alleged) and the created. The ontological creative act that gives rise to temporal differences is eternal, that is, not temporal. The eternal act has the character of containing, among other things, the different modes of time together. The modes of time are temporally distinct. In order for them to be so temporally distinct, they must be eternally together. So, no narrative, even one of creation, can be ultimate in that ontological sense.

The ontological theory of *Philosophical Theology*, however, develops four cosmological ultimates. For something to exist, it has to be something, something determinately this rather than that. The analysis of determinateness shows it to consist in being harmony according to which a thing conditions and is conditioned by the other harmonies with respect to which it is determinate. Any determinate thing, as a harmony, has four traits: form, components formed, existential location, and value-identity. Each of these traits is ultimate in the sense that any thing that exists must have it, and they are interdefined with one another.

Might it not be possible that an apocalyptic narrative is ultimate in the sense of relating to the ultimacy of form, components, existential location, and value-identity? A cosmic history with an apocalyptic ending would, by hypothesis, include within it all the forms as possibilities, as chosen and excluded, and as actualized. The determinateness of possibility would be possible only because of actual components to which formal unity must be schematized, and so all the components of the world that contributed to form would be included in the cosmic history. The cosmic history would include the entire existential field as constituted by the components. And the cosmic history would total up all the value-identity achieved. In this sense the cosmic history would be ultimate, at least cosmologically ultimate.

This is only to say, however, that the creation itself, as the terminus of the ontological creative act, is ultimate, or at least part of the ultimate act, more precisely the cosmological part consisting of the determinate things. What gives meaning to a human life within the cosmic history is not the narrative that history might display, however. Rather it is the elementary fact that the person is a part of the creation. The narrative gives proximate meaning to the person relative to what comes before and after, and to the environment of natural, social, and personal elements. The question has already been raised as to whether the cosmic history can have the form of a narrative. Chances are it can not except in an extremely vague way; the narrative of the move from the Cenozoic to the Ecozoic Era, as Berry argues, gives very little specific orientation to a given individual's life. Scientific theories have just as much place in understanding cosmic history as narratives do.

Furthermore, it is difficult if not impossible to conceive of the creation as a whole history, as totaled up. If the totality is determinate, then it must have a contrast term, something outside it with respect to which it is different. In the case of a totalizing cosmic narrative, that narrative is significant only in contrast to what might have gone before, after, or instead. The beginning of a song is determinate only in contrast to the silence before the first note. What is ultimate about a cosmic narrative is only that it allegedly contains everything, not its narrative form, which is only its form, not the whole.

Why, then, we must ask, are apocalyptic narratives so popular among some major religions for providing ultimate meaning to human life in ways that seem ecstatically fulfilling? They cannot literally be ultimate, although of course they can provide many important kinds of proximate meanings, and give a certain orientation to lives.

A first answer to this question is that narratives of any sort have intimacy for providing meaning. A person can forget about the vast confusing complications of life and identify himself or herself within a larger drama so as to find significance in the roles played in the drama. The drama might be extremely important, for instance, a military struggle to turn back a would-be global dictator or to make the Earth safe from humans. Such intimate symbols provide orientation and play crucial roles in sacred worldviews. But it is very difficult to establish a proper hermeneutical relation between such intimate symbols as apocalyptic narratives that attempt to sum up the meaning of the world and the truly transcendent symbols in which the venue of the world's (and thereby the individual's) ultimate meaning lies.

Perhaps, however, the real reference in cosmic apocalyptic narratives is not so much iconic as indexical. Perhaps believing in the apocalyptic story is not important for the story's truth but rather for the fact that this belief establishes an ultimately meaningful relation to the ontological act of creation itself. Mircea Eliade, among others, argued that many religious ideas of ultimacy, not only narratives "of that time" but also sacred places, people, and singular events, function as signs of an ontological depth that could not be told in finite terms. Part of his argument is that these signs of ultimacy were employed in rituals, the repetitive character of which itself constituted engagement with that which is outside space and time.[8]

This raises the question again of how reference functions in symbolic engagement of ultimacy. The metaphysics of ultimacy aims at literalness, at iconic conventional reference. How many people can find ultimate meaning for their lives through metaphysics? The signs by which ultimate meaning is registered need to have intimate force. *Philosophical Theology* argues throughout that metaphysics provides signs that are corrective of the potentially false implications of other signs that refer only indexically. This point is important to explore as the issue of ultimate meaning is pressed. The form the point takes in the next chapter is the analysis of how eternal meaning, which is where ultimate meaning must lie, can be mapped onto spatiotemporal terms. For now it can be said that the ecstatic fulfillment of life conceived to be within time as in the form of an ultimate narrative can be possible only if the reference actually functions indexically. If the reference in the story is taken iconically, it is idolatry, the confusion of the proximate for the ultimate.

What does this mean for ecstatic fulfillment oriented to the affairs of temporal life? Many people do indeed find ecstatic fulfillment that defines them existentially in ultimate ways in things such as winning a race, perfecting a performance, devoting themselves to a cause such as improving the middle school or saving the planet. Religion shapes these experiences so that they are understood to be ultimately fulfilling in some sense or other, for instance, as being part of a religiously significant story. The ultimacy lies not in the story but in some way by which living according to the story indexically relates the person to some larger context of ultimate meaning, an eternal one.

CHAPTER TEN

Ecstatic Life in Eternity

The previous chapter discussed the attempt to find ecstatic fulfillment regarding the meaning of life in apocalyptic understandings of personal, social, or natural history and argued that such narrative cannot bear ultimacy in the sense required. But a deeper analysis is required of several of the questions at issue. On the one hand, ultimate meaning needs to be tied to what is really ultimate as that best can be engaged. On the other hand, ultimate meaning needs to be intimate to human life so as to be "meaningful." Of course, the meaningfulness of anything as profound as something grasped in ecstatic fulfillment is by no means ordinary. Ecstatic fulfillment in many respects is an achievement of the individual, not an identification of an ultimate meaning. Nevertheless, the question of the meaning of life is fraught with the tension between the transcendent and the intimate. And what is to say that life actually has an ultimate meaning? Perhaps, as so many secularists have argued, life is fundamentally meaningless. But then, if life is fundamentally meaningless, is not that the real ultimate meaning of life?

I. THE PROBLEM OF ULTIMATE MEANING

To address the problem of ultimate meaning it is helpful to reorient the argument with regard to the basic philosophical categories involved. In the previous two parts of this volume, the ways religion addresses the ultimacy of form were discussed in terms of religious ethics (and see *III, 10*). What is ultimate about form is the alternative possibilities it presents for human life, and the fact that this puts human beings under obligation. The previous parts also analyzed the ways religion addresses the ultimacy of components, and the integration of them into wholeness of human life, as a function of spirituality (and see *III, 11*). The fact that human beings lie under obligation integrates with the quest for wholeness of self: only a being under obligation would have an obligation to develop a whole self, and only a being whose norm is wholeness would stand under obligation as such. Religion addresses what is ultimate in the existential field through the problematic of individual and communal engagement of others, also to be discussed in Part IV, under the general rubric of membership and belonging in a complicated existential field with natural, social, and personal configurations. Only individuals lying under obligation and with a norm for their own integrity would find religious concerns for membership for conjoint action in a complicated existential field to be ultimate.

The principal religious orientation to be discussed in Part III is how religion addresses the ultimacy of value-identity. Ultimate ecstatic fulfillment is a function of ultimacy in value-identity. According to the philosophical hypothesis, every determinate harmony whatsoever has some kind of value-identity, resulting from getting its value-laden form to integrate its components in its existential location. Human beings, therefore, have value-identities with both subjective and objective elements whether they want to or not, and these value-identities are ultimate. That is, the value-identities constitute exactly the value-identity that each individual achieves, with good and bad elements and the unique thisness of the individual achievements. Although each value-identity is ultimate in this sense, not everyone approaches value-identity as an ultimate matter.

Religion is the engagement of ultimacy, and so to engage absolute value-identity as an ultimate matter is to be religious in this respect. What religion does is add to the questions an individual might ask about the specifics of personal value-identity an extra question: what does it mean to have this particular value-identity? "What does it mean to have this particular value-identity" has two levels of significance. On one level, common in religions, is the question of the consequence of having this value-identity: will it consign me to Heaven or Hell, to another lousy life or release from suffering, or something else, or nothing? This level of the question supposes that the meaning of one's value-identity is played out within some higher-order cosmological causal structure. What is the larger meaning of this value-identity as that person's life? On another level is the question of the ultimate meaning of having a human value-identity at all. What is the meaning of human life as such? As has been seen in previous chapters, that last question has often been addressed as a question of purpose—is there a purpose to human life? The argument given in *Philosophical Theology* is that there is no externally imposed purpose for human life or for the existence of the cosmos. If there were, that would presuppose a more ultimate ontological context of mutual relevance underlying the relation between the purposer and the world, and hence the question of meaning through purpose is not ultimate enough.

The key to the question of ultimate meaning lies in the dual character of finite/infinite contrasts. The finite side is what actually exists, and the infinite side is the counterfactual state of what would be (or would not be) if the finite side did not exist. In respect of absolute value-identity, the infinite side would be that people had no identity whatsoever. To be sure, much of Buddhism argues rhetorically that there is no absolute value-identity to the individual. But in point of fact this amounts to the claim that the value-identity of an individual is wholly but nothing more than the particular moments of consciousness such as they are and fleeting as they are (in many senses of "fleeting" corresponding to the several schools). The infinite side of value-identity for various Buddhisms is not to have attachment-filled consciousness or the release from it—no consciousness whatsoever.

To engage absolute value-identity ultimately is to take it to be radically contingent. One kind of ecstatic fulfillment is to embrace that radical contingency. In fact, the contingency is so radical that the engagement raises the question of ultimate non-being. To face absolute value-identity ultimately is to face the possibility that one might not be: embrace that possibility is a kind of ecstatic fulfillment. Or, more generally, to face that value-identity in terms of one's own life is to face the question of its local contingency—once it was not and in some (hopefully large) number of years will be no longer; to embrace that is a kind of ecstatic fulfillment. Or, even more generally, the religious engagement of value-identity is to face the question of the very non-being of the cosmos, yet another kind of ecstatic fulfillment.

And yet, the cosmos exists, the human species exists (for better or worse regarding nature), and each individual exists. Therefore the engagement of absolute value-identity comes down to the apprehension of the gratuitous, arbitrary, undeserved, and surprising character of existence itself and of the ontological creative act that is the central reality in determinate existence. At its depths, the question of the "ultimate meaning" of human life, indeed of the cosmos, is answered by the presentation of that which bears meaning as gratuitous, arbitrary, undeserved, and surprising. If Tillich is right that questions of ultimacy become meaningful because of experiences of ontological shock, an even more forceful shock is the presentation of the sheer contingent existence of the cosmos, oneself included, perhaps the most blissful ecstatic fulfillment.

Nevertheless, the gratuitous, arbitrary, undeserved, and surprising existential suddenness of the cosmos is not the only ultimate reality in the absolute value-identity of human beings. Because the world consists of partly determinate harmonies, each human value-identity is given ultimacy by the finite/infinite contrasts in forms, components, existential location, as well as absolute but finite value-identity. Therefore, part of the ultimacy in value-identity is the gratuitous, arbitrary, undeserved, and surprising existence of form, possibilities, and the obligation that defines much of the individual. Another part of the ultimacy in one's value-identity is having some particular components to be integrated into a wholeness of life, and actual groundedness in one's history, facticity, context, and potentialities. Yet another part of the ultimacy of one's value identity is the particulars of one's existential location—the particulars themselves are not ultimate, but having some particulars (and only these particulars are particular to oneself)—as providing the field within which one lives: without that field, nothing—with that field, oneself. Finally, part of the ultimacy of one's value-identity is the counterfactual state of affairs that one would not have existed to achieve anything out of the possibilities given for integrating the component of one's life with respect to engaging the particulars of one's existential field: one might be nothing. Each of these dimensions of ultimacy to be engaged can be the vehicle of ecstatic fulfillment expressed in some terms or other.

So the ultimacy of one's absolute value-identity consists in the radically contingent reality of having that identity. And the meaning of that ultimacy is that one has it rather than not. The ultimate meaning of life is that we have it when there is no reason for it. What life one has, has a certain value, perhaps not what it should be but something. That value has a certain formal shape, and this shape integrates the components of life that one happens to have; this takes place in an existential field in which the interactions with others include ways by which one influences them and so has objective value in them.

The question of the ultimate meaning of life is thus two-faced. Respecting the infinite side of finite-infinite contrasts, it is the question about how there is the world we have. Respecting the finite side, it is the question of recognition of the factually gratuitous, arbitrary, underserved, and surprising singularity of life. Together as a contrast, these elements of ultimate meaning give rise to the answer expressed in awe, joy, bliss, and acceptance that find so many expressions in religions. These are powerful ecstatic fulfillments, and religion trucks with the symbols that make them possible.

II. MAPPING THE INFINITE ONTO THE FINITE

Nevertheless, this abstract embodiment of the answer to the ultimate meaning of life is difficult to express in religion. The metaphysical analysis of the meaning question in the previous section is not intimately available to most people. The religious traditions have provided a multitude of symbol systems that address the ultimate meaning of life in more intimate ways. By and large, those ultimate symbols cannot be literally, that is, iconically, true.

Consider, for instance, the belief common to folk religion in most of the Axial Age religions that the ultimate meaning of this life is to enter into a heavenly afterlife in which one is correctly related to the ultimate.[1] Sophisticated theologians in these religions have interpreted the afterlife notion in different and subtly contradictory ways, for instance, as a function of an immortal soul separate from a mortal body versus a bodily resurrection, perhaps with a body transformed to be immortal. In the folk religion versions, a person in Heaven is in the presence of the ultimate, that is, in some spatial relation with the ultimate, and in the presence of other heavenly rewarded people such as family and friends with whom it is heavenly to be reunited. But here the paradoxes start to arise if this image is taken iconically. What is one's age in Heaven? The age and condition one is in at death (not likely to be an enjoyment)? The age and condition one was in at thirty-three (Augustine's suggestion because that was the age of Jesus at death, and for many people it was a healthy and yet mature time of life)? What about those who died before reaching thirty-three, or who were sick and miserable then? Living forever in Heaven raises questions of aging. Does one get older and older, indefinitely ever more decrepit? Or does one stay an infinitely long time in the condition one was in at entrance into Heaven, an inhuman state of affairs? What would time in Heaven mean if one does not change? And what about meeting people one knows? Will they be the ages they were when they were significant to one in earthly life, or will everyone be thirty three? What about crowding? Can everyone get close to the ultimate, or do some people live in the heavenly suburbs?[2]

In point of fact, people whose piety centers on Heaven rarely ask these questions of what heavenly life really means, at least after the age of fourteen. Instead, their images of Heaven are essentially images of earthly life with bad things negated. Heaven is filled with one's companions because earthly life is so lonely, and friends leave. Heaven is a great rich court of a divine king, or a great feast, or a garden, or a bejeweled city, or a park with many palaces, because for most people life is lived in a mean estate far from pomp and power, with lonely hunger, in dry wilderness or threatening jungles, or in a wretched slum, or on the battleground between warlords. In Heaven the music is always good, no one has to take out the trash, and the nasty neighbors who made one's earthly life miserable are either transformed or in some other place.

Much folk religion that centers on hope for Heaven also centers on fear of Hell. Hell also is inconceivable if imagined literally and in fact is imagined negatively, like Heaven only the reverse. Hell is the worst of what earthly life holds, magnified to the highest imaginable degree and continued without surcease: torment by demons (worse than earthly neighbors); perpetual burning, or freezing, or lonely alienation; or whatever torture seems worst. Dante's *Inferno* is a nuanced view!

Most people with images of Heaven (and Hell) live within those images thinking that their reference is iconic, that is, literally believing in Heaven and Hell. In fact, however, the reference that functions in their lives is not iconic but indexical. The seemingly iconic image cannot be examined too closely without falling into paradox, and the image itself is constructed by negating harms or goods from earthly life. Now, in what can the indexical reference of such images of ultimate meaning consist?

In the semiotic theory of symbolic engagement in *Philosophical Theology*, reference is of three kinds: iconic, in which a likeness is asserted between the signs and their object; indexical, in which a causal relation is established between the signs and their object such that the interpreter picks up on something important in the object; and conventional, in which signs refer to other signs in the semiotic system (I, 3, ii). All interpretations that are expressible in words are at least conventional and involve syntactic and semantic interpretive forms within semiotic systems. But when such an interpretive form is employed intentionally in an actual engagement with an object, it can refer iconically or indexically, or both. If it does not functionally refer iconically, as is the case with images of Heaven and Hell, then it can refer indexically. Now what is the indexical relation involved in belief in Heaven and Hell, and other images of what it is that gives life ultimate meaning?

Although there is no one way for indexical reference to justify the requisite causal relations, at least one logical way can be described that is common in religious symbolism. Kant distinguished between a pure concept, a schema of that concept to experience, and a schema-image of that concept.[3] The pure concept of a circle, for instance, is that of a line in a plane all of whose points are equidistant from a point in the plane outside that line. Its schema is to indicate a point in a plane and draw a line in the plane at a rigid distance from the point, as with a compass or a taut string; the schema is an operation that translates the concept into something in space-time (in this instance). A schema-image for a circle might be a plate, or a tire, or a circle drawn on a blackboard.

How can we schematize the ultimate meaning of life as the right relation to ontological ultimacy? The metaphysical concept of ultimacy developed throughout *Philosophical Theology*, of the gratuitous, arbitrary, undeserved, and surprising character of the ontological act of creation, is rightly related to when it is engaged with philosophical appreciation. But there is no distance between that metaphysical ultimacy and human beings who might engage it so as to find their ultimate meaning. In their very engagement they are elements of that gratuitous, arbitrary, undeserved, and surprising creative act. Except for metaphysicians, most people have to translate this engagement into something that has an existential field, for it is through an existential field that we ordinarily engage things, moving toward or away from them.

So, religious imaginations develop schemata for mapping the immediacy of ultimacy onto experience understood as involving an existential field. The ultimate might be spatialized so as to be something people can journey toward, as in rising up into Heaven. Presence can be schematized in terms of culturally recognized spaces, such as courtrooms, banqueting halls, or gardens. And then religious traditions develop specific schema-images of what Heaven and Hell are like.

Among the schemata in some traditions are the rules that express right relation with the ultimate through the systematic elimination of harms for Heaven and goods for Hell. With respect to the ultimate dimensions of form/possibility/obligation, the schemata might include rules for vindicating the oppressed, rewarding the righteous, and punishing the wicked, although these would need to be supplemented by further rules that create these classes. Most people oppress and are oppressed, and are mixtures of good and bad. Perhaps other schemata would have to describe the ultimate as a judge with perfect discrimination, perhaps with a mixture of justice and mercy.

With respect to the ultimate dimension of components and wholeness of comportment with regard to them, perhaps in a set of afterlife symbols there would have to be rules that would schematize wholeness to a healing of body in Heaven, or to a perfected body, or to a bodiless soul with pure perceptions. The ultimate would have to be schematized as a being or condition that effects healing, or that can be engaged by a disembodied soul.

With respect to the ultimate dimension of engagement of others in an existential field, in such a set of symbols would have to be rules schematizing existential relations to such perfected others. Since there are many cultural ways of understanding both personal wholeness and the engagement of other people, the schematizing rules would have to take these differences into account. Eating or making music together are such schematizing rules. In Chinese and Christian images of heavenly feasting, pork would be served (though of course without the killing of pigs); no pork in the Jewish and Muslim heavenly banquets! Love and affectionate relations are common schemata for engagement in Heaven. When, in Milton's *Paradise Lost* (Book 8, lines 610–630), the angel Raphael is explaining Heaven to Adam and Eve, they ask him about sexual love between angels; Raphael blushes and does not answer. Very few symbol systems for heavenly engagement include engagement of nature beyond what is imagined as the setting for idealized human relations.

With respect to the ultimate dimension of value-identity, in an afterlife system of symbols for ultimate meaning there might be rules for schematizing a peaceable kingdom that includes vast stretches of nature beyond the human sphere. The pure concept to be schematized is the connection one might have with the whole of creation within which one's absolute value-identity might lie. The required schemata would have to depict the wholeness of the created world in some unifying symbols.

All religions have concrete schema-images for depicting in the terms of finite spatiotemporal life the schematized right relations with ultimacy that give ultimate meaning to human existence, insofar as the religions affirm such meaning. Those images, of course, are relative to the cultures, and most religions involve many cultures.

The theological issue with all this is the following. For those people who live within the schema-images of these symbols as if they referred iconically, there is little if any consciousness that they are not literally true or that their functional reference is to the ultimate that can be described iconically only in terms of the metaphysical pure concepts. What are the limits of their belief, then? From what perspective can we say that their beliefs are indexically true? The formula for answering this line of questions is that a determination needs to be made as to whether what is important in ultimacy, in respect of ultimate meaning, is carried over into the interpretive lives of the people. To this question the next two sections turn.

III. ETERNAL LIFE AND ITS TEMPORAL MAPS

The first step in this investigation is to recall the previous discussions of eternal life, particularly in *Philosophical Theology One*, Chapter 12. Next, the argument shall take up a set of four schematic strategies for expressing ultimate meaning in the finite terms of the cosmos.

The eternal life of a human being, like the eternity of the cosmos itself in the ontological context of mutual relevance, is the ultimate and most concrete frame of life. It was argued earlier that life within time, with time passing, presupposes a greater togetherness than the connections afforded by the space-time character of the existential field. In eternity, every moment of our temporal time is together with every other moment of our lives, and in three ways. Each moment is future with respect to some others, each is present and spontaneously happening, and each is past. Moreover, in eternity each date is dynamic: each date as future is being shifted by the decisions that change the elements the future must integrate; each date as present is spontaneously making whatever selections are relevant among the value-laden alternative possibilities; and each moment as past is accruing new identity and value by virtue of what subsequently is actualized. Because human beings are defined by relations with other things—particularly the environing nature, other people, and the institutions of habituated relationships—the dynamism of all temporal interactions is based on and made possible by the eternity of the act of creation. The ontological context of mutual relevance is the eternal context within which finite things dynamically play out their existence in time and space.

Given our created temporal nature, from the standpoint of any given present moment within our lives, our primary experience is that of being a perspective on the rest within our location in the existential field. So we view the future through anticipation, the past through memory and feeling, and the present immediacy of the field through complex, conventionally organized inferences about spatial and other relations of contemporaneity. For obvious pragmatic needs, our primary signs for engaging things fix them in their temporality. Nevertheless, as exhibited here, it is possible to develop metaphysical signs for grasping the eternal context within which temporal flow takes place. And it is possible to develop deep metaphysical, embodied, and grounded signs by which this eternity can be felt (*I, 15–16; III, 15–16*) with ecstatic fulfillment. The discussion returns to the development of virtuosi means of experiencing ultimate meaning in Chapters 11 and 12. The topic here, however, is how eternal life can be schematized to temporality and spatiality so as to be engaged in terms ordinary people understand.

The ways by which religious cultures have symbolized the ultimate meaning of life are multifarious and no classification can chart them without distortion. However, four interestingly related strategies for schematizing the eternity within which the meaning of life consists can be distinguished. Within any given tradition's symbolic repertoire, all four might be functional, although some are paradigmatic for the rhetorical centers of gravity for each tradition. The four are, in technical terms that no one will confuse with the religious symbols themselves: dynamic macrocosmic idealization, dynamic microcosmic idealization, antidynamic macrocosmic identification, and antidynamic microcosmic identification.

Dynamic *macrocosmic* idealization is the schematizing strategy that builds schema-images of the whole cosmos as idealized so that human life is ultimately meaningful. The example of popular religions' belief in an afterlife, heavenly and perhaps hellish, is an example of this. Ordinary life as conceived to fit within a world is symbolized with schematic strategies that make the world morally just, that reward virtue and punish evil, that relate life and afterlife so that ordinary life is no longer absurd, that depict life without harms, and that negatively reward evil in a life depicted without goods. Sophisticated theologians in many traditions have honed these schematizing strategies with great precision, depending on a variety of factors, including their culture's sense of what ordinary life is and its vicissitudes, and some schematized conception of a balancing or right-making agent, such as a judging and rewarding God or inexorable karmic order. The rhetorical center of gravity of the Abrahamic religions is especially adept at these strategies. The strategies discussed for folk symbols are clear enough for present purposes.

Dynamic *microcosmic* idealization is the schematic strategy that idealizes the individual's, or perhaps a group's, place as fitting within an ultimate harmony of the whole. The ultimate meaning of life, despite what it might seem sometimes, is that one is fundamentally at home in the cosmos. Zhang Zai's oft-quoted "Western Inscription" is a classic exhibit of this strategy:

> Heaven is my father and Earth is my mother, and even such a small creature as I finds an intimate place in their midst. Therefore that which fills the universe I regard as my body and that which directs the universe I consider as my nature. All people are my brothers and sisters, and all things are my companions. The great ruler (the emperor) is the eldest son of my parents (Heaven and Earth), and the great ministers are his stewards. Respect the aged—this is the way to treat them as elders should be treated. Show deep love toward the orphaned and the weak—this is the way to treat them as the young should be treated. The sage identifies his character with that of Heaven and Earth, and the worthy is the most outstanding man. Even those who are tired, infirm, crippled, or sick; those who have no brothers or children, wives or husbands, are

all my brothers who are in distress and have no one to turn to. When the time comes, to keep himself from harm—this is the care of a son. To rejoice in Heaven and to have no anxiety—this is filial piety at its purest. He who disobeys [the Principle of Nature] violates virtue. He who destroys humanity is a robber. He who promotes evil lacks [moral] capacity. But he who puts his moral nature into practice and brings his physical existence into complete fulfillment can match [Heaven and Earth]. One who knows the principles of transformation will skillfully carry forward the undertakings [of Heaven and Earth], and one who penetrates spirit to the highest degree will skillfully carry out their will. Do nothing shameful in the recesses of your own house and thus bring no dishonor to them. Preserve your mind and nourish your nature and thus (serve them) with untiring effort. . . . Wealth, honor, blessing, and benefits are meant for the enrichment of my life, while poverty, humble station, and sorrow are meant to help me to fulfillment. In life I follow and serve [Heaven and Earth]. In death I will be at peace.[4]

This strategy first schematizes the conception of the self to the ultimate principles, in Zhang Zai's case Heaven and Earth, which the Neo-Confucians developed into the technical notions of Principle and Material Force. The schematic rule is that the person is the child of the ultimate, and thus finds place as a microcosm of the whole. Additional schemata give ultimate meaning to moral responsibilities, to the development of the wholeness of the self, to the engagement of all others as brothers and sisters and of nature as one's companions, and to the meaning of death—peace in the bosom of the cosmos.

The Confucian traditions have much variety and internal controversy, and not all would accept Zhang Zai's interpretation of Heaven and Earth. But for the most part, Confucians do not look to transcendent sources of ultimate meaning, such as an afterlife of Heaven. In fact, most would regard that as superstitious. Rather, they look for meaning in the ways by which the ultimate principles are intimate in their individual lives. Generally, Heaven is the source of norms and order, and Earth is the source of energy and actualization. The ultimate meaning of life on this view is that one's own life, however painful, wretched, and disharmonious it might be, still takes ultimate significance because it is a microcosm of the ultimate harmony of the cosmos, and can be felt ecstatically to be such.

Antidynamic macrocosmic identification is a strategy that refuses the dynamic play of the cosmos as a whole or of one's own personal life-story within the cosmos as an adequate schematization of ultimate reality. Change itself is the problem. The schematic strategy, rather, is to say that the ultimate meaning of ordinary life that changes, and suffers with change, lies in its truer identity with a deeper, underlying, unchanging macrocosmic reality. The ultimate meaning of life is abandonment of the particulars of life and merging into a deeper ocean of being. Sometimes this is an interpretation of the meaning of death—merging into the ocean of being. But in many schools of Hinduism much more technical symbols are worked out to interpret the identification with an unchanging macrocosmic reality. The ontological rule of schematizing in this strategy is to identify the unchanging reality. In the Hindu traditions alone, not to speak of Western mysticisms, lie a multitude of models, for instance, Brahman with qualities giving way to Brahman without qualities, or Vishnu or Shiva with avatars, or trinities of Godheads. The schematizing rule in these cases needs to say how their unchanging natures relate to change, either change within other aspects of their natures or change in a separate world. Identification of the changing individual with the unchanging also needs rules for schematization, the two basic kinds being complete nondualistic identification or dualistic identification. In the former, the particularities of the self vanish completely; in the latter, the person retains specific identity that still is identified with the macrocosmic unchanging reality. However identification with the unchanging goes, more rules are needed to schematize that identification to issues of moral life, of the cultivation of the self so as to behave properly within temporal life and also to escape to the unchanging, of engagements with others, particularly nature and social institutions as well as persons, and of the assessment of achievement. This antidynamic macrocosmic strategy usually does not stress any ultimate meaning in achievement within time, save that of release from time.

The antidynamic *microcosmic* strategy agrees that time and change are the problem, but instead of finding ultimate meaning in something unchanging, it finds ultimate meaning in identification with the bits of experience that simply are what they are in the moment. Very important for the center of gravity of Buddhist rhetoric, the schematizing rule here has to do with identifying the suchness of things. This is done metaphysically in various ways in the Buddhist schools, and also practically in meditational practices, monastic lifestyles, and the like. The ultimate meaning of the self is that there is no self beyond the dharmas that arise and cease in consciousness. The Buddhist schools give many interpretations of this. But all need to develop additional schematizing rules for constructing images of life within samsara as well as the life of the higher truth. Differences in conceptions of suchness give rise to different rules for meditation. Finding ultimate meaning in suchness is not limited to Buddhism, of course.

The four basic schematizing strategies mentioned here break into two groups, those employing the dynamics of the created order to symbolize the ultimate relative to human meaning, and those rejecting the dynamics in favor of that which does not change, or has no existence as changing. Is there right or wrong between them? Certainly there are different advantages to each side. But neither can be iconically right because neither expresses the eternity that contains temporal dynamism within it. The former steps away from eternity to inscribe certain ultimate traits on the spatiotemporality of the existential field. The latter steps away from temporality to inscribe ultimate traits on the static, not the eternal but simply the unchanging. Static unchangingness is a temporal category. To be sure, the great religions involve reflections that overcome this division. But to the extent that they do, they move to eternity and away from that which is accessible to ordinary people, by and large.

So the question remains, how can we tell whether these schematic strategies give rise to images of ultimate meaning that are true to the ultimate or whether they are false?

IV. THE TRUTH OF FINITE SYMBOLS OF ULTIMATE MEANING

For *Philosophical Theology*'s epistemology of symbolic engagement, truth is the carryover of value or what is important from the object interpreted into the interpreter in the respects in which the signs stand for the object (I, 2–3). "Standing for the object" is a matter of reference, and three kinds are noted.

For iconic reference truth is a correspondence of likeness between the sign (which is a complex extensional formulation within its semiotic system) and the object. Tests for truth in iconic reference often have to do with attempting some kind of comparison between sign and object, although the sign by itself is not the locus of truth; rather, the locus of truth is the purposive role the sign plays within the interpreter. The interpretive engagement itself is true if the interpreter's intentional behavior picks up on the likeness with the object.

For indexical reference, truth is a kind of correspondence between the object and the interpretive engagement that does not necessarily involve formal likeness between sign and object but rather a causal connection. The connection is such that what is valuable in the object, its value-identity, is discriminated in the intentional interpreter and manifest in thought and action. Testing the correspondence is not so much a matter of comparison as it is of identifying the value in the object by some independent means and then ascertaining whether, through the indexical interpretation, the interpreter has registered it and lives as shaped by that registration.

For conventional reference, abstracted from any intentional engagement with real objects, truth is the coherence or consistency of the signs with one another according to their syntax and semantic roles within the semiotic system. But the coherence does not necessarily show itself in terms of the logical or semantic compatibility of the signs themselves. Rather, it lies in how the interpreter can be coherent in the use of several networks of signs at once, even when the networks are not logically compatible. This is where the strength of metaphor lies. A person can know about tulips, and also know about crystal stemware. The crystal is named metaphorically after the flower, and in fact many people forget that it was ever metaphorical.[5] The crystal is not at all a flower. But the sign systems can be used coherently if the interpreter does not try to drink out of the flower, and puts water around the stem of the flower but in the globe of the crystal. The two networks of signs are coherent without being inter-translatable or logically connected when behavior guided by them is coherent.

People's engagement with ultimacy in the search for an ultimate meaning of human existence, especially at the level of ecstatic fulfillment, is rarely a single concrete act of interpretive engagement. Rather, it is a series of such engagements, made in many different contexts, over many years, with a growing and shifting set of symbols. The symbols may come variously from their religious tradition(s) as understood differently at different times in life. Religiously it makes more sense to speak of a life, or a specific period of life, of engaging ultimacy in respect of finding ultimate meaning. The various acts of engagement in the buildup of this habitual interpretive identity involve all kinds of reference: indexical, iconic, and conventional.

For the most part, ordinary people assume (1) that their interpretations are indexical because they look out causally on the real world, (2) that their interpretations are also iconic because the world is simply what they see through them, and (3) that their sign systems are so transparent that their coherence is never an issue. Or, at least this is the model of innocence that philosophers and theologians often have ascribed to ordinary people and their religion. In actual fact, most ordinary people are troubled at one time or another by whether their signs in fact engage the world, whether they are deceived in what they are told they see, and by whether their theologies are coherent.

But assume the innocence model for the moment. A religious person attempts to find ultimacy in signs that refer to ultimacy iconically in ways that are false, that at best are schematizations of the ontological ultimate, or one or all of the four cosmological ultimates. The true ultimate is eternal and the intimate symbols for them treat them as if they are finite and finite only, not finite/infinite contrasts. How can it be determined whether those schema-images are true or false?

The general answer to this is that the truth or falsity depends on the particular cases, the individuals making the meaning-seeking interpretive engagements of ultimacy. In a given case, considering the lifetime stretch of the case perhaps, does the central ontological schematization lead the person to accept and make appropriate responses to the gratuity, arbitrariness, undeservedness, and surprisingness of the radical contingency of the ontological act of creation? Does engagement through the symbols of a finite creator God do this? Or the symbols of being a microcosm at home in the ultimate macrocosm? Or the symbols of merging into a deeper, nonchanging reality? Or the symbols of suchness? Then, with respect to engaging ultimate meaning with respect to form/possibilities/obligation, do the symbolic schematizations of a divine lawgiver, or following Heaven, or fulfilling one's dharma, or the Eightfold Noble Path, carryover the ultimate meaning of obligation? Or, for instance, do they limit justice to one's in-group? With respect to engaging ultimate meaning in the project of comporting oneself toward the components of life, do the schematizing strategies associated with the other schemata lead to an understanding of the ultimate meaning of wholeness, or not? With respect to the ultimacy of engagement in the existential field, do the schema-images lead to accepting the love and care required of that engagement to be of ultimate meaning? Do the schematic strategies of the particular religious culture provide schema-images of absolute value-identity that are ultimately meaningful? These are all empirical questions, to be determined case by case, good work for a spiritual director steeped in the varying symbologies of the world religions and secular cultures. The connections to be checked out include the culture of the engaged interpreter, in terms of which the ultimate must be schematized to be meaningful, the transcendent meanings of ultimacy that answer questions of ultimate meaning, and the embodiment of the interpretive symbols in the person's life.

None of the religious symbols of ultimacy is true or false in itself. Truth or falsity apply only to intentional interpretive engagements, and in the case of religion to the life lived according to them, insofar as they are employed to address the questions of ultimate meaning. The logic of all this dovetails in part with the elaborate discussions of sacred worldviews in *Philosophical Theology*. The difference is that the sacred worldviews need to be true to orient engagements throughout the various mundane domains of life as well as within the domain of the sacred canopy. Here the question is whether the sacred canopy itself can be employed to engage the question of the ultimate meaning of things.

A more specific answer lies at hand to the truth question regarding iconically false but innocently held interpretations of ultimate meaning. In the formula for truth, namely, the carryover of value from the object into the interpreter in the respects in which the signs stand for the object, we now have a small theory of what those "respects" of representation might be. They are the rules for schematizing some aspect of the ultimate into the experiential terms of the person's cultural and semiotic systems; they produce schema-images in the person's intimate terms. For instance, in what respect does the conception of a very large but determinate creator God stand for the ontological act of creation? The answer is, in the respect of schematizing radical contingency, with the gratuitousness, arbitrariness, undeservedness, and surprise that is the way its value is grasped. Now the schema-image of a determinate God, say, Yahweh in the pillar of fire, or in the throne room, or in the still small voice, cannot be iconically true; as determinate, God conceived that way would have to be a creature. But it can be indexically true in leading often, and for many people, to the grasp of the gratuitousness, arbitrariness, undeservedness, and surprise of the contingent act of creating the world. Many of the psalms in the Hebrew Bible employ graphic images of God in determinate form but for millennia have led people to appreciation of the radical contingency of creation. Similarly, theologians can understand how schema-images of justice and obligation, wholeness, engagement of others, and achievement of value-identity, while replete with finite-only culturally defined images, still are schematizations of the various cosmological ultimates. Understanding the rules of schematization is helpful in discerning, case by case, whether the finite images of ultimacy in fact are grasped truthfully so as to carry over truly ultimate meaning.

Chapter 9 here explored the possibility of ultimate meaning being conveyed through apocalyptic narratives that deny the ontological eternity of the created world, and it argued that they cannot. Chapter 10 has explored the possibility of ultimate meaning being conveyed through symbol systems that do not deny ontological eternity but that understand it only as schematized into what roughly can be called the temporal realm, the realm interpreted in terms of the existential field rather than the ontological act of creation. It has developed a notion of schematism, taking off from Kant, and illustrated it with four vague classes of schematic strategies: dynamic macrocosmic idealization, dynamic microcosmic idealization, antidynamic macrocosmic identification, and antidynamic microcosmic identification. Finally, the chapter has asked how schema-images of the ultimate in meaning might be true that are innocently taken to be iconic when in fact they can refer truly only indexically. The answer, as it has been given since the beginning of *Philosophical Theology*, is that this must be decided empirically on a case by case basis. Now, with the theory of schematism, much more detail has been added to the needs of the empirical analysis.

Of course, in theology of this sort, we do not analyze theological truth claims on a case by case basis for each person in each context. Rather, we deal with types, and types of contexts, and types of symbolism. But this means that in theology of this sort we cannot actually determine the truth or falsity of a symbolic engagement for any actual individual.

The argument now moves from the analysis of how ordinary people find ultimate meaning in religious forms that convey ecstatic fulfillment to how religious virtuosi do it, finding ways of transcending the need to translate the eternal into the temporal with literal belief.

Chapter Eleven

Ecstatic Love

The first two chapters of this part discussed how the issues of eschatology, "last things," constitute the problematic of finding ultimate meaning in life, beginning with literal interpretations of last things as apocalyptic narrative and then examining ways by which ultimate meaning is sought in reference to the five ultimate realities articulated philosophically. The engagements with ultimacy in the question of meaning were studied as they are expressed by religious symbols from various religions, as well as through philosophical concepts. Building on the argument in Chapter 9, the claim was made in Chapter 10 that the ultimate meaning of life is gratitude. Gratitude is parsed in four modes, corresponding to the four traits of the ontological creative act as engaged by human beings: gratuity, arbitrariness, undeservedness, and surprisingness. To have a meaningful life, or to see life's meaning, is to engage the ontological creative act, including its terminus in the radically contingent cosmos, with the acceptance of being or existence relative to its gratuity, with acknowledgment of singularity relative to its arbitrariness, with ontological humility relative to its undeservedness, and with self-transcending awe or astonishment at its surprisingness. Most of the Axial Age religions have an abundance of symbols for embracing the ultimate in this sense so as to find ultimate meaning.

At the same time, the religions have indicated that something more is possible for those who commit themselves to religious virtuosity. What have been discussed in the previous two chapters are functions of religious practice within sacred worldviews that at least allege to provide an ultimately meaningful life. These considerations concern finding the signs and contexts for interpretive engagements of ultimacy relative to "last things." Religious adepts or virtuosi attempt to turn themselves and their lives, or at least significant elements in their lives, into concrete signs that connect directly with the ontological creative act. Chapters 15 and 16 of *Philosophical Theology One* develop the point about becoming signs that are at once part of the constitution of the person and also within which the ultimate is present, particularly in forms of mystical development. To a degree limited by the respects in which the signs stand for the ultimate, the intentional causal process from the person to the ultimate ontological reality engaged is the same as the causal process by which the person is created, viewed from opposite directions.

This and the following chapter develop the theme of how being a sign of ultimacy is itself a finite/infinite contrast of being within a semiotic system, including one's own meaningful self, and knowing that the system itself is arbitrary. To be such an achieved sign for engaging ultimacy is to live on the cusp where an achieved sign-status is confronted with its own arbitrariness and inadequacy, something only religious virtuosi are able to grasp and endure. But it is an ecstatic fulfillment. These chapters continue the meditation on religious virtuosi. This chapter addresses some of the issues of obtaining ultimate meaning by becoming ontologically grateful in ways that directly connect with ultimacy. The following chapter addresses the result of this in freedom. Virtuosity, of course, is a matter of degrees. Many ordinary religious people become religious virtuosi in certain respects and to a certain degree. The distinction between ordinary people and virtuosi does not hold in any rigid way. Nevertheless the discussion here concerns heroes.

The general thesis of this chapter is that the interpretive engagement of the ontological creative act with regard to giving ultimate meaning, ecstatic fulfillment, is through cultivating the signs for responding with ontological gratitude, that is, with acceptance of being, acknowledgment of singularity, ontological humility, and astonishment and awe. Beyond this, the virtuoso engagement of the ontological creative act transforms these grateful responses into forms of ecstatic ontological love: the adept becomes a lover of the ultimate in the relevant respects. Everyone can be grateful. Seriously to love the ontological creative act, however, is a special virtuoso achievement.

The sections of this chapter discuss four modes of ontological love.

I. GRATUITY

The ontological creative act creates the world of determinate things for no reason (*I, pt. 3*). The creative act has no determinateness apart from what it creates, because all determinate things require being created. Therefore, there could be no reason to create the world, although the world created has value. The ontological creative act therefore is entirely gratuitous. It is a sheer giving of existence to the world.

One of the principal early uses of the word "religio" meant the duty of gratitude that everyone owes to God for the creation. Thomas Aquinas, for instance, wrote that "*Religio* is a virtue because it pays the debt of honor to God."[1] For Thomas, religion is a duty for all people because all people can understand creation, he thought. Religion in this sense for him did not mean anything having to do with revelation, and so religion does not involve worship of the Christian Trinity, which he thought could be known only through revelation, for instance. Unfortunately for most people, according to Thomas, original sin has distorted their vision of creation and therefore prevents them from being properly religious; Christian revelation is needed to correct original sin and therefore, he thought, only Christians are properly religious.[2] Thomas, of course, overgeneralized his Christian categories. Daoists and Buddhists, each in their own ways, appreciate the radical contingency of the cosmos but would not express this in terms of agency of divine creation. Nonetheless, the radical contingency of the cosmos is a common enough symbol of existence that gratitude for its gratuity can be expected to be widespread.

Gratitude for the givenness of the cosmos, as argued earlier, means the acceptance of the cosmos, or of existence. Without the gratuitous ontological creative act, there would not be anything, and recognition that there is something under this circumstance involves the response of accepting the ontological act.

If life were all pleasant, grateful acceptance would be easy. For some fortunate people, perhaps it is. But for most people life is filled with pain as well as pleasure. Existence has all the predicaments (and more) discussed in *Philosophical Theology Two*. And everyone dies. Job's case was extreme, but not rare. Not all people are easily grateful for being born and some are convinced that the entire cosmos is an inhuman cataclysm of brute heat and cold. In light of the comforts of religion, it is possible but often not easy to develop the capacity to be grateful for existence itself.

To love the gratuitous character of the creative act is a more difficult matter. Jonathan Edwards had perhaps the most succinct analysis of this, which he called "true virtue." Virtue, he says, is a kind of beauty, namely, the beauty of the heart or will. In what does this beauty consist? "True virtue most essentially consists in benevolence to Being in general. Or perhaps to speak more accurately, it is that consent, propensity, and union of heart to Being in General that is immediately exercised in a general good will."[3] He goes on to say that

> Beauty does not consist in discord and dissent, but in consent and agreement. And if every intelligent being is some way related to Being in general, and is a part of the universal system of existence; and so stands in connection with the whole; what can its general and true beauty be, but its union and consent with the great whole.... When I say, true virtue consists in love to Being in general, I shall not be likely to be understood, that no one act of the mind or exercise of love is of the nature of true virtue but what has Being in general, or the great system of universal existence, for its *direct* and *immediate* object: so that no exercise of love or kind affection to any one particular being, that is but a

small part of this whole, has anything of the nature of true virtue. . . . [T]hough, from such a disposition may arise exercises of love to particular beings, as objects are presented and occasionally arise.[4]

Edwards makes many other distinctions that need not be investigated here, including a limitation of Being in general to intelligent beings, not to the whole of nature (a departure from his usual treatment of nature). One further distinction is germane, however. Edwards distinguishes the love of *complacence* from the love of *benevolence*. The former is the love of beauty in the object. Simple gratitude for the gratuitousness of creation might include complacence with the beauty it holds. But benevolence is the beauty of the relation between the lover and Being in general, the consent, propensity, and union of heart. Benevolence wills the well-being of Being in general.

Adopting something of Edwards's account, we can understand ontological love of the created order as consent, propensity, and union of heart toward Being in general, or toward the cosmic realm of determinate things. (*Philosophical Theology*'s analysis of determinate things as harmonies is itself derivative from and consonant with Edwards's analysis of things as harmonies, each with its own beauty and excellence, and in relation to other things.[5]) How can this be understood in the terms of *Philosophical Theology*?

Benevolent love toward the ontological creative act creating the cosmos first needs some symbols for identifying the cosmos, the "whole" of which Edwards speaks. Edwards did not have in mind some specific sense of totality when he wrote. He would probably be happy to say that Being in general consists of anything that has determinate existence, whatever turns up. Benevolence loves this because this is an instance of Being in general. *Philosophical Theology Two*, Chapter 12, discusses some of the issues with developing signs for creation as such. These signs need to be concrete enough, and internalized enough, that they make possible a direct engagement of the cosmos as such, however limited that engagement is to the respects in which the signs stand for it.

Benevolence is a character of the heart, Edwards says. We need not accept his "faculty psychology" to appreciate his point, and can rephrase it as a character of intentionality toward the creation. He gives it three traits: consent, propensity, and union. Consent can be understood (and is by Edwards) as recognizing the creation (as symbolized), agreeing to it (acceptance), and willing it. This is to say, consent involves gratuitous willing of it, just as the ontological creative act is a gratuitous making. Propensity recognizes something of a distance between the human intender and the creation as a whole and signals a leaning toward the creation, not only a gratuitous willing of it but a move toward union with it. The third trait, union, signals the identification of the intender with the intended creation, at least in the respects in which the creation can be signified.

Virtuosity is required for "true virtue" because the ability actually to be in consent, propensity, and union with the creation—the ontological act inclusive of the determinate world created—is an extraordinary achievement. Most people can symbolize the creation only with abstractions, which are not objects of consent, propensity, and union of heart or intentionality except in equally abstract ways. To have love or benevolence of heart requires an object as concrete as the movements of the heart, and for this the adept needs to develop signs internal to the intentional self that deliver up the world concretely. The signs of the creation need to allow the creation to be felt, not only thought about with agreement, approval, and identification. And then the heart, that is, the soul with a wholeness that comes from extraordinary integration of the components of life, needs to develop the habits—the sign-driven behaviors—that constitute benevolence.

The virtuosity of this kind of benevolent love toward the creation itself involves also benevolence toward the four cosmological ultimates. Edwards's principal interest in his book was the development of a theory of ethics, or justice. Mastering the capacity for benevolence toward the creation requires wholeness. Actually being benevolent requires engaging others as creatures within creation. And the value achievement of being benevolent in this sense is the great beauty of being rightly related to the ultimacy of creation.

II. ARBITRARINESS

In the ontological creative act apart from creation, no reason can exist for why this particular world is created. Such a reason would make the ontological creative act determinate, and hence in need of being created along with the world by yet a more profound ontological creative act, which would then have no reason for its creating. Lacking a reason, the ontological creative act is arbitrary. It is free in the sense that nothing in its nature or in preestablished possibilities determines it to create or what to create. That the act is arbitrary in creating anything at all is conveyed in saying that the creation is gratuitous. That the act is arbitrary in what it creates is conveyed in saying that the creation is singular.

Mathematical physicists sometimes are biased to think that the ultimate explanatory principles of the world need to represent it as symmetrical, unitary in its equations, whole in some sense, infinitely full or infinitely empty. The Big Bang is represented as a homogeneous explosion at first, developing differentiation into uneven distributions of gasses that lead to clumpings in differently shaped star systems, in differently shaped galaxies, distributed unevenly through lumpy space-time. The universe as we find it is asymmetrical, and a problem in physics is to show how the original symmetry was broken to produce the asymmetrical universe.

The ontological bias of mathematical physics comes from the nature of the discipline, the assumption that mathematical symmetry must somehow be the ontological foundation for the cosmos.[6] Suppose, however, that the asymmetry of the observed universe is limited by the mathematical symmetry of whatever laws of nature obtain. In the evolution of the universe those events or things that do not find causal and contextual support from other things, as expressed in natural laws, cannot be sustained. So, mathematical symmetry can be found broadly spread across the universe, but only as applying in and across the pockets of order in the asymmetrical structure of the cosmos. The distribution of things in the cosmos is arbitrary, particular, singular. This is so even if, by chance, the Big Bang started out with symmetrical homogeneity. Recognition of the asymmetry or singularity of the cosmos does not need to deny the claim that the Big Bang is best conceived and explained in terms of the symmetrical biases of mathematics. Nor does the recognition of the arbitrary singularity of the universe need to suppose that the Big Bang theory is true, or that the Steady State theory is true, or that the multiple universes hypothesis with many Big Bangs is true. The only thing it supposes, or expresses, is that the ontological creative act creates a particular world. After the fact, given our created capacities to imagine possibilities, and given the created nature of possibility itself, we can imagine a world with a different distribution of stuff.

The singularity of the cosmos has been "known" ever since people noticed that the clear night sky is not a uniform blanket of stars and tried to find patterns (ultimately, explanatory symmetrical laws) in the nonuniform distribution. But the singularity has always been more noticeable at the human scale of things. People are not uniformly alike but differ in millions of obvious ways. Some societies are richer and more powerful than others. Cultures differ in how they do things and even in basic human things to do. Some individuals and groups seem favored over others, sometimes with noticeable rights to the favor and sometimes with the opprobrium of oppression and injustice. How the differences are noticed and interpreted depends on the different perspectives within which they are grasped. Perhaps there are natural laws (with symmetrical mathematics) that explain how certain processes work, for instance, how DNA is passed from generation to generation and expressed phenotypically in biochemical interactions. But to understand a particular person's biology a particular history is required, telling the story of that person's ancestors and biocultural context. The person's neighbor has a different biological nature because of a different history. Who one is, biologically, in the long run is singular and is to be understood only through a story.

Plato was careful never to define a "form" for human nature. People are particular mixtures of variables. There is no such thing as justice or the good life that applies uniformly to all people. The "moral" of Plato's *Republic* is this:

> And this is the chief reason why it should be a main concern that each of us, neglecting all other studies, should seek after and study this thing—if in any way he may be able to learn of and discover the man who will give him the ability and the knowledge to distinguish the life that is good from that which is bad, and always and everywhere to choose the best that the conditions allow, and, taking into account all the things of which

> we have spoken and estimating the effect on the goodness of his life of their conjunction or their severance, to know how beauty commingled with poverty or wealth and combined with what habit of soul operates for good or for evil, and what are the effects of high and low birth and private station and office and strength and weakness and quickness of apprehension and dullness and all similar natural and acquired habits of the soul, when blended and combined with one another, so that with consideration of all these things he will be able to make a reasoned choice between the better and the worse life, with his eyes fixed on the nature of his soul, naming the worse life that which will tend to make it more unjust and the better that which will make it more just.[7]

Note that Plato did not say that everyone could find a person who could help him (Plato was talking only about men, of course, although the point applies to women as well) sort the particulars of his life, or that, when sorted, everyone could necessarily follow through to choose the better life. These things, too, are arbitrary. Heidegger expressed a similar point in his concept of "thrownness." A person, which he called "Dasein," is "thrown" into existence with the particular nature or "facticity" he has: "As something thrown, Dasein has been thrown *into existence*. It exists as an entity which has to be as it is and as it can be."[8]

Just as people are singular—and their groups and circumstances—the powers of ultimacy are singular when they are represented as causing the world. Theistic expressions of ontological creation are rightly represented as arbitrary. The God of the Hebrew Bible plays favorites and is fickle at times. Christians interpret God as somewhat mysterious regarding who or what is saved. Muslims identify Allah with their own cause or say that their cause is Allah's cause. Of course, all these traditions have more sophisticated transcendent conceptions. But there is something right about the representation of God as arbitrary, because the creation is.

Now the singularity of life is noticed by nearly everyone. But most people have differential responses, accepting some of what life has given them but with preferences for other things in many instances. Among Plato's variables most people would rather be beautiful, rich, smart, and high-born rather than the opposite. Sometimes the facticity of life can be changed: a smart poor person might get rich, although a dull poor person is not likely to do so. Most of those variables do change through a lifetime of changing circumstances. But there are some things in the givenness of life that are simply there and must be accepted.

The religious adepts can go beyond accepting to embracing the singular creation. This embrace needs to include acceptance of the unfortunate particulars of life, and of one's fear, dislike, hate, or rejection of the particulars, including psychological denial. This is to say, the adepts embrace the life that kills them, and perhaps makes them suffer a great deal before mortal release.

Whereas the love of benevolence in grasping the gratuitousness of existence consents to "being in General," and to particular creatures, "beings in Particular," because of their relation to the creation as such, the love of the singularity of creation works first through the singular particulars. It is one thing to accept the creation in general as singular. It is a matter of virtuosity to embrace in love each of the important singularities of one's existence. Perhaps that can extend to embracing the singularity of the cosmos as a whole, especially if one has the imagination of a physicist or a poet. The hard part, through which virtuosity comes from building up capacities of loving embrace, is to love the local things.

III. UNDESERVEDNESS

The gratuitousness and arbitrariness of ontological creation are traits of the ontological act of creation itself. Undeservedness and surprise are traits of it in light of human expectations.

The undeservedness of creation means ontologically that there is no potential value in the possibility of the creation apart from the creative act itself. The world does not deserve to be created because of the value in its possibility. Therefore, Leibniz's scenario of God contemplating possible worlds and creating the best one has no metaphysical application.[9]

Nevertheless, the created world is made of determinate harmonies each of which has value. Moreover, the world is interconnected through harmonies of harmonies, and so the values of things are somewhat integrated into other values. Looked at from any perspective within the world, we can imagine how things might be different with different values, for better and worse. By no means are we in a position to say whether this is the best of all possible worlds, or even essay a guess about how valuable the world is. We have far too small a sample of the kinds of things that exist within the cosmos.

Nor can we ask meaningfully about whether the ontological creative act is "justified" in creating the world with whatever value it has. Justification in this sense would suppose that prior to creation the ontological creative act had the possibilities of creating or not creating, or creating this world or some other. Possibilities, being determinate, are themselves created products. Apart from creating them in creating the world, the ontological creative act could not have the possibility of creating or not creating, this world or some other, and so cannot be said to be "justified" by the value of what is created. The application of the notion of justification to the ontological creative act also supposes a strong analogy with human justification in which the agent is taken to know about the possibilities and their value, and to be under obligation to choose the best. But apart from creation, there is no ontological creative act with knowledge and obligation about which the question of justification might be raised. All these anthropomorphic attributions of moral standing to the ontological creative act, as in common conceptions of a monotheistic God, are stricken down by the radical contingency on the ontological creative act of anything determinate. This is what God said to Job, speaking out of the whirlwind, when he told Job that Job had no place to stand in judging God: any stance that would see God as determinate and standing under obligation and the need for justification would put God within the creation and not the creator of it. The anthropomorphizing of the ontological creative act in Job is entirely appropriate, it should be noted: an elaborate literary metaphor that makes its point while undermining any attempt to take it literally. The same literary anthropomorphizing is appropriate in the first creation account in Genesis according to which God just makes the elements of the world and then observes that they are good. Genesis does not suggest that God made them because they are good, or for any other reason either.

To apprehend the full depths of the value-identity of things of the world as undeserving of being created but simply having the value they possess requires a kind of love that includes profound humility. Ontological humility in this sense does not mean undervaluing oneself, or parts of the creation of which one is aware, or even the creation conceived abstractly as a whole. To the contrary it means the accurate and in-depth discernment of just what the value-identity of things is, including one's own. Knowing oneself is perhaps the hardest case because of all the motives for hiding one's faults. As noted, religions have many spiritual exercises such as meditation and confession—and institutionalized offices of self-examination and spiritual direction—that aid persons in coming to deep appreciations and assessments of themselves. The ontological humility that comes with this is the loving observation that "this is what I am and I am created to be this for no reason," and/or "despite the fact that this is what I am, I am created to be this for no reason." Something analogous holds for coming to appreciate the undeservedness of one's social group, and even nature as a whole, however that is symbolized. "My group has its value, and is created for no reason; despite the faults of my group, it is created for no reason." "Nature is a maelstrom of glories and catastrophes—Wow!—and is created for no reason." This is a peculiar kind of humility—accepting creation for what it is without feeling it to be justified or condemned.

Why call this love, and what kind of love is it? It is the "consent, propensity, and union of heart" with the particular parts of the creation loved precisely because of what they are as undeserved in any ontological sense. Virtuosity is required to come to terms with what things are and the fact that value is undeserved. Viewed in the context of other things, any thing is justified or not by all sorts of normative connections—moral, aesthetic, and so forth. But viewed as part of the undeserved status of creation, justification is not an issue. Engaging things with ontological humility is to love them for their own sakes, not for any other reason. Of course there may well be other reasons to love them, or to hate them, and this love and hate relation people have with most things in their ambiguous lives is part of a common human value-identity. Love in ontological humility is to embrace all that and love it anyway.

Gratitude for the undeserved creation turns to love when it masters the density of "consent, propensity, and union" that allows for the embrace of something, perhaps oneself, for its own sake without that being deserved in any sense relevant to the humble position. Most of the time, we love things because they help, fulfill, beautify, or otherwise enhance us. This is so even when we love things for the sheer beauty they have that gives us pleasure. Love in ontological humility mirrors in reverse the ontological creative act. Just as the creation does not "deserve" to be created because of some requirement prior to the act that needs to be fulfilled, so the creation does not "deserve" to be loved out of any human need to love and be enhanced by it. Ontological humility, when it is attained, lets us put aside our need to love the lovely and just love it for and in the created nature it has.

Developing this capacity for ontological love, like the others discussed in previous sections, requires the building up of signs within one's life, like building muscles and a nervous system attuned to playing the piano. These signs are real things, harmonies of a semiotic sort, and they have a material quality to them. If one attends only to the qualitative feel of those signs, as happens so often in the phenomenology of religious experience, then one is likely to lose the sense of intentionality that makes the signs part of symbolic engagements of the ontological act. So, just feeling humble is not enough. Feeling the worth of things in distinction from what they might be worth to oneself is not enough. These feelings of love need to be embedded in a kind of dialectic that keeps their intentional orientation in order.

IV. SURPRISE

The need for a dialectic of intentionality is nowhere more evident than in the case of the ontological love that consists in astonishment and awe at the trait of surprise in the ontological act of creation. Astonishment and awe are feelings of such powerful qualities that it is easy to dislocate them from their interpretive role in engagement with the ontological act. They have what Charles Peirce called "secondness," a kind of shock at resistance, a pushback from reality that does not pay much attention to the character of what is resisting.[10] Peirce said to imagine yourself suspended under a hot-air balloon over an industrial city in the dead of a cloudy night: nothing is heard or seen. Suddenly a super-loud factory whistle goes off, shattering the silence. You quickly come to identify the sound as a factory whistle, that is, interpret it in terms of other things you know. But the initial shock is "secondness," the abrupt obtrusion of a reality that you just have to take into account somehow. Alfred North Whitehead made a similar point when he said that a person seeing Niagara Falls for the first time should say "Wow!" before making any more articulate response.

The surprising character of creation, deriving from its gratuity and singularity and noticed as one assumes a loving humble position, is its "thisness." Thisness, or *haecceity* (the Latin word for thisness), is the absolutely singular character of a thing. In Western philosophy, the idea has been honed through dialectical discussions of the universal character of a thing, asking whether a particular thing can be understood in terms of a specification of all the universals that belong to it. Of course, we can never in practice (or even in theory) know all the universals or properties that a thing might have. But we can know its thisness. The actualization of a possibility, according to the cosmology employed in *Philosophical Theology*, is not merely a matter of excluding all alternatives with a possibility save one, although it is that. It is the making of the possibility chosen a "this." That is part of the meaning of spontaneous creativity in a present moment of actualization. The actualities from the past serve as potentialities for taking on the (new) form in the possibility chosen, and creativity within the moment is the welding of the actual potentialities and the possibility chosen. The possibilities apart from being actualized are universals in the sense that they might be actualized in any number of actual things. But once they are in fact actualized, they become "thises." Duns Scotus pointed out that, while they are actualized in "thises," they still have their universal characters, which he called "common natures." Thus all human beings have (let us suppose for the sake of argument) the common nature of "humanity." Yet no two people are human in exactly the same way: each is a "this human." The common nature is "contracted" into a "this," but still might be common to another "this" that contracts it differently.

Every creature in a space-time existential continuum is, in its actuality, a "this." Even if one knew all the possibilities that go into a thing, its sheer thisness is a surprise. Because we so often approach things looking for the properties that might help or harm us, we pay more attention to "what" things are rather than "that" they are. In fact, to say that we engage things interpretively is to require that the interpretive sign refer to something like a universal property of the thing. The signs themselves are all universal, and insofar as the reference in the interpretation is iconic it treats the object as a congeries of universals. But actual objects are more than congeries of universals. They are each this thing they are with universal properties. They have a secondness to them that sometimes can be noticed. The Scotistic poet Gerard Manley Hopkins extolled thisness in his often-quoted poem "Pied Beauty":

Glory be to God for dappled things—
> For skies of couple-colour as a brinded cow;
>> For rose-moles all in stipple upon trout that swim;
> Fresh-firecoal chestnut-falls; finches' wings;
>> Landscape plotted and pieced—fold, fallow, and plough;
>>> And all trades, their gear and tackle and trim.
All things counter, original, spare, strange;

> Whatever is fickle, freckled (who knows how?)
>   With swift, slow; sweet, sour; adazzle, dim;
> He fathers-forth whose beauty is past change:
>   Praise him.[11]

The point about thisness can be made easily with regard to physical things, because we all know what we mean when speaking of this and that; the philosophical dialectic just rehearsed puts it in a philosophical context. But there also is something like thisness in pure forms. A mathematician knows, of course, that, say, numbers are universals—"two" characterizes every pair. And yet "two" is uniquely what it is, a "this" relative to other numbers. It has properties, being twice "one" and half of "four," but it has its properties because it is exactly this number that it is. This sense of formal "exactness" is a kind of thisness. The creation contains things that, insofar as they are determinate, are "thises" in some sense. Insofar as they are also partly indeterminate, they are possible "thises."

The Scotistic focus on thisness has not been the dominant strain within Western philosophy, although most philosophers get the point between universals and particulars. But in Buddhist philosophy and practice the recognition of "suchness" has indeed been a dominant theme. In some sense, the ability to discipline experience so as to experience things "such as they are" is the goal of most meditative practices. Many Buddhist metaphysical debates have been about just what a dharma is so as to have no own-nature but to be nothing more than such as it is.

The virtuoso's ontological love that consists in grasping things with astonishment and awe at their surprising nature requires cultivation of the experiential powers to grasp things in their suchness. Poets like Hopkins can help many people get the point in certain instances. Years of Zen training can develop virtuoso habits of experiencing with suchness. This training supposes consent, propensity, and union in ontological love of the created things simply in their contingent being. The training supposes ontological love of the singularities in the arbitrary creation, and it supposes the humility of loving things for their own value-identity with one's own interests taken out of the picture. But it is more than all these, or a deeper dimension of them: it is an astonishment and awe, indeed disinterested delight, at the gratuitous, arbitrary, undeserved suchness of creation, part by part.

As has been argued throughout *Philosophical Theology*, virtuoso religious engagement of ultimate things requires the development of special capacities that function as signs that pick up on the deeper elements of ultimacy in order to enable ecstatic fulfillment. These capacities, these signs, have their own material nature. The signs themselves can be stimulated or produced by a variety of means—they are neurological events subject to whatever can cause them. But they do not function as signs except insofar as they are within the intentional stance of engaging ultimacy. In Peirce's language, the quality or firstness of the signs is often so overwhelming that the intentional stance is lost or bewildered, losing the sense of reference to the ultimate as object and the sense of the act of interpreting in some context. The qualitative feel of the signs—awe and astonishment in this instance—might not have any force in interpretive engagement. For it to have that force, for the engagement to be real, the intentional stance must be sustained through the engagement.

In dealing with ordinary objects, even awesome ones such as Niagara Falls or the factory whistle in the dead of night, it is usually possible to move from awe to a more logically spread out interpretation, recovering the intentional stance. In the case of religious engagements, however, the very point of the engagement is to close up the distance between the object, the sign in the interpreter's life, and the interpreter's life itself as it interprets the sign. Experiences of love of the sort under discussion here are powerfully immediate—they drop off distinctions between the objects and the loving engagement of them. But they cannot drop the intentional stance without ceasing to be engagements as such.

The means of maintaining the intentional stance is the dialectical interplay between the experiential engagements and the philosophical interpretation of them relative to the theory of ultimacy. Something like this happens in most of the Axial Age religions, which is why they all have various and often competing philosophical systems. *Philosophical Theology* has developed its own philosophy for this purpose. This chapter has illustrated the dialectic of pointing to the virtuoso experiences and interpreting them relative to the ultimacy of the ontological creative act.

When the monotheistic religions talk about loving God, one connotation of that love is loving God as one would a person. But God cannot be a person without requiring a deeper God to create the ontological context of mutual relevance. So it might seem that it is improper to speak of "loving God." If God is the ontological act of creation, however, determinate only and precisely in the world created, then the ontological love of God can be as complex and deep as described here in reference to the traits of gratuity, arbitrariness, undeservedness, and surprisingness of that creative act.

The dialectical rigor of these reflections matches the strenuous virtuosity of love under discussion. It rises to the high level of a powerful strain of ecstatic fulfillment. Without belying the complexity of what has been said, surely it is true that the ecstatic fulfillment of love has to have an easy moment. The symbols discussed here have been pushed to their transcendent limits. What are their intimate interpretations? Love has the most intimate touch. And perhaps ordinary people with no claim to virtuosity can manage that touch with the properly intimate songs. Consider "Jesus Christ the Apple Tree," a song published in New England in 1784:

The tree of life my soul hath seen, laden with fruit and always green:
The trees of nature fruitless be compared with Christ the apple tree.

His beauty doth all things excel: by faith I know but ne'er can tell
The glory which I now can see in Jesus Christ the apple tree.

For happiness I long have sought, and pleasure dearly I have bought:
I missed of all; but now I see 'tis found in Christ the apple tree.

I'm weary with my former toil, here I will sit and rest a while:
Under the shadow I will be, of Jesus Christ the apple tree.

This fruit does make my soul to thrive, it keeps my dying faith alive;
Which makes my soul in haste to be with Jesus Christ the apple tree.[12]

Not the breathless passion of bhakti religion, this is the intimate slow peaceful passion of one who perceives the world as loving and lovely and in that perception loves back. The song supposes deep knowledge and understanding of the biblical and traditional symbols of Jesus, but in order to put them aside. How outrageous to suggest that Jesus Christ is an apple tree! There is no biblical mention of that. In fact, the tree of the fall in the Garden of Eden in the Genesis story was long called an apple tree. Some legends have it that the tree of the cross on which Jesus died was that same apple tree, and that was not a beautiful sight! Or was it? The crucifixion is part of who Jesus was and that somehow is beautiful. But the crucifixion is not rehearsed in the song. The apple tree as Jesus Christ is the symbol of the gratuitousness of existence, of its arbitrariness and singularity, of the fact nothing in existence is deserved, of its surprising grace. More fruitful than other trees, more beautiful than all beautiful things, more happy and pleasurable than all other things sought, the perfect rest after toil, the apple tree nourishes the soul even in dying "which makes my soul in haste to be with Jesus Christ the apple tree." Ecstatic fulfillment! It can be sensed by just about anyone who thoughtfully sings the song.

CHAPTER TWELVE

Ecstatic Freedom

Love and freedom in their ultimate dimensions, apparently different, are two virtuoso religious achievements that mirror, in a way, the ontological act of creation. They are ways of grasping a person's own reality as part of the end product of that ontological act. Participation in either is a profound kind of ecstatic fulfillment that finds diverse symbolic articulations in many religions and also outside of traditional religions. Love in the highest sense is making something good for no reason: this is the gratuity of the ontological act of creation. Freedom in the highest sense is acting or making without constraints: the arbitrariness of the ontological act of creation. The previous chapter and this one attempt to make these theses plausible through the accumulation of detail.

Freedom, of course, has meant a great many things as applied to human beings. In keeping with the distinction that has been developed throughout *Philosophical Theology*, the various ways of being free within the world can be called "cosmological" freedom, and the ways of being free with regard to the ontological act of creation can be called "ontological" freedom. The main purpose of this chapter is to explore ontological freedom. But this can be done only against a background of cosmological freedom, which is treated in the first section. The exercise or possession of any or all of the elements of cosmological freedom (eight are described here) is not a matter of ecstatic fulfillment unless connected with ontological freedom.

1. COSMOLOGICAL FREEDOM

Cosmological freedom can be divided roughly into two sorts, personal freedom and social freedom. Personal freedom has four main topics: external liberty, intentional action, free choice, and creativity. Social freedom also has four main topics: freedom of opportunity, of social pluralism, of integral social life, and of political life.[1] Each one of these senses of freedom has been taken to be *the* meaning of freedom by some set of authors. In fact, however, freedom involves all of them in various dimensions, and even together they do not exhaust the meaning of freedom, which also involves the ontological senses of freedom.

"Man is born free, and yet we see him everywhere in chains."[2] The first and most obvious sense of personal freedom is to be free of external bondage. To be free is not to be in chains, not to be in jail, not to be a slave where disobedience leads to immediate bondage. Philosophers discussing freedom sometimes neglect this sense of freedom because it is far from their experience. People in prison know about it, however, whether they are there because of criminal misdeeds or political opposition, justly incarcerated or not. Chattel slavery is still practiced in various parts of the world as of this writing. The memory of chattel slavery only 150 years ago is still fresh in the minds of many contemporary African Americans. Some cultures today in the Muslim world and Africa practice a form of slavery for women who are put in bondage for disobedience. The language of bondage has been metaphorized to relate to many other senses of freedom and its lack, but the intent here is to talk about freedom in the literal sense of external liberty or freedom from bondage. Philosophers know that bondage is a kind of dialectical relationship, with the master being bound to the slave in a strange sort of way, needing the slave in order to maintain the identity of being master. Rousseau went on to make this point in the passage immediately after the sentence quoted earlier. Hegel made the point with elaborate brilliance in the "Lordship and Bondage" section of the *Phenomenology of Mind*.[3] Those forms of psychological bondage are real, but are not what is meant by the deprivation of external liberty plain and simple. Many African Americans believe that their ethnic culture puts them in psychological bondage and that this culture is the result of slavery. But the cultural bondage of which they speak now is better understood in the terms of issues of social freedom. Who has external liberty and of what sort is an empirical matter. Although unlikely, it is conceivable that every human being might attain external liberty.

In addition to external liberty is the freedom of intentional action, the freedom to do in fact what one wants. Some causal determinists, such as Spinoza and Jonathan Edwards, believe this is the only kind of personal freedom there is. Spinoza in his *Ethics* described it as "conatus," a will to continue in active motion, limited only by external forces to which one necessarily is passive. He associated happiness with the ability to be active rather than passive. Edwards in his *Freedom of the Will* argued against free choice, saying that true freedom was simply to be able to act on intentions. Empirically, being able to act on intentions is not always natural or easy. Children need to be taught to organize and straighten out their intentions, and to follow through with actions. Edwards distinguished between real actions and mere "wouldings," what one "would do if one were to act." Many people have great intentions but lack the character to act on them, or the skill to act well and successfully (*III, 11*). How free one is in the matter of "getting one's act together" depends on the kind of task at hand, one's stage of life, one's practice, and a variety of other factors. As with external liberties, freedom of intentional action has degrees.

Freedom of choice supposes both external liberties—that is, real possibilities for acting—and competent freedom of intentional action. But it is more. No moral responsibility is possible if the alleged agent does not make the morally relevant difference concerning what happens. If, as determinists say, every intentional action is completely determined by prior conditions, then it is those conditions that are responsible for what happens, not the alleged intentional action. Therefore, choice between live options must be possible in cases of potential responsibility. This means, first, that there must be real live options, alternative possibilities any of which might be chosen. Second, the agent has to be able to recognize and interpret those possibilities; sometimes there are real live options that people miss, and other times they think they have a real option when in fact the outcome is predetermined—elements of freedom empirically to be determined. Third, the agent in a moment of present creativity must be the author of the choice, choosing one option to be actualized and the others excluded. In *Philosophical Theology* this has been a theme of the characterization of the present moment as a spontaneous making of something new out of old actualities and within the limitations of immediately future possibilities. If in fact a free option exists among alternative possibilities, then the past conditions do not wholly determine the choice. The choice is part of the spontaneous coming to be of the agent in the present moment. Among the past conditions are likely to be motives of various sorts coming from past inertia and from previous analysis of what the possibilities are worth. If the motives totally determine the choice, then the choice is not free, only a "mechanical" outcome of the prior motives. Sometimes, as with some addictions, it would appear that a person is free when in fact the motive appeal of the addiction is overwhelming. But in many circumstances a choice is presented with many conflicting motives, none of which is overwhelming. The choice then consists of choosing a possibility and making the motive associated with it *the* motive for the agent in that choice. This is to say, free choice involves adopting a determining motive concomitant adopting the action or possibility associated with it. One gives oneself the moral character of acting on the motive that one chooses. This is the basis of responsibility as that has been discussed throughout *Philosophical Theology*. Thus we can say, regarding the fourth condition of free choice, that one gives oneself the responsible character of being the one who chooses the motives for choice associated with the possibilities chosen. Any free choice not only determines what happens, which would be indeterminate otherwise, but the responsible character of the chooser in respect of that choice.

In addition to the freedom to choose, therefore, is the freedom to choose on the basis of standards. To sort through the values of the alternative possibilities, and the motives associated with choosing any of them, is sometimes possible. One is freer the more one is able to sort through those motives so that the better ones become real possibilities. By understanding the motives better, the values involved, one increases the possibilities that face one for choice—one is free to choose *a*, or *b*, *a—because it is good*, or *b—because it is selfishly bad*. "Standards" is a nontechnical placeholder term for any kind of moral or aesthetic reasoning: standards can be rules, policies, contextual value judgments, senses of dharma and duty—whatever might constitute something of a motive that one can adopt as one's own in making a choice. The better educated one is in these things, the freer one is to make choices on the basis of standards in some sense or other. The current emphasis on virtue ethics emphasizes education in the discernment of the important standards for choices, and the theme of discernment of values relative to standards is at the core of Confucianism.

The best education in these matters, however, is in learning to be creative, to think outside the box, to discern possible connections with motives most people would miss. Living the moral life, as Dewey so often emphasized, is a matter of being creative in seeing value possibilities that most people would miss. This is the limitation of virtue ethics.

Among the social dimensions of freedom, the freedom of opportunity comes first, and is in a rough parallel with the personal freedom of external liberty. A person might be free from jail and able to take any job, but with no job opportunities. A society is freer to the extent that it provides opportunities for people to do what they might want, that is, opportunities for intentional action. A society is freer the more alternative choices it offers people, even when some of the choices are bad (not all kinds of freedom are good). A society is freer the more educational opportunities it offers for learning how to make good choices, and for learning how to be creative in making choices.

At least three dimensions of society are relevant for judging its kinds and degrees of freedoms of opportunity. One is the freedom to participate in culture. It was mentioned earlier that American slavery was destructive of the native cultures of Africans brought to be slaves, and it also denied the slaves access to many dimensions of American culture. This point should not be stressed too much because the slaves created a new culture of their own, which then became a rich addition to the larger polyglot American culture. In our own time, however, we can see the destruction of nearly any effective culture in some of the chaotic, war-ravaged lands of Africa. Moreover, the under classes in many large cities around the world have meager cultures. The main provision a society can make for freedom to participate in culture is education. Societies differ in the freedom they offer in this respect. A second dimension of freedom of opportunity is that of participating in organized society. Many groups are isolated from the political process, and from taking advantage of school systems, judicial systems, and the economy. A society is the more free the more it offers diverse groups the opportunity to participate in its organized structures. A third dimension of freedom of opportunity is harder to state. It is the opportunity to participate in historical action, to be a player in an historical moment. Some societies offer many opportunities to do this, but others do not. As Hegel pointed out, people who are not part of history are somewhat "unreal": if they had not existed nothing would have been different.[4]

The freedom of social pluralism is the freedom a society offers for different cultures to coexist. This is particularly important for minorities, but also important for any group with a distinctive culture. Social pluralism, of course, is itself a cultural matter: a culture for tolerating diverse cultures is a rare thing, although not without historical precedent. The Roman Empire prided itself on having a culture that, within rather broad limits, tolerated many different cultures, including administrative or political cultures, so long as allegiance to the Empire was observed. The ideal is now associated with democracy, and with the facts of modern economic life that require people to be mobile and to work with others whose cultures are different. Freedom is limited for persons, families, or groups that find themselves living in a society that does not tolerate their culture and give it opportunities for vigorous participation in the society, for access to the society's organized structures, and for a place in the society's history.

Cutting obliquely across the drive for social pluralism is the drive for a freedom for integral social life. As discussed at various places throughout *Philosophical Theology*, many people belong to multiple cultures and have memberships in diverse groups. How can they integrate their lives with a style that has integrity? This question has been posed in terms of developing a worldview that integrates different memberships and cultures. Here it is sufficient to note that societies are more or less tolerant of individuals who develop idiosyncratic lifestyles. Monocultural societies, or societies with very dominant cultures, tend to be hostile to those who walk their own way. This is so especially with cultures that emphasize an in-group character with hostility toward out-groups. The freedom one has to live according to an idiosyncratic lifestyle is an empirical matter concerning one's culture.

The freedom of participatory democracy has to do with one's ability to determine the conditions under which decisions are made in one's society. Participatory democracy does not usually mean one-person-one-vote, although it might mean that in small groups. Rather it means participation in setting the conditions for decision-making. This freedom supposes the personal freedoms involved in being an accomplished actor in the social arena. But it also involves avenues of access to power so that one who wants to participate can do so without being excluded for irrelevant reasons. Confusions about democracy, especially the attempts by some historically democratic countries to impose democracy on tribally organized societies, have made the understanding of democracy very difficult. The extent to which one is free to participate in setting the conditions for decision-making is an empirical matter.

All of these conditions for cosmological freedom, and possibly many more, go into an understanding of the various dimensions of human freedom to act in the world. The measurement of whether and to what extent a person or group is free in any of these dimensions is usually an empirical matter. The importance of stressing the empirical character of freedom is that it might seem to be in contradiction to the view that everything determinate is created by the ontological creative act. How can a person's present choices, as well as past actual conditions and future possibilities, be "free" if they are all created eternally together in the ontological creative act? The answer is that they are free in precisely the empirical senses described. The creative act is eternal, which means that at any given present time the future might still be open with viable options; the social context for choosing might allow the free creation of cultural and personal novel ways of life. The eternal creative act is never "at" a time such that it determines the future in advance. Rather, it is the creating of the spatiotemporal field by means of the creating of the harmonies that constitute the field, each in its own existential location. At any given time within the field, a person is more or less free in the dimensions discussed. As products of the ontological act of creation, each moment of every discursive harmony has its dynamics as future, present, and past, in the ways discussed.

But now the question is to be raised of the dimensions of freedom that arise in relation to the ontological act itself. Insofar as the dimensions of cosmological freedom are involved in the freedom that comes in relating to the ontological act, they have ultimacy and can be forms of ecstatic fulfillment.

II. RELEASE FROM ATTACHMENT TO FINDING MEANING

The first issue of freedom in relation to the radical contingency of creation on the ontological creative act is the need to find ultimate meaning itself. That need arises when the question is asked about the meaning of one's absolute value-identity. That identity is what it is, and the question is whether it has ultimate significance. Chapter 9 examined the possibility that absolute value-identity finds ultimate meaning in apocalyptic narratives that seem to offer the advantage of being grasped in intimate ways, and concluded that those narratives cannot be sustained as ultimate. Chapter 10 claimed that the ultimate meaning of life and existence is precisely its gratuitous, arbitrary, undeserved, and surprising character, and that grasping the ultimate meaning of life is the response to this. Most people are not at home with the high transcendence of these metaphysical symbols, and so map the infinite in those finite/infinite contrasts onto finite models. Chapter 11 traced some of the virtuoso attempts to grasp as love the gratuitous, arbitrary, undeserved, and surprising traits of ultimate meaning in the radical contingency of the world on the ontological creative act. The topic now is how this constitutes a kind of ultimate freedom.

The first kind of ontological ultimate freedom is the transcendence of the very need to find ultimate meaning. On the continuum of ultimate concern (I, 5), the most transcendent and intense kind of ultimate concern abandons any *need* for ultimacy on the part of the person and focuses on registering ultimacy itself, for its own sake. Whereas less transcendent forms of ultimate concern seek to grasp ultimate realities in order to prioritize one's life, giving sacred order to one's worldview, the most intense form of ultimate concern gives up the need for prioritizing in any ultimate way. As understood in the present context, this means achieving freedom from the need to find ultimate meaning, or salvation, or release from attachments, or escape from time's flow, or centeredness in the bosom of ultimacy.

How paradoxical that virtuoso success in finding ultimate meaning is to give up on the importance of finding ultimate meaning, salvation, or whatever that "goal" is called! Yet the Axial Age religions have strains within them that recognize the point.

The most direct approach to the point lies in the basic rhetoric of Buddhism, which is to reject attachments per se. Being "ultimately attached" to ending the suffering that comes from improper attachment is thus the worst of situations. The paradox lies in the commitment required to obtain release from attachments. As Sung Bae Park points out, on the one hand the bodhisattva takes a vow to postpone nirvana, which is freedom from all attachments, and on the other hand discovers that he or she is already Buddha, already enlightened, already beyond attachments.[5] Some strains of Buddhism distinguish the truth of enlightenment, which includes nonattachment, from ordinary truth, but then say that the truth of enlightenment is that the ordinary truths are true: nirvana is samsara. This is to say, true nirvana is not some transcendent escape from time but the acceptance of time's flow for what it is, including the attachments required for getting things done. According to this strain of Buddhism, an enlightened, perfectly free, person will look like anyone else with all the troubles, joys, and efforts of daily life, none of them ultimately important over the others.

Similarly, the Hindu ideal of *moksha* means release from the concerns and decay of time. For some strains of Hinduism, *moksha* is not possible within this life and comes only when the person literally dies, never to be reborn again. But for other strains, recognizing the identity of the true self with a deeper unchanging Brahman frees up the person to attend to the dharmas of daily life. The point is to not identify too much with the ego that is involved in ordinary duties, or with the fruit of those duties. To act for the sake of release perverts the release itself, making it an intended fruit of a certain kind of action.

Chinese religions are least amenable to the point at hand, mainly because they do not stress much ultimacy in the effort to find ultimate meaning. Nevertheless, one way of interpreting the Daoist ideal of *wu-wei* is to say that it is perfected nonattachment. When concern for righteousness arises, you can be sure that people have departed from the Dao.[6] This is not the strain of Daoism that gave rise to the symbols of the elaborate heavenly bureaucracy through which one must work to attain fulfillment, but it is the strain that has had the most appeal to philosophers. The Confucian tradition has stressed unrelenting effort, both to improve oneself and to manage affairs well. But much of that effort is the development of internal habits of spontaneous right responses, and more of the effort is to learn to play the rituals of social communication and interaction with spontaneous grace. The emphasis on spontaneity, a skill or way of being in the world acquired with difficulty, is a form of saying that further effort to find meaning is unimportant. As Confucius said, "At seventy I could follow my heart's desire without transgressing moral principles."[7]

Christianity has been deeply conflicted by the paradoxical point about abandoning interest in salvation. Much of the discussion of righteousness, as in Judaism and Islam, has to do with ultimate judgment, from which it has been concluded by some that salvation is to be won by righteous works, and that a failure in righteousness results in damnation. As a counterweight to this, all three Abrahamic religions also stress the mercy of God, balancing out divine wrath at injustice. Within Christianity this point was developed by Paul in his letter to the Romans by saying that we are saved by faith, not works. God's mercy has taken the form, Paul said, of sacrificing Jesus Christ as a justification for or redemption of human sin, and that this justification is accessed by faith. Much debate has taken place about what faith is. Some people say that faith is belief, and that one has access to salvation through believing in Jesus Christ as savior. But this makes salvation dependent on the sinner doing a kind of work, namely, believing. It turns believing into an act of will, not a response to the arguments about truth claims about Jesus. Believing in Christ as a means to salvation is not at all release from the need to find salvation: rather it is a kind of bondage. Instead, by faith Paul could have meant something like living in the spirit of Christ, or belonging to Christ and his way of life. Belonging does not depend on how well one imitates Christ, for Paul, only on accepting that one does indeed belong. Kierkegaard in his *Fear and Trembling* gave one of the most penetrating analyses of faith. For him, faith is not a belief based on evidence: to the contrary, regarding evidence, faith is absurd. Faith rather is a trust in God for no reason and with no expectation of getting something, as Abraham trusted God, who asked him to kill his son. Given the intense, individually defining, subjective act of will to trust, a person of faith goes about doing all the ordinary things ordinary people do. The "knight of faith" is indistinguishable from an ordinary person. As some Christians put the point, salvation is God's business, not a human concern. The human concern is only with how to live in a holy way in light of the divine gift of salvation, a completely practical matter.

The achievement of release from the task of finding ultimate meaning or salvation is extremely difficult, requiring the abandonment of hope for one's value-identity. One takes one's value-identity for what it is, nothing special, but of course what one would like to enhance as much as possible. However good one's value-identity, it is what it is, and this is part of the gratuitous, arbitrary, undeserved, and surprising character of the ontological creation. Having achieved this release, one is then free to worry about other things, the finite things of proximate significance that go into achieving a good value-identity. This is the freedom simply to be oneself, which matches the freedom in the ontological creative act simply to create the world that contains oneself.

The ecstatic fulfillment of the freedom to give up the search for meaning, deliverance, or salvation—however that is understood—is not an early stage in spiritual development. Many people live lives of trivial pursuits, of confusion and contradiction, enslaved to addictions, and unfree in most of the senses of cosmological freedom. For them, spiritual advancement means getting their lives together, finding some priorities based on ultimate realities, and cooking the multifarious ingredients of their lives into a sensible stew of nourishment. They definitely need to organize themselves around a goal of finding meaning, engagement, integration, righteousness, and gratitude for existence. The ecstatic fulfillment of giving up on finding those things is not possible until one has developed the quest to the point it can be given up.

III. FREEDOM IN BECOMING A SIGN OF ULTIMACY

Another sense of freedom relative to the ontological act of creation consists in turning a part of one's life, if not the whole of its intentional character, into a sign of that act. Unlike the previous sense of freedom, which moved *toward* the ontological act in release from need for the act (mirroring the opposite direction of the ontological act itself), the freedom of becoming a sign of the ontological act moves *with* the act. As a literal point, being a sign of the ontological act is really to be just a delimited part of the product of that act, being determinate relative to other things but registering as having the creative act within one. In Spinoza's terms, being such a sign is revealing the *natura naturans* in the *natura naturata* of one's character as a sign.

To be sure, one is only a sign of the ontological act in certain respects. Those respects are limited by the material quality of one's self, the otherness of others with respect to which one is determinate, as well as the capacities of the interpreters. The ontological creative act gives rise to a cosmos vast in space and time and every other measure of scale, and a human being is limited to being an organic body in a certain habitat with a society and culture. Only through long stretches of interpretation could a human being be a sign of the Big Bang or swirling clouds of matter and antimatter. But human beings can become signs of those aspects of ultimacy that bear upon human life.

For instance, a person could work to become paradigmatically and heroically righteous, thus becoming a sign of the ultimacy of the transcendental trait of form/possibilities/value/obligation. Most people are satisfied to be righteous enough. Some religious virtuosi become models of righteousness. Similarly, a person can work to become paradigmatically, heroically, whole, integrated, a model of human dignity. This would be to become a sign of the ultimacy of the transcendental trait of comporting oneself toward the components of life. With regard to the transcendental trait of engaging others in the existential field of life, a person can work to become paradigmatically appropriate, caring, and loving, relating to others with selfless devotion. Religious traditions offer many models of the virtuosi of righteousness, wholeness, and engaged love of appropriate sorts.

With regard to the transcendental trait of absolute value-identity, the problem for virtuoso adepts is to reconcile the inevitable failures regarding righteousness, wholeness, and engagement. Parts I and II discussed at length the problems of fulfilling obligations when sometimes even the optimum choices exclude possibilities of great value. Moreover, righteousness or justice is a matter of imposing a good form on things, when the things themselves have their own integrity that sometimes is necessarily compromised by the forms. Personal wholeness sometimes is in competition with the integrity of the things that are one's important components, particularly one's body, intimate friends, and the institutions one sustains or alters. When it comes to engaging others, it simply is impossible to love all the people the ways they deserve or to care for natural things and institutions as they should be cared for. So even the heroes of righteousness, wholeness, and engagement are compromised, and thus are failures to some extent. The problem for achieving a value-identity in a heroic mode is to learn to live with this failure without anger, bitterness, grief, or sense of failure. Virtuosity in absolute value-identity, paradoxically perhaps, is the ability to accept one's own failings as part of the gratuity, arbitrariness, undeservedness, and surprise of creation. Even Christianity, which deifies Jesus as its model of righteousness, wholeness, and engaged love, represents him as a failed teacher; a healer few of whose patients thanked him; a prophet aiming to purify his religion who was rejected by the religious leaders; a victim of misplaced political worries who was betrayed by his friends, crucified naked in front of his mother, and died young before he could get his movement well organized. Yet at the end he forgave those who hurt or betrayed him and commended his soul to God, a hero at being a finite creature, a sign of victory over the limitations of finitude.

Most of all, a person can become a sign of the gratuity, arbitrariness, undeservedness, and surprisingness of the ontological creative act, living with extraordinary abundance and singularity, celebrating value where it is found and being constantly astonished at the surprising particularity of existence. The richest and most concrete way to do this is through virtuosity in relating to the cosmological ultimates as just mentioned. But even without much virtuosity in those ways, a person can build a life that is manifestly abundant, singular, buoyant in value, and glimmering with delight, replete in ecstatic fulfillments. Most of us know a few people whose lives are like this, even when they are not particularly just, whole, devotedly engaged, or at ease with their own faults.

Signs do not signify unless they are interpreted. The earlier references to religions supplying many models of virtuoso signs of ultimacy supposed that the virtuosi were interpreted as signs by others. But with respect to freedom, the relevant interpreter is the virtuoso himself or herself. The freedom consists in the person engaging himself or herself as a part of the ontological act of creation, hence as embodying the gratuitous abundance, arbitrariness, undeservedness, and surprisingness of the ontological act. This also includes, through some signs or other, feeling oneself to be in and part of the ontological context of mutual relevance, together with others. The feeling of oneself as part of the ontological act of creating is a participation in the freedom of the ontological act itself.

Charles Peirce made the very important point that what is most important about a person is that the person is a sign.[8] By that he meant that at any moment, the person's body, motions, intentional actions, thoughts, and feelings are each and every one an interpretation of previous things. To the extent a person is unified, the unifying elements are interpretations of the things unified. For Peirce, the meaning of the person at a moment will consist in future interpretations, perhaps by a community beyond the person. Peirce's point can be restated as one of the important principles for how human beings are formed with hierarchies of possibilities played out through time—human harmonies are importantly semiotic. The argument of this section is that religious adepts develop themselves into signs that are beyond most people, signs that can be interpreted within their own lives as engagements of the ultimate. Most people cannot engage the ontological act of creation this deeply because they cannot build up within themselves the signs necessary for the engagement. The adepts can feel themselves as engagements with the free ontological act of creation. This is ecstatic fulfillment.

IV. FREEDOM TO LOVE

The feeling of oneself as part of the ontological act of creation is a kind of organization of oneself as a sign interpreting itself that takes place through serious and intense meditation. Mystics sometimes describe their meditation as an intense feeling of freedom. Yet there is another, related, kind of freedom in relation to the ontological act of creation that is exercised in everyday affairs. This is the capacity to love things simply because they are fellow creatures in the ontological context of mutual relevance. Being located in the existential field is the source of this form of freedom relative to the ontological act of creation.

Chapter 11 analyzed dimensions of how human beings can love the creation as the terminus of the ontological act of creation, the dimensions of gratuity, arbitrariness, undeservedness, and surprise. The ontological freedom to love others is different from this, more ordinary in its application. One cannot love everything directly. One can love everything as symbolized collectively in terms of abstractions such as "the existential field," or better yet, "the ontological context of mutual relevance." But the more direct loving of others is aimed at loving the particular others that are around one.

Philosophical Theology Two, Chapters 3 and 7, discussed love as a matter of engaging others in the existential field in terms of what is appropriate to those others. *Philosophical Theology Three*, Chapter 11, discusses the spiritual discipline of learning to do this. But the ontological freedom in loving others involves relating to those others as together with oneself in the ontological context of mutual relevance. The existential field is constituted by the ways by which things mutually condition one another, and insofar as love involves engagement it always takes place in and through the existential field. But the togetherness of things as constituted by the existential field does not include the togetherness of the essential components of the different things that are existentially together. Of course, things could not condition one another if their conditional components were not harmonized together with their own essential components: they would not exist except as harmonies of their own essential and conditional components. But without relating to things including their essential components, one cannot engage them as true others. The ontological context of mutual relevance is the field in which different and separate, though mutually conditioning, things are together inclusive of their own different essential components. The existential field is possible only because of the ontological context of mutual relevance. *Philosophical Theology* argues throughout that only the ontological creative act can be the ontological context of mutual relevance. The ontological freedom of loving others grasps the others as they are in the ontological context of mutual relevance, not only as they are in the existential field.

Of course, this ontological freedom of loving others cannot grasp the others with their essential components directly. This is metaphysically impossible because of the nature of the distinction between essential and conditional components. If the other's essential components were to be grasped, they would be turned into conditional components of the grasper and the other would be reduced to an objectified existence within the one who grasps. So the ontological freedom of loving others works by a special kind of projection onto the others. That projection is mediated by the ontological creative act as the context of mutual relevance. Just as one can make oneself into a sign of the creative act itself, one can make signs for the others that take them to be signs of the ontological creative act. This is to say, one can imaginatively project onto the others what it is like for them to be creatures like oneself and with oneself in the ontological context of mutual relevance.

How can we develop such signs of others so as to grasp them as fellow creatures on their own? A necessary beginning is to know the others as well as we can (II, 3). A further step is to appreciate the metaphysical relations of determinate things to the ontological context of mutual relevance and to one another. This can be done through a metaphysical scheme such as that developed here, or more intimately through the symbols of a viable sacred canopy. These can be integrated in a complex form of engagement in which both the others and oneself are taken to be signs of the ontological act of creation, each in its particular way. The object engaged is not the ontological act of creation but the particular others. The signs involved in engaging the others include their status as signs of the ontological act.

Many kinds and dimensions of love have been discussed in these pages and celebrated in religions, running from desire and need on the part of the lover to efforts to appreciate, help, and care for the needs of the others. What the ontological freedom of loving others adds to all these is the sheer ecstatic delight in the others, in their absolute value-identity. Strictly speaking, this delight is not a function of the lover's need for something delightful, especially not a function of the lover's need for personal fulfillment or something the other can do for the lover. Rather it is delight in the other for simply what the other is created to be. Perhaps Jonathan Edwards had something like this delight in mind when he spoke of "consent to Being in general" over and above its role in defining true virtue. This is a wholly disinterested delight.

Why is this ecstatic fulfillment an ontological freedom? It is a freedom in the sense that it constitutes the engagement of others with total disinterest. The conditioning of others and being conditioned by them define relations in the existential field and to some extent define the value-identity of the others in which one delights. But these things do not matter in the ontological freedom of loving others except insofar as they define the others. It does not matter whether the others are good for the lover or bad: how they are good and/or bad for one is just part of their ontological delightfulness. This is *ontological* freedom because this form of loving others delights in them strictly in their creaturely status, as particular outcomes of the ontological creative act.

What are the others to be loved with this ontological freedom? The language of "love" immediately calls to mind other people as things to be loved. Perhaps the most intense kind of delight is that in one's beloved. But in a strict sense, anything determinate is a creature and can be loved. So, not only other individual people can be loved but also relationships such as friendships of various sorts, collaborations, competitions, hostilities, enmities. From the standpoint of cosmological engagements, friendships are better than enmities, and enmities should be hated rather than be objects of delight. From the standpoint of the ontological freedom to love, enmities are just as much parts of creation as friendships. Their value-identities, though much lower than that of friendships ordinarily, are as much to be delighted in because all are creatures of the ontological creative act.

Beyond individuals and individual relations are social institutions of many kinds, each being an object of possible ontological delight, although cosmologically they should be engaged with due attention to reinforcing the good points and altering the bad ones. Human beings and social institutions are integral parts of nature as the whole of creation. But there are many parts of nature beyond human beings and social institutions. Some of these are gloriously beautiful to the naked eye or to the mathematical understanding. Others are hideous, largely chaotic, and overwhelmingly destructive of many kinds of natural harmonies. Yet all are possible objects of ontological delight. The ontological freedom of loving others is so disinterested that it can take delight in the supernova of one's own sun.

Or is disinterested delight inhuman? Is not the human thing to delight in the good and abhor the terrible and destructive? Perhaps so, according to a certain way of defining humanity, a way that has been explored extensively in these pages. But then ontological freedom is not so much human as it is part of the ontological act of creation. Whereas the ontological act creates the very being of the things created, with their wide range of value-identities including the very bad and destructive, the exercise of the ontological freedom of loving others simply delights in the things created. Human beings are not identical with the ontological act—they delight ontologically whereas the act creates ontologically. But an approximation to the freedom of the ontological act of creation is made through the exercise of the ontological freedom of loving others with sheer delight. Some strains of monotheistic religions say that God's creation of the world is identical with God's loving the world: for God to love is to make something that has value. Human beings do not love by creating, although human creativity sometimes expresses love. But human beings can love in the most nearly divine sense by delighting in each thing as it is. Because this kind of ontological freedom of loving others is not compromised by any interest, it is as close to a pure passion as is possible for human life, a passion that is the obverse of the pure action of the ontological act of creations.

Shiva says, Amen. Krishna has been dancing all along.

Part III

Summary Implications

The chapters of Part III have addressed the question of ecstatic religious fulfillment in four ways. As Chapter 9 discussed, the question is framed in terms of the quest for the ultimate meaning of life, as this is relevant to the choices that people make. The most common religious answer is the symbolic suggestion that ultimate meaning for one's life, or one's people's life, or the cosmos, might be found in a narrative (I, 8). This answer was found wanting for two principal related reasons. First, a narrative presupposes a larger context and therefore cannot deliver ultimacy. Second, all narratives exclude other narratives and therefore cannot be sufficiently inclusive. These limitations are decisive insofar as the narrative is taken with some kind of iconic literalness. But insofar as narratives are construed indexically, it might be the case that they function as orienting mythoi that provide structure for wholeness (II, 2, i).

Chapter 10 moved the question of ultimate fulfillment of meaning within time to the question of ultimate fulfillment of meaning in the sense of eternal wholeness. Ecstatic eternal life finds ultimate meaning in the eternal structure of the ontological creative act, which includes the act itself but also the cosmological ultimates of form, components, existential location, and absolute value-identity. In this sense, the ultimate meaning of life is the creation itself, with its gratuity, arbitrariness, undeservedness, and surprisingness. The metaphysical subtlety of this eternal structure is difficult to make intimate in ordinary life, however, and religious traditions have attempted to map it onto temporal structures. This way, narrative returns as a certain kind of sign for what is not narrative, and ultimate meaning can be found in that narrative form, so long as the wrong inferences are prevented from being made. The situation for ordinary religious life, therefore, is the ambiguous one of dealing with temporal signs for eternal ultimate meaning with a proper interpretation of their limitations and sometimes misleading apparent implications. Coping with the indexical character of such temporal signs for the eternal is a constant trial. Wholeness is interpreted here not so much as an achievement but as a sense of the meaning of one's life set within the context of eternity. Making explicit the contrast between eternity and time enables controls to be set on the iconic versus indexical reference in meaning-giving symbols of the self. Whereas Chapter 9 treated human life in its abstract aspect of merely temporal locatedness, Chapter 10 treated it in its eternal concreteness, paradoxical as that might seem.

The final two chapters of this part analyzed the attempt to find religious fulfillment by means of the attempt to *be* ultimately meaningful through participation in virtuoso ways in the eternal structure of the ontological act of creation. The discussions in Chapters 11 and 12 extended the discussions in *Philosophical Theology One*, Chapters 15–16; and *Three*, Chapters 15–16, all dealing with dimensions of mysticism or the virtuosity of religious genius. Chapter 11 studied the virtuoso development of means of loving the gratuity, arbitrariness, undeservedness, and surprisingness of the ontological creation. Chapter 12 studied ecstatic religious fulfillment through ontological freedom in three dimensions: freedom from the need to find ultimate meaning, freedom in becoming a sign of the ontological creative act, and freedom in loving others with disinterested delight.

Parts II and III have discussed how religion mediates the human responses to predicaments and the venues of ecstatic fulfillment that define people existentially. Religious practices and symbols have been mentioned frequently in giving something of a rich texture to the individual side of this theological anthropology. What has not been thematized, however, is how individuals participate in religion, or in their various religions, so as to access either the deliverances from predicaments or the venues of ecstatic fulfillment. Attention to religious participation is crucial to round out the discussion of religion as important for defining the existential reality of individuals. This is obviously related to but also distinct from the discussion of religion as a social phenomenon in which individuals participate that comes in *Philosophical Theology Three*.

Part IV

Engagement and Participation

Part IV

Preliminary Remarks

How do people relate to their ultimate predicaments and to the deliverances and ecstatic fulfillments offered by religions? They either engage them or fail to engage them. Although the argument of this volume so far has focused mainly on ultimate predicaments and ecstatic fulfillments, for all their existential power they cannot be understood without asking how they bear upon religion that can be accessed. Or, to put the point more adroitly, how can individuals with their ultimate predicaments and their putative paths to ecstatic fulfillment engage them through religion?

In the introduction to this volume we noted, with William James and Alfred North Whitehead, that religion is a matter of interiority, of "solitariness," to use the word they liked. The predicaments and ecstatic fulfillments lifted up in this theological anthropology have been described largely in "inward" terms. But religion offers its deliverances and venues for ecstatic fulfillment at least in socially symbolic terms, in traditions of religious life, and actual community practices. How can the inward access the "external" conditions? The chapters of this part address this question with increasing intensity. The first stage is through participation in ritual; loosest because one can participate without one's inward heart being in it and thus no serious engagement with the ultimate (according to many but not all understandings of ritual). A second stage is through cognitive and emotional commitment to communities and practices that can mediate the ultimates. A third is living a life of faith with others, and the fourth is the intense inhabitation of a sacred worldview. These aspects of religious life lift up the essential components that make genuine religious engagement real.

"Engagement" has been developed as a quasi-technical term in *Philosophical Theology* with two layers of meaning so far. It is the term for interpretive interaction with things (I, 3), distinguishing the epistemology of this project from representationalist epistemologies. It is also the metaphor for normative human intentional interaction with different things in the existential field, the failure of which is estrangement (II, 3, 7). In this latter sense, engagement involves a relationship with something that is other.

"Engaging deliverances" carries both meanings. On the one hand, it involves intentionality that is interpretive in character. On the other hand, there is a reality to the predicaments and to the salvific interventions offered by sacred canopies that stands over and against the intender, so that engaging deliverances means confronting an other. Engaging deliverances involves engaging both the predicaments and their suggested remedies. Similarly, engaging or participating in the paths to ecstatic fulfillment involves both the intent to do so, however symbolically that is articulated, and concrete religious action or enjoyment.

In the typology of predicaments and salvific interventions in Part II of this volume, engagement has to do with the existential field in which a person is located, a field constituted by the other things to which the person is related directly or indirectly through conditional components. When engaging others is problematic, courage is needed. When courage fails and despair predominates, faith is needed. Faith is an underlying condition for engaging problematic things. The predicaments themselves and their respective delivering remedies are problematic. So the existentialist philosophers and theologians such as Tillich and Bultmann were right to emphasize faith, although they were wrong to make it so much more important than obligation, well-groundedness, and the achievement of absolute value-identity. Each of those four is ultimately, that is, religiously, important in its own way. But when it comes to deliverances, other and problematic as they are, faith is central. Here in Part III, Chapter 11, engaging others is a problem of achieving the ecstatic fulfillment of love; faith is a condition for love, but not a sufficient one.

The term "faith," however, has acquired a peculiarly narrow meaning in modern Western philosophy and theology. Anderson Weekes has pointed out that the early modern period in European culture was a time of deep skepticism, especially about religion whose traditions were challenged by the recovery of lost aspects of antiquity and by the Reformation and Counter-Reformation.[1] Earlier Hellenistic skepticism had taken the form of accounting the objects to be known as "shabby," because of their constant changeability. By contrast, early modern skepticism took the human knowing faculty to be shabby because it mixed human will in cognitive judgments, and the will could make mistakes. The modern remedy was to discipline the will, as Descartes argued in paradigmatic ways, so as to limit judgment to what could be known with certainty or with probability within a priori limits, as Kant argued. Cognitive knowledge of ultimate reality was impossible, many argued, and the authority of delivering revelation had to be accepted "on faith." Faith in this sense is an act of pure will affirming something "other" offered as salvific or delivering. Religious commitment cannot be justified cognitively: faith is the form of religious justification, according to Martin Luther, whom Weekes calls "modernity's first great firebrand."[2] So, faith in modern and late-modern Christianity has become peculiarly associated with a kind of fideism that seeks a justification for cognitive religious content that cannot be justified by cognitive means.

But faith need not be given that narrow association. The phrase "people of faith" is given to people who participate in the ritual life of a religious community, with no necessarily explicit, barely even tacit, reference to its detailed theological commitments. Faith also sometimes refers to the inward spiritual journey wherein one seeks wholeness. Tillich's use of faith as a courage to engage the world with its ambiguities has more to do with existential action than with cognitive inquiry or belief.[3] Faith also describes the life of inhabiting a worldview that gives ultimate significance to many if not all of the otherwise mundane affairs of life, and of taking personal value-identity from that inhabitation.

In some strains of Protestant Christianity, powerfully influenced by Luther, faith has been contrasted with works: one is saved by faith, not by works: one cannot earn salvation, only receive it on faith. But this is an extremely complicated notion because it is difficult to ascertain how one acquires faith. Is faith itself a "gift of salvation"? Or is faith a sheer matter of will, as fideists believe? Is willing to have faith the good and necessary work one must accomplish in order subsequently to enjoy some heavenly reward or a better life next time? Or is faith something one has to work to attain? Is faith significantly different for those whom William James called the "once-born" than it is for the "twice-born?"[4] Once attained, what is faith except the enjoyment of the deliverance hoped for? These variant questions indicate some of the dialectical complexity of engaging deliverance. In most of the instances discussed in the first two parts of this volume, being broken and in need of fixing with regard to the ultimate human predicaments means being somehow unfortunately disengaged from what would be salvific. Engagement is not only a state, however, but also and more concretely a process. Religious life, even in secular terms, is an array of processes of engaging more or less with the ultimate realities that define and repair ultimate human predicament, constantly changing the degrees and kinds of engagements. Therefore, it is possible to study basic forms of engagement of deliverance as ways people have of drawing closer to, or farther from, the delivering states and processes.

The analysis here derives from the transcendental traits of harmony that define the ultimate dimensions of human life (and all other life where relevant): form and possibility, components and wholeness, existential location and engagement of others in other places, and value-identity and achievement. Engagement in the first instance means participation in some or many of the religious realities of ritualized life, including special rituals; the rituals are significant because of the meanings that they bear that define ultimately important aspects of possibilities. Rituals form religious living, especially if ritual is understood broadly as semiotic meaning. One crucial dimension of engaging salvation, including entering into ecstatic fulfillment, is participation in religiously significant rituals. This is the topic of Chapter 13.

A second crucial dimension of engaging deliverance and ecstatic fulfillment is through becoming committed. Commitment is a general term for the process of becoming whole (II, 2, 6), where it means acquiring appropriate comportment toward the components of one's life. Commitment means, among other things, identifying oneself with a certain way of being whole, which includes treating rituals, engagements, and the achievement of absolute value-identity as components of one's life. Related to the issues of ultimate concern (I, 5), commitment itself is not a trait everyone possesses, and it involves kinds and degrees. Most likely, the ability to make a religious commitment, and the elements of deliverance and ecstatic fulfillment that might come from that, is an age-specific developmental stage occurring during adolescence. Chapter 14 explores these issues.

A third crucial dimension of engaging deliverance and ecstatic fulfillment is coming to live the life of faith, where this means not so much belief as the faithful engagement of others, particularly, problematic others. "Others" here include situations, institutions, natural and social environments, as well as other people. Becoming faithful and staying faithful is a matter of developing various strengths in a coherent life. It is related to ritual, and to commitment, but is not reducible to them because it consists in engagements across the existential field. Chapter 15 discusses this.

A fourth crucial dimension of engaging deliverance and ecstatic fulfillment is coming to inhabit a worldview in which the mundane things have an ultimate dimension. In this inhabitation one lives out an absolute value-identity. A value-identity is impossible without the world in which it is situated, but often the world is not appreciated in its ultimacy as part of the product of the ontological creative act. The problematic task of achieving an absolute value-identity in an intentional, self-conscious, way requires the development of a worldview that allows for this intentional frame. Chapter 16 analyzes this point.

The discussions of this part anticipate several aspects of the analyses of religion in *Philosophical Theology Three*. Those later analyses bring a more systematic focus on religion as a public phenomenon, whereas the focus here on personal engagement involves individuals engaging public expressions of religion.

CHAPTER THIRTEEN

Ritual

The most public, obvious, and common way of engaging religion's remedies for various ultimate human predicaments and its paths to ecstatic fulfillment is through participation in religion's social manifestations. Children are brought up in a religious social environment if any part of their context is organized semiotically around symbols of ultimacy. This is so even if the symbols in a particular social environment are hostile to traditional religious symbolism and represent themselves as "secular," so long as they involve some reference to what they take to be ultimate.

I. ANTHROPOLOGICAL UNDERSTANDINGS OF RITUAL

Anthropologists and sociologists following Emile Durkheim study religion as essentially a social phenomenon. Durkheim's classic definition is this: "A religion is a unified system of beliefs and practices relative to sacred things, that is to say, things set apart and forbidden—beliefs and practices which unite into one single moral community called a Church, all those who adhere to them."[1] Today this definition seems plainly old-fashioned. We would put heavy qualifications on the notion of "unified system." We would object to the sharp distinction between sacred and profane or mundane things that Durkheim employs, as will be discussed shortly (also I, 7). And we would draw away from calling all those religious communities "united" by certain beliefs and practices a "Church." Nevertheless, we appreciate the force of Durkheim's definition to be that religious beliefs and practices make for a community of their adherents. The scientific reductionism of his position is clear: no reference is made to whether the religious beliefs are true or whether the practices are salvific, ultimately fulfilling, or reflective of ultimacy in any sense. Noting that reductionism for now, we can pass on (but see I, 2; III, 1).

Durkheim's sociology of religion studies how beliefs and practices make for social solidarity. The converse point is that when a community loses the coherence of common beliefs and practices beyond a certain point, the solidarity of the community is shaken. Peter Berger, with a more sophisticated notion of beliefs and practices oriented by a sacred canopy, worried about the decline of community and of people's sense of belonging. He also worried about the rise of moral relativism, social alienation, and anonymity in the modern situation (I, 1).[2] Durkheim thought that religion is best understood in its most "primitive" forms. The need for social solidarity in a hostile natural and human environment was very great in the conditions of the early phases of human evolution and justified the importance of religion to Durkheim. Early twenty-first-century evolutionary biologists studying religion share this sense of justification: socially coherent groups are better able to pass on their genes, and many biologists think religion is thus an adaptive advantage (III, 1).

The identification of religion with its primitive forms, though heuristically convenient, is untenable. Those forms studied by Durkheim and others were just as much the primitive forms of government, education, and medicine as they were of what we now know as religion. The social solidarity argument can just as well be claimed by government or politics as it can by religion conceived separately. The point, of course, is that these projects of human civilization were melded in the rituals and other practices and beliefs of primitive human groups. When critics of religion in our own day decry the violence and bigotry of religion, which they trace back to the in-group/out-group foundations of community solidarity, they should blame government as much as religion. The attempt of Durkheim and his followers to legitimate religion as a socially positive institution in late modernity easily can backfire when it is identified with "primitive" markers that are indeed savage but are just as much markers of the political, educational, and medicinal projects that have come to flourish recently. *Philosophical Theology Three* develops a theory of religion that does not identify religion by its "elementary forms," not even in its early biological and cultural evolution.

Durkheim (and Berger) focused on beliefs and practices as objective social structures characteristic of a society. How do individuals participate in them? Durkheim and most anthropologists would answer, by participating in rituals. Ritual has been studied on many fronts. Victor Turner, following Arnold van Gennep, argued that the ritual process involves moving through a boundary or *limen* from mundane to sacred territory (and sometimes time), then an enactment of something that causes the sacred-mundane contrast to be problematic, and a return to everyday life.[3] The "enactment" is the "rite" itself, which is often identified as the ritual as a whole. Much debate has taken place in the last half-century among anthropologists and other social scientists as to just what that might be, and as to how useful the notion of ritual is in understanding religion. Catherine Bell has summarized and criticized this debate in a classic way.[4]

The most enthusiastic anthropological student of ritual, however, is Roy A. Rappaport, who wrote: "I take the term 'ritual' to denote *the performance of more or less invariant sequences of formal acts and utterances not entirely encoded by the performers.*"[5] "Performance" means that the ritual is intentional action, even if the intentions are not clearly understood by the performers. The "invariant sequences" are ritual roles or forms within which actions take place. That they are "more or less" invariant means that rituals involve some improvisation and are never repeated exactly. The "utterances" are treated as performative acts. "Not entirely encoded by the performers" means that the performers are not the complete creators of the sequence of formal acts but inherit some or most aspects of the ritual form from the past. Nevertheless, as said, they do not just repeat the formal acts: they modify them as they proceed. "Not entirely encoded by the performers" also means that the performers need not know and follow all the inherited rubrics of the formal ritual, and have to make up much of it as they go along. Ritual forms are something like formulated dance steps that each performer has to take in his or her own way, developing recognizable individuality within a generalized form. To participate in a ritual thus means more than acquiescence to doing things the ritual way: it means finding specific ways of doing what the ritual form vaguely prescribes.

Rappaport argued that religious rituals presuppose or embody ideologies that articulate the cosmos within which the ritual performers live and also identify the performers as those who adopt and live within that articulation of the world. He goes so far as to argue that "the making of humanity" requires religious ritual because to be human means to have an identity as an individual within a community of shared (more or less) culture within a world as more or less understood, and that participation in ritual is what effects this humanization. To participate in the ritual, just to participate, is to buy in to the view of individuality, community, and world embodied in the ritual in some profound, if not always conscious and deliberate, sense. This is so, Rappaport said, even if the individual has intellectual reservations about elements in the ritual worldview.

Much more than Durkheim, we are sensitive to the disunified and somewhat haphazard connections among elements in our sacred canopies or religious belief systems. Nevertheless, most religions have rituals that directly or indirectly express the salvific remedies sought by those broken by human predicaments and that celebrate ecstatic fulfillments. Most religions have rituals that express, under appropriate conditions and qualifications, the correction of failures of obligation, the restoration to community membership of those who have betrayed it, the sanctification of those who had refused their personal identity projects, and the purification of individuals and communities from blood guilt. Most religions have rituals of physical and spiritual healing, of the abasement that leads to humility, of comfort for those suffering from time's passage, and the recognition of enlightenment from paths in which people did not know what they were doing. Most have rituals of acceptance after realities had been denied, of purgation of deep-seated biases and distortions, of the exhortations to and celebrations of faith, of reconciliation after conflict. Most have deep, sometimes esoteric, sometimes virtuoso, rituals of renunciation, dedication, submission, and ontological affirmation. Sometimes rituals are the actual contexts of ecstatic fulfillments, and rituals exist that celebrate those and other occasions of fulfillment.

Participation in these rituals is the first line of engagement of what sacred canopies offer as remedies for the brokenness of the human condition and paths to ecstatic fulfillment. In all this it should be remembered that secular sacred canopies might very well attempt to reject the basic symbols of religious traditions but still take responsibility for articulating how they view ultimate realities and the ultimate dimensions of various aspects of mundane life. After all, very few people, at least in the West, fail to celebrate birthdays of people about whom they care. A birthday celebration is the selection of one day a year, arbitrarily affixed to the birth date, to signal the special and ultimate importance of the existence of the person celebrated. By itself that is not a very rich symbol of ultimacy. But it is something.

Writing about rituals bounded by the liminality of the sacred, Rappaport stressed the following point. When a person participates in a ritual, regardless of the person's explicit consciousness, that participation is an implicit commitment both to the ideology underlying the ritual and to solidarity with those who also participate. Rappaport provided a complicated argument to show that, because of this implication of ritual participation, ritual is essential to the "making of humanity," as he put it. It is the practice that enables the group solidarity necessary to fashion and refashion the ideologies that give meaning to human life. In turn, the meaningfulness of human life gives rise to the possibility of participating in rituals that bear that meaning. Of course, meaningfulness, the ideology of the group, and the structure and solidarity of the group are in constant change. Rappaport was acutely aware, like Berger, of the degeneration of community, ritual, and shared meaningfulness in various circumstances, particularly those of late modernity. Rappaport's thesis about the making of humanity has a large truth to it but only when the conception of ritual is expanded to embrace the Confucian vision, as is discussed in Section III.

An implication of Rappaport's point to note here, however, is that participation in liminally circumscribed rituals constitutes the affirmation of membership in the in-group formed by the ritual's solidarity, an in-group with a more or less common ideology and that distinguishes itself from other people who do not participate in the ritual. In the savage conditions of the early evolution of humanity, in-group solidarity had obvious adaptive advantages (*III, 2*). In conditions of competition between small groups for scarce resources, often accompanied by a fairly constant level of warfare, sometimes ritualized, the more cohesive a group's organization and the more readily it could distinguish who is in the group from outsiders the more competitive it is. Although it is not fair to associate ritualized solidarity in primitive conditions more with religion than with government or politics, ritual was a factor in evolutionary adaptive advantage insofar as it played a role in magnifying in-group/out-group distinctions while strengthening the in-group.

Nevertheless, the role of ritual in the making of in-group/out-group distinctions is complex and ambiguous.[6] To be sure, many reasons exist to sustain and attend to in-group/out-group distinctions having to do with family, neighborhood organization, and political organization more generally. Rituals are involved in all of these pockets of human solidarity—family rituals, community rituals, and governmental rituals as broad as the empire when the Chinese Emperor celebrates the rituals for the changing of the seasons. Countless rituals exist in contemporary society that organize business and labor, leisure practices, and the routines of daily life. But insofar as these do not have to do with the ultimate boundary conditions of life that should be symbolized in sacred canopies, they are not particularly religious. The *religious* rituals are those whose important symbols involve the finite/infinite contrasts of ultimate boundary conditions, such as the references to creation and redemption in the Christian Sunday worship rituals (to be analyzed shortly). The religious rituals are sometimes distinguished from others by their liminality, the crossing out of the mundane world into sacred space (and time). In many cultures, the sacred canopy portions of a worldview are sharply separated from the other portions in ways that require special entrance into the sacred context in order to be engaged experientially. But not all cultures make such a sharp separation. And not all religious rituals, even when dealing directly with the ultimate realities in the boundary conditions, require a ritualized passage into sacred space and time. Yet all rituals, religious and otherwise, form some kind of in-group/out-group distinction between those who participate in them and those who do not.

Participation in religious rituals facilitates the engagement with religion's salvific remedies for various elements of ultimate human predicaments and paths to ecstatic fulfillments. Yet, there is a potential existential contradiction insofar as any in-group/out-group distinctions are given ultimacy. The predicaments all involve transcendental characteristics of the cosmos, and hence involve universality. The predicaments coming from obligation because human beings face value-differentiated possibilities mean that individuals are obligated to do the right thing by all people involved in the possibility structures, not only those of their in-group. The predicaments coming from comportment toward the components of life require groundedness with regard to all components, not only those particular to an in-group. The predicaments coming from engaging all those people, situations, and environmental realities in the existential field require proper connection with all those, not only those associated with an in-group. The predicaments coming from achieving an identity through one's existence in the world have to do with the values received from and given to all things, not only those of an in-group. A similar point holds for ecstatic fulfillments. The ultimate realities involved, because they are transcendental conditions of existence, are a refutation of the pre–Axial Age religions insofar as they give ultimacy to in-group/out-group distinctions. They are a demonstration of what the Axial Age religions learned when their founding thinkers reflected on those transcendental conditions (III, 2).

The contradiction in religious rituals thus is that, to the extent they give ultimacy to the in-group distinction of their participants, they compromise the universality of the obligations, grounded wholeness, existential engagement, and achievement of absolute value-identity in the ultimate predicaments they address. The salvific work of rituals is supposed to be to save people from the consequences of their failures of obligations, wholeness, engagement, and mutual identity achievement of "all under heaven."[7] The ritual is counterproductive if its in-group/out-group solidarity leads to less-than-universal comprehension of the scope of obligations, groundedness, engagement, and value-identity. True enough, the ritualized life of many religious communities whose ostensible values include universal love and justice for all often instead leads to bigotry, selfishness, chauvinism, and blindness regarding value-identity. Yet, participation in such rituals is itself a way of engaging whatever religious remedies are offered. It also is a way of engaging ultimacy through the ritual symbols that leads to ecstatic fulfillment. For many people, ecstatic fulfillment comes primarily through participation in rituals.

II. A RITUAL ANALYSIS

The analysis of a complex ritual is a far better illustration of how participation in a ritual is an engagement with a salvific remedy for a human predicament than a thin ritual such as a birthday celebration. Moreover, analysis of a rich, widely used contemporary ritual is better than analysis of an ancient ritual as favored by historians of religion, or a primitive ritual as favored by anthropologists. The methodological advantage of analyzing ancient rituals is that we can trace them to a bounded set of considerations in the texts prescribing them, as in Francis X. Clooney, S.J.'s *Thinking Ritually*, which aims to recover the ritual theory of Jaimini, of the Purva Mimamsa School, underneath the subsequent commentarial and practice traditions.[8] The methodological advantage of analyzing primitive rituals is that the culture to which it belongs can be circumscribed, as in the Australian peoples analyzed by Durkheim or the African community analyzed by Turner. A philosophical analysis of ritual, however, needs to avoid the reductionist boundaries of both history of religions and anthropology and find ways of opening up connections across as many boundaries as possible.

An appropriate contemporary ritual for analysis from the social location of *Philosophical Theology* is Sunday morning Christian worship. Christianity exists in many forms and is spread across every country of the globe.[9] The forms of Sunday morning worship vary by denomination, each of which has its own set of theological interpretations as well as practice traditions.

Within denominations there are variations from the extremely elaborate to the extremely informal or trimmed down. The Orthodox denominations tend to be more elaborate, even with variations within themselves, than the Protestant denominations that also have internal variation on elaborateness and formality. The Roman and Anglican Catholic denominations tend to worship with variations in between the Orthodox and the Protestant. Yet there is an overall structure, vague as it might be, that governs the Sunday morning service in many instances across the field. Occasionally, important elements are eliminated, or other elements introduced. But roughly, the ritual is as follows: entry, praise, confession, word, Eucharist, sending out, and exit. Some Protestant denominations do not celebrate the Eucharist every Sunday, but monthly, or quarterly.

Entry into and exit from the liminal space of worship is usually accomplished by movement into a sanctuary with music, and exit from the sanctuary with music. Sometimes there is no music. Sometimes there is no dedicated sacred place, only the transformation of ordinary space usually used for other things into a sacred place, a transformation often accomplished by music. Typically, entry and exit are accompanied by instrumental music, for instance, pipe organs, pianos, or guitars. The entry can include a musical prelude; special habits of congregational entrance; sitting in pews or chairs; processions by choirs, clergy, and worship leaders; congregational singing of a processional hymn' words of welcome with responsive greetings between worship leaders and the congregation; and a choral introit. The exit picks up from the "sending forth" with the benediction and can include a recessional hymn as the choir, clergy, and worship leaders leave the sacred space and an instrumental postlude during or after which the congregation leaves.

The ritual within the sacred space is modeled after an audience with a king, with God construed in the role of the king. This ritual evolved from earlier Jewish temple worship that likened the King of Israel to God, King of Creation. For over a millennium and a half, Christianity in Europe and in most of the rest of the world developed in contexts where the political organization was some variant on kingship, imperial authority, or the search for a peace-making strongman.[10]

The first part of the ritual proper is to give praise to God as to a king whose glories need to be cited or whom the people simply want to praise. Praise is given in hymns by the congregation—possibly beginning with the processional hymn—by prayers of invocation, by special music, and the like. In some contexts, the priest is dressed in royal robes as a kind of visual stand-in for God or Jesus Christ the King, although the priest or worship leader is never identified with God or Christ. Among the many functions of praise in the liturgy is the giving of expression to the awesomeness of God the Ultimate, the power, the infinity, the sublimity, beauty and glory that are like a great king's but far beyond that. The feelings of praise can be augmented by the majesty of the architectural space and the beauty of the music and liturgical processions and movements. Another function of praise in the liturgy is the people's gaining of access to such an awesome Ultimate Reality. On a crass but obviously functional level, praise of God is intended to render the people acceptable to God's presence. But the people come to the God whom they praise as needy people come to the king.

The second part of the ritual proper is confession of sins on the part of all the participants in the worship, with a petition to God as king to forgive the sins. Confession includes words prayed by the worship leaders, choral petitions such as the Kyrie eleison ("Lord have mercy, Christ have mercy, Lord have mercy"), prayers recited by the congregation, and ritualized moments of silent prayers. Sometimes sinners come forward in the worship for special attention. The minister or priest declares sins to be forgiven in accordance with the atonement in Jesus Christ, and the people respond with thanksgiving. Sometimes the confession ends with a passing of the peace in which the congregants embrace one another as cleansed and ready to approach God the king with a pure heart. This part of the ritual embodies purgation, purification, acceptance, redemption, and restoration, and sometimes renunciation. The deepest meaning of the atonement is the purification of the people in the blood of Jesus.[11] The action of the rite of confession is the admission and confession of fault by the people and the forgiveness and restoration of the people to proper citizenship by God the king.

The liturgy of the word is the proclamation and hearing of the King's intent and consists in prayers for illumination; recitations of scripture, sometimes responsively expressed between the congregation and worship leaders; music based on scriptural or other didactic texts; a sermon or other preaching form. This is the part of the ritual in which the theology of the particular version of Christianity is articulated, very often with an application to practical living, either on a personal and communal level or on the scale of interpreting larger historical and social situations in theological perspective. Preaching is an hermeneutical act, especially in most Christian traditions, in which the symbols are intended to be interpreted with their proper meaning and where misinterpretations of the symbols are prevented. From the standpoint of the people, this is the part of the ritual in which they can come to some intellectual and emotional understanding of what their religion stands for. It usually concludes with the taking of an offering as thanks for the instruction, although the offering can occur at any number of places in the service.

The Eucharist part of the ritual summarizes what has preceded by symbolically uniting the congregation with God and the members of the congregation with one another as a community that has ultimate meaning before God. The Eucharist is a ritualized narrative retelling of the Last Supper that Jesus is reputed to have celebrated with his disciples immediately before his arrest and crucifixion. The Eucharist begins with an invitation to the people to participate; denominations differ in whom they allow to participate. Although there are many Eucharistic forms, most include the following four elements, based on common interpretations of what Jesus did at the Last Supper. First is the presentation of bread and wine on the altar. In most Orthodox communities representatives of the people (not the clergy) bring the bread and wine to the altar as mundane gifts to God, which are then transformed into holy gifts to the people by the action of the liturgy calling upon the action of God. In other communities the bread and wine are brought into the holy space and placed on the altar by worship leaders. In yet other communities they are already on the altar throughout the whole ritual. The second element is the Great Thanksgiving, recited by the presiding clergy (usually after a brief dialogue between the clergy and people), in which thanks are given to God for the salvation sent to the world in Jesus Christ and in which Jesus's words of blessing of the bread and wine are recalled, along with his injunction to remember these blessings whenever bread and wine are taken. The blessing consists of Jesus saying that the bread is his body, broken for the people, and the wine is his blood, spilled for their salvation. Often, the Lord's Prayer is said by everyone as a transition from the Thanksgiving to the third element in the Eucharist, the breaking of the bread and lifting up of the cup of wine. In the breaking of the bread, the priest often recites Jesus's words, "This is my body, broken for you." Lifting up the cup, the priest says something like, "This is my blood, poured out for you." Christian theologies differ radically about what these words might mean, but most conclude that when the people take the elements, eat and drink them, they are participating in Jesus Christ in some sense. The breaking of the bread and lifting up of the cup of wine are invitations to the people to come and partake, the fourth element of the Eucharist. Partaking of the elements has many forms in diverse circumstances, from simply passing around the bread and cup for each person to take some, to the priest and servers placing bread in people's mouths and lifting the cup for them to drink, or to spooning the wine into their mouths. A common method now is for people to file down in front of the altar, receive a piece of bread and dip it quickly (intinction) into the wine, then eat it. Often a congregational prayer of thanksgiving concludes the Eucharistic part of the service. The act of participating in the Eucharist is a form of receiving sanctification, healing, humility, comfort, acceptance, reconciliation, renunciation, dedication to the life and work of Jesus, submission to God, and affirmation of solidarity with God and God's creation.

The conclusion of the ritual proper is the sending forth, sometimes with the taking of an offering and prayers dedicating the people to God's work or to some special way of life. Often there is concluding music such as a going-forth hymn, and a response to the benediction. The benediction initiates the exit from the ritual space and time.

How are we to understand this Sunday morning ritual? Of course, it must be understood historically in terms of the evolution of its elements from early and pre-Christian sources, as contextualized variously throughout history. But what does it mean today for its participants so that participation in it is salvific? To answer that it will be helpful to recur to three of the continua of worldviews studied in *Philosophical Theology One*, especially Chapters 4, 6, and 7.

The first and most important continuum is that within a worldview between, on the one hand, its direct symbols of ultimacy in its sacred canopy and, on the other hand, more mundane aspects of living also symbolized for the sake of orientation within the worldview. In the Sunday morning Christian worship ritual are many references to God, especially in Trinitarian form of Creator Father, Redeemer Son, and Sanctifier Holy Spirit (although some denominations minimize the last). These are embodied and interpreted in prayers, music, scripture, and often sermons, as well as in the central narrative of the Eucharist. But then these direct references to God in the sacred canopy are transferred to many aspects of the mundane world, giving those dimensions of ultimacy. For instance, most praise of God is directed at God being the creator of the world; so praise means that everything in life is to be taken as God's created gift. The mundane itself is holy because created by the praiseworthy God. Confession, for its part, is nearly always for wrongs committed in daily life. All the forms of human predicament discussed earlier are matters of living in the world, and the act of taking them into Sunday worship and asking for forgiveness and restitution acknowledges them to have an ultimate dimension. The elements of the word, in scripture, song, and preachment, include direct expressions of a Christian sacred canopy, but they are usually far more concentrated on how to live in the world in light of the sacred canopy. The life and teachings of Jesus are relevant not only for theologies of symbols in the sacred canopy but for how participants in the worship ritual should understand their own lives and that of their communities.

The Eucharist is a rite of participation in the central realities of the Christian sacred canopy, but its form is to transform eating into a memorial of participation in the ultimate. Although Christians tend to limit Eucharistic consciousness to the explicit ritual, the words of institution in the ritual say to use every occasion for eating (bread) and drinking (wine) to think of eating and drinking Jesus in some participatory sense. The sending forth is obviously a prescription for making the implications of the sacred canopy apply across much, if not the whole, of life as understood in terms of a Christian worldview. So, participation in the Sunday morning worship service is a way of coming to appreciate the ultimate dimensions of all the things in life, perhaps in ecstatic fulfillment, minimally as viewing them with gratitude as God's created gift and maximally as trying to reshape them to conform to the values of love and forgiveness, the repair of broken humanity, and the celebration of freedom that are central to the Christian sacred canopy.

The second worldview continuum to employ in analysis of the ritual is that between sophisticated and folk-religion interpretations of symbols. The same symbols are subject to many positions of interpretation along this continuum. The Christian conception of God as Trinity is one of the most abstract theological notions in any religion, and debates about its meaning over the centuries have included mind-numbing technicalities. Moreover, the very analysis of the worship service in terms of ritual theories is an extraordinarily sophisticated understanding. The Eucharist, for instance, obviously is a symbolic cannibal rite, involving eating (however symbolically or "really") the flesh and blood of Jesus.[12] Yet very few worshippers think about the Eucharist as a cannibal rite, or about worship in terms of ritual theory, or about whether the Holy Spirit proceeds from the Father alone or from Father and Son together.[13] The overall structure of the worship is a begging of favors from God: forgiveness and restitution, a good life, perhaps salvation in heaven, an experience of ecstatic fulfillment. This begging of favors is shamanism. Although a great many people are quite conscious of worship as a begging of favors, few would think of it as shamanism. The commonality of meaning in the worshipping community lies in a range of interpretation of the basic symbols somewhere between the most sophisticated and the most folk-culture oriented. Popular Christianity reaches deep into folk culture, but its symbols resist reduction to that, especially to the shamanic materialism of much folk religion.[14] To understand a Sunday morning ritual in any depth would require analysis of a particular service with contextual explanations of how the various people in the congregation interpret the symbols along the continuum from sophistication to folk culture.

The third continuum within worldviews is between interpretation of the symbols in terms of transcendence and interpretation in terms of intimacy. The symbols are given their most transcendent interpretation in the portion of the ritual devoted to praise, and most of the rest of the ritual requires intimate connections between God and the congregants. A pervasive problem throughout the ritual, however, is that the need for intimate interpretations of the symbols of ultimacy leads to a domestication of those symbols that undermines their reference to the creator of all things. Insofar as the intimate interpretations require the personification of the ontological act of creation as God, and persons are structurally within the created order because of the external reference of intentionality, God is contradictorily represented as creator and created. If sins are of ultimate import and the God who forgives them is less than ultimate, a serious emotional and cognitive dissonance infects the ritual. Therefore, the domesticated intimate interpretations need to be broken—within the liturgies themselves, the interpretations of scripture, and the sermons—in order for the ritual to have coherent salvific efficacy. In practice, interpretations lying on different positions of the transcendence/ intimacy continuum can resonate together, even if they are intellectually exclusive, up to a certain point. Beyond that point, however, the exclusionary interpretations cause the ritual to be ineffective. First naïveté with regard to intimate interpretations needs to be broken and replaced with second naïveté. Sometimes in contemporary worship the breaking of the intimate interpretations simply cannot be followed by a second naïveté that allows the participant into significant engagement; second naïveté is difficult, especially for people who tend to literalize metaphors.

The brief analysis of the typical (in many parts of the world) Christian Sunday worship ritual is an example of the kind of analysis that can be given of any ritual that has boundaries of liminality for the entrance into and exiting from some kind of sacred context. The ritual can be described regarding its components and then analyzed in particular cases in terms of how the ritual employs symbols that lie along the sacred/mundane, sophistication / folk culture, and transcendence/intimacy continua. Of course, many other forms of analysis can be given as well, although these mark out the special concerns of *Philosophical Theology*.

In light of the transcendental universality of the ultimate boundary conditions, religious rituals can build solidarity authentically only when they treat as explicitly nonultimate the in-group/out-group distinction that arises from the distinction between participants and nonparticipants. The Christian Sunday morning ritual focuses a tight sense of solidarity around those who participate in the Eucharist, which is a participation in the body and blood of Jesus, one of the defining marks of being a Christian. This ritual is authentic, however, only if it is construed to be not exclusively ultimate. That is, the ritual ought not to suggest that people who do not participate, who are not Christians (whatever else they might be), are not saved. The function of the Christian ritual is to enable its participants better to repair and fulfill their obligations, comportment, existential engagements, and true value-identity with respect to their universal reach. The ritual should thus teach universal love, for instance, and not have that compromised by loving Christians and not others, or loving Christians more than others. The ritual is salvific, in senses discussed earlier, precisely as it enables the address of obligations, grounded wholeness, engagement, and the achievement of value-identity in their proper universality. Thus, the ritual is instrumental in salvation to the extent that it overcomes any ultimacy regarding the in-group/out-group distinction it embodies. The Christian ritual can be engaged salvifically precisely to the extent that it functions as a training ground, a hospital with remedies, as it were, for participants who otherwise suffer from the ultimate human predicaments and fail the universality of the mutuality of value in the created order. The ritual is a path to ecstatic fulfillment just to the extent that it embraces the ultimate creator who is as close to any other creature as the creative act is close to oneself.

That the Christian ritual is salvific says nothing in itself about whether other religions' rituals are salvific, nor does it exclude other paths to ecstatic fulfillment. Buddhists have many rituals surrounding meditation that leads to enhanced universal compassion. These rituals are different from the Christian ones, with different symbols. To the extent they address the same elements of the human predicament, their symbols are more or less adequate, just as the Christian symbols are more or less adequate. The viability of particular ritual-based communities needs to be judged empirically regarding whether or not participation does indeed engage salvation regarding the human predicament and mark out actions that are paths to or embodiments of ecstatic fulfillment.

To the extent that a religious community does take its existence from rituals, participation in which embeds the symbols of its sacred canopy in the participants and binds them together as a community practicing the remedies of deliverance and the ecstasies of fulfillment, the symbols gain deep existential meaning. Religious symbols mean much more than what they seem to mean, and living with them in ritual and other contexts is necessary in order to live into those meanings. The meaning of the community as such has many levels that are accessed, among other ways (such as theological study), through repeated ritual participation. Without a ritual life within a community, it is difficult for individuals to penetrate to the depths of the symbols that engage ultimacy and that are salvific in the ultimate predicaments of life. Full humanization, as Rappaport might put it, comes with living into the deep meanings of the symbols that allow engagements with ultimacy in depth. Berger and Rappaport are right to worry about societies whose rituals are in disrepair and that contain many people who do not participate.

Here is another difficulty, however. Participation in a ritual community ties one to that community's various rituals' symbols of ultimacy. Participation in that community involves deep appropriation of its symbols. Usually this means that the symbols of other ritual communities are neglected. Of course, there has always been much commerce among religious communities, with borrowings of symbols and ritual practices. In the contemporary world with its public plurality of religions, this borrowing is highly active. Nevertheless, one cannot live into the religious symbols of all religious communities, however eclectic one's ritual (and theological and ecumenical) life. Not all the important symbols of ultimacy can be integrated into consistent rituals. So, religious practice, insofar as it involves rituals, is inevitably particular. Its particularity is its very strength with regard to its depth.

But part of the obligatory, well-grounded, engaged, and value-bearing identity of human life has to do with engaging others on their own terms. This means respecting and perhaps loving them in their own religious particularity. Concern for other people includes concern that they find salvations appropriate for their versions of the human predicaments. This means that one cannot rest, in matters of ultimate salvation, with the achievement of religious depth in one's own particular ritualized community. In order properly to be aware of, appreciate, engage courageously, and love other people, one has to take in their religion as well, for that is where they address ultimate matters (*III, 3, 4*). So, ignorance of other ritual (and theological) communities is a fault, perhaps a necessary and inevitable limitation, but still a fault. Nevertheless, it confirms the point made throughout *Philosophical Theology* that addressing first-order issues in theology or in practice requires a comparative religious base in which the peculiarities of others are understood alongside the peculiarities of oneself. That comparative practice, even in one's own particular religious community's rituals, involves a deeper understanding of ritual, to which we now turn in an examination of Confucianism.

III. CONFUCIAN UNDERSTANDINGS OF RITUAL

Confucianism is the stream of traditions that has most deeply and comprehensively explored the nature and significance of ritual.[15] The most comprehensive of the early theoreticians was Xunzi in the third century before the Common Era. He noted that human beings are endowed by Heaven and Earth, that is, by their natural biological conditions, with vastly underdetermined physical, emotional, and intellectual capacities.[16] For him, "Earth" signified the material processes of nature with varying degrees of crudeness and subtlety, the former being more physical and the latter being more spiritual or mental. "Heaven" signified the organizing principles for the natural processes and was particularly important in human endeavors in which people need to learn how best to organize or harmonize things. We need not press Xunzi's cosmology here, only to accept the general point that human nature as it is given apart from specifically human cultural contributions is underdetermined. What is needed to determine the underdetermined human nature, and so allow for real humanity, is the acquisition of habits that are semiotically formed. These semiotic habits are habits of ritual behavior, and the exercise of those habits in particular circumstances is ritual performance, whatever else it is also.

Thus the Confucian notion of ritual is not limited to special liminally separated rituals as is typical of Western anthropological thinking. For instance, the human body is capable of standing up with the feet angled out from one another, as Westerners stand, or with the feet parallel, as East Asians stand. Before they stand at all, babies can learn to do it either way. But in order to learn to stand, babies have to learn to do it some specific way or another. Learning to stand is to develop interpretive habits in the muscles for resisting gravity in an upright way, and those interpretive habits are semiotically formed. Some particular culture is needed, and so some ritual of standing is taught in every culture with upright folk. Similarly, the human vocal apparatus is capable, in its infantile endowment, of making the sounds of any human language. But to speak at all, some particular language has to be learned, with a semiotics that deals not only with sounds but with grammar, meaningful symbols, and the like. To have some particular language is to have the habits necessary to participate in a linguistic ritual. The ritual of language does not determine what to say—other interests do that. But having a ritual language makes it possible to say something and does affect what can and cannot be said. Every society needs to have some particular forms of greeting; otherwise encounters are likely to be violent or lead to quick separation. Whether greetings are ritualized by shaking hands, by bowing, or by speaking certain words, does not matter so long as there is some ritual for greeting. When people from different ritual cultures meet, their greetings can be confused. Political and religious ceremonial rituals make possible certain kinds of engagement, in these instances, engagements of authority and engagements with ultimate matters. The ritual ceremonies are objectified as rituals, which is what anthropologists notice, and are not largely unconscious habits. But they still are rituals in the same senses, namely, of providing semiotic forms in which an otherwise underdetermined reality can take place. The ceremonial rituals involve many other ritual habits than the explicit ceremony, such as language and posture.

In human life, the semiotically formed rituals are densely layered within each other. When a preacher stands and says something in a Christian Sunday service, the explicitly religious content of the sermon is nested within the entire linguistic system of the community's culture, within the idiosyncratic rituals of the preacher's own thinking, as well as within the rituals of posture and gesture, all of which can be grasped and used at some level by the congregation.

By focusing on human behavior and thought as ritual, the Confucians are able to foster five lines of inquiry: how rituals are learned as elements of interpretive behavior with their own integrity, how rituals condition one another, how rituals change, how rituals are performed, and how the performance of rituals constitutes particular embodiments of humanity.

1. The learning of a ritual, such as learning to stand, to speak, or to sing hymns, creates a new component of a person's life. The component is a habit with a semiotic or meaning structure such that it interprets a reality with a response under certain conditions, often conditions of purpose. Habits of standing interpret the pull of gravity when one wants to stand; habits of speaking English interpret the communication situation when one wants to say something; habits of singing hymns interpret the worship service when the ritual calls for hymn-singing. Without those habits, regardless of the situation and one's intents, to stand, say something, or sing with a congregation is not possible. Being a civilized human being requires a great many habits that are given orientation within a worldview. The ways of acquiring habits are extraordinarily various, from the try-and-try-again method of infants learning to stand, to the rush of new language acquisition when elementary semiotic responses are in place, to transferring secular singing to the worship context.

2. Rituals condition one another in a great dynamic complexity. Rituals are all habits for performance and just about any action involves the performance of a wide array of ritual habits all at once. Suppose a Christian is driving to the golf course on Sunday morning and, feeling guilty for missing church, turns on a broadcast of a worship service, singing along in the car when the hymns come on. Just driving alone involves the performance of interpretive rituals of watching the traffic signs, interacting with other cars, feeling the acceleration and deceleration of the driver's car as it goes around curves, over hills, and up to stop signs. Most of these rituals are performed

unconsciously by experienced drivers whose muscles and nervous systems are habituated, unless some sudden driving emergency calls them to mind. There also are the ritualized emotions of substituting one "good," golf, for another, worship, with attendant guilt or regret, as well as anticipation; states of mind such as this are highly ritualized and can be performed in many circumstances of choice about how to spend time. Then all of the linguistic, religiously symbolic, musical, and community rituals are in play as the Christian drives along, while attention might be focused only on the phrases being sung at the moment. All of these are rituals that interact and make one another possible.

3. Ritualized habits are generally in a constant state of modification. Each performance of a ritual can reshape the ritual form itself somewhat. Rituals are learned through time and exercise, and unlearned through time and failure to be performed. As Charles Peirce pointed out, rituals become more determinate, and also become less determinate. Moreover, the occasions for these modifications of ritual include not only those of their performance but also shifts in their interconnected rituals: learning Latin is likely to modify the rituals by which a Christian takes part in a high church Sunday morning ritual, many of whose phrases are in that language. The constant interaction of a person with a natural and social environment creates a dynamic of changes of ritualized habits.

4. The performance of a ritual is the exercising of a habit. The ritual has a vague form that can be exercised in a variety of ways, just as a dance pattern is vague with respect to just how far to step, how much weight to transfer, and so forth. In musical and dance rituals, the score and directions set the outermost vague form; then there are performance traditions of different ways in which those forms can be performed, allowing different performers to work consistently together; then each performer has a personal style within those performance traditions; and each performance is a specific version of that style. Human life is shaped in many measures by large-scale rituals defining family relations, career development, community life, and so forth. Part of maturation is the individuation of those rituals. A responsible young woman would play the ritual role of a dutiful daughter within the family, but by late middle age would have individuated it to be the ritual interaction specific to the relation between just who she is and just who her parents are. The ritual interactions and changes mentioned previously complicate all this.

5. For the Confucians there are degrees of humaneness or civilized humanity. The baseline is having a body with human capacities (underdetermined) and some culture that provides socializing ritual habits; anyone with these conditions is to be respected as a human being. With this baseline, people become more and more humane and civilized the more they acquire the ritualized habits that enable them to perform in civilized ways. The fundamental complaint Confucius made about his own social environment was that the culture at hand did not offer the rituals that would enable humane living at a high civilized level, and he sought to reinstitute the rituals of the ancient sages so as to make high civilization possible. Without good family

rituals, people can procreate and perhaps raise children to sexual maturity, but they would have no civilized family life. Without political rituals, people might be able to cooperate on the hunt but not have rich community life. Without friendship rituals, people might be able to coexist, but without the joys of deep friendship. Not only do societies differ in the degrees to which they offer the rituals that make for high civilization, according to the Confucians, at any given time each society is changing to offer better or worse rituals in its cultural semiotic store. Because the possession of rituals to be learned through cultural interactions is what makes possible the sorts of behavior that make for civilized life, the focus of ritual has a kind of priority for the Confucians over concerns for other equally important virtues such as sincerity in playing the rituals, moral righteousness, and wisdom, which would have no application if there were no rituals within which they could bear upon the performance of being human.

IV. RITUAL ENGAGEMENT

The Confucians understand how each human individual needs to be more than the biological endowment of the body and its capacities, including intellectual and emotional capacities. Each needs a complex acculturation in rituals at all levels that enable the more or less organic interaction of those capacities that are required for being human, especially for being human in a highly civilized way. The individual is thus formed *as individual* by the acquisition from various social sources and from the individual's own learning within the rituals of society of the rituals enabling humane life. The individual is individuated by learning to perform the rituals with greater finesse and sincerity, even though the rituals do not themselves dictate just how they are to be performed, any more than being able to speak a language dictates what to say, although it affects what can and cannot be said, what is appropriate or inappropriate, and so forth.

The Confucian traditions in many respects stand opposed to the ways many Western philosophical and religious schemes have distinguished the individual from society. For Western thinkers, human individuals are sometimes thought to be more or less human just as "natural" noncultural beings, with culture as an artificial overlay; Rousseau is an extreme instance of such a thinker. The senses in which religion is to be construed as a social or individual matter depend on this distinction, and *Philosophical Theology* builds from the Confucian pattern.

In matters of engaging salvation, the explicitly religious rituals are not the only rituals the performance of which engages salvific remedies and paths to ecstatic fulfillment. Much less is this so for religious rituals that are liminally separated into sacred space and time. As described in Parts I and II of this volume, deliverance regarding the ultimate human predicaments has to do eventually with relating to ultimacy. But the salvific remedies might be spread through a host of interacting rituals required for enabling the performance of rituals that directly deal with ultimate reality. Learning the ritual habit of deep slow breathing might be very important for quieting the soul for meditation about more ultimate things such as the negotiation of change, without supposing that such breathing itself is metaphysically important. Therefore, the anthropological theories of ritual discussed in the first two sections of this chapter are not adequate, however helpful, for understanding how ritual in religion works to remedy ultimate human predicament.

In further chapters in this volume and the next, this discussion of ritual as a dimension of engaging salvation is mapped onto the theory of worldviews developed earlier. Rituals of many sorts are distributed across the whole continuum from the sacred, within the sacred canopy, to the mundane, including activities very far from ultimate realities. Because any human activity that might find orientation within a worldview is semiotically constructed, it is a ritual activity. Because rituals can be connected in the ways discussed, however, rituals at the far end of the mundane extreme might or might not be integrated somehow with rituals arising from the sacred end. This is what gives an ultimate dimension, or dimension of ultimacy, to some of the most mundane things. The understanding of a worldview involves understanding the interconnections of its rituals. The understanding of a religion involves understanding how its rituals play throughout the worldview. The most basic form of accessing religion's deliverances and paths to ultimate fulfillment is through learning to participate in the complex ritual system of a worldview that brings the engagements of ultimacy into touch with daily life.

Because all rituals are vague habits, their forms are vague signs, defined in semiotic systems with other signs. Sometimes these are explicitly verbal, or can be represented in verbal signs, and they include explicitly religious symbols. Thus, to understand the meanings of the rituals that make up a worldview that gives ultimacy to mundane things involves interpreting their symbolic content along the various positions of the continuum from sophisticated expressions to folk expressions. The very same ritual behavior has many different ritual meanings depending on the position along that continuum from which it is interpreted by other rituals. Similarly, the symbols in those rituals that deal with ultimate reality and ultimate dimensions in mundane realities are to be interpreted in terms of the pressures toward greater transcendence and the pressures toward great intimacy.

Playing rituals, especially those formed by religions, is an extremely important dimension of engaging religion's paths to ecstatic fulfillment and remedies for the brokenness of human predicament. Of course, it is not the only way, or even complete by itself. In addition to the role of ritual is the role of commitment. The analysis of worldviews in *Philosophical Theology One*, Chapter 4, noted three continua that bear upon commitment: the comprehensiveness of the worldview with respect to the mundane things of life, the intensity of commitment, and the ways by which different individuals share the worldview. Religious commitment is the topic of the next chapter.

Chapter Fourteen

Commitment

To engage religious paths to ecstatic fulfillment and remedies for various elements of human predicaments requires a commitment to engage them. This is a minimal condition. The commitment might be piecemeal, oriented only to a particular salvific element, such as a kind of healing, for instance, without much attention to the religious system within which the particular approach to healing is embedded. In times of religious eclecticism, such as the present in Western societies, such fragmented commitment is common. How fashionable it is for Americans to seek out sweat-lodge experiences without any serious commitment to the Native American religious systems that employ sweat lodges! But without some embrace of the larger contexts of religious remedies for the human predicament, their salvific effects are likely to be superficial and ephemeral. These larger contexts are analyzed here in terms of worldviews and their religious elements.

Commitment has many dimensions, of which four are discussed here, with reappraisals of the discussions in *Philosophical Theology Three*, Chapter 12. First is the sense in which commitment is to a worldview that has some character of comprehensiveness in the way it orients life. Some worldviews touch on just about everything in life such that commitment to certain salvific religious elements involves commitments across a broad spectrum of activities. At the other extreme are worldviews that orient a few things in life but are irrelevant to a broad spectrum of activities. Most are in between these extremes and have specific characters of comprehensiveness.

Second is the sense in which commitment to a worldview or the religious part of it has some kind of intensity. The intensity of commitment is roughly correlated with the range of intensity of ultimate concern discussed in *Philosophical Theology One*, Chapter 5. Some people are not committed to a worldview with religious elements at all, however much they might admire and want some of the promised salvific effects. Others are strongly committed to certain parts of a religious worldview. Yet others organize their whole lives around the religious commitment. Some are so strongly committed to the religious worldview that they abandon concern for their own salvation in some or all dimensions.

Third is the sense in which commitment is to a religious worldview that is shared, more or less, by a community, such that the commitment is part of community membership. Because of the way classical anthropologists studied their "primitive" cultures, they treated commitment as an act of solidarity with the whole culture whose worldview was embraced. Kathryn Tanner has pointed out that, even within tightly enclosed cultural groups, individuals embrace the worldview with their own modifications.[1] The extent to which commitment is shared is an important dimension.

Fourth, and prior to the other three in this discussion, is the sense in which religious commitment itself is a universal human factor, common in possibility to everyone and necessary for full maturation. Anthropologists have noted that at least 70 percent of the world's cultures have coming-of-age rituals in which adolescents commit themselves specifically to some religious worldview.[2] In many instances, this is a commitment to the worldview in which they had been raised. In late-modern times it is often a commitment to a worldview that is not exactly the parental worldview, a direct rejection perhaps, or a choice of other worldviews made available in a situation of religious pluralism, or an idiosyncratic worldview constructed with elements from many different sources. Given the diversity among cultures in so many other respects, what accounts for the prevalence of adolescent coming-of-age rituals?

I. BIO-DEVELOPMENTAL DIMENSIONS OF COMMITMENT

Some cognitive scientists have suggested that religious commitment is something that is age-specific in the development of the human brain, something associated with brain development during adolescence and crucial for subsequent brain development. Of course, brain development after birth is always a function in part of surrounding environmental and social circumstances, including being in a society that formulates worldviews as possibilities for religious commitment. But the biological factor of brain development helps account for the universality of rituals that embody or symbolize the act of commitment itself.

How might we understand the act of religious commitment as a function of brain development? Candace S. Alcorta likens it to the developmental roles of music and language acquisition in the earlier stage of infancy. She writes:

> Throughout the world, mothers and other caregivers sing to newborns. These songs are sung in hundreds of different languages, but the style in which they are sung is universal. Songs sung to infants are slower, higher

pitched, and have an exaggerated rhythm when compared to noninfant songs. No matter what the language, these are the songs infants prefer. Even two-day-old infants born from congenitally deaf parents who sign and do not speak or sing prefer infant-directed singing to adult-directed singing. . . .

For music, the development of these innate abilities is directly linked to the neural maturation of specific brain areas. The ability of young infants to distinguish pitch is dependent upon the maturation of neurons that make up "tonotopic" maps of the right temporal lobe that associate sound frequencies with pitch. Similar processing of time intervals in music occurs in the homologous region of the left temporal lobe, resulting in perceptions of rhythm. . . .

The development of language capacities occurs slightly after that of music and may actually build on several of the capacities developed during music acquisition. The associations between sound patterns and meaning and the correlations between sound patterns and syntactic structure that are critical elements in language are first developed in relation to music. . . . The pitch, tone, and cadence of speech, collectively referred to as speech prosody, are the first elements attended to in linguistic communication. In contrast to the left-hemisphere processing of all other language components, these elements of language are processed in the right "musical" side of the brain.[3]

The point is that, without the social development of biologically innate musical capacities, the learning of language is very difficult if not impossible.

Something similar seems to be the case with the acquisition of commitment to religion during adolescence. During adolescence the growth of the brain and its connections involves, among many other things, a period when dopamine, a neurotransmitter that suppresses brain activity, is increased in the prefrontal lobe, which results in a suppression of balanced judgment, decision-making, and impulse control. At the same time, dopamine is decreased in the limbic system, which allows for more excited emotions and less well-regulated impulses. Concomitant with this is a set of changes in the neural "reward system," allowing adolescents to find both social bonding and symbolic systems of meaning to be rewarding. Although religion is not the only form of social bonding or symbolic representation of large-scale meaning, it is certainly one of the most central. Adolescence is a time when the brain's development is open to emotionally deep commitment to both social bonding and a symbolic system articulating a worldview. In mature adults, the dopamine delivery system decreases the dopamine in the frontal lobes, thus activating deliberative judgment and executive powers, and increases the dopamine in the limbic system, which calms and steadies emotional responses.

The result of this is that, just as infants who are not sung to do not develop their musical responsiveness, and thus have a much harder time later learning language, adolescents who do not have the opportunities for commitment to a symbolic worldview and the social connections that go with it will not be able to make such commitments later. Or, although they later can make rational choices about worldviews and sometimes act on those choices, they cannot easily do so with the deep commitment of their heart, mind, soul, and strength.

Adolescent commitment, to be sure, is limited to the kinds of symbols and social relations open to adolescents, not just to the limitations of their cultures. In small, homogenous societies, the symbolic content and social organization of the adolescent commitment might not change much later. In more complicated societies, however, the educational development of adolescents is very like to be enlarged with age and more education. So the adolescent symbol system might appropriately be modified or even overthrown as immature. Similarly, the adolescent view of the social world can change radically with greater maturity. Therefore, the content of adolescent religious commitment is very likely to be immature and in need of improvement. Sometimes young adults completely reject their adolescent commitments, as so many Christian individuals do who were raised in narrow religious cultures that provided content for their adolescent commitment. But they still have the developed capacity to make new commitments, shifting the content to more mature material. Adolescents whose social environment or other factors diffused or prevented the opportunities for deep religious commitment have a much harder time making such commitments later, an important lesson for religious communities interested in adolescent education.

More is involved in adolescent religious development than is suggested by the cognitive science material reviewed here. Religion is not the only cultural form that presents systems of symbolic meaning and social organization for adolescent commitment. What makes such commitment religious is the peculiar symbolic activity that has to do with defining oneself as having an ultimate commitment. This is the establishment of a conscious or quasi-conscious sense of self-identity as ultimately committed to the worldview and its social organization (or disorganization). During adolescence a person "chooses" to be an identity through the deep commitment, and this has ultimate significance.

Such a religious commitment is religious because it relates to ultimacy in two places. First, it is a commitment to a worldview that the person takes to establish or represent the boundary conditions for what is ultimately real and important. Second, it establishes the ultimate significance of the individual as the one who takes on the identity involved in the commitment. The adolescent worldview might contain wholly untenable and immature symbols of ultimacy, which the maturing adult might overturn. Similarly, the identity given ultimate significance in the adolescent commitment might be rejected in favor of another. Both senses of religious identity can be changed. Nevertheless, without the adolescent development of ultimate-identity choice in ultimate commitment to the worldview and its social significance, the biological stage passes in which that kind of identity is possible with the force of ultimate commitment.

It is mistaken to identify religious worldviews exclusively with those formulated by religious traditions and to identify the ultimate identity commitment that comes with adolescent commitment to those worldviews involving participation in traditional religious communities. Sometimes those associations obtain. But often they do not. An adolescent, and then the mature person, can be committed to an "antireligious" worldview, as often happens in late-modern cultures. If that "antireligious" worldview provides the ultimate boundary conditions for the person's sense of life and reality, however, it is properly religious in the sense defined in *Philosophical Theology* in terms of ultimacy. And if the commitment does indeed determine a sense of ultimacy about the person's self-identity, then it is an ultimate religious identity however it rejects specific traditional religious social participation.

The issues involved in these senses of ultimacy, even when traditional religious symbols and social membership are rejected, can be explored further with reference to the continua of comprehensiveness, intensity, and sociality of commitment.

II. RELIGIOUS COMMITMENT AND WORLDVIEWS

A self-conscious religious commitment has a dual focus. On the one hand, it is a commitment to an identifiable cluster of symbols that articulates something ultimate, something that defines certain if not all boundary conditions of the cosmos relative to oneself. A formal definition of these boundary conditions as finite/infinite contrasts was given in *Philosophical Theology One*, the introduction and Chapter 1. The boundary conditions for most people are symbolized within a sacred canopy and the commitment is to some central symbols of that sacred canopy and to the life that follows from them. Consider the classic Confucian statement of commitment. "Confucius said, 'At fifteen my mind was set on learning. At thirty I knew the Mandate of Heaven. At sixty I was at ease with whatever I heard. At seventy I could follow my heart's desire without transgressing moral principles."[4] As an adolescent, Confucius "set his mind on learning," which is to say he committed himself to be a sage. What did that mean to him? Of course, we cannot know in much detail because it was presumably after he was fifteen that he worked out the many themes we now know as Confucianism. He likely knew some or many of the prior texts that he went on to edit and give authority, though he was only beginning to understand them. Probably he lived under a sacred canopy with notions such as Heaven and Earth, Dao, the self as special, and questions about how the patterns of human nature relate to ultimate cosmic patterns as microcosm to macrocosm. His religious commitment was to devote himself to their study. At thirty he knew the Mandate of Heaven, which is to say he had worked out his career as a scholar-official-teacher. At sixty he understood enough not to be surprised or hurt by the things he learned. At seventy his desires had been so educated that he could trust them. Tu Weiming's *Humanity and Self-Cultivation* is an extended study of the Confucian decision to become a sage:

> The structure of *li-chih* [to establish the will] is analogous to that of existential decision in the Kierkegaardian sense: it is a fundamental choice that requires an ultimate commitment; it is a qualitative change that affects the entire dimension of one's being; and it is an unceasing process that demands constant reaffirmation. . . . When Confucius says in the *Analects*, "At fifteen, I set my heart on learning," he is describing his early commitment to self-transformation. The decision to learn, which in the classical sense means to be engaged in self-enlightenment, thus symbolizes a qualitative change in the orientation of one's life. . . . Learning so conceived is a conscious attempt to change oneself from being in a state of mere psychophysiological growth to that of an ethicoreligious existence.[5]

The point is that the adolescent commitment is to a task symbolized in ways the implications of which are not clear at that point. As they emerge, the commitment needs to be reaffirmed.

Or consider the adolescent Christian who gives his or her life to Jesus by accepting "Jesus Christ as my Lord and Savior," a formula favored in some conservative forms of Christianity. The focus of the symbols of "Jesus Christ," "Lord," and "Savior" can be highly charged with emotion but without much content. The depth of the commitment can lead to steady learning about those symbols, for instance, through careful and repeated reading of the Bible, further study, and association with other Christians. Sometimes, of course, the more mature meaning of the symbols turns out to be quite different from their meaning to the adolescent.

The other focus of adolescent religious commitment is the self-reflexive definition of the self as ultimately determined by the commitment to the ultimate symbols. So, Confucius took himself to be defined ultimately by his commitment to sagehood. The young Christian takes himself or herself to be defined ultimately by the commitment to Jesus Christ. A similar analysis can be made of the Buddhist commitment to be a bodhisattva. This self-reflexive focus is discussed in the next section.

The comprehensiveness of religious commitment depends on the worldview involved. The symbols in the worldview provide orientation for the host of human activities, situations, and issues spread across the sacred/mundane continuum (*I, 4*). The connections among these symbols articulate how the orientation points of the various aspects of life are connected. Thus the worldview, even if never much brought to consciousness, provides the semiotic meaning structure that relates various parts of human life together and to the larger world, including the ultimate realities. Religious commitment is commitment to the worldview implicit in the focal symbols of the commitment.

Most worldviews include sacred canopies that contain symbols orienting people to what is ultimate, or alleged to be ultimate, in the worldview. Most also contain not-quite-ultimate conceptions of the nature of the physical cosmos and the larger natural environment within which people live. The worldviews also contain orienting symbols for the place of human beings in the world, for the historical and social settings of people, and for the historical and social settings of the individuals at hand, their own group or groups. Toward the more mundane end of the continuum are orienting symbols for the individuals' own local situation, for family, education, and working conditions, for stage-of-life elements, for particular interpersonal relationships, leisure and recreation, and for what to do this week and today.

Worldviews differ among themselves regarding what kinds of things are provided orientation. The aforementioned list is vague and suggestive, although most worldviews say something about most of those elements. To have nothing to say about recreation, or the history of one's group, or nature beyond direct contact, or ultimate reality, is quite possible for a worldview. Worldviews also differ among themselves regarding how much they say about the things they orient. They might provide a great deal of orientation, some, or very little. A worldview might be very determinate about orienting family matters and quite vague with respect to one's place in history; some people suggest that women are more likely than men to have such a worldview, although that caricature should not be trusted. Worldviews also differ in the ways and degrees to which they connect the various clusters of symbols that orient different kinds of things. Some provide loose connection, others tight; worldviews connect some orientation symbols loosely, others tightly. Some have certain kinds of connecting metaphors that range over the whole worldview, as, for instance, in "scientific" worldviews, while others have several different kinds of connecting symbols, perhaps scientific for connecting some spheres, narrative for connecting others, religious for connecting yet others. Worldviews rarely have a consistent logical structure. Rather, their connections are resonances, analogies, traditional associations, and the like, as well as some logical connectives. Sometimes these styles of connection are problematic.

These three points, about the kinds of things a worldview orients, the degree of determinateness in various aspects of orientation, and the degrees and styles with which the different orientation points are connected, constitute some of the most important dimensions of comprehensiveness in worldviews. When a person makes a religious commitment to certain focal symbols, the person makes an implicit commitment to the worldview that orients those symbols. Just how comprehensive that commitment is depends on what kinds of things the worldview orients, how much orientation the worldview provides to those various kinds of things, and the ways in which the orienting domains are connected with one another.

As argued, a commitment is religious if it is focused on symbols of ultimacy and if it self-reflexively gives ultimate definition to the person making the commitment. All sorts of commitments are made that have fairly comprehensive effects throughout one's worldview that are not religious, for instance, commitment to a life partner or a choice of an educational path. Perhaps some people make no ultimate commitments, as there are some people with no ultimate concerns (I, 5). But if a person does make an ultimate commitment (to the Confucian way of the sage, to Jesus Christ, to being a bodhisattva, to submission to Allah, to being an observant Jew, to the way of a Hindu renunciant, to secular humanism, or whatever), the ultimacy of this is articulated somehow in a sacred canopy signifying a view as to what is ultimately real and important. What is ultimately real and important are the finite/infinite contrasts that define the boundary conditions of the world as possibly represented one way or another in the worldview. Where ultimacy is involved in the worldview, the commitment is a religious commitment. Where the worldview has no symbols of ultimacy, lacking a sacred canopy, it provides no orientation or way of engaging the ultimates, real though they are.

The cluster of symbols at the focal point of the initial commitment might not be the whole of the sacred canopy within which those symbols are defined. Young evangelicals committing themselves to Jesus, under the stimulation of an emotional religious commitment worship service, might have no clue at that point about the Christian doctrine of the Trinity. But as they seek to live out the commitment to Jesus, they find themselves exploring a sacred canopy that is responsive to the factors that led ancient Christians to formulate their understanding of God and Jesus in Trinitarian terms. This leads to thinking about what God creating the world might mean, and on and on through the kinds of symbols that make up the astonishingly rich Christian sacred canopy, or family of sacred canopies. So, too, with religious commitments in any of the great religious traditions that have thought theologically about what is involved in ultimacy. As argued throughout *Philosophical Theology*, the things that are really ultimate include: (1) the radical contingency of the world; (2) the nature and ground of form, possibility, and obligation; (3) the nature and ground of the integration of the self; (4) the nature and ground of relations to other things, especially other people; and (4) the nature and ground of absolute value-identity for people. A given individual might not reflect on all these but will indeed encounter traditional ways of symbolizing them and their predicaments. As a relatively innocent religious commitment works itself out in maturing reflection, it has the opportunity to explore all the dimensions of ultimacy, and to fail to do so is to draw back from the ultimate importance of the religious commitment. A religious commitment is not merely to the focal realities symbolized but to the ultimate realities with which they are connected. Moreover, the ultimacy in the commitment includes a commitment to get those realities right.

Moreover, insofar as the ultimate realities to which a commitment is made are connected within the worldview to mundane matters, those mundane matters have ultimate dimensions. Thus, if all determinate things are radically contingent and created, this is an ultimate dimension of anything whatsoever and a worldview should represent this with the appropriate responses to gratuitous creation. If having obligations with regard to the choice among possibilities of different values is an ultimate matter, then every choice in the mundane affairs of life has an ultimate dimension; the choice itself is not ultimate, but having obligations to choose well in that choice is ultimate. If integrating the self is an ultimate condition of life, and this means comporting oneself toward the components of life in a proper fashion, then anything that has to do with the components of life has an ultimate dimension; the components are not ultimate necessarily, but there is a religious dimension to how they are related within the self. If engaging other things in the existential field is an ultimate condition of life, then even the trivial interactions have an ultimate dimension; the interactions themselves might not be ultimate, but the mode of their engagement is ultimate. If achieving a value-identity in ultimate perspective is an ultimate condition, then the worth of everything with value that one causes or bears in oneself or in other things has an ultimate dimension; the values themselves most likely are proximate, not ultimate, but having them is ultimately important. A person with an ultimate religious commitment should have a worldview that expresses at least these if not many other ultimate dimensions in mundane life.

Adopting a richly fashioned worldview from a traditional religion is a shortcut to having a worldview that comprehensively exhibits the ultimacy in mundane things, their ultimate dimensions. But such traditional worldviews might not be adequate, for reasons that are discussed in more detail in *Philosophical Theology Three*, Part IV. Each individual needs to develop an adequate religious worldview that is properly comprehensive as an implication of an ultimate religious commitment (*III, 2, iii*). If it cannot be found ready-made, a point explored in Section IV, it lies as an obligation on the individual. To the extent that a worldview has religious dimensions, it can properly be called a religious or sacred worldview. A given worldview might be sacred in some parts and not in others.

III. INTENSITY OF RELIGIOUS COMMITMENT

The dependence of an ultimate religious commitment on a sacred worldview does not consist only in the meaning structure the worldview provides for the commitment. It consists also in how the worldview in fact orients behavior, actual self-cultivation, actual engagements with others, and the working out in practice of a value-identity. The interlocking meaning structure of the worldview is a problem in itself, as just discussed. But the more practical problems arise in the degree of the commitment to live out the implications of the commitment in the mundane domains of life. The pragmatic meaning of the commitment to a belief or meaning structure of ultimacy is the degree to which a person is willing to act on it.

People might believe that they are committed to something, but if they are unwilling to act on that commitment, the commitment has low intensity. To be sure, people have a great capacity for self-deception regarding ultimate commitments. Most of the great religious traditions include commitments to loving others, all others; yet people committed to them have often acted in nonloving ways. No Jew would believe that Christians are as committed to love as Christians think they are. Nevertheless, reflective people will notice the dissonance between the commitments expressed in a religious worldview and the actions that are supposed to be oriented by them. Sometimes this leads to renewed efforts to act out the religious commitment as expressed in the worldview. But other times it leads to a reconsideration of the worldview itself. If the religious worldview enjoins something that is scientifically untenable, for instance, withholding blood transfusions because of religious belief when a life is at stake, the religious worldview itself might be modified or rejected in favor of some other.

Intensity of commitment is to be measured with regard to comprehensiveness and timing. An adolescent's ultimate religious commitment might have very high intensity in emotional value but this does not guarantee the intensity of practical commitment. The practical commitments are ranged across the religious worldview. A person committing to a traditional religious focus, for instance, to Jesus Christ or to the vow of a bodhisattva, might have very high intensity in commitment to the religious practices that are oriented by the ultimate realities themselves, for instance, participation in church or monastic meditation and training. This high intensity is compatible with low-intensity commitment to the ultimacy of moral obligations, however, or to engaging the environment responsibly in an ultimate way. Or vice versa: particularly in late-modern so-called secular societies, people might have nominal intensity in their commitment to traditional forms of relating to the ontologically ultimate but high intensity in their commitment to morals or the environment as ultimate matters. Surely the intensity varies for any individual with regard to commitment to the different domains within a worldview. Given the various dimensions of comprehensiveness in worldviews, intensity is likely to vary in many ways across different domains.

Intensity also varies in timing. Intense commitment one day is followed by indifference the next, or so it often seems. Intensity also varies with the calendar. Most religions have liturgical calendars with days of special celebration, which are likely to involve an intensification of commitment in some or all the ultimate domains. Life's stages also typically differ in intensity. Adolescence for many people is a time of high intensity of commitment to ultimate matters. The end of adolescence and the beginning of young adulthood frequently is a time of fading intensity of commitment and exploration of new perspectives that might cast doubt on old commitments or elicit new directions of commitment. For many, at least in America, the intensity of religious commitment returns at the stage where adults begin to have families and want to provide an ultimately important context for rearing children. Many older people tend to loosen the intensity of their commitment to their own personal earlier religion and foster tolerance and interest in other perspectives while maintaining or increasing the intensity of their commitment, especially in the domains having to do with achieving value-identity.

How are degrees of intensity of commitment in various domains to be understood? The first level of answer to this is the pragmatic one: the more intense the commitment, the more one is willing to act on it. A corollary is that, when acting on the commitment, the more the action is difficult, requires pain or sacrifice, or increases in difficulty, the more intense the commitment. Some evolutionary biologists argue that religious commitment has adaptive value precisely because group solidarity is fostered when people demonstrate their commitment with "costly signals" such as painful initiation rites, scarification, or unpleasant taboos.[6] A person's overall religious commitment needs to be spelled out in its intensity with regard to each of the domains of ultimacy.

A deeper level of answer to understanding degrees of intensity is through correlation with ultimate concern. *Philosophical Theology One*, Chapter 5, noted a continuum of ultimate concern from little or none through various stages of organizing one's life around ultimate priorities to abandoning concern about oneself altogether in commitment to whatever is taken to be ultimate for its own sake. Assuming that those with little or no ultimate concern make little or no religious commitment, the degree to which one organizes or reorganizes life around the objects of commitment is a measure of intensity. Because of the interconnection of the different domains within a religious worldview, to mark intensity in each one separate from the others is a bit abstract. The organization of commitment through all the religiously significant domains is more realistic for understanding intensity of commitment. The more life's shapes are reordered by the commitment, the more intense it is, particularly when there is opposition or cost involved. The greatest intensity would be the abandonment of concerns for ordering one's life in order to serve the ultimate selflessly, although that is likely also to have an ordering effect on life.

The point of the discussions of the nearly universal biological significance of commitment, of its comprehensiveness, and of its intensity, has been to address questions of how individuals might engage the remedies that religion alleges to offer for the brokenness of the human predicament. Chapter 9 answered the questions with an analysis of participation in religious ritual. But the participation by itself is not the only method of engagement, and in fact might not be very effective if there is not also religious commitment.

Part II discussed the deliverance from human predicament in terms of salvific themes offered by many religious traditions: Justification (redemption, restoration, sanctification, purification), Wholeness (healing, humility, comfort, enlightenment), Connection (acceptance, purgation, faith, reconciliation), and Happiness (renunciation, dedication, submission, affirmation). To think of these as separate and ready to be plucked up for one's predicament at hand is unrealistic, although the effectiveness of religious eclecticism should not be underestimated. Rather, any one religion's version of a remedy is set within a worldview, or family of worldviews, that connects it with much else in life. The argument of this chapter so far has been that seriously to engage any religious salvific intervention or to walk a path aiming at ecstatic fulfillment requires commitment to much of the worldview within which that remedy lies. Not to make that larger commitment is to truncate the meaning of the remedy or the fulfillment. The remedies and fulfillments have specific meaning only within the context of their religious worldviews. A person who goes to a sweat-lodge ceremony for deliverance or ecstasy is likely only to become dehydrated if the larger meaning system of the Native American ritual is ignored and the commitment extends no farther than the duration of the sweat.

IV. SHARING OF RELIGIOUS COMMITMENT

The worldviews involved in religious commitment are all social in their basic meaning elements even when an individual has tailored an extremely idiosyncratic version. The semiotic systems involved in language are enough to guarantee this. For the most part, as they grow up, children are taught a religious worldview, or several of them, or fragments of them, and for many a religious commitment is simply the affirmation of such teachings as defining their own ultimate identity.

Nevertheless, even if a person is taught a religious worldview as a family matter, including being brought up to participate in the religious institutions that carry it, the worldview that is carried in the social and familial culture is inevitably somewhat vague with respect to orienting the individual. Vague meanings are often far more important than idiosyncratic specifications of them. Nevertheless, affirming a worldview requires making it specific enough so as to be able to orient a person's own particular life. Moreover, the activities that find orientation within a worldview often have some feedback effect on the worldview itself, modifying or tailoring the worldview. A person might have a vague appreciation of nature as an ultimate mystery and gratuitous surprise. But that means something different for a Daoist who has traveled down the gorges of the Yangtze River from what it means for a Daoist who has traveled only in the desert. Actual happenings affect the symbolic and metaphoric meanings of the symbols in the worldview domains that orient them. All this is to say that in religious commitment, as in any commitment whatsoever, a dialectical interplay exists between what the society offers as meanings and what the individual takes up to work with. Human beings share meanings vaguely and possess them more specifically.

An added dimension to the sharing of commitment, however, obtains when the commitment involves strong elements of negation. Particularly in late-modern pluralistic societies, hardly anyone accepts a socially constructed and legitimated religious worldview without reservations and changes. The changes might derive from rejection of parental cultures. Or they might arise as one discovers that conflicting implications emerge from an original commitment. Or they might come from a host of components that have to do with plausibility conditions for worldviews (*III, 13–14*). Thus individuals are often put in the position of sharing some but not other parts of their worldview with certain others, and sharing some of those other parts with different others, and sharing yet other parts of their worldview with no one else. The commitments to worldviews are truly social matters because even the rejection of a socially legitimated worldview employs the socially constructed meanings of rejections and of the alternatives affirmed, even when the individual poetically transforms those meanings.

Many grounds exist for rejecting a socially legitimated worldview in favor of an idiosyncratic worldview. These include psychological reasons, family dynamics, being the subject of oppression within the rejected worldview, changing circumstances that render the old worldview inapplicable to the new situation and inadequate to provide orientation, and the like. But the most important reason, the one under obligation, is to change a worldview to make it more nearly true. This includes changing a person's commitment to make it more nearly true. Because of the dynamic character of the relation between a person's commitments, the worldviews symbolizing their focal ultimate realities, the changing circumstances that bring out new things to be oriented, new implications in various domains of mundane life, and the maturation process itself, alternative worldviews are presented as possibilities with different values. A person is always under the obligation, when faced with alternative possibilities, to choose the best, and choosing here means making ultimate commitments to the best. How does a person come to understand the better and worse possibilities for religious worldviews? Through theology, of course (*III, 13–14*)!

Although the intelligence of folk theology should not be underestimated, theological reflection among religious people is rare and even then is a specialized discipline. Why is this? The answer is not exclusively that theology is difficult. Other considerations exist that blunt or deflect intelligent pursuit of a worldview worth an intense commitment. Most people have competing obligations for how to spend time and energy. Perhaps the upset caused by critical reflection on an inherited worldview is such a great disintegrating force in a person's own self that the person is better advised simply to accept the inherited worldview without question and move on. Very often, the questioning of a worldview and the commitment to it is troubling to people's social engagements, threatening family unity and tradition, having the potential to undermine the commitments of others, and being socially disruptive. Going along with a socially legitimated sacred worldview, even if the person suspects it is implausible, might be more important than pursuing the theological truth. Precisely because religious worldviews are about what people take to be ultimately important, the social consequences of breaking off solidarity with a shared religious worldview can be enormous and very costly to the individual.

All this shows that religious commitment to a worldview exhibits the human predicament. Religious commitment can be compromised by competing obligations, by needs for being grounded, and by the associations of social engagement. The intensity of religious commitment is compromised when one does not pay the price for pursuing the truthfulness of the commitment: pursuing the truth regarding what a person should be committed to is a form of costly signaling that marks the seriousness of the commitment itself. In all cases, when the truth of the religious worldview to which one is ultimately committed is compromised by other considerations, more proximate matters are given greater importance than the ultimate matters of ultimate commitment. This is, in effect, a denial of the ultimacy of one's ultimate commitment. For this reason, matters having to do with a person's absolute value-identity can never be in conflict with commitment to pursuing the truth of symbols of ultimacy.

To be sure, the specific content of a person's theology articulating the religious worldview to which the person is ultimately committed is proximate, not ultimate. We know that our religious symbols and theories are partial, broken, and always fallible. The ultimate factor in truth-seeking about ultimacy is the seeking itself: to that, a person should be ultimately committed as a part of the ultimately self-defining commitment to ultimate reality.

The argument of this chapter has been complex. It began with the thesis that engaging the salvific interventions that religion offers requires, among other things (such as ritual, the life of faith, and the inhabitation of religious worldviews), a commitment to what a person can symbolize as ultimate and to the worldview that gives this meaning. This commitment has the dual focus of the ultimate as symbolized and of the self-reflexive act of defining the person's own ultimate identity in the commitment. Part of being fully human is having such an ultimate commitment and the ultimate self-identity it gives. But now it turns out that any old religious worldview will not do. A person needs a religious worldview that the person can believe in with greatest plausibility. Otherwise the commitment to it is compromised. Those other considerations that might pull the person away from the ultimacy of seeking truthfulness about the ultimate would turn the person's religious commitment to a proximate rather than ultimate commitment. Then religion's capacity to remedy the brokenness of human predicament in turn is compromised and ecstatic fulfillments might be only cheap thrills.

In addition to ritual and commitment, another dimension of religion is important for engaging ultimacy: a life of faith.

CHAPTER FIFTEEN

The Life of Faith

Given that rituals are only more or less effective and that truly ultimate commitment is paradoxically difficult, it is wise to recognize that these issues are worked through in the life of faith. The phrase "the life of faith" has many associations in religious writing (*II, pr*). "Faith" often is taken to mean beliefs, and beliefs certainly are involved in faith, shaping its ultimate dimensions. But faith here refers to living out those beliefs in life, hence the phrase "the life of faith." Faith also refers to investment in the practices of a religious community, traditional or not, and so the issues discussed about ritual life in Chapter 9 are taken up here. Faith refers as well to the commitment to the practices of the ritual community. "The life of faith" thus involves living through the rituals of religious life and participating with commitment, as when religious people generally (without special association with a tradition or community) are called "people of faith."

This chapter focuses on an additional dimension to the belief, ritual, and commitment dimensions of the life of faith, namely, life as faithful engagement of the world of the existential field in which a person is located. Given the sociality of belief, the community venue for ritual, and the shared (partly or wholly) character of religious commitment, these other dimensions obviously involve engaging with people, institutions, and nature across some spread of the existential field. This chapter, however, focuses on engagement across that field itself.

How is life lived so as to engage things salvifically and with ecstatic fulfillment? The point under argument in this part is how people can engage the salvific deliverances and paths to ecstatic fulfillment that religion offers, and so this is a question with ironic self-reflexivity. How can people engage things so as to become better engaged?

I. PREPARATION

The first level of answer to this question is through preparation. Much of preparation, of course, is through attaining habits of moral practice and through becoming whole. The special components of preparation here have to do with attaining special skills and habits of engaging the world. Surprisingly, one of the most universal traits of the world's various religions addresses this directly, namely, the elaboration of practices roughly grouped around martial metaphors. In several traditions these apply more readily to men than to women (as explicit traditional practices are often aimed more at men than at women), but even when the martial metaphors do not apply to women, traditions have specialized disciplines for women relative to the roles of engagement the traditions assign.

Consider the range of practices comprehended by military metaphors.[1] Daoism is the home of the "soft" or "inner" martial arts such as taijiquan, and that practice is central to membership in Daoist communities today. Ancient Confucianism, for all its emphasis on literary studies and administrative management practices, insisted on archery and horseback riding as essential components of education; Wang Yangming, the greatest early modern Confucian hero, was a military general for whom meditation was the moving still point in the midst of battle. The most important text common to most or all forms of Hinduism, however they differ in their interpretations, is the Bhagavad Gita, which is a story of how a warrior, Arjuna, is restored to military readiness through the actions and words of Krishna (Vishnu). Buddhism, despite its emphasis on nonattachment (which actually is the first lesson Krishna gives to Arjuna), is the source of the "hard" or "outer" martial arts such as gungfu, attributed legendarily to Bodhidharma, who brought Chan (Zen) Buddhism to China and taught the fighting techniques to his monks in the Shaolin monastery in order to keep them awake for meditation. Many forms of Buddhism depict gods and spiritual adepts as armed warriors. Plato, the most reflective thinker in the Greek pagan world, claimed in the *Republic* that there are three elements of soul: appetite (desires), reason, and aggressiveness; aggressiveness is the source of self-discipline and martial prowess, and he had important principles for the education of such aggressiveness or spiritedness. Israelite religion as well as later Judaism often refers to God as the Lord of Hosts, where "hosts" means army, and where proper relation of people to God often means obedience as to a commanding officer. Notwithstanding extraordinary expressions of the importance of peace and nonviolence (turning the other cheek), Jesus said he came to bring not peace but a sword and checked with his disciples upon leaving the "Last Supper" whether they had enough swords among them (though he repaired a sword wound one of his disciples inflicted wrongly [Luke 22]). The author of the New Testament letter to the Ephesians (traditionally but probably mistakenly said to be St. Paul) urged the following upon Christians:

> Finally, be strong in the Lord and in the strength of his power. Put on the whole armor of God, so that you may be able to stand against the wiles of the devil. For our struggle is not against the enemies of blood

and flesh, but against the rulers, against the authorities, against the cosmic powers of this present darkness, against the spiritual forces of evil in the heavenly places. Therefore take up the whole armor of God, so that you may be able to withstand on that evil day, and having done everything, to stand firm. Stand therefore, and fasten the belt of truth around your waist, and put on the breastplate of righteousness. As shoes for your feet put on whatever will make you ready to proclaim the gospel of peace. With all of these, take the shield of faith, with which you will be able to quench all the flaming arrows of the evil one. Take the helmet of salvation, and the sword of the Spirit, which is the word of God. (Ephesians 6:10–17)

This is the biblical author's prescription for the life of faith, given in conclusion to his letter. Note that the author does not advocate actually fighting people, but treats the metaphor of military readiness as directed against both the external social and cosmic sources of evil and any internal lack of discipline that might threaten the Christian's ability to stand firm while engaging life. Islam elaborated this distinction in its conception of the two jihads: the lesser jihad of fighting God's enemies in a political and military sense and the greater jihad of fighting the elements within each person that prevent living in full submission to Allah, and subduing them.

In one way or another, all these instances express the point that it is ultimately important for a person to prepare to engage the issues of life the way a soldier prepares for engaging battle. Enormous differences distinguish these various traditions, to be sure. Some mean that martial training is literally a part of education (for all men who aspire to spiritual virtuosity, according to the Confucians and probably the Daoists; for the military class, according to the Hindus; and for certain monastic traditions, according to some Buddhist schools). For other traditions, actual military preparation is more of a metaphor for personal preparation to meet the challenges of engaging life, however those challenges are conceived.

Furthermore, other differences result from different conceptions or models of human life. For some, the evil and destructive impulses, mainly desires and angers that are so much part of human life, need to be subdued and brought under control, as in Plato's disciplining of aggression to become the force of discipline itself (*III, 11, i*). For others, desires and angers are themselves the problems that need to be eliminated, resulting in nonattachment and dispassion. For all, however, martial discipline is needed to deal with inner enemies as well as external problematic circumstances, and dealing with the former is a prerequisite for dealing with the latter.

A contemporary rendition of martial preparation for life that sidesteps differences about the nature of the self (and a large number of other issues) is the following.[2]

First, to engage life well people should be physically fit, without stressing much distinction between physical and mental fitness. This means eating healthy food, exercising to maximize strength and grace, and developing the skills to engage things physically, perhaps not archery these days, but sports and other activities in which adept status can be sought. Of course, physical limitations inhibit some people from much physical effectiveness, but this only indicates that physical limitations are unfortunate and should be overcome where possible. Many people are in wretched social conditions without much food, without leisure for careful exercise, and without cultural possibilities for adept activities, which only indicates that part of such wretchedness is that it prevents this point of preparation. Few if any spiritual justifications exist for obesity, not bad diet, not stress, not fashion. Dieting is a spiritual discipline; if one is too stressed to diet, yoga can be an effective preliminary step.

Second, preparation for engagement requires learning effective social skills, administrative skills regarding institutions, and skills for engaging nature. Social skills are not limited to being able to win battles with enemies. Each cultural tradition has ways of articulating and teaching these, although not all are equally effective. The effectiveness of skills for acting in the world depends in large part on what things are in the world on which one should act. A pluralistic society requires different social skills from a monocultural one. Skills for survival in the desert differ from those for the tundra, those for the city from those for the jungle.

Third, preparation for engagement requires education about what is in the world to be engaged. In monocultural, small-group societies lodged in the same environment for long periods, face-to-face social routines address the important educational needs. In more complex cultures, however, more complex and sometimes abstract education is required, including experiences in foreign environments. The need for "higher education" might sound elitist, and it is if limited to narrow cultural definitions. But education adequate to the tasks at hand is not elitist, save in the sense that any religious virtuosity is elitist.

Fourth, preparation for engagement with the field of existents involves a sense of style that integrates the preparation in physical, relational, and educational prowess with the issues, things, and people to be engaged on one's watch. This requires a confident sense of oneself as an actor in engagement, a sense that might not be conscious but that is habituated into the way one acts, behaves, and is. The chief obstacle to developing a confident style of engaging, given baseline accomplishments in physical, relational, and educational prowess, is the ego. The ego is an impediment to integrating the internal and external elements. Some religious traditions respond to this obstacle by teaching that the true ego is the underlying reality common to all things, internal and external. Others respond by saying that the ego as such is a harmful illusion. Yet others respond by dissolving the ego in the harmony of all the elements required for an engagement-ready style. The last position can absorb the insights of the first two.

The discussion of these points of preparation for engagement falls under the general heading of discipline, including educational discipline. Plato argued in the *Republic* that discipline comes from repetitive exercise of graceful movements, which he epitomized as martial arts and dance/music. The discipline internalizes and habituates the readiness to engage the things on one's watch, including appropriate understanding of those things so far as possible. This is preparation in the life of faith. Preparation for the life of faith is not the only context in which spirituality or spiritual formation is important, although spiritual development is crucial for the life of faith. The next step in the analysis of the life of faith is actual engagement.

II. PRESENCE AND ACTION

Actual engagement is only abstractly separated from preparation, because most of the preparation is learned through actual engagements, like sparring to learn the martial arts. Nevertheless, there are dimensions of engagement that appear when readiness issues in actuality.

How shall the actuality of engagement be understood? Behind all the answers to this question should be borne in mind the previous discussions of obligations that are constituted by the possibility structures for engagement, including moral, social, personal, and natural obligations. Insofar as engagement makes the things engaged components of one's own actions and being, actual engagement requires groundedness in the others as others, including appropriation into one's engaged sensibility of their values, deference to their independent integrity, the functions of change, and realism about what is there. Direct engagement requires awareness of the others involved, depending in part on education, appreciation, which comes from learning, courage to stay engaged when costs are involved, and love of the others for their own values and for their being creatures of the ontological act of creation. Actual engagement also involves the many issues of achievement in the existential field, personal and public, and the achievement of ways of facing suffering and treating all things as they are in ultimate perspective. All these points are discussed in Parts I and II.

Taking all these into account, what is the spiritual discipline of actual engagement? An image from the martial art of taijiquan suggests an answer. Traditional taiji practice begins with the learning of an elaborate form of solitary movement. The common full form consists of 108 moves or structured changes, each flowing from a preceding change and issuing in a subsequent change. The overall form has a long history rooted in ancient traditions, particularly the Yijing, and it is learned from a teacher, usually with other students.[3] Thus the "solitary" form is set within deep cultural traditions and social practices. Virtuosity in the form consists in an ability to perform the moves with attention focused exclusively on the move at hand, not thinking ahead or remembering, just doing; there is no meditation on anything other than doing the movement at hand. Ideal virtuosity also consists in feeling the movement at hand to be not only that of one's body but of the body in the larger context, including the physical setting, the local social context perhaps with other players and a teacher, the larger social and natural context, and in fact the movement of the cosmos. Taiji tradition makes much of microcosm/macrocosm relations. The virtuoso player does not think about these other things but rather thinks them in thinking the movement at hand. Attention does not focus on representing these things, or on representations at all. Rather it focuses on the movement as embracing the local environment, the larger environment, and the cosmos in the forms of the movement itself. The movement is not separate from its environing space-time and the things that make up that extension but is constituted by its environing space-time. Of course, this is all ideal. We simply do not have ways of interpretively embodying all things in a single rich movement: we are ignorant of too many things.[4] Moreover, this effort at embodiment of the cosmos in the moving forms of taijiquan amounts to an attempt to harmonize all things in the universe into the singular harmony of the movement. This is a denial of otherness when taken too seriously, a danger that lurks in many Daoist and Confucian images, such as "being one body with the world."

Cousin to the solitary form of taiji, however, is the exercise form called "push-hands," which is played with another person, and is the basis for taijiquan as a martial art. In push-hands, two players face each other with one foot planted forward and the other back, touching usually their forearms or the backs of their hands, mirroring each other's stance left and right. When one rocks forward the other rocks back, turning so that the push is deflected. When the push is finished, the receiving player pushes with his own hand, anticipating the moment to reverse action as well as the avoidance turns of the partner. Every move is a constant change of pressure and retreat, and the motions are generally circular and twisting so that no push meets a stronger obstacle than the small pressure of contact. The discipline of the adept is to be so in synchrony with the other as other that the contact of hands is never broken, never pulled away, never pushed too far. Instead of harmonizing the other into a component of one's own movement, one's own movement is made deferential to the other's. One waits upon the other, respecting the other's freedom of movement and always ready to respect it and respond. The deeper the intimacy of the players in feeling out one another's movements, the deeper the respect for the otherness, integrity, and freedom of the other. In push-hands, one is literally in touch with another as both move freely, but without imposition of the self on the other or loss of self in the face of the other.

This, too, is ideal, of course. At some point, push-hands is competitive, with the purpose of pushing the other off balance. The ideal being-in-touch with the other requires both parties to be equally skilled. As a model for engaging the other things in the existential field as other, with all the requirements of obligation, groundedness, actual engagement, and achievement, push-hands is a broken symbol. Many of our engagements with things are purposive, in which we want to affect an outcome, change something, or achieve a special situation. Not all engagements are like this. Some are almost wholly appreciative, and the engagement is like being in touch but in constant retreat. Given the complexity of the things in the existential field as related to human beings, however, actual engagement is like playing push-hands with "the ten thousand things."

With the push-hands image of reciprocal contact movement in mind, another dimension of actual engagement can be expressed. In the Bhagavad Gita, Arjuna learned that the heart of action is the conviction that he had the right to the action but not to the fruit of the action. As a warrior he should focus on fighting as skillfully as he could with the purpose in mind of winning. But he had no claim on the outcome, whether he won or lost. This intense contrast of martial purpose with all the strength, energy, and violence of a battle combined with studied indifference about the outcome is a difficult notion to absorb. Some schools of Buddhism express it in a slightly different way by saying that one should not be attached to the continuity of things through time; thus, one can attend decisively, energetically, and violently perhaps to the experience of the moment, including strongly purposive behavior on one's own part, without being attached to accomplishing the purpose. One pursues the purpose for all one is worth, but is not attached to achieving it. Michael Raposa points out that this comes to an extreme expression in the Japanese Zen Code of Bushido according to which one is perfectly loyal to the purpose at hand, usually represented by the lord whom the warrior is serving, but not at all concerned with what happens, including one's own death.[5]

Monotheistic religions express something of the same point in saying God's will be done rather than the druthers of the actors. Very strong strains in the monotheistic religions say that with proper loyalty to the right purposes, one is guaranteed a heavenly reward to which one thus has a right. These strains share with shamanism the practice of teaching that many important actions are not so much for the sake of their inherent purposes but for the sake of a reward for undertaking them. Yet other monotheistic strains agree with Krishna in the Bhagavad Gita: there is no divine guarantee of success, and the salvific part of acting on behalf of divine purposes consists only in that acting, not in their accomplishment. That acting itself can be an ecstatic fulfillment.

The ultimate significance of actual engagement, even when it is shot through with purposive intentions to change things, is that things are engaged in their true otherness, with proper attention to all this means with regard to obligation, groundedness, engagement itself, and achievement. The purposes themselves are not ultimate, only proximate. Insofar as engagement involves action, the outcome is only proximally important and the engagement itself is of ultimate significance.

III. RELATIONSHIPS

Yet another ultimately important element of engagement is the development of proper relationships with the things engaged. Most things to be engaged that determine the existential matrix within which people live have contexts and histories. Although some things might be engaged well only as glancing blows, as it were, most things are engaged over time and, even when engaged only once and momentarily, need to be engaged in terms of their history and context.

By "relationship" here is meant a kind of harmony, something like an institution, wherein the individual in the individual's life context is connected with the other thing in the thing's context so that the individual's intentionality of engagement can find expression as adequate to the thing as possible. A relationship is like an institution, and sometimes is an institution, because it is something more than the things encountering one another. Personal relationships, for instance, friendships, are more than the sum of the encounters of two persons. The personal relationship takes on a life of its own and comes to affect the specific encounters. Moreover, the relationship, like an institution, can be nurtured in itself so that it better facilitates the engagement of the persons. Things done to nurture the relationship might not always involve direct encounters, as when a friend schedules time so as to be available to meet, or makes economic arrangements to help the friend, or comes to define crucial aspects of the nurturer's self-identity and way of life in terms of the friendship. A relationship has a reality of its own that is not reduced to the direct interactions of the things related. The shape of the relationship includes not only the things related but whatever is involved to enable the intentionality to engage.

Two reasons are prominent for the importance of establishing proper relationships as an element in engagement. One is that relationships are important for accessing the things engaged, and the other is that they are important for mobilizing people's capacities for engagement.

The ways that are important for accessing the thing engaged are enormously varied. This volume of *Philosophical Theology* has thematized sixteen general rubrics of engagement, and these are only vague rubrics related to ultimately important aspects of engagement. In the first place are the modes of access for engagement per se: awareness, appreciation, courage, and love. Then are the modes of access attendant on the possibilities for engagement, which include moral, social, self-referentially personal, and natural modes. Also are the modes of access for engagement stemming from the wholeness of the individual understood in terms of comportment to the ways in which engagements are themselves components of the individual's life: appropriateness, deference, the negotiation of change, and realism. The modes of access most related to intentionality in engagement, in addition to those of the obligatory sort, are those having to do with achievement, namely, personal goals, public contributions, the facing of suffering, and the relation of all the rest to ultimacy. Previous discussions have clarified, to some extent, each of these. But, of course, they themselves are vague rubrics with many subspecies that interweave in the course of a significant relationship.

Without significant relationships, engagements with things are truncated and limited only to the elements of access that are available at the moment of engagement. Relationships in the sense intended here involve establishing habits of bringing important modes of access into moments of engagement where they might not function otherwise, such as thinking about one's friend's family situation, or career difficulties, when meeting about something else, letting those other considerations shape the whole of the meeting.

A relationship not only enhances access to things but also enhances one's abilities to engage the things. For this reason, a relationship is affected by the intentionalities involved in engagement. Section I of this chapter explored dimensions of preparedness to engage and Section II how to act and be present in an engagement. Without relationships, it is difficult to bring the fullness of one's readiness to engage into a singular encounter. Without relationships, the actions and presence, as in the moving touch of push-hands, are thin and do not allow for the mobilization of the whole person. "Institutionalized" relationships are helpful for making the intentions in engagements rich and wholesome. The Confucians have understood this point better than most religious traditions, although all recognize it.

These very vague discussions of relationships can be illustrated in three spheres already thematized in this volume: personal, social, and natural.

Personal friendship is an obvious illustration of a relationship that facilitates and enriches the intentional interactions of the friends with institutionalized elements that go beyond the sum of direct interactions, although affecting the interactions. Personal friendship also illustrates the dynamic character of relationships, growing through time, needing nurture, sometimes diminishing as things change, eventually perhaps dying out. Most personal relationships, however, are not as intimate and mutual as friendships, marriage, family relations, and the like, in which the potential care for the others is encompassing in powerful ways. Relationships with neighbors are also important to build for the sake of neighborly support and can be mutual. Communities without good neighborly relationships are unsupportive, ready to break into violence, inadequate in their promotion of the local common good such as schools and the aesthetics of the neighborhood, and given to isolation and anonymity. But neighborly relationships also should provide privacy in areas that friendships and family relations would find disengaging. "Fences make good neighbors" is an ironic slogan, but true on both sides of the irony. Individuals relate to many people in their community who are not neighbors and whom they might not know by name but to whom they should be properly related in matters of good citizenship for the sake of all involved in community life. Individuals also have personal engagements with people in other countries with other cultures and whose interests only indirectly intersect. Personal relations of this sort tolerate very much privacy and even anonymity but still should be structured so that engagements, say, through the global economic system, are just. Engagements with others through distantly mediated economic and political encounters can be ignorant, bigoted, and dehumanizing if the proper relationships are not present. Yet another domain of personal engagements is those with functionaries, such as store clerks, street sweepers, and high political officials. The function establishes part of the relationship, and interests of privacy and efficiency limit its outer boundaries. Yet proper relationships with persons related by function still should involve humane treatment, courtesy, and a readiness to see the individuals as more than functionaries when the situation calls for that. Building proper relationships is a crucial part of engaging other people well, and what is "proper" depends on complicated circumstances.

Mention has been made already of the role of social institutions in mediating personal engagements. Institutions themselves are habituated relationships among people and with the natural environment. Most social institutions such as economic, educational, and governmental systems come ready-made to individuals and are built into the social habits of the community in its larger causal relations than individual interactions. Obligations to care for social institutions as well as personal relations are discussed in Chapter 1. The point here is that social institutions themselves need to be engaged, and special relationships with them need to be developed by individuals to engage them well. To go to work, as defined by an economic role, is one thing: to engage one's work as part of an economic system that needs efficiency, productivity, and justice, in ways that fulfill one's own needs for productivity and a good living, is another. The former is spiritually thin, the latter spiritually rich. Work as defined by a job in an economic system needs special relationships beyond the job itself in order for the job to be properly engaged and the work to be fulfilling. The same can be said for going to school, participating in governmental structures (more than just voting!), engaging the police and judiciary. Societies have artistic and other cultural institutions that can be engaged with greater richness through cultivated relationship. The list of institutions can be expanded indefinitely.

Engagement with nature is, of course, mediated by social institutions, especially linguistic and intellectual institutions that direct all the other institutions. Obligations to engage social institutions are shaped in part by the consequences of those institutions on the natural environment. These obligations are becoming increasingly important as people come to understand the footprint of the human species on Earth. But nature is also engaged in ways not wholly mediated by social institutions. "Nature" is a clumsy term here. There are natural things, such as a tree, in a meadow, near a forest, on the seacoast, of a continent consequent on plate tectonics, constituting a planet, in a solar system, in a galaxy in the (or a) cosmos. Engaging nature illustrates the distinction drawn earlier between a thing engaged and its context. The thing is in considerable measure constituted by its context of conditional components (I, 10). To abstract the thing from its larger context is precisely that, to abstract it so that it can be engaged without engaging its context. But this is to fail to engage something in the existential field that is causally constitutive of the very thing one intends to engage, and so is a failure in engagement, or at best a dangerous simplification. Relationships are important to establish with nature so that this abstraction, so obviously necessary for any focus of attention in nature, does not result in estrangement from the context. As in the previous example, the context for one thing might be the focus of engagement with its larger context in another engagement. Relationships with nature, over and above direct encounters, are important to develop in order to engage any part of nature in a proper way. Human purposes might determine most of the focus of attention on various elements of nature, but developed relationships with those elements indicate sometimes when attention should be paid to contextual connections.

The point about relationships that highlight contextual relationships in engagement is obvious in the case of nature, given an ecological sensibility. But it applies as well to relationships for engaging institutions and persons. Parts of the real causal identities of all these things are their larger contexts constituting important kinds of their conditional components. The contexts cannot be reduced to components of the things engaged. Often issues of engagement of externalities within a thing's context are important: each thing's existential location depends on things conditioning it but also being external to it so as to locate it in a larger existential field.

The establishment of relationships in engagement of things is a general point pertaining to the religious significance of engagement itself. Of course, there are proximate justifications for adding the establishment of relationships to engagement, as is illustrated here. The ultimate justification is for the sake of engagement as an ultimate condition of human life.

In three of his most significant writings, Alfred North Whitehead pointed out that all human responses to things, that is, engagements, involve simplification. For him, mathematics is the greatest simplification. But the danger in all simplification is what he called the "fallacy of misplaced concreteness," namely, the mistaking of the simplification for the real thing simplified.[6] Whitehead believed that reality itself involves the infinity of any actual being joined with the abstractions or simplifications of its patterns, and value results from the unification of infinite components with finite pattern. Science, including logic, he said, knows by means of those patterns or abstractions, but through neglect of the infinity of those things they simplify. He wrote,

> Abstraction involves emphasis, and emphasis vivifies experience, for good, or for evil. All characteristics peculiar to actualities are modes of emphasis whereby finitude vivifies the infinite. In this way Creativity involves the

> production of value-experience, by the inflow from the infinite into the finite, deriving special character from the details and the totality of the finite pattern.
>
> This is the abstraction involved in the creation of any actuality, with its union of finitude with infinity. But consciousness proceeds to a second order of abstraction whereby finite constituents of the actual thing are abstracted from that thing. This procedure is necessary for finite thought, though it weakens the sense of reality. It is the basis of science. The task of philosophy is to reverse this process and thus to exhibit the fusion of analysis with actuality. It follows that Philosophy is not a science.[7]

He ends his essay "Immortality" with these words:

> The conclusion is that Logic, conceived as an adequate analysis of the advance of thought, is a fake. It is a superb instrument, but it requires a background of common sense. . . . My point is that the final outlook of Philosophical thought cannot be based on the exact statements which form the basis of special sciences. The exactness is a fake.[8]

All this is to emphasize that the engagement of others on the one hand involves the interpretation of them in some finite respects and on the other hand acknowledges the infinity of their own contexts and self-possession.

The context of the present discussion is the question of how individuals can engage the paths to ecstatic fulfillment and the remedies religion offers for the various aspects and kinds of human predicament. The answers put forward are, in Chapter 9, by engaging religions themselves through participation in their ritualized life and, in Chapter 10, by engaging the process of personal commitment to ways of living in light of ultimate matters. The answer put forward in this chapter is, by cultivating engagement with the things in the world as such. This fostering of good engagement is itself an ultimately important part of living the religious life, which is the topic of the next chapter.

IV. FAITH ENDURING CHANGE AND DEATH

A brief concluding word remains to be said here about the life of faith, with its preparations for engagement, its actual engagements, and its cultivations of relationships to enhance engagements. Things change. If we accept the metaphysical instincts of the East Asian traditions, things are changes. The philosophical cosmology underlying this *Philosophical Theology* accepts this point, common to process philosophies.

Change is good news for the life of faith insofar as it makes possible improvement in preparation for engagement, for actual engagements, and for enriching the field of engagements with ongoing relationships. Change is bad news for the life of faith insofar as nothing achieved lasts. The things engaged change, some as slowly as mountains but most much faster. The relationships established do not last, however effective they might be for the engagements themselves. The readiness of individuals to engage and to engage well does not last: skills diminish, strength fades, and one of the chief pains of old age is increasing, enforced, disengagement. Everyone dies. Every nation dies. The planet, the sun, and the cosmos will vanish in a mix of implosions and explosions. The rich complexity of engaged life will simplify to straight-line inertial order, mutual irrelevance, and the dark. The life of faith has to engage this fact about the cosmos: nothing lasts.

The great religious traditions have all recognized this fact, and also flirted with denials. Nature itself is a constant changing of seasons. The passing of generations of people is obvious to the most locally blinkered group. Most of the great religious traditions have imagined the birth of the cosmos in time, and also its destiny. Some, like the Hindu, have imagined a cycle of birth-expansion-contraction-death-rebirth. Others, like the West Asian monotheisms have imagined a singular birth by a creator God who needs to continue sustaining the cosmos against the forces of chaos, which is not guaranteed.[9] All have seen the predicament of human beings to be in the middle where, whatever the cosmic conclusion, they and their lifeworlds arise and cease. Some have promised escape from time's flow in a changeless heaven, but this does not obviate the fact that people are born, flourish for a while, die, are buried, and their graveyards abandoned or swept away.

The life of faith, for all its emphasis on the engagement of things that constitute the contents of life, needs also to engage the passing away of all engagements. As the worshippers of Shiva know, this passing away is not all bad. Everything has to get out of the way for new things. This is especially true for the generations of people. Nevertheless, for individuals the palpable prospect of change and decay poses a problem for specific engagements. Why try? Why go to the effort to prepare oneself? Why persevere in difficult engagements? Why invest in relationships that are ultimately evanescent? Why not retreat into oneself and ride the process of internal decay to its inevitable conclusion?

Faith is the courage to be, as Tillich said, precisely in response to this challenge to engagement. The way to engage change and death is to give up any false claim to the continuity of our achievements, "the fruits of our actions," and attend rather to engaging the issues of our watch. On our watch we have our families to deal with, our neighborhoods and communities, our particular historical situations, our parts of nature and those more distant parts that might be affected by our behavior. These can be engaged, with attention to the ultimate conditions of engagement itself, with all our heart, mind, soul, and strength. This is enough. When we can engage no more, this is enough.

The reason for this is that engagement is direct and indirect causal contact with the important things in our existential field. The things beyond our causal powers can be contemplated, and engaged in that indirect way, but not affected. Who we are, with respect to the existential field of our engagement, is defined by the causal connections involved.

The desire to control what will inevitably be changed beyond one's control is a kind of denial of the finite determinateness of the creation. A classic monotheistic way of putting the point is to say that human beings have the hubris to wish to possess the creator's simultaneous engaging relation to everything in all times, when no finite thing can have that. To accept change and death is a way of accepting the finite determinate character of our creation.

The courage to accept finitude and give oneself wholly to engaging the issues of one's watch, with no investment in long-term success, is a matter of ultimacy with regard to the radical contingency of the ontological act of creation, the terminus of which is the cosmos of birth, flourish, and ceasing. To perfect the engagement of the issues on our watch in the face of change and death is to embrace, in a summary way, all the remedies of human predicament religion can dispose and to embody ecstatic fulfillment beyond proximate scope.

CHAPTER SIXTEEN

Inhabitation of a Sacred Worldview

One more dimension of the engagement of deliverances and religious ultimate ecstatic fulfillments needs to be addressed. Participation in religious rituals and forming one's life around them was the first dimension of engagement discussed. Making existential commitments that aim at ultimate wholeness of the self was another. Engaging the existential context in which one lives as an ultimate matter, as well as engaging the things in that context, was the third. A fourth, the present topic, is the process of coming to inhabit a sacred worldview. This is perhaps the most serious set of essential components by which a person over the long run organizes the conditions for religious life into a life of engagement of ultimacy, a life of genuine religion.

I. SACRED WORLDVIEWS

Inhabiting a sacred worldview is more than living one's life as oriented by the worldview. Everyone is oriented by the worldview they have, sacred or mundane, with whatever scale of comprehensiveness and sophistication it has, however committed they are to it. Simply to be oriented in some or all domains of life by a worldview is not yet to inhabit it. Inhabitation in the sense meant here is the intentional organization of a person's life so as to embrace the sacred in all the domains of the worldview: the result is that one lives in ultimate perspective in all things, or at least the important ones. This is the engagement of absolute value-identity as part of the ontological act of creation, ultimate reality.

The discussion so far has spoken of worldviews that contain sacred canopies. Not all worldviews do, of course. Of those who do, not all relate the sacred canopy portion of the worldview to all of the other domains. But for those people who aspire to an absolute value-identity, placing themselves in ultimate perspective, the necessity is to develop a worldview in which the sacred canopy touches everything important. The irony is that everyone willy-nilly has an absolute value-identity, for better or worse. But those who possess absolute value-identity without intentionally engaging it are religiously crude, or ignorant, or unfree in this respect, or so disengaged from ultimate reality as to be faulted for not engaging something that, in part, lies outside them. This, despite the fact that what is ultimate in absolute value-identity is constitutive of all things' essential components as much as of their existentially located conditional ones.

The next stage in the discussion requires an explication of how some worldviews are sacred worldviews. The implication is that all worldviews ought to be sacred worldviews and are deficient, if not false, when they are not.

A worldview, as characterized in *Philosophical Theology One*, Chapter 4 and elsewhere, is a more or less coherent set of symbols that provides background orientation for some or all of the various domains of human experience. The coherence may not be logical coherence, but rather a symbolic coherence, and can vary in tightness. The symbols for each experiential domain give contextual meaning for that domain and also contextualize that domain with regard to some or all of the other domains of experience, depending on the coherence of the worldview. Included in many worldviews is a domain of relating to ultimate realities, however the worldview articulates them, and this domain has been called here a sacred canopy. Experiential engagement (including just thinking) of ultimate realities is oriented by the worldview's symbols of ultimacy. Not all worldviews contain sacred canopies, and those that do not provide no orientation for relating to ultimate realities; if people with such worldviews do relate to ultimate realities, it is not with symbolic orientations that provide meaning for those relations or connect them to other domains of life.

Two points need to be recalled from the previous argument.

First, the evolution of complex semiotic systems enables people (and perhaps other beings who possess semiotic systems) to imagine ultimate conditions. These are the conditions without which a significant part of the world, including the world of experience, would be missing. These conditions are characterized as finite/infinite contrasts, with the finite part referring to whatever grounds the significant part of the world and the infinite part referring to what would be without the finite part. The symbolic imagination of ultimate conditions has been astonishingly rich and varied in world cultures. Thus it is possible for anyone with a complex enough worldview to get along in life to have a sacred canopy symbolizing ultimate conditions. That some worldviews do not have such a sacred canopy does not mean that they could not have one.

Nevertheless, the possibility of imaging the ultimate does not prove that there is something ultimate. To say that it does is to fall into what Kant called "transcendental illusion," namely, the mistake of thinking that the possibility of a regress to prior conditions proves there is a totality of conditions that has an ultimate ground.[1] To affirm something about ultimate conditions requires more than the ability to imagine and symbolize them. The symbols by which people think they engage ultimate realities might really be about something else when interpreted properly.

So, the second point to be recalled is that other arguments exist that affirm ultimate realities as ultimate conditions of the world. With this affirmation and the properly defended theory of ultimate realities, theologians then can return to the consideration of whether or not their imaginative symbols are adequate. The other arguments prove that symbols of ultimacy have reference, and the question is whether they are true to that to which they refer. Those other arguments are the metaphysical ones given in *Philosophical Theology One*, Part III. Those arguments give the reasons why the best hypothesis about how determinate things that are genuinely different from one another, but related enough to one another to be determinately different, can exist is that they are created by a singular ontological creative act. The world of determinate things could not exist without being created by such an ontological creative act. Their togetherness in difference is the result or terminus of that act, and this argument applies regardless of what inventory of kinds of created things is believed in or is true, so long as the things are at all determinate. Furthermore, the metaphysical arguments developed a dialectically defended hypothesis about determinateness—regardless of what kinds of things are determinate—that says that to be determinate is to be a harmony. Harmonies have conditional components whereby they connect with each other so as to be determinately different and also essential components whereby they integrate the conditional components into harmony. A harmony necessarily has four traits: form, components formed, existential location, and value-identity. Thus, in addition to the ultimacy in the radical contingency of the world, resting on an ontological creative act, there are four other kinds of ultimate conditions, those having to do with issues of form, with issues of the components, with issues of existential location, and with issues of value-identity. For human beings, these ultimate conditions give ultimacy to having possibilities with alternative forms of value, to issues of comporting oneself toward the components of one's life with well-grounded wholeness, to issues of relating to other things in the existential field relative to one's existential location, and to achieving an absolute value-identity.

These ultimate realities, these ultimate conditions, are real things and need to be interpreted with complex symbol systems, including theologies. One might argue that this is not so, because the ultimate conditions might just be ignored. In fact, this is what many people do. But on the contrary, human beings have the freedom to relate differentially to these ultimate conditions, and ignoring them is just one possibility. Where human beings have such freedom, it is obligatory to consider which is the best possibility (*II, 1*). One cannot consider which is the best possibility for relating to ultimate conditions without interpreting the conditions, and one cannot consider the best possibility well without considering the best interpretations of the conditions. So, ignoring ultimate realities is an unconsidered and fairly stupid thing to do, given the plethora of ways of relating to them with different values.

Therefore, people should have sacred canopies for understanding ultimate realities, and most cultures have fostered thinkers who develop such sacred canopies. To the extent anthropologists such as Roy Rappaport are correct about ritual behavior being a formative condition of humanity as such, all people are heir to worldviews with sacred canopies, however they are forgotten or denied.

Moreover, the sacred canopies should be true interpretations of ultimate realities insofar as this can be determined. Having some sacred canopy or other is not enough where the issue at stake is how to relate to what is really ultimate. With all due respect for the plurality of sacred canopies, and for the variety of different ways they interpret ultimacy, true and false in various respects and always inadequate to the whole job, an ultimate condition of human life is dedication to finding the truth about ultimacy. Most people, of course, are not themselves inquirers into truths about ultimate realities, but they do suppose that the sacred canopy they do have is true, or close to it, or truer than the alternatives they know, or in need of repair by someone if not themselves.

Combining these arguments, ultimate realities are important to interpret well in a sacred canopy that provides orientation for relating to those ultimate realities, and the ultimate realities include the ontological creative act on which the world is radically contingent and the transcendental traits of form, components, existential location, and value-identity. A sacred canopy should include symbolic interpretive elements that refer to these ultimate realities, and one of the principal theses of *Philosophical Theology* is that the major world religions do address them all in various respects and with different kinds of adequacy and inadequacy. The human theological project, carried out in all the religious traditions and also outside of them, is first to develop a most nearly adequate sacred canopy (III, 4).

But to have a most nearly adequate sacred canopy in one's worldview is not enough. How do the ultimate realities relate to the mundane domains of life? Not all worldviews symbolize the connections. But they should. The reason they should is that all the domains of life deal with determinate things. Hence, all that they deal with are creatures together of the ontological creative act. All have form, components, existential location, and value-identity. This is not to say that paying attention to things in each of the domains of life requires thinking about their being created, having form, being composed of components, being existentially located, and having value-identity. But it is to say that all the practical issues of attention should be given orientation by domains within the worldview that are shaped in part by those ultimate conditions. There are in fact ultimate dimensions, at least five, to everything in life (and actual reality). Sometimes it might be important to bring that to bear explicitly on how one behaves in each domain. Should one be grateful for everything created (when some things are very bad)? Should one be attentive to the values things have because of their structures, especially when possibilities for giving them values depends on us? Should one worry about how things, including oneself, are comported as overall harmonies toward their components? Should one worry about how things engage other things in their existential field? Should one worry about the ultimacy of the value-identities of things? The answer is, yes, whenever doing so might make a difference to the value of what one does and the absolute value-identity one achieves.

Therefore, one should have a worldview that not only contains a sacred canopy for orientation to ultimate realities but that also includes within its orientations of everything else symbols of how those things are oriented toward the ultimate realities. An ultimately functional worldview needs to provide orientation to the ultimate dimensions of everything whatsoever, at least insofar as they are significant for human life. Such a worldview then should be called a sacred worldview, because even the mundane domains have sacred dimensions.

The development of such functional sacred worldviews is also part of the human theological task. Of course, one does not need such a worldview to live. Most people do not have sacred worldviews, only worldviews that might have sacred elements. But having a good sacred worldview is necessary for being able to engage one's absolute value-identity in ways to benefit from the paths to fulfillment and the deliverances religion might supply for the ultimate predicaments that are involved with the achievement of absolute value-identity. How is this so?

II. INHABITING ABSOLUTE VALUE-IDENTITY

To inhabit absolute value-identity is to live through the whole array of life, part by part, oriented to the ultimate dimensions in all things. The ultimate reality of the ontological act creating the world is our measure. That measure is difficult to keep in focus as we seek fulfillment as human beings. To inhabit absolutely value-identity is to recover that measure. In part this involves the search for or the adoption of a sacred worldview that is as true as one can find. Most modern people commit themselves to a sacred worldview, find it inadequate, and then spend much of the rest of their life searching for improvements. But also, and more importantly, to inhabit a sacred worldview means learning how to live concretely within the various domains of life with the proper habits and attention that would be appropriate to the ultimate dimensions in their orientation. It is one thing to have a sacred worldview that says one should be grateful for all creation and every creature. It is another thing to know this and pay attention to it. It is yet another thing to develop the habits and means of actually being grateful, especially in light of the tragic ambiguities of many things. "Inhabiting" means coming to dwell concretely in the many domains of life with orientation by ultimate dimensions. "Inhabiting" also means, as the same thing, developing the habits within oneself of living in all domains in ultimate perspective.

How is inhabiting a sacred worldview the same as inhabiting absolute value-identity?

To inhabit a sacred worldview is to be committed to and practiced at engaging in all the affairs of life, however mundane, as if they were also sacred in the sense that the dimensions of ultimacy involved in their worldview orientation are important determinants of the engagement. Of course, the matters that take place within the sacred canopy directly related to ultimate things are heavily oriented by ultimacy. But all the other things in life that are not ultimate themselves also have ultimate dimensions and the inhabiter of a sacred worldview takes those ultimate dimensions seriously. In personal matters, for instance, walking is just walking, eating is just eating, and dressing is just dressing. But in certain sacred worldviews, walking is a way of being present in one's body as a creature in the vast created environment, and so one's posture is held erect as a way of honoring this. In certain sacred worldviews, eating is symbolic of many or all ways in which the cosmos conditions a person to make life possible, and so meals are also celebrations with prayer; sometimes eating is filled within the consciousness that other people do not have enough to eat and are deprived of the conditions that make for health, so that eating is an occasion for compassion. In certain sacred worldviews, how one dresses should reflect great humility and lack of ostentation because of the ultimate dimensions of display. In other sacred worldviews, how one dresses should reflect the beauty of the cosmos and the value-added character of the possibilities for dressing with good style: choice among better and worse possibilities should not be limited to the achievement of functional value but also be determined by how to make things more beautiful.

In social matters, proximate norms govern the vast multitude of interpersonal and institutional engagements, something true on any worldview that orients these engagements. The same thing is true with various engagements with nature. But proper engagement itself is an ultimate dimension of each engagement and so makes each of them potentially sacred. As such, the engagements should exhibit awareness, appreciation, courage, and love, for reasons Chapter 3 discusses. Over and above this, however, one's engagements contribute to one's value-identity. In this sense, one's engagements also include the ultimate dimensions of obligation and of the self-integrating groundedness of oneself. Added to the engagements, already ultimate as engagements, as obligated, and as reflecting groundedness, is the ultimacy of what they contribute to one's absolute value-identity, what one is in ultimate perspective. A monotheist might put this as doing each thing, making every engagement, as something to be done in the sight of God. A Daoist or Confucian might understand each move to be itself a part of the Dao.

Most religious traditions have models for what in English are often called saints. Saints might not be virtuoso adepts in one or several forms of religious virtuosity, such as meditation, service, love, and the rest. But they are people all or most of whose acts and ways of being in the world, including its most mundane parts, are shaped by an intentionality toward ultimacy. The nature of that intentionality depends on how the sacred canopy orients each mundane domain. Saintliness runs from the conspicuous to the hidden. Most religions with monastic traditions foster conspicuous saintliness, in which dress, the organization of daily life, the range of contacts for engagement, and all the rest have prescriptions for reflecting ultimacy. Even outside of regimes with formal prescriptions for behaving in ultimate perspective, individuals exist who are recognized as deeply devoted to ultimacy, expressed in some symbols or other such as God, the Dao, Brahman, or Emptiness, and this devotion shows throughout their whole lives. Kierkegaard, however, wrote of saints as "knights of faith," who live their lives with thorough faithful devotion to the ultimate but in such a way that it does not show on the outside. They live through all the mundane domains of life, enjoying and acting, as anyone else, but always holding on to the fact that they do this because of their faithful relation to the ultimate. Whether conspicuously or inconspicuously, to inhabit a sacred worldview is to be oriented deliberately in all or most things by their ultimate dimensions.

To inhabit a sacred worldview is thus to inhabit one's absolute value-identity. Everyone has a value identity, and its cumulative character including both its subjective elements in oneself and its objective elements in the values one affects in other things is ultimate (*II, 4*). To inhabit that absolute value-identity, however, rather than merely to have it, is to let the project of achieving it be a dimension of everything one does that contributes to it. This project sometimes is described in monotheisms as "giving oneself to God." To be sure, this often is intended to mean putting oneself at the service of some allegedly perceived divine purposes. To speak of divine purposes, however, is extremely problematic, as argued in *Philosophical Theology One*, because the ultimate ontological creative act does not have purposes in any ordinary sense; it only creates purposes as components of finite things. To give oneself to God does not have to mean putting oneself at the service of a deity who tells one what to do. It has a more profound meaning: to have as a transcendental project over all other mundane and ultimate projects (such as related to obligation, grounded wholeness, and engagement as such) the achievement of a worthy absolute value-identity, which is to say, the inhabitation of a sacred worldview that defines the contours of ultimacy throughout life.

The remedies religion offers for human predicaments are fully engaged when one undertakes the project of inhabiting absolute value-identity. So are the paths for ecstatic fulfillment. The quest for ultimacy itself is a way of both engaging the remedies religion offers and identifying oneself as on the path to ecstatic fulfillment. That quest or project does not have to get very far.

It does not have to have high achievements in order to count. The quest or project is a human orientation to the ultimate context in which value-identity lies, the ontological context of mutual relevance, however that is symbolized.

III. THE ONTOLOGICAL SHOCK OF CREATION

The answers given so far in this part to the question of how individuals can engage the deliverances that religion offers for the human predicament and their paths of ecstatic fulfillment have derived from the transcendental traits of all determinate things, which characterize the cosmos. Not only do these traits constitute the major domains of predicament, religions are developed in those domains and are to be engaged there through ritual, commitment, engagement, and the quest for absolute value-identity. Yet a deeper metaphysical point is to be made here. Determinate things, even when conditioning one another causally, together are radically contingent. Nothing could be determinate unless it were defined as different in some respects from something else which, though conditioning it, is essentially different from itself (*I, 9–10*). The togetherness of different things constituted by their mutual conditioning is a cosmological togetherness, to be described in philosophical cosmology. But that togetherness would not be possible if there were not a deeper ontological togetherness in which the essential components of different things could be together without being swallowed up in one another. That ontological togetherness was dubbed the ontological context of mutual relevance. What could that ontological context of mutual relevance be? The only viable answer, it was argued, is an ontological act of creation that produces all determinate things as its terminus. That act is the ontological context of mutual relevance (*I, 11*).

The upshot of this argument is that every determinate thing is radically contingent on the ontological creative act. Each thing, to be sure, is determinately contingent on a host of other determinate things, and the passage of space-time involves all sorts of interplays of determinateness and indeterminateness. But the contingency of one determinate thing on another is not radical contingency. Radical contingency is the contingency of all the things together in their contingent determinate relations. Radical contingency is ontological whereas interdeterminate contingency is cosmological.

The cosmos, then, is gratuitous, arbitrary, undeserved, and absolutely surprising. As gratuitous, the world is something given, a gift, but with no giver except the ontological act of creation that is nothing but the act of making the determinate things that constitute the world. As arbitrary, there is no condition outside the world that would cause it to be created, except the ontological creative act itself, which has no character except in the giving (if it did have a character, it would be determinate and would have to be created). As undeserved, there is no justification for the world as such, only the goodness contained within it, and that goodness is so often if not always ambiguous. As surprising, no reason exists that would lead one to suspect that there should be the world, once one gets a glimpse of how all reason itself is contingent on the ontological act: we are obliged to be right or wrong according to the standards of rationality, but rationality itself is contingent on creation because it supposes determinateness ("a is not non-a" supposes the determinateness of a).

The metaphysics of radical contingency shows up in the human predicaments discussed, and itself locates a deeper ontological predicament.

Facing possibilities, one can realize suddenly that to be in a world where there are possibilities is gratuitous, arbitrary, undeserving, and surprising. When your possibilities all seem bad, the temptation is to ask, "Why was I born at all, if these are my possibilities?" What a shock to realize that the answer is that there is no reason! You just were born with these possibilities. Facing the predicaments of comporting to the components of one's life, especially when they are at odds and are tearing you up inside, the temptation is to ask, "Why should I go on?" What a shock to realize that the answer is that you were given this life to work out, not because it is especially good, but because it is who you are. Facing predicaments of engaging other things in the existential field, especially when the engagements seem always to be violent, ambiguous in moral character, and too often lost, the temptation is to ask, "What can justify my continued struggle with a cosmos that will kill me?" What a shock to realize that nothing justifies the engagement except that you are created a human being in a world that can be engaged. Facing predicaments of achieving absolute value-identity, especially when the misery of your achievements becomes apparent, you are tempted to ask, "Why was I given life so as to have to achieve an absolute value-identity?" No reason, you just were.

Lots of things in life are shocking. Ontological shock is a dimension that can be added on to every other shock that comes from the realization of the radical contingency, the gratuitousness, arbitrariness, undeservedness, and surprise of one's situation as such. Tillich pointed out, as mentioned earlier, that ontological shock is most often triggered by some other shock, such as the death of a friend, or one's life-threatening illness, or a fatal accident narrowly missed, or the destruction of one's home, or of a people. These are the shocks that raise the question being and non-being, as Tillich said.[2] The question of being and non-being is about the radical contingency of the cosmos and one's place in it. The answer to the question of being and non-being is that, as we have being with its beauties and travails, it is gratuitous, arbitrary, undeserving, and surprising.

For human beings, to be alive at all is a surprise. As Heidegger famously said, we are "thrown" into existence.[3] To be sure, we understand the conditions of our lives in terms of the particularities of parentage; of social, cultural, and historical contexts; and of paths through nature. In the moments of reflection on all this, however, we ask rhetorically, Why should this be? That we exist, with all our conditions, is a surprise.

To die is equally surprising. Like being alive, death has its causal conditions—disease, war, accidents, old age, and the rest. As noted in the preliminary remarks to Part I, in some sense death is just a change of elements. Over and above that, however, death is an ending of the surprise at being alive, which is equally surprising. Death is a movement from the being of the creation to non-being. The creation goes on in time, of course, and part of spiritual maturity is to bless the world without one's continued presence. But death does mean that one's ongoing role within creation is not to be.

For this reason, the eternity of one's living days is all the more important. One's identity within the eternal life of the ontological creative act is limited to the days of life one has and the effects of those days on other things. Beyond that is nonentity for the person. So, the finitude of one's life in eternity, glorious though that might be, raises the personal ultimate concern about being and non-being.

IV. CHAOS AND CONTAINMENT

None of this—the surprise of life or the surprise of death—can be engaged without the symbols of a sacred canopy. Even the metaphysics through which it is expressed in these volumes is part of a sacred canopy. Yet all sacred canopies are made of symbols that have been humanly constructed, interpreting ultimate matters in certain respects and not others, and subject to critical reflection. What happens when the integrity of a sacred canopy is threatened? That threat attacks the very core of the engagements of life and death, being and non-being, meaningfulness and chaos, which are matters of ultimate concern. Without some symbols in a sacred canopy, ultimate matters cannot be engaged. But ultimate reality does not sit still for its domestication in a sacred canopy. The gratuitous, arbitrary, undeserved surprise of the ontological act of creation is wild.

Sacred canopies are always in a state of being rent, although more so in some cultural conditions than others. Every major religious tradition has had theologians who say that the meaning of ultimate reality is beyond what their theology says. All religions have apophatic moments, even when those moments are not noticed by people on the folk religion end of the sophistication/folk religion spectrum.

A more profound ultimate human predicament than any discussed in Parts I and II is that of living with rents in the sacred canopies of life. The sacred canopies themselves articulated the predicaments mentioned earlier. But when the sacred canopies are called into question, in whole or part, humanity has a far deeper predicament. For, the death of a worldview, which depends so much on its sacred canopy, is the death of all the orienting meaning that worldview had conveyed when it was living and functional.

The death of a worldview leads to profound terror. One's personal death is inevitable and can be accepted as part of the way of nature. Death for a good cause gives extra meaning to life. Yet the death of one's worldview means that even the meaningfulness of personal death is gone. The result of this profound terror sometimes is that the limits on acceptable behavior are eroded and terrorist methods are tempting to reinforce the authority of the old worldview. But the violence in the defense of the old worldview comes from deep suspicion that those who claim it is implausible might be right. If one were thoroughly confident in one's worldview, there would be no anxiety about its being under attack. Ours, however, is a time of deep anxiety about certain conservative religious worldviews that pushes communities that find meaning in them to extremes of verbal, social, and physical violence, especially in Christian and Muslim communities, although not only there. Consequently, we are in a time of profound ontological predicament, in ontological shock.

Here the argument is brought up short. Up until this point, *Philosophical Theology* has interpreted religion in terms of worldviews with sacred canopies, the present philosophical theology included. But worldviews are fragmentary human constructions. Treated as hypotheses for engaging the ultimate realities and dimensions of things, of course, they might very well carry crucial truths. And yet they are inadequate and easily torn. As an epistemological problem, this is not unexpected, and the proper response is to modify the hypothesis with new and better symbols, and modify practices guided by the symbols. As an existential problem, however, the ontological shock of the radical contingency of the worldview reveals another dimension of worldviews, especially sacred ones.

To be religious under the orientation of a sacred worldview is to be contained, to find containment, within a cosmos that is wildly chaotic to people who have no worldview orientation. Of course, it is impossible to have no worldview orientation whatsoever. That would be the situation in which nothing that happens has a context that relates it to other things that happen at even a slight distance. Eating would not be oriented to finding shelter, which would not be oriented to family life—and the human species would not have evolved because nothing would be contained in such a way as to have meaning. In reality, people do have worldviews, only broken ones in most circumstances. But they realize that their worldviews are constantly having to change, which threatens their authority for those committed to them. Sometimes the changes turn out to be for the worse: this is no mere mistake but a mistake in the meaning structure that gives everything else orientation. In time, people come to appreciate the fact, however much they hate it, that their worldviews are contingent. They are not necessarily false, but not foundationally true.

The structural function of worldviews, particularly sacred worldviews, is to provide orientation for individuals and groups. The existential function, however, is to provide emotional containment for the natural, social, and personal forces (all of which are elements of the natural creation) with which people contend. The cosmic sweep of nature is not scaled to human affairs, and the human niches are fragile: worldviews can make sense of that with a story of divine cosmology or a scientific account of evolutionary niches. The accidental violent encounter of social groups is driven by weather, geography, and migration patterns, and can be contained with meaning provided by worldviews about history, rights to places, and pilgrimages. Personally, people are filled with hungers and rages, passions and disappointments, panics and manias, emotions that without meaningful containment would be utterly destructive. Much emotional illness stems from individuals having no psychological space to contain the effects of trauma, abandonment, inappropriate control, abuse, and many other problems that are simply common parts of life.

The reason people need the orientation that worldviews provide is to contain these hungers, rages, passions, disappointments, panics, and manias directed at internal pressures and the external examples of the fact that nature is not humane: it treats people like straw dogs. To perform this containing function, sacred worldviews need to be accorded an authority that is as powerful as the containment is needy. According authority, in this sense, is one of the inmost acts a person can perform in solitude, on the cusp of defining what it is to be alone. It is an essential component at the heart of organizing life so as to engage ultimacy. When people recognize that their sacred worldviews, however true and helpful, also are contingent, that authority is put in jeopardy. Is it possible for cosmic hungers, rages, passions, disappointments, panics, and manias to be contained by the best hypothesis?

To answer that slightly ironic question with depth it is necessary to move through the dimensions of how to be religious studied in *Philosophical Theology Three*. Chapter 13 of that volume picks up as the continuation of this one.

Nevertheless, it must be noted that the ecstatic fulfillments of religion, when they come and for whom they come, are slightly oblivious as to the plausibility of their sacred worldviews. Life finds meaning in eternity, however inadequately that is symbolized. Simplistic symbols often work just fine. Fulfillment takes the form of ecstatic love and ecstatic freedom. These, too, are a bit loose with regard to their symbolic expressions. The implications of this in some measure are drawn out in the subsequent volume.

PART IV

Summary Implications

The question addressed in this concluding part of *Philosophical Theology Two* is how individuals engage the interventions for deliverance and paths for ecstatic fulfillment that religions offer. Because the nature of religions has not yet been addressed, being the topic of *Philosophical Theology Three*, the question was addressed here in rather abstract ways. Chapter 13 studied how individuals engage deliverance in human predicament through participation in rituals. Chapter 14 studied engagement as religious commitment. Chapter 15 analyzed engagement of religious deliverance through a life of faith lived in connection with others. Chapter 16 read the problems of engagement through the lens of achieving an absolute value-identity. All four of these themes address essential ways by which people organize the potential conditions of their religious life so as to engage ultimacy in relevant respects.

But a great irony has appeared. The argument up until now has been that reality has its structures the engagement of which calls for the development of human cognitive capacities and semiotic symbols. The ultimate realities and the predicaments and fulfillments they contain for human life are among the things with which religion needs to deal; the various religious systems symbolize them in ways many of which have been discussed. These religious symbol systems are important elements of sacred worldviews, and the engagement of religion's various remedies for the human predicament and paths to ecstatic fulfillment all have to do with living into some sacred worldview, through ritual, commitment, faithful living in the world, and direct engagement of ultimacy through the sacred worldview itself. Human predicament and ecstatic fulfillment in their diverse forms have been interpreted in terms of sacred worldviews, including the philosophy employed here. But the worldviews themselves can lose their authority. In fact, they can become implausible, or shown to be contradictory, ignorant, or incapable of orienting certain kinds of existential crises. So, coping with human predicament and finding paths to ecstatic fulfillment are not only what is defined within the sacred worldviews. They also involve living without the authority of a sacred worldview, and this might be an even deeper ultimate predicament than those defined within the sacred worldviews themselves and a great ecstatic fulfillment, as well. The significance of the implosion of a sacred worldview is explored in *Philosophical Theology Three*, Part IV.

This part concludes *Philosophical Theology Two*. The volume opened with the observation that human life is broken in some ultimately defining ways. The brokenness is itself an ultimate, not only proximate, condition of life. One aspect of religion is to fix the brokenness that is termed "ultimate human predicament." Sometimes the text has referred to "predicament" by itself, meaning brokenness in general. Sometimes it has referred to different kinds of predicament in the plural.

The key to the analysis of human predicaments lies in their different kinds of ultimacy. The argument picked up the analysis in *Philosophical Theology One* of the ultimate traits of determinateness—form, components formed, existential location, and value-identity—and the ultimate radical contingency of determinateness as such on the ontological creative act, the most ultimate reality. What do these five kinds of ultimacy mean for human life? For human beings, the ultimacy of form means that people face possibilities that offer alternative actualizations of different value. The ultimacy of components in harmony means that people need to comport themselves toward their components in integrating their lives into well-grounded wholeness. The ultimacy of existential location means that people face issues of genuine engagement of things and people other than themselves. The ultimacy of value-identity is that people are defined ultimately by the value-identity they achieve out of the components of their lives in their existential situation with the forms that define them. These are the cosmological ways in which people face ultimate conditions. The ontological way people face ultimate conditions has to do with the radical contingency of the act of creation, including the existence of determinateness as such.

Part I explored the ways by which each of the cosmological conditions sets up ultimate boundary conditions for human life, each with some kind or other of normative claim upon people. Human beings are defined existentially by how they relate to obligation, the quest for wholeness, engagement of others, and having a value-identity. Part II analyzed how each of these ultimate boundary conditions produces predicaments of a certain type. The predicaments consist in a double condition. On the one hand, the ultimate conditions set up a certain aspect of human identity, and, on the other hand, people fail at those aspects of identity and thus are in a predicament about their very being in respect of that aspect of identity. So, relative to form and possibility, human beings lie under obligation, which they fail and so are in the predicament of guilt. Relative to components, human beings are defined by how well-grounded they are in their components, which takes the form of miscomportment toward them and disintegration. Relative to existential location, human identity is to be engaged with others, which takes the form of estrangement. Relative to absolute value-identity, human beings are what they achieve, which often takes the form of destruction. In the case of each kind of predicament, Part II indicated some typical ways in which religions attempt to remedy or address the predicament.

Part III in a sense reversed the trajectory of the analysis, showing how ecstatic religious fulfillment is possible by engaging the ontological creative act through the four cosmological ultimates. Ecstatic meaningfulness in time, ecstatic life in eternity, ecstatic ontological love, and ecstatic ontological freedom find their convergence as ecstatic fulfillment in the contingency of determinateness as such, which they articulate, on the ontological creative act.

Part IV analyzed how people might access the remedies, that is, participate in the ways in which the remedies address the predicaments. In each of the analyses, the radical contingency of the world as such was shown to provide an opening from cosmological predicaments to the ontological predicaments. These analyses also began to explore the inner essential conditions of religion by virtue of which individuals are able to organize their conditional components so as to engage ultimacy.

The root of the argument here has been philosophical. One of the chief claims of *Philosophical Theology* is that religion is the symbolic engagement of ultimate reality, and that ultimate reality is what it is. Religion struggles to engage ultimate reality, and can be wrong about it. The great historical religions comprise myriads of attempts to symbolize ultimacy. If the philosophy of determinateness and the ontological creative act is a worthy hypothesis, articulating important characteristics of ultimacy, then the great religions are likely to have developed symbolic ways of engaging the various ultimate dimensions—including the predicaments arising from form, components, existential location, and value-identity—as well as radical contingency. In this volume, many examples from the great religions have been given to illustrate the discussions of ultimate human predicaments.

But very little attempt has been made in this volume to discuss religions as actual traditions and institutions. The focus on predicaments and ecstatic fulfillments has been oriented mainly to individuals. Religions are social, or, as Roy Rappaport might put it, societies are religions. Religious individuals are possible only as social religious individuals. The unit of study cannot be only individuals with social attributes or conditions, but also the ongoing historical and institutional development of religions as diverse expressions of religion. Religious individuals are conditions for the overall harmony of religious communities. The study of religion as such is the topic of *Philosophical Theology Three*, which serves as a corrective to the individualistic bias of the study of human brokenness and ecstatic fulfillment. Religion is part of the building of the human, not only repair of its brokenness. Individual ecstatic religious fulfillment is not the whole of religion.

Notes

NOTES TO THE PREFACE

1. See Nishitani's *Religion and Nothingness* where he discusses Sartre, Kierkegaard, Nietzsche, and Heidegger, among others, and uses the term *Existenz* for the fundamental condition of human beings.
2. Although Kelsey and Wildman know one another through the New Haven Theological Discussion Group, these works of theirs were not written in reference to one another, or in knowledge of one another. I am also a long-standing member of that group, know both, and have the privilege of responding to both theological anthropologies.
3. Kelsey, *Eccentric Existence*, p. 8.
4. Wildman, *Science and Religious Anthropology*, p. 28.
5. Kelsey, *Eccentric Existence*, pp. 3ff.
6. Wildman, *Science and Religious Anthropology*, p. xviii and passim.
7. Kelsey, *Eccentric Existence*, p. 9: the hypothesis is contained within the religious community. Wildman, Chapter 1: the hypothesis is definitive of, and yet contained within, the secular academy or, more idealistically stated, the Peircean community of investigators in the long run.
8. See Wildman, Chapter 2 on the definition of naturalism and the context-setting of his project. The distinction between supernaturalism and supranaturalism comes from Paul Tillich, whose texts Wildman discusses in this chapter. Roughly, supernaturalism is belief in disembodied intentional agents or intentional agential properties in natural things that really do not have them, such as trees or storms. Supranaturalism is the belief in a being or beings that transcend the natural cosmos and perhaps create it, the God or gods beyond nature.
9. In another book, *Religious Philosophy as Multidisciplinary Comparative Inquiry*, Wildman embraces the global array of religions as significant stakeholders in the public within which theology (or "religious philosophy") can be written, a position with which *Philosophical Theology* is fully in accord.
10. See Corrington's works in the bibliography, especially *Ecstatic Naturalism* and *Nature's Religion* to which I contributed a foreword. A slight irony lies in the fact that

he interprets religion primarily in terms of ecstasy in face of the sacred, and pays as little attention as Wildman to issues of predicament or "sin." But Corrington is sharply sensitive to pain and suffering and criticizes me for a failure to register that properly. See his "Neville's 'Naturalism' and the Location of God."

11. See *I, intro.*, for a discussion of this treatment of revelation as signs that open engagement to ultimacy in dimensions not otherwise accessible.

12. Another striking recent theological anthropology that lies midway between Kelsey and Wildman is J. Wentzel van Huyssteen's *Alone in the World: Human Uniqueness in Science and Theology*. Like Kelsey, he explicitly construes theology to be Christian theology and develops the theme of *imago dei* at length. But he does not elaborate much of a sense of flaw or fall that might come from Christian reflections on the human predicament. Like Wildman, he surveys extensively findings from several different sciences (including art criticism of Upper Paleolithic paintings) on what might make human beings unique. But he does not elaborate much of a cohesive or systematic sense for what human nature consists in that is theologically relevant, limiting himself mainly, although not exclusively, to questions of the emergence of human beings from evolutionary history as unique in their religiousness.

13. *Philosophical Theology One* is dedicated to Wesley J. Wildman and *Three* to Jay Schulkin. *Ritual and Deference* is dedicated to John H. Berthrong. *The Truth of Broken Symbols* is dedicated to Ray L. Hart, and *Symbols of Jesus* is dedicated to Beth Neville.

INTRODUCTION

1. William James, *The Varieties of Religious Experience*, p. 42; italics in the original.

2. Alfred North Whitehead, *Religion in the Making*, pp. 15–17. The quotation omits comments about character that are very important as well, but not so much for the point at hand about solitariness, a word Whitehead uses in striking parallel to James.

3. Adam Seligman and his colleagues, for instance, entitle their book *Ritual and Its Consequences: An Essay on the Limits of Sincerity*, with a dominant theme being an attack on Protestant individualism and its valorization of sincerity, as in the previous quotation from Whitehead (although they do not discuss Whitehead).

4. See Tu Weiming, *Humanity and Self-Cultivation: Essays in Confucian Thought*, especially Chapter 6, p. 89, where he writes, "The structure of *li-chih* is analogous to that of existential decision in the Kierkegaardian sense: it is a fundamental choice that requires an ultimate commitment; it is a qualitative change that affects the entire dimension of one's being; and it is an unceasing process that demands constant reaffirmation." He goes on to distinguish the Confucian tradition from Kierkegaard in certain respects, but not in respect to inwardness.

5. Some of the topics that would need to be discussed in order to make out this historical generalization are explored in the issues of *Daedalus*; *The Living Tree: The Changing Meaning of Being Chinese Today* 120/2 (Spring 1991); and *China in Transformation* 122/2 (Spring 1993).

6. *Philosophical Theology One* throughout defends the view that the ontological creative act, which is the true ontological ultimate, has been modeled in at least three basic ways, as person, as consciousness, and as spontaneous emergence.

7. Answers to this question mark some of the difference between *Philosophical Theology*'s theological anthropology and that of Wesley J. Wildman's *Science and Religious Anthropology* noted earlier in the preface. Wildman tends to treat religious issues as

presenting situations that need addressing whereas *Philosophical Theology* sees them as predicaments.

8. See, for instance, Serene Jones's *Trauma and Grace* and Shelly Rambo's *Spirit and Trauma*.

9. See his *The Wounded Heart of God*.

10. See S. Mark Heim, *Salvations: Truth and Difference in Religion*.

11. See Wesley J. Wildman's recent summary of the significance of evolutionary biology for religion in his *Science and Religious Anthropology*, Chapter 3. See also *III, pt. 1*.

12. See Robert N. Bellah's discussion of the role of symbolism in the emergence of religion in *Religion in Human Evolution*, Chapter 1.

13. See Bellah's *Religion in Human Evolution* for a comprehensive discussion of Axial Age religion.

14. See his *Systematic Theology*, Volume 1, p. 113.

15. One of the most influential critiques is by Talal Asad, in his *Genealogies of Religion: Discipline and Reasons of Power in Christianity and Islam*. See also the works by Edward W. Said, especially *Orientalism*.

16. Based on deep reflection and much learning, Jaroslav Krejí has written a strikingly imaginative book on the "problems" addressed by the major religious traditions. See his *The Human Predicament: Its Changing Image: A Study in Comparative Religion and History*.

17. From the *Zhuangzi*, Chapter 18. Translated by Wing-tsit Chan in *A Source Book in Chinese Philosophy*, p. 209. For a careful, detailed study of Zhuangzi's views of death, see Mark Berkson's "Death in the *Zhuangzi*: Mind, Nature, and the Art of Forgetting."

18. Job 1:21.

PART I PRELIMINARY REMARKS

1. The philosopher in recent times who most eloquently made the case for a plurality of ultimates was Paul Weiss, especially in his *Modes of Being*. See the discussion of him in *I, 9*. There have been many pluralists, of course, but most of them avoid the question of ultimacy, save in saying that plurality itself is ultimate without explaining how. William James is an example of the latter kind of pluralist.

2. See Berger, *The Sacred Canopy*, especially Chapter 1.

CHAPTER ONE. FORM AS THE CONDITION OF OBLIGATION

1. For a technical analysis of form on which this discussion is based, see Neville, *Reconstruction of Thinking*, Chapter 7; for the analysis of form and time, see Neville, *Recovery of the Measure*, Chapters 6–7, 9–10, and *Eternity and Time's Flow*, Chapters 5–7. For the political theory defining obligation, see Neville, *The Puritan Smile*, Chapters 2–4. On issues of freedom, see Neville, *The Cosmology of Freedom*.

2. See John Dewey's *Experience and Nature* for a defense of the thesis that the "generic traits of existence" (his characterization of metaphysics) are the most practical to know.

3. See Angle's *Sagehood*, Chapter 2. *Li* means, he points out, "the valuable, intelligible way that things fit together," which is indicated by "coherence," p. 32.

4. For a more detailed exposition and defense of this hypothesis about the nature of value, see Neville, *Recovery of the Measure*, Chapter 7. See also Neville, *Realism in Religion*, Chapter 8, and *The Cosmology of Freedom*, Chapter 3. All of these accounts elaborate the treatment of value begun by Whitehead in *Process and Reality*, Part 2, Chapter 3, "The Order of Nature," and Chapter 4, "Organisms and Environment."

5. See Whitehead, *Process and Reality*, pp. 22, 109.

6. See his discussions of the compossibilities making up the "best of all possible worlds" in the *Monadology* and the *Discourse on Metaphysics*.

7. Dewey's *Human Nature and Conduct* is the Western classic on control and its limits, relative to value in the possibilities faced. Wang Yangming's *Instructions for Practical Living* is perhaps the best Confucian (Neo-Confucian) analysis. See also Stephen C. Angle's *Sagehood* and Antonio Cua's *The Unity of Knowledge and Action* and *Moral Vision and Tradition*. On human control relative to interpretable possibilities, see Neville, *Normative Cultures*, Part V.

8. But see Dewey's *Democracy and Education* and David L. Hall and Roger T. Ames's *Democracy of the Dead*.

9. See Hume's *A Treatise of Human Nature*, pp. 469ff. (Book 3, Part I, Section I).

10. See G. E. Moore's *Principia Ethica*.

11. See the analysis in Roy A. Rappaport's *Ritual and Religion in the Making of Humanity*.

12. For the Islamic emphasis, see S. Nomanul Haq's "The Human Condition in Islam: Shari'a and Obligation," in Neville, editor, *The Human Condition*.

13. See his account of hypothetical imperatives and heteronomous ethics in the *Critique of Practical Reason*.

14. See Ludo Rocher's essay, "The Dharmashastras," in Gavin Flood, editor, *The Blackwell Companion to Hinduism*, pp. 102–15.

15. On virtue ethics, see Alasdair McIntyre's *After Virtue*; the more recent book by Robert Merrihew Adams, *A Theory of Virtue: Excellence in Being for the Good*; and Christine Swanton's *Virtue Ethics: A Pluralistic View*. The latter two books are clear that virtue alone is not always (or ever) sufficient for determining what to do. For a comparativist's use of virtue ethics to interpret Confucianism, see Bryan Van Norden's *Virtue Ethics and Consequentialism in Early Chinese Philosophy*.

16. See Stephen C. Angle's *Sagehood: The Contemporary Significance of Neo-Confucian Philosophy*, Chapters 5–8. See also Angle's "Translating (and Interpreting) the *Mengzi*: Virtue, Obligation, and Discretion." The Great Learning is found in Wing-tsit Chan's *Source Book in Chinese Philosophy*.

17. See his *Nicomachean Ethics*, Book 6.

18. See the discussion of resourcefulness in the *Symposium*, for instance.

CHAPTER TWO. COMPONENTS AS THE CONDITION FOR GROUNDED WHOLENESS

1. Karen Armstrong, *The Case for God*, pp. xi–xii.

2. Charles Taylor, in *Sources of the Self: The Making of the Modern Identity*, draws exquisitely on the cultural history of Western Europe to articulate changing mythic models (he does not generally call them that) of the nature, contents, and orientations of human life. For the classical world of Homer, the martial hero such as Achilles provided the ideal in terms of which others measured themselves and whom they

sought to nurture and support. For the literate world of Plato, the critical model of the person with rational distance became the ideal, soon to be modified with the Christian model of the critical heart with a capacity for universal (or at least beyond–the–in-group) love. In the modern democratic world, the mythic ideal is the ordinary person with inner freedom, external rights, whose welfare was to be served by all the other heroes of martial skill, intellect, and saintliness of heart.

3. This author read them to his daughters when they were seven.

4. See Humphrey Carpenter's *J. R. R. Tolkien: The Authorized Biography* for an account of Tolkien's life and particularly his friendship with Lewis.

5. Søren Kierkegaard, *Sickness Unto Death*, p. 146 in Kierkegaard, *"Fear and Trembling" and "Sickness Unto Death."*

CHAPTER THREE. EXISTENTIAL LOCATION AS THE CONDITION FOR ENGAGEMENT

1. From Donne's Seventeenth Meditation.

2. "Contour" is the technical term used by Justus Buchler to deal with this question in his *Metaphysics of Natural Complexes*. His treatment is extraordinarily subtle.

3. The interpretation of Plato here and elsewhere in *Philosophical Theology* is different from some of the more common interpretations, especially those given by thinkers with an Aristotelian bent. Little is original to this author in the present interpretation. Rather it comes from Robert S. Brumbaugh, who with great originality synthesized the (Aristotelian) approach of Richard McKeon with the process approach of Alfred North Whitehead. See Brumbaugh's *Platonic Studies of Greek Philosophy: Form, Arts, Gadgets, and Hemlock*. This author's foreword to that volume explains Brumbaugh's influence as a teacher (on many people in addition to the author). Among the topics of that volume are the reinterpretation of the *Republic* to offset the dualism often ascribed to Plato and to emphasize process, analyses of the interaction of literary and metaphysical features in the dialogues, and a Platonic reading of Aristotle (in contradistinction to the more common Aristotelian readings of Plato). Brumbaugh wrote a popular introductory commentary on all the dialogues of Plato, *The Philosophers of Greece*. He also wrote an extraordinarily detailed analysis of Plato's *Parmenides*, *Plato on the One*, which is a thorough treatment of various interpretations of the so-called theory of forms as well as the problem of the one and the many. His *Western Philosophic Systems and Their Cyclic Transformations* sets Platonism in the context of other systems of Western philosophy. His collection *Unreality and Time* is the source of many of the ideas about time and eternity in *Philosophical Theology*, and his *Whitehead, Process Philosophy, and Education* is the source of much of the theories of moral and spiritual cultivation. See also Neville, *Reconstruction of Thinking*, Chapter 2.

4. This is the sense of otherness associated with the work of Emmanuel Levinas.

5. Tillich's essay is found in his *Theology of Culture*, Chapter 2.

6. See Whitehead's *The Concept of Nature* for his early but most thorough analysis of existential fields, a set of ideas from which the theory in *Philosophical Theology* is descended.

7. See Levinas, *Totality and Infinity: An Essay on Exteriority*.

8. See, for instance, Berry's *The Great Work*.

9. See Dewey's *Experience and Nature*, Chapter 2.

10. Thomas Hobbes, *Leviathan*, Part I, Chapter 13.
11. See Paul Tillich, *The Courage to Be*, and *Systematic Theology*, Volume 1.

CHAPTER FOUR. VALUE-IDENTITY AS THE CONDITION OF MEANING

1. See the classic discussion of anomie in Berger's *The Sacred Canopy*. This is a topic that Tillich dealt with as early as his 1925 *The Religious Situation*. It is a major theme in both Charles Taylor's *Sources of the Self* and in his *A Secular Age*. Hubert Dreyfus and Sean Dorrance Kelly analyze anomie in popular and intellectual culture in *All Things Shining* and offer their remedy.
2. See, for instance, the beginning of this in Talal Asad's *Formations of the Secular: Christianity, Islam, Modernity*.
3. In a recent survey of current scholarly thinking on dharma, and its relation to the texts of the Dharmashastras, see Ludo Rocher's "The Dharmashastras." He raises the important question, which remains unanswered, about the extent to which the dharma structures laid down in the texts actually describe the real situation of their time or are the authors' thought about an ideal situation.
4. See Patrick Olivelle's "The Renouncer Tradition."
5. See James E. Miller's *The Way of Highest Clarity: Nature, Vision and Revelation in Medieval China*.
6. See the discussion in John J. Thatamanil's *The Immanent Divine: God, Creation, and the Human Predicament: An East-West Conversation*, Chapter 3.
7. See William McNeill's *The Rise of the West* for a pioneering comparative study of the "ecumene" across Asia.
8. For a fascinating, if revisionary, account of the separation, see Daniel Boyarin's *Border Lines: The Partition of Judaeo-Christianity*.
9. On the separation of Islam from Judaism and Christianity, see Thomas Sizgorich's *Violence and Belief in Late Antiquity: Militant Devotion in Christianity and Islam*.
10. On Neo-Platonism's movement into Islam, see Syed Nomanul Haq's *Names, Natures and Things: The Alchemist Jabir ibn Hayyan and His "Kitab al-Ahjar" (Book of Stones)*.
11. See his book with that title.
12. See the works on trauma by Shelly Rambo, *Spirit and Trauma*, and Serene Jones, *Trauma and Grace*.
13. See Charles Taylor, *Sources of the Self*.

PART II. PRELIMINARY REMARKS

1. Livia Kohn, editor, *Daoist Body Cultivation*, p. 2. See also Kirk MacGregor's *A Comparative Study of Adjustments to Social Catastrophes in Christianity and Buddhism* for a study of two historical movements from mainly internal remedies to mainly external remedies. He analyzes the move from late-medieval Roman Catholicism to salvation by faith in Luther to salvation by God's grace alone in Calvin, and the parallel (he argues) move from esoteric Tendai Buddhism to Pure Land Buddhism in Hōnen and Shinran.
2. See Neville, *Symbols of Jesus: A Christology of Symbolic Engagement*, for a detailed interpretation of these and more senses in which "Jesus saves" according to Christianity.

CHAPTER FIVE. GUILT AND JUSTIFICATION

1. Many of these issues are sorted in more detail in *Philosophical Theology Three*, especially *III, 9* on "The Reality of Value," and *III, 10*, "Religious Ethics." Particular religions' analyses of many of these issues are discussed in the first section of Chapters 5 through 8 of that volume. The focus in the present chapter is on how religions intervene to repair the rupture when people break under the weight of the predicament of having obligations and failing them.

2. See the analysis of the Confucian and Neo-Confucian educational projects in Stephen Angle's *Sagehood*, Chapter 8 especially.

3. See Tu Weiming's *Centrality and Commonality* for a classic statement of this point from the *Zhongyong*.

4. See Neville, *Ritual and Deference*, Chapters 2–3.

5. See Anthony J. Saldarini with Joseph Kanofsky, "Religious Dimensions of the Human Condition in Judaism: Wrestling with God in an Imperfect World," in Neville, editor, *The Human Condition*, Chapter 5.

6. See the remarkable array of Chinese Daoist myths of origin and fall in Norman Girardot's *Myth and Meaning in Early Taoism*.

7. See the Lotus Sutra for a splendid example of this doctrine.

8. See the comparison of Jewish, Christian, and Muslim interpretations of the Eden story in S. Nomanul Haq's "The Human Condition in Islam: Shari'a and Obligation," in Neville, editor, *The Human Condition*, Chapter 7.

9. For a fine comparison of Buddhist and Hindu notions on this, see Raimundo Panikkar's *The Silence of God: The Answer of the Buddha*.

10. See Francis X. Clooney's *Thinking Ritually*.

11. On sacrifice in Christianity, see René Girard, *I See Satan Fall Like Lightning*; Robert J. Daly, S.J., *Sacrifice Unveiled*, and S. Mark Heim, *Saved from Sacrifice: A Theology of the Cross*.

12. See Neville, *Symbols of Jesus*, Chapter 2.

13. See Paul Ricoeur, *The Symbolism of Evil*.

14. On harmony and disharmony, see *Harmony and Strife: Contemporary Perspectives, East and West*, edited by Shu-hsien Liu and Robert E. Allinson, and also Chapter 4 of Stephen C. Angle's *Sagehood*.

15. See, for instance, the comparative discussion in John J. Thatamanil's *The Immanent Divine*, especially Chapter 2.

16. The New Testament, Paul's letter to the Romans: 7:19.

17. On Edwards's views about benevolence (and malevolence) to being in general, see his *The Nature of True Virtue*.

18. See his *The Symbolism of Evil*.

19. See his discussion in *The Nature and Destiny of Man*, Part I, Nature, pp. 251–264.

20. See Augustine's *Confessions*, Book II.

21. See the subtle and revealing analysis by Carl G. Vaught in his *The Journey toward God in Augustine's "Confessions": Books I–VI*, Chapter 1.

22. See the fascinating account of the enlightened convert Angulimala in David Malcolm Eckel's "With Great Noise and Mighty Whirlpools the Ganges Flowed Backwards," in Neville, editor, *Religious Truth*, Chapter 3.

23. See Hegel's *Philosophy of Right*, pp. 64–81, especially paragraph 101.

24. See Sung Bae Park's *Buddhist Faith and Sudden Enlightenment*.

25. See Paul Ricoeur's *Symbolism of Evil*.

26. On the process of becoming a sage, see Stephen C. Angle's *Sagehood* and Tu Weiming's *Humanity and Self-Cultivation*.

27. Analects 2:4. Wing-tsit Chan translation. See also Neville, *Soldier, Sage, Saint*, the discussions of the sage.

28. On sacrifice in this range of senses, see the works of René Girard and Robert J. Daly, S.J., and S. Mark Heim's *Saved from Sacrifice*. Daly and Heim focus on Christian perspectives.

29. See Francis X. Clooney, S.J.'s *Thinking Ritually* and Michael J. Puett's *To Become a God: Cosmology, Sacrifice, and Self-Divinization in Early China*.

CHAPTER SIX. DISINTEGRATION AND CENTEREDNESS

1. Joseph Grange, *Soul*, pp. 118–119. His citation is from James Joyce, *A Portrait of the Artist as a Young Man* (New York: Viking, 1964), pp. 211–212.

2. See Livia Kohn's *Chinese Healing Exercises* and her book with Robin R. Wang, *Internal Alchemy*. See also her edited *Daoist Body Cultivation*, especially the introduction. On taiji, see Sophia Delza's *T'ai-Chi Ch'uan: Body and Mind in Harmony* and *The T'ai-Chi Ch'uan Experience* for an interpretation of the Chinese approach in Western terms.

3. See the works of Serene Jones and Shelly Rambo.

4. John J. Thatamanil uses the therapeutic or medical model to characterize the central conceptions of Shankara and Paul Tillich in comparison with one another. See Thatamanil, *The Immanent Divine*.

5. See Stephen C. Angle's *Sagehood*, Chapters 7–8.

6. Matthew 25:13.

CHAPTER SEVEN. ESTRANGEMENT AND CONNECTION

1. See Paul Weiss's extraordinary discussion of the logic of different formulations of the Golden Rule in his *Man's Freedom*, Chapter 9.

2. Confucius said, "The man of wisdom delights in water; the man of humanity delights in mountains." Analects 6:21. Wing-tsit Chan, *Source Book in Chinese Philosophy*, p. 30. The author's Chinese given name, Loshan, comes from this passage and means "lover of mountains."

3. See Michael Raposa's discussion of *misogi* in Japanese aikido, a spiritual exercise with a martial base, in his *Meditation and the Martial Arts*, Chapter 1.

4. See the arguments of Huston Smith in *Cleansing the Doors of Perception: The Religious Significance of Entheogenic Plants and Chemicals* as well as those of Patrick McNamara in *The Neuroscience of Religious Experience*.

5. See Chapter 10 of this volume, on commitment, for a richer sense of faith than is analyzed here where the attainment of faith is a form of intervention.

6. See the Bhagavad Gita, Chapter 2, especially Verse 47.

7. See Shelly Rambo, *Spirit and Trauma*.

8. This legend was related to the author at the site by Professor Christopher Chapple, a distinguished Indologist.

9. Charles Griswold has given the most sophisticated philosophical analysis of forgiveness in modern times, surveying and assessing these and many other nuances. See Charles L. Griswold, *Forgiveness: A Philosophical Exploration*.

CHAPTER EIGHT. MEANINGLESSNESS AND HAPPINESS

1. As Michael L. Raposa has shown. See Raposa's *Boredom and the Religious Imagination*.
2. See his *Systematic Theology*, Volume 3, Part 4. He discusses ambiguity in many of his works, including his sermons.
3. Tillich, *Systematic Theology*, Volume 1, p. 189.
4. Bhagavad Gita, Chapter 2, Verse 47. S. Radhakrishnan translation, in Radhakrishnan and Moore, *A Sourcebook in Indian Philosophy*, p. 110.
5. Bhagavad Gita, Chapter 7, Verses 4–12, in Radhakrishnan and Moore, *A Sourcebook in Indian Philosophy*, p. 128.
6. From Buddha's First Sermon, translated by Edward J. Thomas, in Radhakrishnan and Moore, *A Sourcebook in Indian Philosophy*, pp. 274–275.
7. See Michael L. Raposa, *Boredom and the Religious Imagination*.
8. See Tillich's discussion in *Systematic Theology*, Volume 1, pp. 186–210, which is preliminary to his principal discussion of God.

PART III. PRELIMINARY REMARKS

1. See Nishitani's *Religion and Nothingness*, especially Chapters 1 and 3.
2. This transcendent dimension of the meaning of life is akin to what David Kelsey calls "eschatological consummation." See his *Eccentric Existence*, Volume 1, Part 2.
3. See William C. Chittick's discussion of the oneness of God and the multiplicity of creation, and hence the multiplicity of divine names, in his *The Sufi Path of Knowledge: Ibn al-'Arabi's Metaphysics of Imagination*.

CHAPTER NINE. ECSTATIC MEANING IN TIME

1. On the question of what is here called the "material quality" (following Peirce) of experiential signs in religious experience, see Wesley J. Wildman's *Religious and Spiritual Experiences*, especially Chapter 5 where he discusses their interpretive value.
2. See, for instance, his first letter to the Thessalonians 4–5, Second Thessalonians 2.
3. See Paul's first letter to the Corinthians 15.
4. The *Left Behind* series consists of sixteen novels by Tim LaHaye and Jerry B. Jenkins that develop a classical Christian Dispensationalist theology in narrative form.
5. See Altizer's *The New Apocalypse*, *The Self-Embodiment of God*, *History as Apocalypse*, and *Genesis and Apocalypse*.
6. Much of the Lotus Sutra, for example, is the explication of the lives and eons of change of the Buddhas.
7. Thomas Berry, *The Great Work*, pp. 1–3.
8. See Eliade, *The Sacred and the Profane*.

CHAPTER TEN. ECSTATIC LIFE IN ETERNITY

1. See Colleen McDannell and Bernhard Lang, *Heaven: A History*.
2. See Livia Kohn's imaginative, humorous, and truly marvelous article, "Immortality."

3. See Immanuel Kant, *Critique of Pure Reason*, "Schematism." Kant's point is developed in ways systematically connected to *Philosophical Theology* in Neville, *Reconstruction of Thinking*, Chapter 6. The distinction between a concept, schema, and schema-image is the structural basis of the Christology of symbolic engagement in Neville, *Symbols of Jesus*.

4. Zhang Zai, "The Western Inscription," in Chan, *A Source Book in Chinese Philosophy*, pp. 497–498. The text here leaves out the paragraphing in Chan's translation.

5. Who remembers that a "doughnut," originally spelled "dough-naught," is metaphorically named as a zero made from dough?

CHAPTER ELEVEN. ECSTATIC LOVE

1. Thomas Aquinas, *Summa Theologiae*, II–II 80, 2. See the fine history of the term "religio" in Michael S. Hogue's *The Promise of Religious Naturalism*, Chapter 2.

2. See Roger A. Johnson's account of Thomas on religion in *Peacemaking and Religious Violence: From Thomas Aquinas to Thomas Jefferson*, Chapter 2.

3. Jonathan Edwards, *The Nature of True Virtue*, p. 540.

4. Edwards, *The Nature of True Virtue*, p. 541.

5. See Neville, "Philosophy of Nature in American Philosophy."

6. But see the counterargument, unusual among physicists, by Joe Rosen in his "The Primacy of Asymmetry over Symmetry in Physics."

7. Plato, *Republic*, Book 10, 618c–e.

8. Martin Heidegger, *Being and Time*, p. 321.

9. See Neville, *Realism in Religion*, Chapter 13, for a properly philosophical critique of Leibniz on this matter.

10. Peirce wrote: "The act of creation is to be regarded, not as any third object, but merely as the suchness of connection of God and light. The dyad is the fact. It determines the existence of the light, and the creatorship of God. The two aspects of the dyad are, first, that of God compelling the existence of the light, and that of the light as, by its coming into existence, making God a creator." *The Collected Papers of Charles Sanders Peirce*, 1, par. 327.

11. Gerard Manley Hopkins, *The Poems of Gerard Manley Hopkins*, pp. 69–70.

12. "Jesus Christ the Apple Tree," first published in 1784 in *Divine Hymns, Or Spiritual Songs: For the Use of Religious Assemblies and Private Christians*, compiled by Joshua Smith. It is based on a song in the August, 1761, issue of *London Spiritual Magazine* and is attributed to R. H. The version quoted here is commonly sung to music by Elizabeth Poston.

CHAPTER TWELVE. ECSTATIC FREEDOM

1. These divisions follow the analysis in Neville, *The Cosmology of Freedom*.

2. Jean-Jacques Rousseau, *The Social Contract*, p. 5.

3. Hegel, *The Phenomenology of Mind*, pp. 228–240.

4. See his discussions of "the real is the rational and the rational is the real" in *The Philosophy of Right*.

5. Sung Bae Park, *Buddhist Faith and Sudden Enlightenment*, Part I. See the discussion of his theory in *III, 6*. See also his *One Korean's Approach to Buddhism: The Mom/Momjit Paradigm*.

6. See the Daodejing 18 and 38:148 and 158, in Chan, *A Source Book in Chinese Philosophy*.

7. Analects 2:4. Chan, *A Source Book in Chinese Philosophy*, p. 22.

8. See Vincent M. Colapietro's *Peirce's Approach to the Self: A Semiotic Perspective on Human Subjectivity*.

PART IV. PRELIMINARY REMARKS

1. See Anderson Weekes, "Consciousness as a Topic of Investigation."
2. Weekes, "Consciousness as a Topic of Investigation," p. 110.
3. See Tillich's *The Courage to Be*.
4. See William James, *The Varieties of Religious Experience*, Lectures 4–5.

CHAPTER THIRTEEN. RITUAL

1. Durkheim, *The Elementary Forms of the Religious Life*, p. 62.

2. See Peter Berger's classic argument, *The Sacred Canopy*. For a later view, see his *A Far Glory*.

3. See Victor Turner, *The Ritual Process: Structure and Anti-Structure*.

4. See Catherine Bell's *Ritual Theory: Ritual Practice*.

5. Roy A. Rappaport, *Ritual and Religion in the Making of Humanity*, p. 24.

6. See Adam B. Seligman, Robert P. Weller, Michael J. Puett, and Bennett Simon, *Ritual and Its Consequences*.

7. "All under heaven" is a Confucian phrase for "everything important." See John H. Berthrong's *All Under Heaven* for a contemporary analysis of what this might mean for interfaith religious dialogues.

8. See Francis X. Clooney, S.J., *Thinking Ritually: Rediscovering the Purva Mimamsa of Jaimini*.

9. For a sample worship prescription with festival variants, see the *United Methodist Book of Worship*. The Methodist tradition is derivative from the Anglican, and thus is closely allied with both Roman Catholic and Protestant forms of worship. More oriented to the poor and lower-middle-class populations, it is less "high church" than the Anglican or Episcopalian traditions, but more "ordered" than the free church traditions. The United Methodist tradition is also global with strong constituencies south of the equator and hence is not as exclusively oriented to North Atlantic traditions as some other forms of Western Christianity. See Karen B. Westerfield Tucker's *The Sunday Service of the Methodists: Twentieth-Century Worship in Worldwide Methodism* for helpful essays on the variety of worship forms within one tradition. For a general orientation to Christian worship dealing with a range of denominations, see James F. White's *Introduction to Christian Worship*. For an analysis of the contemporary viability of "good" ritual from a Christian perspective intending to revive Roman Catholic liturgy, see Anton Usher's *Replenishing Ritual: Rediscovering the Place of Rituals in Western Christian Liturgy*.

10. Jared Diamond makes an anthropological distinction between bands, tribes, chiefdoms, and states. The first two are egalitarian more or less, and the last two are what he calls "kleptocracies," which means that the governing class takes or steals from the rest. Chiefdoms and states have kings, and can develop toward democracies. See his *Guns, Germs, and Steel*, Chapter 14. The generalization that Christianity developed in

societies that had some form of kingship might find an exception in the flourishing of Christianity along the Silk Road during the first millennium of the Common Era. That would be a large exception because there were more Christians in Asia than in Europe during that millennium. But we know little about the worship liturgies of those Asian forms of Christianity, mainly Nestorian and oriented around traveling trade.

    11. See Robert J. Daly, S.J., *Sacrifice Unveiled: The True Meaning of Christian Sacrifice*, and S. Mark Heim's *Saved from Sacrifice: A Theology of the Cross*. See also Neville, *Symbols of Jesus*, Chapter 2, for an analysis of blood guilt and atonement.

    12. See the analysis of the Eucharist in many levels, including that of cannibalism, in Neville, *The Truth of Broken Symbols*, Chapter 3.

    13. This is the disagreement at the heart of the separation of Eastern Orthodox Christianity and Roman Catholic Christianity in the eleventh century. The former believed that the Spirit proceeds from the Father and the latter from the Father and Son together.

    14. Shamanistic materialism is a subfloor in nearly all branches of Axial Age religions, and each religion has countermeasures for resisting that while accommodating it. See Mircea Eliade's classic study *Shamanism: Archaic Techniques of Ecstasy*, which, however, does not play up the materialism in shamanism.

    15. See Neville, *Ritual and Deference*, especially Chapters 1–3, 8.

    16. See *Xunzi*, Volume 3, Chapters 17, 19. See also Edward J. Machle, *Nature and Heaven in the "Xunzi"*; T. C. Kline III and Philip J. Ivanhoe, editors, *Virtue, Nature, and Moral Agency in the "Xunzi"*; and John H. Berthrong, *Expanding Process*, Chapter 2.

CHAPTER FOURTEEN. COMMITMENT

    1. See Kathryn Tanner's *Theories of Culture: A New Agenda for Theology*.
    2. See the review in Candace S. Alcorta, "Religion and the Life Course," p. 64.
    3. Alcorta, "Religion and the Life Course," pp. 59–60.
    4. Analects 2:4, in Chan, *A Source Book in Chinese Philosophy*, p. 22.
    5. Tu Weiming, *Humanity and Self-Cultivation*, p. 89. "To establish the will" is Tu's translation of *li-chih*; see p. 88. Tu takes pains not to push the analogy with Kierkegaard too far.
    6. See Richard Sosis's "Religious Behaviors, Badges, and Bans: Signaling Theory and the Evolution of Religion."

CHAPTER FIFTEEN. THE LIFE OF FAITH

    1. Michael Raposa's *Meditation and the Martial Arts* is the most philosophically sensitive review of the religious aspects of martial arts, and much of the discussion here derives from this book, and from the author's practice.

    2. See, for instance, Livia Kohn's *Chinese Healing Exercises: The Tradition of Daoyin*, especially Chapter 5.

    3. See Sophia Delza's *T'ai-Chi Ch'uan: Body and Mind in Harmony* and *The T'ai-Chin Ch'uan Experience*. For a more martial application of Delza's Wu-style taijiquan, see Tina Chunna Zhang and Frank Allen's *Classical Northern Wu Style Tai Ji Quan*. More generally, see Michael Raposa's *Meditation and the Martial Arts*.

    4. What really happens with more or less adept players is that certain things "transmute" larger parts of the environment so that a local movement is taken to

represent the rest, with some loss but also with a carryover of the causal feelings of the environment.

    5. Raposa, *Meditation and the Martial Arts*, Chapter 3.

    6. See Whitehead, *Science and the Modern World*, Chapters 3 and 4.

    7. Whitehead, "Mathematics and the Good," p. 681.

    8. Whitehead, "Immortality," p. 700. This essay and "Mathematics and the Good" are Whitehead's last publications, appearing in *The Library of Living Philosophers* volume dedicated to his thought, in lieu of an essay responding to the other contributors; they may be his last compositions, his last words as a philosopher.

    9. See Jon D. Levenson, *Creation and the Persistence of Evil*.

CHAPTER SIXTEEN. INHABITATION OF A SACRED WORLDVIEW

    1. Immanuel Kant, *Critique of Pure Reason*, B349–366.

    2. See Paul Tillich, *Systematic Theology*, Volume 1, pp. 110–113.

    3. See Martin Heidegger, *Being and Time*, Chapter 5. See also Keiji Nishitani's *Religion and Nothingness*.

Bibliography

Adams, Robert Merrihew. *A Theory of Virtue: Excellence in Being for the Good*. Oxford, UK: Oxford University Press, 2006.

Alcorta, Candace S. "Religion and the Life Course: Is Adolescence an 'Experience Expectant' Period for Religious Transmission." In Patrick McNamara, editor, *Where God and Science Meet*, Volume 2, Chapter 4.

Allan, George. *The Importances of the Past: A Meditation on the Authority of Tradition*. Albany, NY: State University of New York Press, 1986.

———. *The Realizations of the Future: An Inquiry into the Authority of Praxis*. Albany, NY: State University of New York Press, 1990.

———. *The Patterns of the Present: Interpreting the Authority of Form*. Albany, NY: State University of New York Press, 2001.

Allinson, Robert E. *Understanding the Chinese Mind: The Philosophical Roots*. Hong Kong: Oxford University Press, 1989.

Allinson, Robert E., and Shu-hsien Liu, editors. *Harmony and Strife: Contemporary Perspectives, East and West*. Shatin, NT, Hong Kong: The Chinese University Press, 1988.

Altizer, Thomas J. J. *The New Apocalypse: The Radical Christian Vision of William Blake*. East Lansing, MI: Michigan State University Press, 1967.

———. *The Self-Embodiment of God*. New York, NY: Harper & Row, 1977.

———. *History as Apocalypse*. Albany, NY: State University of New York Press, 1985.

———. *Genesis and Apocalypse: A Theological Voyage toward Authentic Christianity*. Louisville, KY: Westminster/John Knox Press, 1990.

Anderson, James F., translator and editor. *An Introduction to the Metaphysics of St. Thomas Aquinas*. Chicago, IL: Henry Regnery, 1953.

Angle, Stephen C. *Sagehood: The Contemporary Significance of Neo-Confucian Philosophy*. Oxford, UK: Oxford University Press, 2009.

———. "Translating (and Interpreting) the *Mengzi*: Virtue, Obligation, and Discretion." *Journal of Chinese Philosophy* 37/4 (December 2010), 676–683.

Aquinas, Thomas. *An Introduction to the Metaphysics of St. Thomas Aquinas*. Translated and edited by James F. Anderson. Chicago, IL: Henry Regnery, 1953.

———. *Summa Theologiae*. Latin-English edition. Volume 1, *Prima Pars*, Q. 1–64; Volume 2, *Prima Pars*, Q. 65–119. Scotts Valley, CA: Createspace, NovAntiqua, 2008.

Armstrong, Karen. *The Great Transformation: The Beginning of Our Religious Traditions*. New York, NY: Random House, 2006.

———. *The Case for God*. New York, NY: Random House, 2009.

Asad, Talal. *Genealogies of Religion: Discipline and Reasons of Power in Christianity and Islam*. Baltimore, MD: Johns Hopkins University Press, 1993.

———. *Formations of the Secular: Christianity, Islam, Modernity*. Stanford, CA: Stanford University Press, 2003.

Augustine. *"Confessions" and "Enchiridion."* Translated and edited by Albert C. Outler. The Library of Christian Classics, Volume 7. Philadelphia, PA: The Westminster Press, 1955.

Barth, Karl. *On Religion: The Revelation of God as the Sublimation of Religion*. Translated with an introduction by Garrett Green. London, UK: T&T Clark, 2006. Paragraph 17 of the *Church Dogmatics*, 1.2.

Bell, Catherine. *Ritual Theory: Ritual Practice*. New York, NY: Oxford University Press, 1992.

Bellah, Robert N. *Religion in Human Evolution: From the Paleolithic to the Axial Age*. Cambridge, MA: Harvard University Press, 2011.

Berger, Peter L. With Thomas Luckmann. *The Social Construction of Reality: A Treatise in the Sociology of Knowledge*. Garden City, NY: Doubleday, 1966.

———. *The Sacred Canopy: Elements of a Sociological Theory of Religion*. Garden City, NY: Doubleday, 1967.

———. *A Far Glory: The Quest for Faith in an Age of Credulity*. New York, NY: Doubleday, 1992.

Berkson, Mark. "Death in the *Zhuangzi*: Mind, Nature, and the Art of Forgetting." In Amy Olberding and Philip J. Ivanhoe, editors, *Mortality in Traditional Chinese Thought*, pp. 191–224.

Berry, Thomas. *The Dream of the Earth*. San Francisco, CA: Sierra Club Books, 1988.

———. *The Great Work: Our Way into the Future*. New York, NY: Crown, 1999.

Berthrong, John H. *All Under Heaven: Transforming Paradigms in Confucian-Christian Dialogue*. Albany, NY: State University of New York Press, 1994.

———. *Transformations of the Confucian Way*. New York, NY: Westview, 1998.

———. *Concerning Creativity: A Comparison of Chu His, Whitehead, and Neville*. Albany, NY: State University of New York Press, 1998.

———. *The Divine Deli: Religious Identity in the North American Cultural Mosaic*. Maryknoll, NY: Orbis Books, 1999.

———. With Evelyn Nagai Berthrong. *Confucianism: A Short Introduction*. Boston, MA: Oneworld, 2000.

———. *Expanding Process: Exploring Philosophical and Theological Transformations in China and the West*. Albany, NY: State University of New York Press, 2008.

Bogdan, Henrik. *Western Esotericism and Rituals of Initiation*. Albany, NY: State University of New York Press, 2007.

Boyarin, Daniel. *A Radical Jew: Paul and the Politics of Identity*. Berkeley, CA: University of California Press, 1994.

———. *Border Lines: The Partition of Judaeo-Christianity*. Philadelphia, PA: University of Pennsylvania Press, 2004.

———. *Socrates and the Fat Rabbis*. Chicago, IL: University of Chicago Press, 2009.

Brockington, John. "The Sanskrit Epics." In Gavin Flood, editor, *The Blackwell Companion to Hinduism*, Chapter 5.

Brumbaugh, Robert S. *Plato on the One: The Hypotheses in the "Parmenides"* New Haven, CT: Yale University Press, 1961.

———. *The Philosophers of Greece*. New York, NY: Crowell, 1964; Albany, NY: State University of New York Press, 1981.

———. *Whitehead, Process Philosophy, and Education*. Albany, NY: State University of New York Press, 1981.

———. *Unreality and Time*. Albany, NY: State University of New York Press, 1984.

———. *Platonic Studies of Greek Philosophy: Form, Arts, Gadgets, and Hemlock*. With a foreword by Robert Cummings Neville. Albany, NY: State University of New York Press, 1989.

———. *Western Philosophic Systems and Their Cyclic Transformations*. With a foreword by George Kimball Plochmann. Carbondale, IL: Southern Illinois University Press, 1992.

Buchler, Justus. *Nature and Judgment*. New York, NY: Columbia University Press, 1955.

———. *Metaphysics of Natural Complexes*. New York, NY: Columbia University Press, 1966.

———. *The Main of Light: On the Concept of Poetry*. New York, NY: Oxford University Press, 1974.

Capps, Walter H. *Religious Studies: The Making of a Discipline*. Minneapolis, MN: Fortress, 1995.

Carpenter, Humphrey. *J. R. R. Tolkien: The Authorized Biography*. London, UK: Allen & Unwin, 1977.

Chan, Wing-tsit, editor and compiler. *A Source Book in Chinese Philosophy*. Princeton, NJ: Princeton University Press, 1963.

Chapman, J. Harley, and Nancy K. Frankenberry, editors. *Interpreting Neville*. Albany, NY: State University of New York Press, 1999.

Chapple, Christopher Key. *Yoga and the Luminous: Patanjali's Spiritual Path to Freedom*. Albany, NY: State University of New York Press, 2008.

Chittick, William C. *The Sufi Path of Love: The Spiritual Teachings of Rumi*. Albany, NY: State University of New York Press, 1983.

———. *The Sufi Path of Knowledge: Ibn al-'Arabi's Metaphysics of Imagination*. Albany, NY: State University of New York Press, 1989.

———. *Faith and Practice of Islam: Three Thirteenth Century Sufi Texts*. Albany, NY: State University of New York Press, 1992.

———. *Imaginal Worlds: Ibn al-'Arabi and the Problem of Religious Diversity*. Albany, NY: State University of New York Press, 1994.

———. *The Self-Disclosure of God: Principles of Ibn al-'Arabi's Cosmology*. Lahore, Pakistan: Suhail Academy, 2000.

———. *The Heart of Islamic Philosophy: The Quest for Self-Knowledge in the Teachings of Afdal al-Din Kashani*. Lahore, Pakistan: Suhail Academy, 2004.

———. *Ibn 'Arabi: Heir to the Prophets*. Lahore, Pakistan: Suhail Academy, 2007.

———. With Sachiko Murata and Tu Weiming, and a foreword by Seyyed Hossein Nasr. *The Sage Learning of Liu Zhi: Islamic Thought in Confucian Terms*. Cambridge, MA: Harvard University Press, 2009.

Clooney, Francis X., S.J. *Thinking Ritually: Rediscovering the Purva Mimamsa of Jaimini*. Vienna, AT: Samlung de Nobili, 1990.

———. *Comparative Theology: Deep Learning across Religious Borders*. Oxford, UK: Wiley-Blackwell, 2009.

Colapietro, Vincent M. *Peirce's Approach to the Self: A Semiotic Perspective on Human Subjectivity*. Albany, NY: State University of New York Press, 1989.

Collins, Randall. *The Sociology of Philosophies: A Global Theory of Intellectual Change*. Cambridge, MA, and London, UK: Harvard University Press, 1998.

Corrington, Robert S. *Nature and Spirit: An Essay in Ecstatic Naturalism*. New York, NY: Fordham University Press, 1992.

———. *An Introduction to C. S. Peirce: Philosopher, Semiotician, and Ecstatic Naturalist*. Lanham, MD: Rowman & Littlefield, 1993.

———. *A Semiotic Theory of Theology and Philosophy*. Cambridge, UK: Cambridge University Press, 2000.

———. "Neville's 'Naturalism' and the Location of God." In J. Harley Chapman and Nancy K. Frankenberry, editors, *Interpreting Neville*, Chapter 8.

———. *Ecstatic Naturalism: Signs of the World*. Bloomington, IN: Indiana University Press, 1994.

———. *Nature's Self: Our Journey from Origin to Spirit*. Lanham, MD: Rowman & Littlefield, 1996.

———. *Nature's Religion*. With a foreword by Robert Cummings Neville. Lanham, MD: Rowman & Littlefield, 1997.

Cowan, Douglas E. *Sacred Space: The Quest for Transcendence in Science Fiction Film and Television*. Waco, TX: Baylor University Press, 2010.

Crone, Patricia. *God's Rule: Government and Islam: Six Centuries of Medieval Islamic Political Thought*. New York, NY: Columbia University Press, 2004.

Cua, Antonio S. *Unity of Knowledge and Action: A Study of Wang Yang-ming's Moral Psychology*. Honolulu, HI: University of Hawaii Press, 1982.

———. *Moral Vision and Tradition: Essays in Chinese Ethics*. Washington, DC: Catholic University of America Press, 1998.

Daly, Robert J., S.J. *Sacrifice Unveiled: The True Meaning of Christian Sacrifice*. London, UK: T&T Clark International, 2009.

Dawkins, Richard. *The God Delusion*. Boston, MA: Mariner/Houghton Mifflin, 2006; paperback edition with a new preface, 2008.

Deacon, Terrence W. *The Symbolic Species: The Co-Evolution of Language and the Brain*. New York, NY: W. W. Norton, 1997.

De Lange, Nicholas, and Miri Freud-Kandel, editors. *Modern Judaism*. Oxford, UK: Oxford University Press, 2005.

Delza, Sophia. *T'ai-Chi Ch'uan: Body and Mind in Harmony: The Integration of Meaning and Method*. Foreword by Robert C. Neville. Revised edition; Albany, NY: State University of New York Press, 1985.

———. *The T'ai-Chi Ch'uan Experience: Reflections and Perceptions on Body-Mind Harmony*. Edited and with a foreword by Robert Cummings Neville. Albany, NY: State University of New York Press, 1996.

Dempsey, Corinne G., and Selva J. Raj, editors. *Miracle as Modern Conundrum in South Asian Religious Traditions*. Albany, NY: State University of New York Press, 2008.

Dewey, John. *Democracy and Education*. Volume 9: 1916 of *John Dewey: The Middle Works, 1899–1924*. Edited by Jo Ann Boydston. Carbondale, IL: Southern Illinois University Press, 1980. Original edition, New York, NY: Macmillan, 1916.

———. *Human Nature and Conduct: An Introduction to Social Psychology.* New York, NY: Henry Holt, 1922.

———. *Experience and Nature.* Volume 1: 1925 of *John Dewey: The Later Works, 1925–1953.* Edited by Jo Ann Boydston, with an introduction by Sidney Hook. Carbondale, IL: Southern Illinois University Press, 1987. Original edition, New York, NY: Minton, Balch and Co., 1934.

———. *Art as Experience.* Volume 10: 1934 of *John Dewey: The Later Works, 1925–1953.* Edited by Jo Ann Boydston, with an Introduction by Abraham Kaplan. Carbondale, IL: Southern Illinois University Press, 1987. Original edition, New York, NY: Minton, Balch and Co., 1934.

———. *Theory of Valuation. International Encyclopedia of Unified Science* 2/4 (July 1939), University of Chicago Press.

Diamond, Jared. *Guns, Germs, and Steel: The Fates of Human Societies.* New York, NY: Norton, 1997.

Duns Scotus, John. *Philosophical Writings.* Translated and edited by Allan Wolter, O.F.M. New York, NY: Thomas Nelson & Sons, 1962.

Durkheim, Emile. *The Elementary Forms of the Religious Life.* Translated from the French by Joseph Ward Swain. New York: Free Press, 1965. Original edition, London: Allen & Unwin, 1915.

Eckel, Malcolm David, with John J. Thatamanil. "Cooking the Last Fruit of Nihilism: Buddhist Approaches to Ultimate Reality." In Robert Cummings Neville, editor, *Ultimate Realities*, Chapter 6.

———. "Beginningless Ignorance: A Buddhist View of the Human Condition." In Robert Cummings Neville, editor, *The Human Condition*, Chapter 3.

———. "With Great Noise and Mighty Whirlpools the Ganges Flowed Backwards." In Robert Cummings Neville, editor, *Religious Truth*, Chapter 3.

Eckhart, Meister. *Selected Writings.* Selected and translated by Oliver Davies. London, UK: Penguin, 1994.

Edelglass, William, and Jay L. Garfield, editors. *Buddhist Philosophy: Essential Readings.* Oxford, UK: Oxford University Press, 2009.

Edwards, Jonathan. *The Nature of True Virtue.* In *The Works of Jonathan Edwards,* Volume 8. *Ethical Writings.* Edited by Paul Ramsey. New Haven, CT: Yale University Press, 1989.

Eliade, Mircea. *The Sacred and the Profane.* Translated by Willard R. Trask. New York, NY: Harper & Row, 1959.

———. *Shamanism: Archaic Techniques of Ecstasy.* Translated by Willard R. Trask. Princeton, NJ: Princeton University Press, 1964.

Fakhry, Majid. *A History of Islamic Philosophy.* Third edition; New York, NY: Columbia University Press, 2004.

Ferré, Frederick. *Being and Value: Toward a Constructive Postmodern Metaphysics.* Albany, NY: State University of New York Press, 1996.

———. *Knowing and Value: Toward a Constructive Postmodern Epistemology.* Albany, NY: State University of New York Press, 1998.

———. *Living and Value: Toward a Constructive Postmodern Ethics.* Albany, NY: State University of New York Press, 2001.

Flood, Gavin. *Beyond Phenomenology: Rethinking the Study of Religion.* London, UK: Cassell, 1999.

———, editor. *The Blackwell Companion to Hinduism.* Oxford, UK: Blackwell, 2003.

Frankenberry, Nancy K., and J. Harley Chapman, editors. *Interpreting Neville*. Albany, NY: State University of New York Press, 1999.

Frei, Hans W. *Types of Christian Theology*. Edited by George Hunsinger and William C. Placher. New Haven, CT: Yale University Press, 1992.

Frisina, Warren G. *The Unity of Knowledge and Action: Toward a Nonrepresentational Theory of Knowledge*. Albany, NY: State University of New York Press, 2002.

Girard, René. *Violence and the Sacred*. Translated by Patrick Gregory. Baltimore, MD: Johns Hopkins University Press, 1977.

———. *I See Satan Fall Like Lightning*. Translated, with a foreword, by James G. Williams. Maryknoll, NY: Orbis Books, 2001.

Girardot, Norman J. *Myth and Meaning in Early Taoism: The Theme of Chaos (*hun-tun*)*. Berkeley, CA: University of California Press, 1983.

Grange, Joseph. *Nature: An Environmental Cosmology*. Albany, NY: State University of New York Press, 1997.

———. *The City: An Urban Cosmology*. Albany, NY: State University of New York Press, 1999.

———. *Soul: A Cosmology*. Albany, NY: State University of New York Press, 2011.

Griswold, Charles L. *Forgiveness: A Philosophical Exploration*. Cambridge, UK: Cambridge University Press, 2007.

Hall, David L. *The Civilization of Experience: A Whiteheadian Theory of Culture*. New York, NY: Fordham University Press, 1973.

———. *Eros and Irony: A Prelude to Philosophical Anarchism*. Albany, NY: State University of New York Press, 1982.

———. *The Uncertain Phoenix*. New York, NY: Fordham University Press, 1982.

———, and Roger T. Ames. *Democracy of the Dead: Dewey, Confucius, and the Hope for Democracy in China*. LaSalle, IL: Open Court, 1999.

Haq, Syed Nomanul. *Names, Natures and Things: The Alchemist Jabir ibn Hayyan and His "Kitab al-Ahjar" (Book of Stones)*. Boston Studies in the Philosophy of Science, Volume 158. Dordrecht, NL: Kluwer, 1993.

———. "The Human Condition in Islam: Shari'a and Obligation." In Robert Cummings Neville, editor, *The Human Condition*, Chapter 7.

Harper, Charles L., Jr., editor. *Spiritual Information: 100 Perspectives on Science and Religion: Essays in Honor of Sir John Templeton's 90th Birthday*. Philadelphia, PA: Templeton Foundation Press, 2005.

Harvey, Van A. *The Historian and the Believer: The Morality of Historical Knowledge and Christian Belief*. New York, NY: Macmillan, 1966.

Hegel, Georg Wilhelm Friedrich. *Philosophy of Right*. Translated with notes by T. M. Knox. Corrected edition; Oxford, UK: Clarendon Press, 1945.

———. *The Phenomenology of Mind*. Translated by J. B. Baillie. Second edition revised; New York, NY: Macmillan, 1949.

———. *Lectures on the Philosophy of Religion, Together with a Work on the Proofs of the Existence of God*. In three volumes. Translated from the second German edition by E. B. Speirs and J. Burdon Sanderson. New York, NY: Humanities Press, 1962.

Heidegger, Martin. *Being and Time*. Translated by Joan Stambaugh, revised with a foreword by Dennis J. Schmidt. Albany, NY: State University of New York Press, 2010.

Heim, S. Mark. *Salvations: Truth and Difference in Religion*. Maryknoll, NY: Orbis, 1995.

———. *The Depth of the Riches: A Trinitarian Theology of Religious Ends*. Grand Rapids, MI: Eerdmans, 2001.

———. *Saved from Sacrifice: A Theology of the Cross*. Grand Rapids, MI: Eerdmans, 2006.

Heltzel, Peter G., and Amos Yong, editors. *Theology in Global Context: Essays in Honor of Robert Cummings Neville.* New York, NY, and London, UK: T&T Clark International, 2004.

Hobbes, Thomas. *Leviathan.* New York, NY: E. P. Dutton, 1950. Original edition, 1651.

Hogue, Michael S. *The Tangled Bank: Toward an Ecotheological Ethics of Responsible Participation.* Princeton Theological Monograph Series 89. Eugene, OR: Pickwick Publications, 2008.

———. *The Promise of Religious Naturalism.* Lanham, MD: Rowman & Littlefield, 2010.

Hoopes, James, editor. *Peirce on Signs: Writings on Semiotics by Charles Sanders Peirce.* Chapel Hill, NC: University of North Carolina Press, 1991.

Hopkins, Gerard Manley, S.J. *The Poems of Gerard Manley Hopkins.* Edited by W. H. Gardner and N. H. Mackenzie. Fourth edition, revised and enlarged; New York, NY: Oxford University Press, 1967.

Hume, David. *A Treatise of Human Nature.* Edited by L. A. Selby-Bigge. Oxford, UK: Clarendon Press, 1888. Original edition 1739.

Huntington, Samuel P. *The Clash of Civilizations and the Remaking of World Order.* New York, NY: Simon and Schuster, 1996.

Ivanhoe, Philip J., and T. C. Kline III, editors. *Virtue, Nature, and Moral Agency in the "Xunzi."* Indianapolis, IN: Hackett, 2000.

Jackelen, Antje. *Time and Eternity: The Question of Time in Church, Science, and Theology.* Translated from the German by Barbara Harshaw. Philadelphia, PA: Templeton Foundation Press, 2005.

James, William. *The Varieties of Religious Experience.* New York, NY: Longmans Green, 1902.

———. *"Essays in Radical Empiricism" and "A Pluralistic Universe."* Edited by Ralph Barton Perry. New York, NY: Longmans Green, 1942. Original edition of *Essays in Radical Empiricism*, 1912. Original edition of *A Pluralistic Universe*, 1909.

Johnson, Mark, with George Lakoff. *Metaphors We Live By.* Chicago, IL: University of Chicago Press, 1980.

———. *The Body in the Mind: The Bodily Basis of Meaning, Imagination, and Reason.* Chicago, IL: University of Chicago Press, 1987.

———, with George Lakoff. *Philosophy in the Flesh: The Embodied Mind and Its Challenge to Western Thought.* New York, NY: Basic Books, 1999.

Johnson, Roger A. *Peacemaking and Religious Violence: From Thomas Aquinas to Thomas Jefferson.* Princeton Theological Monograph Series 120. Eugene, OR: Pickwick Publications / Wipf and Stock, 2009.

Jones, Serene. *Trama and Grace: Theology in a Ruptured World.* Louisville, KY: Westminster John Knox Press, 2009.

Kakol, Peter Paul. *Emptiness and Becoming: Integrating Madhyamika Buddhism and Process Philosophy.* With a foreword by Robert C. Neville and a preamble by Purushottama Bilimoria. New Delhi, India: D. K. Printworld, 2009.

Kant, Immanuel. *Critique of Pure Reason.* Translated by Norman Kemp Smith. London, UK: Macmillan, 1929. Original German first edition, Riga: Johann Friedrich Hartknoch, 1781; second edition, 1787.

———. *"Foundations of the Metaphysics of Morals" and "What Is Enlightenment?"* Translated with an introduction by Lewis White Beck. New York, NY: Bobbs Merrill, 1959. Original edition published 1785.

———. *"Critique of Practical Reason" and Other Writings in Moral Philosophy.* Translated and edited with an introduction by Lewis White Beck. Chicago, IL: University of Chicago Press, 1949. Original edition published 1788.

Keller, Catherine. *Face of the Deep: A Theology of Becoming*. London, UK: Routledge, 2003.
Kelly, Sean Dorrance, and Hubert Dreyfus. *All Things Shining: Reading the Western Classics to Find Meaning in a Secular Age*. New York, NY: Free Press, 2011.
Kelsey, David H. *Eccentric Existence: A Theological Anthropology*. In two volumes. Louisville, KY: Westminster / John Knox Press, 2009.
Kierkegaard, Søren. *Purity of Heart Is to Will One Thing: Spiritual Preparation for the Office of Confession*. Translated by Douglas V. Steere. New York, NY: Harper & Brothers, 1938.
———. *"Fear and Trembling" and "Sickness Unto Death."* Translated with an introduction and notes by Walter Lowrie. Garden City, NY: Doubleday Anchor, 1955. Original translation, 1954; original Danish edition published 1849.
Kirkpatrick, Lee A. "Religion Is Not an Adaptation." In Patrick McNamara, editor, *Where God and Science Meet: Volume 1: Evolution, Genes, and the Religious Brain*, Chapter 8.
Kline, T. C., III, and Philip J. Ivanhoe, editors. *Virtue, Nature, and Moral Agency in the "Xunzi."* Indianapolis, IN: Hackett, 2000.
Kohn, Livia. *Seven Steps to the Tao: Sima Chengzhen's "Zuowanglun."* Monumenta Serica Monograph Series 20. Nettetal, DT: Steyler Verlag—Wort und Werk, 1987.
———, editor, in cooperation with Yoshinobu Sakade. *Taoist Meditation and Longevity Techniques*. Ann Arbor, MI: Center for Chinese Studies / The University of Michigan, 1989.
———. *Taoist Mystical Philosophy: The Scripture of the Western Ascension*. Albany, NY: State University of New York Press, 1991.
———. *Early Chinese Mysticism: Philosophy and Soteriology in the Taoist Tradition*. Princeton, NJ: Princeton University Press, 1992.
———, editor. *The Taoist Experience: An Anthology*. Albany, NY: State University of New York Press, 1993.
———. "Immortality." In Amos Yong and Peter G. Heltzel, editors, *Theology in Global Context: Essays in Honor of Robert Cummings Neville*. New York, NY: T&T Clark International, 2004.
———, editor. *Daoist Body Cultivation*. Magdalena, NM: Three Pines Press, 2006.
———. *Chinese Healing Exercises: The Tradition of Daoyin*. Honolulu, HI: University of Hawaii Press, 2008.
———, editor, with Robin R. Wang. *Internal Alchemy*. Magdalena, NM: Three Pines Press, 2009.
Krejí, Jaroslav. *The Human Predicament: Its Changing Image: A Study in Comparative Religion and History*. New York, NY: St. Martin's Press, 1993.
Lakawa, Septemmy Eucharistia. *Risky Hospitality: Mission in the Aftermath of Religious Communal Violence in Indonesia*. A dissertation submitted in partial fulfillment of the requirements for the degree of Doctor of Theology at Boston University, School of Theology, 2011.
Lakoff, George, with Mark Johnson. *Metaphors We Live By*. Chicago, IL: University of Chicago Press, 1980.
———. *Women, Fire, and Dangerous Things: What Categories Reveal about the Mind*. Chicago, IL: University of Chicago Press, 1987
———, with Mark Johnson. *Philosophy in the Flesh: The Embodied Mind and Its Challenge to Western Thought*. New York, NY: Basic Books, 1999.

Lawrence, David Peter. *The Teachings of the Odd-Eyed One: A Study and Translation of the "Virupaksapancasika" with the Commentary of Vidyacakravartin.* Albany, NY: State University of New York Press, 2008.

Leibniz, Gottfried. *Discourse on Metaphysics, Correspondence with Arnauld, and Monadology.* Translated by George R. Montgomery. LaSalle, IL: Open Court, 1902.

Levenson, Jon D. *Creation and the Persistence of Evil: The Jewish Drama of Divine Omnipotence.* San Francisco, CA: Harper & Row, 1988.

Levinas, Emmanuel. *Totality and Infinity: An Essay on Exteriority.* Translated by Alphonso Lingis. Pittsburgh, PA: Duquesne University Press, 1969.

Lewis, C. S. *The Chronicles of Narnia.* New York, NY: Collier Books, 1970. The seven novels were published by Macmillan between 1950 and 1956. Vol. 1, *The Lion, the Witch and the Wardrobe*; Vol. 2, *Prince Caspian*; Vol. 3, *The Voyage of the "Dawn Treader"*; Vol. 4, *The Silver Chair*; Vol. 5, *The Horse and His Boy*; Vol. 6, *The Magician's Nephew*; and Vol. 7, *The Last Battle.* Television shows and films have been made of some or all of the volumes.

Lindbeck, George. *The Nature of Doctrine.* Philadelphia, PA: Westminster, 1984.

Liu, Shu-hsien, and Robert E. Allinson, editors. *Harmony and Strife: Contemporary Perspectives, East and West.* Shatin, NT, Hong Kong: Chinese University Press, 1988.

Lotus Sutra, The. Translation and introduction by Gene Reeves. Boston, MA: Wisdom Publications, 2008.

Machle, Edward J. *Nature and Heaven in the "Xunzi": A Study of the "Tien Lun."* Albany, NY: State University of New York Press, 1993.

McDannell, Colleen, and Bernhard Lang. *Heaven: A History.* New Haven, CT: Yale University Press, 1988.

McDonald, Hugh P. *Political Philosophy and Ideology: A Critique of Political Essentialism.* Lanham, MD: University Press of America, 1997.

———. *Radical Axiology: A First Philosophy of Values.* Amsterdam, NL: Rodopi, 2004.

———. *Creative Actualization: A Meliorist Theory of Values.* Amsterdam, NL: Rodopi, 2011.

MacGregor, Kirk. *A Comparative Study of Adjustments to Social Catastrophes in Christianity and Buddhism: The Black Death in Europe and the Kamakura Takeover in Japan as Causes of Religious Reform.* With a foreword by John K. Simmons. Lewiston, NY: Edwin Mellen Press, 2011.

MacIntyre, Alasdair. *After Virtue: A Study in Moral Theory.* Second edition. Notre Dame, IN: University of Notre Dame Press, 1984.

McNamara, Patrick, editor. *Where God and Science Meet: How Brain and Evolutionary Studies Alter Our Understanding of Religion.* Volume 1: *Evolution, Genes, and the Religious Brain.* Volume 2: *The Neurology of Religious Experience.* Volume 3: *The Psychology of Religious Experience.* Westport, CT, and London, UK: Praeger, 2006.

———. *The Neuroscience of Religious Experience.* New York, NY, and Cambridge, UK: Cambridge University Press, 2009.

McNeill, William. *The Rise of the West.* Chicago, IL: University of Chicago Press, 1963; second edition, 1988.

Marion, Jean-Luc. *God without Being.* Translated by Thomas A. Carlson with a foreword by David Tracy. Chicago, IL: University of Chicago Press, 1991.

———. *Reduction and Givenness: Investigations of Husserl, Heidegger, and Phenomenology.* Translated by Thomas A. Carlson. Evanston, IL: Northwestern University Press, 1998.

———. *Being Given: Toward a Phenomenology of Givenness*. Translated by Jeffrey L. Kosky. Stanford, CA: Stanford University Press, 2002.

Miller, James E. *The Way of Highest Clarity: Nature, Vision and Revelation in Medieval China*. Magdalena, NM: Three Pines Press, 2008.

Moore, G. E. *Principia Ethica*. Cambridge, UK: Cambridge University Press, 1903.

Moores, D. J., editor with a critical introduction. *Wild Poets of Ecstasy: An Anthology of Ecstatic Verse*. Nevada City, CA: Pelican Pond Publishing, 2011.

Muller-Ortega, Paul Eduardo. *The Triadic Heart of Śiva: Kaula Tantricism of Abhinavagupta in the Non-Dual Shaivism of Kashmir*. Albany, NY: State University of New York Press, 1989.

Murata, Sachiko. *The Dao of Islam: A Sourcebook on Gender Relationships in Islamic Thought*. Foreword by Annemarie Schimmel. Lahore, Pakistan: Suhail Academy, 2001.

———, with William C. Chittick and Tu Weiming, and a foreword by Seyyed Hossein Nasr. Cambridge, MA: Harvard University Press, 2009.

Neville, Robert Cummings. *Soldier, Sage, Saint*. New York, NY: Fordham University Press, 1978.

———. *Reconstruction of Thinking*. Volume 1 of *Axiology of Thinking*. Albany, NY: State University of New York Press, 1981.

———. *The Puritan Smile: A Look toward Moral Reflection*. Albany, NY: State University of New York Press, 1987.

———. *Recovery of the Measure*. Volume 2 of *Axiology of Thinking*. Albany, NY: State University of New York Press, 1989.

———. *The Highway around Modernism*. Albany, NY: State University of New York Press, 1992.

———. *God the Creator: On the Transcendence and Presence of God*. Chicago, IL: University of Chicago Press, 1968; reprint with a new introduction, Albany, NY: State University of New York Press, 1992.

———. *Eternity and Time's Flow*. Albany, NY: State University of New York Press, 1993.

———. *The Cosmology of Freedom*. New Haven, CT: Yale University Press, 1974; new edition, Albany, NY: State University of New York Press, 1995.

———. *Normative Cultures*. Volume 3 of *Axiology of Thinking*. Albany, NY: State University of New York Press, 1995.

———. *The Truth of Broken Symbols*. Albany, NY: State University of New York Press, 1996.

———. *Boston Confucianism: Portable Tradition in the Late-Modern World*. Albany, NY: State University of New York Press, 2000.

———. *Symbols of Jesus: A Christology of Symbolic Engagement*. Cambridge, UK: Cambridge University Press, 2001.

———. *Religion in Late Modernity*. Albany, NY: State University of New York Press, 2002.

———. *On the Scope and Truth of Theology: Theology as Symbolic Engagement*. New York and London: T&T Clark, 2006.

———. "Philosophy of Nature in American Theology." In *Theologie Zwischen Pragmatismus und Existenzdenken*, a Festschrift for Hermann Deuser on his 60th birthday. Edited by Gesche Linde, Richard Purkarthofer, Heiko Schulz, and Peter Steinacker. Marburg, Germany: N. G. Elwert, 2006. Pp. 1–11.

———. *Ritual and Deference: Extending Chinese Philosophy in a Comparative Context*. Albany, NY: State University of New York Press, 2008.

———. *Realism in Religion: A Pragmatist's Perspective.* Albany, NY: State University of New York Press, 2009.

———, editor. *The Human Condition: A Volume in the Comparative Religious Ideas Project.* With a foreword by Peter L. Berger. Albany, NY: State University of New York Press, 2001.

———, editor. *Ultimate Realities: A Volume in the Comparative Religious Ideas Project.* With a foreword by Tu Weiming. Albany, NY: State University of New York Press, 2001.

———, editor. *Religious Truth: A Volume in the Comparative Religious Ideas Project.* With a foreword by Jonathan Z. Smith. Albany, NY: State University of New York Press, 2001.

Niebuhr, Reinhold. *The Nature and Destiny of Man: A Christian Interpretation.* One-volume edition. The Gifford Lectures. New York, NY: Charles Scribner's Sons, 1941.

Nishida, Kitaro. *Intuition and Reflection in Self-Consciousness.* Translated by Valdo H. Viglielmo with Takeuchi Toshinori and Joseph S. O'Leary. Albany, NY: State University of New York Press, 1987.

Nishitani, Keiji. *Religion and Nothingness.* Translated by Jan van Bragt. Berkeley, CA: University of California Press, 1982.

Olberding, Amy, and Philip J. Ivanhoe, editors. *Mortality in Traditional Chinese Thought.* Albany, NY: State University of New York Press, 2011.

Olivelle, Patrick. "The Renouncer Tradition." In Gavin Flood, editor, *The Blackwell Companion to Hinduism.*

Olupona, Jacob K., editor. *African Spirituality: Forms, Meanings and Expressions.* Volume 3 of *World Spirituality: An Encyclopedic History of the Religious Quest.* New York: Crossroads, 2000.

Orsi, Robert A. *Between Heaven and Earth: The Religious Worlds People Make and the Scholars Who Study Them.* Princeton, NJ: Princeton University Press, 2005.

Panikkar, Raimundo. *The Silence of God: The Answer of the Buddha.* Translated from the Italian by Robert R. Barr. Maryknoll, NY: Orbis Books, 1989.

Park, Andrew Sung. *The Wounded Heart of God: The Asian Concept of Han and the Christian Doctrine of Sin.* Nashville, TN: Abingdon Press, 1993.

Park, Sung Bae. *Buddhist Faith and Sudden Enlightenment.* Albany, NY: State University of New York Press, 1983.

———. *One Korean's Approach to Buddhism: The Mom/Momjit Paradigm.* Albany, NY: State University of New York Press, 2009.

Peirce, Charles Sanders. *The Collected Papers of Charles Sanders Peirce.* Edited by Charles Hartshorne and Paul Weiss, Volumes 1–6, and by Arthur Burks, Volumes 7–8. Cambridge, MA: Harvard University Press, 1931, 1932, 1933, 1933, 1934, 1935, 1958, 1958, respectively.

———. *The Essential Peirce: Selected Philosophical Writings: Volume 1 (1867–1893) and Volume 2 (1893–1913).* Edited by Nathan Houser and Christian Kloesel, Volume 1, and by the Peirce Edition Project, Volume 2. Bloomington, IN: Indiana University Press, 1992 and 1998, respectively.

Pinker, Steven. "The Evolutionary Psychology of Religion." In Patrick McNamara, editor, *Where God and Science Meet,* Volume 1, *Evolution, Genes, and the Religious Brain,* Chapter 1.

Puett, Michael J. *To Become a God: Cosmology, Sacrifice, and Self-Divinization in Early China.* Cambridge, MA: Harvard University Press, 2002.

Radhakrishnan, Sarvepalli, and Charles A. Moore, editors. *A Sourcebook in Indian Philosophy*. Princeton, NJ: Princeton University Press, 1957.

Rambo, Shelly. *Spirit and Trauma: A Theology of Remaining*. Foreword by Catherin Keller. Louisville, KY: Westminster John Knox Press, 2010.

Raposa, Michael L. *Peirce's Philosophy of Religion*. Peirce Studies Number 5. Bloomington, IN: Indiana University Press, 1989.

———. *Boredom and the Religious Imagination*. Charlottesville, VA: University of Virginia Press, 1999.

———. *Meditation and the Martial Arts*. Charlottesville, VA: University of Virginia Press, 2003.

Rappaport, Roy A. *Ritual and Religion in the Making of Humanity*. Cambridge, UK: Cambridge University Press, 1999.

Ricoeur, Paul. *The Symbolism of Evil*. Translated by Emerson Buchanan. Boston, MA: Beacon Press, 1967.

Richardson, Robert D. *William James: In the Maelstrom of American Modernism*. Boston, MA: Houghton Mifflin, 2006.

Rippin, Andrew. *Muslims: Their Religious Beliefs and Practices*. Third edition; London, UK: Routledge, 2005.

Rocher, Ludo. "The Dharmashastras." In Gavin Flood, editor, *The Blackwell Companion to Hinduism*, pp. 102–115.

Rosen, Joe. "The Primacy of Asymmetry over Symmetry in Physics." In *Physics and Whitehead: Quantum, Process, and Experience*. Edited by Timothy E. Eastman and Hank Keeton. Albany, NY: State University of New York Press, 2004.

Rousseau, Jean-Jacques. *The Social Contract*. Revision of an eighteenth-century translation with an introduction by Charles Frankel. New York, NY: Hafner, 1957.

Rowling, J. K. *Harry Potter and the Sorcerer's Stone*. Illustrations by Mary Grandpre. New York, NY: Arthur A. Levine Books, 1998.

———. *Harry Potter and the Chamber of Secrets*. Illustrations by Mary Grandpre. New York, NY: Arthur A. Levine Books, 1999.

———. *Harry Potter and the Prisoner of Azkaban*. Illustrations by Mary Grandpre. New York, NY: Arthur A. Levine Books, 1999.

———. *Harry Potter and the Goblet of Fire*. Illustrations by Mary Grandpre. New York, NY: Arthur A. Levine Books, 2000.

———. *Harry Potter and the Order of the Phoenix*. Illustrations by Mary Grandpre. New York, NY: Arthur A. Levine Books, 2003.

———. *Harry Potter and the Half-Blood Prince*. Illustrations by Mary Grandpre. New York, NY: Arthur A. Levine Books, 2005.

———. *Harry Potter and the Deathly Hallows*. Illustrations by Mary Grandpre. New York, NY: Arthur A. Levine Books, 2007.

———. Films have been made of all the Harry Potter novels.

Said, Edward W. *Beginnings: Intention and Method*. New York, NY: Basic Books, 1975.

———. *Orientalism*. New York, NY: Random House, 1978.

———. *Culture and Imperialism*. New York, NY: Alfred A. Knopf, 1993.

Saldarini, Anthony J., with Joseph Kanofsky. "To Practice Together Truth and Humility, Justice and Law, Love of Merciful Kindness and Modest Behavior." In Robert Cummings Neville, editor, *Religious Truth*, Chapter 4.

———, with Joseph Kanofsky. "Religious Dimensions of the Human Condition in Judaism: Wrestling with God in an Imperfect World." In Robert Cummings Neville, editor, *The Human Condition*, Chapter 5.

Seligman, Adam B., Robert P. Weller, Michael J. Puett, and Bennett Simon. *Ritual and Its Consequences: An Essay on the Limits of Sincerity*. New York, NY: Oxford University Press, 2008.

Short, T. L. *Peirce's Theory of Signs*. Cambridge, UK: Cambridge University Press, 2007.

Sizgorich, Thomas. *Violence and Belief in Late Antiquity: Militant Devotion in Christianity and Islam*. Philadelphia, PA: University of Pennsylvania Press, 2009.

Smid, Robert W. *Methodologies of Comparative Philosophy: The Pragmatist and Process Traditions*. Albany, NY: State University of New York Press, 2009.

Smith, Huston. *Cleansing the Doors of Perception: The Religion Significance of Entheogenic Plants and Chemicals*. San Francisco, CA: Council on Spiritual Practices, 2000.

Smith, John E. *The Spirit of American Philosophy*. New York, NY: Oxford University Press, 1963.

———. *Purpose and Thought: The Meaning of Pragmatism*. New Haven, CT: Yale University Press, 1978.

———. *Quasi-Religions: Humanism, Marxism and Nationalism*. New York, NY: St. Martin's Press, 1994.

Sosis, Richard. "Religious Behaviors, Badges, and Bans: Signaling Theory and the Evolution of Religion." In Patrick McNamara, editor, *Where God and Science Meet*, Volume 1, pp. 61–86.

Spinoza, Benedict de. *On the Improvement of the Understanding: "The Ethics" and Correspondence*. Translated by R. H. M. Elwes. New York: Dover, 1955.

Suchocki, Marjorie Hewitt. *The Fall to Violence: Original Sin in Relational Theology*. New York, NY: Continuum, 1995.

Swanton, Christine. *Virtue Ethics: A Pluralistic View*. Oxford, UK: Oxford University Press, 2003.

Tanner, Kathryn. *Theories of Culture: A New Agenda for Theology*. Minneapolis, MN: Fortress Press, 1997.

Taylor, Charles. *Sources of the Self: The Making of Modern Identity*. Cambridge, UK: Cambridge University Press, 1989.

———. *A Secular Age*. Cambridge, MA: Harvard University Press, 2007.

Taylor, Mark C. *After God*. Chicago, IL: University of Chicago Press, 2007.

Thatamanil, John J. *The Immanent Divine: God, Creation, and the Human Predicament: An East-West Conversation*. Minneapolis, MN: Fortress Press, 2006.

Thurman, Howard. *A Strange Freedom*. Edited by Walter Earl Fluker and Catherine Tumber. Boston, MA: Beacon Press, 1998.

Tillich, Paul. *The Religious Situation*. Translated by H. Richard Niebuhr. New York, NY: Henry Holt, 1932.

———. *Systematic Theology*. Volumes 1–3. Chicago, IL: University of Chicago Press, 1951, 1957, 1963, respectively.

———. *The Courage to Be*. New Haven, CT: Yale University Press, 1952.

———. *Theology of Culture*. Edited by Robert C. Kimball. New York, NY: Oxford University Press, 1959.

Tolkien, J. R. R. *The Lord of the Rings*, in three volumes: *The Fellowship of the Ring*, *The Two Towers*, and *The Return of the King*. London, UK: Allen & Unwin, 1954, 1954, and 1955, respectively. Popular high-production films have been made of the volumes by Peter Jackson.

Toulmin, Stephen. *The Uses of Argument*. Cambridge, UK: Cambridge University Press, 1958.

———. *Human Understanding: The Collective Use and Evolution of Concepts.* Princeton, NJ: Princeton University Press, 1972.
Tracy, David. *The Analogical Imagination: Christian Theology and the Culture of Pluralism.* New York, NY: Crossroad, 1981.
Tu, Weiming. *Humanity and Self-Cultivation: Essays in Confucian Thought.* Reprint edition with a new preface and a foreword by Robert Cummings Neville, Boston, MA: Cheng & Tsui, 1998; original edition, Berkeley, CA: Asian Humanities Press, 1979.
———. *Confucian Thought: Selfhood as Creative Transformation.* Foreword by Robert Cummings Neville. Albany, NY: State University of New York Press, 1985.
———. *Centrality and Commonality: An Essay on Confucian Religiousness.* A revised and enlarged edition of *Centrality and Commonality: An Essay on Chung-yung.* Albany, NY: State University of New York Press, 1989.
———, with Sachiko Murata and William C. Chittick, and a foreword by Seyyed Hossein Nasr. *The Sage Learning of Liu Zhi: Islamic Thought in Confucian Terms.* Cambridge, MA: Harvard University Press, 2009.
Turner, Victor. *The Ritual Process: Structure and Anti-Structure.* Foreword by Roger D. Abrahams. New Brunswick, NJ: Aldine Transaction Publishers, 1969.
United Methodist Book of Worship. Nashville, TN: United Methodist Publishing House, 1992.
United Methodist Hymnal. Nashville, TN: United Methodist Publishing House, 1989.
Usher, Anton. *Replenishing Ritual: Rediscovering the Place of Rituals in Western Christian Liturgy.* Milwaukee, WI: Marquette University Press, 2010.
Van Huyssteen, J. Wentzel. *Alone in the World? Human Uniqueness in Science and Theology.* The Gifford Lectures, The University of Edinburgh, Spring, 2004. Grand Rapids, MI: Eerdmans, 2006.
Van Norden, Bryan. *Virtue Ethics and Consequentialism in Early Chinese Philosophy.* Cambridge: Cambridge University Press, 2009.
Vaught, Carl G. *The Journey toward God in Augustine's "Confessions": Books 1–6* Albany, NY: State University of New York Press, 2003.
———. *Encounters with God in Augustine's "Confessions": Books 7–9.* Albany, NY: State University of New York Press, 2004.
Wang Yangming. *Instructions for Practical Living and Other Neo-Confucian Writings.* Translated, with notes, by Wing-tsit Chan. New York, NY: Columbia University Press, 1963.
Weekes, Anderson. "Consciousness as a Topic of Investigation." In Anderson Weekes and Michel Weber, editors, *Process Approaches to Consciousness in Psychology, Neuroscience, and Philosophy of Mind*, pp. 73–135.
Weekes, Anderson, and Michel Weber, editors. *Process Approaches to Consciousness in Psychology, Neuroscience, and Philosophy of Mind.* Albany, NY: State University of New York Press, 2009.
Weiss, Paul. *Man's Freedom.* New Haven, CT: Yale University Press, 1950.
———. *Modes of Being.* Carbondale, IL: Southern Illinois University Press, 1958.
Weissman, David. *Truth's Debt to Value.* New Haven, CT: Yale University Press, 1993.
Westerfield Tucker, Karen B., editor with authored chapters. *The Sunday Service of the Methodists: Twentieth-Century Worship in Worldwide Methodism.* Nashville, TN: Abingdon/Kingswood, 1996.
White, James F. *Introduction to Christian Worship.* Third edition; Nashville, TN: Abingdon, 2000.

Whitehead, Alfred North. *The Concept of Nature*. Cambridge, UK: Cambridge University Press, 1920.
———. *Science and the Modern World*. New York, NY: Macmillan, 1925.
———. *Religion in the Making*. New York, NY: Macmillan, 1926.
———. *The Function of Reason*. Princeton, NJ: Princeton University Press, 1929; reprint edition, Boston, MA: Beacon, 1958.
———. *Process and Reality: An Essay in Cosmology*. Corrected edition edited by David Ray Griffin and Donald W. Sherburne. New York: The Free Press, 1978. Original edition, New York: Macmillan, 1929.
———. *Adventures of Ideas*. New York, NY: Macmillan, 1933.
———. *Modes of Thought*. New York, NY: Macmillan, 1938.
———. "Mathematics and the Good." In *The Philosophy of Alfred North Whitehead*. Edited by Paul Arthur Schilpp. The Library of Living Philosophers. New York, NY: Tudor, 1941, pp. 666–681.
———. "Immortality." In *The Philosophy of Alfred North Whitehead*. Edited by Paul Arthur Schilpp. The Library of Living Philosophers. New York, NY: Tudor, 1941, pp. 682–700.
Wildman, Wesley J. "Theological Literacy: Problem and Promise." In *Theological Literacy for the Twenty-First Century*. Edited by Rodney L. Petersen with Nancy M. Rourke. Grand Rapids, MI: Eerdmans, 2002, pp. 335–351.
———. "Global Spiritual Confusion and the Neglected Problem of Excess Spiritual Information." In Charles L. Harper Jr., *Spiritual Information*, Chapter 6, pp. 33–38.
———. "The Significance of the Evolution of Religious Belief and Behavior for Religious Studies and Theology." In Patrick McNamara, editor, *Where God and Science Meet*, Volume 1, Chapter 11, pp. 227–272.
———. *Religious Philosophy as Multidisciplinary Inquiry: Envisioning a Future for the Philosophy of Religion*. Albany, NY: State University of New York Press, 2009.
———. *Science and Religious Anthropology: A Spiritually Evocative Naturalist Interpretation of Human Life*. With a Foreword by Philip Clayton. Farnham, UK: Ashgate, 2009.
———. "Cognitive Error and Contemplative Practices: The Cultivation of Discernment in Mind and Heart." *Buddhist-Christian Studies* 29 (2009), pp. 61–81.
———. *Science and Ultimate Reality: A Multidisciplinary Inquiry*. Farnham, UK: Ashgate, 2010.
———. *Religious and Spiritual Experiences: A Multidisciplinary Inquiry into Their Nature, Functions, and Value*. Cambridge, UK: Cambridge University Press, 2010.
Wilson, David Sloan, and Elliott Sober. *Unto Others: The Evolution of Psychology of Unselfish Behavior*. Cambridge, MA: Harvard University Press, 1998.
———. *Darwin's Cathedral: Evolution, Religion, and the Nature of Society*. Chicago, IL: University of Chicago Press, 2002.
———, editor, with Jonathan Gottschall. *The Literary Animal: Evolution and the Nature of Narrative*. Evanston, IL: Northwestern University Press, 2005.
———. *Evolution for Everyone: How Darwin's Theory Can Change the Way We Think about Our Lives*. New York, NY: Bantam Dell, 2007.
Wilson, Edward O. *Human Nature*. With a new preface. Cambridge, MA: Harvard University Press, 2004. Originally published 1978.
———. *Consilience: The Unity of Knowledge*. New York, NY: Random House, 1998; Vintage Books, 1999.

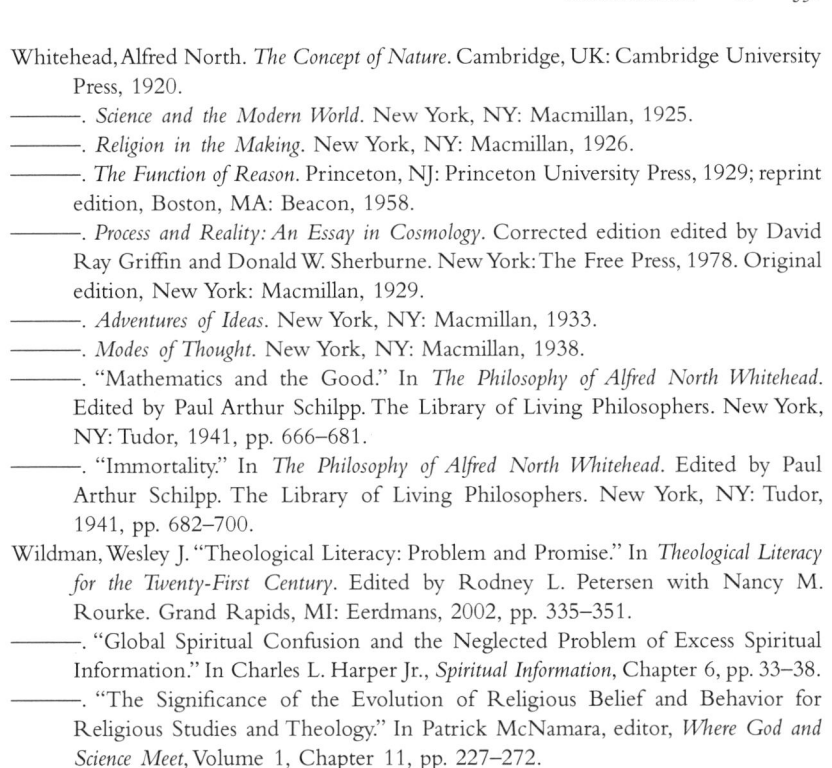

Wolter, Allan, O.F.M., translator and editor. *Duns Scotus: Philosophical Writings.* New York, NY: Thomas Nelson & Sons, 1962.

Xunzi. *Xunzi: A Translation and Study of the Complete Works.* Three volumes. Translated and edited by John Knoblock. Volume 1, Books 1–6; Volume 2, Books 7–16; Volume 3, Books 17–32. Stanford, CA: Stanford University Press, 1988, 1990, 1994, respectively.

Yong, Amos, and Peter G. Heltzel, editors. *Theology in Global Context: Essays in Honor of Robert Cummings Neville.* New York, NY, and London, UK: T&T Clark International, 2004.

Zhang, Tina Chunna, and Frank Allen. *Classical Northern Wu Style Tai Ji Quan: The Fighting Art of the Manchurian Palace Guard.* Berkeley, CA: Blue Snake Books, 2006.

Index

[Citations after **"I"** are to *Ultimates: Philosophical Theology Volume One* and those after **"II"** are to *Existence: Philosophical Theology Volume Two.*]

Abandonment, of self, **I:** 113–18, **II:** 98, 152, 175, 178, 201, 218, 246, 289
Abduction, **I:** xxi, 56
Abhinavagupta, **I:** 327, **II:** 346
Abraham, **I:** 147, 154
Abrahamic religions, **I:** 125, **II:** 147, 157, 200, 204, 217, 246
Absolute, **I:** 195, **II:** 90, 235; Absolute Spirit, **I:** 188–89, **II:** 200; value identity, **II:** 17, 87–99, 102–03, 111, 121, 132, 163, 167, 169, 173, 177–82, 189, 191–93, 210–12, 215, 222, 244, 248, 251–53, 258–60, 266, 286, 292, 307–15, 319, 321
Abstraction, **II:** 303–04; and concreteness in philosophy, **I:** 128–29, 174–76, **II:** 52, 250; metaphysical versus reductionist, **I:** 130; **II:** in religion, 229
Abstractness, of determinateness per se, **I:** 193
Abyss, **I:** 20, 222–25; mystical, **I:** 303, 309–12, **II:** 155; mystical path of, **I:** 323–24
Acceptance, **II:** 108, 124, 149, 155–60, 165, 179, 184, 189, 212, 225–31, 145, 263, 268–69, 289

Accountability, in obligation, **II:** 124; in theology, **I:** 16
Achievement, **II:** 11, 18, 26, 28. 29, 52, 65, 85–89, 96–99, 102–03, 111, 117, 121–24, 132, 137–38, 146, 16771, 173–78, 184–85, 203, 209–10, 219, 223, 226, 229, 239, 246, 254, 258–60, 266, 272–73, 297, 299–300, 305, 311–15
Act of To Be, **I:** 26, 118, 181–84, 217–21, 258, 275, 292–93, 340
Act, of creation, **I:** 309, **II:** 25; *see* ontological creative act, ontological act of creation
Action, **II:** xx, 3, 13, 33–41, 43–47, 51, 60, 93, 99, 101–02, 115, 118, 121, 125, 129–32, 141, 143, 161, 168–71, 174–77, 182, 192, 200, 204, 210, 220, 239–45, 249, 252, 258–59, 263, 268–69, 273–75, 288–89, 294, 297–99, 301, 305, 326
Actual occasions, **I:** 13, 176–66, 195
Actuality, and potentiality. **I:** 181–82, **II:** 67, 304; and possibility, **II:** 32–35, 117, 122–23, 235, 297, 320
Actualization, **I:** 3–4, 36–42, 197–99, 235–41, **II:** 168, 218

Adam, **I:** 274, **II:** 119, 121, 215
Adams, Robert Merrihew, **II:** 326
Adaptive advantage, **I:** 101–02, **II:** 262, 264–65; *see also* Evolution
Adepts, **I:** 251, **II:** 7, 58, 92, 96, 98, 108, 120 154, 195–96, 225, 231, 248–49, 294, 313; *see also* virtuosity
Adequacy, **II:** 226; of metaphysics, **I:** xxi–xxii, 44, 331; of religion, **II:** 310
Adolescence, **II:** 162, 260, 280–82, 288
Advaita Vedanta, **I:** 42, 107, 160, 231, 234, 260, 303, **II:** 93, 127
Aesthetic judgment, **I:** 196, 200
Aesthetic, new for our age, **I:** 165–66
Aesthetics, **I:** 68, 183–86, **II:** 5, 38, 40, 59, 91–93, 233, 244, 301
Affirmation, **I:** 45, **II:** 18, 26–27, 67, 102, 123, 130, 132, 162, 164, 168, 173, 176–82, 185, 190, 264, 269, 284, 289–90, 309, 324
Affordances, **I:** 68
African Americans, **II:** 160, 240–41
Afterlife, **I:** 242–44, **II:** 109, 125, 161–62, 212, 215, 217–18
Age, of persons in heaven, **I:** 242–43
Agency, **I:** 101–02, **II:** 21, 33, 68, 82, 92–93, 114, 129, 131, 227; universal attribution in childhood, **I:** 254
Agents, **II:** 32–34, 49, 93, 113, 123, 131, 171, 176, 241; supernatural, **I:** xix, **II:** 198, 200, 202, 217, 232, 323; *see also* Supernaturalism
Ahura Mazda, **II:** 198
Alcorta, Candace S., **I:** 333, **II:** 280, 334, 337
Alexander the Great, **I:** 55
Alienation, **I:** 25, **II:** 21, 110–11, 135–39, 141–44, 148, 179, 184, 213, 262
Alive, **I:** 305, **II:** 20, 153, 238, 315–16
All under Heaven, **I:** 128, **II:** 266, 333, 338
Allah, **I:** 10; **II:** 2, 94–95, 119, 178, 199–200, 231, 286, 295
Allan, George, **I:** 68, **II:** 337
Allen, Frank, **II:** 334
Allinson, Robert E., **II:** 329
Almond, Gabriel A., **I:** 328

Altizer, Thomas J. J., **II:** 200, 331
American Theological Society, **I:** xxv
Analogy, **I:** 71–73, 321, **II:** 72, 129, 139; of being, **I:** 118, 171, 180–84, 245–46; of human creativity, **I:** 217–18, **II:** 232; of proportion and proper proportionality, **I:** 182–84; in Thomas Aquinas, **I:** 118, **II:** 140, 226, 332, 337
Analytic philosophy, **I:** xix, 14–15, 68, 326
Analytic pragmatism, **I:** 326
Anatman, **I:** 308, **II:** 120, 152
Anderson, Victor, **I:** 68
Angels, **I:** 274, **II:** 215
Anger, **I:** 38, **II:** 248, 295
Angle, Stephen C., **II:** 32, 132, 325–26, 329–30
Anglican, **II:** 56, 267, 333
Angra Mainyu, **II:** 198
Annales School, **I:** 156
Annihilation, **I:** 304–06, 311, **II:** 14
Anselm, **I:** 113, 180
Anthropological ultimacy, **I:** 5, 107–08, 244
Anthropology, **I:** 7, 25, 110, 139, **II:** 3, 266; and colonialism **I:** 50–51; cultural, **I:** 82–83; theological, **II:** xvi–xx, 26, 31, 49, 71, 85, 254, 257, 324
Anthropomorphism, **I:** 27, 85 108, 110–11, 119, 141, 147, 292, 296, 320, **II:** 57, 232–33
Antidynamic macrocosmic identification, **II:** 217–18, 223
Antidynamic microcosmic identification, **II:** 217, 219, 223
Anti-Semitism, **I:** 155, **II:** 63
Apathy, **II:** 168, 171, 173, 177–82, 185
Apocalyptic, **II:** 192, 197–207, 209, 223, 225, 244
Apologetics, **I:** xviii–xix
Apophatic theology, **I:** 2, 19–20, 33, 103, 108–09, 251, 303, 324, **II:** 316
Appleby, R. Scott, **I:** 328
Applicability, **I:** xxi–xxii, 44, 331
Appreciation, **I:** 241, **II:** 79, 81–83, 104, 149–53, 158–60, 168, 184, 214, 222, 233, 290, 297, 300, 312

Appropriation, **II:** 62–69, 135–43, 150, 168, 184, 189, 273, 297
Apsu, **I:** 126
Aquinas, Thomas, **I:** xxi, 5, 26, 34, 77, 86, 118, 130, 170, 180–84, 191, 217–21, 245–46, 258–62, 292–93, 326, 337–38, 340–41, **II:** 140, 226; intentionality in God, **I:** 181; Thomism, **I:** 130, 230
Arbitrariness, **I:** 17, 38, 222–23, 258, 260–62, 267–68, 276–79, 311, 323, **II:** xxii–xxiii, 18, 38, 140, 172, 179–82, 211–14, 226, 229–32, 236, 244, 247, 314–316
Archeology, **I:** 7
Argument, **I:** xv–xvii, xxi, **II:** xix, xx, 4, 12, 17, 26, 41, 101, 109, 183, 210, 256, 309, 314, 317; vs. argumentation, **I:** 56–57; like rope, not chain, **I:** 58, 287
Aristotelianism, **I:** 55, 185
Aristotle, **I:** 14–15, 34, 113, 170, 174, 182, 193, 196, 222, 234, 282, 306, 340, **II:** 45–46, 67, 74–75, 199, 327
Arjuna, **I:** 116–19, **II:** 45, 62, 83, 93, 161, 174, 177, 179, 294, 299
Ambiguity, **II:** 126, 169, 171–73, 180, 190, 331
Armentrout, Kenneth, **I:** xxv
Armstrong, Karen, **I:** 330, **II** 52, 326, 338
Arrogance, **II:** 135–38, 142–48, 179, 184
Art (arts), **I:** vi, 5–6, 25, 58, 82, 87, 130, 200, **II:** vi, 44, 64, 81, 118, 137, 175, 294, 297
Aryan traditions, **I:** 55, **II:** 90
Asad, Talal, **I:** 4, 327, 329, **II:** 325, 328, 338
Asceticism, **I:** 106–07, **II:** 95, 175
Aseity, divine, **I:** 274–75
Asherites, **I:** 291–92
Ashoka, **I:** 341
Aslan, **II:** 54–59
Assumptions, background and foreground, **I:** 46–47
Astonishment, **II:** 18, 156, 225–26, 234, 236–37, 248
Asymmetry, **II:** 229–30; in ontological creative act, **I:** 222–25

Athleticism, **I:** 304–06
Atman, **I:** 39, 85–86, 115, 173–74, 256, **II:** 68, 91, 119–20, 147, 152
Atomism, **I:** 194–95, **II:** 71, 73
Attachment, **I:** 47, 65, 70–71, **II:** 39, 97, 120, 143, 174–75, 201, 211, 244–45, 294–95
Attention, in thinking ultimacy, **I:** 106, 299–300, 302, **II:** 136, 195, 235, 254, 297–99, 303, 305, 310–11
Augustine, **I:** 47, 243, 331, 340, **II:** 2, 125–26, 213
Authenticity, **I:** xvii, 10, 20, **II:** 63, 65, 92
Author of this book, described, **I:** 325
Authority, **I:** xv, xx, 31, 79, **II:** xx, 13, 17, 37, 94, 178, 258, 267, 275, 283, 317–20
Auxier, Randall E., **I:** 333, 336
Avatars, **I:** 19, 116, 255, 315, **II:** 109, 174, 219
Averroes, **I:** 340
Avicenna, **I:** 326
Awareness, **II:** 35, 77, 79–83, 104, 149–52, 155–58, 184, 297, 300, 312
Awe, **I:** 17, 38, 284, **II:** 5, 18, 20, 81, 156, 165, 212, 225–26, 234, 236–37, 267–68
Axial Age, **I:** 4, 16, 32–33, 55, 315, 330, **II:** 14, 16; religions, **I:** 41, 74, 79, 84–87, 113, 127, 161–61, 145, 148, 150–51, 294, 327, **II:** 11, 16, 38, 45–46, 83, 90–96, 130, 149, 158, 160, 164, 193–99, 212, 225, 237, 245, 266, 325, 334
Ayurvedic medicine, **II:** 142

Babette's Feast, **II:** 195
Babylonian religion, **I:** 126–27
Bach, Johann Sebastian, **II:** 140
Banana, **I:** 136, 142–43
Barrett, Nathaniel, **I:** 68, 333, **II:** xxiii
Bartel, T. W., **I:** 326
Barth, Karl, **I:** xx–xxi, 17, 32, 149–50, 152, 157, 325, 327–28, 330, 337, **II:** 60–61, 197, 338
Beauty, **I:** xv, 93, 108, 122, 131, 175, 280, **II:** xxii, 140, 227–29, 231, 234–38, 267, 312; glimpsed from the corner of the eye, **I:** 12

Becoming, **I:** 235–41, **II:** 52, 62, 67. 79, 129, 226, 247, 254, 260, 294
Being (being-itself, *ipsum esse*), **I:** 21, 61, 77, 173–91, 245–47, 297, 321, **II:** xv, xvii, xxi, 19, 21, 26, 28, 65, 67, 76, 102, 108, 123, 141, 155, 168, 172–73, 177, 180–81, 197, 211, 219, 225, 227–28, 232, 251–52, 315–16, 320, 325, 329, 332, 335; analogical or univocal, **I:** 176, 180–84; as common to beings, **I:** 179–80, 184–86, 246; density of, as value, **I:** 199–201, **II:** 34; determinate or indeterminate, **I:** 171–72, 176, 184–91, 246–47; dialectic of, **I:** 176; as dynamic dialectic, **I:** 188–91; as first object of intellect, **I:** 180; one or many, **I:** 176–80; power of, **I:** 311; as a property, **I:** 184–85; question of, **I:** 169–72; as totality, **I:** 186–91, 246; and unity, **I:** 174
Belief, **I:** 6; costliness of, **I:** 46; meaning of, **I:** 45–48; reasons for, **I:** 101–02; religious, **I:** xix, 6, 70, 45–48, 165–66, **II:** 1, 16, 82, 120, 145, 160–62, 198–99, 206, 212, 214–17, 223, 246, 259–63, 287–88, 293, 323; unconscious, **I:** 46
Bell, Catherine M., **I:** xix, **II:** 262, 333
Bellah, Robert, **I:** 32, 330, 336, **II:** 325
Benediction, **II:** 267, 269
Benjamin, tribe of, **I:** 126–27
Berdyaev, Nicolas, **I:** 309, 342
Berger, Peter L., **I:** 29–33, 42, 48, 67, 109, 112, 329–30, 333, **II:** 27, 89, 262, 264, 273, 325, 328, 333
Berkson, Mark, **II:** 325
Bernstein, Richard, **I:** 68, 333–334
Berry, Thomas, **II:** 79, 97, 203–05, 327, 331
Berthrong, John H., **I:** xxv, **II:** xxiii, 324, 333–34
Betrayal, **II:** 43, 98, 102, 114–21, 130–33, 197, 184
Bhagavad Gita, **I:** 117–18, 315, **II:** 45, 55, 62, 174, 177, 197, 294, 299, 330–31
Bhakti religion, **I:** 111, 118, 312, **II:** 238

Bias, **I:** xvii, 6, **II:** 2, 15, 229–30, 269, 321
Bible, **I:** 77, 149–50, **II:** xxiii, 2, 13, 60, 123, 169, 198, 222, 231, 284; *see also* Hebrew Bible, New Testament
Big Bang, **I:** 124, 149–50, 153, 155, 204, 220, 238, 241, **II:** 202, 229–30, 247
Bigotry, **I:** 159, **II:** 151, 158–60, 181, 262, 266
Biochemistry, **I:** 19
Biology, **II:** 64, 230; evolutionary, **I:** xx, **II:** 12, 31, 34, 325; *see also* Evolution
Birthdays, **I:** 92, **II:** 264, 266
Bliss, **I:** 109, 284, **II:** 189, 211–12
Bloch, Ernst, **I:** 327
Blood, **II:** 12, 43, 59, 110, 114, 118, 121, 124, 133–34, 179, 184, 263, 268–72, 288, 294, 334
Bodhidharma, **II:** 294
Bodhisattva, **I:** 106, 312, 226, **II:** 39, 83, 98, 110, 120, 245, 284, 286, 288
Body, **II:** 11, 14, 63–66, 72, 121, 133, 139–44, 161, 164, 212–17, 247–49, 269, 272, 274, 276–77, 280, 297–98, 312, 328, 330, 334; in knowing, **I:** 283; as material quality of symbols, **I:** 304; as metaphor, **I:** 75
Bondage, spiritual, **I:** 20, **II:** 109, 120, 240, 246 *see also* Spirituality
Bosnians, **I:** 8
Boston Theological Society, **I:** xxv
Boundaries, **II:** 17, 77, 140, 272; of disciplines, **I:** xviii; policing, **I:** 8; of religious communities, **I:** 48
Boundary conditions, **I:** 3–4, 31–33, 109–13, 164, **II:** xviii, 14, 320; for human life, **I:** 243, **II:** xxi, 7–8, 11, 13, 16, 18, 21, 25–29, 31, 49, 71, 101–04, 107–11, 183, 265, 282–86; as world defining, **I:** 97–98, 102–93, **II:** 27, 79, 101, 272
Boyarin, Daniel, **I:** 8, 328, 340–41, **II:** 328
Bracketing the truth question, **I:** 20–21
Bradley, F.H., **I:** 195, 338, **II:** 73
Brahma, **I:** 147, 116
Brahman, **I:** xxii, 1, 19, 26, 39, 109, 115, 117–18, 121, 124, 173–75, 220–

21, 229, 231, 234, 255–56, 259–60, 266, 288, **II:** 91, 93, 99, 119–20, 127, 147, 165, 219, 245, 313; Nirguna and Saguna, **I:** 85–86, 132, 273, 291, 308; *see also* Nirguna
Brahmanism, **I:** 2, 106, 115, 17, 132
Brahms, Johannes, **II:** 19–20
Brandom, Robert, **I:** xix, 68–69, 328, 326, 334
Brihadaranyaka Upanisad, **II:**, 91
Brockington, John, **I:** 335
Brokenness, **II:** 4–12, 43, 107–11, 113–15, 118, 121–23, 135, 154, 165, 169–73, 190, 264, 278, 289, 292, 320–21
Broken symbols, **I:** 19–20, 148, 159–61, 280, 324, 327, **II:** 82 *see also* Symbols
Brumbaugh, Robert S., **II:** 327
Buchler, Justus, **I:** 68, 327, **II:** 327
Buddha, **I:** 16, 113–14, 147, 151, 157, 231, 307, 231, **II:** 39, 53, 87, 97, 110–11, 119 175, 179, 198, 201, 245, 331; Buddha-Mind, **I:** 1, 19, 220, **II:** 127–28; teachings of, **I:** 77
Buddhism (or Buddhists), **I:** xvii, 2, 4–5, 7, 8, 10, 18, 26–7, 38, 40, 78, 86–96, 105–07, 111, 119, 127, 129, 137–38, 145, 150, 14–55, 194, 229–32, 234, 242, 303, 308, 329–30, 31, **II:** xvi, 2, 6, 10, 16, 19, 39, 67–68, 83, 91–93, 97, 108, 110, 120, 126–28, 138, 147, 152, 161, 175, 201, 211. 219, 245, 294, 299, 328; concepts of self, **I:** 113–15; ultimate cognitive frame, **I:** 151; *see also* Chan, Madhyamaka, Yogacara, *and* Pure Land Buddhism
Buddhist-Confucian cultures, **I:** 91–92
Bultmann, Rudolf, **I:** xx, **II:** xv, 258
Bureaucracy, heavenly, **I:** 296, **II:** 246
Bushido, **II:** 299

Cabbala, **I:** 86
Cain (and Abel), **II:** 119
Cairns, Huntington, **I:** 338
Calvin, John (or Calvinist), **II:** 36, 61, 195, 328
Cannibalism, **I:** 146, **II:** 124, 271, 334
Capps, Walter H., **I:** 327

Care, **I:** 11, **II:** 44–46, 98, 134, 137, 146, 218, 222, 248, 251, 264, 301–02
Carman, John Braisted, **I:** 340
Carpenter, Humphrey, **II:** 327
Caste, **II:** 40, 90–91
Categories, **I:** xvi, xxi, 26–27, 60–61, 129, **II:** 15, 227; in Peirce, **I:** 334; of *Philosophical Theology*, **I:** 258–62, **II:** 19, 28, 96, 209; religious, **I:** 35–42
Category of the Ultimate, in Whitehead, **I:** 285–86, 337
Causation, **I:** 129, 246–47, **II:** 129; final and efficient, **I:** 50–52; in indexical reference, **I:** 71–72, 288–89; mechanical models of, **I:** 140–41
Celibacy, **I:** 302
Centeredness, **II:** 111, 117, 135–48, 168, 184, 245
Chan Buddhism, **I:** 256
Chan, Wing-tsit, **I:** 220, 340–41
Chandogya Upanishad, **II:** 91
Change, **I:** 912, 233–34, 243, 257–58, **II:** xix, 18–19, 25, 33, 62, 65–68, 74–75, 83, 97–98, 103, 108–110, 119–20, 128, 135, 137–48, 150, 161–65, 168, 184, 200, 202, 213, 216, 218–19, 231, 236, 258, 268, 275–76, 278, 282, 284, 291, 297–301, 304–06, 316–17, 331
Chaos, **I:** 31, 126, 273, **II:** 6, 12, 25, 91–92, 146, 157, 198, 305, 316; needs no explanation, **I:** 225
Chapman, J. Harley, **I:** 325, 334, **II:** 339–40, 342
Chapple, Christopher Key, **I:** 342, **II:** 330–31, 339
China, **I:** 122, **II:** 6, 91–95, 134, 155, 203; and Buddhism, **I:** 55, **II:** 294
Chittick, William C., **I:** 339, **II:** 331, 339
Choice, **I:** 3–4, 39, 41, 201–02, 277–79, **II:** xix, xxi–xxii, 27–31, 33, 38–42, 46, 50–51, 62–63, 96, 101–102, 113–16, 122, 124, 126, 130–131, 137, 191–92, 231, 239–44, 248, 253, 276, 280–87, 312, 324
Chosen People, **I:** 78, 84, 122, 147, **II:** 94

Christendom, **I:** 91, **II:** 89
Christianity (or Christians), **I:** xvii–xviii, 4–5, 8, 11, 18, 26, 31, 50, 46–47, 50–51, 55, 65, 77, 83–84, 86–98, 106, 118, 123, 129, 145, 152, 154–55, 159–60, 170, 174, 230–32, 234, 255, 262–63, 274, 312, 325–26, 330, **II:** 2, 6, 11, 16, 39, 55–56, 60, 67, 82–83, 95–98, 110, 114, 119–23, 126–30, 133, 146, 164, 178, 197, 199, 246–48, 259, 266–68, 271, 284, 329, 333–34; concepts of self, **I:** 114–118; evangelical, **I:** 9, 46–48, 111, and gay rights, **I:** 295
Christ University, **II:** 161
Chrysostom, **I:** 8
Citation, in *Philosophical Theology,* **I:** xxii, **II:** xxiii
Civilization, **I:** 136–37, **II:** 44, 87, 91, 117–18, 203, 262, 276–77; damaged by scientific reductionism, **I:** 53–54
Clarke, Desmond M., **I:** 332
Clooney, Francis X., S.J., **I:** xix–xx, 326, 341, **II:** 266, 239–30, 333
Cobb, John B., Jr., **I:** 279
Cognitive error, **I:** 164
Cognitive science, **I:** 18, 52, **II:** 282; *see also* Science
Coherence, **I:** xxi–xxii, 44, 331, **II:** 32, 50, 129, 220–21, 262, 308, 325; in sacred canopies, **I:** 31–32
Colapietro, Vincent M., **II:** 333
Collins, Randall, **I:** 55, **II:** 340
Colonialism, **I:** 165–66
Colossians, **I:** 255, 274
Comfort, **II:** 142, 145–48, 178–79, 184, 200, 227, 263, 269, 289
Commentary, **I:** 25, 42
Commitment, **II:** 17, 19, 41, 46, 66–67, 83, 132, 33, 182, 257; religious, **I:** 43–44, **II:** 83, 161–63, 175–76, 199, 245, 258–64, 278, 279–93, 304, 307, 314, 319, 324, 330
Common natures, **I:** 198, **II:** 235
Communities, **I:** 41, 47, **II:** 3–4, 8, 43–44, 53, 77–78, 87, 97, 99, 116, 118, 130, 134, 137, 148, 156, 179, 190, 199, 263, 301, 305; boundaries of, **I:** 15–17; and liturgies, **I:** 89; religious, **I:** 18, **II:** 94, 181, 184, 199, 257, 261, 263, 269–73, 282–84, 294, 317–21
Comparative Religious Ideas Project, **I:** 335, **II:** 347
Comparative theology, **I:** xix–xx, 21, 21, 129, 152, **II:** 28, 340
Compassion, **I:** 231, **II:** xxi, 83, 98–99, 149, 154, 170, 177–78, 272, 312
Complexity, **I:** 199–201, 236, 268–69, 271, **II:** 34, 41, 43, 47, 58, 66, 74, 87, 104, 141, 171, 183, 237, 259, 275, 299, 305; needing explanation, **I:** 130–31
Components, **I:** xi, 3–4, 10, 33–34, 97, 197–202, 227, 262–66, 312, 321, **II:** vi, xvii, xix, xxi, 7, 13, 15–17, 21, 25–29, 31, 44, 49–55, 61–69, 71, 85–99, 102–03, 121, 125, 135–54, 163, 170–73, 180–82, 215, 222, 229, 248, 272, 281, 287, 291, 294, 297, 300, 320–21; conditional and essential, **I:** 35–42, 171–72, 178–80, 193–99, 219–21, 227, 146–47, 284–85, 310, **II:** 2–3, 21, 25–29, 32, 72–79, 130, 167, 204–12, 250, 257–60, 265, 303, 307–15; of temporal modes, **I:** 235–41, 263–66, **II:** 14, 32; from Paul Weiss, **I:** 338; as formed, **I:** 137; of harmonies, **I:** 36–42, 201–02; of religion, **II:** 3–6; as ultimate, **I:** 243; and value, **I:** 206–07, **II:** 34
Comportment, **II:** xxi, 45, 50–52, 62–68, 79, 102–03, 111, 135–37, 139, 143–48, 150, 171–72, 215, 260, 265, 272, 300, 321; toward the real, **I:** 43–44
Comprehensiveness, **I:** xxi; **II:** 278–79, 283–85, 288–89, 307
Comprehensiveness continuum, **I:** 43–44, 91–93, 107, 131–32, 320
Computer models of interpretation, **I:** 65–66
Concern continuum, **I:** 106–07, 119; **II:** 7
Concrescence, in Whitehead, **I:** 223, 235, 268

Conditions, **II:** xvi, xviii–xix, xxi–xxii, 2–8, 11–14, 16, 18, 25–28, 44, 63, 67, 74–75, 78, 83, 98, 107–08, 127, 157, 167, 173, 177–78, 191, 205, 230, 241, 243–57, 263–64, 266, 274–76, 291, 296, 305, 307, 312, 315–16, 319–21; for existence, **I:** 35–42; for determinateness, **I:** 3–4; for ultimacy, **I:** 173–76, **II:** 21, 121, 127, 308–10; as unconditioned, **I:** 131, **II:** 116; *see* boundary conditions
Confession, **II:** 2, 233, 267–70
Confessionalism, in theology, **I:** xvi–xvii, xx, 2, 17, 78–79, 175, 325, **II:** xvi; *see also* Theology
Conflict, **II:** 44–45, 52, 61, 63, 66, 77, 109, 121, 128, 134, 157–59, 163, 241, 246, 264, 291–92; among valuable things, **I:** 271, 280
Confucianism (or Confucians), **I:** xvii, xix, 4–5, 12, 63, 75, 77, 82–84, 87, 106, 119, 127, 145, 147, 150–52, 154–55, 171, 228–29, 234, 255, 257, 312–13, 315, 239–30, **II:** xxiii, 2, 40–41, 46, 64, 66, 81, 83, 98, 119, 121, 123, 126, 128, 130, 132, 176, 197, 242, 274, 283, 294, 326; on ancestors, **I:** 137; *see also* Neo-Confucianism
Confucius, **I:** 79, 147, **II:** 3, 62, 81, 87, 92, 119, 132, 246, 276, 283–84, 330
Consciousness, **I:** 26, 64, 106, 114, 128, 147, 173–74, 228–32, 303, 308, 327, **II:** 7, 17, 20, 28, 46, 55, 61–68, 76, 78, 86, 91–93, 98–99, 109, 119–20, 139–41, 154, 156, 165, 203–04, 211, 215, 219, 264, 270, 284, 304, 312, 324, 333; double, **I:** 45–47; indeterminate if pure, **I:** 85–86, 256; metaphors for ultimacy, **I:**1–2, 172, 253–62, 282
Consent to being in general, **I:** 38, **II:** 102, 251
Conservatism, **I:** 9
Consistency, **I:** xxi–xxii, 44, 331, **II:** 27, 111, 116, 220
Connection, **II:** vi, 9, 13, 16, 36, 72, 75–77, 81–83, 91, 97, 103–04, 111, 116, 120–21, 129, 132, 138, 149–65, 168, 170, 172, 176, 181, 184, 196, 198, 215–16, 220, 227, 233, 242, 263, 265–66, 271, 278, 281–85, 289, 303, 306, 310, 319, 332
Consummation, **II:** xix, 331
Containment, **II:** 316–18
Contemplation, **I:** 302–303, 312, **II:** 143; and components of harmony, **I:** 306–09; path of, **I:** 323–24
Context, **I:** 190–91, **II:** xvii–xviii, 2, 6, 9, 32, 40, 43, 51, 64, 75, 81, 93, 99, 109–11, 127, 131–32, 146–47, 151, 157, 161, 168, 170, 176, 178–84, 191–92, 196–97, 201–02, 204, 207, 211, 216, 221, 223, 225, 230, 236–37, 242–45, 253–54, 261, 264–65, 267–269, 271–75, 279, 289–90, 297–300, 303–04, 308, 314–15, 317, 323, 327; of interpretation, **I:** 290, 298–300; of mystical interpretations, **I:** 302, 312; of religious belief, **I:** 48, **II:** xv, xvii; transcendence of, **I:** 128; *see also* ontological context of mutual relevance
Continental philosophy, **I:** 64, 68–69; *see also* Philosophy
Contingency, radical, **I:** 3–4, 12, 16–17, 33–34, 37–38, 74–75, 93, 97–98, 101–03, 113, 116, 122–23, 135, 137, 225, 309–12, **II:** 8, 14, 16–21, 26–29, 108, 124, 153, 173, 181, 211, 221–22, 227, 233, 244, 286, 306, 309, 314–17, 320–21
Continua, in worldviews, **I:** 28, 98, 118–19, 131–32, **II:** 270, 272, 278, 283; *see also* Concern continuum, Comprehensiveness continuum, Intensity continuum, Sacred/Mundane continuum, Sharing continuum, Sophisticated/popular religion continuum, *and* Transcendence/intimacy continuum
Continuity **II:** 65–68, 120, 137–38, 299, 305; of thought and body, **I:** 203
Contradictions, human, **I:** 3, **II:** xviii, 67–69, 122–125, 130, 139, 154, 170–71, 244–47, 265

Contrast terms, **I**: 186–91, **II**: 205
Contrasts, **I**: 33–34, 199–200, **II**: 32, 34, 74, 87, 101, 124, 192, 210–12, 221, 226, 244, 254, 262, 265, 283, 286, 299, 308
Control, **I**: 201, **II**: 15, 17, 35–36, 41, 49–50, 62, 65, 87–89, 92, 102, 116–118, 133, 139, 144, 169, 195, 254, 281, 295, 306, 318, 326
Contour, **II**: 71–77, 86, 140, 313, 327
Conventional reference, **I**: 70–73, 288–90, **II**: 206, 220; *see also* Reference
Conversion, **I**: 47, **II**: 67, 132, 162
Cook, Francis H., **I**; 337
Correction, **I**: 135, **II**: 12, 15, 263; of life, **I**: 103; of meaning-symbols, **I**: 146–48; *see also* Vulnerability to correction
Corrington, Robert S., **I**: xxv, 140, 334, 337, 340, **II**: xviii, 323, 324
Cosmic epoch, **I**; 278
Cosmological ultimates, **I**: 3–4, **II**: vi, xviii–xxi, 7, 18, 27–28, 113, 125, 189, 191–93, 215, 221–23, 229, 248, 253, 321; *see also* Ultimate reality *and* Ontological ultimate reality
Cosmology, **II**: 21, 65–66, 71–73, 92, 140, 180, 235, 274, 325–26, 330, 332; philosophical, **I**: vi, xix, 2, 60, 112–13, 170, **II**: 83, 304, 314, 318; embracing value and fact, **I**: 200, **II**: 123; as metaphysics, **I**: 169; *see also* Philosophy
Cosmos, **I**: 29–30, **II**: 6, 14, 18, 20–21, 39, 46, 57, 60, 64, 79, 89, 94, 97, 108, 120–21, 155–57, 180–82, 201–05, 210–12, 216–18, 227–32, 247, 253, 265, 283, 285, 298, 302, 305–06; conceptions of, **I**: 123, 310
Costly signaling, **II**: 289, 292
Counterculture, **I**: 140–41
Counter-factuals, **I**: 34, 237, 311
Courage, **I**: 147, 208, **II**: 6, 54–57, 79–83, 104, 149–52. 160, 168, 172, 184, 258–59, 273, 297, 300, 305–06, 312, 328, 333
Covenant, **I**: 78, 152, **II**: 130
Created world, **II**: 25, 180, 204, 215, 223, 232; experience of, **I**: 303–06

Creation, **I**: 11, **II**: xix–xxii, 20, 101, 104, 154, 170, 172, 179–82, 193, 197–206, 226–38, 239, 244–52, 287, 304, 306, 311, 328, 331–32, 335; act of, **I**: vi, **II**: 27, 29, 33, 39, 60–62, 75–76, 83, 123, 124, 154–56, 164–65, 191, 214–16, 221, 223, 249–52, 253–54, 265, 267, 269, 271, 297, 307, 314–20; of everything determinate, **I**: 1–4; *ex nihilo*, **I**: 118, 172, 284; story of, **I**: 150; of the world, **I**: 115–16; unintelligibility of, **I**: 311; *see also* God as creator, Ontological creative act, *and* Ontological ultimate reality
Creativity, **I**: 236–41, 264, 284–85, **II**: 168, 235, 239, 241, 252, 303
Creator, **I**: 37, **II**: 19, 36, 61, 65, 94, 129–31, 161, 165, 198, 200, 204–05, 221–22, 231, 270–73, 305–06, 332; character of, **I**: 155–56; not intentional, **I**: 124; *see also* God, Ontological Act of Creation *and* Ontological ultimate reality
Crises, **I**: 295; and ultimate concern, **I**: 107; for worldviews, **I**: 143
Crisp, Oliver D., **I**: 326
Crosby, Donald A., **I**: 333
Cua, Antonio, **II**: 326
Cultivation, of religious virtuosity, **I**: 301–17, **II**: 40, 57–58, 118, 129, 131–33, 147, 155, 158, 163, 219. 236, 284, 287, 304, 324, 327–28, 330, 334
Culture, **I**: 13, 71, 101, 110, **II**: xx–xxi, 3, 6, 12–16, 35, 42–46, 52, 57, 60–66, 72–73, 77–78, 85–90, 95–96, 99, 107–111, 118–24, 134, 140–41, 151, 154–62, 170, 180–82, 190, 215–17, 222, 230, 240–43, 258, 263–66, 271–77, 280–83, 290–96, 302, 308–10, 326–28, 334; evolution of, **I**: 102–03; habits of changed, **I**: 63–64; and linguistic systems, **I**: 48; resisted in the name of religion, **I**: 54; and scientific reductionism, **I**: 49–52
Cumulative value-identity, **I**: 207, **II**: 14, 16–17, 181; *see also* value-identity
Curiosity, **I**: 142
Curley, Edward, **I**: 332

Daly, Robert J., S. J. **II:** 329–30, 334
Damnation, **I:** 68, **II:** 114–21, 124–27, 179, 184, 246
Daniel, book of, **II:** 198
Dao, **I:** xxii, 1–2, 19, 25, 33, 42, 75, 83084, 86, 102, 115, 121, 123–24, 128–30, 132, 138, 151, 155, 170, 173, 175, 191, 205, 220, 228–29, 255, 257–62, 267, 296, **II:** 40, 99, 189, 246, 283, 312, 313; as river, **I:** 159; transcendent and embodied, **I:** 257
Daodejing, **I:** 124, 228, 257, 336, **II:** 333
Daoism (or Daoists), **I:** xvii, 4–5, 37, 77–78, 87, 115, 119, 125, 127, 137–38, 145, 147, 151, 154–55, 160–61, 171, 173, 228–29, 233–34, 255–57, 291, 296, 315, 339, **II:** 2, 7, 17, 40, 57, 64, 66, 92, 119, 126, 147, 179, 227, 245–46, 290, 294–95, 298, 312, 329
Darfur, **I:** 88
Dates, in time, **I:** 239–41, 265, 277–79, **II:** 216, 264
Davaney, Sheila Greeve, **I:** 333
David, King, **I:** 127, 147, 342; and Bathsheba, **I:** 295–96
Davidson, Donald, **I:** xix, 70, 334
Dawkins, Richard, **I:** 328, **II:** 340
De facto character of world, **I:** 227–28; 52
Deacon, Terrence **I:** 334, **II:** 340
Death, **I:** 12, 38, 65, 74, 107, 119, 131–32, 311, **II:** 6–7, 10, 14, 18–21, 26, 54, 58–60, 66, 71, 81–83, 93, 117, 119–20, 124–25, 133–34, 138–39, 153, 161, 174, 178, 199–201, 213, 218–19, 299, 304–06, 315–17, 325; and life after, **I:** 144
Decentering, **I:** 113
Decision points, **II:** 32–33; and intelligibility, **I:** 278, 285–86
Decisions, **I:** 198–99, 247, 284–85, **II:** 31–33, 45, 52, 88, 116, 122, 216, 243
Deconstruction, of self, **I:** 308–09, **II:** 158
Dedication, **II:** 168, 173, 176–82, 185, 264, 269, 289, 310

Deduction, in Peirce, **I:** 57
Deely, John, **I:** 340
Deep grammar, **I:** 48
Deer Park Sermon, **I:** 113
Deference, **II:** 50–52, 62–69, 79, 92, 103, 110, 135, 137–148, 150, 168, 184, 297, 300, 324, 329, 334
Definiteness, **I:** 268
Deism, **I:** xviii
Delighting in, as love, **I:** 314, **II:** 61, 83, 164, 252
Deliverance, **II:** xviii, 5, 8, 107–14, 121, 127, 130–36, 139, 142, 144–49, 153, 157–61, 168, 173–81, 183–85, 190, 247, 254, 257–60, 273, 277–78, 289–93, 307, 311, 314, 319
Delusion, **II:** 17, 135–36, 142, 147–48, 179, 184
Delza, Sophia, **II:** 330, 334
Demonic, **II:** 9, 96. 200; in symbols, **I:** 90, 293–96
Demons, **I:** 255, **II:** 213
Demonstration, in Peirce, **I:** 57
Denial, **I:** 10, 38, 203, **II:** 71, 78–79, 82, 108, 114, 120, 123, 149–61, 169–73, 179, 184, 231, 292, 298, 305–06
Dennett, Daniel, **I:** 328
Density, of being, **I:** 199–201, **II:** 34, 234
Dependent co-origination (*pratitya samutpada*), **I:** xxii, 86, 194
Depth, **I:** 268, 279, **II:** 6, 16, 61, 76, 83, 92, 101, 108, 110, 161, 165, 178, 196, 206, 211, 233, 273, 284, 318; **I:** infinite, 321; of intension in nature, **I:** 135–38; of nature, **I:** 103, **II:** xvi–xvii, 157; in Tillich, **I:** 270
Descartes, **I:** 53, 55–56, 59, 63–68, 193, 219, 327, 331–32, 339, **II:** 258
Despair, **II:** 11, 57, 68, 116, 123, 149–55, 160–62, 173, 175, 179, 184, 258
Destiny, **I:** 147, 229–30, **II:** 19, 305, 329
Determinate distance, in analogy, **I:** 182–83
Determinateness, **I:** vi, 1–4, 112–13, 121, 184–91, 275–76, 278–79, **II:** xxi, 8, 25, 205, 285, 306, 309, 320–21; in God, **I:** 96; and indeterminateness, **I:**

Determinateness *(continued)*
133, 177–80, **II:** 314–15; and modeling, **I:** 254–62; in ontological creative act, **I:** 259–60, **II:** 226; presupposed universally, **I:** 58, 60–61; respects of, **I:** 35; theory of, **I:** 21, 35–42, 171, 193–209, 246–47, 321; traits of, **I** vi, **II:** 8, 13, 27, 49, 102, 320; in ultimacy, **I:** 2, 243–44; of world, **I:** 227–31, 309

Determinations of being, **I:** 170–72

Determinism, **I:** 49–52, **II:** 16, 119

Development, in worldviews, **I:** 93, **II:** xx, 132, 148, 236, 246, 260, 282, 311, 319

Devotion, **I:** 314, **II:** 44, 248, 313, 328

Dewey, John, **I:** 68, 169, 327, 332, 337, 339, **II:** 81. 242, 325, 27

Dharmas, **I:** 114, 138, 151, 194, **II:** 2, 7, 39, 65, 90–93, 114, 119–21, 126, 136, 175. 201, 219, 221, 236, 242, 245, 328

Dialectic, **I:** 85–86, 130, 151, 166, 169–72, 232, 256, 273, 284–87, 289, 329, **II:** 46, 120, 146. 164, 196, 234–37, 240, 259, 290, 309; of being, **I:** 174; defined, **I:** 112–13; in metaphysics, **I:** 57–61; of one and many, **I:** 224–25; of ultimate reality, **I:** 245–47

Dialectical illusion, **I:** 56

Dialogue, interreligious, **I:** 48

Diamond, Jared, **II:** 333

Diaspora, **I:** 154, **II:** 94

Dickens, Charles, **I:** 72, 253

DiDonato, Nicholas, **II:** xxiii

Diet, **I:** 292, 294, 302, **II:** 63, 111, 117, 133, 152, 196, 296

Dignity, **I:** 41, **II:** 113–14, 248

Discipline, **II:** xvii, xx, 2, 229, 291 spiritual, **I:** 118, **II:** 40, 92–98, 108, 111, 150, 160, 165, 236, 250, 258, 294–98, 325

Discrimination, **II:** 111, 215; through signs, **I:** 65

Disgust, **I:** 73

Disharmony, **I:** 146, **II:** 17, 122, 329; *see also* Harmony

Disintegration, **II:** 17, 110–11, 135–48, 150, 168, 184, 321

Dispensationalism, **I:** 96

Distortion, **II:** 10, 26, 142, 149–53, 158, 161, 179, 184, 217, 263

Distraction, in meditation and contemplation, **I:** 307

Diversity **II:** 13, 34, 44 religious, **I:** 7, 199–200, 263, **II:** 147, 184, 191, 280

Divine intentionality, not indicated by known world, **I:** 124

Divine life, **I:** 266–69, **II:** 20

DNA, **I:** 136–37, **II:** 8, 12, 230

Doctrine of the Mean, **I:** 151, **II:** 40

Doctrine, **I:** 15–17, 77, 165, **II:** 16, 68, 120, 152, 286, 329

Domains, within worldviews, **I:** 82–84, 107, 142, **II:** 7, 53, 103, 110–11, 141, 156, 168, 181, 191, 222, 285, 287–91, 307–14

Donne, John, **II:** 71, 74, 327

Dostoyevsky, F., **II:** 123

Doubt, **I:** 111, **II:** 197, 288

Dravidian traditions, **I:** 55

Dream worlds, **I:** 139

Dreyfus, Hubert, **II:** 89, 328

Dualism, **I:** 115, **II:** 198, 327

Durkheim, Emile, **I:** 54, 331, **II:** 261–63, 266, 331

Duty, **II:** 65, 90–91, 161, 226, 242

Dyad, **I:** 218, 224, 234, 340, **II:** 332; *see also* One, the

Dynamic macrocosmic idealization, **II:** 217, 223

Dynamic microcosmic idealization, **II:** 217, 223

Dynamism, **I:** 234; of eternity, **I:** 241–44, **II:** 88, 216, 219 of existential field, **I:** 265; in sacred canopies, **I:** 131; of temporal modes, **I:** 238–41, 322

Ea, **I:** 126

Earth, **I:** 135, 155, **II:** 12–13, 60, 81, 97, 140, 174–202, 206, 213, 217–18, 274; 283, 302; as cosmic center, **I:** 123

Ecclesiastes, **I:** 242, 341, **II:** 169

Eckel, Malcolm David, **I:** 47, 330–31, 335, **II:** 329

Eckhart, Meister, **I**: 309, 342
Ecology, **I**: 19, **II**: 50
Economics, **I**: 25, 50
Ecozoic Era, **II**: 203–05
Ecstatic fulfillments (*or* ecstasy), **I**: xv–xvi, 12, 20–21, 58, 107, 133, 148, **II**: vi, xv, xviii–xxiii, 4–9, 15, 18, 20–21, 25, 83, 173, 178, 185, 189–93, 195–207, 209–12, 216, 221, 223, 226, 236–39, 244, 247, 249, 251, 254, 257–60, 263–65, 270–73, 277–79, 290, 292–93, 299, 304, 306–07, 313–14, 318–21
Education, **I**: 160, **II**: 2, 17, 35–36, 40, 44, 75, 81, 118, 128, 133, 136–37, 150, 242, 262, 282, 285–86, 294–97, 302, 326–27, 329
Edwards, Jonathan, **I**: 38, **II**: 36, 123, 227–29, 240, 251, 329, 332
Ego, **I**: 308–09, **II**: 41, 126, 137–39, 144, 152, 157–58, 175–76, 245, 296
Egypt, narrative of, **I**: 156; religion of, 229
Eightfold Noble Path, **I**: 114, **II**: 39, 221
Ein Sof, **I**: 124
Einstein, Albert, **I**: 53, 204
Eliade, Mircea, **I**: 32, 40, 138, 150–51, 165, 335, **II**: 13, 183, 206, 331, 334
Ejaculatory birthing, **II**: xxii
Elwes, R.H.M., **I**: 331, **II**: 349
Emanation, **I**: 193
Embodiedness, **I**: 39–40, **II**: 4
Emergence, **II**: 120, 324–25; double meaning of, **I**: 257–62; spontaneous, **I**: 1–2, 151–52, 228–32, **II**: 7, 17, 28, 33, 61–62, 76, 92–93, 99; as metaphor for ultimacy, **I**: 253–62, 282
Emotional tone, of symbolic engagements, **I**: 312, **II**: 118
Empires, and Axial Age religions, **I**: 122
Empirical reality, **I**: 49–50
Empiricism, and intelligibility, **I**: 285–86; in *Philosophical Theology*, **I**: 6–7; in religious truth, **I**: 42–44
Emptiness, **I**: 48, 84, 116–18, 231, 288, 291, **II**: 99, 198, 313
Enemies, **I**: 115, **II**: 14, 18, 55, 82–83, 157, 165, 294–96

Engagement, **I**: xix, 4, 6, 15–17, 69–72, 107, **II**: xv–xvi, xix, xxiii, 3–9, 17–18, 28–29, 40–46, 66, 71, 79, 81–84, 99, 102–04, 108, 114, 121, 132, 144, 149–65, 168, 170–72, 180, 183–85, 189–93, 196, 206, 210, 215, 218–23, 225–28, 234–37, 247–51, 257–60, 264–66, 272–73, 275–78, 287–308, 312–16, 319–20, 324, 328, 332, 346; defined, **I**: 67; with existential field, **I**: 203; versus truth, **I**: 67–68; of ultimates, **I**: 131–33, 287–90
Enlightenment, **I**: 146, **II**: 18, 93, 109, 120, 126, 128, 142, 147–48, 177, 179, 184, 190, 201, 245, 263, 284, 289, 329, 332; European, **I**: 25, 140–41, **II**: 37, 124, 200
Enuma Elish, **I**: 126
Environment, **I**: 265, **II**: xviii, xxi, 2, 6, 12–17, 31, 44, 46–47, 51, 63–66, 71, 74, 77–80, 85–94, 97, 103, 117, 137, 142, 144, 151–57, 160, 170, 202–05, 260–65, 276, 280–82, 285, 288, 296, 298, 302, 312, 326, 334–35; social, **I**: 136–37
Ephesians, letter to, **II**: 295–96
Epistemology, **I**: 21, 54, 68, 309; pragmatic, **I**: 320; of symbolic engagements, **I**: 297, **II**: 220, 257
Eschatological consummation, **II**: xviii
Essential components, **I**: 178–80, 291, **II**: 3–5, 26, 50, 65, 72–79, 86–88, 149, 153, 167, 182, 204, 250, 257, 294, 307–09, 314; of modes of time, **I**: 235–41; *see also* Components, Conditional Components, *and* Harmony
Estrangement, **II**: 18, 79, 110–11, 139, 148–65, 168–69, 184, 258, 303, 321
Eternity, **I**: 21, 133, 144, 205, 247, 322, 339, **II**: xix, 10, 192–93, 203, 223, 325, 327; hostility to, **I**: 235; imagined, **II**: 55; of ontological creative act, **I**: 172, 219–220, 232–35, 262, 266–69, 277–79, **II**: 88; of a person's life, **I**: 239–40, **II**: 88, 167, 254, 316–18, 321; as togetherness of

Eternity *(continued)*
  modes of time, **I:** 238–41, **II:** 216–19; as ultimate, **I:** 243
Ethics, **I:** 58, 68, **II:** 40–45, 64, 209, 229, 240, 242, 326, 329
Eucharist, **I:** 146, **II:** 121, 124, 267–72, 334
Europe, **I:** 55, **II:** 200, 203, 258, 267, 334
Evangelical Christianity, *see* Christianity, evangelical
Evidence, **I:** 7, **II:** 81, 110, 246
Evil, **I:** 42, 152, **II:** 13–14, 54–63, 68, 116–18, 123–27, 134, 143, 163–64, 190, 198, 200, 217–18, 231, 294–95, 303, 329–30, 335
Evolution, **I:** 10, 20, 153, 308, **II:** xviii, xx, 5, 12–15, 35, 61, 80, 83, 117, 124, 195, 202, 204, 229, 262–65 269, 289, 308, 318, 224–25, 334; biological and cultural, **I:** 101–03; in the human body, **I:** 135–38; as mechanism of creation, **I:** 124
Evolutionary biology, **I:** 7, 18, 41, 52, 139, **II:** 12, 325
Excellences, in God, **I:** 275–76
Exclusivism, religious, **I:** 7, 10
Exhibition, in philosophy, **I:** xxi–xx
Exile, **I:** 127, **II:** 94, 198
Existential continua, **I:** 91–93; *see also* Worldviews
Existential decisions, **I:** 294–95
Existential definition of the self, **I:** 27, 105, 108, 153–55
Existential dimensions of religion, **II:** 1–8
Existential field, **I:** vi, 3–4, 11–12, 40–41, 202–209, 237–41, 39–12, 327, **II:** xix, xxii, 6, 14–17, 26, 43, 71–86, 97, 99, 103, 110, 121, 139, 141, 149–76, 180, 191–93, 205, 210–16, 219, 222–50, 258–62, 265, 287, 293, 297–99. 303, 306, 309, 311, 315, 327; and intelligibility, **I:** 283; non-spatiotemporal, **I:** 202–03
Existential location, **I:** 3–4, 36–42, 97, 115, 137, 147, 202–09, 227, 237–41, 262–66, 312, 321, **II:** xix, xxi, 7, 13–29, 49, 71–100, 102, 111, 125, 149, 153, 167, 176, 180–81, 205, 210–11, 244, 253, 259, 303, 309–10, 320–21; of human body in evolution, **I:** 135–38; relative to ontological creative act, **I:** 269–71; as ultimate, **I:** 243
Existentialism, **I:** 5, **II:** xv
Exodus, **I:** 19, 154, 333
Experience, **I:** 4, 18, 28, 69, 135, 148, **II:** xviii–xxiii, 1, 9–10, 25, 27, 34, 41–44, 54, 62, 68, 73, 78, 80–83, 85, 97–98, 138, 143, 147, 150–55, 170, 178, 184, 189–93, 195–96, 203, 211, 214, 216, 219, 234, 236, 271, 279, 296, 299, 303–04, 308, 324–325, 327, 330–31, 333–34; of ontological act of creation, **I:** 298–99; and pressure for transcendence, **I:** 131; religious, **I:** xv, 139, 247; adaptive in evolution, **I:** 308; through theological theory, **I:** 284; of ultimacy, **I:** 5, 300
Explanation, **I:** 102–03, 112, 135, 139, 164, 284, 323; as complex or simple, **I:** 130; of ontological creative act, **I:** 223–25; in philosophy, **I:** 127–31
Explication of the hypothesis, **I:** 57
Extension, **II:** 20, 66, 77, 142, 190, 220, 298; of cosmos, **I:** 19, 64, 135, 138, 155–58, 233, 265, 279; of interpretation, **I:** 71–72; ultimate in, **I:** 269–71
Extensive continuum, **I:** 232, 340, **II:** 77
Ezra, **I:** 294, **II:** 94

Fact/value distinction, **I:** 13–14
Facticity, **I:** 227, **II:** 211, 231
Failure, **II:** xxi, 7–10, 27–28, 49, 61, 82–83, 97, 107–08, 113–26, 130–31, 135–39, 142, 147–55, 163, 167–71, 174, 176, 182, 246, 248, 258, 263, 266, 276, 303, 324
Faith, **I:** 46, 203, 262, **II:** xvi, 67, 82, 110, 127, 129, 140, 150–55, 160–65, 168, 172, 179, 184, 198–99, 238, 246, 257–64, 289, 292, 293–306, 313, 319, 328–30, 332
Fall, **I:** 311, **II:** xix, xxi, 8, 10, 55, 60–61, 119, 123, 154, 164, 168, 197, 200, 238, 324, 329, 342

Fallacy of misplaced concreteness, **II:** 303
Fallibilism, in metaphysics, **I:** 58–61, 324; in science, **II:** xix–xx
Falsity, **I:** 10; **II:** 221–23
Families, **I:** 40, 93, 118–19, 206, **II:** 14, 18, 43–45, 50, 63–64, 77–78, 82, 87, 90–91, 94, 96–99, 115, 130, 133, 136–37, 141, 143–45, 160, 164, 172, 174, 190, 199, 213, 243, 265, 276–77, 285–88, 290–301, 305, 317; for learning love, **I:** 313, **II:** 117
Fantasy, **I:** 72–73, **II:** 53, 56–58
Feeling, **I:** 305, **II:** 1, 9, 126, 140, 155, 159, 163, 171, 173, 177–78, 189–91, 216, 233–34, 249, 267, 275, 297–98, 335
Feminism, **I:** 295
Feng shui, **I:** 140
Ferre, Fredrick, **I:** 68, **II:** 341
Feuerbach, L. **I:** 327
Fiction (literary), **I:** 202–03
Filial piety, **I:** xxii, 313, **II:** xxiii, 40, 62–63, 218
Film, **I:** 88, **II:** 56–60, 196, 340
Final Dissipation, **I:** 241
Finite/infinite contrasts, **I:** 33–40, 73–79, 83, 93, 97–98, 107–08, 111, 113, 115–118, 132–33, 173–76, 234, 304, 311–12, 319, **II:** 124, 192, 210–11, 221, 226, 224, 265, 283, 286, 308; and ultimate mystery, **I:** 44
First object of intellect, **I:** 184
First Person, of Trinity, **I:** 261–62; *see also* Trinity
First principles, **I:** 284, 323
First Samuel, **I:** 127
Firstness, **I:** 15, 70, 224, 334, 340, **II:** 237
First-order, claims, **I:** 6; issues defining theology, **I:** xv–xxi, 79, 251; ultimate realities, **I:** 16–17
First-person, **I:** 146–48
Fitting together, **I:** 195–99, 246
Flint, Thomas P., **I:** 326
Floch, Bethany Joy, **II:** xxiii
Flood, Gavin, **I:** 329, **II:** 326
Florensky, Pavel, **I:** 342
Flow, temporal, **I:** 197–99, 235–41, 266–69, 276–79, **II:** 19, 216, 245, 305, 325

Folk, culture, **I:** 88, 159, **II:** 271–72; religion, **I:** 108, **II:** 200, 212–13, 270, 291, 316; religion on life after death, **I:** 144; science versus university science, **I:** 87–90; symbols, **I:** 44, **II:** 217, 278
Form of the Good, **I:** 86, 112, 130, 197, 235; creating the world, **I:** 273
Form, **I:** vi, 3–4, 13, 36–42, 97, 116, 197–202, 205–09, 227, 236–41, 262–66, 312, 321, **II:** xix, xxi–xxiii, 7, 13, 16, 19, 21, 25–29, 31–47, 49–53, 62, 66–67, 71, 74–75, 85–87, 102–03, 114, 122–25, 129, 135, 141, 180–81, 191, 205, 209–11, 214, 221, 235–36, 248, 253, 259, 286, 309–10, 320–21, 325, 327, 337, 339; as future possibilities, **I:** 246; and intelligibility, **I:** 283–83; as ultimate **I:** 243; with value, **I:** 206–07, 271, **II:** 31–47, 85–89
Formal reality, **I:** 338
Founders, of religions, **I:** 91
Four causes (in Aristotle), **I:** 222
Fourfold Noble Truths, **I:** 114, 151, 307
Framing theology, **I:** 149–61
Frankenberry, Nancy K., **I:** xix, 325–6, 333, 332, 337, **II:** 339
Freedom, **I:** 111, 133, 221–22, 260–62, 323, 326, **II:** xix, xxii, 18, 20, 33, 36, 133, 193, 226, 239–52, 254, 270, 298, 309, 318, 321, 325, 327, 330
Frege, G., **I:** 14–15
Frei, Hans, **I:** 48, 331, **II:** 342
Freud, Sigmund, **I:** 51, 327, **II:** 139
Friendship, same-sex, **I:** 83–84
Frisina, Warren G., **I:** 333, **II:** 342
Fulfillments, *see* ecstatic fulfillments
Fullness of being, **I:** 275–76
Fundamental dilemma of ontology, **I:** 184–91
Fundamentalism, **I:** 9–11, 147, **II:** 60
Funerals, **I:** 92, **II:** 14
Future, **I:** 3–4, 197–99, 207, 235–41, 247, 263–66, 277–79, 322, **II:** 13–21, 32–36, 41–42, 66, 88, 126, 161, 172, 216, 241, 244, 249, 337; *see also* Temporal modes, Time, Past, *and* Present

Gabriel, the angel, **II:** 198

366 ❋ INDEX

Galaxies, **II:** 156–57, 229, 302; in collision, **I:** 123
Ganesh, **I:** 116
Gays, **I:** 11, 295
Genealogy, **I:** 4
Generic traits of existence, **I:** 169, **II:** 325
Genetic division, **I:** 13
Genius, **I:** 16–17, 51, 79, **II:** 119, 254
Gentiles, **I:** 154, 158; **II:** 94
Genus/species, **I:** 14
Geomancy, **I:** 140
Gilson, Etienne, **I:** 337
Girard, Rene, **II:** 329
Girardot, Norman, **II:** 329
Glory, **I:** 284, **II:** 55, 61, 235, 238, 267
Go, Yohan, **II:** xxiii
Goals, personal, **II:** 96, 104, 168–69, 174–76, 185
God, **I:** 1–2, 5, 37, 40, 48, 75, 84, 86–88, 116, 124, 132, 141, 152–53, 170, 191, 208, 220–21, 269–71, 279–86, 288, 291, 295, **II:** xvi–xvii, xix–xx, 2, 10, 55, 61, 67–68, 76, 83, 85, 94, 97, 99, 108, 119–21, 126–29, 133–34, 145–47, 154–56, 161, 164–65, 174, 78, 189, 195, 198–202, 217, 221–22, 226, 231–35, 237, 246, 248, 252, 267–71, 286, 294–95, 299, 305, 312–13, 323–26, 328–32; as agent, **I:** 269–70, 341; backside of, **I:** 255; beyond gods, **I:** 230; blessing from, **I:** 132; as boundary condition, **I:** 123; as creator, **I:** 115, 123, 260, of non-human nature, **I:** 126; as determinate or not, **I:** 175, 233, 260–62; and evil, **I:** 42; as father, **I:** 20, 118, 300; as fellow sufferer, **I:** 279; as free, **I:** 260–62 (*see also* Freedom); not in genus, **I:** 259–62; as good, **I:** 118; as Ground of Being, **I:** 5, 150, 340; High, **I:**310; image of the invisible, **I:** 274; infinite in contrast to finite things, **I:** 80–84; as intelligent, **I:** 219; as king, **I:** 123, 125; as Lord, **I:** 125; as malleable or unchangeable, **I:** 234; and metaphors for ultimacy, **I:** 256–62; name of, **I:** 290; nature of, **I:** 118, 322–23; and ontological creative act, **I:** 229–32; as partisan, **I:** 125; personal, **I:** 38, 161, **II:** 17, 36–40, 53; present to, **I:** 232–35; as a player in human narrative, **I:** 155–58; purposes of, **I:** 9; referred to as common noun and proper name, **I:** 260–61; revelatory, **I:** 16–17; as rock of salvation, **I:** 61, 124, 159; as shepherd, **I:** 255; as simple, **I:** 183; as temporal or eternal, **I:** 232–35; for Whitehead, **I:** 177; will of for retribution, **I:** 296
Godhead, **I:** 309, **II:** 219
Gods, **I:** 1–2, 33, 39, 121–24, 292; household, **I:** 73, 146; personal, **I:** 34, 137–38
Goffman, Erving, **I:** 335
Golden Egg (Hiranyagarbha), **I:** 19, 22, 153, 310, **II:** 201
Goldstein, Jonathan, **I:** 336
Good, **I:** 175, **II:** 13, 19, 37, 39, 54, 56–61, 83, 117–18, 123, 125, 143, 145, 170, 198, 231, 242, 248, 303, 3214, 335; and evil, **I:** 146; Plato's lecture on, **I:** 14, **II:** 75
Goodness, of harmonies, **I:** 263–64, 280
Grace, **I:** 17, **II:** 238, 246, 296–97, 325, 328
Grange, Joseph, **I:** 68, **II:** 140–41, 330
Gratitude, **I:** 11–12, 17, 38, 75, 169, 314, **II:** xxi, 8, 18, 20, 82–83, 102, 152, 163–64, 173, 181, 225–28, 234, 247, 270
Gratuitousness, **I:** 38, **II:** (*or* gratuity) 179–81, 211–14, 221–32, 236–38, 244–50, 253–54, 287, 290, 314–16
Great Ultimate, (taiji), **I:** 25, 37, 130, 151, 173–74, 228–89, 234, 258–60, 267, 273, 309
Greece, **I:** 55; philosophy of, **I:** 127, **II:** 327; religion of, **I:** 229
Green, Garrett, **I:** 328, **II:** 338
Grief, **II:** 53, 59, 145, 161, 248 over, Christendom, **I:** 165–66
Griffin, David Ray, **I:** 332, 340
Griswold, Charles L., **II:** 331
Ground of Being, *see* God, as Ground of Being

Groundedness, **I:** 111, 116, 205–07, 270–71, **II:** (and grounded wholeness) 13, 17, 29, 49–69, 71, 79, 99, 102–03, 110–11, 121, 135–48, 150, 153, 168–72, 180–82, 184, 191–92, 211, 216, 258, 265–66, 272–73, 292, 297–99, 309, 312–13, 320; in components, **I:** 39–42, 201–02; and intelligibility, **I:** 282–83

Guanilo, **I:** 180

Guanyin, 230, 312

Guidance, **II:** 7, 111, 178; from metaphysics, **I:** 247

Guilt, **II:** 6, 11, 17, 43, 59, 61, 113–34, 163, 168, 184, 275–76, 320; blood, **II:** 43, 110, 114, 118–21, 124, 133–34, 179, 184, 263, 334

Gurus, **I:** 84, 303–04, **II:** 39, 62, 110–11, 147, 195

Habits, interpretive, **I:** 63–68, **II:** 35–36, 40, 42–45, 51, 118, 137, 146, 162, 190–92–202, 211, 229, 231, 236, 246–47. 257, 267, 274–78, 293–302, 311–12

Haecceity, **I:** 198–99, 264–65, **II:** 141, 235

Hahn, Lewis Edwin, **I:** 333, 336

Hall, David L., **I:** 68, **II:** 326

Hamilton, Edith, **I:** 338

Han Dynasty, **I:** 86

Happiness, **II:** 55, 61, 111, 158, 167–82, 185, 195–96, 238, 240, 289

Haq, S. Nomanul, **II:** 326, 328–29

Hardwick, Charley D., **I:** 333

Harmony, **I:** 3–4, 21, 33–34, 97–98, 106, 137–38, 146–48, 171–72, 176, 78, 231, 246–47, 262–66, 278–79, 311–12, **II:** vi, 3–4, 17, 32–35, 41, 50–52, 64–68, 71–79, 85–90, 102–04, 109, 118, 121–22, 125, 129, 135–43, 147–48, 154, 181–82, 205, 210, 217–19, 244, 259, 296, 298, 300, 309, 320–21, 329–30; de facto, **I:** 266; defined, **I:** 35–42, **II:** 3–4, 26; discursive, **I:** 36, 266; not always good, **I:** 197–98; in nature, **I:** 160–61; in Plato, **I:** 14; synchronic and diachronic, **I:** 200–201; theory of, **I:** 193–209, 321; transcendental traits of, **I:** 197–209

Harrell, Bert, **I:** 337

Harry Potter, **II:** 58–60

Hart, Ray L., **II:** xxiii

Hartshorne, Charles, **I:** 68, 224–25, 233, 284, 339–41

Harvey, Van A., **I:** 328, **II:** 342

Hasler, Joshua, **I:** xxv, **II:** xxiii

Hassidism, **I:** 312

Hate, **II:** 76, 102, 116, 118, 143, 149–55, 160, 163, 169, 171, 179, 184, 231, 233, 251, 317

Healing, **II:** 5–6, 115, 130, 141–48, 179, 184, 215, 263, 269, 279, 289, 330, 334

Heaven, **I:** 65, 74–75, 82, 141, 175, 242–44, 260, 288, **II:** 10, 19, 40, 61, 76, 82, 99, 117–18, 132–33, 140, 146, 156, 161–62, 179, 199–202, 210–18, 221, 259, 266, 271, 283, 295, 299, 305, 331, 333–34; bureaucracy in, **I:** 125, **II:** 246; and Earth, **I:** 25, 37, 83–84, 86, 115, 129–30, 255, **II:** 274; is my father, **I:** 269–70, **II:** 217–18; and straw dogs, **I:** 124, 336

Heavenly Principle, **I:** 191

Hebrew Bible, **I:** xxii, 61, 122, 124–27, 152, 156–58, 242, 255, 274, 342, **II:** 13, 169, 198, 222, 231

Hegel, G. W. F., **I:** xviii, 15, 59, 112–13, 188–91, 193, 246, **II:** 127, 200, 240, 243, 329, 332; Hegelianism, **I:** 69, **II:** 67

Heidegger, Martin, **I:** 59, 61, 149, 170, 174, 337, **II:** 173, 231, 315, 323, 332, 335

Heim, S. Mark, **II:** 12, 109, 325, 329–30, 334

Hell, **I:** 65, **II:** 109, 199, 202, 210, 213–17, 258

Hellenism, **I:** 122

Heltzel, Peter G., **I:** 325, 335, **II:** 343

Hermeneutics, **I:** 2

Hierarchy, in form and value, **I:** 199–201, **II:** 34, 41

Highlands Institute for American Religious and Theological Thought, **I:** xxv

Hillman, Anne, **I:** xxv
Hinduism, **I:** xvii, 4–5, 10, 18, 40, 86–87, 115–16, 127, 145, 147, 154–55, 234, 273, 291, 330, **II:** 2, 39040, 91, 97, 119–20, 126, 147, 161, 178, 219, 245, 294, 326
Historicism, **I:** 17–19
History, **I:** 25, **II:** xx, 3, 21, 59, 77, 85, 101, 119, 136, 167, 177, 196–205, 209, 211, 230, 243, 266, 269, 285, 297, 300, 318, 324–26, 331–32; of religions, **I:** 6; **II:** 184
HIV/Aids, **I:** 206–07
Hobbes, Thomas, **I:** 50, 193, **II:** 81, 328
Hocking, William Ernest, **I:** 68
Hogue, Michael S., **II:** 332
Holiness Code, **I:** 294, **II:** 94
Holocaust, **I:** 147, 329
Holy One of Israel, **I:** 84
Holy Spirit, **I:** 20, 95, 152, 263, **II:** 61, 270–71
Homo religiosus, **II:** xviii, xx
Homosexuality, **II:** 151, 158–61
Honen, **II:** 328
Hong, Jong Wook, **II:** xxiii
Hoopes, James, **I:** 334
Hope, **I:** 262, **II:** 55, 59, 61, 75, 115, 145, 151, 160–62, 175–76, 213, 246, 259
Hopkins, Gerard Manley, **II:** 235–36, 332
Human Condition, **I:** xvi, **II:** vi, xv, xvii–xxiii, 5, 9–15, 17, 20–21, 39, 41, 49, 67, 100–04, 107–08, 122, 125, 127, 169, 190, 264, 326, 239
Humaneness (*ren*), **I:** 312–13, **II:** 62, 92, 276
Humanism, **I:** 11–12, 328, **II:** 286
Humanity, **I:** 128, **II:** xvii, xx, 43–45, 53, 65, 127, 171, 177, 218, 235, 252, 263, 64, 270, 274–76, 284, 310, 316, 324, 326, 330, 330, 334
Hume, David, **I:** xviii, 193, **II:** 38, 326
Humility, **I:** 38, 324, **II:** xvii, 18–20, 110, 141–48, 179, 184, 225–26, 233–36, 263, 269, 289, 312
Husserl, Edmund, **I:** 332
Hutagalong, Toar, **I:** xxv
Hwa Yen Buddhism, **I:** 151

Hyperactive agency detection, universal in children, **I:** 139; *see also* Supernaturalism
Hypothesis, **I:** xxi, 6, 282–86, 332, **II:** xxiii, 9, 21, 49, 182, 183, 205, 210, 230, 317–21, 323, 326; about determinateness, **I:** 278–79, **II:** 3, 309, (*see also* Determinateness, theory of); metaphysical, **I:** xxi, 56–61, 76, 169–72, **II:** 41–42; about ontological creative act, **I:** 222–25, 319–24, **II:** 25–28; of *Philosophical Theology*, **I:** 1–4; about ultimacy, **I:** 245–47, 287–90, 297–300

I Jing, **I:** 218
Iconic reference, **I:** 15, 70–73, 144, 282–86, 288–90, **II:** 220; in metaphysical theories, **I:** 293–96; in narratives, **I:** 157–58
Ideal language, **I:** 326
Ideal types, **I:** 50, 142
Idealism, **I:** 71; absolute, **I:** 186, **II:** 73; German, **I:** 81, 105–06
Identity, **II:** xxii, 21, 44, 65, 67, 71, 74, 79, 85, 87, 92, 94, 113, 125, 130, 137–47, 174, 180, 240, 245, 263, 265, 282–83, 290, 300, 320–21, 326; in Barth's theology, **I:** 150; individual, **I:** 41–42, **II:** 192–93, 216–18; religious, **I:** 8, 10, 153, 324, **II:** 158, 169; ultimate, **I:** 4; *see also* value-identity
Idolatry, **I:** 85, 135, 164, **II:** 206; as pressure for transcendent symbols, **I:** 124–27
Ignorance, **II:** 36, 116, 123, 150, 152, 155, 158, 273harmful, **I:** 146, **II:** 19
Illusion, **I:** 132, **II:** 17, 67–68, 109, 119–20, 127, 135–38, 147, 296, 308
Imagination, **I:** 101–02, 329, **II:** 21, 41, 60, 111, 156, 159, 202, 214, 232, 308, 331
Immediacy, **II:** 190, 214, 216; in material signs, **I:** 306; of ontological creative act, **I:** 223
Immensity, **I:** 135, 207, 232–35, 270, 339; of ontological creative act, **I:** 172, 219–20

Imperative (hypothetical or categorical), **II:** 37, 64, 83, 326
Imperialism, in the study of religion, **I:** 18, **II:** 348
Implosion, of sacred worldviews, **I:** 19–20, 146–47, **II:** 320
Importance, of interiority, **II:** 3; in object of interpretation, **I:** 72, **II:** 151; ultimate, **I:** 73, **II:** 96, 99, 264, 286
Impotence, **II:** 108, 168–69, 173, 179, 182, 185
Impurity, **I:** 146, **II:** 121, 128, 159, 163
Incarnation, **I:** 19, 274; *see also* reincarnation
Inclusivism, religious, **I:** 7
Incommensurability of values, **I:** 208–09
Indeterminateness, **I:** 33–34, 44, 184–91, 263; of being; in Brahman, **I:** 117; in ontological creative act, **I:** 1–4; in pure consciousness, **I:** 256; in temporal flow, **I:** 277–79, **II:** 314
Indexical reference, **I:** 70–73, 144–45, 159–60, 253, 282–86, 288–92, 317; in narratives, **I:** 157–58
Individuality, **II:** 93, 263; in religion, **II:** xx–xxi, 1–5; of ontological creative act, **I:** 259–60
Individuals versus kinship groups, **I:** 55; versus societies, **I:** 32
Individuation, **II:** 171, 276; of worldviews, **I:** 91–93
Indra, **I:** 6
Induction, in Peirce, **I:** 57–58
Inferentialism, **I:** 69
Infinite, bad, **I:** 188–89
Infinitesimals, in ontological creative act, **I:** 223–4, 280
Infinity, **I:** 44, **II:** 267, 303–04, 327; *see also* Finite/infinite contrasts
In-groups, and out-groups, **I:** 11, 41, 158, 164, **II:** 117
Inhabitation, **II:** xviii, 44, 196, 257, 259–60, 292, 307–18
Innocence, **I:** 145, **II:** 54, 60, 221
Inquiry, **I:** xxii, 43–44, 56–61, **II:** xx, 1, 8, 21, 25, 81, 102, 163, 259, 275, 323
Insiders, **I:** 52

Instrumentation, **I:** 53
Integration, and contemplation, **I:** 307; of the self, **I:** 235–41, 265, 267, **II:** xxii, 13–17, 26–29, 31, 50–52, 60–64, 74, 79, 89, 110–11, 129, 135–48, 150, 168, 184, 209, 229, 247, 286, 321
Intellect, **I:** 180–84, **II:** 27, 101, 118, 160, 161, 263, 268, 274, 277, 302, 327–28
Intelligent design, **I:** 130, 132, 280–81
Intelligibility, **I:** 222, 278, 322; with antecedent potentials and future possibilities, **I:** 284–85; as created, **I:** 218–21; and decision points, **I:** 85–86; four dimensions of, **I:** 282–86; of ontological creative act, **I:** 323–24
Intending the ultimates, **I:** 302
Intension, of cosmos, **I:** 19, 135–38, 148, 155–58, 164–65, 279, **II:** 77; ultimate in, **I:** 269–71
Intensity continuum, **I:** 91–93, 98, 107, 131–32, 320
Intention, **II:** 33, 41–42; of interpretation, **I:** 71–72, **II:** 34–35
Intentional fulfillments, **I:** 303
Intentionality, **I:** 139, 268, 316, 330, **II:** 22, 86, 120, 141, 153–54, 168–75, 190–91, 214, 220–22, 226, 228–29, 234–41, 47–49, 258, 260–63, 271, 299–301, 307–08, 313, 323; attribution of, **I:** 254–56; divine, **I:** 175, 280–86, **II:** 39, 58, 75, 198; in interpretations, **I:** 66–67, 74–75; and reductionism, **I:** 49–50; for engaging ultimacy, **I:** 309–12; in thinking ultimacy, **I:** 298–300
Interests, human, **I:** 275, **II:** 22, 156–57
Interpretation, **I:** 15–17, 33–34, 63–68, 288, 293–96, **II:** xvi–xvii, xx, 4, 35, 78, 160–62, 191, 214, 220–22, 235, 237, 249, 271, 304, 310; always in context, **I:** 160–61; as act, **I:** 66; defined, **I:** 66; theory of, **I:** 28, 97–98; and orientations, **I:** 81–84
Interpreters, **I:** 288–90, **II:** 42, 109, 247
Intimacy, **I:** 84–87, 97–98, 102, **II:** 298; in symbols of ultimacy, **I:** 135–48,

Intimacy *(continued)*
164–65, 281–82; 297, 320–21, **II:** 54, 206, 271–72, 278
Intuition, **I:** 332; and intelligibility, **I:** 285–86
Iran, **I:** 9
Ishvara, **I:** 116, 132, 231, 309
Islam (or Muslims), **I:** xvii 4–5, 7–8, 10–11, 18, 55, 77, 86–87, 123, 129, 145, 150, 154–55, 170, 174, 230, 234, 260, 273–74, 290, 330, **II:** 2, 6, 39, 67, 89, 95, 109, 119, 123, 126, 178, 191, 199–200, 246, 295, 325–26, 328–29
Isolation, **II:** 168–82, 185, 301
Isomorphism, **I:** 1, 253
Israel, **I:** 150, 154, 156, **II:** 94, 128, 133, 175, 199, 267, 294
Israelites, **I:** 122, **II:** 121
Ivanhoe, Philip J., **II:** 334

Jack Frost, **I:** 159
Jaimini, **II:**, 266, 333
Jainism, **I:** 107, 127, 154–55, **II:** 2, 91
James, Thomas A., **I:** 341
James, William, **I:** 32, 45, 51, 68, 331, 337, **II:** 1–5, 190, 257, 259, 324–25, 333; on metaphysical pluralism, **I:** 175–76
Jang, Jaehu, **I:** xxv
Jaspers, Karl, **I:** 330, **II:** xv
Jenkins, Jerry B., **II:** 331
Jerusalem, **I:** 40
Jesus Christ, **I: 19–**20, 46, 70–71, 115, 118, 124–25, 147, 152, 243, 255, 262, 274, 293, 315, 328, 333, **II:** 53–54, 61, 83, 87, 94, 109–10, 120–21, 128, 133–34, 140, 147, 164–65, 169, 175–79, 196–200, 213, 237–38, 248, 267–72, 284–86, 294, 324, 328–29, 332, 334; historical, **I:** 262; as sacrifice, **I:** 65, **II:** 128, 246
Jesus Christ the Apple Tree, **II:** 237–38
Jnana yoga, **I:** 118
Job, **I:** 123, 154, 342, **II:** 19, 145, 227, 233, 325
Johnson, Mark, **I:** 75, **II:** 343
Johnson, Roger, **II:** 332

Jonah, **I:** 9
Jones, Judith, **I:** 68
Jones, Serene, **II:** 325, 328, 330
Joseph, **I:** 157
Joshua, **I:** 126
Journalism, on religion, **I:** xvii
Joy, **I:** 20, 111, **II:** 8, 20, 52, 140, 168, 177, 182, 189–90, 212, 245, 277
Joyce, James, **II:** 140–41, 330
Judah, **I:** 154
Judaism (or Jews), **I:** xvii, xxii, 4–5, 8, 11, 18 40, 55, 77, 83–84, 86, 123, 129, 145, 147, 150, 154–55, 158, 170, 174, 230, 234, 255, 273, 312, 329–30; **II:** 6, 39, 67, 94–98, 118, 121, 123, 130, 146, 178, 197, 199, 246, 294, 328–29
Judges, **I:** 126
Judgments, **I:** 208, **II:** 49, 203, 242, 258 divine, **I:** 205
Justice, **I:** 11, 41, 206, 242, 281, **II:** 11, 44, 64–65, 75, 98, 115–17, 126–28, 135, 202, 215, 221–22, 229–30, 246, 248, 266, 302; universal, **I:** 84
Justification, **II:** 8, 18, 37, 85, 111, 113–34, 168, 173, 181, 184, 232–33, 246, 259, 262, 289, 296, 303, 314

Kabala, **I:** 234
Kali, the Goddess, **I:** 72, 76; Kali-Yuga, **II:** 201
Kanofsky, Joseph, **I:** 335, **II:** 329
Kant, Immanuel, **I:** 49–52, 58–60, 70, 145, 193, 235, 327, 330–32, 336–37, 341, **II:** 37–39, 214, 223, 258, 308, 332, 335; causation in, **I:** 222; on concepts as rules, **I:** 33; failed critique of metaphysics, **I:** 55–57, 174–75; on the sublime, **I:** 131
Kantian Captivity of the religious imagination, **I:** 17–19
Karma, **I:** 26, 74, 123, 143, 243, 254, **II:** 67, 124, 126–29, 198; Yoga, **I:** 118
Kataphatic theology, **I:** 19–20
Kaufman, Gordon D., **I:** 341
Kelly, Sean Dorrance, **II:** 89, 328
Kelsey, David, **I:** 337, **II:** xvi–xx, 323–24, 331

Kierkegaard, Soren, **I:** 106, 336, **II:** 2, 67–68, 246, 284, 313, 323–24, 327
Kim, Chanhong, **I:** xxv
Kim, Sungrae, **I:** xxv, **II:** xxiii
Kindness, **I:** 281
King, God as, **II:** 267–68
Kinship, **I:** 128
Kline, T. C. III, **II:** 334
Knight of faith, **I:** 106, **II:** 246
Knowledge, **II:** 35, 52, 76, 81, 156, 230, 232, 258, 323, 326, 331; as form, **I:** 282; of ontological creative act, **I:** 322–23; for its own sake, **I:** 308
Kohn, Livia, **I:** 78, **II:** 108, 328, 330–31, 334
Kreji, Jaroslav, **II:** 325
Krishna, **I:** 116–19, 147, 255, 315, **II:** 45, 174, 252, 294, 299
Kuehn, Manfred, **I:** 331
Kurtz, Paul, **I:** 328

LaHaye, Tim, **II:** 331
Lakawa, Septemmy Eucharistia, **II:** 11
Lakoff, George, **I:** 75
Lamont, Corliss, **I:** 328
Lang, Bernhard, **II:** 331
Language, **I:** 334, **II:** 3, 13, 38, 200, 274–77, 280–82; of philosophy, **I:** 127–29, **II:** 26; and semiotics, **I:** 64–65
Laozi, **I:** 147
Leaving, **I:** 208
Legends, **I:** 293, **II:** 52–53, 62, 123, 161–62, 238294, 330
Legitimation, **I:** 31, **II:** 60
Leibniz, Gottfried, **I:** xviii, 13, 56, 194–95, 204, 219, 280, 331–32, 339, **II:** 34, 232, 332
Lesbians, **I:** 11
Leuba, James H., **I:** 51, 331
Levenson, Jon D., **I:** 336, **II:** 335
Levinas, Emmanuel, **II:** 78–79, 327
Leviticus, **I:** 333, **II:** 94
Lewis, C. I., **I:** 68
Lewis, C. S., **II:** 55–60, 82, 160, 327
Liberalism, **I:** 9, **II:** 2
Life, **I:** 311, **II:** *passim;* as symbol for the ontological creative act, **I:** 266–67

Liminality, **II:** 264–65, 267, 272, 274, 277
Lindbeck, George, **I:** 48
Linguistic turn, **I:** 7054
Lisbon earthquake, **I:** 42
Literacy, **I:** 88; theological, **I:** 329
Literalism, **I:** 10, 293
Literature, **I:** 18, 25, 72, **II:** 44, 127; as iconic, **I:** 253–54
Liturgy, **I:** xx, 73; Christian, **I:** 88–89, **II:** 267–69, 267–69, 333; world of **I:** 293
Liu, Shu-hsien, **II:** 329
Liu, Xinjun, **I:** xxv, **II:** xxiii
Liu Zhi, **I:** 339
Location, **I:** 3–4, **II:** 7, 164; in existential field, **I:** vi (*see also* Existential location); historical and social, **I:** xvii, **II:** 15, 55, 170, 266, 3424; religious, **I:** xv–xvi
Locke, John, **I:** xviii, 50
Locklin, Reid B., **I:** 326
Log, in rapids, **I:** xxi
Logic, **I:** 14, 68
Logo-centrism, **I:** 51–52, 59–61
Logos (Wisdom), **I:** 220, 255, 262–62, 274, 279–80, **II:** 52
Lord of the Rings, **II:** 55–60
Lotus Sutra, **I:** 137, 310, **II:** 329, 331
Love, **I:** 17, 109, 115, 133, **II:** xxi, 18, 56, 59, 79–83, 102, 104. 110, 118, 124, 134, 143, 149–55, 163–65, 168, 184, 215–218, 222, 248–52, 270–73, 288, 297, 300, 312–13; ecstatic, **II:** xix–xxii, 20, 192–93, 225–39, 244, 258, 318, 321; of enemies, **I:** 315; of God and neighbor, **I:** 314, **II:** 189; mystical path of, **I:** 303, 312–17, 323–24; universal, **I:** 84, **II:** 266, 327
Loving God and God loving, **I:** 324, **II:** 76, 189; virtuoso, **I:** 314–15
Lucas, George, **II:** 57–60
Luckman, Thomas, **I:** 29
Luther, Martin, **II:** 2, 259, 328

Machle, Edward, **I:** 335, **II:** 234
Madhyamaka Buddhism, **I:** 26–27, 47, 105, 114, 231, 208, **II:** 68, 120

Magic, **II**: 54–60
Mahabharata, **I**: 19, 74, 125, 154, 156–57, **II**: 13, 197
Mahayana Buddhism, **I**: 84, 106, 114, **II**: 83, 127
Maimonides, Moses, **I**: 78
Maitreya Buddha, **I**: 151–53, **II**: 119, 201
Making, sheer, **I**: 216–21, 227–32, 281
Mammalian humor, primordial, **I**: 64
Mandate of Heaven, **I**: 87, 147, 151, 255, **II**: 132, 283
Maps, **I**: 72, **II**: 216–20
Marduk, **I**: 86, 126, 157, 336
Marginalization, **I**: 59–61; in sociology of religion, **I**: 30–33
Marriage, **I**: 294, **II**: 61, 301
Martial traditions, **I**: 106, 304, **II**: 12, 57, 64, 118, 139, 142, 160–62, 175–77, 294–97, 326–27, 330, 334–35
Martyrdom, **I**: 10, **II**: 163
Marx, Karl, **I**: 51, 54, **II**: 200, 204; Marxism, **I**: 11–12, 327–28, **II**: 15
Masuzawa, Tomoko, **I**: 327, 329
Material force (*qi*), **I**: 310, **II**: 19, 218
Material quality, of signs, **I**: 65–66, 289–90, 300–03, 309, 323–24, **II**: 9, 191, 234, 247, 331
Mathematics, **I**: 129, 140–41, 200, 203, 263, **II**: 75, 230, 303, 335; as iconic, **I**: 253–54; as interpreting world, **I**: 13–15; and scientific reductionism, **I**: 50–52
Matter, **I**: 196, **II**: 67
Maturation, **II**: 41, 61, 133, 276, 280–81, 291 in worldviews, **I**: 93
McDannell, Colleen, **II**: 331
MacGregor, Kirk, **II**: 328
McIntyre, Alasdair, **II**: 40, 326
McKeon, Richard, **II**: 327
McNamara, Patrick, **I**: 308, 329, 331, 336, 342, **II**: 195, 330
McNeill, William, **II**: 328
Mead, George Herbert, **I**: 68
Meaning, **I**: 3–5, 11, 31–33, 68, 71, 103, 107, 142, 203, 231, **II**: xxi–xxii, 6, 708, 12–13, 18, 20–29, 31, 37, 39, 41, 43, 53, 55–60, 65, 73, 82, 85–99, 104, 107, 114, 118, 152, 162, 189, 192–93, 195–207, 209–23, 225–26, 244–47, 253–54, 264, 268, 290, 316–18; network and content, **I**: 299–03
Meaningfulness, **I**: 141–46, 164–65, **II**: xix, 71, 189, 321, 331
Meaninglessness, **I**: 109, **II**: 6, 167–82
Meat brains, **I**: 65, 298
Mediation, of carryover in truth, **I**: 298–99
Meditation, **I**: 35, 302, 209, 312, **II**: 40, 92, 139, 219, 233, 249, 272, 278, 288, 294, 297, 313, 327, 330, 334–35; path of, **I**: 323–24; and unity, **I**: 303–06
Medium, between world and creative act, **I**: 220–21, 274
Membership, **I**: 92, 154, **II**: 94–95, 116, 130, 147, 151, 159, 210, 243, 263–65, 280, 283, 294
Mencius, **I**: 79; **II**: 40, 118
Mental health, **I**: 5
Mercy, **I**: 230, 281, **II**: 76, 94, 118–19, 128, 163, 199, 215, 246, 268
Messiah, **I**: 46
Metaphor, **I**: 71–75, 148, 293, **II**: xix, 4–7, 18, 20, 28, 46, 66, 76, 91, 94, 127, 134, 139, 142–43, 149, 158, 163, 192–93, 220, 233, 240, 257, 272, 285, 290, 294–95, 332
Metaphysics, **I**: xix, xxi, 7, 18–19, 32, 44, 54–61, 68, 76–79, 113, 128–31, 145, 169, 242, 270, 319, 325, **II**: 3–4, 25, 32, 38, 41, 197, 206, 315–16, 325–27, 331; apriori, **I**: 58–59; empirical, **I**: 97–98; foundational, **I**: 58; hypothetical, **I**: 174–75; of ontological ultimacy, **I**: 173–91, 244–27, 251, 260–66, 287–90; pluralism in, **I**: 171; as rhetorical frame, **I**: 149–53; the control on symbols, **I**: 169; as system, **I**: 61; tested, **I**: 58–61; as theological frame, **I**: 157–58; and universal adequacy, **I**: 130
Methodism, **II**: xvi, 2, 333
Methodology, in religious studies, **I**: xx, 21
Michelangelo, **I**: 76
Microbes, **I**: 136, 156, **II**: 154

Microscopes as signs, **I:** 65
Microstudies, **I:** 52
Miller, James E., **I:** 78, 337, 341, **II:** 328
Milton, John, *Paradise Lost*, **II:** 215
Mind, **I:** 1, 64, **II:** vi, 11, 59, 73, 110, 127–28, 132, 143, 163, 170, 174, 177, 203, 218, 227, 240, 271, 276, 282–83, 305, 325, 330, 332, 334
Minjung, **II:** 11
Miracle, **I:** 140
Models, of ecstatic fulfillment, **II:** 195, 219, 244; of ontological creative act, **I:** 1–3, 253–62, **II:** 7, 76
Modern science, and metaphysics, **I:** 60; reconciling with personifying religion, **I:** 255–56; *see also* Science
Modernity, **I:** 140–41, **II:** 259, 262, 264, 328
Modes, of being, for Paul Weiss, **I:** 177–80; of time, essential and conditional components, **I:** 247; *see also* Temporality, modes of.
Moments, **I:** 277–29, **II:** vi, 19, 32, 88, 192, 211, 316
Monads, **I:** 13, 194, **II:** 326
Monasticism, **I:** 114, 304–05, **II:** 2, 177
Monotheism, **I:** xxii, 2, 17, 42, 51, 83–84, 110–11, 116, 125, 127, 147, 160–61, 255, 260, 273, 291, 322, **II:** 19, 305, 313; and consciousness, **I:** 256
Montgomery, **I:** 331
Moore, Charles A., **II:** 331
Moore, G. E., **I:** 184, **II:** 38, 42, 326
Moores, D. J. **II:** 190
Moral character, **II:** 38, 241, 315; none in God, **I:** 280–86
Moral identity, **I:** 277–79
Morality, **I:** 201, **II:** 45, 92, 123, 126, 131, 137, 171
Mortality (or immortality), **II:** 6, 45, 53, 66, 85, 199, 212, 231, 304, 331, 335
Morphological division, in Whitehead, **I:** 13
Morse, Christopher, **I:** xx–xxi
Moses, **I:** 78, 122, 147, 154–57, 255, **II:** 179
Motivation, in creation, **I:** 323

Mozart, Wolfgang Amadeus, **II:** 169
Multidisciplinary studies, **I:** xx, 54, **II:** 323
Mundane, the, in worldviews, **I:** 83–84, 90, 244, 287, **II:** 7, 222, 259–78, 284–91, 307, 310–13
Mungre, Divine, **I:** xxv, **II:** xxiii
Murata, Sachiko, **I:** 339, **II:** 339
Musement, **I:** xxi, 56–57
Mutazilites, **I:** 291–92
Mutuality, **I:** 196–99, 204–08, 215–21, 233–34, 275–76, **II:** 272; as ultimate, **I:** 243–44
Mysterium tremendum et fascinans, **I:** 32, 68, 139
Mystery, **I:** 44, 132, **II:** 35, 76, 290
Mysticism, **I:** 1, 20, 133, 225, 251, 301–17, 323–24, **II:** 95, 219, 254; and the abyss, **I:** 315–16; immediacy in, **I:** 256
Myth (*or* mythos), **II:** 10, 13, 52–68, 253, 326, 327, 329; of reference, **I:** 47, 334

Nagarjuna, **I:** 151
Naiveté, **I:** 145, 159–60, **II:** 271–72
Narayana, **I:** 116, 147
Narnia, **II:** 54–61
Narrative, **I:** 19, 31–32, 34, 38–39, 96, **II:** 86–87, 99, 179; broken, **I:** 159–61; comparative, **I:** 158; and conflict, **I:** 8, 156; all symbolically false, **I:** 155–58, **II:** 192; and intimacy, **I:** 153–55; as rhetorical frame, **I:** 149–53, **II:** 60–62, 179, 196–206, 209, 223, 225, 244, 253, 270, 285, 331; truth in, **I:** 157
Narrowness, **I:** 13
Nasr, Seyyed Hossein, **I:** 336, 339–40
Nationalism, **I:** 11–12, 328
Native American religion, **II:** 65, 180, 279, 290
Natura naturans and *natura naturata*, **I:** 221, **II:** 247
Natural history, **I:** 137
Natural science, **I:** 19
Naturalism, **I:** 69, **II:** 200, 323–24, 332; in anthropology, **I:** 54; ecstatic, **II:** xviii; in pragmatic epistemology, **I:** 64–68; in religion, **I:** 328, **II:** 180

Nature, **II:** 31, 34–47, 51, 64–66, 77–86, 91–97, 102–04, 116–19, 124, 129–33, 137–58, 168, 170–73–76, 180, 201, 211. 215–237, 252, 274, 290, 293, 296, 302–05, 315–18, 323, 342; depths of, **I:** 156–58, 164–65; not always harmonious, **I:** 42–43; human, **II:** xvi–xx, 14, 33, 189, 274, 283, 286, 324–42; of ontological creative act, **I:** 321–22, **II:** 25, 27, 204; *see also* Extension *and* Intension, *and* humanity
Nazis, **I:** 8, 42, 84, 123, 328
Negation, **I:** 132, 276, **II:** 18, 20, 102, 142, 173, 200, 290
Nehemiah, **I:** 294, **II:** 94
Neo-Confucianism, **I:** 130, 151, 173, 228, 255–57, 273, 291, 303
Neo-Platonism, **I:** 26, 34, 37, 55, 74, 102, 118, 130, 133, 170, 193, 219, 230, 234, 258, 275, **II:** 95, 328
Neo-pragmatism, **I:** 68–70
Network meaning, **I:** 65–66, 309, 312
Networks, of signs, **I:** 70–79, 163, **II:** 220; social, **II:** 64
Neuroscience, **I:** 52, **II:** 195, 330
Neville, Beth, **I:** vi, xxv, **II:** iv, vi, xxiii, 324
New Age spirituality, **I:** 141
New Haven Theological Discussion Group, **I:** xxv, **II:** 323
New Testament, **I:** xxii, 125–27, 152, 274, **II:** 199, 294, 329
Newsome-McLaughlin, Imani-Sheila, **II:** xxiii
Newton, Isaac, **I:** 53
Nicholson, Hugh, **I:** 326
Niebuhr, Reinhold, **II:** 125
Nietzschean transvaluation, **II:** 113, 323
Nine/eleven, **I:** 9
Nineveh, **I:** 39
Nirguna Brahman, **I:** 26, 102, 117; *see also* Brahman *and* Saguna Brahman
Nirvana, **I:** 41, **II:** 245
Nishida, Kitaro, **II:** 2
Nishitani, Keiji, **II:** xv, xix, 9, 189, 192, 232, 331, 335
Noah, **I:** 126, 154, 119, 201, **II:** 119, 201

Nominalism, **I:** 19
Nomos, **I:** 29–31
Non-action (*wu-wei*), **I:** 233–34
Non-being (*wuji*), **I:** 131, 151, 173–75, 268, 311, **II:** 155, 168–71, 172–73, 177, 180–81, 185, 211, 315, 315–16; equivalent to being, **I:** 171; *see also*, Ultimate of Non-Being *and* Great Ultimate Non-dualism, **I:** 42, 115, 193, 260
Normative claims, **II:** 8, 28, 38, 101, 320
Normative measure, **I:** 273
Norse gods, **I:** 157
Nothingness, **I:** 222–23, 227–28, **II:** 172, 189, 192, 323, 331, 335
Novelty, **I:** 217–25, 236, 275–76, 279, 323, **II:** 33; creation of, **I:** 285–86
Numinous, the, **I:** 32, 68, 139
Nygren, Anders, **I:** 327

Obedience, **I:** 125, **II:** 17, 37–38, 109, 126, 178, 240, 294
Objectification, **I:** 29–30, **II:** 150
Objective reality, **I:** 338
Objectivity, **II:** 68, 79, 86; in science, **I:** 49–2
Obligation, **I:** 3–4, 10–11, 39, 68, 107, 201, 231, 241–42, 277–79, **II:** xxi, 6–8, 13, 17–18, 26–29, 31–47, 49–51, 62, 64, 71, 79, 97, 99, 102–03, 107–08, 111, 113–34, 136, 150, 152–54, 168, 170–72, 180, 184, 191–92, 209–14, 221–22, 232–33, 248, 258, 263, 265–66, 272, 286–91, 297–99, 302, 312–13, 320, 325–26, 329
Odin, Steve, **I:** 337
Odysseus, **I:** 88
Oil on the ocean, **I:** 137
Old Testament, xxii; *see also* Hebrew Bible
Olivelle, Patrick, **I:** 336, **II:** 328
One and many, **I:** 21, 28, 56, 170–91, 245–47, 285–91, 297–98, 321, **II:** 327; not a theological problem, **I:** 175–76
One, the, **I:** 26, 34, 86–87, 102, 118, 235, 275, 340, **II:** 327, 331

Ontological act of creation, *see* Ontological creative act
Ontological context of mutual relevance, **I:** 37–38, 171–72, 179–80, 190–91, 207–09, 227–28, 233–25, 246–47, 258–62, 266, 284–86, 291, 297–98, 310–13, 316–17, 321–24, **II:** 20–21, 62, 75–76, 88–89, 92, 94–95, 155–56, 167, 182, 204–05, 210, 216, 237, 249–51, 314; containing the modes of time, **I:** 240–41
Ontological creative act, **I:** 1–4, 17, 21, 33–34, 159–61; 246–47, 256, 258–62, 291, 298, 301, 309, 311–12, 315, 321–22, **II:** xxi–xxii, 18–21, 25, 28, 39, 75–76, 88–89, 94, 104, 108, 122, 129, 132, 145, 155, 164, 172–73, 181–83, 191–93, 204–05, 211, 225–34, 237, 244–51, 254, 260, 309–16, 320–21, 324; argument for summarized, **I:** 170–72; eternal and dynamic, **I:** 242–44 as free, **I:** 276–69; as God, **I:** 229–32; as good, **I:** 263–66; hypothesis about proved, **I:** 218; intelligibility of, **I:** 284–86; as loving, **I:** 313–17; cannot be modeled, **I:** 225; nature of created, **I:** 225–32, 322–24; personified, **I:** 76; singular, **I:** 230–31; no stages of, **I:** 280; theory of as symbol for engaging ultimates, **I:** 288–300; as ultimate, **I:** 243–44
Ontological principle, in Whitehead, **I:** 225, 285–86
Ontological shock, **II:** 9, 14, 211, 314–17
Ontological status, of properties, **I:** 184–86
Ontological ultimate reality, **I:** 3–5, 27, 36–37, 153, 227–44, **II:** 25, 33, 94, 101, 189; no nature apart from creation, **I:** 273–76; not a person, **I:** 279–86, predicting, **I:** 275–76
Ontology, **I:** vi, 21, 58, 60, 149–52, **II:** 21, 25, 172; in metaphysics, **I:** 169; as rhetorical frame, **I:** 149–53
Order, **I:** 176, **II:** 6, 39–40, 43, 46, 51, 60, 134, 156–58, 178, 195, 198, 200, 217–18, 245, 289, 304–05, 326, 333;

created, **I:** 281, **II:** 60, 82, 120, 167, 180–81, 219, 228, 271–73; needs explanation, **I:** 225; intentional, **I:** 309; pockets of, **I:** 69, **II:** 230
Organism and environment, **I:** 63, 69, **II:** 326
Orientalism, **I:** 51, **II:B 325**
Orientation, **I:** 5, 81–93, 106, 123, 139–40, 142–46, 289, 292–96, **II:** vi, xix, 5, 7, 13, 16, 41, 51–53, 60, 97, 104, 159, 205, 206, 234, 270, 275, 278, 284–86, 290–91, 308, 310–14, 317–18, 326
Orsi, Robert A., **I:** 89
Orthodoxies, **I:** 92, **II:** 36, 267, 269, 334
Others (or Otherness), **I:** 3–4, 41, 68, 121–24, 190, **II:** vi, xix, xxii, 6–8, 11, 13–18, 26–31, 33, 40, 43, 46, 58, 65, 71–75, 78–88, 90–94, 97–102, 107, 115–17, 126, 133–34, 141, 144–46, 149–65, 168–72, 176–77, 182, 191–92, 210, 212, 215, 218–19, 229, 243, 247–52, 254, 258–60, 272–73, 287–88, 291, 297, 301–04, 319–21; love of, **I:** 314–17
Otto, Rudolf, **I:** 32, 139, 327
Own-being, **I:** 47, 186, 193
Ozone layer, bone of my bone, **I:** 136

Paganism, **I:** 2, 123, 170, 234, 291, 330, **II:** 39, 67
Paleogalactic Age, **I:** 254
Paleolithic Age, **I:** 254, **II:** 324
Panikkar, Raimundo, **II:** 329
Pannenberg, Wolfhart, **I:** 220, 340
Pantheons, comparative, **I:** 25
Park, Andrew Sung, **II:** 10–11
Park, Sung Bae, **I:** 336, **II:** 127, 245, 329, 332
Participation, **II:** 4, 9, 20, 38, 79, 94–95, 103, 131, 143–44, 172, 193, 197–98, 239, 242–43, 249, 254, 257–70, 272–74, 278, 283, 288–90, 293, 304, 307, 319, 321
Paschal lamb, **I:** 70–71
Past, **I:** 197–99, 207, 235–41, 277–79, 322, **II:** 13–17, 31–32, 35, 46, 53, 63,

Past *(continued)*
66, 85–88, 98, 108, 145, 203, 216, 235–36; *see also* Modes of time *and* Temporal modes
Paths, **I:** of religious engagement, 303–17, **II:** xxii, 5, 18, 21, 39–41, 108–09, 123, 126–29, 132, 175, 178, 192, 221, 257–58, 261, 263–65, 272–73, 277–79, 290, 293, 304, 311, 313–15, 319–20
Patience, in love, **I:** 314–15
Pattern, **I:** 33, 197–201n **II:** xvi, 3, 25–26, 32–34, 41, 43, 50, 66, 74, 86, 92, 102, 122, 140–41, 167, 230, 276, 281, 283, 303–04, 332
Paul, **I:** 150, 152, **II:** 68, 123, 147, 198–200, 246, 294, 329, 331; on eating meat sacrificed to idols, **I:** 159–60, 241–44, 263
Peace, **I:** 8, **II:** 20, 177, 196, 202, 215, 218, 238, 267–68, 294–95; that passes understanding, **I:** 20
Peer pressure, **I:** 46
Peirce, Charles, **I:** xxi, 15, 59, 68–70, 72, 194, 224, 283, 327, 329, 332–34, 340, 342, **II:** 41, 234, 236, 249, 276, 323, 331–33; on metaphysics as hypothetical, **I:** 56–57
Perennial Philosophy, **I:** 37, 74, 133, 234, 336, 331
Persian religion, **I:** 55, 86, 229; *see also* Zoroastrianism
Personhood, **I:** 40–41, 153, 228, 277–79, 323, **II:** 108; divine, **I:** 155–58; as metaphoric system, **I:** 172, 254–62; as model of ontological creative act, **I:** 1–2, **II:** 28, 33
Personification, **I:** 26, 102–03, 159–61, 229–32, 257–58, 274–75, **II:** 271
Peters, Richard, **I:** xxv, **II:** xxiii
Pharaoh, manipulated by God, **I:** 156–57
Phenomenology, **I:** 15, 32–33, 59–61, 165, **II:** 183–84, 234, 240, 332; normative, **I:** 151
Phenomenon, **II:** xviii, 7; religion as, **I:** 6, **II:** 5, 260–61
Philebus, **I:** 14, 196

Phillips, D. Z., **I:** xviii
Philosophical cosmology, **I:** 68, 112–13, 170, **II:** 72, 83, 304, 314
Philosophical Theology (this three-volume project), **I:** xvii–xviii, 2, 4–6, 17–21, 31, 69, 112–138, 152, 189, 230, 244, 242, 254, 310, **II:** vi, xv–xvi, xviii–xxi, xxiii, 3–9, 12, 15–17, 19, 21, 25–28, 31–32, 35, 38–40, 51, 53, 55, 60–61, 68, 72, 74–79, 83, 96, 99, 102, 108, 129–31, 140, 158, 162–63, 171–72, 182, 183–84, 192, 197, 203–06, 210, 213–14, 220, 222–25, 227–28, 235–37, 239, 241, 243, 250, 254, 257, 260, 262, 266, 270, 272–73, 277–79, 283, 286–89, 300, 304, 308–10, 313, 317–21, 323–25, 327, 329, 332
Philosophical theology, **I:** xv–xxi; defined for this project, **I:** xx–xxii, **II:** see *Philosophical Theology* above; three layers of, **I:** 251
Philosophy of nature, *see* Philosophical cosmology
Philosophy, **I:** xv, 12–15, 20, 25, 86, 325, **II:** xv, xvii, 9, 26, 35, 75–79, 132, 142, 177, 201, 235–38, 258, 304, 319, 321, 323, 325–27, 329–34; as critic of worldviews, **I:** 294; Confucian, **I:** xix; and contemplation, **I:** 308; controlling for reductionism, **I:** 52–54, **II:** 304; defining religion, **I:** 5–11; of existence (existentialism), **II:** xv; Indian, **I:** 12; origin of, **I:** 127–28; in *Philosophical* Theology, **I:** xvi–xvii; of religion, **I:** xviii–xx; and religious symbols, **I:** 166; of science, **I:** 170; seduced by science, **I:** 53–54; systematic, **I:**68; *see also* Analytic Philosophy, Continental Philosophy, Process Philosophy, Cosmology (philosophical)
Physics, **I:** 232; and reductionism, **I:** 53
Piety, **I:** 40, 206–07, 262, **II:** 40, 62–63, 135, 137, 213, 218
Place, **I:** 40–41, **II:** 12–13, 15, 20, 51, 72, 76–81, 136, 143, 146, 152, 160, 163–64, 168, 181, 204, 206, 213, 217–18, 233, 259, 267, 295, 315, 318, 333

Plantinga, Alvin, **I:** xviii
Plato, **I:** 14–15, 75, 86, 106, 113, 120, 170, 174, 193, 196–97, 206, 235, 273, 228–39, **II:** 36, 39, 46, 67–68, 74–75, 230–31, 294–97, 327–29, 332
Platonism, **I:** xix, 55
Plausibility, **I:** 42, 46, 287–88; **II:** 110, 183, 291–92, 318
Plotinus, **I:** 170, 174, 218, 224, 234, 339, 341
Pluralism, **I:** 32, 96, 152, **II:** 239, 243; metaphysical, **I:** 175–81, **II:** 73; religious, **I:** 7, **II:** 280, 350
Poetry, **I:** 16
Poise, **I:** xxi
Politics, **I:** 58, 125, **II:** 66, 152, 190, 262, 265
Polke, Christian, **I:** xxv, **II:** xxiii
Popular culture, **I:** 87–90, **II:** 140
Positivity, of all things, **I:** 311
Possibilities, **I:** 3–4, 10, 36–42, 73, 97–98 147, 205–09, 235–44, 263–66, 276–79, **II:** xix, xxi, 11–17, 21, 26–29, 31–47, 49–52, 67, 77, 88, 102, 113–17, 121–29, 138, 168, 180, 205, 209, 211–12, 216, 221, 229–32, 235, 241–44, 248–49, 259, 265, 280, 287, 291, 296, 300, 309, 311–12, 315, 320, 326
Possible worlds, **I:** 276–79, **II:** 232, 326
Postmodernism, **I:** xvi, 17–18, 51–52, 59–61, 165–66, **II:** 15
Poston, Elizabeth, **II:** 332
Posture, **I:** 302
Potentialities, **I:** 26, 215–21, **II:** 36, 68, 172, 211, 235
Power, **I:** 139, **II:** xix, 9, 15, 36, 49, 54, 56–62, 66, 68, 76, 95, 108, 127, 140, 142, 172–73, 198–200, 236, 257, 267, 294–5, 306, 325; dynamics, **I:** 51
Practice, religious, **I:** xix, 20, 25, **II:** 3, 126, 195, 225, 254, 273, 288
Pragmatism, **I:** xix, 43, 45–48, 63–70, 320, 326; analytical, **I:** xix, 69–70; in Berger's sociology, **I:** 30, metaphysical, **I:** 12–15; and the self, **I:** 106–09
Prakriti, **I:** 303

Pratitya samutpada, **I:** 194, **II:** 19, 120, 128, 152
Prayer, **I:** 35, 292, 302, **II:** 140, 267–70, 312; at meals, **I:** 84, 87, 109; employing metaphysical theory, **I:** 290
Pre-Axial Age religions, **I:** 41, 74, 121–24, 158, 165, **II:** 38, 158, 266
Predicaments, **I:** xv, 11–12, 20–21, 58, 103, 133, 146–48, **II:** vi, xv, xviii–xxiii, 4–12, 18–21, 25, 27, 49–52, 76, 78–79, 89–95, 99, 101–02, 107–11, 113–14, 118, 121–26, 131, 134–43, 149–50, 153–65. 168–85, 189–91, 195, 227, 254, 257–59, 261, 263, 265–66, 270, 272–73, 277–79, 286, 289, 292, 304–06, 311, 313–17, 319, 319–21, 324–25, 328–29; first person, **I:** 147–48
Predication, **I:** 182–83
Premises, **I:** xvii, **II:** xvi–xvii, 74
Preparation, **II:** 144, 293–97, 304
Presence, **II:** 91, 128, 133, 203, 212–14, 268, 297–301, 316 to consciousness, **I:** 184
Present, **I:** 197–99, 207, 235–41, 247, 277–79, 322, **II:** 13–16, 32–33, 88; *see also* Past, Future, *and* Modes of time
Pre-Socratics, **I:** 128
Presuppositions, **I:** 112–13; metaphysical, **I:** 58
Pride, **I:** 115, **II:** 137, 171
Principle of the ontological equality of reciprocal determinations, **I:** 187–91, 196, 246
Principle of the ontological ground of differences, **I:** 185–91, 246
Principles, **II:** xvii, 42, 98, 132, 218, 229, 246, 274; first, **I:** 222, 224–25
Priorities, **I:** 107–10, 117, 164, 299, 301, 320
Probation, in Peirce, **I:** 57
Problematics of ultimacy, **I:** 34–42
Process philosophy, **I:** xix, 68–69, 170, 284–85, **II:** 327
Process theology, **I:** 191, **II:** 146
Prochnik, George, **I:** 331
Proofs for God's existence, **I:** 326
Prophet, **I:** 19, **II:** 5, 248

Propositional functions, **I:** 14–15, 328
Propositions, **I:** 70–73
Protestantism, **I:** 9, 78–79, **II:** 2
Psalms, **I:** 61, **II:** 222
Psychology, **I:** 25, **II:** 2, 31, 56, 190, 228; physiological, hermeneutical, and empirical, **I:** 51
Public, **I:** xxii, 15–18, **II:** xvi, xx, 27, 93, 95–97, 113, 160, 169–170, 176, 185, 260–61, 273, 297, 301, 323; multicultural for philosophy, **I:** 55
Puett, Michael J., **II:** 330, 333
Pure Land Buddhism, **I:** 87, 111, 312, **II:** 108–10, 133, 328; *see also* Buddhism
Purgation, **II:** 133, 149, 155, 159–60, 165, 179, 184, 263, 268, 289
Purification, **I:** 147, **II:** 67, 114, 121, 128, 133–34, 175, 179, 184, 263, 268, 289; of consciousness, **I:** 17, **II:** 62, 92
Purity, **I:** 146, 95, 102, 111, 121, 128, 139, 159, 163, 174; of heart, **I:** 106
Purpose, **II:** 33, 41, 80, 303 and context of interpretation, **I:** 299–300; divine, **I:** 38, 41,**II:** 19, 158, 198, 201, 210, 299, 313 and interpretation, **I:** 66–67, 81–82
Purusha, **I:** 303
Purva Mimamsa, **II:** 266, 333
Pyysiainen, Ilkka, **I:** 341

Quantities vs. qualities, **I:** 14
Quarks, **I:** 53
Quest, spiritual, **I:** 305–06, **II:** 40, 45, 53, 57, 61, 85, 133, 135–36, 209, 247, 253, 313–14, 320
Qur'an, **I:** 19, 77, 127, 274, **II:** 199

Racism, **I:** 11
Radhakrishnan, S., **II:** 331
Rahab, **I:** 126
Ramanuja, **I:** 221, 340
Ramayana, **I:** 19, 125, 154, 157, **II:** 13
Rambo, Shelly, **II:** 10, 161, 325, 328, 330
Raphael, the angel, **II:** 215
Raposa, Michael, **I:** 334, 342, **II:** 177, 299, 330–31, 334–35

Rappaport, Roy A., **I:** 53–54, 331, 335, **II:** 262–64, 273, 310, 321, 326, 333
Rationalism, **I:** 284–85
Rationality, of world, **I:** 263–64, **II:** 315
Rea, Michael, C., **I:** 326
Realism, in comportment, **II:** 62–69, 103, 135, 142, 150, 168, 184, 297, 300; in worldviews, **I:** 139–40
Reality, **II:** 109–11, 116, 119–21, 126, 136, 138–39, 151–52, 167–73, 234, 239, 275, 283, 296, 303–04, 326–27, 329; corrects theory, **I:** 297; as disruptive, **I:** 5–6; existential, **I:** 12, **II:** xv–xvii, 179, 189, 254; formal, **I:** 181–82; as phenomena in experience, **I:** 59–60; ultimate, **II:** xviii–xxii, 3, 7, 91–94, 96, 98–99, 101–04, 126–29, 132, 162, 169–73, 180–85, 191–93, 196, 198, 211–12, 218–221, 226, 258, 268, 278, 285, 292, 307–11, 316, 319–21; universal structures of, **I:** 101
Receptacle, **I:** 194
Reconciliation, **II:** xviii–xix, 11, 111, 129, 150, 155, 163–65, 179, 184, 196, 264, 269, 289
Redemption, **II:** 57–61, 114, 121, 127–29, 164, 179, 184, 197, 199, 204, 246, 265, 268, 289
Reductionism, **I:** 6, 45–54, 66, 320; price of, **I:** 53–54; in identifying religion, **I:** 90; in sciences of religion, **I:** 97–98, **II:** 261
Reference, **I:** 20, 43–44, 66, 70–73, 90, 97–98, 144–46, 160–61, 288–89, **II:** vi, xvi, 74, 78; direct and indirect, **I:** 71; iconic, indexical, and conventional, **I:** 28, 320, **II:** 206, 213–15, 220–21, 254 (*see also* Iconic reference, Indexical reference, *and* Conventional reference); literal, **I:** 2; in narratives, **I:** 157–58, **II:** 206; of religious symbols, **I:** 27–28, **II:** 89, 110–11, 190, 200, 225, 235–37, 261, 265, 270–71, 309
Reformed epistemology, **I:** xviii
Refusal, existential, **II:** 114–21, 131–33, 179, 184
Regularities, **I:** 130
Rehman, Adnan, **I:** xxv

Reincarnation, **I:** 132, 243, **II:** 126–27
Relationships, **II:** 65, 86, 103, 137, 143, 216, 251, 285, 300–05
Religion, **I:** xv–xvi, 58, 68, 244, 251, **II:** xvii, 9–15, 19, 26–27, 38–41, 45–46, 52, 64, 68, 81–83, 87–98, 101, 107–10, 113–14, 118, 121–22, 125–35, 139, 142–49, 154–65, 167–77, 180–85, 195–200, 206–07, 217–22, 225–27, 233, 237–39, 245–54, 257, 260–73, 277–82, 287–94, 304–19, 323–26, 329, 331–35; approaches to, **I:** xviii; authentic, **I:** 9–11; as belief in supernatural agents, **I:** 6; as cultural, **I:** 4, 102–03; as defined, **I:** 4–9, 18–19, 84, 95–98, **II:** xvi, 3; defined by Durkheim, **II:** 261–62; defined in the popular press, **I:** 9; distorted, **I:** 9–11; essential components of, **II:** 3–5, 257307–08;existential reality of, **II:** xv, xviii, 1–9, 31, 189–92, 195; as individual vs. social, **II:** 1–5; origins of, **I:** 52; quasi-, **I:** 9–12; versus religions, **I:** 17–19; scientific study of, **I:** 49–52; as dimension of society, **I:** 9–10; theories of, **I:** xviii, 21, 29–30, 79, 297, 326; as engaging ultimacy, **I:** 20–21, **II:** 209–15; as universal, **I:** 4, 17–19, 35–36, 165, **II:** 15–18; as worship of gods, **I:** 25
Religions, Abrahamic, **I:** 40; diverse, **I:** 101–03; symbolized, **I:** 102–03; world, **I:** xviii, 42–44
Religious philosophy, **I:** xx, **II:** xvii, 323
Religious situation, **I:** 7, **II:** 89, 91, 95, 158–59, 328
Religious studies, **I:** 20
Remedies, **I:** 146, **II:** xviii, 4, 8, 12, 21,, 107–11, 133, 185, 258, 261, 263–66, 272–73, 277–79, 289–90, 304, 306, 313, 319, 321, 328
Renouncer traditions, **I:** 106–07. 111. 336, **II:** 2, 7, 91, 96, 126, 131, 286, 328
Rents, in sacred canopies, **I:** 31–33
Renunciation, **II:** 131, 168, 173–79, 182, 185, 264, 268–69, 289; of proximate concerns, **I:** 107

Representationalism, **I:** 63–64
Representations, **I:** 300, **II:** 7, 64, 78, 180, 292; subjective and objective, **I:** 49–50, **II:** 150
Republic, Plato's, **I:** 206, **II:** 36, 74, 230, 294, 297, 327, 332
Resentment, **I:** 38, **II:** 8, 54, 126
Resonance, of symbols, **I:** 71, **II:** 57, 285
Resources, **II:** 10, 35, 42, 133, 264; religious, **I:** 9
Respect, **II:** 46. 50–52, 65, 79, 93–94, 98, 127m 139, 143–45, 148–51, 159, 171, 204, 212; of comparison, **I:** 26; of determinateness, **II:** 3–4, 25–29, 75, 88, 103, 204–05; of interpretation, **I:** 43, **II:** xiii, xxi, 21, 35–37, 102, 109, 162, 215
Responsibility, **I:** 145, 276–87, **II:** 39, 46, 57, 61. 67, 87–88, 96, 117, 123–24, 133, 136, 168, 178, 241, 264
Restoration, **II:** 111, 114, 129–132, 163, 179, 184, 263, 268, 289
Revelation, **I:** xv, xx, 16–17, 77–79, 95, 110–111, 152, 326, 328, **II:** xvi, xx, 95, 1290, 198–99, 227, 258, 324, 328; Book of, **II:** 199
Revelatory frame, **I:** 149
Rhetoric, **I:** 2, 103, **II:** 10, 67, 99, 109–10, 129, 168, 197, 211, 315; center of gravity of, **I:** 86–87, 146–47, **II:** xix, 6, 17–18, 39, 109, 217–19, 245
Richardson, Robert D., **I:** 331
Ricoeur, Paul, **I:** 45–46, 337, **II:** 124, 133, 329–30
Righteousness, **I:** 39, 201, 241, 262, **II:** 17, 40, 109–11, 113–14, 135, 189, 245–48, 277, 295
Ritschl, Albrecht, **I:** 327
Rituals, **I:** 25, 46, 82–83, 132, **II:** xvi, 1–4, 13, 38, 42, 44, 62, 64–66, 90–94, 111, 117–21, 124, 131, 133–34, 160, 171, 190, 206, 246, 257, 259–78, 280, 289–93, 304, 307, 310, 314, 319, 324, 326, 329–30, 333–34; and interpretation, **I:** 66–67; and sacrifice, **I:** 257
Road rage, **I:** 336, **II:** 117

Rocher, Ludo, **II:** 326, 328
Rohr, David, **II:** xxiii
Roman Catholics, **I:** 8–9, 89, 146, **II:** 56, 328, 333–34
Romanticism, **I:** 13, 140–41
Rome, **I:** 55
Roots, religious, **I:** 92, **II:** 168
Rorty, Richard, **I:** xix, 68–70, 326, 333–34
Rose thorns, **I:** 137
Rosen, Joe, **II:** 332
Rosenthal, Sandra, **I:** 68
Ross, James F., **I:** 326
Rousseau, J-J, **II:** 240, 277, 332
Rower, **I:** 304–06
Rowling, J. K., **II:** 58–60
Royce, Josiah, **I:** 68
Ruth, Book of, **I:** 342

Sacred canopies, **I:** 19–20, 27–33, 34, 36–48, 54, 67, 73–79, 96–98, 107–09, 119, 131–33, 138–39, 146, 153, 159–60, 160–64, 231–32, 242–44, 287–90, 292–94, 297, 319–20, 329–30, **II:** 13–21, 27–28, 53, 54, 76, 82, 101, 104, 114, 118, 127, 142, 161–62, 184–85, 222, 251, 258, 262–65, 270, 273, 278, 283–86, 307–13, 316–17, 325, 328, 333; as domains within worldviews, **I:**83–84, **II:** 6
Sacred folds, **I:** 140
Sacred history, **I:** 145
Sacred, the, and the uncanny, **I:** 138–39
Sacred/mundane continuum, **I:** 28, 81–84, 98, 119, 131–32, 139, 143–44, 320–23, **II:** 284
Sacredness, **I:** xix, 30–33; in worldviews, **I:** 83–84
Sacrifice, **I:** 40, 146, 257–58, **II:** 40, 55, 58, 97, 120–21, 124, 128, 134, 145, 329–30, 334; Jesus Christ as, **I:** 70–71, **II:** 110, 128, 164
Sagacity, **II:** 129, 131–34, 184
Sagehood, **I:** 106, 151, **II:** 40, 132, 284, 325–26, 329–30
Saguna Brahman, **I:** 117; *see also* Brahman *and* Nirguna Brahman
Said, Edward W., **II:** 325

Saints, **I:** 118, 146; **II:** 2, 98, 195, 313, 327, 330
Saldarini, Anthony J., **I:** 335, **II:** 329
Salvation, **I:** 46–47, 152, **II:** 6, 12, 95, 109–10, 143, 175, 197, 245–47, 259–60, 269, 271–73, 277–80, 295, 325, 328
Samkhya, **I:** 231–32, 256, 303, **II:** 138
Sample-size, of knowledge of creation, **I:** 281, **II:** 232
Samsara, **I:** 74, 114, **II:** 128, 219, 245
Sanctification, **I:** 20, **II:** 114, 132, 179, 263, 269, 289
Santa Claus, **I:** 159
Sartre, Jean-Paul, **II:** 323
Saul, King, **I:** 127
Scale, **I:** 135, **II:** 47, 68, 81, 132, 157, 161, 169, 183–84, 230, 247, 268, 281, 307, 317; of cosmos, **I:** 121–24, 164–65, **II:** 128
Scapegoat, **I:** 70–71, **II:** 63, 134
Schematism, **I:** 145, **II:** 223, 332; of finite to infinite, temporal to eternal, etc., **II:** 216–23
Schleiermacher, F., **I:** 327
Schulkin, Jay, **I:** xxv, **II:** xxiii, 324
Schuon, Frithjof, **I:** 336
Science, **I:** 6, 13–15, 31, 40, 42, 58, 87, 153, 170, 269, 336, **II:** 25, 44, 60, 69, 145, 155–56, 180, 195, 202–03, 282, 303–4, 323–25, 330, 335; ancient, **I:** 310; cognitive, **I:** xx; and contemplation, **I:** 308; and fact/value distinction, **I:** 200–01; and meaning, **I:** 142–43; modern, **I:** 137; studying religion, **I:** 27–28, **II:** xvi–xx; and value, **I:** 129
Scientific study of religion, **I:** xvi
Scotus, John Duns, **I:** 183, 191, 198, 338–39
Scriptures, **I:** xx, 25, 42, **II:** xx, 111, 178, 268, 270–71
Seasons, in orientation, **I:** 82
Second Isaiah, **I:** 127
Second Person, of Trinity **I:** 118, 261–62, 293, **II:** 110; *see also* Jesus Christ
Second Samuel, **I:** 342
Secondness, **I:** 15, 69–70, 224, 283, 334, 340, **II:** 234–35

Sectarianism, **I:** 154–55
Secularism, **I:** 8–9, 92, 257
Self, **I:** 10, 105–09, 113–18, 243, 301, 208, **II:** xv, xxi, 2, 18, 33, 51–52, 62, 67–69, 77–81, 91–94, 99, 111, 113–20, 122–24, 128–34, 136–48, 152, 162, 168–72, 176–77, 190–93, 209–12, 218–19, 226, 229, 245, 247, 254, 283–84, 286–87, 291, 295, 298, 307, 324, 326, 328, 330, 333–34; deconstructing, **I:** 306–09; losing, **I:** 266; -love, **I:** 315
Selfishness, **I:** 12, **II:** 41
Seligman, Adam, **II:** 324, 333
Sellars, Wilfrid, **I:** 69, 334
Semantics, **I:** 70–71, 101–02, **II:** 38
Semiotics, **I:** 4, 16, 70–73, 101–02, 270, 301–03, 312; in nature, **I:** 64–68; pragmatic, **I:** 43–44
Serbia, **I:** 8
Sex, **I:** 302, **II:** 151, 158–60, 192, 215, 277; birthing and ejaculation as symbols of divine love, **I:** 316–17; images for ontological creative act, **I:** 314, **II:** xxii
Shaivism (or Shaivites), **I:** 109, 111, 263, **II:** 120, 161; Kashmir, **I:** 8, **II:** 20
Shakespeare, William, **I:** 238
Shamanism, **II:** 64, 299, 334; in Christianity, **I:** 89; and philosophy, **I:** 86, **II:** 271
Shangdi, **I:** 86, 254–55
Shankara, **I:** 107, 303, **II:** 330
Shanqing Daoism, **I:** 256–57, 341, **II:** 92, 147; *see also* Daoism
Sharia, **I:** xxii
Sharing continuum, **I:** 91–93, 98, 131–32, 320
Shinran, **II:** 328
Shiva, **I:** 1, 26, 124, 175, 229, 242, 255, 263, 266, 279, 327, **II:** 19–20, 65, 120, 161, 201, 219, 252, 305; Shiva/Shakti, **I:** 116, 147
Shock, ontological, **I:** 17, 144, **II:** 9, 14, 211, 314–17
Short, T. L., **I:** 334
Signifier/signified, **I:** 71

Signs, **I:** 73–79, 101–03, **II:** xx 15, 34, 42, 80, 87, 109–10, 129, 150–51, 155, 158, 206, 220–29, 234–37, 247–53, 275, 278, 324, 331; in interpretation, **I:** 64–68, **II:** 213–16, 220–29; material quality of, **I:** 65–66, **II:** 9, 191, 234; in Peirce, **I:** 334, **II:** 249; physical, intellectual, and emotional, for unity, **I:** 306; not true or false in themselves, **I:** 66, **II:** 249; for wholeness of world, **I:** 310–12; in worldviews, **I:** 81–84, **II:** 52
Silk Road, **I:** 55, **II:** 334
Simon, Bennett, **II:** 333
Simple location, 236
Simples, 36, 196
Simplicity, **I:** 236, 268–69, 271, 199–201, **II:** 34, 41, 74, 87, 141
Simultaneity, **I:** 233–34
Sin, **I:** 147, **II:** 11, 61, 109, 121, 125, 128–29, 134, 164, 227, 246, 263, 271, 324
Sincerity, **I:** 115, **II:** 1, 3, 41, 92, 277, 324
Singularity, **I:** vi, 38, 259–62, 279, 315–16, 322 **II:** 141; of ontological creative act, **I:** 230–24, **II:** xxii, 212, 225–26, 230–32, 235–38, 248
Sirach, **II:** 20
Sisera, **I:** 126
Sivan, Emmanuel, **I:** 328
Sizgorich, Thomas, **I:** 8, 328
Skepticism, **I:** 111, **II:** 258
Slavery, **I:** 159, **II:** 240–42
Smith, Huston, **I:** 336, 339–40, **II:** 330
Smith, John E., **I:** 11, 18–19, 68, 328, 333
Smith, Joshua, **II:** 332
Social class, **I:** 159, **II:** 56
Social construction, **I:** 109–13, 112–13; of reality, **I:** 29; of religion, **I:** 17–19, 42–43
Social constructionism, in pragmatism, **I:** 69
Social contract, **I:** 50, **II:** 332
Social order, **II:** 10, 131, 133; and religion, **I:** 20, 39
Social sciences, **I:** 17–18, **II:** 2; *see also* Science

Socialization, **I:** 45
Sociology, **I:** 25, 51, 110, 261; of knowledge, **I:** 29–33, **II:** 27
Solitude, **II:** 1–2, 5, 81, 257, 297–98, 318, 324
Song, Bin, **II:** xxiii
Sophistication, **II:** 16, 307, 316; in intellectual life, **I:** 87–90
Sophistication/popular culture continuum, **I:** 87–90, 98, 119, 131–32, 144, 291–93, 295, 320, 323, **II:** 271–73
Sosis, Richard, **II:** 334
Soul, **I:** 206, **II:** 45, 54, 67, 76, 99, 119, 123, 139–41, 147, 174, 199–200, 212, 215, 229, 231, 237–38, 248, 278, 280, 294, 3–5, 330
Source, **I:** 261–62, **II:** xvii, 147, 153, 165, 193, 218, 249, 295
South Asia, **I:** 55, **II:** 17, 62, 66–68, 89–109, 122, 131, 138, 144, 168, 195, 198, 201–02
Space-time, **I:** 194–95, 219–21, 232–41, 264–65, 72–73, 214, 216, 229, 235, 298, 314; created, **I:** 322
Spenta Mainyu, **II:** 198
Spinoza, Baruch, **I:** xviii, 56, 193, 221, 331–32, 340, **II:** 145, 240, 247
Spirit world, **I:** 138–41
Spiritual paths, **I:** 21, **II:** 175
Spiritual practices, **I:** 47, **II:** 7, 108, 128, 136
Spirituality, **II:** 95, 190, 209, 297; cultivation of virtuosity, **I:** 290, 299–317
Spontaneity, **I:** 235–41, 275 277, 279, **II:** 33, 62, 76, 88, 92–93, 99, 156, 216, 235, 241, 246, 324
Spontaneous emergence, *see* Emergence
Stability, **I:** vi
Stace, Walter, **I:** 340
Stain, **I:** 146, **II:** 118–224, 128, 133
Starbuck, Edwin Diller, **I:** 51, 331
Starry skies above and the moral law within, **I:** 131
Star Wars, **II:** 57–60
State of nature, **I:** 50
Stone, Lucian W., Jr., **I:** 336
Stout, Jeffrey, **I:** 68, 326
Straw dogs, **II:** 318; *see* **I:** Heaven, and straw dogs

Structuralism, **I:** 51
Subject/object, 148
Subjectivism, in postmodernism, **I:** 51–52
Subjectivity, **II:** 2, 42, 68, 76, 78, 146, 149, 333; divine, **I:** 124
Submission, **II:** 2, 168, 173, 177–79, 182, 185, 264, 269, 286, 289, 295
Substance, **I:** 195–96, **II:** 67, 74, 160; in Descartes, **I:** 63–64; as model of creation, **I:** 275
Suchness, **I:** 117–18, 138, **II:** 18, 93, 219–21, 236, 332
Suchocki, Marjorie, **I:** 279, 341
Suffering, **I:** 42, 47, 107, 140, 146, 264, **II:** 6, 9—15, 18–19, 53, 67, 83, 96–99, 104, 120, 135–38, 142, 144–48, 150, 153, 157, 165, 167–70, 175–82, 184–85, 190, 210, 245, 263, 297, 301, 324; in Buddhism, **I:** 27, **II:** 39, 175
Sufism, **I:** 111, 312
Supernatural agents, **I:** 102, 139; **II:** 200
Supernaturalism, **I:** xix, 2, 25, 139, 254, **II:** 200, 323
Superstition, **I:** 73, 160
Supranaturalism, **II:** 323
Surprisingness, **I:** 38, 311, **II:** (or surprise) xxii, 15, 20, 33, 54, 179–80, 211–14, 221–22, 225, 232, 234–38, 244–50, 253–54, 284, 290, 294, 314–16; in orientation, **I:** 82
Swallows, **I:** 306
Sweat lodges, **II:** 279, 290
Symbol systems, **I:** 147, 294–95, **II:** 16, 20–22, 28, 109–10, 185, 196, 212, 215, 223, 282, 309, 319; *see also* Semiotics *and* Network meaning
Symbolic engagement, **I:** 4–5, 15–17, 59–60, 72–73, 79, 97–98, 160–61, 165, 251, 301–03, 316, **II:** xvi, xxiii, 5, 183, 193, 206, 213, 220,. 223, 234, 321, 328, 332; defined, 63–68; through metaphysical theories, **I:** 287–300; of ultimates, **I:** 18–19, 319–20
Symbolic reference, **I:** 70, 136–38, 282–86, 51–54, 60–65, 73, 76
Symbols, **I:** vi, 32, 43, 122–24, **II:** vi, xvii, 13–18, 20–21, 25, 27–28, 87,

89–96, 99, 101, 109–33, 142, 154–62, 169, 180, 264–74, 278–86, 290–92, 299, 308–21, 324–24, 328–30, 332, 334; broken, **I:** 1–2, 9–10, 76–79, 137, 228, 230, **II:** 82; engaging and/or true, **I:** 67–68, 288; engaging transcendence, **I:** 131–33; of eternity, **I:** 242–44; higher and lower levels, **I:** 299–300; metaphysical, **I:** 19; religious, **I:** 61, 65, 329, **II:** xxi, 3, 12; iconically false and indexically true, **I:** 72–73; theory of, **I:** 287–300 (*see also* Semiotics); of ultimacy, **I:** 11, 125, 245, 253–62, **II:** xvi, 5–6, 33, 179–85, 189–98, 206, 212–23, 225–29, 233–38, 244, 246, 250–51, 253–54, 258, 261; under pressure from reality, **I:** 251

Symmetry, in concept of ontological creative act, **I:** 222–25, 280–81, 289, **II:** 229–30, 332

Syntax, **I:** 70–71, **II:** 38, 220

System, **I:** xvi **II:** 3 10, 12–16, 20–28, 34, 35, 43, 45, 52, 65, 76, 78, 81, 91, 97, 109–11, 116–17, 128, 149, 155–58, 185, 190–96, 203, 212–16, 220–29, 234, 237, 242, 260–63, 275–82, 290, 302, 308–09, 319, 324, 325, 327, 328, 331–32, 335; testing of, **I:** xxii; in *Philosophical Theology*, **I:** xxi–xxii; in theology, **I:** 44, 111–12, 153, **II:** xix, xxiii

Taiji, **II:** 140, 142, 294, 297–98, 330, 334; *see also* Great Ultimate
Tanner, Kathryn, **I:** 54, 331, **II:** 280, 334
Taste, **II:** 174; in theology, **I:** 175–76
Taylor, Charles, **II:** 89, 99, 326, 328
Taylor, Mark C., **I:** 5–6, 328, 330
Teleological argument, **I:** 130
Telos, **I:** 196
Temporality, **I:** 172, 232–35, 246, 259–62, 276–79, **II:** 25, 216, 219 modes of, **I:** 219–21, 322, essential and conditional components of, **I:** 263–66, eternal togetherness of, **I:** 267–69; real only in eternity, **I:** 241–44; theory of, **I:** 235–41; as ultimate, **I:** 243

Tendai Buddhism, **II:** 328
Terminus, of ontological act of creation, **I:** 1, 218–22, 231, 261–62, 268
Terror, **I:** 29, 68, **II:** 126, 316–17
Thangaraj, M. Thomas, **I:** xxv
Thatamanil, John J., **I:** 47, 330–31, 339, **II:** 328–30
Theism, **I:** 2, 117–18, 138, 279, **II:** 57; personal, **I:** 2, 123; *see also* Monotheism
Theodicy, **I:** 31, 110, 123, **II:** 10
Theological aesthetic, **I:** 172
Theological anthropology, **II:** xvi–xx, 26, 31, 49, 71, 85, 254, 257, 324
Theological circle, **I:** xx
Theology, **I:** xv–xxi, 44, **II:** xv–xvi, xxiii, 1, 10–11, 28, 56, 60, 102, 114, 146, 159, 161, 163, 171–72, 175, 179, 183–84, 190, 192, 196–201, 223, 258, 268, 273, 291–92, 316–17, 323–29, 331–32, 334; and the metaphysics of being, **I:** 174–75; biblical, **I:** xx; breaking symbols, **I:** 160–61; comparative, **I:** xix–xx, 42, 96; as creation and critiques, **I:** 77; as deep grammar, **I:** 48; disinterest in certain questions, **I:** 190–91; as engagement of ultimacy, **I:** 251; practical, **I:** 295–96; framing rhetoric of, **I:** 103; secular, **I:** xx; as a sign, **I:** 287–300; sophisticated, **I:** 90; systematic, **I:** 90, 78–79, 90, 95, 293–96; *see also* Confessionalism
Theravada Buddhism, **I:** 114.
Thinking the ultimate through thinking theory of ultimacy, **I:** 290–300
Third Person, of Trinity, **I:** 261–62
Third term, **I:** 186–87
Thirdness, in Peirce, **I:** 15, 70, 224, 334, 340
Thisness, *see* haecceity
Thomas Aquinas, *see* Aquinas
Thomas, Edward J., **II:** 331
Tiamat, **I:** 126, 157
Tillich, Paul, **I:** xx, 5, 26–28, 32, 77, 93, 96, 102, 105–06, 108, 111, 149–50, 152, 203, 230, 258, 270, 309, 311, 325, 327–28, 330, 336, 339–40, 342, **II:** xv, xix, 6, 8–9, 14, 60, 76, 82, 89, 171–72, 180, 192, 197, 211, 258–59,

384 ❊ INDEX

Tillich, Paul *(continued)*
305, 315, 323, 327–28, 330–31, 333, 335
Timaeas, **I:** 14
Time, **I:** 21, 133, 197–99, **II:** xix, xxi, 19, 25, 32, 38, 55, 57, 61, 65, 68, 72–73, 77, 81, 86, 88–89, 93, 103, 119, 161, 182, 192–93, 196–98, 203–07, 213–16, 219, 229, 235, 244–49, 253–54, 262–63, 265, 269, 277, 281, 298–301, 305, 314, 316, 321, 325, 327, 332, 335; created, **I:** 322; flow of **I:** 235–41, **II:** 19; modes of, **I:** 235–41; *see also* Temporality
Togetherness, **I:** 177–80, 215–21, 237, 247, 267–71, **II:** 72, 76, 82, 86, 204, 216, 250, 309, 314; de facto, **I:** 284, **II:** 52; ontological and cosmological, **I:** 286, **II:** 314
Tolkien, J. R. R., **II:** 55–60, 327
Torah, **I:** 77–78, 149–50, 154–55, 273, **II:** 94, 114; *see also* Hebrew Bible
Toulmin, Stephen, **I:** 328
Traditions, **I:** xv–xvi, 5, 7, 18–19, 21, 25, 32, 86–87, 109, 152, 157, 284, 319, **II:** xvi, xx, xxiii, 3, 6, 11–12, 16–17, 25, 28, 36, 38, 42–44, 53, 57, 60, 63–68, 73, 75–76, 81–83, 85, 87, 90–99, 101, 109, 114–22, 126–31, 134, 136–48, 152, 155–59, 171, 175–84, 190, 195, 198, 201–04, 212, 214, 217–19, 231, 248, 253, 257–58, 264, 266, 268, 274, 276–77, 283, 286, 288–89, 294–97, 301, 304–05, 310, 313, 321, 325, 333; with differing symbol systems, **I:** 288–300; membership in, **I:** 165–66
Transcendence, **I:** 84–87, 97–98, 102, **II:** 7, 19, 21, 244–45, 271–72, 278; signals of, **I:** 330; in symbols of ultimacy, **I:** 121–33, 163–65, 282–82, 297, 320
Transcendence/intimacy continuum, **I:** 84–87, 98, 119, 131–32, 290–92, 320–23
Transcendental conditions of mind, **I:** 56–57
Transcendental ideality, **I:** 49–50
Transcendental philosophy, **I:** 235

Transcendental traits of determinateness (or of Harmony; *see also* Harmony), **I:** 2–3, 36–42, 169, 175, 197–209, 231, 261–69, 312, 321, xxi, 8, 13, 21, 25, 27, 29, 71–75, 85–86, 101–04, 121, 125, 181, 183, 191, 205, 219, 225, 232, 259, 309–10, 314, 320; as logos, **I:** 220; as ultimate, **I:** 243–44
Transfiguration, **I:** 117
Transformation, **I:** 118, **II:** 10, 19, 61, 63, 67, 92, 126, 159, 175, 218, 267, 284, 324, 327
Transgenders, **I:** 11, **II:** 159
Translation, **I:** 66, 302
Transmutation, **II:** 155
Trauma, **II:** 7, 10–11, 98, 143, 161, 318, 325, 328, 330
Triadic structure of interpretation, **I:** 66
Tribes, **I:** 121–22, 155, **II:** 333
Trinity, **I:** 118, 261–62, **II:** 110, 227, 270, 286; and shamanism, **I:** 88–89
Triumphalism, **II:** 10
Triviality, **I:** 13
True believers, **I:** 10
Truth, **I:** xv, xvii–xviii, 97–98, 122, 175, **II:** 53, 97, 109–10, 120, 138, 162–63, 174–75, 197, 206, 219–25, 245–46, 264, 291–92, 295, 310, 317, 324, 329, 334; as carryover of value, **I:** 43–44, 144, 293–96, 342; in religious engagement, **I:** 20, 28, 42–44, 90; in folk religion, **I:** 89; in indexical reference, **I:** 159–61; and intimacy, **I:** 141; in narratives, **I:** 157; ontological, **I:** 47; and reference, **I:** 45–54; in symbols, **I:** 288, 293–96, 319–24; in theology, **I:** 15–17, 67–68; in worldviews, **I:** 138–39
Tucker, Karen Westerfield, **II:** 333
Tu Weiming, **I:** 106, 336–37, 339, 342, **II:** 3, 284, 324, 329–30, 334
Turner, Victor, **II:** 262, 266, 333
Twenty-third Psalm, **I:** 255
Two truths, in Buddhism, **I:** 111, 114
Tylor, E. B., **I:** 32, 138

Ultimacy, **I:** 4–9, 42–44, 5, 84, 149–50, **II:** vi, xvi, xviii–xxii, 3–9, 15–21, 28–29, 40, 49, 51, 53, 57, 86, 95, 99,

101–04, 113, 122, 125, 127, 129–32, 158, 168, 170, 181–85, 191, 195–98, 205–07, 209–15, 221–23, 225–26, 229–31, 236–37, 244–49, 253, 260–61, 264–66, 270–73, 277–78, 282–83, 285–89, 292, 301, 306–13, 318–21, 324–25; anthropological, **I:** 75; bearing on human life, **I:** 21; conceptualizing, **I:** 21, 95–98, 149–53; as conditioned and unconditioned, **I:** 131; cosmological defined, **I:** 193–209; defined, **I:** 109–13, 297; domesticated, **I:** 132; and explanation, **I:** 128; heuristic definitions of, **I:** 297; as knowable and unknowable, **I:** 21, 251; metaphysics of, **I:** 21, 70; in mundane things, **I:** 83–84, 119; as mystery, **I:** 273–86; orientation to, **I:** 75–76; and pressure on symbols, **I:** 319; and possible worlds, **I:** 276–79; in supernatural agents, **I:** 2; in the sacred, **I:** 33–34; symbols of, **I:** 65, 90, 101–03, 159–61; true, **I:** 113–18; in uncanny things, **I:** 141

Ultimate concern, **I:** 5, 11, 105–119, 294–95, 301–03, 327, **II:** 7, 110, 199, 245, 260, 279, 286, 289, 316; defined, **I:** 27; individual and social, **I:** 118–19; as normative, **I:** 110; versus proximate concerns, **I:** 105–06; *see also* ultimate realities

Ultimate concern continuum, **I:** 163–64, 320, **II:** 7

Ultimate of Non-Being (wuji), **I:** 25, 220, 228–29, 234, 257–58, 260, 273, 291, 309

Ultimate realities, **I:** xi, 1–4, 9–12, 20–21, 44, 72–73, 84–87, 131–33, 269–71, 287–90, 319–24, **II:** xv–xvi, xviii, xx, 3, 14, 21, 25, 33, 43, 54, 58, 62, 91, 94, 96, 98–99, 101–04, 107, 121, 127–29, 132, 162, 168–71, 180–81, 183–84, 189, 191, 193, 196, 211, 218, 225, 245, 247, 258–59, 264–68, 278, 284–88, 291–92, 307–11, 316–17, 320–21; closer to me than I am to myself, **I:** 138; defining, **I:** 25–28; interpreted as finite/infinite contrasts, **I:** 33–34, 72–79 (*see* Finite/infinite contrasts); good or just, **I:** 275–76; ontological **I:** 173–91, 253–62, and anthropological, **I:** 102–06, and cosmological, **I:** 3–4; receding from grasp, **I:** 108–09; the unconditioned conditions, **I:** 173–76; *see also* Ultimacy *and* Ultimates

Ultimates, **I:** 9–10, 16–17, **II:** vi, xv, xviii–xix, 7, 41, 61, 113–14, 125, 189–93, 205, 221, 223, 229, 248, 253, 257, 286, 321, 325; anthropomorphic, **I:** 85–87; five in number, **I:** 4, 169–72, **II:** 11, 18, 27–28; as objects of metaphysical inquiry, **I:** 169–72; ontological, **I:** 85–86; ontological and anthropological, **I:** 153–66; ontological and cosmological, **I:** 169–70; positive knowledge of, **I:** 253–71; *see also* Ultimacy *and* Ultimate realities

Uncanny, the, **I:** 32, 103, 135, 138–41, 148, 321

Understanding, **I:** xxii, **II:** xvii, 13, 43, 56, 78–81, 156, 161, 174, 183, 190, 203, 205, 215, 222, 244, 278, 286, 289, 310

Undeservedness, **I:** 38, **II:** 221–22, 225, 232–34, 237, 248–50, 253–54, 315

Uniqueness, **I:** 264, **II:** 141, 324

Unity, **I:** 175, 197–201, 235–41, 262–67, 280, **II:** 3, 27, 32, 51, 155, 191, 326; and being, **I:** 174; of body and intentionality, **I:** 305–06; de facto, **I:** 176, 178–80; underlying diversity and change, **I:** 256; with God, **I:** 342; of ontological creative act, **I:** 259–60, 303–06; with the ultimate, **I:** 302

Universality, **I:** 129, **II:** xxiii, 4, 15–18, 159, 265–66, 272, 280; of ultimate concern, **I:** 105–06

Univocity of being, **I:** 171; demonstrated, **I:** 182–84

Upanishads, **I:** 256, **II:** 91

Usher, Anton, **II:** 333

Vagueness, **I:** xxi, 13, 194, 198, 258, 329; defined, **I:** 26–27; of religious categories, **I:** 42, 96

Value, **I:** xvii, 3–4, 11–15, 26–27, 38, 41–42, 75, 122, 129, 137, 147, 184,

Value *(continued)*
202, 235–42, 146–47, 262, 276–79, **II:** vi, xx, xxiii, 5, 8, 13–16, 31–47, 53, 61, 63–67, 73–77, 81–82, 102–04, 107–11, 113–26, 131–33, 136–44, 151–58, 161–65, 167, 173, 180, 190–92, 203, 216–23, 226, 229, 232–36, 241–44, 248, 265–73, 303, 326, 329, 331; in depth, **I:** 271; in form, **I:** 198–201; of harmonies, defined, **I:** 205–07; and intelligibility, **I:** 283; and interpretation, **I:** 84; modalities of, **I:** 206–08; in nature, **I:** 170; of persons, **I:** 265–66; in ultimacy, **I:** 68; *see also* value-identity

Value-identity, **I:** xi, 36–42, 97, 106, 111, 116, 148, 204–09, 227, 241, 262–66, 312, 321, **II:** xix, xxi, 6–7, 16–21, 26–29, 49, 108–11, 203–16; of persons, **I:** 313, **II:** 85–99, 102–04, 167–82, 189, 244–47, 251–60, 286–97, 307–15, 320–21; subjective and objective, **I:** 3–4, 49–52, 09, 339; as ultimate, **I:** 243

Van der Leeuw, Gerardus, **I:** 32, 138
Van Gennep, Arnold, **II:** 262
Van Huyssteen, J. Wentzel, **II:** 324
Van Norden, Bryan, **II:** 326
Vasubandhu, **I:** 151
Vaught, Carl G., **I:** 331, **II:** 329
Vedas, **I:** 77, 147, **II:** 17, 174
Verstehen, **I:** xxii
Virgin Mary, **I:** 292–93
Virtues, **II:** 41, 46, 52, 62, 119, 142, 158, 277; of traits of harmony, **I:** 208
Virtuosity, religious, **I:** 4, 133, 251, 301–17, 323–24, **II:** 22–23, 95–96, 132, 153, 155, 162, 195–96, 216, 223–26, 228–29, 232–37, 244–49, 254, 264, 295–98, 313
Vishnu, **I:** 26, 116–18, 147, 229, 255, 279, 315, **II:** 161, 174, 201, 219, 294
Visualization, **I:** 309, **II:** 92
Vulnerability, **II:** 178; to correction, **I:** xvi–xvii, 58–59, 113, 324

Waltemyer, Seth, **I:** xxv
Wanderer, Jeremy, **I:** 334

Wang, Robin R., **II:** 330
Wang Yangming, **I:** 106, **II:** 3, 147, 294, 326
Wangbi, **I:** 173, 228
War, **I:** 84, **II:** 33, 45, 58, 81, 102, 117, 198, 213, 242, 264, 294, 299, 316
Ward, Keith, **I:** xviii, 181, 326, 228
Watchmaker, **I:** 130
Watson, Lancelot, **I:** xxv, **II:** xxiii
Weber, Max, **I:** 50
Weekes, Anderson, **II:** 258–59, 333
Wegter-McNelly, Kirk, **I:** 339
Weiss, Paul, **I:** 68, 171, 177–80, 245, 333, 337–38, **II:** 325, 330
Weissman, David, **I:** 68
Weller, Robert P., **II:** 333
Wesley, John, **II:** 2
West, Cornel, **I:** 68, 333
White, James F., **II:** 333
Whitehead, Alfred North, **I:** xxi, 13, 33–34, 59–61, 68, 96, 140–41, 170, 193, 195, 199, 204, 223, 225, 232–236, 263, 268, 278–79, 282, 285, 328, 330–32, 335, 337–41, **II:** 1–5, 34, 77, 79, 155, 234, 257, 303, 324, 326–27, 335; on metaphysical pluralism, **I:** 176–77
Whitney, Lawrence, **I:** xxv
Wholeness, **I:** 3–4, 10, 68, 97–98, 107, 231, 141, **II:** xix, xxi–xxii, 6–8, 13–18, 26–29, 35, 40–41, 45, 49–69, 71, 79, 93, 102–03, 108, 111, 114, 121, 132, 135–36, 139–50, 168, 171–72, 180–82, 184, 189, 191–92, 209–22, 229, 248, 253–54, 259, 266, 272, 289, 300, 307, 309, 313, 320; of world, **I:** 310
Width, 13
Wildman, Wesley J., **I:** v, xx, xxv, 139, 326, 328–29, 331, 336, **II:** xvi–xx, xxiii, 180, 190, 323–25, 331
Wildness, in divine life, **I:** 261 267, 271, 281
Will, **I:** 130, **II:** xix, **II:** xvii, 119, 132, 277, 330
Wilson, David Sloan, **I:** 335
Winkler, Ulrich, **II:** xxiii
Wisdom, **I:** 280; Wisdom literature, **I:** 154

Wittgenstein, Ludwig, **I:** 18, 326
Witzel, Michael, **I:** 335
Wood, William, **I:** 326
Wonder, **II:** 5
Word, divine, **I:** 110–11
Works righteousness, **I:** 46–47
World religions, **I:** xxii, **II:** 89, 101, 113, 121, 139, 162, 222, 310
World Soul, **I:** 234
World, **I:** 2–3, 16, **II:** xxi–xxiii, 8–15, 19–20, 25–29, 31, 34, 38–42, 51–57, 60–62, 71–76, 79, 82–84, 89, 95, 101, 104, 113–24, 129, 133–34, 136, 147–57, 160–78, 180, 190, 198–206, 210–12, 217–23, 226, 229–38, 239, 242–60, 263, 265–70, 273, 293–98, 304, 307–18, 320, 326, 329, 335; conceptions of in Axial Age religions, **I:** 122–24; defining, **I:** 33–34, 43–44, 74, 107, 109–13, 116 132; as determinate, **I:** 284–85; as kingdom, **I:** 125; images of, **I:** 121–24; other possible, **I:** 276–79; religions, **I:** 96; as terminus of ontological creative act, **I:** 218–21, 322, transcendentally defined, **I:** 59; within worlds, **I:** 9, 137
Worldviews, **I:** 19, 31, 97–98, 103, 107, 109, 131–32, 138–39, 141–46, 163–64, 244, 257–58, 283, 287, 290–92, 294–96, 320, **II:** 6–7, 51, 82, 107, 260, 263, 270, 275, 278–92, 318–20; comprehensiveness of orientation, **I:** 92–93; continua intersecting, **I:** 87–88; defined, **I:** 28, 81–93; minimalist, **I:** 143; as shared, **I:** 91–93
Worship, **I:** 18, 132, **II:** 111, 121, 161, 189, 227, 265–76, 286, 305, 333–34

Wrong (or wrongness), **II:** xviii, 5, 10–12, 15, 17, 97, 127, 270, 315
Wu, Kuang-Ming, **I:** 341

Xunzi, **I:** 79, 141, 335; on orientation, **I:** 82–83, **II:** 40, 117–18, 157, 274, 334

Yahweh, **I:** 86, 122, 126, 150, 254–55, 261, 336, **II:** 94, 222; among other gods, **I:** 127
Yale School, **I:** 4
Yin/yang, **I:** 1, 10, 38, 12, 131, 151, 171, 193, 218–19, 233–35, 258, 260, 267; vibratory patterns, **I:** 228–29
Yoga, **I:** 118, 231–32, 303–06, **II:** 64, 142, 296
Yogacara Buddhism, **I:** 114, 231, **II:** 120
Yong, Amos, **I:** 325, 335
Yugoslavia, **I:** 8

Zanetti, Nikolas, **I:** xxv, **II:** xxiii
Zazen, **I:** 73
Zen Buddhism, **II:** 108, 147, 236, 294, 299; *see also* Chan Buddhism
Zeus, **I:** 86
Zhang, Tina Chunna, **II:** 334
Zhangzai, **I:** 341
Zhou Dunyi, **I:** 37, 130, 173, 228–29, 234, 257–60, 273, 309, 327, 340
Zhuangzi, **I:** 269, 341, **II:** 18, 66, 68, 117, 325
Zionism, **II:** 94
Zoroastrianism, **I:** 86, 123, 127, 255, 330, **II:** 198